DOCUMENTARY FILMMAKING

DOCUMENTARY FILMMAKING

in the Middle East and North Africa

EDITED BY
VIOLA SHAFIK

The American University in Cairo Press
Cairo New York

First published in 2022 by
The American University in Cairo Press
113 Sharia Kasr el Aini, Cairo, Egypt
One Rockefeller Plaza, 10th Floor, New York, NY 10020
www.aucpress.com

ISBN 978 9 774 16958 8

Library of Congress Cataloging-in-Publication Data

Names: Shafik, Viola, 1961- editor.
Title: Documentary filmmaking in the Middle East and North Africa / edited by Viola
    Shafik.
Identifiers: LCCN 2021043232 | ISBN 9789774169588 (hardback)
Subjects: LCSH: Documentary films--Middle East--History and criticism. |
Documentary films--Africa, North--History and criticism. | Motion picture producers and
    directors--Middle East. | Motion picture producers and directors--Africa, North.
Classification: LCC PN1995.9.D6 D5756 2021 | DDC 070.1/80956--dc23 LC record
    available at https://lccn.loc.gov/2021043232

1 2 3 4 5   26 25 24 23 22

Designed by Adam el-Sehemy

CONTENTS

Aesthetics/Politics of Representation

CONTRIBUTOR PROFILES

Ali Abdulameer is a contributing writer for Al-Monitor's Iraq Pulse and a correspondent for Al-Hayat. A writer, journalist and TV presenter residing in Amman and Washington, he was editor-in-chief of a number of cultural magazines and Iraqi newspapers, and was the managing editor of Iraqi news in the Arabic-language American Al-Hurrah. Abdulameer presented a television show entitled *Seven Days* from 2004 to 2010.

Hend F. Alawadhi is assistant professor at the College of Architecture in Kuwait University. Her dissertation on gender, memory, and erasure in contemporary Arab cinema earned an award from the Susan B. Anthony Institute for Gender, Sexuality and Women's Studies. Alawadhi's research includes the history of moving image in the Arab world, feminist media activism, and gendered representations of disability and illness in Arab media.

Jamal Bahmad is assistant professor at Mohammed V University, Morocco. He has published widely in the fields of Moroccan and Maghrebi cinema. Bahmad co-edited a special issue of *French Cultural Studies* (SAGE, August 2017) on trash cultures in the Francophone world. He co-authored a book on Moroccan transnational cinema (Edinburgh University Press, 2020), and is working on his first monograph on Moroccan cinema and globalization.

Ahmed Bedjaoui is professor of audiovisual communication and cinema at Algiers University 3, artistic manager of the Algiers International Film Festival, and author of *Cinéma et guerre de libération, des batailles d'images* (2014), *Littérature et cinémas arabes* (2016), *La Guerre d'Algérie dans le cinéma mondial* (2016), and *Cinema and the Algerian War for Independence* (2019). He received the 2015 UNESCO Féderico Fellini Medal for his contribution to global film culture.

Dore Bowen is research professor in the Department of Art, Art History & Visual Studies at Duke University. Working at the intersection of media art history, phenomenology, and cultural theory, she co-authored *Bruce Nauman: Spatial Encounters* (with Constance Lewallen, University of California Press, 2019), and is currently completing a manuscript on the diorama. She has curated several exhibitions with the Arab Image Foundation.

Donatella Della Ratta is a scholar, writer, performer, and curator specializing in digital media and networked technologies. Donatella managed the Arabic speaking community for Creative Commons (2007-2013), and in 2012 she co-founded the website SyriaUntold, recipient of the Digital Communities award at Arts Electronica. *Shooting a Revolution: Visual Media and Warfare in Syria* (Pluto Press, 2018) is her latest monograph.

Yasmin Desouki is a film archivist and programmer who worked as the artistic director at Cimatheque-Alternative Film Centre in Cairo, Egypt from 2013 to 2019. She studied cinema studies and moving image archiving at NYU's Tisch School of the Arts, and came to Egypt in 2011, where she first worked at Misr International Films, managing their archival collections. She is currently the collections manager at Chicago Film Archives.

Kay Dickinson teaches Film and Television Studies at the University of Glasgow. She is the author of *Arab Cinema Travels: Transnational Syria, Palestine, Dubai and Beyond* (2016), and the editor of *Arab Film and Video Manifestos: Forty-Five Years of the Moving Image Amid Revolution* (2018), as well as co-editor of *The Arab Archive: Mediated Memories and Digital Flows* (2020). She has published widely on Arab popular and revolutionary culture in anthologies and journals.

Ali Essafi, born in Morocco, studied psychology in France, then entered the world of filmmaking. His works as a director include *General, Here We Are*, *The Silence of the Beet Fields*, *Ouarzazate Movie*, and *Shikhat's Blues*, which have been screened internationally. He has been researching North African film & visual archives since 2013. One of his latest films, *Crossing the Seventh Gate*, premiered at the Berlinale's Forum Section in 2017.

Nouri Gana is professor of comparative literature & Near Eastern languages and cultures at the University of California. He authored *Signifying Loss: Toward a Poetics of Narrative Mourning*, and edited *The Making of the Tunisian Revolution*, and *The Edinburgh Companion to the Arab Novel in English*. His second monograph, *Melancholy Acts: Defeat and Cultural Critique in the Arab World*, is forthcoming with Fordham University Press (2023).

Mohannad Ghawanmeh is a film scholar and cineaste. His cinema practice has included production, project development, and curation. A recipient of multiple awards, Mohannad's writing engages cinema in relation to migration, religion, and song. A PhD candidate in cinema and media studies at UCLA, his dissertation investigates the political economy of silent and early sound cinema in Egypt, 1896–1934.

Olivier Hadouchi is an independent film curator and researcher affiliated with IRCAV/Paris 3. He has a PhD in film studies on cinema and the tricontinental movement, and has published on solidarity with the Third World, Algerian cinema, and Jocelyne Saab. He has curated film programs for various festivals (Amiens, CorsicaDoc), art centers, and museums (Reina Sofía, Jeu de Paume).

Ahmad Izzo is a postdoc scholar at the Department of Geography, Johannes Gutenberg University in Mainz. His dissertation *Die syrische Gesellschaft in den Filmen von Omar Amiralay* (2017) deals with film geography, a branch of cultural geography. Izzo's research focuses on migration and community studies. He is currently working on the DFG-research project "Communities of Syrians in Germany."

Alisa Lebow, professor of screen media at the University of Sussex, is a leading scholar of documentary film, innovating in practice-led research with her interactive database meta-documentary, *Filming Revolution* (2018). Her books include *A Companion to Contemporary Documentary*, *The Cinema of Me*, and *First Person Jewish*, and her films include: *For the Record: The World Tribunal on Iraq*, *Treyf*, and *Outlaw*.

Peter Limbrick is professor of film and digital media at the University of California. He is the author of *Arab Modernism as World Cinema: The Films of Moumen Smihi* and *Making Settler Cinemas: Film and Colonial Encounters in the U.S., Australia, and New Zealand*, and has published on postcolonial and transnational cinemas in *Framework*, *Third Text*, *Camera Obscura*, and other journals.

Florence Martin is professor of French transnational studies at Goucher College, Baltimore. Her most recent publications on Maghrebi cinema include *Screens and Veils: Maghrebi Women's Cinema*, *Les Cinémas du Maghreb et leurs*, *Transnational Crossings: Terrorism on Maghrebi Screens*, and *Moroccan Cinema Uncut*.

Irit Neidhardt is director of Mec film, an international distribution and sales company for films by Arab directors. She has co-produced several award-winning feature documentaries, and authored various articles related to cinema and the Arab World, focusing on cooperation and financing. Neidhardt is currently researching the cooperation of the two Germanies and the PLO in the field of cinema and TV.

Stefan Pethke is a filmmaker, author, translator, subtitler, consultant, lecturer, and program coordinator of UNERHÖRT! – International Music Film Festival Hamburg. He was a founding member of "ENTUZIAZM – Friends of Mediation between Film and Text." Pethke has been a jury member in Rabat (Festival International de Cinéma d'Auteur), Torino (See You Sound), and Paris (F.A.M.E.).

Mathilde Rouxel is a French PhD candidate in New Sorbonne University. Her thesis deals with the representation of peoples in struggle in women filmmaking in Egypt, Lebanon and Tunisia from 1967 to 2017. She published her monograph *Jocelyne Saab, la m*émoire indomptée *(1970-2015)*, and coordinates the Lebanon-based scriptwriting residency "Films Femmes Francophones Méditerranée."

Viviane Saglier is a Mellon postdoctoral fellow at McGill University. She holds a PhD in film and moving image studies from Concordia University.

Viola Shafik is author of *Arab Cinema: History and Cultural Identity* (1998, rev. 2016), and *Popular Egyptian Cinema: Gender, Class, and Nation* (2007). She taught at the American University in Cairo, Zürich University, Humboldt University, and Ludwig Maximilians University. She has worked as a consultant for numerous international film festivals and film funds. Her most recent documentaries are: *My Name is not Ali*, and *Arij – Scent of Revolution*.

Ella Shohat is professor of cultural studies at New York University. Her books include *On the Arab-Jew, Palestine, and Other Displacements*; *Taboo Memories, Diasporic Voices*; *Israeli Cinema: East/West and the Politics of Representation*; *Talking Visions: Multicultural Feminism in a Transnational Age*; *Dangerous Liaisons*; *Between the Middle East and the Americas*; *Unthinking Eurocentrism*; *Flagging Patriotism*; *Race in Translation*, and *Multiculturalism, Postcoloniality, and Transnational Media*.

Mohamad Soueid is head of Al Arabiya news channel's documentary department, and has directed *The Insomnia of a Serial Dreamer*, *Civil War*, *Nightfall*, and *Tango of Yearning* (winner of Best Documentary Director Prize at Beirut International Film Festival, 2000). He published two essay books, *Postponed Cinema - Lebanese Films During the Civil War*, and

O Heart - A Film Autobiography On the Late Movie Theatres of Old Beirut, and a novel, *Cabaret Souad*.

Hanan Toukan is Associate Professor of Politics and Middle East Studies at Bard College, Berlin. Her book *The Politics of Art: Dissent and Cultural Diplomacy in Palestine, Lebanon and Jordan* (2021) is published with Stanford University Press.

Oraib Toukan is an artist and EUME fellow at the Forum Transregionale Studien in Berlin. Until Fall 2015, she was head of the Arts Division and Media Studies program at Bard College at Al-Quds University, Palestine, and was visiting faculty at the International Academy of Fine Arts in Ramallah. Toukan is author of *Sundry Modernism: Materials for a Study of Palestinian Modernism*, and the essay film *When Things Occur*.

Stefanie Van de Peer is a researcher of African and Arab film cultures, and works for Africa in Motion. She is a lecturer in film and media at Queen Margaret University. Van de Peer's monograph, *Negotiating Dissidence: The Pioneering Women of Arab Documentary* and award-winning collection *Animation in the Middle East*, were both released in 2017. She co-authored *Women in African Cinema: Beyond the Body Politic*.

Nadia Yaqub is a professor in the Department of Asian Studies at the University of North Carolina. Her research has treated Arab cultural texts ranging from medieval literature and contemporary oral poetry to modern prose fiction and visual culture. She is the author of *Pens, Swords, and the Springs of Art: Palestinian Oral Poetry Dueling in the Galilee*, and *Palestinian Cinema in the Days of Revolution*, and co-editor of *Bad Girls of the Arab World*.

Alia Yunis is currently completing a book on creating national identity in the UAE through film. A former associate professor of film and media at Zayed University in Abu Dhabi, she has also worked as a writer, journalist, and filmmaker on five continents and her work has been translated into six languages. Her feature documentary, *The Golden Harvest*, recently won Best of the Fest at the Minneapolis St. Paul International Film Festival.

Hady Zaccak is a Lebanese award-winning filmmaker and professor at IESAV Film School-Saint-Joseph University, Beirut. He has directed more than twenty documentaries, including *A History Lesson, Marcedes, Kamal Joumblatt-Witness and Martyr, 104 Wrinkles*. He is also the author of two books on cinema: *Lebanese Cinema, an Itinerary Towards the Unknown (1929-1996)* and *The Last Film Screening-A Biography of Cilama Tripoli*.

ACKNOWLEDGMENTS

Many of the chapters in this volume emerged out of the 2017 conference "Histories of Arab Documentary," held in Munich at the Ludwig Maximilians Universität (LMU). For this reason, I am highly indebted to the conference participants and all the contributors for their great efforts, as well as to my colleague Kerstin Pinther, then still at the Art History Department of the LMU, who hosted me, my project, and the conference. I am likewise grateful to the Deutsche Forschungsgemeinschaft, who generously funded the project, and contributed to financing both the conference and the translation costs of the book. My thanks go also to the Goethe Institut Cairo, Johanna Keller, and Ghada El-Sherbiny for the financial support, and to the Film Museum Munich, where accompanying screenings were held. Similarly, I would like to express my gratitude to Laura Gribbon, the editor of this book, and her team at The American University in Cairo Press, to whom I am very indebted for the thorough revision of the very diverse contributions of this volume, some of which were kindly translated from French or Arabic by Najat Abdulhaq, Kevin St. John, and Stefan Pethke.

ILLUSTRATIONS

INTRODUCTION: HISTORIES OF 'ARAB' DOCUMENTARIES OR DOCUMENTARY FORMS SOUTH AND EAST OF THE MEDITERRANEAN?

Viola Shafik

Instead of an Introduction

The working title of this book, "Histories of Arab Documentaries," was changed to "Documentary Filmmaking in the Middle East and North Africa" for promotional reasons. The original concept of diversity and pluralism is still inscribed within it, though. In fact, I have been imagining this volume as a poem, but without meter or rhyme, a sort of expressive mosaic—I am borrowing here Michael Renov's notion of the "poetic documentary" (Renov 1993, 25)—a discourse quite unlike a meta-narrative suggesting one big continuous and consistent "Arab" film history, which in turn could be blown up into an essentialist legend. I prefer to speak, therefore, of "history" in the plural; in other words, multiple, diverse and subjective histories of a likewise hard to define, if not amorphous, cinematic format, namely the documentary.

As it is impossible to pin down documentary to one single form, so one can hardly speak of a clearly identifiable Arab identity, or—as advocated by pan-Arabism—an Arab *umma* (nation), unified by ethnic, geographic, linguistic and religious characteristics. This is not to deny numerous historical, infrastructural, and political co-relations and commonalities among the countries of North Africa and the Middle East, or south and east of the Mediterranean.

Little wonder it was hard to find a satisfactory title for this book. I had thought to use the term "Arabic-speaking countries," as it seemed less forced than the notion of "Arab" peoples, but this also has evident shortcomings. Which Arabic language am I referring to? The classical Arabic of the Quran and Quranic studies, or rather Modern Standard Arabic that is used in science and media but not on the streets? Both of these elevated forms of Arabic are in fact unable to accommodate the wealth of the often mutually unintelligible colloquial languages and jargons used in the many different regions of the Arab East and West, Mashriq and Maghreb.

1

What then? Eventually a friend and expert on the region suggested the title "South and East of the Mediterranean," borrowed from 'Abd al-Rahman Munif's novel *East of the Mediterranean* (*Sharq al-Mutawassit*, 1975). With its strong critique of authoritarian rule and political oppression, it certainly resonates with some of the topics raised in this volume, and the title sounds poetic enough to match my own intentions for this book even though in the end it did not appear in the title.

"South and East of the Mediterranean" is a geographic description, but one that also implies ancient history and the routes of cultural exchange among all countries united by the Mediterranean, or those in direct exchange with it. Permeability, diversity, and a fragmentary character are surely the most adequate descriptions of the region's culture, and a prerequisite for any sincere exploration of its documentary filmmaking. Yet, what about the—often unacknowledged—African roots in countries like Mauritania, Sudan, Algeria, Morocco, and Egypt? Perhaps, in the end, we should settle for the slightly technocratic term MENA (Middle East and North Africa) to accommodate these frequently denied African elements as well? I still don't feel enthusiastic about the final title, *Documentary Filmmaking in the Middle East and North Africa*, but at least it avoids some of the above-mentioned pitfalls.

Against a backdrop of such considerations, this volume has been developed to offer some basic, but definitely incomplete, observations on the main historical developments in the field of documentary filmmaking in the region. This collection of essays, interviews, and academic studies examines and presents some of the unrecognized scholarly or filmic endeavors in the field, and is reflective of the region's immense cultural, human, linguistic, and ethnic diversity. It also attempts to provide a long-overdue contextualization of regional production within a wider history of international film and cinema, using relevant theoretical frameworks of analysis. This edited volume sits alongside my own DFG- (Deutsche Forschungsgemeinschaft) funded research project, "Subversive Spring? Arab Non-Fiction and Its Revolution(s)," and is a collective endeavor to tackle what I consider to be some of the main obstacles in the writing of a history of Middle Eastern and North African documentary filmmaking, namely the scarcity of relevant academic research and publications, and the difficulties in finding and accessing the films themselves, particularly early productions.

Structure and State of Research

This volume has three main focuses: firstly, the general historical development of documentary film, including frameworks, practices, and social and political implications; secondly, the analysis of individual works and filmographies; and thirdly, structural and formal specificities as analyzed

through different thematic perspectives, such as the politics of representation, reception, narration, aesthetics, avant-gardism, revolution, new
media, and the like. Consequently, these topics are grouped into three thematic sections, namely: "Histories and Structures," "Aesthetics and Politics
of Representation," and "Individual Works and Filmmakers."

The topics the various chapters span are varied, and as inclusive as
possible in terms of geographical and cultural representation. The intention was to pay tribute to the diversity of the region, as well as to different
schools of analysis and the writing of filmic history. For this reason, the
book includes chapters by film professionals, critics, and artists, alongside
more traditional academic analyses. Thus this volume seeks to explore a
number of important aspects of documentary filmmaking in the region,
such as in the early days the reception of newsreels—discussed by Mohannad Ghawanmeh in chapter one—as well as the subsequent appropriation
of documentary film by nascent nation-states, and the roles they played
in constructing an Orientalist image of the region and its inhabitants—as
tackled by Yasmin Desouki and Mohamad Soueid in chapters ten and two
respectively. Also discussed is documentary filmmaking during the wars
of liberation from the 1950s to the 1970s, and its relation to history, by
Ahmed Bedjaoui (chapter six), Olivier Hadouchi (chapter eighteen) and
Irit Neidhardt (chapter four), as well as the development of the oeuvre
of individual filmmakers—namely Jean Chamoun and Mai Masri—in
the framework of the Lebanese civil war, by Hady Zaccak (chapter
twenty-three) or Emirati female director Nujoom Alghanem (Nujum
al-Ghanim) by Alia Yunis in chapter twenty-eight. Theoretical queries as
well as matters of political and aesthetic representation are obviously of
prime importance to the composition of this volume, and I will return to
them at the end of this introduction.

Notwithstanding, I need to underline that the immense wealth and
long history of local filmmaking cannot be represented in one volume.
Some of the most knowledgeable researchers and authors in the field could
not commit to contribute to this volume due to other obligations, though
many of them are cited in the reference list. Consequently, not all countries, key aspects, periods, and filmmakers could be discussed. Notably
missing are articles on Jordanian, Mauritanian, and Sudanese filmmaking,
and most of the Gulf region, most pertinently Kuwait. There is also a lack
of basic infrastructural data, numbers, and statistics, as the focus of this
book is more on general developments, individual films, filmmakers, and
textual analysis.

Many pioneering documentary directors and their oeuvre are not
given sufficient attention here. Among them, to name just a few: Michel
Khleifi, Rashid Masharawi, Norma Marcos, Azza El-Hassan and Nizar

Hassan from Palestine; Jocelyne Saab, Ghassan Salhab, Khalil Joreige, Joana Hadjithomas, Eliane Raheb, Mohamad Soueid, and Borhane Alaouié from Lebanon; Hala 'Abdallah from Syria; Mahmoud al-Massad from Jordan; Qais al-Zubaidi from Iraq; Suleiman Mohamed Ibrahim El-Nour from Sudan; Attiat El-Abnoudi, Ali al-Ghazuli, and Tahani Rached from Egypt; Mustapha Hasnaoui from Tunisia; Azzedine Meddour and Belkacem Hadjadj from Algeria; Ahmed El Maanouni, Ali Essafi, and Dalila Ennadre from Morocco; and many, many more.

Also absent from this volume are a number of films that I personally cherish from the late 1970s and 1980s, a decade that witnessed a new wave of well-achieved and innovative documentaries replacing older documentary schools of thought, such as: Maroun Baghdadi's *The Best of Mothers* (*Ajmal al-umahat*, 1978), *Permissible Dreams* (*al-Ahlam al-mumkinna*, 1983) by Attiat El-Abnoudi, *Fertile Memory* (*al-Dhakira al-khisba*, 1980) by Michel Khleifi, *Trances* (*al-Hal*, 1981) by Ahmed El Maanouni, *Ezzitouna in the Heart of Tunis* (*al-Zaytuna fi qalb Tunis*, 1981) by Hmida Ben Ammar, *The Dream* (*al-Manam*, 1987) by Mohamed Malas, and Med Hondo's (full name: Muhammad 'Abid Maddun Hondo) two films on the Polisario, among others.

Moreover, the field itself is changing. Many regional films produced since the digital turn have been featured at international festivals, are therefore easier to access, and have been analyzed and discussed in the media, or in individual academic studies. To name just a few: Hanan Toukan's film review of Jumana Manna's *A Magical Substance Flows into Me* (*Fi ithr madattin sihriyattin*, 2017), Peter Limbrick's (2012) study of Kamal Aljafari *The Roof* (*al-Sath*, 2006), and Mark Westmoreland's work on experimental film and video in Lebanon (2009), among others. Also, documentary filmmaking within Palestinian cinema has been well covered in several English publications, including *Dreams of a Nation* (2006), edited by Hamid Dabashi, and the incredibly thorough and well-researched *Palestinian Cinema in the Days of Revolution* (2018) by Nadia Yaqub. Similarly, documentaries by female directors are prominent in Rebecca Hillauer's *Encyclopedia of Arab Women Filmmakers* (2005), and Stefanie Van de Peer's *Negotiating Dissidence: The Pioneering Women of Arab Documentary* (2016), dedicated to the works of seven female film directors. The same author edited, in co-operation with Mathilde Rouxel, *Refocus, the Films of Jocelyne Saab* (2021). In 2015, the latter had already dedicated a French volume to the same Lebanese director (Rouxel 2020). Laura Marks' *Hanan al-Cinema* (2015), which deals in depth with experimental Arab filmmaking from the last two decades, touches upon several important documentary oeuvres, first and foremost those of Mohamad Soueid. Donatella Della Ratta's *Shooting a Revolution: Visual Media and Warfare in Syria* (2018), focuses on internet practices and documentation and was followed by Joshka Wessels' highly informative *Documenting Syria* (2019) on early documentary filmmaking and recent video activism. Other contributors, including myself, as well as Kevin Dwyer, Jeremy Randall, Iman Hamam, and Terri Ginsbery, have dealt with selected countries, such as Morocco, and individual oeuvres, for instance Maroun Baghdadi, or other aspects of documentary film within the context of larger studies in a special edition of *Framework* (2002), Alisa Lebow's *The Cinema of Me* (2012), *Arab Cultural Studies: History, Politics and the Popular* (2013) edited by Anastasia Valassopoulos, and *Uncommon Grounds: New Media and Critical Practice in North Africa and the Middle East* (2014), edited by Anthony Downey, and Terri Ginsberg's and Chris Lippard's *Cinema of the Arab World* (2020), to name just a few.

The relatively late interest of Anglophone academia in nonfiction in the region is striking given that, since the late 1980s, Anglophone film theory and historiography has found the documentary format to be a fruitful field of informed, sophisticated, and often interdisciplinary investigation. Numerous publications have appeared dedicated solely to Asian and Latin American documentary. In contrast, researchers based in the MENA region have far too often confined themselves to systematic data collection and chronicling, rather than grappling with the different waves of film theory that were informed by other cultural disciplines such as psychoanalysis, structuralism, linguistics, ethnography, feminism, gender and queer studies, affect theory, multiculturalism, and postcolonial studies.

It needs to be noted that there is an abundance of Arabic publications on Egyptian documentary, but little to nothing on other countries in the region. One of the few Arabic exceptions is *Documentary Film in Egypt and the Arab World* (*al-Sinima al-tasjiliya al-watha'iqiya fi Misr wa-l-'alam al-'arabi*, 1982) by Mona al-Hadidi, and *Documentary Film in the Arab Homeland* (*al-Sinima al-tasjiliya fi-l-watan al-'arabi*, 2010) by Mahmud Sami 'Atallah. Al-Hadidi presents a thorough study of history and infrastructure, but offers only rudimentary information on the rest of the region, given its early publication. It is not entirely clear why 'Attalah's more recent publication focuses primarily on Egypt, despite its title. In contrast, Khalil al-Hady's *Tunisian and International Documentary Cinema* (*al-Sinima al-watha'iqiya al-Tunissiya wa-l-'alamiya*, 2012) displays knowledge of the history of international documentary, but his choices in discussing just three filmmakers from his own homeland, along with two from Lebanon and one fairly unknown TV director from Egypt, seem likewise limited and haphazard.

As already stated, there is an abundance of data collection on Egyptian documentary and newsreels from the silent era to the present. The most comprehensive work in Arabic is probably *The History of Documentary Film in Egypt* (*Tarikh al-sinima al-tasjiliya fi Misr*, 2003) by Diya' Mar'i, which is an expanded version of his 1978 master's thesis. This text, Mona al-Hadidi's study, and Ilhamy Hasan's *The History of Egyptian Cinema* (*Tarikh al-sinima al-misriya*, 1976), have become the main sources for several other studies, such as Hashim al-Nahas' *The Future of Documentary Cinema in Egypt* (*Mustaqbal al-sinima al-tasjiliya fi Misr*, 1990). Ali Abu Shadi's (est. 1980) *Documentary Film in Egypt* (*al-Film al-tasjily fi Misr*) is a useful collection of interviews and film critiques, featuring some of the most renowned filmmakers at the time. Also, *Studies in Moroccan Cinema* (*Abhath fi-l-sinima al-maghribiya*, 2001), by Mustafa al-Misnawi, is a thorough study of early Moroccan history until the 1990s, including documentary films but not focusing on them specifically.

The aforementioned major impediment to any study of the early stages of documentary in the region is the inaccessibility of much of what was produced before the digital age—that is, before the 1990s—including newsreels, information, propaganda, and educational films, as well as travelogues and more artistic or radical formats, such as direct cinema and film essays. Some films are considered to be exclusive state property, and are therefore often threatened by extinction, or have even disappeared altogether, due to the disastrous lack of film archiving in the region, which is usually related to war and conflict and/or inadequate state intervention. In one such sad account old films were sold off by the kilo when the Egyptian Studio Misr was nationalized, along with its biggest shareholder Banque Misr, in the 1960s (Mar'i 2003, 29). Luckily, some individual and pivotal works have been pirated and circulate today in low-quality copies online, for instance most of Omar Amiralay's films and those of other more recent Syrian directors, as well as works by Ali al-Ghazuli, Hashim al-Nahhas, Ahmed El Maanouni's film *Trances* (1981), and some of Hichem Ben Ammar or Nadia El Fani's films. Yet this should not mask the fact that many originals on celluloid, particularly public sector productions, are neither available for projection, nor have they been digitized properly (the latter process is in no way a substitute for sustainable film archiving). For instance, some of the Egyptian films discussed in this volume could not be brought to the Munich Film Museum for a screening. The copies the National Film Center in Cairo made available were digitized versions of poor VHS (!) copies of films originally shot on 35mm. It is much the same picture in Tunisia: the version of *Ezzitouna, in the Heart of Tunis* (1981) by Hmida Ben Ammar, which was projected at the Carthage Film Festival in 2017, was an incomplete, defective electronic television copy.

Anyone who wants to get an impression of the horrific state of some of the archives in the region should watch Suhaib Gasmelbari's (Qasam al-Bari) reportage for Aljazeera English *Sudan's Forgotten Films* (2017). It portrays 'Awwad and Benjamin, two Sudanese film veterans who have been fighting for years to preserve a collection of 13,000 copies—according to the film, the largest in Africa—originating before the Islamist turn and Omar al-Bashir's ascent to power in 1989. What Gasmelbari shows are stacks of dusty film rolls, some of which have simply disintegrated into powder. It is made clear that authorities are concerned neither with film nor with cinema archives. The veterans' pleas for rescue call out. Eventually, the two men themselves fall prey to administrative neglect; 'Awwad is fired, and Benjamin receives inadequate medical care at a public hospital and dies.

This is not to say that all is lost. In 2014, the Living Archive Project, initiated by the German Arsenal Institut für Film und Videokunst e.V., started with the restoration and digitization of films by Sudanese camera-man and documentary filmmaker Gadalla Gubara, who ran a private film studio from 1974 until its confiscation by al-Bashir's government (Arsenal 2014). Even though Gubara's cinematic vision falls short of that of some of his colleagues—most notably Suleiman Mohamed Ibrahim El-Nour and al-Tayyib al-Mahdi, initiators of the Sudan Film Club, who have received more attention recently with Suhaib Gasmelbari's documentary *Talking about Trees* (2019)—the necessity of preservation remains unquestionable.

The Sudanese example shows clearly the extent to which the ques-tion of film archives is linked and subject to governmental arbitrariness, authoritarian rule, and hegemonic policies. This applies also to the colo-nial period. As Mohamad Soueid illustrates in this volume (chapter two), the only surviving moving pictures from early twentieth-century Lebanon stem from foreign (European) lenses, and are clearly tainted by colonial and Orientalized visions of what the region looks like and stands for in Western imaginaries. This, however, has generated subsequent attempts at deconstructive counter-representations, and at reinterpreting the colo-nial archives. The most impressive cinematic attempts at this rewriting are discussed in this volume by Ahmed Bedjaoui and Ali Essafi (chapters six and seven), most notably Azzedine Meddour's *I Love You So Much* (*Kamm uhibbuk, Combien je vous aime*, 1985), and Assia Djebar's *The Zerda and Songs of Forgetting* (*al-Zarda wa aghani al-nisyan, La Zerda et les chants de l'oubli*, 1982) from Algeria, as well as *Memory 14* (*Dhakirat arba'at 'ashar, Mémoire 14*, 1971) by Ahmed Bouanani from Morocco. There are likely similar interventions that have been made in other countries in the region that are outside the scope of this volume.

Islands of History

To give a coherent summary of the overall development of documentary filmmaking in the region is an impossible undertaking for the reasons sketched out above, and, in the end, may even seem pretentious. For that reason I appreciate very much Laura Marks' Sufi-inspired metaphor of historical "enfolding and unfolding" (Marks 2015, 8). So much of our knowledge of history is masked over the course of time, and our attempts to recover or unfold some of it often result in new waves of enfolding, whether intentionally or not.

The spectrum of contemporary nonfiction films from the MENA region is huge, as can be seen from a cursory glance at the catalogs of many international and local festivals—their role within a transnational mediascape is analyzed in chapter nine, by Stefanie Van de Peer. Such works range from interventionist fly-on-the-wall, guerrilla-type filmmaking methods, to "expository" or rhetorical agitprop, as well as observational, poetic, performative, and self-reflexive modes—I have obviously borrowed Bill Nichols' (2001) terminology here—and more avant-garde approaches. More recently, autobiographical-inspired films, historical reenactments, and fake documentaries have completed the picture. The reasons for such diversity are certainly numerous and complex and invite a similarly wide range of theoretical considerations and methodological approaches that can only be touched upon in this volume. This is why I have chosen to ask a number of open questions in the following sections, rather than giving premature explanations.

One of the queries I would like to pose regards the correlation between the provisional categories mentioned above and specific historical periods, which has been discussed by writers like Eric Barnouw (1993), Bill Nichols (2001), Michael Chanan (2007), and many others with regard to Europe and filmmaking in the Americas. Yet, as other film historians have contended before me (Chanan; Bruzzi 2006; Renov 1993), such categories should be regarded as neither exhaustive nor self-explanatory. Moreover, to correlate them with specific periods in a sort of chronology of appearance as Nichols does—namely poetic, expository, observational, participatory, reflexive, and performative—is a mode of analysis that can be easily challenged. There is a question, for example, about whether the early newsreels (which appeared around 1910) weren't promotional, but in that sense were already expository. Robert Flaherty's staged documentaries also contained elements of ethnographic observation, while John Grierson's productions—for example Basil Wright's *Song of Ceylon* (1934)—were expository in motivation, but no less poetic in their realization. And, of course, Dziga Vertov's revolutionary *The Man with Movie Camera* (1929) seems to me as poetic and self-reflexive as it is performative.

Naturally, most of these categories would need to be more closely investigated in terms of how they were adopted in specific contexts in the MENA countries, and what motivated them. For, at their core, self-declared documentaries acknowledge two issues: firstly, how they use evidence and the indexical nature of the cinematographic image as an argument about history and reality, and secondly, how they resolve the basic dynamics of communication among subject, filmmaker, and audience. In the end, what counts is the motivation for the work, and the aesthetic tools deployed to either affirm or contradict projections of reality and the "truth."

With regard to the historical development of film in general I suspect that, in our region, nonfiction formats have developed similar traits to elsewhere, just perhaps in a temporally delayed manner (for instance, as I point out in my chapter, the British-inspired Egyptian documentary school started more than a decade later than its model). This observation, however, should not mislead us in assuming the same motivations or similar sociopolitical contexts. Many Egyptian documentarists who were trained by the British and admired John Grierson—the so-called architect of the British documentary movement of the 1930s—were at the same time nationalists, opposed to British domination, though they used the same cinematic means for their anticolonial and anti-imperialist counter-propaganda. This may also apply to a number of first-generation filmmakers from the Maghreb concerning their attitude toward their French colonizers, for example the Algerian Ahmed Rachedi and the Moroccan Ahmed Bouanani.

As for periodization: for the time being, I would like to suggest makeshift divisions based on film technology: firstly, the founding years during colonialism, when filmmaking (not so much exhibition) was mostly confined to Egypt and to the French-colonized Maghreb, to 35mm and extradiegetic sound; secondly, the era of national liberation, the anticolonial and pan-Arabist struggle up until 1970, the spread of portable light 16mm and synchronous sound equipment; thirdly, the advent of neoliberalism, television, beta cam and video; and fourthly, the end of the Cold War and the spread of new media in the 1990s, followed by the digital turn with new forms of aesthetics, transnational exchanges, and structures, including the advent of the Gulf region as a player in the field of media production (Shafik 2016, 249-258).

Within this protracted development, documentary filmmaking has been confronted by huge obstacles: colonial domination, lack of infrastructure and know-how, and later, appropriation by young nation-states and their ideologies, poor governmental planning, bureaucracy, censorship, and eventually a dependency on globalized international distribution circuits. This is not to deny or disregard local specificities, and the fact that Egypt, as the host of the first film industry in the region since the end of the 1920s, was able to conquer the film markets of its neighbors, whose "national" cinemas emerged, by and large, only after decolonization in the 1950s and 1960s. Egypt indeed attempted at first to engender a sort of anticolonial, state-sponsored film culture.

While numerous aspects of fiction film during the interwar period have been relatively well studied, there is still much to learn about the making and use of nonfiction, particularly newsreels, travelogues, and information and propaganda films, which were dominant at the time, at least in terms of their number and audience. Film pioneers like Albert Samama Chikly in Tunisia, and Mohammed Bayoumi—Egyptian cameraman, director, and founder of the Egyptian newsreel *Amun* (1923)—have already been well studied (Farid 1994; Disuqi and Hilmi 2010). Others, like Hassan Murad, a cameraman responsible for Egyptian newsreels from 1925 to 1970 (Mar'i 2003, 59), have received attention only lately (Farid 2003). Yasmin Desouki's contribution to this volume (chapter ten) focuses on the later stage of newsreel production in Egypt—that is, after independence—and investigates the role it played in cementing national identity.

No in-depth study of the British–Egyptian War Pictorial News, produced at Studio Misr from 1939 to 1945, has come to my attention so far. It would certainly be illuminating to learn more about this cooperation. The same applies to the Shell Film Unit, established in 1952 (al-Hadidi 1982, 26-7), and the Iraqi Oil Company film unit, active in the 1950s (al-Hadidi 1982, 171), mentioned also in Ali Abdulameer's chapter (three). The lack of reliable sources due to war and dictatorship is particularly evident in this case. Delving into British and European archives, in a manner similar to how Irit Neidhardt did for her contribution to this volume (chapter four) on the cooperation between the former GDR and the PLO (Palestinian Liberation Organization), can produce much useful information on motivations, scope, and the formats produced in these frameworks. The cooperation agreement between the Gulf States and Iraq in 1976 to create a body for the production of television programs and documentaries in Kuwait would likewise be interesting to investigate further.

According to Arabic publications, the first locally produced nonfiction films, dating back to 1912 (or possibly 1914–16), were set in a series produced by movie theater owner De Lagarne, titled *In the Streets of Alexandria (Fi shawari' al-Iskandaria)*, along with some promotional films (Mar'i 2003, 51; Farid 1984). Mohannad Ghawanmeh's contribution to this book on the reception of newsreels through the Egyptian film magazine *The Motion Pictures (al-Suwwar al-mutharikka)*, 1923–25, shows that much can also be discovered by sifting through the printed press. Such research might also be applied elsewhere. Ahmad Fayad al-Mufrajy compiled an inventory of all publications on cinema in Iraq, but little is known about their content and orientation (al-Mufrajy 1981). In chapter three of this volume, Abdulameer provides more detail about Iraq's vivid early film culture, even though some of its data needs to be cemented more through reliable archival sources.

Likewise, foreign, nongovernmental, and early amateur filmmaking has hardly been studied in the region. Film critic Ibrahim al-Ariss stated during a private conversation in November 1917 at the Carthage Film Festival that it is very likely that some of Lebanon's Armenian photographers may have also shot films in his homeland. Elsewhere, amateur filmmakers made an important contribution, for example Mohamed Osfour in Morocco from 1941 (al-Misnawi 2001, 48-50), and others in Kuwait as early as 1948 (al-Hadidi 1982, 163). These are all trails to interesting research that only few have followed thus far. While the silent era in North Africa was much more dominated by colonial cinema, and even became a center for colonial film production, to compete with the increasing popularity of U.S. and Egyptian cinema, and to enhance France's self-proclaimed humanist and civilizing mission (Bloom 2008, 151), there were also private enterprises. Some of the above, particularly fiction film, has been well studied by Maghrebi authors (Benali 1998); however, it would be of tremendous interest to learn more about the local impact of French colonial documentary, the raison d'être for which Bloom (2008) has already so well investigated.

There is no doubt that early documentary film in Algeria and Palestine was born out of the resistance movement for national liberation, as Ahmed Bedjaoui illustrates in chapter six. There are, however, also films made by engaged Western avant-gardists, some of which for instance may be considered part of a tradition of Jewish and Israeli voices critical of Israel that are still being silenced, as described by Hanan Toukan in chapter 16. A recent Palestinian essay film by Mohanad Yaqubi, *Off Frame: Revolution Until Victory* (*Kharij al-itar aw thawra hatta al-nassr*, 2015), presents some of the most remarkable so-called solidarity films involved in shaping a "revolutionary" discourse of Palestinian liberation. A similar militantism was underway with regard to female liberation, as shown in *The Hour of Liberation Has Arrived* (*Sa'at al-tahrir daqqat*, 1974), by Lebanese filmmaker Heiny Srour. Another example is Selma Baccar, whose state-produced film *Fatma 75* (1975) was banned by authorities, according to Mathilde Rouxel's argument in this volume (chapter seventeen), because it contradicted official representations of former president Habib Bourguiba as the first liberator of women in Tunisia (see also Van de Peer, 2018).

After independence, documentary in most MENA countries developed within the embrace of the young nation-states, economically as well as ideologically. Public or semi-public sectors were introduced in Syria, Iraq, Egypt, Tunisia, and Algeria (not in Lebanon). They monopolized the industry at different stages, whether in totality or just in the production of fiction or nonfiction films, and had similarities to the socialist model. Contrary to what we might think, however, top-down decisions and implementation were often haphazard, and came sometimes only after pressure from below, namely from the filmmaking community itself. What the exact conditions were, what role nonfiction production played in each context, and what purpose it served over the years, remains to be learned in more detail.

These institutions also had different legacies, which were reflected in their varying involvements in the field. The state-run Moroccan CCM (Centre Cinématographique Marocain), founded in 1944, was inherited from the colonial administration (al-Misnawi 2001, 53). It continued to cater to foreign productions orientalizing Morocco for years after independence, rather than fostering a genuine film culture (al-Misnawi 2001, 36). Thus, the creativity of a whole generation of talented and critical Moroccan filmmakers was stalled. Among them was Ahmed Bouanani, whose still unpublished manuscript of a first history of Moroccan cinema is discussed in this volume by Ali Essafi (chapter seven). Bouanani's study helped discover cinematic gems like Mohamed Afify's film essay *Return to Agadir* (*al-'Awda illa Aghadir*, 1967). Unlike the Sudanese case mentioned earlier, this at least is a success story, as the manuscript has enabled the rediscovery of some amazing films and filmmakers from the 1960s—archived by the CCM, presented in a retrospective at the Berlinale in 2017, and lauded in Essafi's documentary *The Seventh Gate* (*al-Bawaba al-sabi'a*, 2017).

Works from the 1960s and 1970s—not just in Morocco, but also in Tunisia—are still waiting to be studied in greater depth, such as the ethnographic films by Sophie Ferchiou, for instance *The Mistresses of Agriculture* (*Rabbat al-manzil fi-l-fillaha*, Les Ménagères de l'agriculture, 1975), touched upon in chapter seventeen by Mathilde Rouxel. Subsequent important and prolific Tunisian documentary filmmakers have said that Ferchiou's films had great influence on their own practice, for example Hichem Ben Ammar (private conversation, November 2016). This era saw the creation of a number of bodies interested in adopting the documentary format. Iraqi officials, and a number of filmmakers from Egypt, Syria, and Iraq, among others, were backed by the Leipzig Film Festival (GDR) in 1975, during the foundation of the Arab Documentary Film Association (Ittihad al-Tasjiliyyin al-'Arab) (al-Hadidi 1982, 171; Abd al-Fattah 2014, 40). Some of these filmmakers came from a leftist background and were placed under state scrutiny, like the Egyptian Fouad al-Tuhamy (Abd al-Fattah 2014, 38). Generally, dissident and innovative filmmakers have had to cope with direct and indirect censorship and state paternalism, among other ailments such as clientelism, bureaucracy, and a general lack of resources, if they wanted to achieve anything within the confines of the given system. Possibilities to escape these restrictions have been found through economic independence, and/or looking for alternative financing sources, such as foreign (largely European) funding, television, or civil society—options that emerged more strongly in the 1980s.

Filmmakers who opted for these solutions appeared in the 1970s and 1980s. They also embraced new film technologies (16mm and mobile synchronous sound recording), which in turn paved the way to a more observational or participatory style. Egyptian filmmaker Attiat El-Abnoudi was probably the first filmmaker from her country to acquire her own 16mm equipment. She resorted to European coproduction and the support of a number of NGOs to be able to finance her films. Syrian Omar Amiralay did similarly in the second phase of his career, when he started making films for French television, such as antenne2. Ahmad Izzo's chapter (twenty-six) details Amiralay's complicated and critical relationship to the state, which was at the same time the financier of his two early masterpieces, *Everyday Life in a Syrian Village* (*Haya yawmiya fi qarya suriya*, 1974) and *The Chickens* (*al-Dajaj*, 1977).

Others, like Tahani Rached and Safaa Fathy from Egypt, who were or still are based abroad, have relied almost entirely on their host countries, in this case Canada and France, in the production of their documentaries. The same applies to other diasporic filmmakers, among others the Palestinian directors Michel Khleifi, Norma Marcos, Rashid Masharawi, and Kamal Aljafari, and the Tunisian Mustapha Hasnaoui. Algerian filmmakers generally became dependent on France during the 1990s, after the outbreak of the civil war. Today's most acknowledged Algerian documentarist, Malek Bensmail, whose work is discussed by Peter Limbrick in chapter nineteen, is based abroad, as is Moroccan director Hakim Belabbes, whose cinematic vision in and on displacement is referred to by Stefan Pethke (chapter twenty-seven). Another reason for filmmakers to seek foreign coproduction is because of forced or self-chosen exile as a result of war or occupation, like in the Palestinian and now Syrian case. Lebanese filmmakers, such as Heiny Srour, Jocelyne Saab, and Maroun Baghdadi, left because of the civil war that erupted in 1973.

Unlike in Germany, France, and the United Kingdom, where certain public TV channels, such as ZDF, la sept, or Channel 4, played a major role in supporting and producing creative documentaries—whether on the national or transnational level—most national broadcasters in the Arab world did little or nothing to produce or air critical or innovative films, with the sole and laudable exception of Algerian ENPA, or more recently 2M (Moroccan TV). The introduction of transnational Arab TV channels in the 1990s, most notably Al Jazeera and MBC, gave rise to the launch of specific documentary channels, boosting production, but confined largely to TV reportage and didactic infotainment.

The acceleration of digital technology led to a steep reduction in production costs and so, I suspect, contributed to the spread of independent video art or experimental works, as well as deconstructive, subjective, and self-reflexive approaches. Akram Zaatari, interviewed in this volume by Dore Bowen (chapter twenty-four), along with others like Mona Hatoum, Walid Raad, Lamia Joreige, Hassan Khan, Wael Shawky, 'Ammar El-Beik, Mounir Fatoumi, and Bouchra Khalili, have been partly discussed in *Hanan al-Cinema* (2015) by Laura Marks, and testify to a wealth of experiences. The conceptual ideas of these media artists certainly need to spread more among filmmaking communities because of their inspiring, innovative, and deconstructive approaches.

At the same time, the Gulf region, particularly the United Arab Emirates and Qatar, has started developing its audiovisual sectors further, by establishing festivals, coproduction markets, and film funds, and adding to already existing private training initiatives created in the 1990s in Egypt and Lebanon—Semat and Beirut DC. Other collectives followed in the wake of the Arab rebellion or earlier, like Idioms Film (Palestine), Rufy's, FigLeaf, Hassala, and Mosireen (Egypt), and Abun-addara (Syria). Due, among other factors, to these initiatives, and to the new funding opportunities available during and after the so-called Arab Spring, a proliferation of documentary film production occurred, with Tunisia a prime example, as the chapter (five) by Nouri Gana exemplifies. In exceptional cases, documentaries even ended up in movie theaters, like *The Jews of Egypt* (*'An yahud Misr*, 2013) by Amir Ramsis in Egypt (Shafik 2016, 222). This, however, is a rare exception. As Kay Dickinson and Viviane Saglier show in chapter eight of this volume, the complicated interplay between international politics and regional funding institutions at times has placed film and its producers in situations of having to cater to hegemonic power struggles of representation, as is the case with the virulent issue of immigration and refugee existence, instead of responding to the needs of their own regional audiences.

The extent to which documentary film, its topics, and its aesthetics may be tied to these kinds of representational, racialized, and confessional struggles is examined in Ella Shohat's contribution (chapter fifteen), which focuses largely on Zionist politics and questions of Jewish–Arab identity in film. These kinds of struggles are also reflected in pivotal works of the Western avant-garde, as the chapters by Oraib Toukan and Hanan Toukan show in deconstructing, among others, Godard's and Susan Sontag's films on Palestine (chapters fourteen and sixteen respectively).

By compiling these contributions, this volume seeks to address a variety of topical film-theoretical questions, for instance: transnational identities in music documentaries by Maghrebi women filmmakers, tackled by Florence Martin (chapter twenty); opacity as a means of cinematic deconstruction and as a response to a situation of occupation, as proposed by Nadia Yaqub (chapter twenty-five), and the use of the voice-over and its questionable association to didactism and authoritarianism, which I discuss myself (chapter eleven).

Ahmed Bedjaoui investigates the documentary effect of fiction films in chapter six. So does Hend Alawadhi in her analysis of two correlated films on AIDS in Egypt, one fiction and one documentary, in chapter twelve. Shohini Chaudhuri has taken the opportunity to study slow cinema by looking closely at one Iraqi documentary in chapter twenty-nine, while Alisa Lebow has used her analysis of contemporary Egyptian first-person documentaries to investigate the triangle of revolution, subjectivity, and the collective in chapter thirteen. And last but not least, what are the limits that the web—formerly regarded as a democratizing medium—poses to the representation of a just cause, as in the case of the Syrian revolution? Donatella Della Ratta asks this question critically in chapter twenty-two. Complimenting this study, Jamal Bahmad (chapter twenty-one) has examined the online practices of a politically mobilized rural Amazigh community, which, in cooperation with Moroccan filmmaker Nader Bouhmouch, has added a new word to our vocabulary: "artivism."

I am sure there is still a lot more out there in the film histories of the areas south and east of the Mediterranean that is waiting to be explored further.

Transcriptions and Film Dates

Finally, I need to add a few practical remarks for the reader. Arabic transcription in this volume follows the *IJMES* (*International Journal of Middle Eastern Studies*) transcription standard, without any diacritics. It applies this system also to Amazigh (Berber) names, using their most common Arabic transcriptions to avoid any confusion. Generally all film titles are either translated into English or represented by the most common English title. The original titles, if in Arabic, have been transcribed once and placed in parentheses upon first mention. The same applies to names. Particularly in the case of North African productions, French titles are mentioned either alternatively, in case of the absence of an Arabic original title, or in addition to it, to facilitate the tracing of films. Moreover, original film titles are normally accompanied by the year of production or release (which are at times difficult to distinguish). In some exceptional cases, such as in Abdulameer's article on Iraqi documentary, not all dates could be identified due to the nature of the available sources.

References

Abd al-Fattah, Muhammad. 2014. *Fu'ad al-Tuhami: dhikrayat la mudhakkirat*. Cairo: Sunduq al-Tanmiyya al-Thaqafiyya.

Abu Shady, Ali. 1980. *al-Film al-tasjily fi Misr*. Cairo: al-Thaqafa al-Jamahiriyya.

Arsenal. 2014. "The Film Holdings of Gadalla Gubara." *Arsenal Institute for Film and Video*. arsenal-berlin.de.

'Atallah, Mahmud Sami. 2010. *al-Sinima al-tasjiliya fi-l-watan al-'arabi*. Cairo: al-Majlis al-A'la li-l-Thaqafa.

Barnouw, Eric. 1993. *Documentary: A History of the Non-Fiction Film*. New York: Oxford University Press.

Benali, Abdelkader. 1998. *Le cinéma colonial au Maghreb*. Paris: CERF.

Bloom, Peter. 2008. *French Colonial Cinema: Mythologies of Humanitarianism*. Minneapolis: University of Minnesota Press.

Bruzzi, Stella. 2006. *New Documentary*. London: Routledge.

Chanan, Michael. 2007. *The Politics of Documentary*. London: Palgrave Macmillan.

Dabashi, Hamid, ed. 2006. *Dreams of a Nation*. London: Verso.

Della Ratta, Donatella. 2018. *Shooting a Revolution: Visual Media and Warfare in Syria*. London: Pluto Press.

Dissuqi, Ibrahim, and Sami Hilmi. 2010. *al-Sinima al-misriya al-samitta al-watha'iqiya/al-tasjiliya (1897–1930)*. Cairo: al-Majlis al-a'la li-l-Thaqafa.

Downey, Anthony, ed. 2014. *Uncommon Grounds: New Media and Critical Practices in North Africa and the Middle East*. London: I.B. Tauris.

Farid, Samir. 1984. "Naissance et développement du cinéma égyptien (1922–1970)." In *À propos du cinéma égyptien*, edited by Khémaïs Khayati, Tahar Chériaa, and Robert Daudelin. Québec: Les dossiers de la cinémathèque, no. 13. collections.cinematheque.qc.ca.

———. 1994. *Safahat majhula min tarikh al-sinima al-misriya*. Cairo: al-Majlis al-A'la li-l-Thaqafa.

———. 2003. *al-Sinima al-tasjiliya: ihtifal fi-l-dhikra al-ma'awiya li-mawlid Hasan Murad*. Alexandria: Bibliotheca Alexandrina.

Framework: The Journal of Cinema and Media. 2002. Special edition, 43(2).

Ginsberg, Terri and Chris Lippard eds. 2020. *Cinema of the Arab World. Contemporary Directions in Theory and Practice*. London: Palgrave Macmillan.

al-Hadidi, Mona Sa'id. 1982. *al-Sinima al-tasjiliya al-watha'iqiya fi Misr wa-l-'alam al-'arabi*. Cairo: Dar al-Fikr al-'Arabi.

al-Hady, Khalil. 2012. *al-Sinima al-watha'iqiya al-Tunissiya wa-l-'alamiya*. Tunis: Dar Afaq.

Hassan, Ilhamy. 1976. *Tarikh al-sinima al-misriya*. Cairo: Matbu'at al-Jadid.

Hillauer, Rebecca. 2005. *Encyclopedia of Arab Women Filmmakers*. Cairo: AUC Press.

Lebow, Alisa, ed. 2012. *The Cinema of Me: The Self and Subjectivity in First Person Documentary*. New York: Columbia University Press/Wallflower.

Limbrick, Peter. 2012. "From the Interior: Space, Time and Queer Discursivity." In *The Cinema of Me*, edited by Alisa Lebow, 98–120. New York: Wallflower.

Mar'i, Diya'. 2003. *Tarikh al-sinima al-tasjiliya fi Misr*. Alexandria: Bibliotheca Alexandrina.

Marks, Laura. 2015. *Hanan al-Cinema: Affections for the Moving Image*. Cambridge: MIT Press.

al-Misnawi, Mustafa. 2001. *Abhath fi-l-sinima al-maghribiya*. Casablanca: al-Zamman.

al-Mufrajy, Ahmad Fayad. 1981. *Masadir dirasat al-nashat al-sinima'y fi-l-'Iraq 1968–1979*. Beirut: al-Mu'assasa al-'Arabiya li-l-Dirasat wa-l-Nashr.

al-Nahhas, Hashim. 1990. *Mustaqbal al-sinima al-tasjiliya fi Misr*. Cairo: al-Markaz al-Qawmi li-l-Sinima.

Nichols, Bill. 2001. *Introduction to Documentary*. Bloomington: Indiana University Press

Renov, Michael. 1993. *Toward a Poetics of Documentary*. In *Theorizing Documentary*, edited by Michael Renov, 12–36. London: Routledge.

Rouxel, Mathilde, and Stefanie Van de Peer. 2021. *ReFocus: The Films of Jocelyne Saab*. Edinburgh: Edinburgh University Press.

Rouxel, Mathilde. 2015. *Jocelyne Saab – La mémoire indomptée*. Beirut: Dar An-Nahar.

al-Sabah. 2017. *Fadhil Khalil wa ta'sis ittihad al-tasjiliyyin al-'arab*. November 2.

Salti, Rasha, and Gabrielle Chomentowski. 2018. *Saving Bruce Lee: African and Arab Cinema in the Era of Soviet Cultural Diplomacy*. Berlin: Haus der Kulturen der Welt.

Shafik, Viola. 2016. *Arab Cinema: History and Cultural Identity*. Cairo: AUC Press.

Toukan, Hanan. 2017. "Music, Border, and the Sensorial Politics of Displacement in Jumana Manna's 'A Magical Substance Flows into Me.'" *Jerusalem Quarterly* 67. 117–23.

Valassopoulos, Anastasia, ed. 2013. *Arab Cultural Studies: History, Politics and the Popular*. New York: Routledge.

Van de Peer, Stefanie. 2018. *Negotiating Dissidence: The Pioneering Women of Arab Documentary*. Edinburgh: Edinburgh University Press.

Wessels, Joshka. 2019. *Documenting Syria. Film-making, Video Activism and Revolution*. London: I.B. Tauris.

Westmoreland, Mark. 2009. *Post-Orientalist Aesthetics: Experimental Film and Video in Lebanon*. Rochester: University of Rochester Press.

Yaqub, Nadia. 2018. *Palestinian Cinema in the Days of Revolution*. Austin: University of Texas Press.

1

TRACING EARLY NEWS CINEMA THROUGH THE PAGES OF EGYPTIAN MAGAZINE *AL-SUWAR AL-MUTAHARRIKA*

Mohannad Ghawanmeh

The newsfilm is the longest-lived topos of Egyptian nonfiction cinema during the silent era. Thus, I find it generative to explore how this form of nonfiction cinema in Egypt set the stage for the production of narrative films, works that would stand for the Egyptian film industry in the cultural imaginary and in pervasive film histories of the Egyptian cinema's classical era. Further, our perceptions of modern history can be enriched through acquiring greater knowledge about the early newsfilms, even if we cannot watch most of its representative works because they have been lost. The titles of the newsfilms made and exhibited in Egypt during the country's first two years of nominally independent nationhood indicate which events mattered to audiences, or which were at least expected to matter to them according to the producers and exhibitors of newsfilms, during the nationally momentous years of 1923–25.

This chapter traces the history of newsfilm production and exhibition as it relates to Egypt, by rigorously examining *al-Suwar al-mutaharrika (Motion Pictures)*, the first Arabic-language cinema magazine, for its coverage of news cinema and its reception of this form. The magazine's publication began in 1923 and concluded in 1925, the year of the founding of the Misr Company for Acting and Cinema (Sharikat Misr li-l-tamthil wa-l-sinima), a subsidiary

1.1. Cover of the first issue of *al-Suwwar al-mutaharrika (Motion Pictures)*, the first cinema magazine in Arabic, May 10, 1923.

19

incorporated as one of the companies of the Banque Misr companies (Sharikat Banque Misr). The Misr Company for Acting and Cinema pursued varied production and coproduction interests and projects, but sputtered for a decade, before an unprecedented capital investment relocated it, in 1935, from its original location on the second floor of the Misr Printing Company building to the relatively mighty Studio Misr, a bona fide studio, large and equipped to undertake all phases of filmmaking at a rate that deserves the ascription *industrial*.

Newsfilms, Newsreels and the Appeal of Illusory Proximity

Before embarking on a historical analysis of the news cinema of the silent era in Egypt, a rich and vital history, I wish to clarify the object of this examination conceptually and linguistically. This is important for a readership that may have never experienced such cinema, considering it is a lapsed form at this point in history. The term *newsfilm* came into use in 1915, to describe a form of nonfiction, event-capturing short film. Prior to this, it had been referred to as the "topical"(Peterson 2012, 283), though the term would remain current as a synonym to newsfilm, as reflected in the name of one of the major British newsreels: *Topical Budget* (1911–31) (McKernan, n.d.). A 1921 British guide to the film industry, cannily titled *The Film Industry*, introduces topical films by mentioning that they are not in need of explanation, since they are familiar to all who go to the cinema, adding, "They are pictorial records of the important topical events taking place in all parts of the world."[1]

If a newsreel is a publication, then a newsfilm may be considered an issue, or more likely a story within an issue. Yet, instead of "newsreel," which was in use titularly and descriptively by 1921, the British guide opts for "screen newspapers," a term I have not encountered in English elsewhere, but one that I find curious, considering that *journal*, "newspaper" in French, had been used to name the very first and instantly popular *Pathé Journal*, which debuted in Egypt in its first year of publication, 1908 (Abu Shadi 2004, 12)[2] The precedence of *Pathé Journal* in Egypt may explain why *jarida*,[3] Arabic for "newspaper," is the term I have seen most frequently in popular and fan press coverage, and in advertisements for screenings placed in these publications by Egyptian exhibitors, during the silent era.

The Film Industry also alerts its reader that the major screen newspapers publish distinct editions in different countries.[4] Indeed, a variety of newsreels, possibly even multiple editions from the same producer, screened in Egypt. Topicals and newsfilms that were not a part of newsreels, as they commonly were not, screened in large and coastal cities, to be sure, but also in smaller cities and towns, such as Tanta and Shubra. Moreover, where relevant to the central discussion of newsfilms, I note education films or episodes of film magazines, which were serial like newsreels, but concerned with covering general-interest subjects instead of events.[5]

Newsfilms date back to the second month following the arrival of the cinema in Egypt. The first screening took place in Alexandra, on November 5, 1896, and was carried out by Lumière photographer/projectionist/emissary Henri Dello Strologo. On December 9, 1896, Strologo screened in Cairo the newsfilm *Procession to the Wedding of Princess Maud* (original title: *Cortège au mariage de la princesse Maud*, 1896), in Hammam Schneider, where the first cinema screening in Cairo had taken place on November 28.[6] The newsfilm had arrived early and would become a mainstay, thriving at first-, second- and third-run venues.

I have located in American exhibition trade magazines the crux of the sales pitch made to exhibitors by newsfilm producers and distributors—prestige. The very word appears in advertisements for two of the most established producers, Gaumont and Pathé. In the first issue in 1920 of the weekly *Exhibitors Herald*, the Chicago-based distributor Celebrated Players Film Corporation placed a full-page advertisement that boasts "prestige" in larger font than any of the other verbiage on the page, separated from the rest of the text near the top of the page, below which is the boast: "The best theatres in Chicago, New York, London, Paris—throughout the entire world—show the *Gaumont News Service*. No matter what other picture is on the program, any theatre will add PRESTIGE by showing Gaumont News and Graphic. *The News Reels and Real News*" (original caps and italics).[7]

In a 1925 issue of the New York weekly *Exhibitor's Trade Review*, there is a similar illustrated advertisement. Mostly made up of a color painting of a cinematographer taking footage, from a propeller plane bannered "PATHÉ NEWS" [original caps], of military ships sailing in caravan below, a relatively small text box below the drawing reads, "It rivals the newspapers in its swift generation of the news. For many years the standard of film quality. Undoubtedly the best-known motion picture in the world. With it you buy prestige that means better business and more profits; and a service that is truly incomparable. ONE REEL TWICE A WEEK."[8] Prestige as pitch was common in promoting an assortment of facets integral to the cinema industry—from production houses, to shopfront designs, to movie stars. Nevertheless, prestige made sense in justifying arguably the most serious of popular film forms, fiction and non—the newsfilm. Moreover, whereas the cinema in the United States was derided for its vulgarity or frivolity, in Egypt these criticisms accompanied suspicions of foreign influence on Egyptian values.[9] Newsfilms perhaps stood out as serious offerings that appealed to concerned national and world citizens, the very citizenry that a modernizing and industrializing Egypt wished to cultivate, as did cinemas vying for respectability. Audiences likely did not go for newsfilms in order to leave cinemas feeling more prestigious. Rather, they sought proximity to personages and topical events, people they could never see up close and personal, and places they could not afford the time or expense to visit. This appeal was not lost on at least one Egyptian cultural observer: "Cinematic newspapers have created a significant facet that has made connecting with the greats, simple and available to all, for it has shortened the distance between us and them and has made us view them as if they were near us" (Jum'a 1930, 234).

Beside prestige, Pathé's advertisement above promises exhibitors something that has come up in my research as a point of appeal for audiences as well—speed of news delivery. Producers may have wished to churn out newsfilms as swiftly and regularly as daily newspapers, but never managed to do so on a sustained basis,[10] nor was their ambition helped by the success of radio, the first broadcast of which began in 1924 in Egypt (Stanton 2012, 355), a nation that at the turn of the century enjoyed several dailies in multiple languages.

There is no reason to think that the programming windowing typical for the three tiers of exhibitors—first, second, and third—did not apply to newsfilms as it did to fiction titles. It was moreover a custom, at least in Britain, to discount newsfilms every few days, so that exhibitors, including those in Egypt, may have been motivated to hold off on newly available newsfilms. Nevertheless, speedy delivery could only heighten interest in a newsfilm based on a dated event, as evidenced by the proprietor of the *Cinematograph Pathé* in Alexandria announcing to the press a new contract signed with the mother company, allowing his cinema to receive and exhibit newsfilms no later than eight days after their screening in Paris. According to Ahmad al-Hadari, newsfilms particularly appealed to European residents during the war, because they illustrated events that they had probably only read or heard about (al-Hadari 1987, 128). I have located advertisements for two Egyptian exhibitors, dating to the First World War, that include a newsfilm relating to the Great War. The first is *Handing Out Medals to Heroes of the Battle of Verdun*, screened in Cairo's Cinematograph Shedovar, whose site was Salle Kléber, dated March 1917.[11] The second is *Britain's Bulwarks, No. 11: The Duke of Connaught Visits the Western Front* (titled Ziyarat sahib al-sumuw al-muluki al-Duke of Connaught li-Faransa, 1918), screened in Cairo's Cinema Ideal.[12] How could newsfilms not have thrived during the Great War when they were so well suited by their format to propaganda, for these productions reported on particular current events in a selective manner. British imperial authorities were concerned with which films were exhibited in Egypt, and they were subjected to the censor's scrutiny, first by way of inspecting a given print upon its arrival at

Egyptian customs, then by instructing police to monitor them as they were exhibited in houses of entertainment (Ali 2008b, 200–202).

Following the Great War, newsfilm production would flourish in Egypt, as evidenced by the number of domestically produced titles over the course of the 1920s.[13] Moreover, cinemas in Egypt continued to exhibit newsfilms after the war, as seen in the pages of the short-lived Egyptian cinema magazine *Motion Pictures*.

Newsfilms as reported in *Motion Pictures*

Nonfiction films, including newsfilms, were certainly not discussed in the press in the 1920s and early 1930s as much as their fictional counterparts. More specifically, it was the stars of the cinema and theater, mostly foreign but also domestic, whose news and images took up the greatest space in popular and fan publications. Nevertheless, newsfilms appeared regularly in exhibitor advertisements, enabling us to glean some idea of the presence of this form in the exhibition industry, which by then comprised over fifty cinemasnationwide.[14]

I have endeavored to identify exhibited titles. Common and contentious was the custom of showing features in parts over successive weeks, so that a film advertised and denoted "part four," for example, would not necessarily mean the fourth film in a series as produced. In addition, exhibitors often translated titles they screened inaccurately, and at times renamed them deliberately, so as to better appeal to local targeted audiences (al-Hadari 1987, 125). A notable example is the programmed newsreel advertisement for *Jaridat al-barq*[15] in *The Domestic/Indigenous Cosmograph (al-Kusmugraf al-ahli)*,[16] a nationalist response to the American Cosmograph cinemas that had opened in Alexandria and Cairo in 1913 (al-Hadari 1987, 121). Al-Ahli Cosmograph screened the *Jaridat al-barq*, which turned out to be the name lent to the French *Éclair* newsreel, for a couple of months before switching to the mighty Pathé newsreel in July.[17]

Ahmad al-Hadari reports the screening of a number of domestic newsfilms in 1922. He qualifies that he was able, however, to find details about one, details restricted to the event captured—*King Fouad's Visit to al-Azhar Mosque (Ziyarat al-malik Fu'ad li-l-jami' al-Azhar)*. Otherwise, al-Hadari provides no more than names: *Alexandria (Iskandariya)*, *On the Shores of the Nile ('Ala difaf al-Nil)*, *The Great City of Egypt (al-Madina al-'azima fi Misr)*, *From Cairo to the Pyramids (Min al-Qahira ila al-Ahram)*, and *The Vesture Caravan and the Mahmal's Travel (Mawkib al-kiswa wa safar al-mahmal)* (*mahmal* being the apparatus used to transport the Kaaba's cover, *al-kiswa*) (al-Hadari 1987, 161). The last of these may well have been one of the titles included in an advertisement for domestic films in *Motion Pictures*, published nearly a year after the film's initial release. The advertisement is not for a particular venue's program, but for three films said to comprise "the first Egyptian reel made by Egyptian hands," under the heading "To Egyptians."

The advertisement and the films it names were likely the work of Egyptian film pioneer Mohammed Bayoumi, not least because his name appears elsewhere in the very same issue of the magazine, as a member of the newly elected board of directors of the recently established *Motion Pictures* Club (Nadi al-Suwar al-Mutaharrika). Bayoumi refers to himself as the first Egyptian filmmaker in his papers and in reference to his newsfilm, *The Nation Welcomes Saad Zaghloul (Tarhib al-umma al-misriyya bi-istiqbal al-ra'is Sa'd Zaghlul Basha)*, into the beginning of which he inserts a card: "The first reel managed and made by an Egyptian national."[18] In addition to *The Vesture Caravan and the Mahmal's Travel*, identified as *The Mahmal's Travel (Safar al-mahmal)* in the advertisement,[19] there is the mention of two films—*Visit by Lord Headly and His Colleagues to Cairo (Ziyarat al-Lord Headly wa zumala'ih li-l-Qahira)*, and *The Mahmal's Return Without Performing the Hajj ('Awdat al-mahmal bidun ta'diyat faridat al-hajj)*, which is the title of a Bayoumi film.[20] It would seem that Bayoumi had decided to advertise in the same magazine that had successfully launched a cinema club, the first meeting of which had been held a mere nine days prior to the operative edition's publication, and on whose all-Arab board of directors Bayoumi sat.[21] The advertisement promises that the reels[22] in question would be screened along with superlative "tales" (*riwaya*, a term used to mean novel, play, and fiction film), then concludes in relatively large print, "So wait and watch and judge." A follow-up advertisement confirms the exhibition venue for these "Egyptian reels"—Cinema Magic, located in the famed theater and entertainment district of Emad al-Din Street—for two nonfiction films, presumably Egyptian—*Crossing the Gulf (Qat' al-Khalij)* and *Scene of the Festival's Rockets (Manzar sawarikh al-mahrajan)* (*Motion Pictures*, August 30, 1923, 24).

Bayoumi's endeavor was opportune, for Egyptians had already been expressing resentment over their country's depiction in Western films. Because of the ostensible veracity and authenticity of nonfiction films, such imports were subjected to more biting censure than narrative Western films. A unique mode of analysis that I have encountered in examining pages of *Motion Pictures* is that of the reception of reception. In most cases, readers wrote to the film magazine to convey frustration with what they had learned from the mighty daily *al-Ahram* about Egypt's depiction in Western films. In one case, the complaint was over a newsfilm—*What Egypt Offers*. In the regular feature "Around the World," a letter from a reader using the moniker "Who is about to Disown . . ." appears in full, supplanting the typical collection of around-the-world trivia blurbs. As

had become typical, the feature begins with its editor's lead-in, informing readers that the letter has been published so that they may deliberate
about it. The letter itself, originating in Milwaukee, and dated December 15, 1923, opens with an alert to the frigid conditions from where the
author writes, indicating temperature and snowfall in Imperial measure-
ments (degrees Fahrenheit and feet), thereby denoting the foreignness of
the account. The appalled reader goes on to mention that, having noticed
in a cinema's program a film featuring the most recent news from Egypt,
he rushed to attend, hoping it might assuage his longing and warm his
insides. The reader identifies the film as a Pathé title, *What Egypt Offers:
Tanta, Egypt. Celebration of the Birthday of Sayed El-Babawi* [sic], referring to
the Sufi saint al-Sayyid al-Badawi, then describes the newsfilm's content:
*gallabiya*s, turbans, and Sufi (specifically Shadhili) worship circles. The correspondent expresses particular disdain ("may God uglify her face") for
a fallahi dancer, "one of those who cadge in the streets," whose body is
covered in reflective copper ornaments, shaking her belly as she dances,
a barefoot boy blowing an arghul at her side. The correspondent alerts
readers to the meaning of *offer* in the film's title, that it entails the best that
Egyptians have. The appalled correspondent concludes with repudiation:

> I cannot describe my embarrassment and was about to disown Egypt,
> the Egyptian who shot these scenes if he was Egyptian, and the one
> who permitted such a film to leave Egypt. I thanked God that I
> entered without any of my American friends who know my national-
> ity, so does this please you? And is this all there is in Egypt? (*Motion
> Pictures*, January 17, 1924, 23)

As early as the beginning of the 1920s, we may note a sensitivity for
an identified mode of representing Egypt in Western cinema—an exoticized, Orientalized one. How could Egyptians trust declarations by
Western authorities about their interest in developing Egypt, in aiding its
modernization, when their countries' cinemas continually exhibited little
interest in a modernizing Egypt? Western newsfilms could be indicted in
this regard more than other forms of nonfiction film, and certainly more
than fiction cinema, because the form was concerned with development a
priori. Why were Western newsfilms about Egypt predominantly about
old news? Producing a film about the celebration of a saint's birthday does
appear to comport with the impetus for news cinema, because its title
refers to an event, but a film like *What Egypt Offers* must have struck Egyptian viewers as hardly different from the travelogues and education films
that Western producers made about Egypt, since all three forms favored
similar subject matter.

Another instance of the reception of reception marks an issue of *Motion Pictures* a few months prior to the published letter above. In a remark published in the "*Motion Pictures* Parliament," under the title "Propaganda Against Egypt," a reader writes:

> I read in *al-Ahram* newspaper on August 21 an article by this title about a cinematograph film exhibited in London by the name of *The Streets of Cairo*. These streets were among our filthiest streets and meanest, showing the filthy side, neglected and lacking care, showing our blind and wretched men. How long am I to remain silent about such works. and why do we not fight them by directing films that depict our civility and civilization whereby they would know the degree of our advancement? (*Motion Pictures*, September 13, 1923, 21)

This Fox release was slated among a year's worth of "educational and instructional" films ("Special Sales Force" 1922, 1). Such an ascription would have hardly impressed Egyptian readers and viewers, who questioned the interest in showing images of Cairo's sordid streets. Having lived through the 1919 Revolution only a few years prior to this, a revolution that had delivered (nominal) independence, they might have conjectured that such a film served the argument that Egyptians were incapable of keeping their streets clean, let alone effectively running their nation. Egyptian readers might also have surmised that Western film production companies were keen to promote their own nations indirectly, by showcasing the wretchedness of others. No wonder readers of *Motion Pictures* wrote to the magazine to voice their support for a domestic production effort with invocations of Egyptian independence, empowerment, and

1.2. Special report on newsreels in *al-Suwar al-mutaharrika*

advancement. A reader named Ali Isma'il, who wrote in from Mansura, articulated the vague desire—explicit or implicit—in many of the calls for preparing Egyptians to produce their own films—"so that Egypt appears in its true appearance." The reader did not go on to describe what such an appearance may entail, but it was evidently not what was being depicted in Western films as a matter of course.[23]

As if in response to letters from disgruntled readers about newsfilms, *Motion Pictures* published a one-and-a-half-page essay on the cinematic form titled "What Do You Love about the News of Newsreels?" It began by affirming the valuation of newsfilms by audiences, whose viewing of them "fulfills the cinema-going experience," even though newsreels and newsfilms are not advertised in and of themselves. Rather, audiences find appeal in these motion pictures based on the news stories they present, the article contends. The best-known newsreels produced in the United States, according to the essay, are *Pathé*, *International* (produced by Universal), *Fox*, *Kinograms*, and *Paramount*; in France, *Gaumont* and *Éclair*. The piece singles out *Pathé*, *Selznick* (a Canadian newsreel), and *International* for having captured singular and especially important events. It then informs the reader of the challenges involved in capturing royalty-centered events, particularly negotiating their fear and distrust of photography, and the protocols for photographing maritime events, which entail oversight and censorship by the militaries involved. These newsfilms about maritime activity had been particularly popular during the Great War, the article states, before reporting on the popularity of newsfilms about sports, singling out football, because, it notes, the feats recorded will have been actual, unlike in narrative films. Also popular was reportage featuring animals: the piece notes the marked success of a newsfilm depicting the transport of elephants from ship to port. The essay concludes by asserting the dangers of newsfilm cinematography, though it closes whimsically by quoting a cinematographer saying that "the hardest job in the world is to make beautiful celebrities appear as described in newspapers" (*Motion Pictures*, March 20, 1924, 20–21)!

This article, the most substantial on the subject of any in *Motion Pictures*' run, proposes that newsfilm photographers are of two sorts: those in the employ of newsreel producers, and freelance photographers who sell their films by the foot. Two Egyptian freelance cinematographers are named Mohammed Bayoumi and, appropriately enough, Hassan al-Halbawi, both of whom had been elected to the defunct *Motion Pictures* Club, founded by *Motion Pictures* (*Motion Pictures*, August 23, 1923, 20). Al-Halbawi is a mysterious figure in the annals of Egyptian cinema, his name appearing first in *Motion Pictures* by way of his involvement in the first and third iterations of the ill-fated *Motion Pictures* Club. He is then cited as the cineaste to whom 'Aziza Amir, actor/producer of *Layla* (1927), the film mentioned at the outset of this essay, had assigned the task of improving the original cut of the film, then titled *Nida' Allah (God's Call)*. This was reportedly because al-Halbawi had been the most critical of the original cut, which had disappointed the audience at its first screening. He could not continue in this task, however, because his employer, the Ministry of Agriculture, had been alerted that he was engaged in a film project while in its employ (al-Hadari 1987, 212).

By 1925, Bayoumi had already made twelve newsfilms, and had sought to collaborate with Banque Misr to establish a cinema division. The extent of his affiliation with them, however, is unclear, because he was not named as an employee at any point. Yet Bayoumi's own papers, published by his posthumous biographer Mohammed al-Qalyubi, do include a letter of invitation sent from Misr Printing, one of the Banque Misr Group affiliates, as well as an invoice recording its purchase of used equipment from Bayoumi (al-Qalyubi 2009, 140). This equipment presumably was used at the outset of the operations of the Misr Company for Acting and Cinema, an affiliate of Banque Misr established in 1925.

Domestic Newsreel Assembly and Newsfilm Production Industrializes

Bayoumi's contribution to the cinema in Egypt is among the most notable of any of the country's cineastes of the silent era, warranting a more extensive discussion that cannot be provided here. Yet I do wish to note that it was nearly a year after the magazine's final and definitive discussion of news cinema, "What Do You Love about the News of Newsreels?," before *Motion Pictures* would print anything else on the topic. Fittingly, this issue, dated April 23, 1925, marks a locally branded, assembled newsreel, as well as the beginning of the industrial production of Egyptian newsfilms.

As mentioned above, Bayoumi claimed to have worked for the Banque Misr affiliate Misr Company for Acting and Cinema, though no such relation is confirmed by historical papers of the Banque and its affiliate companies, which have been closely examined.[24] A full-page piece titled "Banque Misr and Moving Images" reports that Banque Misr had already asked Bayoumi to produce films, assisted by others, and that the team was currently working on "news, descriptive, and educational reels."[25] Its author, presumably publisher and editor Mahmud Tawfiq, writes that he had already watched three "scenes," produced by the Misr Company for Acting and Cinema: one a documentary of sugar manufacture in Egypt, the other two newsfilm clips—one of the opening of parliament, and the other of guests at the international geography conference. Bayoumi's collected papers mention only the third of these films. Bayoumi, according to his own papers, had made a film, now lost, about a visit by members of the geography conference, as al-Qalyubi notes, having learned of this film from Bayoumi's documents and from three photos relating to it. Al-Qalyubi elsewhere tells of a telegram that Bayoumi sent to Banque Misr about a promotional film he had made, *Al-Mahalla Train Engine (Wabur al-Mahalla)*, in the same year, 1925 (al-Qalyubi 2009, 61).

It would seem that Bayoumi was working independently and was attempting to sell his films to Banque Misr, as he had anticipated joining the company after selling his equipment to it a couple of months earlier (for what his papers deemed a pittance) (al-Qalyubi 2009, 20). As for *Motion Pictures*'s identification of Bayoumi as head of the photography crew of the newly established Misr Company for Acting and Cinema, it is worth noting that the article also refers to him as a "colleague," which hints that the article's author, Mahmud Tawfiq, learned of Bayoumi's alleged hiring from Bayoumi himself (*Motion Pictures*, April 27, 1925, 20)!

The other notable mention of news cinema in the same issue of April 27, 1925 is an advertisement for Cairo's Cinema Triumph, presenting the cinema's program for the coming week, including the Westi newsreel (*Motion Pictures*, April 27, 1925, 23). Westi Film Consortium was an agent for nearly a dozen American and French producers that distributed their films domestically, as well as in Palestine and Syria (the Levant, essentially). It seems that this outfit assembled its signature newsreel from newsfilms for which it owned distribution rights, a unique arrangement in Egypt during this era, as far as I have gathered. *Motion Pictures* was back in the business of printing advertisements for exhibitors, including one for Cinema Gaumont, which placed ads for its weekly programs in all four of the May 1925 editions of the magazine, each program including a newsreel issue.[26] Although no advertisements for newsfilms appeared in the magazine's final issue of June 4, 1925, Egyptian producers and distributors had decidedly cast their lot with the newsreel business, the cultural impact of which would persist in Egypt well into the sound era. Indeed, the new nation was poised to join the modern film-producing nations, but it would first aim to tell its own news.

References

Abu Shadi, Ali. 2004. *Waqa'i' al-sinima al-misriya*. Damascus: Ministry of Culture Press.

Ali, Mahmud. 2008a. *Fajr al-sinima fi Misr*. Cairo: Egypt Ministry of Culture, Cultural Development Fund.

———. 2008b. *Ma'at 'am min al-raqaba 'ala al-sinima al-misriya*. Cairo: The Higher Council of Culture.

Beinin, Joel, and Zachary Lockman. 1993. "1919: Labour Upsurge and National Revolution." In *The Modern Middle East: A Reader*, edited by Albert Hourani, Philip S. Khouri, and Mary S. Wilson, 395-429. Los Angeles: University of California Press.

Boughey, Davidson. 1921. *The Film Industry*. London: Isaac Pitman and Sons.

Davis, Eric. 1983. *Challenging Colonialism: Bank Misr and Egyptian Industrialization 1920–1941*. Princeton: Princeton University Press.

"Duke Visits Battlefields." 1918. In "Short Subjects in Review." *Motion Picture News*, July 27. archive.org.

France, Leys A. 1935. "Revision of World Motion Picture Data: Answering Mr. Burke's Memo of September 13." November 18, 1935. 4. Box 195. Records Relating to Commercial Attaché's Reports. Records of the Bureau of Foreign and Domestic Commerce. The National Archives at College Park, Maryland.

Griffith, Linda. 1917. "Early Struggles of Motion Picture Stars: When David W. Griffith, the Brilliant Director, Was Just Beginning to Shine." *Film Fun*, February. archive.org.

al-Hadari, Ahmad. 1987. *Tarikh al-sinima fi Misr, al-juz' al-awwal min bidayat 1896 ila akhir 1930*. Cairo: The Cinema Club.

Hasan, Ilhami. 1986. *Mohammed Tal'at Harb: rai'd sina'at al-sinima al-misriya, 1867–1941* (Mohamed Tal'at Harb: Pioneer of the Egyptian Cinema Industry, 1867–1941). Cairo: The Public Egyptian Organization for Books.

Hughes, William. 1976. "The Evaluation of Film as Evidence." In *The Historian and Film*, edited by Paul Smith, 49-79. New York: Cambridge University Press.

Jum'a, al-Sayyid Hasan. 1930. "Jara'id al-sinima: kayfa tasdur wa kayfa tajma' akhbariha." *al-Hilal*, December 1. archive.sakhrit.co.

McKernan, Luke. n.d. "Topical Budget (1911–1931)." *Screenonline*. screenonline.org.uk.

The Memory of Modern Egypt. Special collection. Digital. Main Library. Bibliotheca Alexandrina.

Mould, David H. 1983. *American Newsfilm 1914–1919: The Underexposed War*. New York: Routledge.

Motion Pictures [al-Suwar al-mutaharrika]. May 10, 1923–June 4, 1925. Microfilm. Main Library, American University in Cairo.

"Pathé News." 1925. *Exhibitor's Trade Review*, June 25. archive.org.

Peterson, Jennifer. 2012. "Educational Films and Early Cinema Audiences." In *A Companion to Early Cinema*, edited by André Gaudreault, Nicolas Dulac, and Santiago Hidalgo. 277-297. Hoboken: John Wiley & Sons.

"Prestige." 1920. *Exhibitors Herald*, January 3. archive.org.

al-Qalyubi, Mohammed. 2009. *Mohammed Bayoumi: al-ra'id al-awwal li-l-sinima al-misriya*. Cairo: The Public Organization for Books.

"Special Sales Force." 1922. *The Film Daily*, July 24. archive.org.

Stanton, Andrea L. 2012. "Radio." In *Cultural Sociology of the Middle East, Asia, and Africa: An Encyclopedia*, 337-339. Los Angeles: Sage Publications.

Vertov, Dziga. 1984. "I Wish to Share My Experience." In *Kino-eye: The Writing of Dziga Vertov*, edited by Annette Michelson, 119-122. Los Angeles: University of California.

2

DOCUMENTING LEBANON

Mohamad Soueid

Cinema documentation includes every film that has been screened or obscured, each work that was banned or forced to remain in drawers and basements, no matter how short, or what type of film.* Every document or paper that is found completes a missing element in cinematic history, or has the potential to correct postulated theories. There is a plethora of formal documented and inherited or experiential information about cinema in the Arab region, including reference books and encyclopedias that are often circulated and taken for granted as solid reference points, without necessarily being questioned or updated. An example is a collection of articles and data on Arab cinema by French film historian George Sadoul, *The Cinema in the Arab Countries*, published by the Interarab Centre of Cinema & Television in 1966. Documenting and historicizing cinema is not a linear process, but rather a web of tangled trajectories that intersect at various points. It is an endless mode of discovery that challenges preconceived ideas, one in which doubt on the part of the researcher should outweigh supposed certainty.

When I first considered the title of this chapter, "Documenting Lebanon," I assumed it would be an overview of the country's history through discovery of its documentary films, and thus a process of sorting them by director and year of production. After careful consideration, I concluded that the material available is not sufficient to add anything meaningful to what has already been presented about Lebanese cinema, as the gaps in data and lack of information are too substantial for a thorough historicizing process. This text is a perspective; its point of departure is that documenting Lebanon through cinema does not depend solely on documentary film, but must include fiction and advertisements, whether commercial, government propaganda, political party advertisements, or

---

* translated by Najat Abdulhaq

33

what has been written about these films and published in the media. An example: In summer 2017, the ARTE channel released a documentary using fiction films produced during the revolution as its source material. Following this path, the natural assumption might be that "Documenting Lebanon" should be a journey back to cinematic practices from the founding of the nation. Lebanon was established in 1920, and Greater Lebanon became the Republic of Lebanon in 1926.

The aim of this study is not to examine a particular political era as such, as films related to the mandate era and the immediate period post-independence did not greatly change; rather, it is to study cinematic and video practices. Combined, they create a comprehensive atlas of Lebanese history through audio and visual materials. It is instructive to look at early films and newsreels produced by the French mandate authorities, or under its instruction and control. No doubt, it would have been better to start before the era of Greater Lebanon and before the French mandate, when Lebanon was a province under Ottoman rule (until the First World War). Sadly, the documents on the beginnings of cinematic activities in the late nineteenth century and early twentieth century in the region under Ottoman rule are not available. I have chosen for the purpose of this chapter to examine newsreels produced by the French company Pathé. In so doing, I quote two lines from the French commentator announcing the birth of the new state, as they represent the start of the official historical narrative on modern Lebanon: "General Gouraud announced, on behalf of the French Mandate Authorities, the birth of Greater Lebanon on September 1st 1920, succeeded by the Republic of Lebanon that was set under French mandate in 1926."

The migration of the Turk Wedad Orfi (Vedat Örfi Bengü) to Egypt, and his involvement as an actor in the first Egyptian silent film—he was also its co-director with 'Aziza Amir (1927)—means that, despite his somewhat ambiguous persona in his homeland, cinematic activities already existed. Did the Sublime Porte (the central government of the Ottoman Empire) follow its Western enemies in recognizing the new invention of the Lumière Brothers as a good investment for political campaigns? Many of the visual references to the Ottoman era, and the filming of daily life in its Arab provinces, among them Lebanon, are archived in the West. Most major films are owned by the Lumière family company and their film-developing laboratories in Lyon. After launching their invention on December 28, 1895, and commercial success in France, the Lumière Brothers decided to discover the world and introduce cinema to its people. The missionary expedition sent cameramen overseas to bring back films about the other side of the world, among them the Frenchman Alexandre Promio (1868–1927), who was, like the Lumière Brothers, from Lyon. Promio was tasked with filming in Europe, the United States, and particularly the

Levant and Maghreb, which were under Ottoman rule. He shot dozens of documentary films in the countries of the Sultanate between 1896 and 1904, among them: *Muezzin Prayers, Government Square in Algeria, Coal Market in Sousse/Tunisia in 1896, Constantinople, Bosporus Banks Panorama in Istanbul, Bethlehem, Leaving Jerusalem by Railway, The Holy Sepulcher in Jerusalem in 1897 (Jérusalem, le saint sépulcre* [1897]), and *The Tunisian Bey and His Entourage Going Down the Bardo Stairs (Le Bey de Tunis et les personnages de sa suite descendant l'escalier du Bardo)* in 1904. Lebanon was also represented in Promio's travels, in his short, *Beirut: Cannons Square (Place des Canons*, 1897), a 45-second, fixed-shot film, showing pedestrians and donkey riders in the square—which later became "Martyrs' Square," in honor of those who were executed by Jamal Pasha on August 21, 1915, and May 6, 1916.

Promio's depiction of Beirut is not like the other vivid cities he filmed during the same period, like London, New York, and Venice. Cannons Square appears uncrowded through his lens, people appear to be in a hurry rather than enjoying a walk, and the roads are bumpy—as can be deduced from the shaking film, which gets more extreme when a carriage or cabriolet passes by. Despite some modern sights, such as buildings and an ancient house—most probably a worship house—in the background of the shot, here we see the people of Ottoman Beirut looking more like nomads in a position of hardship, which is made clear by the austerity of the view: men in *djellaba* (traditional clothes), and women holding baskets on their heads; curious gazes at the camera lens; and the labored walk of an older man with a white beard and white turban leaning on a child. Was the past as Promio filmed it? Was Beirut as he saw it?

Due to the scarcity of resources and the need to scrutinize the availability of other sources, *Beirut: Cannons Square* is in fact the only cinematic recording of Beirut during this period, and Alexandre Promio's camera was the first to record it. It is unlikely that his visit to Lebanon was limited to Beirut, but if he recorded in other locations, these films have been lost. One might assume that 1897—two years after the Lumière Brothers invented the cinematograph—was the first time a camera was used to record in Lebanon, as Promio's filmography does not include any traces of the country before this. It is difficult to find film material from the Ottoman era in general, particularly the last years. One exception is the archival shots screened as part of the short video documentary *1916–1918: Famine Mont-Liban* (2015), produced by the French online newspaper *Orient XXI*, documenting the historical famine that caused Lebanese waves of migration to Africa, Australia, the Americas, and Europe.

The footage of the First World War famine reveals a unique collective misery that was not witnessed again for decades in Lebanon. It shows the viewer the harsh reality of Lebanese life since the famine and the end of the Ottoman era, and the dichotomy between staying and being pushed into the diaspora. While recalling this dark chapter of Lebanese history, I tried in vain to find a cinematic shot by a Lebanese cameraman from the transitional period between the end of the Ottoman Empire and the French mandate. There is no evidence that I could find, however, of the documentation of daily life in Lebanon at this time, in contrast to other countries in the region. Having searched the French state's archives, company archives, and those of the military institution—which is full of unclassified film material—from the beginning of the twentieth century, I came across a narration by the cinema production elders, stating that Giordano Pidutti, the director of the first Lebanese film, *The Adventures of Elias Mabrouk* (*Mughamart Elias Mabrouk*, 1929), was a cameraman in the French army in the years before directing his film. This account has not been verified, but even if we assume it is true, it does not change the fact that the French army was the sole producer of a variety films in Lebanon at this time, and that Pidutti, like other local cameramen, was a functionary of the French media machine. Going back to the newspaper archives of the thirties, in particular *al-Nahar* newspaper, it is clear from the announce-ments that short French films, mainly about the mandate army, were screened in Lebanon before fiction films. During the mandate era, these films were not limited to propaganda. Some were professional commer-cial films depicting Beirut as a flourishing modern city, with its buildings, transportation, and fashion; a beautiful land between sea and mountain, compared to its rural past, and in contrast to the misery of Promio's film. In these representations, there is a seeming harmony of old and new: the tram alongside the cabriolet, modern suits and ties with the traditional vest and wide trousers, or the meeting of a man in a fez with another in a modern overcoat. These films reflect a totally different image of Beirut—a modern flourishing city in the twenties (INA 1920).

Did Promio miss this moment of the city? Or was his film, shot twenty years earlier, limited to a specific camera angle? Did all these changes occur in twenty years to reveal a city image that we got used to seeing in the films that followed; were we restricted by the collective memory of our forebears? Photographs of Ottoman Beirut in the late nineteenth century refute the cinematic image Promio introduced in *Cannons Square*. Beirut and Lebanon boasted several splendid edifices during the Ottoman era, as well as a functional transportation system, and architecturally beautiful buildings—with their red tiled roofs and modern infrastructure. Local his-torical sources and historians corroborate that Beirut was one of the most beautiful Ottoman provinces, and the cleanest. The square that Promio filmed soon had cinemas, a theater, and entertainment centers. This image complements other films on Lebanon and its capital since the mandate. Observers at the time commented: "Trade is flourishing in the city," "that corniche walk beside the Raouché rock is special," the "city is the central post and telecommunication center in the orient," a "crossroads for Asian and African pilgrims on their way to Mecca," and "an important intellectual center, the French University includes medicine and a dentistry school besides law and engineering." A French film of more than eleven minutes, *Les circuits touristiques du Liban* (*Touristic Highlights in Lebanon/al-Matafat al-siyahiya fi Lubna*, 1920–29), produced by the National Audiovisual Institute (INA 1920), depicts highlights from the country, from Beirut to Aley via the Damour road, passing by Deir al-Qamar, Beit Eddine, Barouk, Sawfar, Bhamdoun, and Suq al-Gharb. There are noticeable mistakes in the French pronunciation of some cities on screen. Shortly before the end of the film, there are shots of ships and small boats, and of a visit from the French High Commissioner Auguste Henri Ponsot, showing him drinking coffee with leading personalities of the city. This leads to the assumption that filming took place when Ponsot was high commissioner, between August 1926 and July 1933 (INA, n.d.). The film reflects a positive image of French Beirut, as local historians did with Ottoman Beirut. Both the film and historians' accounts contradict the image Promio delivered in 1897. Out of a personal desire to defend Promio, however, it is worth saying that those who projected a solely positive image of Beirut perhaps also missed its darker side and misery; one is not complete without the other. Furthermore, the image Promio captured is an honest moment of reality, and holds a responsibility with regard to the moment in which it was filmed. Promio was a cameraman, a director, and a producer, and was committed to the content he captured, more than to the form of documentary. The cameramen after him allowed themselves to be instrumentalized to serve the form over the content of their work. Was what they produced a new documentary on the French mandate, or an eye-catching work limited to the stunning nature of Beirut as a tourist attraction? In this sense, the cameraman, director, and producer became tour guides.

Similarly, in the British newsreel, *The Trouble in Lebanon* (British Pathé 1943), the commentator cites the arrest of President Bishara al-Khuri as the reason for the protests, mispronouncing his name "Bekara Kauri." The film is produced by the British Pathé Company, the archives of which include many recordings of events and social phenomena that give a general impression of the country from the 1920s until the mid-1970s.

More pertinent than the differences between their misspellings is the variation in political tone between the French and British films from the mandate era to independence, and their use of cinema newsreels and films as propaganda tools. While the French newsreels depicted stability and flourishing tourism, the British films underscored the existence of the Lebanese opposition and the detention of its leaders. British–French tensions were known under their mandate in the Levant. Britain encouraged the seekers of Lebanese independence, up until the country declared its independence on November 22, 1943.

After independence, the news and crisis reporting decreased and was replaced by films on the high life in Lebanon: images of the sea, bikinis, skiing, green mountains, the archaeological sites of Baalbek, Sidon and Tyre, Alb Elleil, Phoenicia Hotel, San George Bay, and Casino du Liban. A short civil war broke out in 1958, so again the news focused on street fights, tanks in the streets, and the Marines in Beirut. The British Pathé actively produced news reports on the Lebanese crisis (British Pathé 1958a) and the intervention of 14,000 U.S. Marines, who landed in Beirut on June 16, 1958, and controlled the harbor and the airport (British Pathé 1958c). These troops left Lebanon on October 25, 1958, after President Camille Chamoun ended his presidency on September 22. The British Pathé films produced post-independence were not anti-French. Their propaganda adopted Cold War politics in their pro–United States stance, in opposition to the Soviet Union and its communist camp of alliances with Nasserite Egypt, Ba'thists in Syria, and other nationalistic powers calling for pan-Arab unity (British Pathé 1958b). The British Pathé reports were like special editions of cinema newsreels covering the Lebanese crisis and the turbulent situation in the region.

After the end of the Ottoman Empire and the French mandate, through the Cold War and after, Lebanon was not only a space for proxy wars; it was, and still is, a stage for many different battles. During the mandate, the propaganda and counter-propaganda were limited to British and French cinema newsreels. After independence, Western reportage decreased, and Arab reporting gained a huge space, shifting the propaganda and counter-propaganda onto Arabs themselves. The Egyptians introduced cinema newsreels to the Arab world. In 1923, pioneer Mohammed Bayoumi established Amun Newsreel (Amun Newsreel 1923), the first films of which survived in a collection by Mohammed al-Qalyubi. Gamal Abd al-Nasser's visit to Lebanon in 1959 was the reason for introducing Egyptian newsreels. A cinema newsreel documenting the "Tent Meeting" of 1959 was combined with the voice of an Egyptian commentator. This was the voice of the Nasserite era, supported by the radio station Voice of the Arabs *(Sawt al-arab)*, which collected Arab peoples in large numbers around Nasser's speeches, just as it had brought them together around Umm Kulthum. The words of its famous presenter Ahmed Said reading the military declaration of the Arab armies' victory against Israel, however, turned out to be misleading, as the Jordanian, Egyptian, and Syrian armies were defeated in the June 1967 War. The Nasserite voice emerged simultaneously with an increase in the media activities of the Palestinian resistance, in particular the Democratic Front, led by Nayef Hawatmeh, and the Popular Front, led by George Habash. Both movements have their roots in the Arab Nationalist Movement.

On the official side, there were Syrian state TV and the cinema department of its army—both produced films on the war in Lebanon—as well as the Iraqi media, which were anti-Syrian. The different Arab media outlets were split between the two poles of the Lebanese cold war: one supporting Sadat and Egypt, and the other the Front of Endurance and Resistance, which rejected the Camp David Accords, and the Rejection Front, which refused any peaceful compromise. This media battle was funded by the petrodollar countries in various ways, according to their interests. Gulf money was particularly strong in funding the printed press, while Iraqi and Libyan financial support went beyond this and reached the cinema. Several Palestinian factions loyal to the governments in these countries benefited from this funding.

Oil is the malediction of the Middle East, and has contributed to its corruption, with the enemy and its allies both benefiting from it. The Palestine Liberation Organization (PLO) and its largest faction, the Fatah movement, played this game to their benefit, guaranteeing them a kind of political independence to establish their own institutions, like the Palestinian Film Institute, which produced many films, the majority of which are closer to propaganda than to solid documentary films.

Lebanon hosted all kinds of propaganda, and had its own newsreel, *Lebanese Events (al-Ahdath al-lubnaniyya)*, covering key political and cultural events. It was a replica of the official media's news program, upholding the governmental line in promoting stability, diversity, and tourism. *Lebanese Events* was shown in all cinemas before the main feature film, and was mostly black and white (with some color exceptions), in French and Arabic, and often accompanied by music rather than narration. The advertisement industry also flourished alongside the newsreel, particularly the official advertisements on tourism and heritage, funded by diverse ministries. Antoine Mushahwar is the pioneer of professional films, especially those documenting trade and industry, known as corporate films. His works are inscribed in Lebanese collective memory, even with the demise of documentary cinema. Among the most famous productions from that time are the heavily debated investigative documentaries of the Lebanese Television Company from 1974, aired on Channel 7. These investigative documentaries, titled *Seven Thirty*, were the earliest productions by the late director Maroun Baghdadi and his friend, the journalist Fu'ad Na'im. Compared to the competing company, Television of Lebanon and the

Orient, on Channel 11, Channel 7 was exceptional in its courage, and for creating a space for freedom and creative cooperation between its program director, Paul Tannous, and the best of Lebanon's creative authors, theater professionals, and cinema specialists. There is no question that the war suppressed these growing experiments, and its onset in spring 1975 ensured the end of all official and nonofficial cinema forms. A few months later, *Lebanese Events* ceased to exist, and the unclear suicide of Antoine Mushahwar dominated the news.

The image did not die because of the war, however. To the contrary, the war caused the explosion of the image, and turned it into a propaganda tool. The stage was West Beirut, bastion of the Palestinian fighters and their allies—the Lebanese leftist and nationalist militia, along with the Islamist forces. East Beirut was the bastion of the Christian militia and their parties, who mostly used the radio as their media outlet. The Voice of Lebanon (Sawt Lubnan) broadcasting was the most influential, and had a wide reach, including among its enemies. East Beirut was isolated, reinforcing a belief, held mostly by leftist Lebanese and Palestinian factions, that the Palestinian–Lebanese leftist experiment had failed due to the Israeli invasion in 1982. This led to the complete collapse of the image. When cinema left West Beirut, a new television era dominated the scene, mainly from East Beirut. It emerged first as an analog station, and later a satellite broadcaster that was established on August 23, 1985, by Lebanese forces under the name Lebanese Broadcasting Corporation International (LBC). This new station shared news options that were not controlled by the employees of the media ministry, as it was not the official state medium. Official state television was Lebanese Television, created in 1977 by merging channel 7 and channel 11. Its priority was controlling the news to avoid the propagation of any sectarian views that might inflame tensions. But controlling official television created a high demand for freer media, and a desire for other sources of information. LBC closed this gap. Generally speaking, the channel adapted the style of privately owned television, and changed the Lebanese media scene from analog to satellite broadcasting. The number of private stations mushroomed across the country, to a point at which nearly everyone could broadcast from a tiny room with basic techniques and equipment. This ended after the war, when a new law was promulgated to systematize the television scene, issuing licenses according to specific stipulations, including balancing the media outlets of the political powers in the country. The relative independence they had experienced previously was manipulated by special interests, and used to support one political power against another.

Neither the systematization nor the increased censorship and limitations could stop the explosion. In the second decade of the new millennium, digital inflation contributed to the explosion in Lebanon, going beyond all previous cinema borders and forms. Instead of noting the beginnings of documentary film in the first shots of Beirut by Promio in 1897, the digital age created its own beginnings, and redefined cinema and its meaning and usefulness, as if digital media were the "Big Bang," opposing the path of image creation. The birth of cinema at the end of the nineteenth century was supposed to be the big bang. In the case of Lebanon, I feel as though Promio's first shots were like labor pangs for a long cinematic history that followed. Lebanese film, first coopted by the Egyptians, then by Palestinian organizations, and later by political propaganda, was, in a way, colonized just as the country was.

Maroun Baghdadi's feature films about the war are more liberated than his previous documentary films, largely produced for the Communist Action Organization, and maybe more so than his first feature film, *Bayrut ya Bayrut (Beirut, O Beirut)*, which took the same path as the leftist documentaries he produced later. His war films are a liberation from a certain kind of cinema, from Maroun Baghdadi himself, and from the limiting reputation of a committed filmmaker. When it became difficult to continue, he migrated to Paris, where he continued his work with French producers featuring the civil war. The war was the reason for his departure, but it was not the reason for his liberation, or the impetus for him to make films.

Videos and audio recordings reached their peak during the war, with the cassette tape becoming a popular new medium for communication. Amin Gemayel, who was elected to follow his assassinated brother to the presidency, chose to deliver his first public speech to the Lebanese people through a videotaped documentary depicting the political, social, and economic challenges facing the country. This documentary speech was made by Maroun Baghdadi, but was uncredited at the time. The popular Friday sermons of the Sunni sheikh 'Abd al-Hafiz Qasim also made the medium of the casette tape more prominent. The sheikh became famous for his emotional preaching at Abd al-Nasser Mosque in the Corniche al-Mazraa region in 1986, during which he expressed widely held feelings of defeat, the injustice of occupation, and frustrations over the Christian militia's control of the country. Many thought that he would be a passing phenomenon, but, while the sheikh may have been forgotten, the mosque became a new communication and broadcast medium, marking a shift from the defeated Leftist past to an Islamist future. Sheikh 'Abd al-Hafiz Qasim was cheered on in Beirut, young people followed religious classes, and sermons by the Ethiopian sheikh 'Abdallah al-Harari, known as "al-Habashi," at the Burj Abi Haydar Mosque became more popular, just as the Tawba mosque in Tripoli became the bastion of Sheikh Sa'id Sha'ban, the founder of the Islamist Unification Movement, in 1982. Shi'a Muslims also had their spiritual leaders, including al-Sayyid Mohammed Hussein Fadlallah and his open religious classes at Bi'r al-Sabi' Mosque in South Beirut, as well as more sermons at the Husseiniyat mosques and eulogy gatherings. The Christian model was to have a live broadcast on Sundays as a political stand, in particular during the era of the late Maronite patriarch Nasrallah Sfeir.

In the 1980s, Lebanon became a laboratory for the region's politics, and a prototype of its coming wars. Decades before the rise of al-Qa'ida, the Afghani Emirate, and the caliphate of Abu Bakr al-Baghdadi in Iraq and Syria, Sa'id Sha'ban created his Islamic Emirate in Tripoli. Before Zarqawi and ISIS published online videos of the forced confessions of their captives, the kidnappers of Western citizens—like Terry Anderson, Terry Wait, and Michel Seurat— were sent from Lebanon to news agencies and newspapers, which broadcast them and accompanying threats of execution if the kidnappers' conditions were not fulfilled. Terror tactics, means of communication, and video techniques were all in correlation: video went beyond being a simple technology, and became synonymous with politics and security and digital armies. Controlling communications became part of the war machine (the occupation of Iraq in 2003, the hybrid wars, control of the Crimean Peninsula, and the alliance between international militias and the Russian Army in Syria). An unstable Lebanon missed the hybrid wars, but invested early in virtual images. The general secretary of Hizbullah, Hassan Nasrallah, communicated virtually with a wide audience through the screen—a source of broadcasting, and a means of reception at the same time.

As mentioned, documenting Lebanon went beyond the cinema newsreels to include audio and visual recordings, religious preachers, political figures, and videos by terrorist groups, all of which became creators of news and events. The political demand for technology did not decrease the degree of cinema production and audiovisual arts. The 1980s were the biggest and most extensive cinema and visual production years since the migration of Egyptian film to Beirut, with the added difference that the content was more Lebanese in terms of form, themes, production, and language. This was proof that Lebanese filmmakers could finance and produce their own work, instead of relying on Egyptian and foreign teams that considered Lebanon to be a suitable shooting location and a convenient way of smuggling their money out of the Egyptian nationalized economic system.

The producers of the 1980s worked in close cooperation with a government apparatus that had been weakened by sectarian wars, foreign interference, and the control of militias. The films were largely motivated by a mission to show that there is no weapon but that of the state, and no matter how long the darkness may prevail, there would be a new dawn of the state, national army, and internal security forces. The majority of these works are commercial and similar to American action films, depicting a bad gangster who is defeated by an honest figure, supported by legitimate powers. The Lebanese legitimate power (the authorities) facilitated the production of these films, provided any required tools, and honored their filmmakers. For example, *The Decision* (al-Qarar), by Yusuf Sharaf al-Din, was endorsed by the late President Elias Sarkis, and was screened at the presidential palace one day before its official launch at the Strand Cinema in Alhamra on December 6, 1981, with Prime Minister Shafik Wazzan as the guest of honor. The 1980s films made up for the collapse of state media, the breakdown of documentary supply, and the shutting down of the newsreel production *Lebanese Events*. These films gained widespread notoriety, as they were feature length and screened in cinemas all over the country, despite the barriers and barricades. Due to the absence of documentaries presenting the history of Lebanon during the 1980s, *The Decision* became almost like a document recording the history of that period.

The documentaries made during the 1950s, 1960s and mid-1970s by Europeans and Americans along with Egyptian and Lebanese filmmakers also form a Lebanese archive of these decades, and are part of the individual and collective memory of those who arrived to work in Lebanon, especially during the 1960s. From Egypt to Syria, Iraq, Iran, and Turkey came directors, actors, producers, and scriptwriters. Beirut was welcoming to all. And we could say that by time fiction films necessarily turn into documents of their times.

As the years pass, films seem to be aging like people. In their senility, they can appear childish. A film at heigh age looks archaic, its fresh image slides into primitivity, as if going back to the childhood of cinema at the time of the Lumière Brothers, or back in Beirut's history to the first shot by Alexandre Promio. Returning to the 1980s is a return to practices that document Lebanon amid an absolute absence of documentary cinema, empowered by the emergence of home video and its use as a public civic practice. This is a story that I have to precede with another, about the start of my personal experience in making movies.

At the peak of commercial television movies and series productions using video, I tried to make my first film. I wrote a script for a short feature film, *Merry-Go-Round (al-Malahi)*, about the meeting of a man and a woman—who hardly knew each other previously—during the night in an amusement park in Beirut. I filmed part of it, and then the production stumbled. One of the actors faced a security problem and had to leave the country, and the producer took this as a reason to abandon the project, as the making of the film exceeded the modest planned budget. I have to admit, the reason I needed more time to film was due to my hesitation regarding an experiment that I did not handle well in terms of both its tools and its human elements, after years of working as an assistant on commercial movies shot largely on 35mm cameras, following the tradition since the 1960s. I was about to abandon filmmaking altogether, but the desire to try resurfaced in the last year of the war, in 1989. I had the idea to make a long documentary called *Absence (Ghiyab)*, about death during the war, but with no direct reference to the war, summarizing my ambition to make a film beyond the television categorization. I wanted to make a film with intense cinematic language, in which feature and documentary are interwoven, closer to *cinéma vérité*. I was encouraged to do so in a time when Lebanese productions had discovered audiovisual and autobiographical works, the "Cinema of the Self"—films including self-expression.

Those who migrated to Gulf countries at the beginning of the war (1975–78) often replaced written letters to their families with audiotapes, telling them about their successes or failures, their lives and new friendships in the countries they migrated to. They created indirect physical contact with their voices, allowing their families to listen to them, and making the task of reading behind the lines with formal letters a little easier. Audiotapes were replaced by videotapes, as the first generation of video cameras emerged, moving closer to simulating real-time physical contact. These tapes linked camera use to the "cinema of reality." A lot of people tend to connect this practice to the use of 8mm cameras, commonly used to film individuals, families, and their memories, and often referred to as "home movies." This title again is perhaps misleading, as 8mm cameras, or video cameras, can adapt to diverse forms of cinematic narrative. The difference between the two practices is mostly technical: using an 8mm camera as an amateur individual looking to archive personal memories, for example, is a disadvantage in terms of sound quality—unless one can afford the cost of a separate sound recording device, which should be transferred to a magnetized tape, then edited to synchronize the pictures and sound. This usually requires a team of people, and the intention is to achieve a film with consistency. The increased use of the 8mm camera by individuals, while providing ease of use and control over the footage, has led to the rise of mediocre directors and filmmakers. The scriptwriter claims he has an idea; the director claims he has a vision; the actor claims it matches his character; and the producer claims he will provide inaccessible facilities. The film is the sum of a mediocre collective claim.

Another encouragement for me to undertake my first work, *Absence*, was "Studio Clemenceau," the only Lebanese cinema devoted to artistic and experimental movies. The golden era of the cinema was in the years prior to the war, when it opened its doors and introduced great filmmakers to the country, such as the Soviet director Andrei Tarkovsky, the Swedish Ingmar

Bergman, the Italians Pierre Paolo Pasolini, Federico Fellini, Luchino Visconti, and Michelangelo Antonioni, the French–Swiss Jean-Luc Godard, the Japanese Akira Kurosawa, the French François Truffaut, the Egyptian Youssef Chahine, the British Lindsay Anderson, and many others from the seventh art's prominent figures. Studio Clemenceau received local support from the National Cinema Centre, and international moral support from independent artistic and experimental cinemas. It was distinctive, and sustained itself in opposition to commercial cinemas. Financial support for the cinema ceased during the war, as did its communication with similar cinemas worldwide, and local audiences deserted it. Formally, it kept the slogan "art and experimentation," but its content became dependent on local offers from American distribution companies, or the rerunning of previously screened highlights. The original film strips were not usable any more, and the owner could not afford to renovate and maintain the building. He resorted to private rentals by word of mouth, which did not ultimately prevent it from meeting its fate and closing. What interests me in the tragic story of this cinema is that it was mostly rented by Kurdish cultural and social clubs for private events, usually wedding parties, which had a tradition of filming, the cost of which often exceeded that of the television works. After I watched a sample of tapes from these Kurdish weddings in the 1980s, I discovered a popular practice of making documentaries that preceded the mastering of video to produce them. Apart from their poor quality, these wedding tapes still required postproduction processes of shooting, editing, copying, and distribution. The voice recordings and documentations of those in diaspora, and the videos documenting Kurdish celebrations, both show another type of documentation that goes beyond political and war propaganda, and the official media outlets and policies. They document memories, feelings, and traditions, a kind of repetitive meditation on the past. In his special film *My Father Is Still a Communist* (*Abi mazal shuyu'iyan*, 2011), Ahmad Ghossein used the private archives of his mother, who had kept the cassettes his father used to send her from the Gulf region, where he was forced to migrate for work during the war. This film is similar to other documentaries in which the filmmakers distanced themselves from "committed cinema" and produced a historical take based on proximity to the protagonist and their experiences.

Before the video and digital boom, it was easy to count the films produced in a year and their makers on one hand. In the twenty-first century, this process changed, and it became almost impossible to track or collect all of them. The increase in cinema and audiovisual arts schools has produced a huge number of young filmmakers and technicians that are not bound by the classical film or cinema academy. The Syrian revolution provides a unique example: it failed to end a despotic regime, but its citizens made an unprecedented number of documentaries with minimal tools, often just digital cameras and smartphones.

The digital revolution may have failed to democratize a tense world, but it managed—along with other means of communication—to democratize the film industry. If we consider the history of moving images, Lebanon would be a cinematic foundling in that waif shot by Frenchman Alexandre Promio at the end of nineteenth-century Beirut. In the era of cinema and wars of the twenty-first century, a struggle ensued as to the parenthood of this foundling; whether by serious, alternative, committed cinema on the one hand, or commercial mainstream cinema on the other. Today's Lebanon, despite the wars of the last decade, has realized that cinema does not belong purely to its founding fathers, but to a new generation of filmmakers who are willing to adapt with the times and grow with their films.

References

Amun Newsreel. 1923. "Al-'adad al-awl min jaridat Amun." YouTube video.

British Pathé. 1943. "The Trouble in Lebanon." YouTube video.

———. 1958a. "Eisenhower's Statement on Landings in Lebanon." YouTube video.

———. 1958b. "Marines Begin Lebanon Exodus." YouTube video.

———. 1958c. "U.S. Marines Landing in Lebanon." YouTube video.

INA (National Archive Institute). n.d. "Les circuits touristiques du Liban 1921–1929." YouTube video.

———. 1920. "Lebanon Beirut 1920." YouTube video.

Orient XXI. 2015. "1916–1918: Famine Mont-Liban." YouTube video.

Promio, Alexandre. 1897. "Beirut 1897 Place des Canons." YouTube video.

Sadoul, Georges. 1966. *The Cinema in the Arab Countries*. Beirut: Interarab Centre of Cinema & Television.

3

A CONCISE HISTORY OF IRAQI DOCUMENTARY FILMMAKING

Ali Abdulameer
Translated by Najat Abdulhaq

There is no comprehensively documented history of Iraqi cinema, despite the fact that the seventh art of filmmaking has played a crucial role in the cultural life and aesthetic education of numerous Iraqi generations, especially between the 1940s and 1970s, a period that witnessed the emergence of documentary film in Iraq. This golden era was not just a historical moment; it reflects the struggle for modernity in a society that suffered for a long time from oppressive Ottoman rule, followed by British military occupation (1914–21), and then by an emerging national state, as it fought to establish new features of its own in a post–Second World War culture and society. The relationship of Iraqi audiences to all forms of cinema, however, started long before this.

In this chapter, I will give an overview of Iraqi film history and the development of documentary in the country, as well as a compendium of Iraqi filmmakers who have been involved in documentary work, and a list of some of their films.

A Brief Introduction to Iraqi Cinema

Some consider the cinematograph screenings that started in summer 1909 to be the beginning of film history in Iraq, when Baghdadi merchants presented so-called fantasy plays *(al'ab khayaliya)*, in a highly frequented public park in the city, at an affordable price. In the year 1911, the shows presented different types of documentaries: those with educational content, and those with information about wildlife and nature, such as *Leopard Hunting (Sayd al-fuhud)*, *Rough Sea (Bahr ha'ij)*, *The Search for the Black Pearl (al-Bahth 'an al-lu'lu'a al-sawda')*, *The Balloon Race (Sibaq al-manatid)*, *Predatory Birds (Tuyurun muftarisa)*, and historical films, like *The Funeral of King Edward the Seventh (Tashyi' janazat al-malik Edward al-sabi')* (*al-Mada* 2014).[1] The location in the park was later called Cinema Blocky, after the name of a well-known Iraqi machine importer and must be considered the first cinema in Iraq. Between 1910 and 1920, more movie theaters were opened. According to Kamal Salim, the historians Abbas Baghdad and Fakhri al-Zubaydi mention that Cinema al-Iraqi was located at the Maydan and Cinema Royal at Bab al-Aga (Agha Gate), while Cinema Central lay in al-'Ammar, near the Takiyyat al-Badawy in Ra's Jisr Mawd (present-day al-Ahrar), Olympia in al-Muraba', and Cinema National in Sayyid Sultan 'Ali. Cinema Royal was the first to show imported silent movies. In addition to the big screen, it had a smaller one which provided explanations for what was seen on the larger one (Salem 2017). It was, moreover, the most luxurious movie theater, with its elegant hall and furniture. Cinema Iraqi, in contrast, opened in 1922, but was not favored by the middle classes for being located near al-Manzul, the public brothel. Many cinemas were financed by Jewish-Iraqi businessmen.

The late 1920s and early 1930s witnessed two crucial events: the first was the screening of sound films at Cinema Central, and the second was the projection of documentaries that were filmed in Iraq, like *The Spring Celebration of the Iraqi Army* (*al-Hafla al-rabi'iya li-l-jaysh al-'Iraqi*) said to be screened in 1927 (*al-Mada* 2014), and the inauguration of a civil airplane in Baghdad. At the same time, Egyptian musicals found their way to Iraq. Cinema National screened *The White Rose* (*al-Warda al-bayda'*) on December 6, 1934, starring Egyptian singer Muhammad 'Abd al-Wahhab. Also screened for months were historical films like *Dananir* (1940), set during the rule of the Abbasid caliph Harun al-Rashid, with many songs about Baghdad.

Toward a National Film Industry and First Steps in Documentary Filmmaking

Baghdad Film Company Ltd. (Sharikat aflam Baghdad al-mahduda), established in 1942, was the first Iraqi film production company, but it did not produce any films. The real beginning of the film industry was in the post–Second World War era, when most films were coproduced with Egypt, starting with *The Son of the East* (*Ibn al-sharq*, 1946), produced by al-Rashid Iraqi Egyptian Company, and directed by the Egyptian Niazi Mustafa. A number of other films followed. In 1953, 'Ali al-Nasir founded Dunya al-Fann Company (Sharikat Dunya al-Fann), which was dependent on Iraqi facilities. Its first film was *Fitna and Hassan* (*Fitna wa Hasan*, 1955), directed by Haydar al-Omar. Another cinema company was Sumer (Sumar), which produced the first full-length feature film *Who Is Responsible?* (*Man al-mas'ul?*, 1956), by 'Abd al-Jabbar Wali. The 1950s was a decade of huge political, cultural, and social changes. Actor Ibrahim Jalal, known for his performances in the films *Cairo–Baghdad (al-Qahira–Baghdad, 1947)*, *Alia and Issam ('Aliya wa 'Isam, 1948)*, and *Laila in Iraq (Layla fi-l-'Iraq, 1949)*, left Iraq in 1952 to study cinema in Italy. He was trained by the famous directors Rossellini and De Sica. Jalal made a short documentary, *The Door (al-Bab,* most probably between 1950 and 1952), which is considered to be the first Iraqi documentary, despite the fact that it was produced abroad, and mostly because of the Iraqi nationality of its director (Jalal) and author, Yusuf al-'Ani. The British Iraqi Oil Company established a film unit, as did the American Information Service. Several Iraqi cameramen joined these two units and gained modern filming experiences. The oil company unit produced a newsreel, *Our Homeland (Biladuna),*[2] in addition to other films such as: *The Iraq Savior (Munqidh al-'Iraq),* about the 1954 flood; *Controlling the Water (al-Saytara 'ala al-miyah),* about the irrigation project; and *Our Sport Generation (Jiluna al-riyadi).* The Ministry of Education was also committed to the medium through a special educational unit that worked on producing short films and news reflecting its educational activities. Karim Majid, the first Iraqi cameraman, was one of the employees of this unit.

Two Iraqi scenarists, Mohammed Shukri Jamil and Sahib Haddad, had a cardinal role in Iraqi documentary and fiction cinema, and participated in producing the film *The Living Legacy (al-Turath al-hayy,* 1952) in Britain with Majid Kamil. The commentary to the film was written and spoken by Palestinian–Iraqi Jabra Ibrahim Jabra. This film is an example of a progressive documentary with a high level of artistic skill that was produced by the oil company unit, even if through a British cinema company like Centre Film. Another cinema unit was founded by the Railway Corporation at the beginning of the 1950s, and managed by the artist Khalil Shawqi beginning in 1959.

The Documented News Portfolio *(al-Haqiba al-ikhbariya al-watha'iqiya)* summarized the country's news every week. This was one of the first experiences that brought audiences closer to documentary cinema, and the cinema showrooms were always keen on screening them prior to the main feature film.

The Image of Society or a State Narrative?
In the 1950s, Iraqi documentary, assisted by the oil company, began to present a narrative on reality that followed that of the ruling regime, but this official history did not mean there were no influential works offering a progressive documentation of Mesopotamia and the depth of its civilization alongside the promises offered by transformations within the modern nation-state. A fundamental innovation occurred in the genre,

thanks to a number of returning directors, camera operators, and writers, who had gathered great knowledge from countries with more prominent cinema experience. Thus, some documentaries started to go beyond the news style of documenting an event, to reach a level where the artist is both observer and documenter, and can express their views and opinions through film. By 1975, Iraqi film had reached a level that enabled participation in many international film festivals, like Leipzig (East Germany), Moscow, Karlovy Vary, Tashkent, and Carthage. More than forty documentaries were produced on many scientific, educational, and cultural topics in that year alone.

The first state corporation for cinema, the Cinema and Theatre Administration (Maslahat al-Sinima wa-l-Masrah), was established in 1966, a few years after the end of the royal era in 1958, producing, among others, *The Tax Collector* (*al-Jabi*, 1966), by Ja'far 'Ali. Until the 1980s it produced a number of important news and documentary films. Examples include:

- *The Dawn of Civilization* (*Fajr al-hadara*, 1977), about ancient Iraqi civilizations, by the acknowledged Egyptian director Tawfiq Salih, who worked in Iraq.
- *Journalism Photography in Iraq* (*al-Taswir al-sahafi fi-l-'Iraq*), by Kazim al-'Umari.
- *Civilizations Valley* (*Wadi al-hadarat*), by 'Abd al-Latif Salih.
- *The End* (*al-Nihaya*), by Kamal 'Akif.
- *The Collective Farms* (*al-Mazari' al-jama'iya*) and *Life's Lovers* (*'Ashiqu al-haya*), by 'Abd al-Hady al-Rawi.
- *The Sniper* (*al-Qannas*, 1980), by Faysal al-Yasiri.
- *Yes, No* (*Na'am, la'*, most probably 1972), by Faruq al-Qaysi; the film received an award at the Palestinian film festival in Baghdad in 1972. The director made two other documentaries: *Shatt al-Arab and the Pulse of Life* (*Shatt al-'Arab wa nabad al-hayat*) and *Suspended Assassination* (*Ightiyyal ma' waqf al-tanfidh*).
- *The Beginning* (*al-Bidaya*), by Carlo Hariton.
- *Tales of Beautiful Hours* (*Hikayat al-sa'at al-jamila*), by Tariq 'Abd al-Karim.
- The works of 'Abbas al-Shalah: *Storyboard* (*Qissa musawwara*), *Triumph Road* (*Tariq al-nasr*), *Wondering* (*Tasa'ul*), *A Feather and a Knife* (*Risha wa sikkin*), *The Circle* (*al-Da'ira*), *Feasts* (*A'yad*), and *Baghdad in the Mirror* (*Baghdad fi al-mir'at*).
- The works of Egyptian director Fu'ad al-Tuhami, who worked in Iraq from 1973, and documented aspects of the military operations at the Syrian front during the October War in 1973. Tuhami's well-known films are *Down with Silence* (*Yasqut al-samt*, 1974), on the Dhofar rebellion in Oman, and *Iraqi Workers' Song* (*Ughniyat 'amal 'iraqiya*, 1977).

During the 1970s, the private sector still played a big role in producing films, for instance the beautiful film *The Curve* (*al-Mun'ataf*, 1975) by Ja'far 'Ali, inspired by the novel *Khamsat aswat* (*Five Sounds*, 1967) by the father of the contemporary Iraqi novelist Gha'ib Tu'ma Farman. Yet the official narrative, particularly under the republican regime, gradually put an end to the independent cultural sphere. From the establishment of the General Institution for Cinema and Theatre until the fall of Saddam Hussein's regime in 2003, state-produced documentaries were prisoners of the propagandist formula, and were limited to the news style. Hence documentary filmmakers steered clear of any analysis or dramatic plots, except for exceptional cases, such as *Marshlands* (*al-Ahwar*, 1975), by Qasim Hawal, and *The Sniper*, by al-Yasiri, who was a pioneer Arab director in docudrama portraying the Lebanese civil war.

As soon as the Iran–Iraq War broke out in 1980, Iraqi documentary productions became even more dominated by propaganda, projecting what Iraqis have come to know as "images from the battle," showing the atrocities of the war as a victory anthem that every citizen was expected to sing. By the end of the dictatorship in 2003, amid the abolition of regulations and censorship, many people expected the opening of closed doors for cinema lovers. It was anticipated that democracy would lead to a new era of Iraqi documentaries and cinema, reflecting the peculiarity of the Iraqi reality and critically analyzing its dialectic.

Unfortunately, these expectations collapsed dramatically. The documentaries produced by the state were still expected to reflect the official narrative on events and challenges. This was also adopted by non-official Iraqi institutions that were connected to political parties hidden behind commercial and media façades. The propaganda and fomenting discourses flourished, in stark opposition to documentaries that distinguished themselves more through their objectivity and dramatic structures. In the post-2003 era, the basic concept of documentary—"to be an analysis of reality in order to know and explore what is behind, without ignoring the artistic and avoiding superficial journalistic reporting" (al-Rashid 2008)—vanished.

Exile and Return Films: The Land's Image, Delights, and Sorrows

Studying the state of Iraqi cinema after 2003, one can notice the huge challenges the cultural scene as a whole faced, due to the deterioration of security and destruction of cultural structures, in particular the movie theaters (Halil 2013). One of the impacts of this change is that millions of Iraqi youth were unaware of their country's film history, and had never seen an Iraqi film. This was not just a result of the absence of cinemas, but also the miserable fact that local channels, with very few exceptions, never aired any Iraqi films. Egyptian film critic Samir Farid is reported to have stated, in his work on a history of documentary film in Iraq, that between 2004 and 2009, Iraq produced 400 short films (mainly documentaries), 150 of them political propaganda films (1959 to 2011), 50 produced in exile, and 200 independent production films (Reuters 2011).

After the fall of Saddam Hussein's regime, many Iraqi film artists returned from exile, and a new feature and documentary film movement began. Many of them won awards at international film festivals. One of these films, the 155-minute feature *Life after the Fall* (*al-Haya ba'd al-suqut*, 2008), by Kasim Abid, was about life after the fall of Hussein. The director is one of the filmmakers who lived in exile and returned to Iraq to participate in a new era of Iraqi cinema through the Baghdad Film School, which he helped found. The wave of Arab and Kurdish return films after the fall of Saddam includes: *16 Hours in Baghdad* (*Sittata 'ashar sa'a fi Baghdad*, 2004) by Tariq Hashim, *Iraq My Homeland* (*al-'Iraq mawtinni*, 2004), by Hadi Mahud, and *The Return to Kirkuk* (*al-'Awda ila Kirkuk*, 2005), by the Kurdish Karzan Shira Biyani.

Between Documentary and News?

The writer Mohamed al-Rashid argues: "Whoever follows the movement of Iraqi cinema will have no difficulty in noticing the failures of this journey. The Iraqi culture as a whole has been exposed to a deliberate alienation according to a pre-designed plan, creating a path which can be easily used by the destructive projects of the authority (the regime of Saddam Hussein) as it promoted the travesty of culture, and it was very active in this, especially during the 1980s" (2008).

Though a low number of films were produced in the years following the occupation, Iraqi cinema during the four years post-2003 was characterized by a clear and distinctive approach. Directors were very much interested in producing documentaries reflecting the suffering of the Iraqi people, and experiences of repression, injustice, and iniquity. These films were aimed at an international audience. Among them are documentaries such as the Swiss production *al-Anfal* (*Al-Anfal. Im Namen von Allah, Baath und Sadam*, 2005) by Kurdish director Mano Khalil, and *Baghdad Days* (*Layali baghdadiyya*, 2005) by Hiba Basim. *Al-Anfal* shows the suffering of survivors searching for relatives in mass graves, and the disastrous effects of chemical weapons on the flora and fauna in the region.

Then there are films produced in this period (2004 to 2008) that prompted discussion on documentation in film, such as *Underexposure* (*Ghayr salih li-l-'ard*, 2005) by 'Uday Rashid, *Going to Paradise* (*al-Dhihab ila al-janna*) by director and actor Miqdad 'Abd al-Rida, and *Iraq: The Song of the Missing Men* (*Aghani al-gha'ibin; Irak: Les chants des absents*,

2006), by Layth 'Abd al-Amir. These films document a living reality, or a realistic theme that is embedded objectively in the tools and techniques of fictionalized cinema, under the condition that the mise en scène does not affect the real essence of the final product.

The film *Iraq: The Song of the Missing Men* by the Franco-Iraqi director Layth 'Abd al-Amir discusses the question of Iraqi identity via a journey across the country, exploring many sites and people from different backgrounds and classes, in an attempt to observe the effects of war on people's perceptions of identity. The film tries to record the status quo in the country, and the effects of the American occupation starting in 2003. The director himself makes a journey, stopping in al-Ahwar in the south, then following the stream to Karbala, in a new documentary-style approach that differs from other productions of the time. The director says, "I tried to keep distance from the political or philosophical discourse, which makes the tape heavier, and I used a cinematic language I found suitable for me in which I presented signals for the audience to receive according to their awareness mechanisms, culture, and perspective" (Agence France-Press 2006).

In the same vein, the France-based Iraqi director Abbas Fahdel presented his film *Homeland: Iraq Year Zero* (*al-Watan: al-'Iraq sanat sifr*, 2015). After he made the feature film *World's Dawn* (*Fajr al-'alam*) in 2008, critics blamed him for presenting the Iran–Iraq war from a one-sided perspective, claiming that Iraq—then under Saddam Hussein—shattered the happiness of the Iraqi people by sending men to war, tearing families apart, and turning the delight of love between happily married couples into misery. The film failed to critique Iran for its provocation, and focused solely on what the director refers to as "the Iraqi mistake."

It seems Fahdel avoided this controversy in *Homeland*. He appeared to have more empathy with Iraqis as Iraqis first, despite their awareness of the cruelty of the former regime in managing their lives amid its atrocities. On the eve of the American attack on Iraq, the director makes room for his characters—in a well-studied, slow pace—to exchange news about the growing possibility of conquest from a purely nationalist stance, in which all announce their loyalty to the homeland. This approach helped Fahdel's new film to overcome many of the failures of his previous depiction, and to adopt a wider comprehensive vision.

Despite the existence of dozens of important Iraqi film experiments, there are some critics who judged Iraqi filmmakers hastily, saying, "the Iraqi documentary has not sufficiently invested in the means to narrate the Iraqi story. Unlike documentary filmmakers in neighboring Arab countries and other countries, we have not yet narrated many moments in our lives and our contemporary history" (Omar 2015). In the same

vein, the author of this hasty judgment advises Iraqis to watch important international films and take them as models before proceeding
to innovation.

Compendium of Directors
Qasim Hawal
Hawal co-founded the Palestinian Film Unit in 1970 after he joined the
Palestinian resistance in Beirut. He made several films, among them: *The
Cold River* (*al-Nahr al-barid*, 1971), *Our Little Houses* (*Buyutuna al-saghira*,
1974), *Why Do We Plant Roses . . . Why Do We Carry Weapons?* (*Limadha
nazra' al-wurud . . . limadha nahmil al-silah?* 1974), and *The Guns Will Not
Be Silent* (*Lann taskut al-banadiq*, 1974), produced by the Palestinian Film
Institute. He returned to Iraq in 1976, and made his film *Marshlands*, which
became a distinctive landmark in Iraqi and Arab documentary cinema.

3.1. Qasim Hawal

Victor Haddad
Haddad's career started in the film unit of the British-Iraqi Oil Company,
where he acquired advanced skills and techniques that opened doors for his
academic studies. In 1974, he was commissioned by the Iraqi Radio and TV
Agency to establish a film unit, which produced dozens of documentary and
feature films. In 1978, the Administration of Cinema and TV Affairs was
established as a department of the Ministry of Culture and Communications.
Haddad was assigned to carry out this task. He later became a lecturer and
trainer at the Centre of Radio and TV Research of the Arab League in Tunis,
where he lived between 1990 and 1993. His success was due to his unique
ability to maneuver around the red lines and limitations of producers (usually

state institutions), and deliver excellent work without scarifying its aesthetics, whether filming, editing, or writing the musical score. He passed away in 2011 in Cairo. Some of his works are: *Baghdad Through the Centuries* (*Baghdad 'abr al-'usur*, 1962), *Blessed Ramadan* (*Ramadan mubarak*, 1962), *Jawad Salim* (1962), *Shaping Silver* (*Siyaghit al-fidda*, 1963), *White Gold* (*al-Dhahab al-ab-yad*, 1964), *Days in Iraq* (*Ayyam fi-l-Iraq*, 1966), *Rotating Wheels* (*Dawalibuna al-da'ira*, 1969), *Inquiry* (*Tasa'ul*, 1969), *Floating Tanks* (*al-Saharij al-'a'ima*, 1971), *Cache of Treasures* (*Makman al-kunuz*, 1971), *Generations Harvest* (*Hasad al-ajyal*, 1972), and *Wonder Country* (*Balad al-'aja'ib*, 1980).

Mohammed Shukri Jamil

Jameel started his career in 1953, following the path of Victor Haddad in the film unit of the British-Iraqi Oil Company. In 1964, he left for Cairo to work with the General Company for Arab Film Production, which was run by the prominent Egyptian director Salah Abu Seif. It was there that he made the documentary *Family Picture* (*Sura 'a'iliya*), portraying the realities of Egyptian women, and another film, shown at Alexandria's Biennale, *The Sculptor Mahmoud Moukhtar* (*al-Nahhat Mahmud Mukhtar*).

Jamil was called back to Iraq in 1967, and worked with the Cinema and Theatre Administration, where he directed a musical that had no success. He also made several documentaries: *A Return to Basra* (*'Awda ila al-Basra*), *A Nation's Tragedy* (*Ma'sat sha'b*), *Land's Yearning* (*Hanin al-ard*), and *The Blue Suit* (*al-Badhla al-zarqa'*), which had an air of solid professionalism, even though soaked in ideology, if not propaganda. His technical capabilities enabled him to move naturally toward fiction filmmaking, in which he achieved a number of masterpieces, such as *The Thirsty* (*al-Zami'un*, 1973), and eventually *King Ghazi* (*al-Malik Ghazi*, 1993), which turned out to be the last Iraqi feature film until 2003.

3.2. Mohammed
Shukri Jamil

Sahib Haddad

Haddad was born in 1939 in al-Muraba', a popular quarter of Baghdad, and passed away in Baghdad in 1994. His first experience of acting was at the age of thirteen, years before joining the Institute of Fine Arts. He worked as an actor and assistant to director 'Abd al-Hadi Mubarak on the film *Euphrates Bride* (*'Arus al-Furat*, 1958). Then he joined the Artistic Modern Theatre Group, and later the Free Theatre Group. In Hungary he studied film editing, which became his main career, and edited numerous Iraqi films. Haddad returned to Iraq with the intention of establishing a film production company, but the heavy presence of the regime and its control and censorship pushed him to leave for Beirut, where he stayed for twelve years and produced more than twenty-five Lebanese, Egyptian, Syrian, and Iraqi films.

Later on he returned to Iraq to head the *Film Journal, al-Jaridat al-sinima'iya*, which was a weekly newsreel, shown in all Iraqi movie theaters before the feature film. Haddad transformed this space into a real workshop, where the best Iraqi camera operators, like Yusuf Michael, Salman Maz'al, Shikib Rashid, and William Danial, among many others, were trained and hired. He also edited many international and national fiction films by Samir Khuri, Kamiran Husni, 'Atif Salim, Youssef Chahine, Ja'far 'Ali, Faysal al-Yasiri, and Mohammed Shukri Jamil, among others. He directed several full-length fiction films, the best-known of which is *Another Day* (*Yawm akhar*, 1979), which became a landmark in Iraqi cinema. Sahib Haddad managed "to narrate the events in an artistic style through a clear cinematic expression free of needless fillings, presenting an artistic work with humanistic elements; the struggle between the landlords in a feudal system and the authority on one side and the peasants burdened by debts on the other" (Halil 2013). His films are shot beautifully and edited courageously: *Mutawi' and Bahiyya* (*Mutawi' wa Bahiyya*, 1982), *Building 13* (*'Amara 13*, 1987), and his war epic *Fire Borders* (*al-Hudud al-multahiba*, 1984) on the Iran–Iraq War, which was only shown after the war.

3.3. Sahib Haddad

Fire Borders bridged two cinematic styles: the documentary (known facts about the war with Iran and its crucial battles), and a narrative structure that goes beyond the front lines of the battle to introduce characters and their stories. The authenticity of the film prompted the ruling authority to ban it from 1982 until the war ended in 1988, due to a concern that it would influence the morale of the fighters because of its portrayal of a strong enemy.

Bassam al-Wardi

Al-Wardi, who passed away in 2007, is one of the most renowned Iraqi directors of documentary film, and the maker of the most controversial film in Iraq, which was banned for more than twenty-five years. His feature film *Travel Night* (*Laylat safar*, 1990) prompted widespread debate when the Saddam regime banned it because its star, Ghazwa al-Khalidi, joined the Iraqi opposition in exile. Al-Wardi was born in 1942, in al-Kazimiya neighborhood in the north of Baghdad. He dropped out of studying biology at Baghdad University for the sake of cinema, and joined the film department at the Institute of Fine Arts in 1961. His documentaries were largely cultural, including the biographies of prominent Iraqi artists, like the sculptors Mohammed Ghani Hikmat and Khalid al-Rahal and the painter 'Atta Sabri. His films have been described as lucid cinema works for their sharp vision and expert construction. Al-Wardi won great success for his main documentary film *A Story for the Magnitude* (*Hikaya li-l-mada*, most probably 1979), about the life of artist and writer Yahya Jawad. The film won several festival awards and has to be considered one of the most important in the history of Iraqi documentary films.

Faysal al-Yasiri

Faysal al-Yasiri was born in 1933. His work as a journalist (since 1948) and writer—he published a short-story collection, *Fi-l-tariq (On the Road)*, and a novel, *Kanat 'adhra' (She Was a Virgin*, 1952)—allowed him to bring a broad perspective to his work in cinema. In 1958, al-Yasiri was awarded a degree in the Art of Filmmaking and TV Programming in Vienna, and returned to Baghdad to become a TV director in 1958. He left Iraq again between 1959 and 1962 to work as a TV director in the German Democratic Republic. Then, after nearly a decade in Syria as a film and TV director, al-Yasiri returned to his homeland and made the films: *The Head* (*al-Ra's*, 1976), *The River* (*al-Nahr*, 1977), *My Beloved Babylon* (*Babil habibati*, 1987), and finally *Baghdad, a Rosy Dream* (*Baghdad hilm wardi*, 2013), which was banned in Iraq, despite the fact that it was produced for the event "Baghdad, the Capital of Arab Culture" in 2013. Two of al-Yasiri's documentaries became landmarks of Iraqi film and television history.

The first is *The Sniper* (*al-Qannas*, 1979), which was shot in Lebanon to portray the civil war through the actions of a sniper (actor Roger Asaaf), who targets his victims mercilessly. The film unveils numerous social contradictions and conflicts during the civil war—a restless, bloody struggle between the different parties, with no determination to stop the blood flow. It shows how the rival powers turned their followers into either amateur or professional killers. The second prominent work by al-Yasiri was the television program *The File* (*al-Malaf*, most probably 1991), in which he led a team that brought Iraqi TV out of its monotony and banal propaganda, to address the horrors caused by hundreds of thousands of bombshells dropped by the allied states on Iraq after the war of 1991, as punishment for Saddam's occupation of Kuwait. He interviewed state officials and military leaders in a style that had not been experienced by Iraqi audiences before, and engaged in discussions and debates, not just repeating stagnant ideas. It was not only the content that was new, but also the directing style, the presentation, and even the musical themes he deployed.

Khayriya al-Mansur

Director Khayriya al-Mansur grew up in a leftist family in al-Diwaniya, a city in the middle Euphrates region. She was not just the first female filmmaker in Iraq, but was also trained by the famous Egyptian filmmaker Youssef Chahine. Al-Mansur made her first short documentary, *The Girl of Mesopotamia* (*Bint al-rafidayn*, 1984), after she presented the script to Chahine, who made some corrections. It won several local awards and was the second-prize winner at the Tashkent film festival in 1984. Al-Mansur also has an extensive record of about 78 other films, among them: *The Magic Fingers* (*al-Anamil al-sahira*), about female artists in Iraq, and *Churches in Iraq* (*Kana'is al-'Iraq*). Her last documentary feature film, *Snow Does Not Erase the Memory* (*al-Thalj la-yamsah al-dhakira*), is about the occupation of Iraq. It was the first Iraqi–Egyptian production presenting the horrors of the American occupation. After the occupation of Iraq in 2003, al-Mansur worked for the Egyptian al-Nahrayn TV channel as the head of documentaries, and she presented a series of TV films produced by the channel called Profile. The series included sixty films about Iraqi artists, the most prominent of which were about Yusuf al-'Ani, Ja'far al-Sa'di, 'Abd al-Khaliq al-Mukhtar, Asya Kamal, and others. She also made a series of films called *Fine Art Story* (*Hikaya tashkiliya*), about the most prominent Iraqi artists.

Maysoon Pachachi

Maysoon Pachachi is a director, editor, and producer. She was born in 1947, the daughter of the politician and diplomat 'Adnan Pachachi. She studied in

Iraq, the United States, and the United Kingdom. Besides cinema, Pachachi holds a degree in philosophy, and has taught directing and cinema editing in the United Kingdom, Iraq, and Palestine (Jerusalem, Gaza, and Birzeit University). She is the co-founder of Working Together: Women Against Sanctions and War in Iraq, a group created in 2000 that opposed the sanctions and war on Iraq and is currently involved in supporting independent feminist initiatives in Iraq. She also ran the Baghdad Film School, together with Kasim Abid. Among her documentaries are: *Iraqi Women: Voices from Exile* (*al-Mar'a al-'iraqiya: aswat min al-manfa*, 1994), *Iranian Journey* (*Rihla iraniya*, 2000), *Living with the Past: People and Monuments in Medieval Cairo* (*al-'Aysh ma' al-madi: al-nas wa-l-ma'alim al-athariya fi-l-Qahira fi-l-qurun al-wusta*, 2001), *Return to the Land of Wonders* (*al-'Awda ila ard al-'aja'ib*, 2004), and *Our Feelings Took the Pictures: Open Shutters Iraq* (*Masha'iruna tal-taqit suwar: al-'Iraq maftuh 'ala misra'ayhi*, 2008).

Samir Jamal Aldin

Samir Jamal Aldin's documentary *Forget Baghdad* (*Insa Baghdad*, 2002) presents a controversial case, as it documents the lives of Jewish Iraqi writers living in Israel who were experiencing racism, and who recall their expulsion from Iraq. Though Jamal Aldin is half Swiss, his approach to this film is very Iraqi, in terms of how he presents an issue of fundamental Iraqi transformation. The film recalls the memories and thoughts of three famous Jewish Iraqi writers from the first generation: Shimon Ballas, Samy Michael, and Samir Naqqash, together with Moshe Houri, the former real estate trader, and Ella Habiba Shohat, an expert in Israeli cinema from the second generation of Iraqi immigrants. Ten years later, the director returned with *Iraqi Odyssey* (*'Udisiya 'iraqiya*), a documentary film that follows the journeys of five of his family members who left Iraq in three stages to different destinations all over the world, exposing stories of deprivation, fragmentation, and disappointment. He opens the files of the political left in Iraq, and explores modern Iraqi history, from the British occupation to the end of the Ba'th regime in 2003. While he criticizes the lack of freedom and democracy, and authoritarian trends at all stages, he devotes most of his critique to Saddam Hussein's regime.

Kasim Abid

Kasim Abid graduated from the Institute of Fine Arts in Baghdad and holds an MA from VGIK-All Union State Institute of Cinematography, Moscow. He moved to London in 1982, where he continues to live and work as a filmmaker. In Abid's opinion, the cinema is "the voice of those without voice" (Hady, 2009), particularly when it is independent and influenced by directors like himself with painful life experiences. He studied in Baghdad and Moscow, then fled to London, before returning to his city after the fall of Saddam and trying to reestablish himself. During his first months back in Iraq, he joined Maysoon Pachachi in establishing the nonprofit Independent Film and TV College in Baghdad. Here he organized three courses, each of them graduating twenty students, who produced eleven short documentaries among them. He was forced to leave Iraq in 2006, after the deterioration of the security situation in the country. Throughout his time in Iraq, he was collecting material for his film *Life After the Fall*, which won the best film award at the Munich International Documentary Film Festival. He recalls: "When I returned to Iraq after thirty years of absence, I met three generations of my family from different ages and moods; each of them is a possible main character in an artistic work. I had no clear idea about making a film or writing a script. But the idea came to me and developed gradually. In four years I observed the transformations of the family and the whole society it lives in. I had neither a script nor a working plan. I was only collecting material to rediscover the family I left in my youth. It became clear to me that I am shooting a story that is becoming clearer with the development of events in Iraq. Paradoxically, the family, which had been solid under the dictatorship, began to fall apart after the occupation. I realized later on, especially after the murder of my younger brother in an ambiguous way, that I cannot add anything. All that I add is meaningless" (Hady 2009)."

Despite dozens of important Iraqi cinematic experiments, some critics commented hastily: "The Iraqi documentary is still in its infancy and has not served in any significant way to narrate the Iraqi story. Unlike in other neighboring Arab countries, it has not narrated many moments of our lives and our contemporary history" (Omar 2015). In fact, there are still many stories,

3.4. Kasim Abid

big and small, old and new, that Iraqis could dig out for themselves and for the world. This holds true not only for potential stories that may serve as material for Iraqi documentary filmmaking but also for the history of Iraqi documentary as a whole. Thus, this article should not be considered more than a concise but incomplete contribution to a unfinished historiography.

References

Agence France-Press. 2006. "Taqrir thaqafy fi-l-wakalat al-sahafiya al-firinsiyya." *Al Jazeera*, June 20. aljazeera.com.

———. 2010. "Uns Baghdad yaftah malaf al-yahud al-'iraqiyin al-muhajjarin." December 11. elaph.com.

Hady, Sa'd. 2009. "Qasim 'Abid: Hall hunak haya 'iraqiya ba`d al-suqut?" *Al-Akhbar*, Beirut, March 12. al-akhbar.com.

Halil, Sa'dun. 2013. "Hiwar ma'a al-bahith al-duktur Ahmad Isma'il 'Abud." *Markaz al-dirasat wa-l-abhath al-'ilmaniya fil-l-'alam al-'arabi*, May 8. m.ahewar.org.

al-Mada. 2014. "Hadith 'an al-sinima fi-l-'Iraq: min dar al-shifa', tamuz 1906 illa film ghayr salih li-l-'ard 2005." Issue 3220. almadapaper.net

Omar, Ali. 2015. "Limadha la nusawiq li al-hikaya al-'iraqiya' watha'iqqiyan?" *al-Mada*, November 26. almadapaper.net

al-Rashid, Muhammad. 2008. "Al-film al-tasjily: bayn al-watha'iqiya wa-l-siyaq al-ikhbary." *Mudawannat al-sinima al-tasjiliya*. February 7. cdsagher.blogspot.com.

al-Rawi, Nizar. 2012. "Sinima bilad al-rafidayn qaddamat aflaman naw'iya hasaddat jawa'iz 'alamiya wa-'arabiya." *al-Shabiba*, July 2.

Reuters. 2011. "Bahith: al-'Iraq antaj 400 film tasjily nisfaha ba'd suqut Sadam." May 12. ara.reuters.com.

Salim, Kamal Latif. 2017. "Kayf dakhalat al-sinima li-l-mara al-ula illa Baghdad." *al-Mada*, May 21. almadapaper.net

4

PALESTINE FIGHTS: BEHIND THE SCENES OF PLO–GDR COOPERATION IN FILMMAKING

Irit Neidhardt

In recent years, and especially within the realm of discourses about archives, there is an increasing interest in films made by the Palestinian Liberation Organization (PLO) between the late 1960s and the early 1980s. Due to the claim that the (unspecified) archives have been lost, the debates and related research on the cinema of the Palestinian Revolution are based on the supposedly lost films themselves, and on oral history.[1] The legal and official political context of the making of the films is rarely of interest, though documents of this nature are available, due to the fact that most of the PLO films are international coproductions made through standard bilateral agreements. This article focuses on one such agreement and the two documentary films[2] that were based on this dossier.

Palestinian filmmaking started in exile in the late 1960s. As film production is always regulated by national law, only the PLO, which is widely acknowledged as the sole representative of the Palestinian people, produced films that were internationally considered Palestinian. Michel Khleifi's highly acclaimed feature documentary *The Fertile Memory* (*al-Dhakira al-khisba*, 1980) was not made under the umbrella of the PLO, and is thus regarded as the first independent Palestinian film. Since the PLO had to move its headquarters from Beirut to Tunis in the early 1980s and reduced its filmmaking immensely, almost all Palestinian films are independent in the sense that they are not produced within the framework of Palestinian public bodies.

As an exile organization, the PLO depended on cooperation with states that provided the liberation movement with access to the means of film production. Though it worked on its foundation, the PLO itself never had proper laboratories. The film lab that the PLO's economic institution, Palestine Martyrs Works Society (SAMED), had set up in 1980 was destroyed in the Israeli war on the PLO in Lebanon in 1982.

The Rock Cinematographic Industries (RCI) was, according to written sources, another SAMED institution that was destroyed in 1982 (Adams 1986, 86–89; Wright 1981). It is recorded to have been a dubbing studio translating martial arts and Hollywood films for the Arab market. Filmmakers related to the PLO, however, remember that it was actually a joint venture the PLO made with a partner (though they do not remember whom), that operated well into the 1980s. RCI appears as one of the coproducers of Mai Masri and Jean Chamoun's 1983 documentary *Under the Rubble (Taht al-anqad)*.

An important partner with regard to film, and later also TV, was the German Democratic Republic (GDR) (1949–90). A relatively high number of records about its almost twenty years of collaboration (1974–90) with the PLO can be found in various official German archives. Not all the documents have been de-classified and made accessible yet. One of the files archived in the Foundation Archives of Parties and Mass Organizations of the GDR in the Federal Archives (SAPMO) in Berlin is labeled *Working Title: PLO, Final Title: Palestine Fights (AT: PLO, ET: Palästina kämpft)* (SAPMO-BArch, DR118/3658).[3] It records the first contacts and agreements made between the PLO Department of Culture and Information (DCI) and the DEFA's Department for Documentary Film.[4] The title *Palestine Fights* is used to name both a film project and a broader cooperation scheme between the DCI and the DEFA that was initially planned for the years 1975 to 1978. The dossier stands out from other folders due to its quite unusual variety of documents, ranging from newspaper clippings to official letters, drafts of a bilateral contract, pay slips, a film scenario, lists of archival footage viewed for the production of a PLO film, reports to the foreigners' police, notes for the file, minutes of meetings, delivery notes, and film budgets. Therefore it allows a comprehensive insight into the fundamentals of the cooperation between the PLO and the GDR in film and TV. While in later records on cooperation between the two partners the production of an individual film can be studied or bilateral contracts read, this file allows one to observe the conceptual setup of the DCI-DEFA collaboration: their respective interests and actual difficulties, their organizational and bureaucratic structures, and the PLO's long-term vision of its film and TV policy and infrastructure, as well as the GDR's political and economic interests and needs.

This article follows the entire path of *Palestine Fights*. As archives are rarely as complete as one might wish, the file with the label *Working Title: PLO, Final Title: Palestine Fights* ends rather abruptly in 1976. The project title, however, appears again in dossiers of other GDR institutions. Thus this text keeps track of additional accessible documents until this project's apparent end in 1980.

Historical Context: Diplomatic Recognition and New Political Roles

The earliest document in the *Palestine Fights* folder is a typed copy of a newspaper article from December 13, 1974, about visits of GDR prime minister Horst Sindermann to several new nation-states, including a meeting with the chairman of the PLO, Yasser Arafat, in Damascus in November 1974. The passages on Syria, Iraq, and the PLO are highlighted. December the same year is the date of an exchange of letters between the PLO Department of Culture and Information and the DEFA Department for Documentary Film.

In order to understand the documents in the file, some information about the political context seems indispensable. After the Arab defeat in the June war of 1967, which resulted in the Israeli occupation of the West Bank—including Jerusalem, the Gaza Strip, the Sinai Peninsula, and the Golan Heights—the PLO, launched by the Arab League in 1964, turned into a mass organization. At its summit in October 1974, the Arab League affirmed the right of the Palestinian people to self-determination, as well as "the right of the Palestinian people to establish an independent national authority under the command of the Palestine Liberation Organization, the sole legitimate representative of the Palestinian people, in any Palestinian territory that is liberated" (UNISPAL 1974). Since then, the liberation movement has represented Palestine at various supra-national organizations, like the United Nations and the Movement of Non-Aligned Countries, to name only two.

This strengthened position and new diplomatic role of the PLO, which was internationally approved by over one hundred states, shows some parallels to the situation of the GDR during those same years. The socialist Germany, founded in 1949, was recognized only by its fellow socialist states in Central and Eastern Europe. The Federal Republic of Germany's Hallstein Doctrine of 1955 had declared the establishment of any diplomatic relations with the GDR a hostile act to the capitalist German state; the Soviet Union was regarded as an exception. Since no text of the doctrine ever existed,[5] the countermeasures were not clearly defined. Yet the rich, high-tech West German state used the tool of economic pressure, especially against young nation-states that considered building official ties with the socialist Germany. In 1969–70, five states broke the doctrine and entered full diplomatic relations with the GDR: Iraq, Syria, Egypt, the Congo, and Algeria. As a result, as well as due to new West German politics under Chancellor Willy Brandt, more than one hundred states recognized the smaller Germany diplomatically in 1972–73; in September 1973, the GDR became a member of the United Nations. This pressed the country to instantly find and define its role on the international political stage. In a constitutional amendment of October 1974, the parliament of the GDR newly codified its anti-imperialist conviction and years-long support of national liberation movements. In part one, "Foundations of Social and State Order," chapter one, "Political Foundations," it now said that "the German Democratic Republic supports those states and peoples that fight against imperialism and colonialism and for national freedom and independence in their struggle for social progress" (Gesetz vom 7. Oktober 1974, 2012).

With regard to the media cooperation between the PLO and GDR, it is important to note the role of Syria. Since 1956, the GDR had a trade mission in Damascus, as well as a consul general; hence official relations existed between the two small states[6] far before diplomatic recognition. Syrian TV, which started broadcasting in 1960, and the National Film Organization, founded in 1963, both had good relations with the corresponding institutions in the GDR. Since the mid-1960s and until the change of leading state personnel following the military putsch of Hafez al-Assad in 1970, the Palestinian Abdallah Hourani was director general of the General Organization of Radio and TV–Syria. In 1969, he had also started to work with the PLO. When the DCI set up its first collaboration with the DEFA Studio for Documentary Film in 1974, Hourani was the deputy chairman of this highest Palestinian cultural institution. Though the PLO was based in Beirut, he kept his office in Damascus.[7] In his new position, Hourani's German partners were the same people he had worked with as head of Syrian television.

Two more aspects explain the fast, though difficult, procedures of cooperation and the generally strong ties between the Department of Culture and Information and GDR media institutions, which lasted until the fall of the Berlin wall in November 1989. The DCI was the only supra-party institution of the PLO that was not controlled by the strongest and rather bourgeois party Fatah, but by the Marxist-Leninist Democratic Front for the Liberation of Palestine (DFLP). Among the political parties under the umbrella of the PLO, it had the strongest ideological proximity with the Marxist-Leninist Socialist Unity Party of Germany (SED), which ruled the GDR for forty years. The DFLP operated from Damascus. In 1973, Yasser Abed Rabbo became the head of the Beirut-based DCI. He was deputy secretary general of the DFLP, and the party's representative on the PLO Executive Committee, the body acting as the PLO's government. Furthermore, cameraman-editor-director Qais al-Zubaidi had worked with both Syrian TV and the Syrian Film Organization before serving as the film delegate of the PLO Department of Culture and Information for some twenty years. Al-Zubaidi had studied at the state-run film school of the GDR in Potsdam, near Berlin, in the 1960s, had a good command of the necessary languages, was familiar with the East German system, and had excellent networks.

The *Palestine Fights* Folder

Two documents in the *Palestine Fights* folder shed light on the DCI's long-term plans in the field of film and TV, as well as on the interests each partner had in the cooperation. In 1975, a PLO delegation from Beirut came to East Berlin to work on the first film with the working title *PLO*, based on a cooperation agreement that was still under negotiation. In the delegation was the head of the PLO Department of International Relations and International Information, who, despite being part of the film team, functioned as a messenger of the PLO Executive Committee. A note about a meeting between members of the DEFA Studio for Documentary Film and the guests from the PLO, dated July 28, 1975, reports, inter alia, on the ideas and wishes of the PLO Executive Committee regarding further cooperation. 1. Collaboration with the DEFA Studio for Animated Film regarding the production of animated films for children by PLO filmmakers. 2. The construction of a film studio by the PLO in the GDR. It seems from the memo that the PLO negotiated with the Czechoslovak Socialist Republic (CSSR) about installing TV studios there.

> For the production of documentary and eventually fiction films there is the wish to construct a respective studio with modern technology in the GDR. If possible, the necessary requirements shall be made by the beginning of 1976. The needed valuta [free convertible foreign currency] are said to be already approved by the executive committee of the PLO and are available.
>
> The director of the Department of Information and National Education and his deputy are willing, as authorized representatives of the PLO, to come at any time to the GDR to negotiate the issue.[8]

In addition to their common ideological interests, the PLO and GDR each had concrete needs the other could provide, if not mutual dependency. While the PLO needed to collaborate with states that gave access to means of production and permitted the Liberation Organization to set up autonomous institutions on their soil, the GDR needed valuta. As the GDR currency, the mark, was not convertible on the international market (including banks, hotels, or currency exchange offices), the state was constantly searching for options to get hold of valuta, preferably U.S. dollars or West German Deutsche Marks (DM), which were both strong currencies at the time. The PLO in those days was affluent and paid in U.S. dollars. Cooperation agreements that provided for the expenses abroad to be covered by the partners allowed DEFA teams to make films outside the GDR.

While this first document points at the PLO's media strategy, the second document, the above-mentioned cooperation agreement, gives insight into its tactics and operational ideas. The first draft that is filed in the *Palestine Fights* dossier was proposed by the PLO and is not dated in the Arabic version, yet it is signed. The receipt stamp on the German translation is August 4, 1975, thus a few months after the beginning of the war in Lebanon.[9] The German version is not signed. In sixteen articles, the draft defines the cooperation and mutual support in the production of a total of 1600 meters of 35mm film (roughly one hour) by each side within the period of three years. As a first work, the PLO intended to realize a compilation film based on archival material that was partly owned by the PLO, but mainly existed in GDR archives. According to their employees, the PLO film archives in Lebanon mainly stored footage of current political and military events of the party, as well as moving images that were handed over by the United Nations Relief and Works Agency for Palestine Refugees in the Near East (UNRWRA). Historical film material from Palestine since the invention of film was not in the hands of the Palestinians. It was mainly made by Western film teams (the Lumières shot in Palestine as early as 1896), the British Mandatory Forces, or Zionist organizations. In the first decades of the twentieth century, this footage was traded for the production of newsreels or other kinds of films and therefore can be found in most European public film archives.

The contract draft in the *Palestine Fights* folder suggests that the DEFA Studio for Documentary Film was to bear the costs for the postproduction: machines, technical and creative personnel, translations, and positive copies. In return, the PLO intended to facilitate and assist the DEFA Studio with shooting in Lebanon,[10] given that the DEFA team brought its own technical equipment and bore all the costs for the postproduction back in East Germany. As far as the expenses were concerned, the suggestion was not to pay the mutual aid in foreign currency, to agree that the DEFA Studio would cover more expenses than the Information Department, and that in case of a PLO overdraft, the sum would be credited to the DEFA Studio for another production. If in case of vis major, which explicitly included war, the PLO could not carry out its duty toward the DEFA Studio, the two sides were to find a solution for how to use the values at the Information Department until the end of 1978.

A second draft of the cooperation agreement, dated March 11, 1976, typed in German and with handwritten remarks added to it, is filed in the dossier. This draft is obviously a proposal from DEFA. Above it is a paper with three different handwritten notes, signed twice with the same initial. The exchange is dated between November 5 and 8, 1976, and consists of short comments and questions. It was not clear to the German side who were the proper signing parties of the agreement. On the one hand, the documents suggest that the issue was moved to ministerial ranks in the GDR state hierarchy, as both valuta and traveling abroad were involved. On the other hand, the PLO now had an office in East Berlin, yet its status was unclear in the first couple of years (see Maeke 2017, 124, 137). Some formal exchange between the DEFA and the PLO's Berlin office, as well as between the DEFA and the headquarters in Beirut, can be found. In the new contract draft, the shooting of the DEFA Studio for Documentary Film in Lebanon was questioned, with regard to both time and place. The dates were no longer specified as being at the end of 1978; the wording was now "upon further agreement," and the shoot was not to take place in Lebanon, where the PLO had autonomy over the refugee camps, but should be "conducted in countries in which the support of the PLO is fully granted" (Cooperation Agreement, March 11, 1976), this being questioned in view of the war. The new version speaks about financial claims of the DEFA Studio, instead of overdrafts being credited to future film productions. A completely new paragraph is added, stating that "in the credits of the films, both sides name only their own studio as producer without mention of the contracted partner" (Cooperation Agreement, March 11, 1976). Thus, without knowledge of the production files and/or the cooperation agreements, it is not possible to trace films that were made with a share from, or under significant control of, the PLO.

While contract negotiations continued, however, a film was completed under the project scheme *Palestine Fights*. Its production is carefully documented in the *Palestine Fights* folder, under the working title *PLO*; the final title became *Born in Palestine/From Palestine* (*Geboren in Palästina/ Min Filastin*). The twenty-two-minute black and white film was directed by the Lebanese director Rafiq Hajjar.[11] It is framed by the story of Ahmad al-Jammal, the narrator and political staff member, as he is called in a DEFA document from September 9, 1975 that lists the PLO guests. *Born in Palestine* consists mainly of archival film footage, as well as some still photographs. The film begins with contemporary street scenes from a Palestinian refugee camp in Lebanon. The camp is composed of makeshift homes for the newer refugees from 1967, and simple houses belonging to the refugees from 1948. The narrator walks along a street toward the camera, and we hear his story from the off. The footage from Lebanon is silent, and when Ahmad al-Jamal introduces himself with his full name, the frame freezes. He says he was born in 1940 in Lubya, near Tabariya in Palestine. Then we see the film's title, and the scene cuts to al-Jamal in a park in a completely different geographical area. From the *Palestine Fights* dossier it is understood that the shoot took place in Potsdam, near Berlin. At the beginning of the film, the narration is strictly in the first person.

It is the childhood memories of the narrator, until the Nakba in 1948. The archival footage of the first scenes consists of well-known historical newsreel material about the war in Palestine in 1947–48. While the narrator became a refugee, as the viewer has already learned, the story focuses on the lost Palestine, and the voice-over becomes politically analytical. The analysis starts with the First Zionist Congress in Basel, Switzerland in 1897, and ends with Yasser Arafat explaining the goal of the PLO to build a democratic Palestinian state for all citizens. The central texts of Zionist politicians regarding their economic and military cooperation with imperial powers are cited from a Leninist perspective, and at times contextualized, at times visualized with film footage. Zionist activities in Russia at the time of the October Revolution in 1917 are analyzed from the perspective of the working class, with the argument that propagating the Zionist religious-nationalist concept was dividing the working class and weakening the revolutionary movement. The murderous Nazi policy against the Jewish population in Europe is talked about and condemned, and the cooperation between the Zionist movement and the Nazi government is analyzed. Imperialist and colonial violence in Vietnam, on the African continent, and in Latin America is equated with the Zionist settlement in, and the occupation of, Palestine. The narrator repeatedly reminds the viewer that Jews, Muslims, and Christians have been living together in the Middle East for centuries, and that hostilities did not arise because of different religious beliefs or fate, but by using religious sentiments to spur political mobilization. The last quarter of the film deals with class- and race-based violence inside the Jewish community in Israel, and features Jewish voices against Israeli politics. Jewish immigrants from Arab countries talk to the camera about their social conditions, and a trade union meeting of Arab Jewish and Palestinian workers is attended. As the PLO was prohibited in Israel, and thus the shooting of film in the country was made impossible for the liberation movement, Western camera teams were sent to make the required moving images, or clips from existing films were used. As an accompanying document, *Planning for the Finishing (Endfertigungsdisposition* 24.9.1975), shows, in the case of Geboren in *Palästina*, the footage is from the film *Israel 74* by the Group Dr. Sabine Katins of the GDR-Television. Austrian-born political poet Erich Fried, who was filmed for this documentary in London where he lived since escaping the Nazis, is reciting his poem "Hear O Israel" ("Höre Israel")[12] from his poetry book *Hear O Israel: Poems against Injustice (Höre Israel: Gedichte gegen das Unrecht*, 1974). Testimonies from the Arabic translation of the book *With My Own Eyes (Be'am 'eayni, 1975)*, by the Israeli human rights lawyer Felicia Langer, about the situation of Palestinian prisoners she defended, are also read out and more or less affirmed by the Palestinian teacher and ex-prisoner Latifa Hawari, who narrates her story in a highly reflective and analytical way. In the last frame, al-Jamal, who is in the park in Potsdam, asks the audience if they have ever asked themselves why Palestine vanished from the world map.

Born in Palestine was completed in November 1975, and shown in the official competition of the Leipzig International Filmweek for Documentary and Short Film, where it won the Silver Dove (Mauersberger 1997). The festival, which still continues today, is the oldest documentary film festival in the world, and at that time was the biggest and most important. In 1973, the festival was nationalized by the GDR government, and that same year, filmmakers from the PLO participated as a delegation for the first time. Some of them had been in Leipzig before, but as individuals or representatives of their parties or institutions. Showing the film and receiving an award at this outstanding festival drew attention to it, yet the story of *Born in Palestine* ends rather abruptly here. A file memo from October 20, 1975 (File Memo Regarding the Problem of the Cooperation Agreement with the PLO/*Aktenvermerk zum Problem des Kooperationsvertrages mit der PLO*), declares without further explanation that, due to unanswered questions, the cooperation agreement is now regarded as invalid. The matter was placed in the hands of the directorates of the Ministry of Culture and the Ministry of Foreign Affairs. No new working orders were to be accepted, and no direct talks with the PLO were to be conducted, until the PLO solved the problem. An internal note from October 28, 1975, states that the final work on the film *Born in Palestine* has been completed, and the English- and French-language versions can now be finalized the following week. The question asked in this memo is whether the agreed-upon copies will now not be made, following the note from October 20. The copies were to be: two Arabic 35mm, two German 35mm, two English 35mm, two French 35mm, and two Arabic 16mm. The same question was forwarded to the Ministry of Culture on November 3, 1975. A bill of delivery from December 4, 1975, from the DEFA Studio to the office of the PLO in the GDR, states that forty-two canisters with negatives for the film *Born in Palestine* were handed over, and hence the delivery of material was complete. The story, though, was not yet over.

The *Palestine Fights* Scheme in Ministerial Hands

Despite this delivery bill, a few months later a five-page letter from Abdallah Hourani, dated April 13, 1976, was addressed to the Afro-Asian Solidarity Committee, GDR—Berlin. It is preserved in a dossier of the Solidarity Committee of the GDR (Solidaritätskomitee der DDR), an institution comparable to a Ministry of Development Aid within a capitalist state (SAPMO-BArch DZ8/178). The accompanying cover letter is to be found in another folder of the Solidarity Committee's files (SAP-MO-BArch DZ8/215), and states that, due to the war in Beirut, Hourani's letter was transmitted to East Berlin by the Embassy of the German Democratic Republic in the Syrian Arab Republic. Copies were sent to the Central Committee of the Socialist Unity Party of Germany and the Ministry of Culture.[13] In the letter, Hourani expresses his thanks for their support and cooperation, affirms the importance of the partnership, and asks why the agreement came to a standstill: to date, he writes, the PLO has not received any copy of the film, despite repeated requests. The film therefore could not be presented at festivals that were important for the PLO, such as Tashkent, Krakow, the Palestinian Festival in Baghdad, and others. Regarding the cooperation agreement, Hourani stresses its significance to the PLO, stating that the PLO Department of Culture and Information was interested in signing an agreement similar to those the DEFA was signing with cultural institutions of other Arab countries. He also wonders why the delegation of the DEFA Studio that was supposed to visit in November 1975 neither came nor answered letters. He reinforces this invitation, expressing his desire to welcome a delegation in either Beirut or Damascus.

Indeed, the DEFA Studio had previously accepted the invitation, and also sent a list of the delegation's names and requests to the PLO Department of Culture and Information in Beirut on March 5, 1975 (SAP-MO-BArch, DR118/3658). An internal note without date is titled, "In relation to possibilities given by the invitation of the PLO, the following productions are suggested," and gives an idea about the DEFA's production interests with regard to the cooperation agreement. The authors propose to interview Yasser Arafat during the mission in Lebanon. Five subjects to ask him about are listed, the duration of the interview is projected to be forty minutes, and it was suggested that parts of it might be used for either currently planned or future documentary films or broadcast on television. "The Anti-Imperialist Struggle for the Legitimate Rights of the Palestinian People" could have been another film project, or "The Teacher and Her Family," dealing with the question of how a family lives in a refugee camp, based on the story of a female teacher who is a daughter at home but who at school serves as a father figure for many of her pupils. The mission would also have been used for shooting a DEFA children's film on "The Oldest City in the World"—Byblos in Lebanon. A work envisioned for 1976, "Petrol in the Struggle of the Arab Peoples" could have been prepared, and would have also required shooting in Iraq and Egypt.

An answer to Hourani's letter can be found in the files of the Ministry of Culture's Department for International Relations/PLO (SAP-MO-BArch DR1/11647 1/2). It is written by the head of the Department of International Relations at the Ministry of Culture, dated May 24, 1976, and addressed to the embassy of the GDR in the Syrian Arab Republic, which transmitted Hourani's letter. It briefly informs the embassy about the incident, saying that the DEFA Studio for Documentary unilaterally bore enormous costs, and therefore a film team from the DEFA should travel to Lebanon or Syria at the expense of the PLO. All of these matters, the author says, are regulated by a contract that has been confirmed by the ministry and is ready to be signed. The embassy is asked to inform Mr. Hourani that the DEFA Studio is interested in signing the agreement and is expecting a representative of the PLO to sign it in Berlin. Only after concluding the contract could the delivery of copies of the film *Born in Palestine* be negotiated. A document from November 1, 1976, states that Abdallah Hourani, plus two additional people, would arrive in Berlin on November 3, 1976, and stay until November 6. It details that the guests' languages are Arabic and French, and the purpose of their visit is to sign a contract between the DEFA Studio for Documentary Films and the PLO. Applications and directives for two official trips by a DEFA film team of director Kurt Tetzlaff[14] and his colleagues are also documented. A research visit took place in 1978, and a second trip for the actual shooting of the film, with the working title *Palestine Fights*, was undertaken in 1979.

A note for the file by the Solidarity Committee of the GDR from September 19, 1978, about a meeting with the Ministry of Culture's Department for Asia/Africa/Latin America (AAL) (SAPMO-BArch DZ8/215), lists the exchange with the PLO and PLO activities in the GDR in the field of the arts for 1979. One item on the list is the information that the DEFA Studio for Documentary Film had begun working on a film called *Palestine Fights*. The attendees of the meeting were advised to learn more about it, and "to examine if the Solidarity Committee could use this film for its purposes."

The film was finally called *The Children of Palestine (Die Kinder Palästinas)*, directed by Kurt Tetzlaff. This 54-minute color movie opens with three small children wearing the blue shirt of Fatah's Lion Cubs,[15] posing for the camera and making the victory sign. The youngest of them, practically a toddler, cannot coordinate his fingers, so one of the older kids helps him out. The question of why children are trained to fight is the subtext of the film, and is explained verbally at the end by Yasser Arafat. Within this frame, the German guests of the PLO ask what the liberation struggle means for the daily lives of Palestinians, and how it influences the reality of children. The film is mainly shot in the Bourj al-Barajneh, Rashidiyyeh, and Tel al-Za'tar camps, with the film team spending most of its time in the latter, at the House of Steadfast Children (Bayt Atfal al-Sumud), one of the PLO's orphanages. Throughout the film, Tetzlaff and his cameraman, Jürgen Greunig, observe the daily routine from a respectful distance. They observe and introduce family life, as well as institutional setups, taking time to allow the audience to grasp a sense of the place. Their status as outsiders, as visitors who want to learn, and who are at times overwhelmed by what they see, is never hidden. The sporadic commentary is reminiscent of a travelogue, and is always subjective, something that was very unusual in DEFA films. Apart from the scenes of the military training at the Lion's Cubs, nobody ever poses for the camera. In the opening minutes of *The Children of Palestine*, a funeral is shown. The German team had asked to talk to the widow, who refused, telling them that journalists always filmed the misery of Palestinians but did not help. It appears as if her message echoed throughout the entire DEFA team's visit.

4.1. *The Children of Palestine* (1980), directed by Kurt Tetzlaff.

The production file for *The Children of Palestine* has been so far untraceable. The folder of PROGRESS, the distribution arm of the DEFA, containing the documents regarding the release permit, is, however, available (SAPMO-BArch DR1/Z 3572). The final permit for *The Children of Palestine* is dated December 19, 1980, and allows the film to be shown in cinemas in the GDR for a period of five years (Protokoll Nr. 0503/80). It did not permit children under the age of fourteen to watch the film. On the permission form, a handwritten note from December 23, 1985, reads "no extension." All documents in the file mention the film's final name, as well as the working title *Palestine Fights*. While in the opening credits of *The Children of Palestine* the names of the Palestinian team members are mentioned, and Palestinian friends of the film are thanked, no coproducing country is indicated in the application for the release permit, just as was agreed in the second draft of the cooperation agreement between the PLO Department of Culture and Information and the DEFA Studio for Documentary Films. The three-page film assessment from November 15, 1980, which is enclosed with the documents of the permission, echoes the new paragraph of the 1974-amended GDR constitution, as it concludes: "The film *The Children of Palestine* is a moving document of our solidarity, makes our solidarity with the Palestinian people more concrete, gives it a name, an address, a face."

Even though Hourani visited with a delegation of three people to sign the contract in 1976, it did not seem to have solved all the problems. Since 1976, several minutes of meetings with the head of the Section for Culture of the PLO, a Fatah-controlled organization—this body must not be mistaken for the PLO Department of Culture and Information that was headed by the deputy secretary-general of the DFLP but was often confused by the Germans, as several people from the DEFA recount— mention the *film problematic* (die Filmproblematik), but it is only discussed once. In a note for the file about a conversation with the head of the Section of Culture of the PLO on March 15, 1979, at the Ministry of Culture (Aktenvermerk über ein Gespräch mit dem Leiter der Sektion Kultur der PLO am 15.3.1979 im Ministerium für Kultur), it says (on page 3):

> On this occasion he informed us that the film *Born in Palestine*, which was awarded the Silver Dove at the Leipzig International Filmweek for Documentary and Short Film in 1975, is still at the PLO mission in Berlin and has not yet been shown in Lebanon. He further mentioned that in a few months there would be a change in the PLO office in Berlin.

The film's title appears in some filmographies of Palestinian cinema, mainly as *Mawlud fi Filastin*, the literal translation from the German title, rather than the original Arabic title, *Min Filastin*, from the film itself (Cine Palestino 2011; Hosny 2014; Saleh 2013—but only Saleh provides some limited information on the film's content). Actual screenings, apart from individual presentations in Germany in the context of this research, could not be traced. In the Palestinian Audio-Visual Archive, only the German copy is stored, whereas usually several language versions of the PLO-produced films exist.

The small glimpse this text provides into the extraordinary richness of the accessible archival material about the cooperation in film between the PLO and the GDR shows that the collaboration goes far beyond the production of movies. As film laws always follow political, economic, and technological interests, the *Palestine Fights* folder suggests that further research of the joint filmmaking might help us to understand crucial elements of the (re-)construction of Palestine, of how the socialist German state consolidated itself temporarily, as well as the ways in which solidarity was spelled out in practical terms. It thus calls for a more comprehensive political reading of these films.

References

Adams, James. 1986. *The Financing of Terror: Behind the PLO, IRA, Red Brigades and M19 Stand the Paymasters.* New York: Simon and Schuster.

"Bratpfanne vor der Sonne." 1965. *Der Spiegel/12*, March 3. 29–33.

Buali, Sheyma. 2012. "A Militant Cinema: Mohanad Yaqubi in Conversation with Sheyma Buali." In *Contemporary Visual Culture in North Africa and the Middle East.* Ibraaz. 2 May. ibraaz.org.

Cine Palestino. 2011. "Biofilmografías: Rafiq Hajjar." cinepalestino.com

Darwish, Ibrahim. 2011. "al-Sinima al-filastiniyya: arshif al-da'i' mahatthu al-hurub wa-l-sha'i' at" (The Palestinian Cinema: A Lost Archive Erased by Wars and Rumors). In *Al Quds Institution for Culture and Heritage.* 22 March. alqudslana.com.

Donia al-Watan. 2015. "Tilifisyun Filastin yatamakkan min ihdhar arshif al-thawra al-filastiniyya min Almanya" (Palestinian Television Brings the Archive of the Palestinian Revolution from Germany). *Donia-al-Watan,* 15 March. alwatanvoice.com.

Fourest, Laure. 2012. "Un cinéma palestinien 'en mal d'archive.'" *Ateliers d'Anthropologie* (36). ateliers.revues.org.

"Gesetz vom 7. Oktober 1974." 2012. In *Geschichte und Geschehen Oberstufe Online, 6.2: Die DDR und der Westen: Standpunkte zu Staat und Nation. Zusatzmaterial.* 290–95. Stuttgart: Ernst Klett Verlag.

al-Ghul, Asma. 2012. "Ghalib Sha`th: al-Suriyyun akhadhu arshif al-sinima" (Ghaleb Shaath: The Syrians Took the Palestinian Cinema Archive." *Al Jazeera Documentary,* May 6. doc.aljazeera.net.

Grey, William Glen. 2003. *Germany's Cold War: The Global Campaign to Isolate East Germany, 1949–1969.* Chapel Hill: University of North Carolina Press.

Habashneh, Khaijeh. 2008. "Palestinian Revolution Cinema." *This Week in Palestine.* thisweekinpalestine.com.

Hosni, Dia. 2014. "Cinematic Thoughts, the Palestinian Cinematography." *Al-Ahram al-masa'i,* December 25.

Jacir, Annemarie. 2007. "Coming Home: Palestinian Cinema." *The Electronic Intifada,* February 27. electronicintifada.net.

Maeke, Lutz. 2017. *DDR und PLO: Die Palästinapolitik des SED-Staates*. Berlin: De Gruyter Oldenbourg.

Mauersberger, Kerstin. 1997. *Weiße Taube auf dunklem Grund: 40 Jahre Internationales Leipziger Festival für Dokumentar- und Animationsfilm*. Berlin: Henschel Verlag.

Filastin Assafir. 2012. "Hal indatharat al-aflam al-filastiniya?" (Did the Palestinian Films Disappear). March. palestine.assafir.com.

Saleh, Jihad Ahmad. 2013. "History of the Fictional and Documentary Palestinian Cinema." *Algerian Scientific Journal Platform*. asjp.cerist.dz.

UNISPAL (United Nations Information System on the Question of Palestine). 1974. "Resolution on Palestine." *Seventh Arab League Summit Conference*. October 28. Rabat, Morocco: League of Arab States (LAS).

Wright, Robin. 1981. "PLO's Pinstripes, Money Behind Fatigues and Guns." *The Christian Science Monitor*, October 1.

Archives accessed

Palestinian Audio-Visual Archive at the Palestine Broadcast Corporation, Ramallah, Palestine.

SAPMO-BArch Foundation Archives of Parties and Mass Organizations of the GDR in the Federal Archives (SAPMO), Berlin-Lichterfelde, Germany.

5

DOCUMENTS WITHOUT DOCUMENTARIES? FILMMAKING IN POSTREVOLUTIONARY TUNISIA

Nouri Gana

There are a great number of war films with pretensions of denouncing war which at the same time are great spectacles of war; and in the
end the spectacle is what you enjoy about them. So to speak clearly:
art is essentially a disinterested activity, but if we're in a phase when
we have to express interests, then let's do it openly and not continue
to camouflage it. And therefore, if art is substantially a disinterested
activity [*actividad desinteresada*] and we're obliged to do it in an interested way, it becomes an imperfect art. (Espinosa 1997b, 84)

In a recent book, *Documentary Filmmaking in Tunisia and Beyond* (2012),
Tunisia's premier film critic, Hédi Khélil, laments the postrevolutionary
paucity of fictional and documentary masterpieces of cinematographic
creativity despite the unprecedented explosion of visual works of various
kinds following the Tunisian Revolution of Freedom and Dignity (December 17, 2010–January 14, 2011). This quantitative leap in productivity is
seen as too impulsive and clumsy to make a qualitative and artistic shift,
or a turning point of sorts, worthy of the historic popular mass uprisings
that shook Tunisia and the rest of the Arab world in the wake of Mohammed Bouazizi's self-immolation on December 17, 2010. For Khélil, the
plethora of visual works that resulted are, more or less, subsumable under
the category of (TV) reportage writ large, rather than that of aesthetically
accomplished and artistically rounded documentary filmmaking.

Khélil argues that the documentary proper and the reportage are two
different animals, insofar as the former "is based on an idea, a vision, and a
position or a stance which surpasses the surface level of things to delve into
invisible matters without sophistry or banal sloganeering while the latter
is concerned exclusively with the transmission of the info without the kind
of vision that enables the reconfiguration of reality and its contingencies

in new ways" (Khélil 2012, 166). Obviously Khélil is weary of the will to expose, and even wearier of the willing suspension of the aesthetic imagination that has come to characterize most postrevolutionary films produced under the broad category of documentary, even by such renowned filmmakers as Mourad Ben Cheikh, Mohammed Zran, Hichem Ben Ammar, and Sonia Chamkhi. If, for Khélil, documentaries must deliver an artistic vision capable of transforming reality by raising awareness rather than by scoring cheap political points, then it may be the case that, with the exception of a few endeavors, there are no documentaries yet in postrevolutionary Tunisia. What we have are mostly visual documents without documentaries.

Undoubtedly, postrevolutionary politics has cast a long shadow on documentary filmmaking in Tunisia insofar as the label "revolutionary" itself has become a sort of a litmus test for what would count as a good film, be it documentary or fictional. In the first three years following the revolution, not only films but all sorts of works of artistic and cultural production had to pass this litmus test to be able to succeed or, at least, survive in a polarizing postrevolutionary public sphere, tirelessly discriminating between what is pro-revolutionary and what is counterrevolutionary, applauding the former and demonizing the latter. No wonder, then, that both professional and amateur documentarists hastened to hitch their wagon to the only train in town named the revolution. They were obliged, to borrow Espinosa's words from the epigraph above, to make documentaries in an interested way—that is, documentaries that may have been "imperfect," yet not necessarily inconsequential politically (a condition to which the majority of prerevolutionary documentaries have been consigned despite their artistic rigor).

The proliferation of documentary films in the aftermath of the revolution may have come at the expense of artistic quality writ large (as Hédi Khélil claims), but it has, I would argue, contributed to the democratization and dissemination of art and artistic creativity. The acute urge to visualize and expose the invisibilized practices of Zine El Abidine Ben Ali's authoritarian regime far superseded the concomitant artistic exigencies. Cinematic engagement has become increasingly the occupation of amateur documentarists and not exclusively that of professional filmmakers, as was the case in the prerevolutionary period. In a country that does not boast much of a postcolonial documentary filmmaking tradition, apart from the quasi-nationalist works of a dozen or so documentarists, it has been able to produce, according to the Ministry of Culture, eighty-nine documentary films in the first three years alone following the revolution. These include fifty-six long documentaries and thirty-three short ones (Jemli 2014). I do not currently have the exact number of all the documentaries produced thus far since the revolution, but it may very well be twice that number. When it comes to fictional films, including docufictions, the numbers are even more striking. According to some statistics, Tunisia produced thirty films in the first five years after the revolution alone, while it has produced only 102 films in the whole fifty years after independence.

The loosening of the state's grip on freedom of expression has indeed proven magical for documentarists (as was most notably the case for rappers and other cultural actors, artists, and producers), but one may wonder about the extent to which these seemingly revolutionary documentaries are consequential politically (despite their imperfection artistically). On the one hand, Khélil may be right in contending that documentaries ought to have an artistic vision beyond everyday politics, but the real tragedy of these works is that while they may have sacrificed the exalted artistic vision for the sake of politics, they end up counting for little to nothing politically. On the other hand, this may indeed be an unfair question since the role or agency of a work of art does not necessarily revolve around progressive politics writ large or opposition to the state per se. I guess what I am trying to suggest here is that denunciatory artistic expression under dictatorship had higher value precisely because it was virtually synonymous with death, or at least with some form of punishment such as imprisonment and torture.

This does not mean that there is absolute freedom of speech in postrevolutionary Tunisia, but that the plethora of documentaries—not to mention the proliferation of other artistic forms of expression—has resulted in the devaluation of art insofar as its political edge has almost been reduced to nothingness. In fact, successive postrevolutionary governments have routinely pointed to the enormous quantity of protests and demands to justify doing little to nothing. A Tunisian adage has it best: Before the revolution, you speak you die; after the revolution, you may go on speaking until you lose your voice (and die). The pun works much better in the Tunisian dialect: *Iqbbal i-thawra tit-kallim, itmut, w-ba'd i-thawra itkallim hatta itmut.*

There is a real concern, therefore, about the extent to which the acute urge and irresistible will to expose the vagaries of dictatorship, which best characterizes the majority of postrevolutionary documentary films, may be able to maintain itself or be retained by documentarists if it continues to be inconsequential politically. I will be arguing that this will to expose that characterizes the work of documentarists—and which involves investigative journalism and field research of the highest caliber, as in the work of Sami Tlili and Habib Ayeb, two university professors turned documentarists—must indeed continue to develop. The adage or slogan here would have to be the one adopted by cyberactivists in the ongoing fight against corruption: *Partaji w-afdah li-kwazi*, which literally means, "Share and expose these assholes."

Bearing these generic observations in mind, it may be possible to chart the trajectory of documentary filmmaking in Tunisia from independence to the present as a movement from consent to dissent in which the 2011 revolution constitutes a major turning point. This is not to say that the pioneers of documentary filmmaking in postcolonial Tunisia were apolitical, but that they were state documentarists, political only in the sense of being anticolonial but not anti–state politics. The new Tunisian state was indeed behind the foundation of a national cinema, and so did not perceive the medium in any form other than affirmatively nationalistic and patriotic. It bears pointing out in passing that the very creation of ERTT (Tunisian Radio and Television) in 1961, and SATPEC (Tunisian Production and Cinematographic Expansion Company) in 1964—and later the Carthage Film Festival for Arab and African Cinema—was spurred early on by the refusal of a French laboratory to return the processed film of the massacre (of 1,300 Tunisians) committed by the French army in Bizerte in 1961.

The lost footage of the massacre, which would have constituted the first documentary film, gave rise to the postcolonial need for documentary filmmaking that recorded and transmitted the story of independence for future generations. No wonder then that the early documentary films—which emerged from the amateur film movement and which mixed heroism and fantasy with historical reality—were nationalist by design, seeking to document and represent the realities of the anticolonial struggle of Tunisia against French colonialism, especially after the Second World War. Notable examples include Omar Khlifi's films, especially *The Dawn* (*al-Fajr*, 1966), which was arguably the first Tunisian feature film, and Abdellatif Ben Ammar's *Sejnene (Sijnan)*. *The Dawn* delved—documentary-style—into the national struggle against French colonialism, while *Sejnane* focused on the role of the UGTT (Tunisian General Labor Union) in the events of 1952–54 that led up to independence.

It was not until 1976 that Salma Baccar's *Fatma 1975* turned the critical gaze of the early documentarists inward—that is, not only to the colonial situation and its aftereffects, but also to the national situation and the plight of Tunisian women before and after independence. Like its precedents, the film is not a documentary proper but makes use of the features of documentary montage, newsreel footage, and interviews to map the critical role of women during the anticolonial struggle and their patriarchal impasse after independence. Despite the fact that Baccar's feminist critique does not normally contradict the alleged agenda of state feminism adopted by Bourguiba since the foundation of the Personal Status Code in 1956, the film was banned for thirty years because of the shockingly graphic imagery of one sex education scene (see van de Peer 2010). Ironically, the film was both funded and banned by the state, compelling filmmakers and documentarists ever since to ponder self-censorship.

Still, while fictional feature films continued, with Nouri Bouzid, Ferid Boughedir, and others, to break taboos—especially around religion, sexuality, and gender—documentary filmmaking chose to focus on the richness and glory of Tunisian folklore, heritage, and traditions, not to mention Tunisia's religious, ethnic, and architectural history. Although documentary filmmaking is conventionally the vehicle par excellence for political contention and dissent, it has not been the case with the two generations of documentarists in postcolonial Tunisia. While fictional filmmaking, through its rhetorical and visual twists, may be said to have challenged the patriarchal norms of intelligibility on which postcolonial authoritarianism hinged (Gana, 2017), the same cannot be said of documentary filmmaking, which was forced to thrive in the apolitical realm of Tunisian culture and lore. There had been a reversal of roles of sorts in which fictional filmmaking assumed (at least timidly) the role of political engagement, which was normally associated with the genre of the documentary.

The early trailblazers—notably Abdelhafidh Bouâssida, Sophie Ferchiou, and Hmida Ben Ammar—made the kind of films that revolved around ancient and modern Tunisian history, society, and culture, as well as around the ethnic and racial diversity of Tunisians, including the various indigenous or settler colonial minorities who lived and died in Tunisia. Of note here is Ben Ammar's beautifully textured and historically rounded feature documentary on Zitouna Mosque, *Zitouna at the Heart of Tunisia* (*al-Zaytuna fi qalb Tunis*, 1981), and Bouâssida's provocative feature documentary, *Lotus Island*, about the islands of Djerba and Djersis, mapping the local customs and ancient monuments, such as the Ghriba Synagogue, one of the oldest Jewish pilgrimage sites in North Africa.

The generation of documentarists that followed includes most notably Hichem Ben Ammar and Mahmoud Ben Mahmoud, but also Mokhtar Laâjimi, Fatma Skandarani, Kalthoum Bornaz, and Hichem Jerbi. These documentarists zeroed in on particular individuals rather than on locales and monuments, and while Ben Mahmoud focused on foreigners who chose to live in Tunisia, and on Italians and Tunisians on both sides of the Mediterranean, Ben Ammar delved into the archives of obscure figures that were legends not so long ago but had been thrust into oblivion. Ben Mahmoud's fiction *The Crossing* (*'Ubur*, 1982) delivers a spirited critique of racial and ethnic discrimination, and points toward a more capacious concept of Tunisian citizenship that is more cosmopolitan and worldly. Ben Ammar's *And I Saw the* Stars (*Shuft al-nujum fi-l-qayyila*, 2006) showcases the stories of celebrated boxers from 1911 to the present, at times weaving beautifully the entanglements between the individual stories of these boxers and the bigger national picture of Tunisia as it went from colonialism to independence, as if implying that the boxers are national allegories par excellence.

Just two years separate Ben Ammar's *And I Saw the Stars* and the 2008 uprising at the mining region of Gafsa in southwest Tunisia that compelled amateur filmmaker Sami Tlili to start filming what would be his feature documentary *Cursed Be the Phosphate!* (*Yil'an bu-l-fusfat!*, 2012). The film is about the six-month-long mass protest and civil disobedience movement that started in January 2008 against the Compagnie des Phosphates de Gafsa (CPG), in response to the company's announcement of the results of a recruitment competition, which turned out not to be based on merit, as most competitions are, but on clientelism and nepotism. In fact, CPG did not extend the rightful and much-needed job offers to local unemployed youth, but to the highest bidders or those highly connected to the ruling oligarchy. Met by a total media wall of silence, not to mention complicity with the Ben Ali regime, the protest was in the end crushed by special police forces and army units. In a concerted effort, the police and the army raided the city of Redeyef, dispersed the protesters, and arrested, detained, and tortured numerous militants from the whole region. Astonishingly enough, the regime sent a powerful army of 30,000 police officers to Redeyef alone (a town of only 25,000 inhabitants) to ruthlessly crush the protests.

5.1. *Cursed Be the Phosphate* (2012), directed by Sami Tlili.

Sami Tlili documents the tragedy of the local inhabitants, whose phosphate brings foreign currency and significant revenues to the state. In return, they gain zero benefits except further economic marginalization, structural underdevelopment, and environmental degradation—such as air and water pollution and desertification, not to mention the numerous health hazards resulting from the extraction of phosphate. As one of the interviewers in Tlili's film says, "Cursed be the phosphate that I extract and that only enriches others . . . we never benefited from this wealth that lies under our homes." Throughout the film, Tlili contends that this crucial episode amounts to the black box of the 2011 popular uprising. The Revolution of Freedom and Dignity ought therefore to be understood "as an episode in a long series of social and environmental micro-struggles fought by workers mostly without centralized, top-down union control" (Rousselin 2018, 31). As it happens, even Tlili's *Unleaded* (*Bidun rasas/Sans Plomb*, 2006) is premonitory, precisely because it is about a Bouazizi-like character who pours gas on himself in an attempt to self-immolate. *Cursed Be the Phosphate!* was filmed partly before and partly after the revolution, and thus delves into the origins of the mass revolt that eventually sent Ben Ali packing. The same can be said about Ridha Ben Halima's twin films on the demonstrations in the same mining region: *Leila Khaled, the Tunisian* (*Layla Khalid al-tunisiya/Leila Khaled, la Tunisienne*, 2009), and *Caught Red-handed* (*Fi halat talabbus/En flagrant délit*, 2010). The first focuses on the story of a Tunisian activist and wife of the respected syndicalist Béchir Labidi, who happens to bear the same name as the renowned Palestinian militant and veteran hijacker Leila Khaled; it documents Leila's testimony and her everyday struggles while her son and husband, along with other strikers and demonstrators, are detained, tortured, and imprisoned. The second, which is a sequel to the first, is about eyewitness accounts of torture.

Cursed Be the Phosphate! is in the end a film that delves into the political economy of the uprising, and serves as a record in the national archive of the continuities between colonialism at home and imperialism abroad, or by proxy—in short, the continuities between the confiscatory practices of local resources at the national level by authoritarian regimes, and at the global level by multinational corporations, foreign investors, and financial institutions backed up by imperial powers that aspire for global domination (Rousselin 2018, 36). Like Ben Halima's films, Tlili's film represents a much-needed account of the political memory of corruption, exploitation, and the marginalization of entire regions in the interior and southern parts of Tunisia. While prerevolutionary documentary films dealt mainly with historical and cultural memory, postrevolutionary documentaries have focused on the taboo topic of political memory, the censorship of which in postcolonial Tunisia threatened the very raison d'être of documentary filmmaking. It is not for nothing, therefore, that there is a postrevolutionary upsurge of films that not only try to map the uncharted territory of political memory from the post-independence moment to the present, but that also zero in on the survivors of political oppression, imprisonment, and torture. The politics of exposure that drives most of the cinematic documentary production in postrevolutionary Tunisia is undergirded by a twofold gesture: the recovery *of* and the recovery *from* the forgotten or concealed and erased atrocities of pain and suffering perpetrated by the authoritarian regimes of Bourguiba and Ben Ali against any form of political or critical opposition to their runaway legitimacy.

Surely postrevolutionary documentary filmmaking in Tunisia is a multidirectional endeavor but there is no question that the (investigative) inquiry about and the exposure of the wrongs of the past has emerged as one of the more crucial and urgent orientations of documentary filmmaking. All the more so with the establishment of the Truth and Dignity Commission (TDC) in 2013, which would then take over the official effort of collecting testimonies from both victims and perpetrators, and of setting the stage for national recollection and reconciliation. While the TDC would not hold its first public hearings until November 2016, several amateur and professional documentarists had by then already made their own documentaries about the political victims of the authoritarian regimes of both Bourguiba and Ben Ali. Their efforts must have surely eased the path of the TDC, but it is also significant in its own right. For while the TDC's role may be largely reparative, that of the camera may be therapeutic: the camera may help suture the wounds of injustice and offer victims of torture the dignity of recognition in ways that material reparations alone cannot possibly fulfil.

Both experienced and inexperienced documentary filmmakers have realized the importance of the camera not only in addressing and redressing the cruelties of the past but also in trailblazing the path for transitional justice. Mahmud al-Jimni is one of those directors who quickly seized on the liberal apertures opened up by the revolutionary public sphere to broach the taboo topic of torture. In 2012, a year or so after the ouster of Ben Ali, al-Jimni came out of retirement as a school inspector to make a feature documentary titled *Colocynth (Hanzal/Coloquinte)*. Foregrounding content over artistry, the film chronicles the personal testimonies of some of the political prisoners who were the victims of torture in Tunisian prisons. The film aspired to be comprehensive in terms of its in-depth coverage of the topic of torture from independence to the 2008 uprising in the mining region of Gafsa; in the end, however, it only managed to be eclectic, even though the testimonies are quite substantial in their own right. It staged fourteen eyewitness accounts of political dissidents of various persuasions and ideological affiliations, including Youssifists, Leftists, Islamists, syndicalists, and activists writ large. Al-Jimni even reached out for the testimony of a torturer and the perspective of a psychiatrist. As the title of the film aptly suggests, the memories recounted by the interviewees were as bitter as colocynth; despite the many years that have gone by, they left indelible marks not only on the bodies of the showcased political militants but, above all, on their psyches.

Through their tears and sighs, the victims opened up to the camera, making visible their invisible pain and suffering. The camera allows the otherwise private experience of invisible pain to become public and, above all, imaginable, recognizable, and visible, which would in the end help soothe it. Herein lies the therapeutic and human significance of documentary filmmaking about torture. Following in the footsteps of Mahmud al-Jimni, the visual artists and amateur filmmakers Arbia Abbassi and Marwan Trabelsi made a short documentary in 2013 titled *Stateless (al-Mugharrabun/Les apatrides)* on the very same topic of torture and its psychosomatic imprint. The film inquires about the fate of political prisoners, all the while highlighting the sacrifices they made and the atrocities they suffered during the post-independence period. Unlike *Colocynth*, the film does not focus on high-profile political prisoners, but weaves together the testimonies of everyday Tunisians, male and female, young and old, and from different parts of the country: Jendouba, Nabeul, and Gafsa. Interspersed with the poetic recitations of Mahmoud Darwish and Nizar Qabbani, the victims recount the inhuman treatment they have been subjected to by the regimes of Bourguiba and Ben Ali. Like *Colocynth*, the film ends by inquiring about the possibility of forgiveness and more particularly about the unfolding process of transitional justice, intimating that forgiveness is in the end as difficult to realize as the experience of torture itself.

These two films—which aimed at full-scale coverage of a wide variety of former political prisoners—preceded two other films that engaged directly with specific victims of torture. The first of these films is Hichem Ben Ammar's *Black Memory: Testimonies against Forgetting (al-Dhakira al-sawda': shahadat did al-nisyan/Mémoire noire: Témoignages contre l'oubli,* 2013), which focuses on the leftist movement Afaq (Perspectives), and brings together the testimonies of four of its imprisoned and tortured militants. The second is Ghassen Amami's *Barraket Essahil* (2014), which focuses on the victims of the alleged military coup d'état of January 1991 against Ben Ali's presidency. Barraket Essahil is the name of a hamlet near Hammamat where the alleged Ennahda-inspired scheme to overthrow the regime of Ben Ali was concocted. As a result, hundreds of military officers were rounded up, detained, imprisoned, and tortured systematically in the months that followed. It turns out afterward that the "entire Barraket Essahil affair was made up by Ben Ali to discredit the Islamists," his formidable political opponent at the time (Wolf 2017, 75). Indeed, "the whole thing was made up. There was no plot. There was no coup. It was all a decoy, a pretext to allow the dictator to crack down on legitimate opposition within Tunisia. Ben Ali was worried about a coup being launched by either Islamists or ambitious, competent military officers. To kill two birds with one stone, he concocted the Barraket Essahil Affair to discredit both" (Klaas 2016, 123). What baffles the imagination is that, even after it was discovered that the Barraket Essahil Affair was a complete fabrication, the fate of the victims hardly changed, if at all. Produced by the Association Insaf (Justice), Amami's documentary calls for the rehabilitation of the 244 former military personnel, especially the ninety-three of them who were at the receiving end of the abominable purge, detention, and torture perpetrated by Ben Ali's regime.

The rehabilitation of Barraket Essahil victims has been long overdue, even after the ouster of Ben Ali, after a torture case about the whole affair was launched before military courts in 2011 and after the case resulted in the conviction of, among others, former interior minister Abdallah Kallel and former president Ben Ali in absentia. What is important about Amami's documentary is that it has taken upon itself the cause of these former military officers, who were unjustly terrorized and tortured so that Ben Ali could consolidate power and neutralize his political opponents. The victims of Barraket Essahil were in the end nothing but cogs in Ben Ali's propaganda machine, and the mainstream media were too overawed by the former president and his overnight rise to power to offer a podium for any form of dissidence. Amami's documentary is perhaps the first and only one so far to gain access to the headquarters of the Tunisian army. The poignant testimonies of Colonel Moncef Zoghlami, Lieutenant Colonel Mohamed Ahmed, Commandant Hedi Tijani, and captains Mongi Jghirim and Hbib Khdimallah, among others, highlight the cynicism and sadism of the security apparatus of Ben Ali's regime. Amami's documentary came at a time when the counterrevolutionary current had become strong, and, indeed, at a time when Nida' Tunis (The Call for Tunisia), a party that appealed to and embraced former Ben Ali supporters, had gained center stage in the parliamentary and presidential elections of 2014.

Transitional justice may in the end boil down to forgiveness, and to the abandonment of all feelings of bitterness and resentment, but it cannot be reduced to forgetting. The so-called Reconciliation Law (Qanun al-musalaha), which was approved by parliament on September 13, 2017, has, however, extended amnesty to corrupt businessmen and public officials who committed crimes in prerevolutionary Tunisia. Under the banner of reconciliation, and in an attempt to encourage investment in Tunisia's cash-strapped economy, the bill was initially proposed by then president Béji Caïd Essebsi, and has been met by "vociferous objections of peaceful protests, social movements, civil society groups and opposition forces" (Aliriza and Chettaoui, 2017). And no wonder: it was Béji Caïd Essebsi himself and his ilk who brazenly opposed an opposite draft bill that aimed to protect Tunisia's nascent democracy from the encroachments of counterrevolutionary forces, including former regime officials and old-guard agents (Fordham 2013). Fortunately, though, the law has reawakened the revolutionary instincts of a great number of Tunisian youth, and resulted in the birth of a sobering protest movement, Manich Msameh ("I will not forgive"). "This decentralized and diverse grassroots movement has brought together several civic organizations and interest groups into a highly vigilant, active coalition that pushed legislators to water down the bill and remove amnesty for businessmen and those who committed financial crimes. In the best case, their experience with this law will help Tunisians better tackle future projects that threaten the democratic transition" (Aliriza and Chettaoui, 2017).

"Manich msameh" is a very suggestive slogan that expresses the desire of young protesters to retain their right to remember the atrocities of the past, a right that the Law of Reconciliation attempts to confiscate and delegitimize, wittingly or unwittingly. It is from within this embattled public sphere that the full significance of Amami's *Barraket Essahil* becomes clear. There can be no forgetting-inducing-forgiveness that would lead to forgetting, even though the victims of torture will need to be rehabilitated and eased back into society. Indeed, it was partly thanks to the calls for rehabilitation of the victims of torture made by these kinds of documentaries that the Tunisian Institute of Rehabilitation and Dignity was founded. At the inauguration of the institute on December 5, 2015, a cultural event was organized in which Hichem Ben Ammar's *Black Memory: Testimonies against Forgetting* was shown at the Agora cinema in the northern suburb of Tunis. Produced by 5/5 Tunisian Productions, in collaboration with the Berlin Stasi Memorial and the German Ministry of Foreign Affairs, the film focuses on the testimonies of leftist militants of GEAST (Groupe d'Etudes et d'Action Socialiste Tunisien). Later known as Perspectives, this was a largely leftist movement that opposed Habib Bourguiba's centralization of all powers in his own hands, and expressed the growing disenchantment of Tunisians with the authoritarian outlook of his project of modernity.

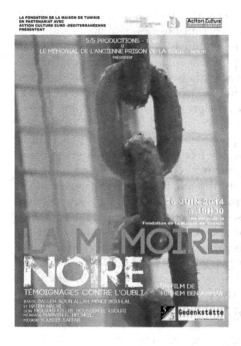

5.2. *Black Memory* (2013), directed by Hichem Ben Ammar.

The four chosen militants whose testimonies are presented in a refracted visual fashion—with measured intercuts, dark shades and light—are fairly well known, albeit not in a highly mediatized sense. They are Hachemi Troudi (analyst, journalist, and author of a biography of the Perspectives movement; he was imprisoned and tortured first in March 1968–January 1970, and then in March 1973–August 1979); Ezzedine Hazgui (editor; he was imprisoned and tortured first in March 1968–January 1970, and then in November 1973–April 1979); Fethi Ben Hadj Yahia (former school director, Marxist pamphleteer, and author of the critically acclaimed memoir *al-Habs kadhab* or *Prison Does Not Exist, We Always Return Home: Fragments of the History of the Left under Bourguiba*; he was imprisoned and tortured from March 1975 to June 1980); and Simone Lellouche (founder of the Tunisian section of Amnesty International in 1981 and spouse of Ahmed Othmani, the leader of Perspectives as of 1964; she is an indefatigable human rights militant, which is why she was expelled from Tunisia in 1972 and condemned in absentia). Generally, the charges leveled against the dozens of Perspectivists range from the serious (membership in an illegal organization and conspiracy against state security) to the ridiculous (distribution of leaflets against the regime and the defamation of President Bourguiba). Most Perspectivists suffered solitary confinement, humiliation, and torture, as Nouri Bouzid had poignantly shown in his docufiction *Golden Horseshoes* (*Safa'ih min al-dhahab/Les sabots en or*, 1989).

Ben Ammar's *Black Memory* succeeds in juxtaposing self-reflexive, sensitive, and heart-wrenching testimonies; the four witnesses speak about their political affiliations, their agenda, their ambivalent rapport with Bourguiba (who imprisons them while calling them sons), their experiences of torture, and their survival techniques, as well as the cell-smart tactics they developed inside prison to communicate with each other and with the outside world. They conclude by offering touching reflections on the relationship between themselves and their torturers inside and outside prison, and on the question of forgiveness and transitional justice. After *Tunisia Votes* (*Tunis tantakhib/ La Tunisie vote*, 2011)—which is, as Hédi Khélil would argue, closer to TV reportage than to documentary filmmaking—*Black Memory* is a tour de force of sorts, in that it marks perhaps the first time that Ben Ammar engages so forcefully with the topic of political memory, a topic he only gestured toward in his prerevolutionary films. "Compared to his lively and amateur previous films, which are full of technical 'flaws' (image definition, sound quality, color balance), *Black Memory* appears very sober, mature, even classical" (Pierre-Bouthier 2018, 232). Perhaps the issue with testimonial documentaries such as *Black Memory* is not the lack of art—much less of narrative—but of its inevitability. "Audiovisual testimonial utterances are always already mediated at the level of the speaking subject whose narrative is a product of selection, ordering, interpretation, partisanship, prohibition, character, reflection, and the vicissitudes of memory" (Sarkar and Walker 2010, 7). Perhaps the issue with the postrevolutionary testimonial documentaries I have so far been discussing is not—*pace* Khélil—the fact that they are documents without documentaries, but rather that they are documentaries aspiring to become documents. They reveal the tragic desire of documentarists in their attempt to reclaim the past, all the while remaining as truthful as possible to the reality of what happened in those prison cells, in spite of the entanglements of subjectivity, narrative embellishments, and the pitfalls of memory. They are then imperfect documentaries, or, more precisely, *documentaries without documentariness*—if by "documentariness" we mean the aesthetic quality that makes a documentary a documentary and not a TV reportage, report, or newsreel.

These testimonial documentaries, from Tlili's *Cursed Be the Phosphate!* to Ben Ammar's *Black Memory*, belong to a category of documentaries that can be called "what went wrong," the scope and aim of which are to address, however retrospectively, the root causes of the revolt and the reasons behind the continuation of popular demonstrations in the postrevolutionary phase. There are several other films that belong in this same category, ranging from Mourad Ben Cheikh's *No More Fear after Today* (*La khawf ba'd al-yawm/Plus jamais peur*, 2011) and Kaouther Ben Hania's *The Challat of Tunis* (*Shallat Tunis/Le Challat de Tunis*, 2012) to Nadia El Fani' *Sons of Lenin* (*Awlad Lenin/Ouled Lénine*, 2007), a biography of her father, who was one of the militant leaders in the Tunisian Communist Party. Documentary filmmaking after the revolution did not, however, remain fixated on what went wrong during the presidencies of Bourguiba and Ben Ali, but took on more presentist directions that addressed what happened during the revolt and afterward. Hence, apart from the "what went wrong" category, there are arguably two other categories of documentary film.

The second category could be called "the revolt." It seeks to document and expose what happened during the uprising, relaying the experiences of those who witnessed it firsthand, while remaining attentive to the various transformations that shook and continue to shake the political, cultural, social, and public spheres. There is a large number of films in this category, some of which documented the first few days and weeks after the ouster of Ben Ali, and the reactions of different people in various neighborhoods and cities across Tunisia. Films such as Ilyas Baccar's (Bakkar) *Red Word* (*Kalima hamra/Parole rouge*, 2012), and Abdallah Yihaya's *We Are Here* (*Nahnu huna/ Nous sommes ici*, 2012), represent attempts to capture the event of revolt and the unyielding spirit of brotherhood and solidarity that maintained it. This spirit of conviviality is emphatically displayed by Rafik Omarani's and Abdallah Chamekh's *Fallega 2011*—a film that documented the famous mass sit-in around the government headquarters in the Qasba of hundreds of young men and women who marched to the capital from marginalized regions in southern Tunisia to ask for, among other things, a new constitution and a new temporary government. A different kind of influx of people into impromptu camps is documented by the two-hour-long and audacious *Babylon* (*Babil*, 2012), a film by first-time directors Mohamed Ismail Louati, Youssef Chebbi, and Ala Eddine Slim. The film focuses on life inside and outside a refugee camp (that hosted thousands of displaced foreign workers from Libya pouring into neighboring Tunisia in the wake of its bloody revolution), from the moment of its construction to its demolition and desertion.

Still in this same second category, there are films that documented the artistic transformations that shook the cultural scene by a diverse number of (amateur) artists, as is the case with Ridha Tlili's *Revolt Minus Five Minutes* (*Thawra ghayr draj*, 2012), which zeroed in on the rise of the provocative graffiti group People of the Cave (*Ahl al-kahf*); others delved into the risky work of war reporters, like Mohamed Amine Boukhris' *War Reporter* (*al-Hay yirawah*, lit. "The living will go home," 2014). Others documented the so-called transition to democracy and covered the various political processes that unfolded, including the first democratic election, such as Ben Ammar's *Tunisia Votes* and Nedjib Bilkadhi's *Seven and a Half* (*Sab'a wa nuss*, 2014). While some chose to focus on taboo topics such as homosexuality in Tunisia, like Nada Mezi Hafeidh's *Upon the Shadow* (*Fi al-zill*, 2017), still others documented the life and death of political figures, such as Lahbib al-Mistiri's *The Happy Martyr* (*al-Shahid al-sa'id*, 2013), which takes as its topic the assassination of Chokri Belaid, a leftist politician who was assassinated in front of his home in February 2013. Others were not content with purely documenting events, but called for a new revolution, such as Kamo Hmaid's *We Need a Revolution* (*Yilzimna thawra/Il nous faut une révolution*, 2011), or advocated for a postrevolutionary secular Tunisia, like Nadia El Fani's controversial documentary film *Laicism, God Willing!* (*Laikiya in sha' Allah/Laïcité, Inch'Allah!*, 2011).

Finally, there is a third category of documentary films, which are quite diverse and open-ended in terms of their scope and substance. Their point of departure is approximately three years after the revolution, and they might be called "the aftermath," because of their interest in mapping the consequences—positive and negative—of the revolt. This broad category includes a diverse number of documentaries that range from films about nostalgia for Ben Ali's regime of police brutality (understood as respect for law and order), to films about economic inequality, unequal development, social ills, irregular migration, and others on environmental disasters and food insecurity. Take, for instance, the case of the Franco-Tunisian feature documentary *Seven Lives* (*Saba' arwah*) by Lilia Blaise and Amine Boufaïed. Its central aim is to understand the overwhelming return of the dictator to the minds and hearts of a large segment of disenchanted Tunisians three years after his departure. The film betrays the ambivalence of Tunisians vis-à-vis the dictator, as some identify strongly with him while others do not. Yet the nostalgia that some Tunisians express toward Ben Ali must not be understood reductively as a mere nostalgia for dictatorship, although some observers acknowledge a dependency complex at work. On the contrary, it ought to be understood as a form of disillusionment and dissatisfaction with the postrevolutionary present and the dangerous slide of the country into an ever-deepening economic crisis. Admittedly, there is also a deep-seated nostalgia for law and order, which in the minds of some Tunisians is viscerally associated with a firm grip on power by an authoritarian figure.

Perhaps Hichem Ben Ammar's latest, *The Return of Bourguiba* (*Bu-Rqiba, al-'awda/Bourguiba de retour*, 2017), also falls into this same category of aftermaths, political nostalgias, and ghostly returns of various kinds. The film is not about the return of Ben Ali, but that of Bourguiba, the founder of independent Tunisia and the figure that Ben Ali almost banished from public memory. The film covers part of an otherwise wide-ranging dialectical effort to purge the rotten legacy of Ben Ali and his extended family, to rehabilitate the legacy of Bourguiba, and to build on it what was once touted by the then president Essebsi as the "Second Republic." Surely Bourguiba is the sculptor of modern Tunisia, but the film focuses instead on the sculptor of his infamous statue of leadership and victory. It takes its cue from Bourguiba's popular return from forced exile under the French colonial regime more than six decades ago, to shed light on the curious history of his "Supreme Combatant" statue (the "Za'im"), which was placed in downtown Tunis on avenue Bourguiba in 1978, displaced to La Goulette by Ben Ali in 1988, and rehabilitated and returned to its original place by Essebsi in 2016.

Other documentarists have not paid particular attention to the nostalgia for Ben Ali, much less to that of Bourguiba, but to the postrevolutionary conditions of regionalism, corruption, and nepotism that combine to make possible the rise of nostalgia for the two defunct regimes of authoritarianism. Of note here are such films as Ridha Tlili's *Controlling and Punishment* (*al-Muraqaba wa-l-mu'aqaba*, 2014) and *Forgotten* (*Tunsa ka'annaka lam takun*, 2017), as well as Hamza Ouni's *El Gort* (*Jammal al-baruta*, 2015), Hinde Boujemaa's *It Was Better Tomorrow* (*Ya min 'ash/C'etait mieux demain*, 2012), Riadh Laabidi's *Do You Have Connections?* (*'Andik-shi shkun?/ Nécrose*, 2016), and Abdallah Yahya's *On This Earth* (*'Ala hadhihi al-ard/Un retour*, 2014). The closure of the horizon of the possible during and after the revolution resulted in the intensification of irregular migration, a topic that has been the focus of numerous TV reports, but also of two poignant documentaries: Fethi Saïdi's *Behind the Wave* (*Wara' al-mawja/Derrière la vague*, 2016) and Fedia Ben Henda's TV documentary, *Vapore* (*Babur*, 2016).

5.3. *All is Well in Gabes* (2014), directed by Habib Ayeb.

5.4. *All is Well in Gabes* (2014), directed by Habib Ayeb.

Meanwhile, there are films that have paid attention to the economic and ecological realities of Tunisia, and warned about impending environmental and food disasters. The work of Habib Ayeb is salutary in this regard. In his *All Is Well in Gabes* (*Gabis là-bas/Tout va bien à Gabès*, 2014), Ayeb shed light on the environmental and human consequences of the pollution that has been produced by various firms around Gabes since the construction of the phosphate-refining plant in 1972. The industrial-chemical complex (including oil refineries and petrochemical plants) expanded into what used to be the seaside oasis of Gabes, and resulted in the confiscation of agricultural land and the dispossession of traditional peasantry and small family farms. Ayeb's documentary paints Gabes as

> an almost ideal typical-case of the contemporary confiscatory practices of extraction industries in the global South: a region experiencing high levels of poverty and unemployment hosted a lucrative but polluting industry in the confidence that it would generate export revenues and boost local development. And yet, local job creation remains limited and is even offset by the destruction of traditional economic sectors such as farming or fishing brought about by pollution while local populations and ecosystems are plagued by environmental and health hazards. (Rousselin 2018, 27)

Documents without Documentaries?   95

Not unlike Tlili's *Cursed Be the Phosphate!*, Ayeb's *All Is Well in Gabes* is, above all, a film that is highly sensitive to the increasingly tragic predicament of Tunisia as a dependent economy, one in which phosphate was transformed overnight from a much-envied asset into a curse that deepened and cemented its economic dependency. Not surprisingly, Ayeb's more recent documentary, *Couscous: Seeds of Dignity* (*Kuskusi: hubub al-karama/Couscous: Les graines de la dignité*, 2017), zeroes in on this growing dependency on the international economic order. Focusing on agricultural sovereignty, *Couscous* explores what it would take for Tunisia to become self-sufficient in terms of its grain needs, especially wheat, which has been gradually supplied by Western corporate-capitalist agribusiness profiteers. The film exposes the nonchalance of the successive postrevolutionary governments toward the concerns of small farmers, such as their need to preserve traditional agricultural methods and local seeds, and reduce the dependency on pesticide-dependent GMO seeds and grains imported from Euro-American agrochemical corporations.

Couscous is beautifully shot and aesthetically well-rounded, alternating between long takes and extreme close-ups effortlessly, and weaving together a decolonial narrative that is both sober and fresh. This is clearly a documentary film that does not lack documentariness, although its content is laudable in its own right. It shows the extent to which postrevolutionary documentary filmmaking has matured in a very compressed period of time, and become not only a tool of targeted criticism (for example, of the former dictator and his regime), but also a tool of critique that examines the complicated web of power dynamics within present-day, economically dependent Tunisia. It is this promissory direction of postrevolutionary documentary filmmaking—with its focus on Tunisia's strategic national interests and its cultural and economic sovereignty—that may end up winning all accolades.

The politics of exposure that has so far dominated documentary filmmaking may no longer have to be associated with the exposure of the past crimes of Bourguiba and Ben Ali—however vital that role continues to be for the unfolding process of transitional justice—but rather with the postrevolutionary practices of successive governments, given that they have so far failed to apprehend the character of the changes that have taken place, and even more importantly still need to take place, lest Tunisia should bounce back into authoritarianism, or worse, descend into bankruptcy and poverty. If this task necessitates the production of documentaries without documentariness, so be it!

References

Aliriza, Fadil, and Ouiem Chettaoui. 2017. "Tunisia's Parliament Just Cast a Vote Against Democracy" *The Washington Post*, September 19. washingtonpost.com.

Espinosa, Julio García. 1997a. "For an Imperfect Cinema." Translated by Julianne Burton. In *New Latin American Cinema: Theory, Practices and Transcontinental Articulations*, edited by Michael T. Martin, 71–82. Detroit: Wayne State University Press.

———. 1997b. "Meditations on Imperfect Cinema . . . Fifteen Years Later." Translated by Michael Chanan. In *New Latin American Cinema: Theory, Practices and Transcontinental Articulations*, edited by Michael T. Martin, 83–85. Detroit: Wayne State University Press.

Fordham, Alice. 2013. "Tunisia's 'Immunisation of the Revolution' Draft Legislation Fiercely Debated." *The National*, June 28. *www.thenational.ae.*

Gana, Nouri. 2017. "Sons of a Beach: The Politics of Bastardy in the Cinema of Nouri Bouzid." *Cultural Politics* 13, no. 2 (July): 177–93.

Jemli, Aymen. 2014. "Tunisian Cinema after the Revolution: The Birth of the Documentary Filmmaking School." *al-Quds al-'arabi*, May 17. www.alquds.

Khélil, Hédi. 2012. *Al-Sinima al-watha'iqiya al-tunisiya wa-l-'alamiya* (Documentary Filmmaking in Tunisia and Beyond). Tunis: Dar Afaq.

Klaas, Brian. 2016. *The Despot's Accomplice: How the West Is Aiding and Abetting the Decline of Democracy.* New York: Oxford University Press.

Pierre-Bouthier, Marie. 2018. "Documentary Cinema and Memory of Political Violence in Post-Authoritarian Morocco and Tunisia (2009–2015)." *The Journal of North African Studies* 23, no. 1–2: 225–45.

Rousselin, Mathieu. 2018. "A Study in Dispossession: The Political Ecology of Phosphate in Tunisia." *Journal of Political Ecology* 25: 20–39.

Sarkar, Bhaskar, and Janet Walker, eds. 2010. *Documentary Testimonies: Global Archives of Suffering.* New York: Routledge.

Van de Peer, Stefanie. 2010. "Selma Baccar's *Fatma 1975*: At the Crossroads Between Third Cinema and New Arab Cinema." *French Forum* 35, no. 2–3 (Spring/Fall): 17–35.

Wolf, Anne. 2017. *Political Islam in Tunisia: The History of Ennahda.* New York: Oxford University Press.

6

ALGERIAN WAR FOR INDEPENDENCE: DOCUMENTARIES QUESTIONING HISTORY

Ahmed Bedjaoui

Those who fail to learn from history are doomed to repeat it. (Winston Churchill)

Depictions of Algerian contemporary history have been heavily divisive, with documentary film at the heart of many people's conceptions of the struggle for independence. A war of images was waged that began in 1832 and continued beyond July 1962.

In the late 1930s, Tahar Hannache made the documentary *Aux Portes du desert* (*Abwab al-sahra'*, 1938), the negatives and prints of which have since completely disappeared. The first truly Algerian film with traces remaining is the silent documentary *The Divers of the Desert* (*Ghattasin al-sahra'/Les Plongeurs du désert*, 1952–54), also by Hannache, assisted by Djamel Chanderli.

As Algerians slowly gained access to artistic professions and imagined representations, certain leaders of the colonial system learned the lesson of May 1945, and started to use cinema as a weapon of propaganda as well. Alexandre Promio, one of the most renowned veteran reporters of Lumière, was appointed Chief of the Photography and Colonial Cinema Service between 1919 and 1924. This service included the Itinerant Cinema Center, which was equipped with a cine-bus that traveled throughout Algeria, proposing short documentaries to Algerians in order to promote the "advantages" of colonialism. The role of the SCA (Army Cinema Service)[1]—created later, in 1948—was to complete the propaganda machine of France. This service was redefined in 1954 to allow it to participate in the psychological aspect of the war.

Cameramen, often those doing their national service, accompanied soldiers on their "combing operations," as those murderous raids of modern times were called. Hundreds of thousands of kilometers of film were shot in this way, with the aim of displaying the vigor of the colonial military

99

apparatus. Certain researchers, such as Sébastien Denis, have more recently been able to study these images, which were stashed away in the bunkers of the French army. After their success, and despite their limited means, Algerians got to wear for the first time the cloak of the victor. This was thanks, in part, to the news and short documentaries they managed to broadcast on television channels in socialist, Anglo-Saxon, and Latin-American countries, at a time when television was in the process of becoming the dominant media. Alongside arms, audiovisual communication played an important role in stirring people's consciences everywhere in the world.

Filmmaker Pioneers

The year 1956 was a turning point in the use of visual images by the National Liberation Front (FLN). Filmmakers offered their services to the FLN and National Liberation Army (ALN) (Helal 2011, 16). They came not only from Algeria, as in the case of Djamel Chanderli, but from around the world. Much was said after 1962 about the role of each of these "militants" of the camera—both men and women—in combat (Mehdaoui 2009). In reality, some of them were enrolled in the ranks of the ALN, while others were more involved in propagating ideas. Regardless of their approach, they all delivered images to the information service, which later became the Cinema Service when the Provisory Government of the Republic of Algeria (GPRA) was created. These images can be seen in footage taken by the GPRA's cinema service, or integrated into reportages shown on international television channels—among them CBS in the United States, and other channels in Mexico and Australia, as well as socialist Eastern European countries (*L'Introduction du visuel* 2013).

Djamel Chanderli and the "Image and Sound" Service

As an independent filmmaker, Chanderli already had extensive experience of the profession. He had coproduced *The Divers of the Desert*, directed by Tahar Hannache, with whom he collaborated from 1942 onward. In Algiers, he had worked as a cameraman and freelance photographer for various agencies, especially for French News. He provided the ALN with the first embryo of the photographic, then cinematographic, service in Tunis. In 1958, he returned to the maquis (resistance movement) north of Constantine, and filmed ("by chance," he said) a bombardment with napalm in the region of El Milia in a place called Beni Sbih (Chominot 2012b). Given the importance of these images, Chanderli decided to return to Tunis, and, as he said, "send this material personally to my brother Abd al-Kader Chanderli at the United Nations, to develop and utilize the images immediately to confront the French army, who claimed not to be using napalm in Algeria" (Chanderli 1990, 16). Among the films he shot, Chanderli mentions *Yasmina, The People's Voice (Sawt al-sha'b/La voix du peuple), The Refugees (al-Laji'un/Les réfugiés)*, and *The Guns of Freedom (Banadiq al-huriyya/Les fusils de la liberté)*.

The credits of *Yasmina* and *The Guns of Freedom* bear the joint signatures of Chanderli and a future winner at Cannes, Mohammed Lakhdar-Hamina, whose "touch" is also recognizable. If Chanderli was doubtless the precursor and founder of Algerian cinema in the maquis, the name of René Vautier must also be linked to its birth. Vautier filmed *Algeria in Flames (al-Jaza'ir multahiba/Algérie en flammes)*,[2] a collaboration between the staff of the ALN and the DEFA collective studio,[3] at the beginning of 1957 in the Aurès-Nememtchas. The film was edited in East Germany, and had considerable impact in America and Eastern Europe, where several sequences—including one added later to the film showing the blowing up of a train in the mining region of El Ouenza (shot by Moudjahine under the direction of René Vautier)—served to show that what was happening in Algeria was not a case of simple domestic French affairs, but was clearly a war of national liberation.

Other filmmakers from various countries constituted a real "international cinematographic brigade" for the freedom of Algeria. Among them were Pierre Clément (France: *Sakiet Sidi Youcef* and *The Refugees*); Stevan Labudović (former Yugoslavia), who shot a lot of war sequences; Karl Gass (former GDR: *Forward Children . . . for Algeria/Auf Kinder . . . für Algerien*), Cécile Decugis (France: *The Sharing of Bread/Taqasum al-khubz/Le partage du pain* and *Refugees*; and Yann LE Masson (France: *I Am Eight Years Old/J'ai huit ans*, based on children's drawings provided by Franz Fanon).

The Algerian war also became an attractive subject for Western television news. Between 1956 and 1958, the "Algerian question," including the debate at the United Nations and the eight-day general strike in 1957, took up more and more space in American national political life. The Democrats, through the voice of young Senator Kennedy, put pressure on the Republican administration to recognize the Algerian insurrectional movement as an irreversible reality (de Person 1995–96, 209). American television, NBC in particular, began to devote regular magazines to the war in Algeria (Connelly 2002, 133). If we attempt to imagine the impact of real images of war shown in households by a still-novel medium, we can understand that propaganda had become a crucial part of this conflict (Blidi 2003, 5). While the French were trying to insist on their "crop and health" actions and banish images of war, the FLN produced a much firmer action, consisting of upending French propaganda as it was presented to the world (Maatoug 2012, 112). The shock was immediate in the media, and contributed to discrediting French policies in Algeria (Connelly 2011).

The greatest achievement was accomplished when the leaders of the Algerian resistance invited American news reporters behind battle lines. Peter Throckmorton and Herb Greer were escorted by ALN fighters across the border in the region of Nedroma. For nearly five months, from September 1956 to January 1957, the two reporters lived in the mountains among ALN combatants, in the region stretching from Nedroma to the edge of the Saharan Atlas. They photographed and filmed scenes that a few months later became unprecedented scoops, and a source of torment for the upholders of French war propaganda. They were able to film the everyday lives of the freedom fighters, and even accompanied them on ambushes, which allowed them to film the human and material losses suffered by French troops (Mehdaoui 2009).

In January 1957, the two reporters were accompanied back to Tangiers, from where they returned to the United States, while the reels of film they shot were sent separately by *moussabilines* (liaison agents). These rushes were developed and, in line with the agreement previously reached, a copy of all the filmed images remained in the hands of the ALN/FLN. The iconographic documents were widely exploited by the information services of the revolution. In particular, they destroyed the image presented by colonial authority propaganda that the fighters of the FLN were just a few isolated groups of *fellagha*s (bandits), with no popular support. On the contrary, the images taken by the two American reporters show an army in uniform, organized, disciplined, and more than effective in combat. Certain images were rushed across the border well before the two American reporters left the maquis of Wilaya V. Once developed, they served to influence international opinion, American perspectives in particular, just before the eleventh session of the U.N. General Assembly.

From 1956, the leaders of the revolution carefully followed each session of the General Assembly. The FLN office in New York, with the help of Abd al-Kader Chanderli and Mohammed Yazid, the two major lobbyists on the American scene, succeeded in getting sequences—filmed by the two reporters in the maquis—shown for the first time on October 28, 1956, in the televised news bulletins of the NBC channel. "The world abroad has never seen visually the resolute men who oppose French law. The film that we have here is a rare exception (a film actually made from the insurgent lines somewhere in northwest Algeria)" (Chominot 2012a). Stills taken from the films of Throckmorton and Greer were also used in a special edition of *Résistance algérienne*, with four pages of photo illustrations. In the meantime, their images had a large impact on the world of Western media, which were still reticent about displeasing Paris.

The consecration of Throckmorton, and even more so of the Algerian independence cause, coincided with NBC's screening in June 1957 of the thirty-minute documentary *Life Behind the Lines*, on *Outlook*, the top-rated program of Chet Huntley, who presented the televised evening news. This media success owes much to Throckmorton, to be sure, but also to the duo of Abd al-Kader Chanderli and Mohammed Yazid. For the television channels, images of the Algerian conflict provided a spectacle of war, and were the subject of an edition of the program *60 Minutes* called "Algeria in Flames,"[4] shown in October 1957, presenting the arguments of both sides. "The French refused to admit that they were at war and did not have the decency to recognize their adversary's right to debate with them" (Connolly 2002, 133).

In 1960, the GPRA moved its production to Tunis, where the provisional government was based, making two films aimed at informing international public opinion for the debate on the Algerian question at the General Assembly of the United Nations. For Mohammed Yazid, then minister of information of the GPRA, *Djazairouna* (*Djaza'iruna/ Our Algeria*, 1960) was intended to speak to the mind, and *Yasmina* to the heart. Both films were produced in 1960 to be screened on the fringes of the U.N. General Assembly, and both were directed by Djamel Chanderli and Mohammed Lakhdar Hamina. *Yasmina* was designed "to be a real tear-jerker" (Mehdaoui 2009). The choice of the little girl as protagonist was an intentional symbolization of the suffering Algeria faced against the French Goliath. The commentary, presented as a monologue, was written to move Western spectators: "My name is Yasmina and I'm seven years old. I'm Algerian and this is my hen, Mina. She's frightened." Yasmina speaks of the long march from her village across the mountains, and the bomb that destroyed her house: "We don't have a house any more. . . ." These factors—the artistic approach, representations of emotion and displacement, and the manner of conveying a message—make *Yasmina* the first documentary film about Algerian liberation. Many global films produced since 1962 about the liberation war have used sequences from this film, giving Algerian cinema a key role in the arts in its post-independence period.

On their return from Tunis, filmmakers of the maquis, such as Ahmed Rachedi, Abderrahmane Sidi Boumediene, Mohammed Guennez, and others, as well as those trained by French television, such as Nasredine Guenifi, found themselves in 1962 in the Audiovisual Center at Châteauneuf, Ben Aknoun, run by René Vautier.[5] In 1962–63, they participated in the first effort of collective production, with a feature documentary *People on the Move* (*Sha'b fi tariqihi/Peuple en marche*), the aim of which was to promote the socialist construction of the new state. The film also included a sequence filmed at the Tunisian border before the end of the war, by Vautier and Rachedi, about landmines.

Three million landmines out of the eleven million laid by the French army are still buried along these borders. Eighteen months after independence, they had already caused more than a thousand deaths and two thousand injuries. Even the French engineers recorded 120 killed among their ranks when the bombs were being laid.[6]

The question of the mines and the victims they continued to produce well after the end of the war is the subject of a few Algerian films post-independence. One of these is *Hands Like Birds (Ayadi mithl al-tuyur/Des mains comme des oiseaux)*, a thirty-minute documentary about the de-mining operations at the borders, completed in 1964 by Ahmed Rachedi, based on a script by René Vautier.

During the same period, Marcel Herz also filmed a fifteen-minute documentary on the Moroccan border, *Attention, Mines (Mantiqa mal-ghuma*, 1965) devoted to this tragic problem of de-mining that has taken forty thousand lives since independence. *Steel Harvest (al-Hadiyya al-akhira*, 1982), by Ghaouti Bendeddouche, is the only Algerian fiction feature film to show the period after the war in a village at the border, in particular the insecurity relating to mines.

The First Steps

While documentaries were prioritized during the war of liberation, and also in the first decades following independence, Algerian filmmakers generally favored fiction at the expense of documentaries. There was, of course, the usual commemoration coverage on television, and occasional reporting by the Algerian News Office. Most of the documentaries dealing with the War of Independence, however, remained didactic and conventional. The making of documentaries was often regarded as a simple step to be taken before making fictional feature films, which most directors seemed impatient to undertake.

In the wake of the commemorations, Ahmed Rachedi made his first personal fifteen-minute documentary, *Tebessa, Year Zero (Tbessa, sanat sifr/Tebessa, année zero*, 1963). Back from Tunis, Rachedi described daily life during the first months following Algeria's independence, in the city on the Algerian–Tunisian border where he was born. After having set up the Algerian News Office, Mohammed Lakhdar Hamina, this time on his own, made *Suddenly a November Day (Mais un jour de novembre*, 1964), a sixty-minute documentary about the preparation of the liberation struggle.

In 1966, Ahmed Lallem directed a remarkable twenty-two-minute documentary, *The Women (Fatayat/Elles)*, in which he interviewed secondary-school girls on their daily lives and hopes in post-independence Algeria.[7]

When producing *The Battle of Algiers (La Bataille d'Alger)*, Saadi Yacef had planned to precede the film with a documentary that would explain the history of the resistance of Algerians against the French occupation. Gillo Pontecorvo suggested Ennio Lorenzini to do this. Thus was born *Free Hands (Hurr al-yadayn/Mains libres)*, shown at the Cannes Film Festival in 1965, and then officially presented in August the same year in Algiers and Rome, before disappearing to resurface only in 2021. It was originally to be called *Trunk of the Fig Tree (Jis' shajarat al-tin/Tronc du figuier)* (Bedjaoui 1966, 65). Here is what its brochure said about it: "From sea to desert, from 1830 to 1962, from Abd al-Kader to Larbi Ben M'Hidi, the struggle of an entire people, the resistance of a world clinging to its dignity as its last chance of survival."

The Archive Documentary

The few documentaries that were made in Algeria during the sixties and seventies were commissioned feature films, made with archival material to commemorate anniversaries or political events. This was the case for *Dawn of the Damned (Fajr al-mu'azzabin/L'aube des damnés)*, commissioned in 1963 by the Algerian state to mark the opening in June 1965 of the Afro-Asian summit, which actually never took place because of the military coup d'état that overthrew Ahmed Ben Bella. Actually, most of the native Algerian filmmakers trained on the battlefields were dreaming of leading positions that would allow them to achieve their Hollywoodian dreams of personal achievement, while ascending the steps of the Cannes festival. In their perceptions, this dream could only be realized through fictional blockbusters. The archive film seemed to be more oriented toward television, and did not attract the powerful new men of the national film sector. Only three films based on archival stock shots were produced during the first two decades following independence. All of them were commissioned to celebrate the anniversary of independence, or the beginning of the armed struggle.

During the first decade after liberation, the treatment of history by audiovisual means was mostly taken up by French researchers and journalists. Yet the issue was not easy in France, as the Algerian war was taboo in the French establishment, which even refused the terminology "war in Algeria," using instead the phrase "events in Algeria." Until the 1990s, it was difficult to show violent scenes of repression or torture. As a consequence, archival films appeared as an alternative to censorship or self-censorship.

Yves Courrière was a correspondent in Algiers for Radio-Luxembourg during the war. In 1972, when Algeria was commemorating the tenth anniversary of independence, he made a film with Philippe Monnier, using archival material and lasting two hours and thirty-seven minutes, also called *The Algerian War (al-Harb al-tahririya/La guerre d'Algérie)*. For the first time, it was French documentary filmmakers who were producing images that Algerians could and should have made themselves. Although Algerian Newreels (les Actualités Algériennes), under the direction of Mohammed Lakhdar Hamina, were unable to obtain permission to record meetings with the leaders of the revolution present in Algiers, Yves Courrière took full advantage of this to get the major protagonists of the war to talk, including all the members of the GPRA, subsequently removed from power. Thanks to their revelations, and in spite of their sometimes incomplete or anecdotal nature, the work of Courrière continues to be one of the basic historical references about how the war of independence unfolded.

To respond to the film by Courrière, the Ministry of Information asked a young filmmaker, Farouk Beloufa,[8] to coordinate the editing of an archival film called *Liberation War (al-Harb al-tahririya/La guerre de libération)*. The semantic nuances connoting the titles should be noted in passing here: "*Guerre d'Algérie*" *(Algerian War)* for Courrière and "*Guerre de libération*" *(Liberation War)* for the Algerians.[9] The version presented by Beloufa was largely considered to be too far removed from the dominant current at the time. The reworked version by Ministry of Information officials was refused by the director, and the film was credited to an anonymous body. The socialist and ultra-centralist management of the state cinema led to the first Algerian cinematic failure in this war of documentary images between the two countries.

The treatment of the war by way of the documentary remained sensitive for a long time in Algeria. A long silence took hold in France following the film by Courrière and the documentary *French People, If You Only Knew (Français, si vous saviez)*, made the same year by Jacques Brissot, Alain de Sédouy, and André Harris, about de Gaulle and the chaotic history of decolonization.

As usual, the production of archival films was meant as a plain response to French initiatives, which also coincided with anniversaries, leading to funding support. In 1979, on the occasion of the twenty-fifth anniversary of the outbreak of the war of liberation, the Algerian Office of the Cinema (ONCIC) commissioned the writer Mouloud Mammeri to produce a scenario entitled *Morte la longue nuit (Wafat al-layl al-tawil* or Death of the Long Night). The production was commissioned to Ghaouti Bendeddouche and Slim Riad jointly. This eighty-minute documentary about struggles against neocolonialism around the world had no lasting effect. The failure of the film might also be explained by lack of financing for films based on archives in Algeria. Most of the archives related to the war had been transferred to France, and the collection gathered by the Algerian Provisory Government was scattered when they were transported from Tunis to Algiers during the summer of 1962.

Archival Documentary and Public Television

To find a space for creativity and audacity, the Radio Télévision Algérienne (Algerian Radio and Television Broadcasting, RTA) was the place to go, in contrast to the ONCIC. Since 1973, it had developed a very dynamic film production department. This national channel was the first in Algeria to allow an Algerian woman to carry out a film project, in 1978. The writer and historian Assia Djebar, a militant of the liberation war, was thus able to produce *The Nouba of the Women of Mont Chenoua (Nawbat nisa' jabal Shinuwwa/ La nouba des femmes du Mont Chenoua)*, a feature film linking documentary and fiction. The following year, Djebar produced her second feature film, *The Zerda or the Songs of Oblivion (Zarda aw Alhan al-nisyan, La Zerda ou les chants de l'oubli)*. This documentary used archival film relating to visits by French dignitaries to Maghreb countries during the thirties, to mark the centenary of the invasion of Algeria by colonial troops. For many, it was difficult to admit that a woman writer had been able to attract fame worldwide and bring to her work the independence of spirit that they themselves were lacking. Using the sense of commitment she acquired during the struggle for liberation, Djebar brought to the cinema a mature interpretation and account of history. Entirely based on stock footage, *Zerda* is an accomplished work about memory—analytical, in contrast to former Algerian archival films, which were largely descriptive and conventional. Djebar's film successfully combines historical research with a rich literary text that supersedes representation. The film was first called *The Maghreb in the 30s (Maghreb, les années trente)*, because the author was principally interested in these *zerdas* (festivities) and the fantasias organized at the time by colonial forces, with natives dragged in to cheer during the visits of French political figures to the three countries of the northern Maghreb.

After producing a series of ten programes of edited archives, each an hour long, devoted to the history of decolonization, Azzedine Meddour made his masterpiece *How Much I Love You*. To achieve this, he reviewed television news programs filmed between 1957 and October 1962 by the regional station of French television in Algiers. Meddour's tour de force thus consisted in appropriating the rhetoric of these images (designed to explain the policy of the occupier), thereby turning the tables and making a mockery of the political class engaged in the war against the Algerian people. In 1985, after two years of intense editing, the team delivered a film, lasting one hour and forty-five minutes, of such an exceptional quality that it has become one of the rare pearls of Algerian cinema. No feature documentary has made better use of filmed archives to testify to the recent history of Algeria.

Mouny Berrah wrote an article in 1997 in which she pinpointed an essential aspect of the representations that could be made of the War of Liberation, depending on the viewpoint, Algerian or French. Meddour "ventured into the corridors of colonial power and deconsecrated the role of persons high up in the hierarchy . . . It is a national view observing the political arena of the other, with all that that supposes in terms of contradictions, antagonisms between the different currents, the differences in the positions taken, struggles and confrontations between the various conceptions of the Republic and the State of Law" (Berrah 1979, 15).

Above all, it was the case of the Algerian prisoners who were used in 1960 as guinea pigs during an atomic test near Reggane that provoked a tremendous reaction in French official spheres. In fact, the sequence of the prisoners of the ALN tied to poles at the firing site was taken from German documents provided by Karl Gass, who came to the RTA in 1982 at my request, to make a film recalling his role within the cinema service of the GPRA. At the end of the film, a former German legionnaire declares that he served in Reggane at the time the events took place. He confirms having seen 150 Algerian prisoners tied to poles. As has already been stated, this passage was already present in the film by Karl Gass, made for the East German DEFA in 1961 and completed in 1962.

Azzedine Meddour, and before him Assia Djebar, were obliged, when portraying the colonial period, to use news sequences filmed or bought principally by two companies, Pathé Cinema and Gaumont. These companies still own and control a significant part of Algerian and French historical visual memory from colonial times. Our film directors are therefore reduced to buying the rights to this material at extremely high prices. One way to begin appeasing hurtful memories would be with healthy cooperation on the question of joint ownership of these images. This would perhaps make it easier to extract the colonial period from the darkness in which it remains plunged.

Documentaries Question History

After independence, the use of documentaries was rare. By limiting artistic documentaries in the cinematic sphere, the leaders of the sector also deprived Algerian audiences of any active role in the closed debate about the relationship between the country's past and recent history. There were two types of production format: fictional productions were marked by an outstanding creativity, while the reports and documentaries produced by the news department of Algerian television were rather poor, preventing the genre from reaching any great artistic level. Fifty years later, there are debates within Algerian cinema as to the best way to tackle a liberation fight that was in many ways at the origin of the modern Algerian nation. Until recently, fictional works had avoided mentioning by name the protagonists of the liberation war, with the exception of *The Battle of Algiers* (*Ma'rakat al-Jaza'ir*, 1967) by Pontecorvo, which is situated between a neorealist political film and a docudrama. In *Chron-icle of the Years of Amber* (*Waqa'i' sanawat al-jamr/Chronique des années de braise*, 1975) and *Outside the Law* (*Kharij 'an al-qanun/Hors-la-loi*, 2010), the documentary was at the service of fiction. Lakhdar Hamina tells the story of the national movement from the 1930s to the start of the libera-tion war. Bouchareb largely used interviews of the various players within the armed struggle to prepare a well-documented scenario.

These films (including *The Battle of Algiers*) demonstrate admirably that the secret of the cinematic narrative as applied to contemporary his-tory resides in a magical mixture somewhere between documentary and fiction, while using an analytical approach rather than a purely descriptive one. It is for historians to write history and for filmmakers to promote it by using the two essential weapons that they master best: movement and emotion.[10] Historians document histories, but filmmakers have the power to humanize it and popularize it by using the best of their talent, a pano-ply of the techniques of expression that cinematic art can offer. Benjamin Stora insists on the role of fiction in the work of memory: "Whether it is in a documentary or in a film, what counts is the portrayal of an event" (Stora 2010). Unfortunately, this mixture is more present in films that are primar-ily identified as fictional works, while most documentary films (essentially the archival ones) are devoid of this touch of fantasy. The Algerian film industry has produced a significant number of long documentary films. Ironically, this documentary dimension is mostly found in historical fea-ture films, at least in the cinema sector.

The Fiction-Documentary and the "Outlaws"

Alongside these fictional works that appeal to the imagination, another type of audiovisual production dealt with history. These films were the reconstruction documentaries/fictions that tackled the cases of those who were once called "outlaws," and who played an intermediary role in the resistance against injustice and the *hogra*, or abuse of power.

The first in this series, *The Outlaws* (*Kharij 'an al-qanun/Les hors-la-loi*, 1969), was made by Tewfik Fares.[11] He was already the screenwriter for *The Winds of the Aures* (*Rih al-Awras/Vent des Aures*), in which he set out to recount how, during the colonial period, the code of honor and the law of an-eye-for-an-eye had survived Napoleonic law in certain regions. At the time it was presented as the first "Alge-rian Western." This aroused some negative reactions. *The Outlaws* is a film presenting a prerevolutionary awakening of consciousness in some individuals, through the inhumanity and indignity of their condition. Their tragic end is the collective catalyst that allows the idea to spread and advance.

The subject is a very fine one and does not deserve having the description of "Western" attached to it. . . . Trying to get an Algerian film liked, by saying it is a Western, amounts to condoning the value and the justice of the "cowboys" law, when our place is closer to that of the Indians in history. (Koussim 1968, 12)

The theme of the outlaw was abandoned by the cinema sector until the beginning of the 1980s, to be taken up by TV directors. Two of them succeeded in getting around this hurdle linked to the theme of the "unstructured" rebel: Belkacem Hadjadj and Abderrezak Hellal chose the fiction-documentary format to recount popular resistance efforts dating from the previous century.

Hadjadj reconstituted the feats of arms of two "outlaws," *Bouziane el-Kala'i* (1979) and *Djillali el-Guetta'a* (1982). A talented actor, Boumediene Sirat, played the majority of the roles, the convention of the genre allowing him, with a good dose of humor, to multiply points of view on the history of this period.

As for Hellal, thanks to the same methods, he revived the story of the life of an outlaw, *Benzelmat* (1983), using reconstitution to mix fiction, documentary, and history. His visual scenes are rarely accompanied by narrative and are often set to songs by Aissa Djarmouni. Benzelmat became famous between 1917 and 1921 for his rebellion against the colonial order, executing *caid*s (local chiefs) and the agents of the French administration.

A Generation of Franco-Algerian Documentarists

At the end of the 1990s after the Black Decade which was marked by terror, a new generation of documentary filmmakers appeared. For the most part they were talented individuals from the emigrant community in France, with dual nationality, working and living in France.

May 8, 1945, is a key date in French history. While the world was celebrating the victory over Nazi Germany, Algerians dared to display their flag, openly claiming the independence of a free Algeria. Thousands of demonstrators were slaughtered. Both in France and Algeria, film documentarists kept silent on a major event, which obviously lies at the origins of the war in Algeria (Tabet 2002, 10).

Mention should be made of the films of Yasmina 'Adi, *The Other 8 May 1945* (*L'autre 8 mai 45*, 2008), and also the recent version of the demonstrations of October 1961 in Paris, titled *Here, We Drown Algerians (Ici, on noie les Algériens*, 2011). A precursor to the documentary school of French Algerians was Mehdi Lallaoui, who made several films about the repression of May 1945, and also about the demonstrations of October 1961 in Paris. In his latest film, *The Moudjahida and the Parachutist (al-Mujahida wa al-muzali/La moudjahida et le parachutiste)*, he confronts a combatant of the war of liberation with a parachutist haunted by remorse for having committed acts of torture during *his* war of Algeria. Another highly talented documentary maker, Malek Bensmaïl, born in Algeria, emigrated to France, where he has made numerous films, almost all devoted to Algerian history. Three of his films dealing with the War of Independence are *China Is Still Far Away (al-Sin lazalat ba'ida/La Chine est encore loin*, 2008), *FLN Secret Wars in France (Guerres secrètes du FLN en France*, 2010), and *The Battle of Algiers, a Film in History* (2017).

It has previously been shown that the question of the Algerian Sahara influenced the Evian negotiations.[12] For General de Gaulle, the nuclear tests represented a priority in his strategy to provide France, before withdrawing from Algeria, with a nuclear strike force, allowing it to remain a world power. Fifteen years after Azzedine Meddour, two Franco-Algerian filmmakers—Djamal Ouahab with *The Blue Jerboa (Gerboise bleue*, 2009) and Larbi Benchihawith *Sand Wind (Rih al-rimal/Vent de sable*, 2008) and *De Gaulle, Algeria and the Bomb (De Gaulle, al-Jaza'ir al-nawawiya/De Gaulle, l'Algérie et la bombe*, 2010)—addressed the question of the nuclear tests and their permanent effect on health and the environment. Unlike the emotions aroused by *How Much I Love You (Kayf uhibuk/Combien je vous aime*, 1985), these three films hardly provoked a reaction between the two countries. On the contrary, they contributed, by way of discussion of a very sensitive subject through images, to bringing an end to forty years of silence and the unspoken.

The Battle of the Fiftieth Anniversary in Documentaries

At the beginning of 2010, French television channels launched an appeal for projects commemorating the fiftieth anniversary of the end of fighting in Algeria. The French national channels—mainly in March and April 2012—succeeded in presenting dozens of films (the majority of which were documentaries) devoted to the war of Algeria. They chose to observe the official end of hostilities marked by the signature of the Evian agreements on March 18, 1962, and not the actual date of Algerian independence, which occurred officially on July 5, 1962.

On the fringes of these nostalgic evocations, the five French public channels involved in the project presented the views of authors and personalities known for their sympathy toward the Algerian cause. It is thus that that in 2012 Hervé Bourges, a former companion of Ahmed Ben Bella, presented his documentary in two parts, *Algeria, the Test of Power, 1962–2012 (L'Algérie à l'épreuve du pouvoir, 1962–2012)*. Numerous filmmakers of Algerian origin were also invited to contribute. Two of these were Ben Salama, with *An Algerian Story (Une histoire algérienne)*, and Bensmaïl, who coproduced a film with Marie Colonna, born like him in independent Algeria, *From French Algeria to Algerian Algeria (De l'Algérie française à l'Algérie algérienne)*. In 2012, Lallaoui assembled a box set of the various documentaries he had made on the war of Algeria, which he entitled *Finish with War (En finir avec la guerre)*. Along with *For Memory's Sake*, Lallaoui decided to approach the conflict from the angle of *The History and Multiple Memories of the Algerian War (L'Histoire et des mémoires plurielles de la guerre d'Algérie)*, part of the box set.

It was a French filmmaker, François Demerliac, who in 2010 made an investigative film on the death of the Algerian militant Maurice Audin. The documentary was soberly titled *Maurice Audin, the Disappearance (Maurice Audin, la disparition)*. It recounts how in Algiers, in June 1957, Maurice Audin, a twenty-five-year-old mathematician, was arrested by the French parachutists of Massu and taken to an unknown destination. His wife Josette and his three children never saw him again. This investigation relies essentially on research by the historian Pierre Vidal-Naquet, published in 1958 (Vidal-Naquet 1958), and also makes use of testimonies from Algerian militants, French militants for Algerian independence, such as Henri Alleg, lawyers such as Robert Badinter, historians such as Mohammed Harbi, and even some soldiers.

Time for Assessment and a New Start
Algerian filmmakers are still attracted by the documentary genre. During the last two decades, and apart from the fifty-two–minute film designed mainly for television, there has been an average of three to five feature-length documentaries produced every year in Algeria. Only a few among the twenty documentary films selected for the fiftieth anniversary of independence proved to be creative and successful. Until the end of the millennium, most of these documentaries were commissioned and produced directly by public film companies. Since then, private producers have initiated the majority of long documentaries, which have received financial support from the Algerian film fund (FDATIC).

In the first decade of the millenium, a few films seemed to reconcile documentary and fiction: *The Yellow House (al-Bayt al-asfar,* 2007) by Amor Hakkar, and *Mascarades (Maskhara,* 2007) by Lyès Salem. But again, the production of expensive biopics dedicated to leaders of the war for independence failed on both levels: fictional and documentary. They appeared to be an attempt to legitimate the rule of an old generation, rather than a contribution to the writing of a national narrative in which the ordinary citizen is the real hero.

It seems that the new generation of Algerian filmmakers is no longer attracted by the theme of the war. Some of them have produced films of exceptional value. After *Half of Allah's Sky (Nisf sama' Allah/La moitié du ciel d'Allah,* 1996), on the participation of Algerian women in the War of Independence, Djamila Sahraoui turned her research to the difficulties encountered by teenagers in Algerian society: *Algeria, Life after All* (*al-Jaza'ir, al-haya raghmahum*/*Algérie, la vie quand même*, 1999) and *Algeria, Life Always* (*al-Jaza'ir al-haya da'iman*/*L'Algérie la vie toujours*, 2001).

Another female filmmaker, Bahia Benchikh El Fegoun, made three shorts before directing three successful feature-length documentary films. In *We Outside* (*H'na bara*, 2015), she explored the issue of wearing or not wearing the veil through the experiences of three young women. In 2017, *Fragments of Life* (*Ajza' min al-haya*/*Fragments de vie*) conveys adolescent frustrations and desires for freedom. The younger generation is trying to evaluate daily life, with its social difficulties and obstacles. This has led to a comeback of this mixture of fiction and social documentation. The best examples of this are: *A Roundabout in My Head* (*Fi rasi rond point*, 2016) by Hassen Ferhani, *Until the Birds Return* (*Tabi'at al-hal*, 2017) by Karim Moussaoui, and *The Blessed* (*al-Su'ada'*, 2017) by Sofia Djema. These three films were produced outside the official cinema system, and seem to announce a new brand of creators who wish to observe their society with a mixture of realism and fantasy.

A Roundabout in My Head reveals the daily lives of two young men living entirely at the central abattoirs of Algiers, with surprisingly good aesthetic results. Ferhani gives the floor to twenty-year-old Yusuf, a pure product of the Arab Spring, and middle-aged Ali Bey, who is the memory of postcolonial Algeria. Both are very much products of their historical moment: Ali feels confused and desperate, and Yusuf is part of the Arab Spring generation, feeling lost in a bewildering multiplicity of potential options, some of them dramatic.

The Algerian War of Liberation still continues to generate divergent and relatively personal cinematic depictions. Two generations later, there is still an acute awareness of the question of transmitting memories and taking responsibility for them. Born during the struggle for independence, the Algerian film documentary for decades expressed a national dream of justice and freedom. However, the new documentarists are willing to express the difficulties of their daily lives, as they question the "Algerian dream" that emerged from an exemplary struggle for national freedom. Born during the "black decade" of the 1990s (which some describe as a civil war, while others prefer to define it as "resistance to Islamic terrorism"), the filmmakers of the recent generation are more concerned by the trauma generated as a result of this conflict, and seem more inclined to display in their works the collapse of the national dream.

References

Bedjaoui, Ahmed. 1966. *Réalités et perspectives du cinéma en Algérie*. Paris: IDHEC.

———. 2014. *Cinéma et guerre de libération*. Algiers: Chihab.

———. 2016. *La guerre d'Algérie dans le cinéma mondial*. Algiers: Chihab.

Berrah, Mouny. 1979. "L'enjeu des fictions: Mouny Berrah." *Le Monde diplomatique* (July): 15.

Blidi, Amel. 2003. "L'intense lobbying des hommes du FLN aux USA." *al-Watan* [Algiers], December 2.

Chanderli, Djamel. 1990. "Chanderli Djamel to Boudjemaa Karèche." *L'Hebdo libéré* 22 (21–27 November).

Chaulet, Pierre, and Claudine Chaulet. 2012. *Le choix de l'Algérie*. Algiers: Barzakh.

Chominot, Marie. 2012a. "1956–1957: L'ALN sous l'objectif de deux reporters américains." In *Histoire de l'Algérie à la période coloniale*, edited by Abderrahmane Bouchène, 610–13. Algiers: La Découverte–Barzakh.

———. 2012b. „La Révolution par l'image: Les services d'information du FLN pendant la guerre d'indépendance algérienne." *La vie des idées* (April 4, 2012). laviedesidees.fr.

Connelly, Matthew. 2002. *A Diplomatic Revolution: Algeria's Fight for Independence and the Origins of the Cold-War Era*. Oxford: Oxford University Press.

———. 2011. *L'Arme secrète du FLN: Comment de Gaulle a perdu la guerre d'Algérie*. Paris: Payot.

Denis, Sébastien. 2009. *Le cinéma et la guerre d'Algérie: la propagande à l'écran (1945–1962)*. Paris: Nouveau Monde.

de Person, Maxime. 1995–96. "Kennedy et l'Algérie." In *Recherches contemporaines* no. 3/1997 (January–March). 144-145. Paris: L'Université Paris Nanterre.

Hellal, Abderrezak. 2011. *Le Refus d'une mise en images*. Algiers: Rafar.

L'Introduction du visuel dans la guerre de Libération nationale: L'Image et la Révolution. 2013. MAMA Symposium, Algiers, May 15–16, 2013. Reported by APS on May 15, 2013.

Koussim, Reda. 1968. "Le cinéma algérien en mouvement." *El Moudjahid*. October 24.

Maatoug, Fredj. 2012. *John F. Kennedy, la France et le Maghreb*. Paris: L'Harmattan.

Mehdaoui, Said. 2009. *Les Cinéastes de la liberté*. Full-length documentary, 70 minutes, December. ENTV Production.

Stora, Benjamin. 2010. "En France, certains n'ont toujours pas accepté la décolonisation." Interview with Caroline Venaille. *Le Monde*, May 21. lemonde.fr.

Tabet, Ainad. 2002. *8 Mai 45, le Génocide*. Algiers: ANEP.

Vidal-Naquet, Pierre. 1958. *L'Affaire Audin*. Enlarged edition 1989. Paris: Editions de Minuit.

7

A BRIEF HISTORY OF DOCUMENTARY FILM IN MOROCCO

Ali Essafi

I feel obliged to write this chapter in the first person in order to make clear from the very start its partial and subjective[1] character, far from the perfections of academic works, or rather because of the lack of and restrictive nature of academic works.* The young history of cinema in Morocco is still largely unwritten. Researchers and critics have tried to fill the void, but have rarely reached the level of a comprehensive and seriously documented survey. The only existing book—as yet unmatched—was accomplished by a filmmaker, Ahmed Bouanani, but his work has remained unpublished since its completion in 1986.[2] Bouanani was the first to have ventured into the field of research because nobody had done so before him, and because he feared no academic researcher would ever bother to do it, as he told me toward the end of his life. He probably managed to finalize his own investigation due to his position in the CCM (Centre Cinématographique Marocain, the Moroccan Cinema Center), where he worked officially as an editor, which gave him extremely privileged access to the country's film archives. This was the basis for his *Film History of Morocco*, the only one giving a detailed account of the local production of documentaries or related formats, in addition to an illuminating critical analysis. Bouanani's work sets the course for exploring the rich facets of Moroccan cinema and a stream of history that runs, as we shall see, between missed opportunities and the fight against censorship—leading to the disappearance of that particular cinema in the early 1980s. Is that the reason why Moroccan cinema was disregarded so much by the critics and rare film historians?[3]

Like most filmmakers of my generation, I began training in the 1990s, in almost absolute ignorance of the history of national cinema. At that time, I only knew of one nonfiction film from Morocco: *Trances* (*al-Hal/ Transes*, 1981). Many Moroccans know the film up to this day, even if only

---

* translated by Stefan Pethke

by hearsay, because it narrates the trajectory of the legendary band Nass El Ghiwane. I must point out that no one at the time referred to the film as a documentary, or gave it any other attribute. It was talked about as a "film," just like the others!

Only much later, in the mid-2000s, after having finally managed to meet Bouanani, did I begin to affiliate myself with the sinuous and untold history of Moroccan nonfiction film. In crossing Bouanani's *Seventh Gate*, I discovered sources that allowed me to proceed in my quest.[4]

My fondness for Bouanani was largely determined by the discovery of *Six and Twelve* (*Sitta wa ithna 'ashar/Six et douze*, 1968) and more particularly of his *Memory 14* (*Dhakirat arba'at 'ashar/Mémoire 14*, 1971). Back then, I thought these were the first Moroccan nonfiction films. To my great surprise, however, my mentor told me of another pioneer who inspired his own first attempts: Mohammed Afifi. Like everyone else, I had never heard of him.

Afifi is part of an initial host of Moroccan filmmakers who were stifled by the colonial system. When they did emerge, this half-a-dozen-or-so men were to become the first generation of directors from independent Morocco, mostly trained at IDHEC (Institut des Hautes Études Cinématographiques, the most prestigious film school in Paris; Afifi was part of its so-called twelfth promotion, which means that he graduated in 1957). Bouanani declares the date of release of Afifi's first film, *Of Flesh and Steel* (*Min lahm wa fulaz/De chair et d'acier*, 1959), the date of birth of the "first short film of value . . . [and the] only documentary of the time noticed by Georges Sadoul in his *Histoire du cinéma mondial* (History of World Cinema)." Given the conditions of film production at that time, this film is really heroic. The CCM, the institution that controlled all film activity, only allowed newsreels covering royal and governmental activities, or films commissioned by ministries and other official agencies. These commissions were sometimes reinterpreted by young filmmakers who, like Afifi and later Bouanani, could not wait any longer, and were brimming with projects and imagination. But before we go on to explore the modern era and grasp its complexity and challenges, let us go back even further.

In Search of Our Ghost Images

In Morocco, in contrast to its neighboring countries, it is difficult to find a trace of a figurative image culture before colonial penetration at the beginning of the twentieth century. Both production and consumption seem to have been nonexistent, or anecdotal, both in the realm of official representation and in private spaces. And there is no record of any law or jurisprudence regulating or forbidding the use of the image, nor was there any statutory provision which would have explicitly legalized the image when it was officially and definitively adopted by the authorities.[5] This suggests that Moroccans were deprived for a long time of any governmental support in engaging with artistic modes of self-reflection. Many of us still remember the difficulty our grandparents had in looking at their own photographic portraits on the spot and not upside down. With the exception of some notables in contact with Algeria and other countries under Ottoman domination, or with certain European countries, Moroccans did not know the figurative image until after its dissemination under French and Spanish colonization. And when the photographic and cinematographic cameras made their appearance in Morocco, they were largely associated with and used by colonial power, just like so many other modern devices like the steam train, the plane, or the tank.[6] This exclusion prevented the "natives" from representing themselves during most of the colonial period.

Just like other film historians, Ahmed Bouanani could not find any trace of a significant nonfiction film from Morocco made in the period of colonial cinema. Yet "several thousand documentaries [were] shot in the three countries of the Maghreb," as Pierre Boulanger recounts in his reference book *Le cinéma colonial* (Colonial Cinema, 1975). But films that were summarily labeled as documentaries were in reality quite often propaganda reels or so-called educational films primarily addressed to France and its colonies. Similar productions conceived by the Spanish colonial regime were documented by another film historian, Moulay Driss Jaïdi, who is the only one to record the Spanish legacy (Jaïdi 2001, 12).

Researchers cannot help but notice that we did not have visitors such as Robert Flaherty or Jean Rouch in Morocco. The ethnographic film wave nonetheless touched the country as early as the 1930s, but the results never went beyond the scope of the commissioners' objectives, and were rarely freed from the colonial tone of the time. This is the case, for example, with Jean Benoit-Levy's *Morocco, Land of Contrasts (Maroc, terre des contrastes)*, a commission from the Ministry of Agriculture that he made in the wake of his famous feature film, *Itto* (1934). According to Maurice Bardèche and Robert Brasillach's "Histoire du Cinéma" (1935), *Itto* would have been the first film in the history of French cinema to bring Western publics closer to "the native and his customs." They also describe the film as a "documentary on Morocco made of a series of admirable images" (Bardèche and Brasillach 1935, 119).

It is curious to note that historians of French cinema have always labeled any colonial films about indigenous people and their culture as documentary, whether fictional or not. Boulanger did exactly this when talking about Marcel L'Herbier's *The New Men (Les hommes nouveaux,* 1936) and *The Soul of the Countryside (L'Âme du bled)*, pioneering films in this genre: "Sometimes . . . the tale gave way to documentary style, just like in *The Soul of the Countryside*, first film by Jacques Séverac (in 1928) . . . It was a movie focusing on the capital city of the South, embellished with a rather tenuous, secondary structure . . . . This was just a pretext to show a village still little known" (Boulanger 1975, 54).

This trend seems to have persisted in the decades that followed, when well-known young figures in postwar French cinema took the lead. Even the unclassifiable André Zwoboda, one of the few filmmakers of the colonialist era to whom Bouanani gave credit—so much so that he borrowed the title of Zwoboda's film *The Seventh Gate* (*La septième porte*, 1947) for his own survey on the history of Moroccan cinema[7]—fails to stand out from the crowd. Zwoboda's *Berber Symphony* (1947), however, which was shot in parallel to *The Seventh Gate*, adopts the same formula as the other short films of the time, such as Robert Vernay's *At the Doors of the World of the Sahara* (*Aux portes du monde saharien*, 1947), or *Hello Casablanca* (*Salut Casa*, 1953) by Jean Vidal. These films all depict a French traveler (sometimes a couple), through whose eyes we see the countryside, a gaze that inevitably commits itself to the colonial discourse venerating its modern progress in contrast to the archaic indigenous world. However, these films did not seem to lack reputation, since all of them were part of the official competition at the Cannes Film Festival, sometimes even under the banner of Morocco. But we should note that they did not age well and have vanished into the dungeon of cinema. The great historian Jean Lacouture, who praises these two films in an article on Moroccan cinema in 1948 (Lacouture 1948, 59), evokes with the same enthusiasm other similar productions of which I could not find any trace. In the same manner, a list of films available in the cinemathèque of the CCM, dating from the 1960s, reveals more than forty short documentary films produced between 1947 and the year of independence in 1956. Surprisingly, only around ten of these exist in an Arabic version, meaning few of them were intended for an "indigenous" audience, including didactic films such as *Childcare (Puériculture)* or *B.C.G.* (BCG, an anti-tuberculosis vaccine).

In terms of films for an Arabic-speaking audience, Mohamed Osfour, the pioneer of national cinema, shot his first 9.5mm amateur reels from 1942 onward: "remakes" of Tarzan, Robin Hood, and similar heroes, in which this brave, self-taught filmmaker seems to have searched primarily for the magical effect of cinema that fascinated him in his childhood. He also filmed and photographed his social environment or significant events, such as demonstrations for independence and the return from exile of the royal family. But, apparently, this footage has never been used for a potential film.

Osfour's ambitions are in contrast to those of a fellow "native" he met while shooting colonial films: Tahar Hannache, a pioneer of Algerian cinema, over whom history continues to unjustly cast a veil of silence. Hannache has produced nothing but nonfiction films. He remains a legend as the director of the first Algerian film, entitled *The Desert Divers (Ghat-tasun al-sahra'/Les plongeurs du désert*, 1953). But his first attempts as a film director were actually shot in Morocco, from the early 1940s on. In the few utterances about Hannache's career, he is said to deplore the disappearance of at least two short films of that period: *Casablanca* and *Port-Lyautey*.[8]

A Documentary Cinema without Tomorrow
In the absence of a new vision, independent Morocco pursued the policies of the Centre Cinématographique Marocain (CCM), effective since 1944, in an almost identical way to the colonial period, with the notable difference that the production of fiction films ceased. It was fourteen years until the emergence of the first local fiction films. Must we conclude that the Moroccan nonfiction film was born out of deficiency? Bouanani asserted this to me plainly, explaining that his first films, as well as the films of Afifi, came into being because of a lack of any possibility to make fiction films.

The inaugural film of independent Morocco is an eleven-minute-long educational film, titled *Our Friend, the School (Sadiqatunna al-madrasa/Notre amie l'école*, 1956), directed by Larbi Benchekroun. Dozens of films followed for more than a decade, all commissioned by governmental organizations. As for the quality of these so-called documentary productions, of which I have only been able to watch some, I cannot evaluate this as eloquently as someone with the advantage of seeing them all and even participating in some of them:

> In fourteen years, about eighty reports are made in the anonymous style of Moroccan News. . . . Invariably, the takes are glued together (the term of "editing" is not appropriate here), in continuity (the "cut-in" becomes the major element of the syntax), a radio commentary with the most impersonal voice, added to bits of music transferred from records, constitutes the foundation of the soundtrack. Even in elaborate documentaries, dialogues and sound effects are rare. One is tempted to believe that the technicians responsible for the productions wished to escape from the real. For the vast majority of these films, camera movements do not reflect any specific expression; most of the time, the cinematographic vocabulary is reduced to questions of framing, going from the extreme long shot to the wide shot, from the medium long shot to the medium close-up. Close-up shots are rarely used, and if so, they are by definition descriptive.[9]

This terse record does mention exceptions, as rare as they are.[10] But Bouanani cannot help but rightfully exclaim:

In the long run, one could have expected the emergence of a documentary school, just like those that came into existence in other parts of the world in different times. Nothing came of it, even though no real obstacle was set to the development of artistic expression and sensitivity. This is attested by examples such as *Of Flesh and Steel* (1959) and *Return to Agadir* (*al-'Awda ila Aghadir/Retour à Agadir*, 1967), both made by Mohammed Afifi. They make us say that talent was not esteemed, and neither was audacity.[11]

This frustration seemed to me even more justified when I found out coincidentally in my research that the first independent film from Morocco to participate in the competition of the prestigious Cannes Festival was a documentary titled *Souls and Rhythms* (*Arwah wa iqa'at/Âmes et rythmes*, 1962), directed by Abdelaziz Ramdani,[12] whereas Bouanani ranks this film in the aforementioned category of productions and qualifies it as "a soulless assemblage where the only rhythms are those of folk dances."[13]

7.1. *Memory 14* (1971), directed by Ahmed Bouanani.

A Brief Documentary School

Bouanani considers the two short films by Mohamed Afifi, *Of Flesh and Steel* and *Return to Agadir*, to have influenced the next generation of filmmakers, who made *Six and Twelve* in 1968, *Forest (Ghabat/Forêt)* in 1970, *Mémoire 14* in 1971, and *Shining (al-Buraq/Al bouraq)* in 1972.[14] These are the first films made—individually or collectively—by Bouanani and two fellow students at IDHEC (eighteenth graduating class, 1963), Majid Rechiche and Mohamed Abderrahmane Tazi. They represent the second generation of filmmakers, although barely five years lay between their respective school classes.

7.2. *Six and Twelve* (1968), directed by Mohamed Bouanani, Majid Rechiche and Mohamed A. Tazi

So, who was the disregarded master of this "brief school," the memory of which has completely vanished from the young history of our national cinema? Bouanani was the only one trying to save Afifi from oblivion. He dedicated an entire chapter in his aforementioned book to him, titled "Sound and Fury." This chapter reports the scant information available on Afifi's work and career.

During our conversation, Bouanani shared with me that when he applied for the IDHEC scholarship, Afifi, who was a CCM executive at that time, had him take his oral exam personally. But when Bouanani returned to Morocco after graduation, Afifi had already left the CCM. According to Bouanani, Afifi could not stand producing newsreels and covering state visits any more. Subsequently, he and Bouanani met each other only occasionally, without ever getting to know each other really well.

Incidentally, when Afifi later made his second and last film, *Return to Agadir* (1967), it was Majid Rechiche who was his camera operator. Obviously, this collaboration made Bouanani and his acolyte's plans with film take another turn. This is evidenced by the radical change in the writing of the films they would shoot from that date onward, compared to their first attempt: *Tarfaya or The March of a Poet* (*Tarfaya aw masiratu sha'ir/Tarfaya ou La marche d'un poète*, 1966), with Bouanani listed as its director. Although rarely mentioned by its maker, this film clearly goes beyond just executing the governmental order to show the commitment of the state in the development of the city of Tarfaya, recently liberated from Spanish colonization. Bouanani tried to divert the assignment by imposing a sense of fiction on it. This resulted in almost two separate films: one a documentary on Tarfaya, the other fictional—The March of a Poet.[15] Here, Bouanani introduced one of his recurring topics, rituals of initiation, demonstrating his attachment to popular culture. Aside from the main role, played by Ahmed Naji, the favorite comedian of this generation, all the parts are played by non-professional local actors. The scenes have no dialogue, but there is a voice-over in French.

This first attempt proves once again that documentary film was a choice Bouanani made as a result of its deficiency, and his desire to narrate in a fictional mode is almost physical.

Let us return to Afifi and his "school" films. These were also commissioned works: one on the activities in the harbor of Casablanca, the other on the reconstruction of Agadir five years after an earthquake had destroyed it. But rather than diverting them by imposing a personal story on them, as was done in *Tarfaya or the March of a Poet*, Afifi reacted to the commission by informing the film with a subjective gaze and a sensitive tone. First, he managed to liberate himself from using talkative commentary, which burdened every CCM production back then. When commentary is needed, it remains brief, and Afifi never elaborates on what the images show anyway. On the contrary, the commentary transcends the images, to give its tale more meaning and more depth. Thus, the soundtrack ceases to be merely illustrative and becomes a narrative segment in its own right.

Afifi successfully did away with the diktat of linear narration, and his sophisticated construction of visual expression enabled the core of the film to emerge. While embodied in a very real time and a very real space, the tale evolves into an autonomous and coherent universe, where it can roam around, without beginning or end, beyond conventions.

The freedom afforded by Afifi's approach no doubt had a decisive impact on Bouanani and his comrades-in-arms, as films of such force were not common at that time in emerging or newly independent countries. This can be seen clearly in their second collective attempt, *Six and Twelve*, made in 1968, in the wake of *Return to Agadir*. The film has no comment or dialogue. It casts a glance at Casablanca through the changes in light and rhythm between six o'clock and noon, a concept halfway between Dziga Vertov's *Man with a Movie Camera (Chelovek s kino-apparatom)* and the "school" films of Afifi. Bouanani elaborates extensively on the genesis and the conditions of production of this project. He is critical of the film's imperfections, which he blames on the lack of symbiosis in the collective approach. Subsequent films produced under the influence of Afifi were made individually from this point on. However, one can note a surprising disparity in the style and writing of these films, which Bouanani puts under the same banner of Afifi's "brief documentary school." *Memory 14*[16] is a montage film that somehow continues the experimentation of *Six and Twelve*, except that it is transposed to the processing of archival footage. To my knowledge, this film is the first attempt to deconstruct (colonial) archives ever under-taken by an Arab-African filmmaker. As for Majid Rechiche's *Forest* and *Shining*, they are rather unconventional fiction films that successfully try to express the atmosphere of fear and confinement that reigned at the time. But what these four films have in common above all is the search for a creative narrative form and a dominating soundtrack. Bouanani told me that he, and probably also his filmmaker friends, had understood that censorship mainly focused on the image and was less concerned with sound.

7.3. *Return to Agadir* (1967), directed by Mohamed Afifi.

Afifi and his two films sank into oblivion for a long time, until Bouanani revealed their existence to me. During a tribute to Bouanani organized by the Cinémathèque of Tangier, I wanted to program them both and invite their author, but at the last moment, the CCM claimed that the prints of these films were not available. On hearing the news, Afifi reportedly said, "I am not surprised!" and consequently canceled his trip to Tangier. This was doubtless his last chance for a reappearance, because soon after, I received a message from his daughter informing me of his passing away (in November 2014). Subsequently, I managed to program his films in other events. Now they circulate in Morocco again, as well as abroad. May they continue to carry the breath of the "brief school" and inspire new talents.

Skipping the School of Sociology

Bouanani strangely failed to include in the lineage of the "brief school" a film made a few years later by Mohammed Abouelouakar, *The City of Remembrance* (*Madinat al-dhakira/La cité du souvenir*, 1977).[17] Trained at the Moscow film school VGIK from 1966 to 1971, this new recruit of the CCM soon became close with Bouanani. Abouelouakar asserts that, after his arrival at the CCM, he spent a lot of time in the archives, watching the films of Afifi and his descendants, among others *Memory 14*.[18] Abouelouakar admired this film so much, as he told me, and he watched it countless times, including the reels of those sequences that had fallen victim to censorship.[19] In *The City of Remembrance*, the influence of the "brief school" is not only manifest, but whole sound fragments borrowed from *Mémoire 14* can be found in it. The outcome is a portrait of Marrakesh, the filmmaker's hometown, made in a way this city has rarely been depicted.

But perhaps it was the right thing for Bouanani to do, not to put Abouelouakar's film in the succession of the "brief school"? Indeed, *The City of Remembrance* seems to have been exposed to both the influence of Afifi's "brief school" and to that of another school, never revealed to date, the school of the ethno-sociological film. The lack of appreciation for this school is quite incredible, considered it was the most durable and most prolific. As we will see later, this school is the foundation for the most outstanding films in the history of Moroccan cinema throughout the 1970s to the early 1980s. I only became aware of it myself through conducting the research for this book. Obviously, several films from this sociological school have benefited from some attention here and there, but only on a case-by-case basis, and not in the context of an evaluation of it as a movement in its own right, taking into account all of its surrounding circumstances. Two reasons seem to explain this failure. First, some of the films were made by Moroccan directors operating abroad, often at the service of foreign television stations or other foreign institutions, and were therefore never distributed in Morocco. Secondly, some of them were wholly or partially censored. Yet we find traces of the beginnings of this movement, started in parallel to the "brief school," or even a little earlier. These are a few films from the mid-1960s that Bouanani said stand out in a decade of insignificance, such as *Sin Agafaye* (1967) by Latif Lahlou. This film reports on a practice of the management and distribution of water that was almost primitive, but was still utilized in certain places at that time.

In the same year, the young researcher Mohammed Aït Youssef, who had completed a class with Jean Rouch, made a film based on a thesis in ethnology written by a French student at the University of Montpellier. The result is an ethnographic film of rare maturity titled *The Tanners of*

Marakesh (Dabbaghi Marrakish/Les tanneurs de Marrakech). However, in his book, Bouanani points out this director for another film: *Nostalgia of the Naive (Nostalgie du naïf)*, produced ten years later, "during a brief stay at the CCM, a documentary on a craftsman from Rabat, unfortunately in black and white, is a very touching experience that went unnoticed at the first National Film Festival in Rabat in 1982."[20] Bouanani does not seem to know of Youssef's previous work, which also is not mentioned anywhere else. Deceased in the prime of his life, Youssef could only finish these two films, in addition to his work as a painter, often confused with the work of his father, Saïd Aït Youssef, who was known as a painter of naive art who lived in Marrakech.

In 1968, another young director by the name of Mohammed Abbazi tried to make a film for his graduation, having started his studies at the University of California Los Angeles and completed them at Harvard. The film was supposed to be about the day-worker cleaning women of Casablanca. But Abbazi abandoned the project while still at the stage of the often clandestinely shot rushes, because he could not get the permission to film his protagonists in the informal settlement they were living in.[21]

Who knows how many more attempts have not reached us or are still out there in the wild? Bouanani mentions a newsreel format called "Vu pour Vous" (Seen for You), which offered filmmakers who were part of the CCM the opportunity to suggest a personal project of four to seven minutes' length, to be broadcast at the end of the weekly news.

> Various subjects are addressed in these films, through which the young filmmakers could gain experience: small businesses, endangered traditions, museums, forgotten crafts, manuscripts, *moussems* [translator's note: a harvest celebration with economic, cultural, and social functions] etc.—everything can be used as a pretext in order to practice and search for a cinematographic expression beyond the beaten path. This is how Majid Rechiche produced the mini-documentary *The Cameleers of Azemmour (Jamalin 'Azimur/Les cameliers d'Azemmour)*, about an original guild providing the entrepreneurs of small towns with sand; Mohammed Abderrahmane Tazi filmed wrought-iron-working craftsmen; Mohammed Laâlioui made known the traditional fight of 'Mchaoucha', a sort of Japanese wrestling, Moroccan style, forgotten today."[22]

Among the films lost forever, Bouanani evokes a group of short films, produced in the early 1970s, abandoned by the management of the CCM in a Parisian laboratory. His own film about the legendary marabout Sidi Ahmed O'moussa, filmed in 1972, is part of the damage.

Once upon a Time There Was a Moroccan Named Paul Pascon

Paul Pascon is another name struggling to remain in the collective memory of Moroccan film, despite the fact that this son of a colonizer, who chose to remain in the country and acquired citizenship, only died in 1985. Pascon is recognized as the uncontested father of the Moroccan school of social sciences. From the early years of independence onward, he put heart and soul into dedicating himself to several major projects related to the research and development of rural Morocco as well as its working class. He involved dozens of students in these projects, many of whom still represent the best of the nation's intelligentsia, permanently marked by the methods of this creative sociologist, who combined field research and action. His pioneering work is appreciated, but was also closely watched by the regime until his death in an accident, an event that more or less coincided with the prohibition on teaching sociology and philosophy in Moroccan universities.

Meanwhile, Paul Pascon's role in the introduction of sociological film has never been subject to serious and complete study, as far as is known. In the register of film, Pascon's name is officially associated with only one film of this period, the emblematic *The Children of Haouz* (*Abna' al-Hawuz/ Les enfants du Haouz*, 1970), directed by Driss Karim,[23] an x-ray of rural youth unemployment, famous for having first been censored first and then disappearing completely. Pascon is also linked to *Rites of the Bound* (*Ma'ruf n'tamijlusht/Rite du ligoté*, 1980), a Hamid Bensaid film for which he had written the commentary. However, the direct and indirect involvement of Pascon in cinema seems to have been more important than that, and more sustainable. The testimonies of his disciples attest that he introduced the use of photography and film to his work at a very early stage. While encouraging his students to take an interest in these techniques, he also appealed to young filmmakers outside the discipline who were attracted by the social sciences. For instance, it was at the urging of Pascon that Mohammed Abouelouakar left for the Moscow film school. At the age of fifteen, Abouelouakar had joined the National Office of Irrigation in Marrakech, which the master sociologist Pascon headed in the mid-1960s. Abouelouakar remembers having worked as the assistant of Latif Lahlou, the director of the above-mentioned *Sin Agafaye*, dealing with archaic water management. Driss Karim assisted Lahlou with his previous film *Feed* (*'Alf al-mashiya/Fourrage*, 1966), before directing *The Children of Haouz*. Lahlou, who belongs to the first generation of Moroccan post-independence filmmakers to attend the Parisian film school IDHEC (1959/ fourteenth graduating class), simultaneously studied sociology at the Sorbonne. Was this a coincidence? Not really, if one takes a closer look. The Moroccan filmmakers of that time, especially those of the third generation, seem to have had a lot of enthusiasm for the social sciences. And

Pascon's students were in close contact with these filmmakers via certain "ciné-clubs" (film clubs), which were, like al-Azaim in Casablanca, hubs of exchange on culture and arts.

It should be pointed out that the enthusiasm for social sciences had also seized the "brief school," both teachers and disciples. It could be argued that Mohammed Afifi's first film, *Of Flesh and Steel*, is in line with the socio-ethnographic film.[24] Ahmed Bouanani is probably the filmmaker who has conducted the most research on culture and popular arts in Morocco, including fieldwork, some of which was published in the first issues of *Souffles (Anfas)*, the cult magazine of the 1960s and 1970s (Bouanani 1966). But unlike the "school of sociology," which engaged in a frontal exploration of the real, the "brief school" preferred to extract the imaginary and the poetry from it.

The Golden Age of Moroccan Cinema

It is interesting to establish the connections between our two documentary schools and the fiction films that their proponents were able to produce, for better or worse. Indeed, these connections are behind the most beautiful chapter of the national cinema of fiction. After funding the first three Moroccan feature films in 1968–69,[25] the CCM stopped its support of film production right away. Ahmed Bouanani and Mohammed Abderrahmane Tazi of the "brief school" reacted by joining two new IDHEC graduates—Hamid Bennani and Mohammed Sekkat—to create the first Moroccan filmmakers' collective: Sigma 3. The collective's aim was to allow the self-production of the first films of each of its members. With very limited funds, *Wechma (Washma/Traces)* by Bennani was finalized in 1970, becoming the first cult movie in Moroccan film history, and receiving critical acclaim on an international scale. But the collective perished soon after, preventing the shooting of Bouanani's project *The Miracle (Le Mirage)*, scheduled to immediately follow *Wechma*. In the end, *The Miracle* would take ten more years to come into existence. Just as *Wechma* did before, *The Miracle* entered the pantheon of Moroccan masterpieces. Perhaps Moumen Smihi's singular early works, including his distinguished *El Chergui (al-Sharqi/Vent d'est/East Wind*, 1975) and *44 or the Legend of the Night (44 aw Usturat al-layl/44 ou Les récits de la nuit*, 1981), should also be affiliated with the "brief school"? But with this atypical artist of the third generation, there is no way of telling whether such a genealogy would be genuine or just spiritual. In his own writing about film, Smihi never mentions any filmmakers from the "brief school," or any of their films. But just like the school's main figures, he claims to have been influenced by Dziga Vertov and Flaherty, and confesses his admiration for André Zwoboda's Moroccan films (Smihi 2005).

As for the "school of sociology," its connections with fiction bring out another path in which fiction is nothing but a protective shield at the service of filming reality. However, the foundational film for this connection, *Spring Sunshine* (*Shams al-rabi'/Soleil de printemps*, 1969), was still wide off the mark in terms of its use of fiction. Obviously, this first feature-length fiction of Latif Lahlou, the same director who was a documentary pioneer with *Sin Agafaye*, fell victim to the commission's official objective. The film is nonetheless distinguished by Bouanani as the only sincere work out of the first three fiction films commissioned and produced by the CCM. But after this hesitant start, the "school of sociology" freed itself by delivering docu-fictions, essays, and special research, carried out with full commitment.

The first feature-length fiction film of the 1970s, *Thousand and One Hands* (*Alf yadd wa yadd/Mille et une mains*, 1972–73), was directed by Souhail Ben Barka, freshly trained at the Centro Sperimentale di Cinematografia in Rome, after having also obtained a degree in sociology at the University of Rome. His film is the first to have dared to explicitly show the exploitation of child labor and other everyday miseries. Built around a rather minor plot, its strength lies more in quasi-documentary sequences describing the hard work of carpetmaker artisans and the small trades revolving around them. In the wake of this production and with the same technical team, Ben Barka shot a short documentary about the little worker who embodies one of the fiction's main parts: *Malika, the Dyer's Daughter* (*Malika bint al-dabagh/Malika, la fille du teinturier*). Obviously, that film went unnoticed after the international (and commercial) success of *Thousand and One Hands*. Ben Barka's filmography also mentions a first short documentary titled *Water* (*al-Ma'/L'eau*, 1970), and another one released in 1975, *Those of the Moussem* (*Ashab al-mawsim/ Ceux du Moussem*), which none of my contacts remembers having seen. With a pioneering strategy, Barka secured the survival of his cinema by managing to liberate himself from the help of the CCM at all stages of production through privately funded coproductions with Italy and other European countries.

Bouanani cites the case of another Moroccan trained in Italy whose films have never circulated in Morocco: a certain Boughaleb Bouriki, whom Bouanani apparently was the only one to remember. This out-of-sight filmmaker also shot several documentaries in the 1970s on behalf of RAI (Italian public broadcaster), including *In the Name of Civilization* (*Au nom de la civilisation*, 1978), selected in 1979 for the Festival des 3 Continents (Festival of Three Continents) in Nantes, France, and two more, one on Iraq, the other on Kuwait, to which I found access to in the Cinémathèque québécoise.

Immediately after *Thousand and One Hands*, a new film became a talking point, for its conceptualization process as much as for its total and absolute ban: *About Some Meaningless Events* (*Ahdath bidun dalala/De quelques évènements sans signification*, 1974). Like *Thousand and One Hands*, this film is built around a secondary plot serving as a pretext for the documentary aspect. The plot allowed the camera to roam freely where it had never gone before in Casablanca, immortalizing snippets of atmosphere in popular bars, with some of Morocco's best future wordsmiths, beards and hair in the wind, chanting the revolution. It includes interviews filmed in the streets, the first of their kind in Morocco, asking people about their preferences for a national cinema. The project is credited to Moustafa Derkaoui, but it is in fact a collective work, to which a beautiful blend of third-generation filmmakers contributed, most of them trained at the National Film School in Łódź (Poland). Several of these filmmakers began making short documentaries at the end of their studies and for some time afterward, but only a few of their films were shown in Morocco. One of them, directed by Noureddine Gounajjar, remains in the annals for having obtained two awards at the National Film Festival, including best director for *Ensemble* (*Rukkam/Agrégats*, 1984). The film was finished for the festival's second edition, held in 1984, even though its footage had been shot in 1972. *Ensemble* is a purely ethnographic film about the ritual of trance in the Aissaoua brotherhood, "shown in their mystery (which may appear daunting) and their symbolic opacity, through the eyes of a child who is surprised at first, then amused, and then frightened. Such explorations of the various realities of our society, especially the ones that the current urban 'culture' knows least of and represses most, should multiply" (Jibril 1985, 32). The director of the film confessed to me that he was convinced, at the time, that the censors would never pass the shocking images of the trance, which are reminiscent of Jean Rouch's *The Mad Masters* (*Les maîtres fous*). So he edited them a good ten years later, when a brighter period offered more favorable conditions.

After the experience of *About Some Meaningless Events*, and despite the censorship, Moustafa Derkaoui and part of his team joined forces with some newcomers around another project, *The Ashes of the Closed* (1976). On this occasion, the director's task was taken on by Mohammed Reggab, another great figure of the cinema of this generation formed at the Moscow film school VGIK. But Reggab eventually gave up the project.[26] The final result is a docu-fiction, also born under the influence of the "school of sociology," in which the so-called fictional aspect tries to cover what the Direct Cinema approach in the other parts could not catch, in order to give a stark account of the waste of the rural exodus. *The Ashes of the Closed*, for once, managed to pass the censorship. Despite weak distribution, the film benefited from a strong response, and still holds interest to this day. This film was quickly out-rivaled by *Alyam, Alyam (Ô les jours!/O Days!*, 1978), a feature debut by Ahmed El Maanouni. Conceptually more accomplished, this film addresses the same topic as El Maanouni's predecessor Reggab, but ventures further in terms of Direct Cinema, thus giving the whole film more strength and coherence. *Alyam, Alyam* quickly achieved critical success internationally, thanks to which it continues to circulate to the present day. El Maanouni built on this, and in 1981 released the notorious *Trances*, his cult film that I mentioned at the very beginning of this chapter as the only Moroccan documentary film I knew before starting my research.

7.4. *Alyam Alyam* (1978), directed by Ahmed El Maanouni

The school of socio-ethnographic showpieces continued to emerge until the mid-1980s, and even beyond. In 1984, the CCM set up a funding system to support film production, an event that significantly affected the development of the country's young art of film. It ended in beauty, with two major films: *The Barber of the Poor Neighborhood (Le coiffeur du Quartier des pauvres*, 1982) by Mohammed Reggab, who managed to deliver his first and only feature-length fiction film at last; and finally *Hadda* (1984), another first and last feature-length fiction film, directed by the already mentioned Mohammed Abouelouakar. Again, as in *The City of Remembering (La Cité du souvenir)*, he seems to have achieved a perfect synthesis of the "brief school" and the "school of sociology." The originality of this work left such a strong impact on the second edition of the National Film Festival in 1984 that it garnered the majority of the awards.

But from then on, documentary cinema of all schools combined disappeared from the scene, depriving fiction films of the freshness and singularity they had emerged from. Later, Moroccan documentary films would return in a different form, and sometimes on other shores, but with no connection at all to the experiences accumulated by these first schools.

In 1985, Paul Pascon died, shortly after the teaching of sociology, restricted to the universities of Fes and Rabat, was banned in 1981. The mistrust of the regime toward this discipline, perceived for a long time as a source of subversion, had already led to the closure by royal order of the Institute of Sociology of Rabat as early as 1970.

As for *Our Friend, the School*, the title of the first film of independent Morocco, the state never developed an educational institution dedicated to the teaching of cinema until very recently, when the ISMAC (Institut supérieur des métiers de l'audiovisuel et du cinéma, or Institute for Higher Education in the Professions of Audiovisual and Film), based in Rabat, opened its doors in 2013.

This text was conceived and written in Casablanca, 2018.

References

Bardèche, Maurice, and Robert Brasillach. 1935. *Histoire du cinéma*. Paris: Denoël et Steele.

Bouanani, Ahmed. 1966. "Pour une étude de la littérature populaire marocaine." *Souffles* 3: 3–9. clicnet.swarthmore.edu.

Boulanger, Pierre. 1975. "Affabulation et documentaire." In *Le cinéma colonial: De L'Atlantide à Lawrence d'Arabie*, edited by Pierre Boulanger and Guy Hennebelle. Paris: Seghers, p. 53–56.

Jaïdi, Moulay Driss. 2001. *Histoire du cinéma au Maroc: Le cinéma colonial*. Rabat: Al-Majal.

Jibril, Mohammed. 1985. "Les cinéastes marocains sur la sellette." *Lamalif* 162. January, p. 27–32.

Lacouture, Jean. 1948. "Cinéma marocain." *Revue Plaisir de France*, June, p.57–59.

El Messaoudi, Bouchaib. 2011. *al-Wathaqi'i asl al-sinima*. Khouribga: al-Waraqa al-muttahida.

Ould-Braham, Ouahmi. 2012. "Itinéraire singulier d'un cinéaste algérien en France à l'époque coloniale." *Migrance* 37, p. 38–56.

Smihi, Moumen. 2005. *Parler cinéma (Hadith al-sinima)*. Tangier: Editions Sliki Ikhwan.

8

FUNDING THE "CREATIVE DOCUMENTARY": AN ART CINEMA OF REFUGEES

Kay Dickinson and Viviane Saglier

S pending time with the closing credits of any contemporary Arab art documentary will quickly reveal one simple fact: that these works "come" from multiple places at once. Emerging from an intricate congregation of far-flung funding and coproduction, the Arab art documentary of today demands examination according to the prerogatives of transnational funding regimes.

In order to better trace these out, this essay follows a group just as itinerant, although beholden to often radically dissimilar conditions: refugees. Films seeking to represent displaced peoples must often nest within the same geopolitical and financial structures that mold the legal and social framing of "the refugee." The refugee is increasingly tracked by visualizing technologies, from drones and other militarized devices to online, shareable charity videos encouraging aid donations, to stereotypes from the popular press, with their emphasis on unstoppable tides of unwanted arrivals. As such, the refugee becomes a highly documented figure caught up in the cross-border currents of modern filmed culture. The focus for this chapter is the Arab "creative documentary," which also arises out of, as part of, and helps constitute this surveilled and controlled landscape. Once they are completed, creative documentaries lead itinerant lives through distribution and exhibition circuits, comparable, in some ways, to those of refugees. However, this chapter involves itself more with the origins of funding for Arab documentary films, which is at once regional and foreign or, more particularly, a telling and highly geopolitical amalgam of both.

Since the 2000s, the capital invested in producing and promoting documentary films in the Arab world has diversified, accruing from regional and private media groups, international art cinema funds, international human rights foundations, and regional nongovernmental organizations

(NGOs). Symptomatic of a global tendency, the reconfiguration of the economy surrounding Arab documentaries has paralleled a trend in documentary filmmaking at large toward the more authorial and hybridized form of the *creative* documentary, a genre which increasingly experiments with innovative narrative structures allowed by access to new technologies (de Jong, Knudsen, and Rothwell 2012, 3–4). Deemed "not very common in the Arab world" (Ajroudi and al-Tahhan 2014, 286) in comparison to more lucrative genres like commercial dramas or comedies, the traditional Arab documentary has readily been accused of lacking credibility altogether, oftentimes reduced to "either propaganda, or dull touristic docs [produced] under the thumb of the regime in each country" (Hamilton 2014). In contrast, the emergence of the creative documentary in the international film market has provided new avenues for rebranding the unpopular genre in the Arab world and expanding the reach and penetration of the Arab media industries' financial networks.

If low profitability and lack of popular trust have shaped Arab investors' relationship to documentaries in the past, then it is significant that the intensification and the diversification of funding injected into Arab creative documentaries has coincided with a certain faith in the growing independence and democratization of the "new Arab public sphere," following the rise of satellite TV more particularly (Lynch 2006). We can also wonder what role the increased penetration of art cinema's financial networks into the region plays in this scenario. In what follows, we will examine the input of the Arab Fund for Arts and Culture (AFAC) and the Dubai International Film Festival (DIFF) in developing creative documentaries made by Arab filmmakers. On further inspection, the many works dedicated to the prominent figure of the refugee that these institutions foster beg questions about their integration into broader streams of international capital and human movement.

To be specific, refugees support an entire economy of human rights organizations on the ground who strive to provide the care and freedoms these populations have been denied by their own national regimes (so the rhetoric goes). At the same time, refugees spark gestures of solidarity the world over. The international interest in learning about refugees' stories has thus pointed to the possibility for expanding markets. Taking refugee films as symptomatic of the current economy of Arab creative documentaries, the upcoming sections argue that local industries involved in developing nonfiction filmmaking are obliged to strategically negotiate an international politics of art cinema that is entangled within a broader Western politics of aid, most pressingly the "democratizing forces" of human rights organizations that propose to fully realize the potential of documentaries to beget social change.

Negotiating Social Change Through the Creative Documentary

Founded in 2007, a regional grant-making project, the nonprofit and philanthropically oriented Arab Fund for Arts and Culture (AFAC), emerged at the same moment satellite TV began to thrive, when the Al Jazeera Documentary channel and the Gulf-based film festivals were hitting their strides. Active in a variety of cultural fields (including cinema in general, literature, dance, and music), the Fund's mission prevails, for executive director Rima Mismar, to "fill a gap in public funding and private investment" in the realm of cultural affairs (Mismar 2017). The Fund's primary objective with respect to documentaries was to balance out the investments of TV stations like Al Jazeera and Al Arabiya. According to AFAC's perspective, TV documentaries limit themselves to illustrating current affairs rather than exploring creative expression. It deems these stations tainted by agendas deriving from their Qatari and Saudi funding, despite those networks' efforts to brand themselves as independent media. In contradistinction, AFAC declared "transparency in the grant giving process and independence through a diversity of funding sources" (AFAC 2011, 6) as its guiding principles. In fact, Arab filmmakers like Annemarie Jacir have celebrated AFAC's unique support for political topics, free of "any conditions or artistic censorship," which responds to "the need to break the reliance on European funding to have a strong and independent film community" (Jacir 2013). In 2009, the Fund fashioned a program specifically dedicated to nonfiction filmmaking in partnership with the Sundance Documentary Institute: the Arab Documentary Film program (ADFP). In the first three years, the program supported forty-four documentaries, and then remodeled itself as the AFAC Arab Documentary Program (ADP) in 2013. That year, the ADP represented 10 percent of AFAC's budget (AFAC, "6 Years") and projected support of fifteen films per year with a maximum grant amount of US$50,000 each (AFAC, "AFAC's Documentary Program"). Although the sum seems modest, this type of starting budget was intended merely to facilitate filmmakers' access to coproduction, allowing them to negotiate agreements from a position of strength in exactly the sorts of film market contexts proliferating at events like the Dubai International Film Festival (which we discuss toward the end of this chapter) (Mismar 2017).

Following a widespread ambivalence toward foreign funding in the region, AFAC has both criticized dependence on foreign donors[1] and encouraged cooperation with international artistic funds. In 2009, the Sundance Documentary Institute provided funding, consultation, networking, and training opportunities for documentary filmmakers (AFAC 2011). Many partnerships with art cinema institutions have also taken the shape of workshops, which both serve the interests of the foreign art funds and remain flexible enough to adapt to local infrastructures. Workshops have become markedly representative of the power negotiation between Arab cultural institutions and temporary foreign investments in art. They provide provisional training spaces sometimes attached to larger events, such as the film festivals (DIFF included) that drive the economy of creative documentaries; they provide a quick turnover of grantees; and they do not require a long-term investment from partners, although they do constitute a formidable tool to expand these partners' spheres of influence at a low cost through pedagogy.

In 2011, the AFAC workshop held at Leipzig's DOK Festival established networking opportunities for Arab filmmakers with Berlinale's World Cinema Fund and Berlinale's coproduction market representatives, thus generating attachments that reinforced the centrality of European festivals as the institutions setting the creative standards for documentaries. The advisors animating the workshops hailed from both the Arab world and Euro-Western countries. Throughout the program's existence, advisor and jury membership has comprised film workers from regional organizations such as Lebanon's Beirut-DC, Tunisia's ATAC, and Egypt's SEMAT, with some also originating from TV. One example would be the director of the Al Arabiya–backed company O3 Production, Mohamad Soueid, also a renowned experimental filmmaker. The Arab Documentary Program's network of Euro-Western art cinema organizations and Arab TV producers thus reveals the continuing mechanisms of interdependence (rather than outright independence) at work in shaping a space dedicated to creative documentary in the regional film industry. This tension also points to the dual interest in catering to a thriving Western documentary market with film festivals as an endpoint, and the instrumentalization of that market for building a regional platform for funding and distributing documentaries.

The focus on refugees, furthermore, exposes creative documentaries' influence within the intersection of art cinema and human rights economies. The conjunction of these financial networks is not unique to AFAC; it persists, for example, in the conceptualization of creative documentaries by European funds that target "developing countries" and thereby perpetuate a continuity of aid fed through national politics. Such a case is the prestigious IDFA Bertha Fund, embedded in the International Documentary Festival of Amsterdam, which defines creative documentary as, on the one hand, innovative and upholding cinematic quality and market potential, and, on the other, empowering films that tackle "controversial issues," including social and economic justice (or injustice), freedom of expression, human rights, poverty, and education (IDFA, n.d.). In parallel, the National Film School of Denmark (NFSD) has inaugurated their own "Middle-East project" dedicated to documentary training in collaboration with national and nongovernmental organizations already involved in capacity and institution-building in the region, such as the International Media Support (IMS), which helped establish the Arab Film Institution in Amman (now Screen Institute Beirut) (Hjort 2013, 132). The bleeding of human rights discourse and its institutional apparati into art cinema thus materializes in film funding partnerships. AFAC's independence and diversifying endeavors very much rely on seed money provided by the Open Society Foundations, a U.S.-based international grant-making network founded by the philanthropist George Soros. Apart from Open Society, AFAC's main donors include the Netherlands-based DOEN Foundation and the Ford Foundation, the latter pitching into AFAC's documentary program through its Just Films initiative, a fifty-million-dollar program that also funds the Doc Corner at Cannes' Film Market. All three donors propose a vision for political change and a society based on "the rule of law; respect for human rights, minorities, and a diversity of opinions; democratically elected governments; and a civil society that helps keep government power in check" (Open Society Foundations, n.d.), consistent with AFAC's mission of transparency and independence. AFAC's and its partners' emphasis on democratization processes—and a binary notion of independence which seems to unilaterally equate oppressive structures with authoritarian Arab regimes—is, however, also deeply rooted in some of these organizations' imperialist histories, and testament to a certain configuration of human rights politics that is familiar from the late 1970s and then the fall of the Soviet Union. The Ford Foundation, among others, assumed a significant role in shaping an anti-communist "culture of freedom" during the Cold War (McCarty 1987, 93–117), competing with the non-aligned interests of the third world.

For AFAC board member Oussama Rifahi, the philanthropic model is key, but it is crucial that it develops at the local level precisely because of the region's various histories of Western dependence (AFAC 2011). Drawing lessons from European philanthropy's "mixed-economy funding model" and the decentralized and corporate-driven imperatives of the United States, AFAC has devised its own "strategic philanthropy," which concurrently draws on a regional culture of charity and endowment (Farouky 2015). The Fund has thus striven to establish a sustainable regional culture of giving to the arts that can systematize local donations through lobbying, fundraising events, and media campaigns that valorize the impact of culture on society (AFAC, "6 Years"). The Fund's efforts also aim to attract the region's numerous wealthy donors, and, to a lesser extent, corporations, who often include charity in their branding strategies. By mobilizing, among others, topics such as the life conditions and histories of refugees, AFAC's Arab Documentary Program strategically bridges a regional tradition of charity to the destitute, pressing human rights issues, international marketing interests, soft power strategies, art cinema's interest in situated subjectivities, and documentary's claim on social change.

The Ford Foundation is now central to funding numerous initiatives that support Arab cinema in general, as well as isolated documentary film projects that address issues of freedoms and rights in contexts where the Foundation underlines democratization as a central project. For example, the British–Yemeni documentary *Fatherland* (renamed *The Mulberry House* (*Bayt al-tut*), Sara Ishaq, 2013) weaves together Yemen's attempt at emancipation during the 2011 uprising with the filmmaker's own emancipation from her father and grandfather in a self-defined effort to "challenge patriarchy" (Takieddine 2012); through *In the Last Days of the City* (*Akhir ayam al-madina*, 2016), Tamer El-Said confronts the imminent exile and death of his loved ones, wandering the streets of Cairo in search of a new apartment, while the city sits poised on the brink of uprising (Ford Foundation, n.d.). These two films examine migrant histories, feelings of estrangement, and the challenges of returning home, thus cohering with AFAC-funded films that deal more directly with refugees' experiences in the context of political unrest. Mismar has defined creative documentary as akin to "an auteur film [promoting] an individualistic [and] unique gaze" (Mismar 2017) and, correspondingly, AFAC's documentaries place the subjectivity of various scales of exile and homelessness at the center of their narrative. Mais Darwazah's poetic account of her return to Palestine in *My Love Awaits Me by the Sea* (*Habibi biyistanani 'and al-bahr*, 2013) is also an ode to a fantasy lover; in *Broken Record* (*Qawanah*, 2012), Parine Jaddo returns to Iraq in search of a Turkman song interpreted by her late mother; Tamara Stepanyan's *Those from the Shore* (submitted to AFAC as *Limbo*, 2016) stems from the filmmaker's own experience in exile, and explores the welfare of Armenian asylum seekers upon their arrival in France; Samer Abu Qatmeh's *194. We, the Children of the Camp* (*194. Nahnu awlad al-mukhayyam*, 2016) details the complicated politics of Palestinian refugees in Syria after the uprisings; in *A Drowning Man* (*Rajul yaghraq*, 2016), Mahdi Fleifel continues his investigation of the hardships of Palestinian refugees' attempts at emigrating to Europe; Rami Farah's project, tentatively called *A Comedian in a Syrian Tragedy* (Fares Helou. *Hikayat mumathil kharaj 'an al-nass*, 2019), observes the absurdity of exiled existence. All these films, by prioritizing a personal understanding of what it means to be a refugee, reclaim and redefine an appellation that has many times been used to dehumanize refugees at the expense of their human rights of shelter, dignity, and security. By promoting social change and the empowerment of refugees, these films thus negotiate two distinct but seemingly compatible agendas: the artistic expression of individual experiences of forced displacement through the creative documentary, while also conforming to IDFA's claims and philanthropy's promises.

Marketing Refugee Subjectivity: Toward an Aesthetic of Relevance

Refugee films open a tappable market within the genre of creative documentary. We now turn to how refugee topics are articulated within the economics of art cinema aesthetics. Refugee films are in demand across various art cinema networks because they spotlight a population that makes the headlines. These works simultaneously convey unique experiences that challenge, and experiment with, common representations of forced migration. Creative documentaries on or by refugees thus potentially encapsulate three out of the four criteria set by AFAC in its evaluation process: quality, creativity (these two being inherent to the genre), and relevance to the Arab region (AFAC 2013). Highlighting AFAC's interest in "relevance" here points to the criterion's wider function as a marketing compass for art documentaries in general, and starts explaining how privileging the point of view of the refugee subject may become a commercial asset for Arab documentaries internationally. We can wonder to what extent the festival-driven film market runs the risk of placing upon refugees, or Arab filmmakers by proxy, the burden of having to render their condition, and the context of what is readily called "the refugee crisis," legible to international audiences. These audiences in turn expect and request "human stories" that coincide with creative documentaries' interest in personal narratives. This tapering down to singular protagonists can be seen to close out the possibility of representing certain core dimensions of the refugee experience, most particularly the sheer magnitude of affected populations, or the communality of, for instance, transit and camp life. Non-Arab filmmakers have also tapped into this market as a gesture of solidarity, while also at times dangerously flirting with the exploitation of their subjects, such as in the hyper-aestheticized *Requiem for Syrian Refugees* (Richard Wolf, 2014), and the intrusive investigation that spawned *A Syrian Love Story* (Sean McAllister, 2015).

Aaron Bady has raised these concerns about legibility with respect to depictions of the so-called Arab Spring that oftentimes did their utmost to impart upon the uprisings a "rhetorical consistency." The convergence on Tahrir Square in particular promoted a vision of popular resistance that could be grasped by Western media and accorded with Western liberal values of nonviolence, secularism, and technological liberation (Bady 2012, 129). Art cinema has indeed responded to the call for legibility, conjuring a space where refugees can tell their stories and share their individualized subjectivities through both the so-called universal language of cinema and, in effect, the unproblematized cosmopolitan language of *art* cinema. This bears consequences for the way filmmakers' work is defined. For humanitarian organizations such as the Ford Foundation's Just Film program, legibility also increases the impact of a story's message and becomes a distinguishing quality of leadership among filmmakers who are dedicated to social justice.

Because of the individual-driven refugee subjectivity that promises to guarantee the films' legibility, the art refugee documentary also provides humanitarian organizations with the tools they need for their own promotional agendas. In a one-day conference on "Refugee Voices in Film" at the Cannes Film Market's Doc Corner, sponsored by the UNHCR (United Nations High Commissioner for Refugees/UN Refugee Agency) and IEFTA (International Emerging Film Talents Association), UNHCR-Cairo representative Ragnhild Ek advocated for her organization's commitment to art cinema in the following terms.

> The real lives of refugees are by far more dramatic than anything a fictional film script can provide. So it does not come as a surprise that filmmakers all over the world are taking up the issue in documentaries and fictional films. UNHCR seeks the cooperation of the cinematic world. We intimately know the issues and have experience in communicating with individual refugees without doing harm. The filmmakers bring their stories to an influential audience. It is a perfect match. (Levine 2016)

Filmmakers' familiarity with dramatic structures is thus necessary to communicate refugees' hardships and hopes. While the conference introduced itself as an invitation to "witness the diverse use of film in addressing the most pertinent global humanitarian crisis of our time" (Doc Corner), the marketing of refugee films in effect contributes to the mobilization of compassion through the global circulation of images, which translates into donations for humanitarian organizations, especially in a space like Cannes' Film Market, whose very purpose is to stimulate investment. For an organization like the UNHCR, budgets can be counted in billions of dollars, the Middle East's being the second most funded refugee program in 2017 after Africa's and amounting to US$1,246,956,859, against the third largest program, Europe's, which stretches to around $760,000 (UNHCR, n.d.). The UNHCR's hunger for strong stories will therefore condition its systematic penetration of various cinema networks. Along with the non-credited short humanitarian film *Raghad's Dream*, the 2016 program included the aforementioned multi-award-winning *A Syrian Love Story*, and Zahra Mackaoui's *Hany's Story* (coproduced by the UNHCR, the BBC, and Channel 4), which documents the resettlement in Canada of a young blind Syrian artist after a long exile. Because the success story of Hany relies on his talent as a photographer and the eloquence with which he shares his suffering, the film hammers home the direct impact of telling stories.

In addition to encouraging new markets, the criterion of relevance, upheld by AFAC but articulated in distinct ways, for example by the UNHCR, also functions as a counterpoint to TV's alleged biased and normative treatment of current affairs. However, such a definition of creative documentaries still promotes an engagement with contemporary politics, thus following John Grierson's 1930s credo that documentary film is the "creative treatment of actuality." Here, the point of view of the refugee subject both proposes an intimate vision of an inherently political and situated experience, and potentially can become a vehicle for human rights advocacy for the universalist and unquestionable value of human life. The refugee experience allows for visual experiments and holds a strong potential for telling "good stories." It may thus function as a conduit for greater narratives of despair and hope in the face of a political crisis that are naturalized through the transfer of political responsibilities onto refugees (when talking about a "refugee crisis," for example).

In this multifaceted context, the creative aspect of documentary risks functioning as a measure for good politics, all the while constituting artistic institutions' proclaimed discursive political neutrality. AFAC's grantees are free to tackle any topic, "without any limit or red lines related to politics, religion, [or] sex" (Mismar 2017). However, AFAC's report on its AFAC Express program, which was tailored in 2011 to respond to the exceptional needs encountered by filmmakers willing to document and reflect upon the Arab uprisings, points to the challenges the program met at the moment of its implementation because it had no choice but to define how it would deal with politics. True to its promise of transparency, the report explicates the jury selection process and justifies its choice not to support films that would show "overzealous patriotism," because such projects would carry "an unoriginal and propagandistic quality with little analytical or creative depth." The report continues: "upholding openness and critical awareness in parallel with artistic creativity and authentic expression were important in the jury selection process" (AFAC 2012). Symptomatic of ongoing debates around film selection, the discursive displacement of good politics to good aesthetics, to what is "creative enough," both provides a strategy to privilege proclaimed progressive narratives in the region and contributes to establishing creative documentary's aesthetic relevance to international art cinema markets as an ethical and political compass.

Creative Subjects and Creative Workers: DIFF's Circumscription of Refugees

We turn now to the film markets where these works circulate in order to examine the part these contexts also play in initiating similar brands of refugee-centered creative documentary. Since 2007, exactly the same year as AFAC's birth, the Dubai International Film Festival has extended significant support, both professional and financial, to Arab documentary filmmaking. In this respect, it replicates, with a number of welcome alterations, the activities of its (mainly European) forebears, most particularly the IDFA Bertha Fund mentioned previously, the Hubert Bals Fund, which is run out of the International Film Festival Rotterdam, and the Berlin International Film Festival's World Cinema Fund. DIFF confers production and postproduction bursaries (via the Dubai Film Connection and Enjaaz), while also hosting the region's most attended opportunity for negotiating coproduction deals, the Dubai Film Market. A decade into these initiatives, over three hundred film projects, long and short, have benefited, with documentaries numbering a good fifty to date. DIFF was born into an era when the national (sometimes once nationalized) funding prospects of yesteryear had been decimated, where European support, at best, assimilates debilitating restraints on how Arabs are to present themselves for a foreign audience and, at worst, still harbors the embedded geopolitical hierarchies of their colonial heritage (France's discontinued Fonds Sud, now Aide aux cinémas du monde, for instance, has weathered this critique). Unsurprisingly, then, DIFF's regionally grounded opportunities appear to offer succor and an alternative.

With an approach akin to AFAC's professed criteria, Jane Williams, DIFF's first Industry Office Director, once declared of their selection process "there are no restrictions on subject matter" (Williams 2009). Yet a film festival, and one based in a very specific kind of city-state, is bound, consciously or not, to harvest documentaries of a particular persuasion. Firstly, as has been stated, festivals largely plow a certain kind of field, namely global art cinema. Then there are the local economic contexts to consider, digressing as they do from the aid prerogatives detailed above. DIFF runs through the Dubai Creative Clusters Authority, a grouping of economic free zones dedicated to ramping up the proportion of the Emirate's GDP deriving from the creative industries. As part of this mission, DIFF aims to place Dubai on the map, to route film production through a location that has never previously been considered a hive for (Arab) cinema, and to foster a space where expatriates of artistic persuasions can feel catered to by the city. The festival requires right of first refusal for the work it backs, thereby nourishing the quality of movies in its repertoire. And, as each of its winning films travels the world, the DIFF logo features in the opening idents, branding Dubai internationally. DIFF benefits from partnerships with already established sectors of its economy: transport (the Emirates airline) and tourism (the Madinat Jumeirah resort), both, like DIFF, government-owned concerns. All these structural characteristics have a bearing on the types of documentaries that emerge from the festival.

Because Dubai was a significant port for centuries, and is now a global shipping and logistics center with some of the world's most trafficked airports in terms of people and freight, the theme of border-crossing runs strong within DIFF, in terms of the support it offers, the topics it champions, and, as will become evident, in how it marshals an especially transnationalizing approach to cinematic production. We might start with some basics and practicalities. Dubai's sectorial strongholds allow flights and accommodation to figure easily as part of the packages winning film-makers receive. With an eye to the fact that the most crucial help that independent cinema requires is a leg-up in exhibition, rather than produc-tion, DIFF's branded Distribution Program secures screenings for a select repertoire of its funded movies around the region.

In terms of film content, however, if its European competitors had, for years, all but insisted on output that was, to quote the Hubert Bals Fund stipulations, "original, authentic and rooted in the culture of the applicant's country,"[2] DIFF's espousal of films that not only travel, but deal with mobility as a core concern, comes as a welcome relief. Certainly, DIFF embraces material dealing with steadfast heritage, such as *Nearby Sky* (*Sama' qaribah*, 2014) by Nujoom Alghanem, with its treatment of an Emirati woman's entry into the circuits of camel beauty pageants. Yet no longer is Arab documentary funding shackled to provisos that insist upon falsely static and state-based snapshots conceptualized for, one could argue, primarily Western delectation of a potentially exoticized locale. The authenticity of mass movement and migration also plays a role, and, moreover, comes as no surprise as a priority vision, in a country where an estimated 89 percent of the workforce are themselves non-nationals, DIFF personnel included. Thus, for example, *Gate # 5* (*al-Hawd al-khamis*, 2011) by Simon El Habre and *Guardians of Time Lost* (*'Araq*, 2013) by Diala Kachamr tackle displacement and internal migration in Lebanon, while the portmanteau structure of *Family Albums* (*Mawsim hasad*, 2012) by Nas-sim Amaouche, Sameh Zoabi, Mais Darwazah, and Erige Sehiri, via its fractured directorial stewardship, takes dispersal into the very heart of its exploration of four different sites within the region.

Amid all this motion, though, what of the refugee? While AFAC-spon-sored narratives negotiated from within the aid economy traverse this space, even supplement their startup budgets within it, DIFF's prevailing objectives digress appreciably from AFAC's. How might a refugee figure

in documentaries assisted by the government-supported festival of a country whose majority population are noncitizens, but which refuses to offer
itself up, in declared and outright humanitarian terms, as a haven for asylum seekers? A healthy fifteen or so DIFF documentaries treat the topic of
refugees—one of any number of possible themes filmmakers could have
pitched. The broad historical span of the refugee experience and its legacies
range across DIFF's output, from *23 Kilometers* (Noura Kevorkian, 2014)'s
foregrounding of an Armenian Lebanese protagonist to *Taste of Cement*
(*Ta'm al-asmant*, 2017) by Ziad Kalthoum, an examination of the contemporary conditions endured by Syrian construction workers displaced to
Beirut. Palestinians and their complex and persisting experience of exile
feature prominently in the corpus, including within *The Council* (*al-Majlis*,
2014) by Yahya Alabdallah, a portrait of life in a UNRWA school for Palestinian refugees in Jordan, and *Off Frame AKA Revolution Until Victory* (*Kharij
al-itar aw Thawra hatta al-nasr*, 2016) by Mohanad Yaqubi, which pains-
takingly compiles archive footage to reveal how Palestinian expulsion and
liberation has been narrativized for screen. This latter initiative was simultaneously supported by AFAC, pointing out the interweave between the
two institutions. Kamal Aljafari's *Port of Memory* (*Mina' al-dhakira*, 2009),
Searching for Saris (*Bahthan 'an Saris*, 2013) by Jinan Coulter, *Coffee for All
Nations* (*Qahwa li-kul al-umam*, 2014) by Wafa Jamil, and Salim Abu Jabal's
Roshmia (2014) all, in their various ways, detail the devastating impact of
Palestinian dispossession within the homeland itself, and with implications
for the broader diaspora. Given that, globally, internally displaced people
far outnumber refugees outside their country of origin, this contribution
to discourses on refugee life is of crucial importance for nuancing what we
have just highlighted as the mainstays of the aid-driven narrative. These
representations rise above what asylum scholar Aimé Claude Ndongozi
rebukes as the sensationalist stereotype of "hungry refugees wandering with
dying children along dusty paths in war-torn countries. . . . [Images that]
seek to shock rather than inform" (Ndongozi 2007, 269).

Yet, since migrants—but migrants who are treated exclusively as an
economic and labor force and not welcomed as outright asylum seekers—
are the principle demographic in the UAE, there is much to learn about
this context from probing how refugee narratives are handled aesthetically
and generically in DIFF's film portfolio. Central to DIFF's declared priorities for funding is, again, the "creative documentary," defined by them as
expressing "the personal vision of the maker . . . [highlighting] insights into
the world around us; but . . . also characterised primarily by artistic qualities: innovation, originality, professional skill, expressiveness and cultural/
historical value" (Dubai International Film Festival, n.d.). Jane Williams
elaborates DIFF's impetus to find

the more personal voice . . . to encourage filmmakers from the region to develop their work from being very issues-based and politics-based to stories that have emotional relationships in the foreground, rather than politics in the foreground. . . . the politics is of course an integral part of it, but the story that plays out in the foreground is much more to do with the characters than their beliefs or their politics. (Williams 2009)

Within Williams' own and DIFF's more official definitions, creativity absorbs a number of additional characteristics that bear implications for migrant interpellation.

Firstly, and once more: the personal. It cannot go unacknowledged that a large number of the documentaries that garner financial assistance from DIFF are small-scale stories dealing with a sole protagonist, from *The One-Man Village* (*Sam'an bi-l-day'a*, 2008) by Simon El Habre, *Red Blue Yellow* (*Ahmar azraq asfar*, 2013) by Nujoom Alghanem, and Noura Kevorkian's *23 Kilometers* (2015) to Aseel Mansour's *Uncle Nashaat* (*'Ammu Nash'at*, 2011), the already mentioned *Coffee for All Nations*, and *Those Who Remain* (*Mayyil ya ghzayyil*, 2016) by Eliane Raheb. There is certainly a dignity to the characters distinguished by these sorts of documentaries, but one that speaks to the liberal bourgeois values of individual rights and even, ultimately, individualism itself. We have noted how this emphasis attracts foreign audiences and, with it, donations to the aid economy. In Dubai, such principles also buttress the Emirate's concerted drive to enlarge its creative economy; the UAE needs to foster this kind of worker self-conception in order to compete successfully within this sector.

These are exactly the sorts of tenets upheld within a policy document pivotal to this economic expansion. The UAE's "National Innovation Strategy" lays out that

Innovation is defined as the aspiration of individuals, private institutions and governments to achieve development by generating creative ideas and introducing new products, services and operations that improve the overall quality of life. Innovation is key to promoting economic growth, increasing competitiveness and providing new job opportunities. (United Arab Emirates Ministry of Cabinet Affairs 2015)

"Innovation and professional skill," it should be remembered, figure in DIFF's official delineation of the "creative documentary." Within the broader context of the UAE's planned economy, initiatives such as DIFF clearly figure as cogs in the machinery of economic growth, powered by neoliberal principles such as competition and entrepreneurialism.

As noted earlier, the festival runs out of the Dubai Creative Cluster Authority, a grouping of economic free zones that comprises Media City, Studio City (which provides resources for film and broadcast production), and Internet City, to name a few. Each free zone is tailored to the particular needs of the sector in which it wishes to excel and often runs counter to the legislation governing the immediate outside world. Freedom of expression allowances, for instance, differentiate the free zones of the Creative Cluster Authority, prompting Williams' declaration that "there are no restrictions on subject matter" presiding over the festival's selection procedure. Be that as it may, the program or the funding roster has yet to witness a documentary investigation of the migrant workers who underpin the functioning of the free zones—or the UAE at large—namely, the close-to-indentured contract workers in sectors such as construction and domestic labor. These are the people who live nearest to the conditions we might associate with refugees, often within the cramped quarters of workers' camps. In fairness, it may well be that such topics are not even proposed to DIFF, an absence that speaks to a broader recognition of what is and is not condonable in such a context, instead regulated by cautious self-censorship or comfortable obliviousness.[3]

These Creative Cluster free zones also promise (as Dubai's free zones in general do) tax-exempt earnings and partial ownership to skilled foreign workers, as well as rapid work-permit arrangement (within a mere day) for anyone a company wishes to hire from outside.[4] Such provisions stand in stark opposition to the refugee experience, with its typical suspension of life in liminal zones like camps or migrant detention centers for any amount of time. Conversely, a precarious existence, albeit with diverging incomes, is common to all. Within the free zones and the festival's creative employee rosters, there work any number of migrants from countries that register a high refugee or stateless population—people from Syria, Iraq, and Palestine. It should be stressed, though, that such personnel are welcomed into the UAE purely on an individual and competitive basis by dint of their training and skills, not at all in response to recognition of unbearable conditions elsewhere.

Film Festival Markets and the Commodification of Refugees

This privileging of the entrepreneurial self is compounded further by the structures through which DIFF promotes a commodified film culture, most particularly via its Film Connection, which serves as an umbrella for its funding initiatives. While its Enjaaz scheme gives over money for production (now only for Gulf projects) and postproduction, support provided under the rubric of the Dubai Film Connection points recipients most adamantly toward networking and hustling within the international media marketplace. Here filmmakers are presented with a tailor-made program of meetings with industry professionals, including local and international buyers, best envisioned to realize their potential, either within the region or globally. They are also invited, as are other industry attendees, to the types of workshops familiar from AFAC's international festival activities. A level of professionalization that coalesces with the standards of the market is required by the application procedure, which demands a financial plan that foresees where funding can be secured (as for AFAC, it is not DIFF's job to provide the lion's share) and a signed-on producer who can adequately handle such investments.

DIFF's role here therefore becomes one of a *broker*, rather than a solid backer, an expertise long established in Dubai, courtesy of its status as an entrepôt port, a meeting point of commercial cultures for centuries, with cinema simply a newcomer recipient of this treatment. Within this matrix, film's significant monetary requirements are not actually delivered by the Emirate. Rather, DIFF logistically draws together within its borders the necessary international backers, thereby benefiting its flourishing transportation and tourism industries. Jane Williams pictures the festival as similar to a clearinghouse, a physical space where deals are negotiated without the host taking on an active role in the exchange of goods, services, or capital. She explains the comparison thus: "We go through over a hundred, 120, 150 projects and we select fifteen to twenty. We're like a clearing-house; we do a selection. And we have an international group of people who do that selection, who are operating in the international marketplace, so they have an idea of what to look for and what might find partners on the international market" (Williams 2009). What, then, are the leading priorities engendered by the brokerage occurring in this particular space and, in the end, what sorts of documentary projects rise to the top?

The terms of selection become decisive in this instance given that, as scholars of festivals have contended, these events increasingly assume curatorial duties that, at the same time, shape cinema's financing, their traction augmented if their "brand" comes to be associated with the quality of selection and end product.[5] How this understanding of "quality" plays out in terms of advantage and disadvantage for particular documentary endeavors places them within the tides of the international art film festival and sales circuit's prerogatives, which are governed by their own specific laws and power relations.

The international-film-festival-as-broker not only abides by the competitive ambits of the market, but also concomitantly prides itself on a rhetoric of "discovery" that arguably carries with it the taint of imperialism.

The festival might be likened here to an updated World's Fair, where the spoils of far-flung and mysterious nations are gathered in one space for the delectation of a curious and comfortable clientele. Wealth enshrines the status of arbiter, who is also framed as a benefactor; when the relationship becomes one of dependence, the financier's presumed elevation is also materialized and bolstered by the participation of a subordinated other. Within such a picture, Dubai's magnanimity reigns supreme. At the very least, a filmmaker will have to reach a deal at the DFC with its assembled financiers, most likely pandering to these coproducers' inclinations, tastes, and priorities. A project will not be green-lit if it cannot conform to any number of their stipulations, including, often most centrally, those in step with the aid paradigms outlined above. Film festival scholar Tamara Falicov itemizes often-told stories of this nature, all easily overheard from directors as they play the Dubai Film Market. In her experience, these encounters readily become

> one of neo-colonialism, and one of the filmmakers having the "burden of representation" to write storylines about marginalization for the benefit of wealthy viewers or what has been deemed "poverty porn (*pornomiseria*)." Others have catalogued instances where producers have been asked to make their films look more "authentic" (e.g., "more African") and examine a kind of "global art house aesthetic" that Global South filmmakers may conform to. (Falicov 2016, 218)

Such constrictions regularly recur when cinema is configured first and foremost as a commodity, and thus the obligation to unravel the geopolitical implications of the selection and funding processes endure. The makeup of the international presence at DIFF is illuminating. In the earlier years of its Film Market, Jane Williams observed that attendees came "particularly from Europe. That's still the biggest market and the potential for finding money from some of the schemes that run in Europe and also from some of the broadcasters etc." (Williams 2009). This much we garner from AFAC's international dealings, meaning both institutions have elected to get into bed with an art cinema that would see its core audiences, backers, and standard-setters based in that continent. It is telling that Dubai's hallmarking of its emerging creative industry aspires to these registers and accepts the ramifications for documentarians hoping to gain from such delimiting provisions.

Triggered by exactly these kinds of critiques, the DFC, like AFAC, has been motivated to appeal to more local revenue streams. As Williams continued,

If you spoke to most of the Arab filmmakers, they're desperate to raise money from this part of the world. Because as soon as they have a European partner on board, then the perspective of the film changes and then they have to say "in my country we do it like this." That's the kind of voice that goes on a lot of the time when they're developing their projects for an international audience. (Williams 2009)

Given the burgeoning media market of the MENA region, particularly across the wealthier Gulf states, avoiding backers who insist on so much cultural translation was easily within the realms of possibility.[6] In search of more Arabic-language content for their audiences, it has been the region's commercial broadcasters, networks often based in the Gulf, like ART and Rotana, who have invested most. These stations' own movement away from cultural and economic dependency upon Western production centers such as Hollywood pairs well with the policy aims fueling the acceleration of a creative economy in countries like the UAE. Although such networks' support can figure as pleasingly "local," more attuned to Arab values, it is still necessary to be cautious about the capitalist models all these institutions absorb, including, as stressed, their attendant marshaling of migrants, both on screen and off.

These new, largely Gulf-headquartered corporate arrivals on the media scene, moreover, proclaim significant disparity from historical precedent. In the period just after many Arab nations' postcolonial liberation, cinema had been nationalized to one degree or another. Such was the case, for example, in Syria, Egypt, and Algeria. Massive public divestment from this sector mutates the period in which DIFF and the Gulf broadcast networks ascend, their commercial priorities standing in stark contrast to the funding regimes of old, distinguished as they were by secure employment, not-for-profit agendas, and dedication to local concerns. International aid agencies have also filled the gap across a plethora of sectors, including basic provision of housing and food, as well as, as we have noted, national cultural production. Frequently based outside the creative team's country of origin, the brokers and traders of the international festival circuits conversely maneuver national designation first and foremost as marketplace differentiation and advertising ("a new discovery from Syria," or the like). The inclination to screen a funded documentary where it might have started its life becomes minimal.

Given the impossibility of even entering a country like Dubai except as a worker, or of accessing somewhere as glitzy as Cannes, where AFAC has made a home for itself, a refugee cinema easily becomes a genre that is *about*, but not necessarily *for*, its subjects. A careful dissection of how aid, creativity, and "the refugee" are geopolitically circumscribed both inside and outside film culture exposes the motivations for this exclusive and excluding state of affairs.[7]*

---

* Since writing this chapter, DIFF has ceased to exist. The last edition was in 2017.

References

AFAC. n.d. "AFAC's Documentary Program."arabculturefund.org.

AFAC. n.d. "6 Years of Strategic Philanthropy for Arts and Culture in the Arab Region." arabculturefund.org.

———. 2011. "The First Four Years." March. arabculturefund.org.

———. 2012. "AFAC Express, Program Brief." September. arabculture-fund.org.

———. 2013. "AFAC Grantee Survey." arabculturefund.org.

Ajroudi, Asma, and Zena al-Tahhan. 2014. "'Our Festival Is Our Window onto Others': An Interview with Abbas Arnaout, Director of the Al Jazeera International Documentary Festival." In *Film Festivals and the Middle East*, edited by Dina Iordanova and Stefanie Van de Peer, 285–98. St Andrews: St Andrews Film Studies.

Bady, Aaron. 2012. "Spectators to Revolution: Western Audiences and the Arab Spring's Rhetorical Consistency." *Cinema Journal* 52, no. 1 (Fall): 137–42.

de Jong, Wilma, Erick Knudsen, and Jerry Rothwell. 2012. *Creative Documentary: Theory and Practice*. London and New York: Routledge.

Dickinson, Kay. 2016. *Arab Cinema Travels: Transnational Syria, Palestine, Dubai, and Beyond*. London: BFI Palgrave.

Doc Corner, Marché du Film. n.d. "Schedule." marchedufilm.com.

Dubai International Film Festival. n.d. "FAQs." https://dubaifilmfest.com/en/page/214/faqs.html.

Falicov, Tamara L. 2010. "Migrating from South to North: The Role of Film Festivals in Funding and Shaping Global South Film and Video." In *Locating Migrating Media*, edited by Greg Elmer et al., 3–22. Lanham, MD: Lexington Books.

———. 2016. "The 'Festival Film': Film Festival Funds as Cultural Intermediaries." In *Film Festivals: History, Theory, Method, Practice*, edited by Marijke de Valck et al., 209–29. London: Routledge.

Farouky, Naila. 2015. "Trends in Philanthropy in the Arab Region: Beyond a Charity-Based Model." *State of Civil Society Report*. civicus.org.

Ford Foundation. n.d. "All Grants since 2006." https://www.fordfoundation.org/work/our-grants/.

Hamilton, Peter. 2014. "Al Jazeera Documentary Arabic: What's the Strategy? And the Deal?" January 20. documentarytelevision.com.

Hjort, Mette. 2013. "Art and Networks: The National Film School of Denmark's 'Middle East Project.'" In *The Education of the Filmmaker in Africa, the Middle East, and the Americas*, edited by Mette Hjort, 125–50. New York: Palgrave McMillan.

Hubert Bals Fund. n.d. "Selection Criteria." http://archive.dokweb.net/en/documentary-network/producers-calendar/hubert-bals-fund-3785/

IDFA. n.d. "About the IDFA Bertha Fund." www.idfa.nl.

Jacir, Annemarie. 2013. "Why I Make Films." AFAC. November 27. arab-culturefund.org.

Levine, Sydney. 2016. "Refugee Voices in Film: An All Day Event at 2016 Cannes Film Festival." *IndieWire*, May 5. indiewire.com.

Lynch, Marc. 2006. *Voices of the New Arab Public: Iraq, Al Jazeera, and Middle East Politics Today*. New York: Columbia University Press.

McCarty, Kathleen. 1987. "From Cold War to Cultural Development: The International Cultural Activities of the Ford Foundation, 1950–1980." *Daedalus* 116, no. 1, "Philanthropy, Patronage, Politics" (Winter): 93–117.

Mingant, Nolwenn. 2015. "A Peripheral Market?: Hollywood Majors and the Middle East/North Africa Market." *Velvet Light Trap* 75 (Spring): 73–87.

Mismar, Rima. 2017. Interview by Viviane Saglier. February 8.

Ndongozi, Aimé Claude. 2007. "Ambiguous Voices: Western Media and Refugees." In *Transnational Lives and the Media: Re-imagining Diaspora*, edited by Olga G. Bailey et al., 268–73. Basingstoke: Palgrave Macmillan.

Open Society Foundations. n.d. "About Us, Mission Values." opensociety-foundations.org.

Ross, Miriam. 2011. "The Film Festival as Producer: Latin American Films and Rotterdam's Hubert Bals Fund." *Screen* 52, no. 2: 261–67.

Takieddine, Zena. 2012. "Challenging Patriarchy." July 20. arabculture-fund.org.

UNHCR, The U.N. Refugee Agency. n.d. "Financials." reporting.unhcr.org.

United Arab Emirates Ministry of Cabinet Affairs, Prime Minister's Office. 2015. *UAE National Innovation Strategy*. Dubai: Ministry of Cabinet Affairs.

Williams, Jane. 2009. Interview by Kay Dickinson. December 9.

9

ARAB DOCUMENTARY LANDSCAPES: TRANSNATIONAL FLOW OF SOLIDARITY AT FESTIVALS

Stefanie Van de Peer

In response to the global commodification of culture and neoliberal, capitalist tendencies, political filmmaking and specifically documentary have taken on an increasing urgency, with creative as well as political ideas and idealism central to the form. Documentary and political cinema is also increasingly present in the world on television, cinema, and smaller screens. In the Arab world, audiences' growing attachment to the nonfiction form is reflected in the establishment of new documentary TV channels, the introduction of extra documentary slots on existing channels, and the increasing number of specialized documentary film festivals.

Likewise, in the past, festivals often did not accept documentaries on their programs, or if they did, these films were part of a sidebar: cheaper to program due to lower screening fees, screened in smaller or off-site venues, not accompanied by director or producer but by local activists or specialists in a topic, screened to smaller audiences, and awarded fewer and less valuable prizes. This has changed dramatically in the last decade, as even the biggest festivals in the world generally,[1] and in the Arab world specifically, are increasingly awarding top prizes to creative documentaries.[2]

For a long time documentary was the overlooked relative of fiction film, and often seen as a training ground for the "real" work in fiction feature filmmaking. But documentary's long dip in popularity was remedied with the digital revolution and its increased democratization of the medium of film, and now, in the age of fake news and reporters under pressure (physically and morally), creative documentaries are gaining traction. Likewise, the Arab revolutions have seen a rapid change in attitudes toward Arab documentary both in and beyond the Arab world. This urgency and change are reflected in film festivals' programs and their missions. Festivals are first and foremost celebrations of an art, but documentary festivals dedicate themselves entirely to a specific form, as an act of resistance to the underrepresentation of the form, often with ideals serving as inspirations for a gender, generation, or ethnic group.

In this global growth of documentary appreciation and the urgency with which the form is increasingly regarded, this chapter will bring together some of the rare scholarship on Arab documentary and festivals and on the increasing ability of a global audience to see and listen to politically relevant documentaries from the Arab world, and draw an overview of documentary festivals located throughout the MENA. In this chapter I address questions such as: How and when were documentary festivals established in the MENA region and what has their development been? If historically documentaries may have been more keenly suppressed or censored, which are the institutions and individuals dedicated to screening documentaries at festivals now? How do Arab documentaries feature on the global festival network? Has the changing global flow of culture had an influence on the increasing production of documentary?

Looking at and comparing six festivals in the MENA dedicated entirely or mainly to the documentary form, this chapter reveals a lively network that runs counter to the glamour of the Arab world's most established international film festivals. International festivals such as those in Marrakech, Carthage, Cairo, Doha, and Dubai are perhaps more widely known for their star-studded atmosphere and the big-budget markets, red carpets, and production networking events, but the documentary festivals in the region, like DoxBox from Damascus (Syria), Doc à Tunis (Tunisia), Fidadoc in Agadir (Morocco), DocuDays in Beirut (Lebanon), Ismailia Documentary Festival (Egypt), and the Al Jazeera International Documentary Festival in Doha (Qatar), show how a strongly congenial and collaborative nature can stand up against these larger festivals that are gobbling up budgets and markets. Fostering transnational coproductions, collaboration, and solidarity movements in film, networked (as opposed to networ*ing*) events shape documentary communities that are concrete, creative, and often nomadic hubs on the global festival network.

Film festivals and film festival studies have long outgrown their European cradle and are now a global phenomenon. Some of the largest and most respected film festivals are no longer located in the so-called West but in previously marginalized places such as Eastern Europe (Karlovy Vary), East Asia (Busan), Africa (FESPACO), and the Arab world (Carthage and Cairo). Similarly, the significance of the international festival network as an outlet for Arab documentary and independent cinema is growing exponentially, as some of the largest documentary festivals in the world, like IDFA (International Documentary Festival Amsterdam) in the Netherlands, CPH:DOC (The Copenhagen Documentary Festival) in Denmark, and Sheffield Doc/Fest in the United Kingdom, are embracing more and more Arab films for their expanding audiences. The study of festivals must be central to understanding the sociocultural dynamics of global cinema and international cultural exchanges at large, especially in a study of Arab documentary. No longer a marginal region or a marginal film form, Arab documentary needs to be inscribed in its region and history, at festivals that are sustained moments where time and space are condensed and intensified and where audiences expand.

Documentary Film Festival Studies: Scoping a Field

In their pioneering work on film festivals, Marijke De Valck and Dina Iordanova both theorize the global network of film festivals, and festivals' roles as alternative distribution channels for cinema. They propose that festivals act as "special" occasions or nodes on the transnational network in which films circulate. Anderson's understanding of "imagined communities" is central to Iordanova's ideas. While I am not, as Iordanova is, looking at migrant communities, or, as De Valck is, discussing globally central red carpet events, I do regard the documentary festival as a strong and increasingly confident transnational moment dedicated to a specific audience in and of itself. Indeed, in my view, through the convergence of documentary and its audience, a documentary festival creates a momentary unity among a diverse audience that comes together in the spirit of a shared experience, a moment of solidarity in the cinema, where time and space on the screen construct that shared experience. In an explosively globalizing world, especially when we speak of media like cinema, perhaps a more useful term than "imagined community" is "imagined world," as Appadurai theorizes it through various "landscapes" (Appadurai 1990, 295–310). In particular, the ideoscape and the mediascape are relevant here, as a film festival is a space where diverse individualities from a myriad of landscapes converge in the spirit of solidarity with a form of filmmaking (in the case of documentary festivals), and with the attitude of shared experiences that such a space provides.

Indeed, Appadurai's extension of Anderson's imagined community into an overlap of imagined worlds might be more useful in looking at festivals as moments of networks of kinship, of friendship, of work and leisure. Festivals as part of the global cultural economy flow are "mediascapes": metaphors by which people live, that subvert center–periphery models and instead blur the lines between nations and cultures. They bring together the "multiple worlds, which are constituted by the historically situated imaginations of persons and groups spread around the globe" (Appadurai 1990, 297). Likewise, documentary is not a genre, but a form of filmmaking and as such does not carry strong implications of state or nationhood. Rather, it is a transnational (aspirational) form of filmmaking that encourages cross-border and supra-national thinking and also creates a more obvious opportunity for solidarity, for seeing and hearing beyond the border, and for transnational understandings of humanity. This idealistic element crosses boundaries and creates imagined worlds at festivals, between the international audiences, in ideoscapes rather than an ethnoscape. As people come together and cross boundaries in communicative mediums like cinema, hearing and seeing one another become increasingly central to the globalization of culture (Appadurai 1990, 300). In my approach to documentary festivals, this idea of achieving an approximation through an art form that enables a more democratic "hearing" and "seeing" is central to the conceptualization of a networked, collaborative platform for solidarity. Documentary festivals offer a sense of place through communication, media, and shared responsibilities.

As stated, festivals act as celebrations of films or a theme, as alternative networks for distribution, and as showcases for ideas and ideals, for or in the service of an audience and a group of practitioners and professionals who are part of a shared experience. Audiences and programmers involved with the festival are invited to experience themselves, by an "undisguised act of imagination, as an extension of a community . . . to which they, by virtue of their very attendance at the festival, now relate through a mental image of affinity and through the act of their very real togetherness" (Iordanova 2010, 13). My interpretation of this imagined world shaped through documentary flows is perhaps more specific: I want to show that it is not only the screening but also the making of documentaries that conjures up a specific atmosphere, a particular abstract experience that is enacted within an imagined world of festivals. Any film festival provides a suitable context for causes that thrive on solidarity and togetherness. A documentary festival does this even more, as it brings together diverse audiences to experience an imagined togetherness, in the spirit of acceptance of a reality on screen that seeks empowerment, and to benefit from exchanging images, narratives, and especially ideologies.

Events that focus on documentaries, and where documentary makers, documentary subjects, professionals, and docuphiles gather, create a very specific idea of imagined togetherness, a mix of people and topics that are interested in the same ideals and ideas: the shaping of a platform for "real" voices—usually people who are perhaps more concerned with the reality of the sociopolitical world than with red-carpet events and star-studded shows, in films that pose moral dilemmas and ethical questions that consider the "real" world and a lived experience. In the live space of the festival, organizers and audiences form an identity that comes alive in the act of watching a film and imagining fellow human beings becoming part of one's own lived experience. Thus, the festival's setup extends an invitation to engage in what is essentially a political act of imagined belonging, with the films' subjects and with fellow audience members: a shared experience that considers a lived experience, and where those who share it can progress to a newly lived experience. Perhaps then we can consider that the "imagined" turns into a "real" documentary world at documentary festivals.

Marking documentary festivals as networked events, and as platforms for workshops, meetings, and opportunities, is both an inherently ethical part of the festivals' missions and visions, and also crucially relevant for the business structure of the festival. Likewise, the business proposition is directly linked to the creation of an ephemeral "imagined world" or a fluid mediascape that becomes the fan base niche for transnational film distribution of special-interest material (Fischer 2013). This concrete togetherness is also always already related to funding streams: often, documentary festivals are funded or sponsored with official and/or grassroots money, and ultimately do serve specific business purposes if they wish to become sustainable. A festival is a part of the film business and industry, and is run by managers, CEOs, producers: people who need to manage large sums of money in order to keep the festival going. However much the artistic directors aim to visualize their ideals and their aspirational approach to film, ultimately a festival cannot run without a financial structure.

If documentary is often associated with ideals and activism, so are social and digital media, in particular since 2011, the year of revolutions in Tunisia, Egypt, and across the MENA region. As I have argued elsewhere (Van de Peer 2012, 297–317), the interest since 2011 in the Middle East carried the potential to open up opportunities for Arab voices to be heard elsewhere, and documentary emerged as a tool to confront the media over their limitations and prejudices. Documentary festivals around the world have taken the images that emerged from the revolutions (both the digital one and the sociopolitical ones) seriously and present them as alternatives to mass media images. Documentary from the Arab world has become producer and product of these progressive social movements, and has paved a way for itself within worldwide documentary and other film festivals. Likewise, within the Arab world, documentary festivals have gained confidence and increasing relevance, as I will show.

Documentary and digital and social media thrive on one another: more and more of the content on social media consists of nonfiction or documentary content, as documentary makers increasingly use social media platforms to spread their subjects. The global trend of an increasing interest in "causes," and the trendiness of activism online, have, next to the increased global awareness of larger groups of people, also given shape to online shared experiences. This awareness of preaching to the converted has led to some critical studies of commodified activism, or "slacktivism."

The commodification of culture and the increasing immateriality of the body are by-products of the exponential rise of social and digital media. As Klausen argues, organizations "strategically use the visually mediated body as an effective tool on social media to both commodify the imaginary and create 'spreadability' as well as to channel followers' engagement" (Klausen 2017, 372–84). Likewise, a festival of documentary film interested in the ethics of filmmaking and the engagement of audiences uses the form as a commodity in order to create a tool that inspires. The contemporary commodification of culture and of activism have been shown to be a struggle over representation (Markus 1996, 10): image is everything, and part of a very strong and increasingly "imagined" *and* "real" identity.

Thus it is useful, if not always practicable, to distinguish between festivals that enjoy the endorsement of official policy and those organized by (grassroots) activists committed to specific causes. The divide between "official" and "activist" agendas links to different funding streams and sponsorship arrangements where public and private interests intersect or diverge. But these streams often overlap and certainly influence each other, as they commodify one another. Commitment and commodification increasingly become partners in the furthering of social and cultural engagement and sustainable projections, in particular with documentary festivals (or all festivals that focus on non-mainstream forms of filmmaking for that matter, such as short film festivals, animation festivals, themed film festivals). Each festival devoted to the particular form of documentary encapsulates its vision through various event details, either through their film programmers, the festival's title, or their mission statement. Often devoted, as we shall see, to solidarity and engagement through documentary, festivals explicitly phrase an agenda of ideals in their ambitions and initiatives, where they almost without exception mention concepts like solidarity, collaboration, meeting place, and networked events—in other words, in the space where the documentary "landscape" brings people together. It is in the ideals behind documentary festivals, conceptualized by their directors or programmers, that personal political stances and priorities shape the festival and the audiences' expectations and contributions.

This chapter looks at film festivals that specialize in documentary and that over the last two decades have come to represent an important regional (and international) cinematic phenomenon. I will show how newer Arab documentary film festivals, as well as those that have been established for a while, are growing in size and ambition in parallel with the world opening up toward individual voices, subjective points of view, and increasingly shared (social media) stances toward politics. Social media and mobile technology have undoubtedly contributed to the opening up of the Middle East and its documentaries to the rest of the world, but also to itself, through fluid landscapes of film and documentary. The question remains, of course, whether documentaries and festivals can actually change sensibilities, and how sustainable these political and financial ambitions are. Some of the festivals under discussion are more successful than others at mediating between the local and the global and in negotiating national and transnational interests. And that is often also where the nexus of their success is located. Ultimately I hope to show that the congenial atmosphere or the aim to share and open up subjective voices to the collective ear is a particular strength of documentary festivals in the Arab world, and that here we have platforms for change, for ideology, for solidarity rather than for stars, glamour, and the myth of the individual.

Arab Documentary Festivals
DoxBox, Damascus, Syria

One of the most activism-focused and aspirational documentary organizations from the Arab world is DoxBox, established in Syria in 2008 as an annual documentary film festival organized by two Syrian filmmakers, Diana El Jeiroudi and Orwa Nyrabia from the production company Proaction Film (which, since 2018, has been artistic director of one of the biggest documentary festivals in the world, IDFA in the Netherlands). It was a nonprofit, free-admission event that aimed to spread awareness and increase interest in documentaries, a form of filmmaking that had been practiced by few but very important and widely respected documentary makers like Omar Amiralay, who had been and continues to be highly appreciated outside of Syria. With its free admission for local audiences and an audience award, it was the first festival in Syria to highlight audience participation.

2012 marked the first anniversary of the uprising in Syria, and would have seen the fifth year of the DoxBox festival. All over the Arab world, filmmakers have documented their uprisings and are paying for it with their freedom and lives. So in 2012 the DoxBox organizers decided to make a statement against the Bashar al-Assad regime by not holding the festival in Syria; instead, they planned a DoxBox Global Day to be held in twelve countries, from Sudan to the United Kingdom to Kosovo, as a gesture of continued support for these filmmakers amid fears that media interest in the conflict was waning. In 2012 and 2013, DoxBox Global Day for Syria was the festival's international showcase of Syrian documentary films, organized in solidarity with the festival at venues around the world. In 2014, the festival transitioned into the DoxBox Association, a nonprofit association registered in Berlin, aiming to support and train documentary filmmakers from the Arab world.

In another oppressive context (China), Tit Leung points out that, for documentary and political films, regional cultural and political conditions can mean "run-ins with authorities" and having one's festival "shut down" in one place, only to be "regrouped and quietly moved to an unobtrusive location" elsewhere (Leung 2012). Nornes describes this resilience as independent documentary filmmakers playing a "cat-and-mouse game with the government" (Nornes 2011, 105). This is exactly what happened with DoxBox: the festival could not take place in 2012 due to the Syrian government's disregard for human rights, which ran counter to the festival's ideals. Instead, these shared ideals—along with urgent Syrian films—found another, global audience. As such, the festival's ideals have become even more central to the association's core values that have become increasingly important in documentary making worldwide.

Before this, Syrian cinema had been known for its "refined and sophisticated system of metaphors and symbols" (Halassa 2012), as Charlotte Banks explains, and described as a culture of paradoxes (Salti 2006, 30). The revolution and then war in Syria became a manifestation of the government's failed suppression of a popular will for change, expressed more and more urgently in a changed visual language, as observed in documentaries by older as well as younger generations, like Amiralay's own work but also in work by people he had trained or collaborated with, such as Reem 'Ali and Hala al-Abdallah. Banks describes this as a "freer language," where artists first became activists and then evolved into different kinds of artists with a new identity.

Both as a festival and as an association, DoxBox aims to nurture a community, or a landscape of filmmakers that make impactful films. It now wants to

> re-build an active and independent community of filmmakers from the Arab World based on mutual solidarity and trust; to empower this community through various avenues of networking and support, including completion and promotion of films; to celebrate and acknowledge the achievements of community members at both regional and international levels. (DoxBox, n.d.)

The Association supports documentary filmmakers in and from the Arab world, promoting the values and principles of justice, dignity, and human rights. It does this through seven avenues: education (the academy); resources (a library); publications (a catalog); a residency; funding; by influencing policy; and through an award called The Amiralay. It is evident that the ideals and structure of the association are positioned around ideals like solidarity, support, sustainable networks, and development or education. This spirit is inspired not only by the production company that originally set up the festival, but also by Omar Amiralay. His personal, subjective, almost testimonial documentary films laid the groundwork for what Syrian documentary has become since 2011–12: a collaborative, aspirational, and transnational example of documentary solidarity. Civil society was central to Amiralay's understanding of the future of Syria and the road toward a democratization of the country and its arts, reflected in the prize awarded by DoxBox in his name, presented to those making documentaries that illustrate direct, active, and lasting impacts on, and for, their societies.

As is the case with other documentary film festivals and organizations, DoxBox works in close collaboration with other festivals: for example, the director of FIDADOC in Agadir in Morocco sits on the board for DoxBox. DoxBox also works closely with IDFA and CPH:DOC and the European Documentary Network. Support and grants for DoxBox come from The Netherlands' Prince Claus Fund, Denmark's KVINFO, Germany's Goethe Institute and Heinrich Böll Foundation, and the Arab Fund for Art and Culture (AFAC), among others. Significantly, DoxBox runs a fund for documentary production, specifically for those documentary makers working in dangerous conditions. Like some of the more established international film festivals, such as IDFA, DoxBox is developing its ability to support more documentary production.

Doc à Tunis, Tunis, Tunisia
Revolution has had an enormous impact on the cultural flow in Tunisia. But documentary has not been very popular in the past in the country. Tunisian film history emphasizes its Golden Age of filmmaking in the late 1980s and 1990s, with filmmakers like Nouri Bouzid, Férid Boughedir, and Moufida Tlatli. Hédi Khélil notes that because documentary making has political implications and consists of unavoidable subject choices, its long absence in Tunisia is due to the fact that no individuals have dedicated themselves completely to documentaries (Khélil 2007, 80). Documentary filmmaking, if it exists, is mainly seen as a prelude to a more sustainable and profitable career in fiction. Tunisia, he claims, as a land of fictions and myths, has not been comfortable with documentary presentation. Hillauer agrees that documentaries have had a bad reputation, as Tunisians are not accustomed to discussing their problems in public (Hillauer 2005, 363). Boughédir adds to this that in Tunisia there is a ruling "tendency to synthesize influences, . . . transforming them in a nice, happy, moderated way. It's a culture that smoothes off the sharp edges" (Barlet 1998). But Tahar Chikhaoui notes the growing importance of documentary.

> Partly as a result of their freedom from many of the social and political concerns which were so vital to their elders, the newcomers have

shown more confidence in the camera and in reality, from which stems the place accorded to the suggestive force of the image, liberated from the process of narration, and the growing interest in the documentary. (Armes 2006, 156)

Nowadays the country is one of the most prolific documentary producers in the region, with production houses like Nomadis really engaging with the pre- as well as the post-revolution realities. These filmmakers, their films, but also their ideals—which had to be hidden or censored until recently—grew out of the collaborative spirit of the cine clubs.

While in most Tunisian films there was a tendency to move away from social realism into pure fiction and magic, the amateur movement moved in the opposite direction in the late 1960s. Amateur cinema contributed to the development of documentary in Tunisian film culture. The FTCA (Fédération Tunisienne des Cinéastes Amateurs) was set up in 1962. There was no greater plan for the federation than to bring together amateurs in order to enable them to make films. The amateurs reacted against the system, fashioning militant films and mobilizing a cultural and intellectual environment or "landscape" for artists (Khélil 2007, 26). The result was a body of films that engaged with the reality of the present and opposed it to the hagiography of the past. It is, then, with the continued efforts of particular individuals and amateur organizations dedicated to the documentary that the form has steadily become a more appreciated and respected art.

Doc à Tunis was established in 2006 by the cultural organization Nas al-Fann ("People of the Arts"), and the first festival director was François Niney, a French philosopher and a writer for *Cahiers du cinéma*, specializing in documentaries. The main vision of the founding organizers was to develop the dialogue between cultures and peoples; to link artistic and pedagogical dimensions by highlighting the present and future of encounter and exchange in their program education, creation, and dissemination through workshops and specialized training; and to become part of a global conversation on the world and its realities. Indeed, the mission statement of the organization emphasizes that the festival's goal is to form a view of the world through inclusion and exchange: "We cannot develop a relevant point of view on the world on our own; it is shaped by putting it to the test with other points of view, by encounter and exchange" (Nas al-Fann 2006). Likewise, Niney has said about documentaries that they "show the real from a point of view born not of submission but of analysis and change, initiation, encounter and reflection" (Na al-Fann 2006). Documentary, for him, opens up the dimension, artistic as well as political, of our freedom. In this way, he meant to create an awareness of the heritage of a documentary tradition from Africa and Europe at the first edition of the festival: he did not focus only on the newest releases in 2006, but programmed a panorama of documentaries through an international selection, as well as a retrospective of Tunisian documentaries.

From 2007 until 2017 Hichem Ben Ammar was the festival's artistic director. He is a teacher of cinema and audiovisual culture, a cine-club organizer, a film critic, and a festival organizer. As a critic, in his filmmaking, and also in his programming, he is interested in promoting creative documentaries that are relevant to the present moment in the particular contexts of the southern Mediterranean countries, and that are, as he said, handicapped by the absence of a production and dissemination framework. He also states there is a real urgency to preserve a northern African/southern Mediterranean identity, to focus on local and independent filmmaking. Ben Ammar is interested in the ethics of the documentary, and sees Doc à Tunis playing a central role. With the festival he wishes to remind the audience, filmmakers, and politicians that the documentary is "dissident, dissonant and discordant" (Ben Ammar 2007) and that the documentary unveils, denounces, and distills ideas, defends diversity, demolishes dogmas. As such, Doc à Tunis—located at the heart of the Mediterranean—is to be the link of solidarity and dialogue between East and West. Once again, this reminds us of the idea of bringing together, for a brief and specific moment in time, a space for artists and admirers of documentary, in a landscape of likeminded, open, and fluidly linked metaphorical networks.

With Ben Ammar, Doc à Tunis became a non-competitive festival that focuses on young people and students. It is thus not only a dissident but also a very inclusive festival, where the development of the form and its growing confidence take center stage. Throughout the years, Ben Ammar's director statements, with which he opens the festival annually, emphasize ideals such as justice and democracy, and a fervent belief in young people. In 2009, the festival included, for example, a workshop that introduced children aged ten to fifteen to shooting techniques. In 2010, Ben Ammar stressed the importance of locating Tunisia and its documentary making within the Arab world, by reflecting on its membership in the Mediterranean. From this flowed an interest in the idea of a Documentary Caravan, which saw the light of day in 2011, with the aim of disseminating the values of citizenship through documentaries in Tunisia's rural cinema regions.[3] Ben Ammar recognized how "the real" was becoming increasingly important in 2011 with the statement that "the urgency is tangible," as it is, according to him, "through art that we collectively learn how to build an identity." This became even more the case in 2012, and at this edition of Doc à Tunis, he noted:

Documentary cinema will never have had the importance it has had this past year. With the historical upheavals that the world has witnessed, a new dimension of the documentary is outlined. The documentary is the art of making visible the complexities of the human, to discover its hidden facets at the bend of a glance stolen by the camera lens. A new breath is given to the documentary which not only captures the real and transmits the truth but also acts on it. (Ben Ammar 2012)

As a result of the changes brought about by the Tunisian revolution in 2011 and 2012, the 2013 edition of the festival downsized, as it wanted to break with the profusion of screens and titles of previous years in order to concentrate on what it considered essential: decoding reality and developing debates with filmmakers, interest in students, and sessions with professors from FEMIS at l'Ecole des Arts et du Cinéma (EDAC). The program thus revealed a focus on documentaries from and about countries like Syria and Algeria, and with an interest in the consequences of terrorism globally, but most specifically and urgently in the Arab region.

In June 2017, the Tunisian Ministry of Cultural Affairs announced that Hichem Ben Ammar had been named the director of the new Tunisian Cinémathèque (Mahdaoui 2017). Ben Ammar has thus expanded his interest in documentary, having developed the art form into a respected and valued way of filmmaking, and guiding the festival successfully through the Jasmine Revolution. With documentary festivals, young people are given the opportunity to finally express themselves on political issues and to criticize previous generations for not doing so. Documentary cinema in Tunisia allows young filmmakers to give their views on their environment and to question the historical period with their own vision.

Fidadoc, Agadir, Morocco

Like Tunisia, historically Morocco has produced comparatively few documentaries, as financial, political, and social limitations, as well as a lack of producers interested in the form, have hampered the development of a viable documentary culture. The CCM's influence on cinema in the country has resulted in a very lively filmmaking scene, to the detriment of documentaries. But this is rapidly changing. Documentary makers like Leila Kilani,[4] Dalila Ennadre, and Jawad Rhalib are making their mark on the global documentary scene. Farida Benlyazid, one of Morocco's most important female filmmakers, also increasingly focuses on documentary films. Simultaneously, a new generation of young documentary makers with strong activist tendencies is also finding its feet with anti-establishment and independent films and practices; see, for example, the work of Nadir Bouhmouch, Saïda Janjague, and Mahassine Massi.

Since 2008, Fidadoc, a film festival in Agadir that is entirely dedicated to documentary, has also played a significant role in the popularization and appreciation of the form. In collaboration with TV channel 2M and several regional and international partners, this festival is putting all its efforts into stimulating new national production. Due to a lack of experienced producers in the country in general, documentary production is very often a matter of coproductions with European producers, and in order to remedy this situation, Fidadoc develops and encourages local and regional work, focusing on a pan-Arab and pan-African inspired approach. As such, their programming and events envisage the development of a real documentary industry in Morocco, positioning themselves at the helm of South–South collaboration.

Fidadoc was founded by producer Nouzha Drissi, who specialized in documentaries. With Drissi's vision, Fidadoc's vocation has always been fundamentally plural: educational, developmental, cultural, and professional. She wanted to develop a culture in Morocco that was more open to documentary (Van de Peer 2017, 168–93), to introduce to a wider audience a cinematographic form of writing rooted in reality. The festival still emphasizes her words:

> We believe there is no economic development without a social and cultural one. An ideal channel to raise awareness among the citizens about humanist values, documentary filmmaking meets this need to build and assert an identity. (Nouzha Drissi)

The general manager of the festival is Hicham Falah, who is also artistic director of the international Women's Film Festival in Salé and sits on the general assembly of DoxBox. Fallah has held on to Drissi's ideals for the festival. Since Drissi passed away in 2011, the festival is run by ACEA (Association de Culture et d'Éducation par l'Audiovisuel), and, like Drissi, ACEA runs on the idea that documentary cinema constitutes an ideal means for education and development.

The educational focus is not only on young people and children watching educational films, but also on developing new talent in documentary filmmaking. Since 2012, the festival boasts the Documentary Hive, a series of workshops that help develop young people's capacities and projects. The Hive invites fifty young documentary makers from the many film schools around Morocco, thus contributing to a "landscape" of Moroccan documentary professionals. During the festival they attend workshops and film screenings, and present their work to professionals who critique their projects. Fifteen of these young people are then selected for more intensive, thirty-minute, one-on-one meetings with professionals. At the end of the festival, a few of them are invited to a Writing Workshop in Safi. ACEA is also associated with the Rencontres Tënk de coproduction de Saint-Louis (Senegal), organized in the context of the AFRICADOC network. The best young filmmakers from the Hive get to attend "Tënk" ("pitch" in Wolof) in Senegal, with aspiring sub-Saharan documentary filmmakers. However, while these intentions are certainly admirable, a young filmmaker told me anonymously that its usefulness is limited, and that the vision and discourse sound better than the practice: Moroccan mentors are not as interested in the new talent as they could be.

In line with its founder's ideals, next to education, the festival is also interested in humanistic values such as mutual respect and tolerance. As part of a much larger effort to revitalize film production and reception in Morocco, Fidadoc deploys digital cine-mobile units to local communities. The festival's mission is to "remain faithful to the spirit of sharing and openness that characterizes its focus and identity, and to continue to create a congenial atmosphere" (Fidadoc 2014), something we see returning in the missions and visions of most of the documentary festivals under discussion here.

While the educational developments focus on young Moroccan filmmakers and the cine-mobile units emphasize the national distribution of film, the festival also has an interest in wider pan-Arab and pan-African collaborations and outreach projects. MenaDoc is a program of film screenings that focuses on creating a network for Maghreb producers. Ideally located at the crossroads of Africa, the Arab world, and the Euro-Mediterranean area, the Fidadoc platform of exchanges aims to become the central rendezvous for creative documentary makers in the region. The festival's wider interest lies in its pan-African associations with sub-Saharan countries like Senegal, Mali, and Niger. AfricaDoc organizes a coproduction workshop, "Produire au sud Agadir-Sahara," and is the festival's newest step in establishing itself as a platform for collaborations across the Sahara. In fact, Fidadoc is the only north-Saharan member of AfricaDoc, a network for documentary professionals from more than fifteen countries in Central and West Africa.[5]

In the wake of the popular uprisings of the Arab Spring, there has been an explosion of interest in documentary filmmaking in the Maghreb and the Middle East. In some countries, this has stimulated a documentary renaissance, while in others a documentary impulse has newly emerged. This bears on festival programming, and in 2012 and 2013, Fidadoc's program focused on Tunisia's new wave of documentary and paid homage to Syrian filmmakers. In 2013 Syrian producer Orwa Nyrabia attended Fidadoc: he co-founded DoxBox and won the 2014 Grand Prix of the Sundance Festival for his production *Return to Homs*. A contingent of young

Algerian documentarists contributed to the Hive, and in 2014 the selection highlighted the originality of documentary filmmaking in Lebanon and Palestine.

With its focus on expanding the affiliations with other Arab and African countries and documentary organizations, Fidadoc is one of the most active, creative, and expansive festivals today. Its emphasis on regional transnational landscapes and its negotiation of different shifting audiences makes it one of the most interesting festivals. With Falah, who is richly connected, at its helm, this festival reveals in its structure the strength of a transnationally networked experience for documentaries and their makers. The central support for Fidadoc comes from Moroccan TV channel 2M. Since Fidadoc's first edition, 2M has offered a prize for the International Competition and ensures complete media coverage of the festival. This collaboration has resulted in an active partnership that encourages the screening and promotion of documentary on national TV. For example, 2M's weekly documentary program, *Des histoires et des hommes* (Men and Their Histories), offers films screened during Fidadoc the chance to reach bigger audiences on TV. This television program has been known to set new audience records. 2M and Fidadoc work together to develop Moroccan documentaries and their audiences by contributing to a successful model for partnering on increasing the visibility of documentary, aspiring to raise a national interest in the form.

Fidadoc is an important local player, working toward making documentary more popular in the growing Moroccan film industry, developing an interest in the form with producers, directors, and audiences in Morocco. At the same time the festival is of crucial importance regionally, in the Maghreb, the MENA, and in Africa at large, with a focus moving away from Europe, away from the (past) "center" and toward a pan-African and pan-Arab network of collaborations and coproductions, working both with very young and aspiring filmmakers on the African continent, and with professionals who are developing increasing confidence and establishing a regional transnational network of documentary aficionados.

Docudays, Beirut, Lebanon

Docudays was founded in 2001 in Beirut by siblings Mohamed and Abir Hashem, after they started up their documentary production company Solo Films, with offices in Doha and Beirut. Solo Films specializes in producing television and corporate documentaries in and about the Arab world. At the head of the company is Mohamed Hashem, who also assisted with the launch of the Al Jazeera Documentary Festival in Qatar in 2005 as senior consultant. In parallel with DocuDays, Hashem launched the Beirut Documentary Encounter, a networking event where filmmakers, producers, and funders meet, and Beirut Documentary Forum, a "more theoretical space, aimed at both the study of and the contribution to the advancement of the industry in the region" (DFI Blog. 2011). His sister Abir is a filmmaker, teacher, producer, and film festival director. She acted as the managing director of DocuDays Beirut International Documentary Film Festival for five years. In 2011 they aimed to create the Arab Documentary Network, an online portal that aims to serve the Arab documentary world by creating an online network for films, filmmakers, and film professionals. But this never materialized, and the festival has in fact not taken place since 2011.

Again, in the Arab world in general and in Lebanon specifically, the years 2011–12 changed the face of the arts and cinema. In Lebanon, several festivals were suspended in 2012 due to the threat of the Syrian conflict spilling over into Lebanon, and so 2011 was the last edition of the festival. For the manager and director of the festival, filmmaking and producing became more important, and perhaps because of the increased democratization of the digital age and the expansion of storytelling methods and storytellers due to the revolutions and the war in Syria, there are simply more films to make: films that are increasingly coveted by film festivals around the world. Ambitious as they were with DocuDays, the Hashems' Encounter and Forum as well as the festival folded due to external political pressures, and to their personal ambitions in more corporate filmmaking, as evidenced by their interest in the Qatar office expansion. Mohamed runs his company in Doha, and Abir is focusing on making films rather than running the festival in a volatile and vulnerable city. While visions and missions, and revolutionary moments, are crucial to the impetus to create urgent documentaries, festivals as events that are condensed in time and space remain subject to outside factors beyond the control of the organizers and their individual ambitions.

Ismailia International Film Festival for Documentaries and Shorts, Ismailia, Egypt

Egypt was the first country on the African continent and in the Arab world to establish a film industry that remains popular. While documentary was long regarded a minor form of filmmaking next to the hugely popular melodrama and the realist turn in the late 1960s and early 1970s, since the revolutionary year of 2011, realism in film and documentary has become increasingly important for Egyptian film's international reputation. It was in the 1980s that Egypt's first festival entirely dedicated to documentary was established: the Ismailia Festival for Documentaries and Short Film.[6]

Since 1988, the Ismailia festival has celebrated documentary and short film—forms of filmmaking that can be described as non-mainstream, especially in Egypt. The first edition of this new national film festival saw, in addition to the films participating in the official competition, the screening of a selection of classical films from the national archive, to commemorate documentary filmmakers from the past, with discussion panels. From originally being a festival dedicated to national documentary production, in 1991 it was transformed into an international film festival and expanded from a three-day festival into a celebration of film that lasts six days.

From its very beginnings, the festival's founder Hashim al-Nahhas, then-director of the National Cinema Center, was very clear in phrasing the festival's mission and vision. He did not want to merely add another event to the busy calendar in Cairo, but "to promote dialogue between cultures [through] films that deepen the understanding of others' social visions, values, and thoughts" (al-Nahhas 2018). He found Luxor uninterested but the governor of Ismailia showed an interest in developing the appeal of his city and province, and thus al-Nahhas set up a competitive festival.

Until 1993 the festival had Hashim al-Nahhas at the helm, but in 1994 Samir Gharib, director of the Culture Development Fund, took over for the fourth international film festival and appointed film analyst Samir Farid as festival director. Gharib merged the festival with the National Film Festival in Cairo. Thus the Ismailia Film Festival was not held until Ali Abu Shadi was selected as director of the National Cinema Center; he brought the festival back into action in 2001 in Ismailia, where it was first launched. The festival became better organized and bigger as it gained wider recognition and the number of guests, audiences, and films grew. Under the subsequent director, 'Isam Zakariya, a Cairo journalist, the program was based on an international competition for long and short documentaries. The festival noticeably suffers from the constant changing of directors and the obligatory collaboration with the Ministry of Culture.

In addition to the film screenings and competitions, the festival also organizes networking events and debates between filmmakers and the audience, journalists, and professionals, and film workshops in collaboration with other film festivals and organizations that provide opportunities for young filmmakers to advance their experience and knowledge. Again, we see an emphasis on the development of networks, on the learning process, and encounters between established filmmakers and other professionals with younger, newer directors and students. This is also reflected in the non-competitive strands of the festival, where tributes to film personalities and distinguished filmmakers from around the world aim to feed the historical and formal knowledge and context within which younger up-and-coming documentary directors work. This educational aspect of the festival confirms, again, that documentary festivals often tend to focus their efforts on development and training, in a context of congenial events.

In this respect, 2013 was a significant year in the history of the festival, run then by writer and producer Mohamed Hefzy, as the Ismailia Co-Production Platform was inaugurated. It was the first coproduction forum in the MENA region dedicated entirely to documentaries. The collaborative nature of documentary is emphasized in the exchange process and germination of ideas where, as the festival says, "it is best not to walk alone" (Hefzy 2013). The Platform was expanded in 2014, when Beirut DC Lab and the Screen Institute Beirut collaborated to develop the workshops. These workshops focused on storytelling and writing techniques, pitching, and production, run by pioneering Arab documentary makers Hala al-Abdallah and Viola Shafik, both in group sessions and in one-on-one meetings. Simultaneously, Shafik also ran a one-time pitching workshop for the German Documentary Campus. The years when the festival was run by Hefzy's Film Clinic were very productive in their collaborative approach and educational focus, where young people were central to their view for the development of documentary in the region.[7]

But funding and space have become an issue for the festival, as Zakariya admits: "The lack of budget and lack of space is sufficient to present an important obstacle for the festival management" (Zakariya 2017). Having been launched in 1988 under the jurisdiction of the National Cinema Center, it continues as one of three film festivals coordinated by Egypt's Ministry of Culture. But even presenting itself as the oldest focused festival in Egypt and in the region, this festival struggles to maintain its ambitions. Having been merged with the Cairo Festival and returned to Ismailia, and now continuing to struggle with financial and spatial demands, its outlook is increasingly international and establishment, in contrast to what the two editions in 2013 and 2014 promised with their focus on young people and the development of local talent. Perhaps then the many switches at the director's level, the dependence on the Ministry, and the competition aspect, with substantial money prizes, become too heavy a burden for relatively small festivals. These obstacles, combined, are becoming increasingly complex and prohibitive for the festival to continue running confidently as part of the regional and transnational flow of global cultures.

Al Jazeera International Documentary Film Festival, Doha, Qatar

The year 2005 marked the inauguration of the Al Jazeera International Documentary Film Festival. The festival has managed to carve out a name for itself within the Middle East and North Africa, and globally, perhaps mostly due to its association with the Al Jazeera Media Network and its growing reputation. The festival was developed and is still mainly supported by the government-funded news broadcaster Al Jazeera, in order to "add a cultural aspect" (Ajroudi and al-Tahhan 2014, 287) to the organization's heavy news substance. Al Jazeera also established a documentary channel in 2007 and has really carved out a niche for itself as a globally respected news and documentary network. Since the start, the festival has been run by Abbas Arnaout, its founder and director. A Jordanian TV drama producer and documentary director, Arnaout joined Dubai TV in the United Arab Emirates. In 1996, he moved to Al Jazeera, where he established the production department for the then-infant Al Jazeera Satellite Channel.

The first edition included participants from Arab countries only. Participation included TV productions, such as news programs and documentary films. After the success of the first edition, it was decided to expand the festival and make it an international event where Arab and non-Arab participants were allowed to take part. This was in line with the orientation of Al Jazeera Network, as are Arnaout's values of neutrality and honesty in his festival's journey to credibility. He sees the festival as a "window" that works both ways: for locals to open their eyes to foreign productions, and for foreign filmmakers to discover local productions and local culture when they visit. This touristic and marketing aspect of the festival (and other festivals in the area) is often criticized: Qatar being such an expat-rich community, the festival is seen as too "international" and not open or receptive enough to local productions. This limitation, in addition to some other taboos and indirect censorship issues, have been the main restrictions to the festival's growth and directly caused its limited international reputation. Arnaout himself admits that "there are some topics that we cannot pursue in the festival; for example, a topic that verbally attacks celestial religions, or a specific religion or a specific race or nationality" (Ajroudi and al-Tahhan 2014, 287).

The festival sets a special theme every year. The first theme was "Welcome," and later editions have been organized around themes and concepts such as "Communication," "Peace," "Together," "Hope," "Freedom," "Dialogue" for 2011, then "Future," "Windows," and "Steps." The 2016 edition of the Al Jazeera International Documentary Film Festival was themed "Horizons," to express the progressiveness of Al Jazeera. All these themes are highly idealistic but also very broad concepts that can be interpreted in a variety of ways and that are flexible enough to encompass all types of documentaries. They are also, notably, optimistic terms that emphasize once again the congenial nature of documentary festivals, or, as the festival's critics would have it, vague ideals. Trying to fit into a global festival network and remaining conservative at the same time has not provided the festival with a clear vision or agenda for the future. Mostefa Souag, acting director general of Al Jazeera Media Network, announced that the twelfth edition of the Al Jazeera International Documentary Film Festival, which was to take place in 2016, would be postponed to 2017, due to multiple activities planned for the twentieth anniversary of the network. This was a year in which some other big festivals were canceled, interrupted, or postponed (e.g., Cairo, Marrakech). While Cairo temporarily thrived under the directorship of Mohamed Hefzy, and Marrakech restarted in 2018, so far the Al Jazeera International Documentary Film Festival has not taken place since this announcement. However, since 2018, the Al Jazeera Balkans Documentary Festival has worked in close collaboration with the Al Jazeera Media Network and Al Jazeera Media Institute, to showcase international documentaries, and develop young filmmakers' skills and opportunities to work on projects of interest to the Al Jazeera Media Network (AJB, 2018). The festival takes place both in person and online, offering opportunities for large international audiences to benefit from online streaming events. Al Jazeera's interest in international documentaries is, thus, developing but literally moving away from prohibitively complex conservative value systems.

Conclusion

What I have highlighted in this paper is the particularly democratic nature of documentary film festivals, with values like solidarity, collaboration, education, and training at the forefront of their programs. I have also emphasized the nature of documentary festivals as collaborative, and as spaces and moments in time where documentary professionals come together in order to embody and develop the worldwide documentary landscape as part of a global cultural flow. This is evident in the visions of their directors or founders, and in the programs of the festivals, where ideas of solidarity and flexibility are highlighted. Likewise, I have painted a broad picture of documentary festivals in the Arab world as spaces for collaboration and networked events, where the emphasis lies on truly hearing and seeing one another in light of these sensibilities, in a congenial atmosphere where young as well as established filmmakers interact with democratic and common goals: working toward a better world and an adequate, truthful representation of that better world. This ambitious and aspirational nature of Arab documentary in my description and analysis of Arab documentary festivals aims to highlight the intensified moments within which festivals take place, and the spaces they construct for competing flows of ideas, culture, media, and finance. These transnational flows of different constructs of congeniality are not homogenizing, but rather shifting over space and time as a consequence of human creativity and its priorities. And while the idea of the congenial nature of documentary film festivals is hard to use as "evidence," it is experienced at festivals in the sense one gets as an audience member or invitee, and as part of the flowing network of documentary festivals.

Likewise, the people at the helm of these organizations and festivals embody these ideals with their own presence at their festivals and at others. Hicham Falah from Fidadoc in Morocco, for example, also works with DoxBox as a member of the board. Mohamed Hashem from the Beirut DocuDays was involved with the Al Jazeera Documentary Festival as a senior consultant. Indeed, almost all founders, directors, or presidents of the festivals discussed in this chapter are closely affiliated with three central transnational organizations: IDFA, AFAC, and/or DoxBox, not just for funding or sponsorship but also for training and networked exchanges. This in itself beautifully illustrates the shifting flows of transnational culture and the global landscape of documentary festivals.

Overlaps in visions and missions are very clearly rooted in solidarity, learning, dialogue; in a sense of idealism to topics and approaches; and in dedication to a regional transnationalism, with a special interest in either pan-African collaborations and coproductions (for example, Agadir) or pan-Arab networked opportunities (for example, DoxBox). The congenial nature of documentary festivals is a transnational characteristic, and in the Arab film festivals under discussion I have highlighted the focus on training, networks, exchanges, and the fast-paced development of confidence in young people and the support they receive from those more established in the field. All this, combined with the general tenor of documentary production, distribution, and exhibition—less preoccupied with glamour, corporate interests, or escapism— reveals a transnational network of support and solidarity among documentaries, documentary makers, and those who manage them. Even if the flows and connections between documentary events can at times also be regarded as hierarchical, the success and sustainability of the smaller, non-competitive festivals is remarkable. Perhaps this more democratic approach to festival celebrations of the documentary is also reflected in the fact that some of these festivals are supported not by national interests but by television stations, independent production companies, or cultural organizations: Agadir works with 2M and Qatar with Al Jazeera; Doc à Tunis is supported by a cultural organization; DoxBox and DocuDays are or were supported by independent producers and developed into different organizations; and Ismailia has undergone many different incarnations under different ministries and the Ismailia Governorate, depending on their focus, but has been most consistently supported by the National Center for Cinema. Another factor might be the non-competitive nature of the most productive and sustainable of the festivals. The two competitive festivals that award monetary prizes, Ismailia and Al Jazeera, are struggling to keep going.

There is no doubt that 2011–12 was an absolutely crucial sea change in the documentary world. Even more, arguably, than the digital revolution, the 2011 revolutions have marked a considerable switch in focus on the MENA region and in its attitude toward documentary. In addition, and likely because of this, since 2013 most of the films, festivals, and organizations under discussion here have benefited from a new type of support, the AFAC Documentary Program. This program supports and funds creative documentary films that address social realities in the Arab region. AFAC recognizes the changing reality and shifting sociopolitical circumstances for filmmakers in the Arab world. These changes and shifts are unlocking and creating new creativity throughout the region. Where oppressive governments have in the past challenged filmmakers to be creative within their permissible circumstances, newfound freedoms since the turning point of 2011–12 across the Arab region have opened the eyes and ears of international festivals and audiences, in order to welcome these new creatives and their films at documentary festivals. In particular, documentaries from the MENA have outperformed their counterparts at global players like IDFA and CPH:DOC. While there is no space here to engage in depth with how Arab documentaries have performed, these European festivals certainly benefit from increasingly programming the many innovative and revolutionary documentaries coming from the Arab world since 2011–12.

As AFAC points out, "Documentaries from the Arab region address critical topics, and yet they continue to suffer from limited funding, underexposure, and alienation from regional and worldwide audiences" (AFAC, n.d.). But the digital revolution and evolution, and the Arab revolutions and wars, as well as the depositions of a number of dictators, have also opened up routes to a freer self-expression. Due to the explosions of digital media, revolutionary minds, and citizen journalism, and the democratization of technology for access and distribution, far more content is available. While it remains a challenge for documentary filmmakers from the Arab world to find financial support for their work, the increasing creativity and the persistent presence of Arab documentaries at international festivals around the globe and in the Arab world certainly challenges these limitations.

References

AFAC. n.d. "Special Programs: AFAC's Documentary Program." arabculturefund.org.

Ajroudi, Asma, and al-Tahhan, Zeina. 2014. "'Our Festival Is Our Window onto Others': An Interview with Abbas Arnaout, Director of the Al Jazeera International Documentary Film Festival." In *Film Festival Yearbook 6: Film Festivals and the Middle East*, edited by Dina Iordanova and Stefanie Van de Peer. 285-296. St Andrews: St Andrews Film Studies.

Appadurai, Arjun. 1990. "Disjuncture and Difference in the Global Cultural Economy." *Theory, Culture and Society* 7: 295–310.

Armes, Roy. 2006. *African Filmmaking North and South of the Sahara.* Edinburgh: Edinburgh University Press.

Barlet, Olivier. 1998. Interview with Férid Boughédir, "The Forbidden Windows of Black African Film." *Africultures* 5327. www.africultures. com.

Ben Ammar, Hichem. 2007. "Editorial 2007." www.nesselfen.org.

Ben Ammar, Hichem. 2012. "Doc à Tunis Editorial 2012." nesselfen.org.

DoxBox. n.d. "Our Story." www.dox-box.org.

Fidadoc. 2014. "Presentation 2014." www.fidadoc.org.

Fischer, Alex. 2013. *Sustainable Projections: Concepts in Film Festival Management.* St Andrews: St Andrews Film Studies.

Halassa, Malu. 2012. "Syrian Art Comes of Age." Ibraaz.com, November 21. www.ibraaz.org.

Hillauer, Rebecca. 2005. *Encyclopedia of Arab Women Filmmakers.* Cairo: American University in Cairo Press.

Iordanova, Dina. 2010. "Mediating Diaspora: Film Festivals and 'Imagined Communities.'" In *Film Festival Yearbook 2: Film Festivals and Imagined Communities*, edited by Dina Iordanova and Ruby Cheung. 12-44. St Andrews: St Andrews Film Studies.

Khélil, Hédi. 2007. *Abécédaire du cinéma tunisien.* Tunis: Simpact.

Klausen, Maja. 2017. "The Urban Exploration Imaginary: Mediatization, Commodification, and Affect." *Space and Culture* 20, no. 4: 372–84.

Leung, Tit. 2012. "Extending the Local: Documentary Film Festivals in East Asia as Sites of Connection and Communication." PhD diss., Lingnan University, Hong Kong. www.commons.ln.edu.hk.

Mahdaoui, Anissa. 2017. "Hichem Ben Ammar nommé à la tête de la Cinémathèque tunisienne." HuffpostMaghreb, June 14. www.huffpostmaghreb.com.

Markus, George E. 1996. *Connected: Engagements with Media.* Chicago: University of Chicago Press.

al-Nahhas, Hashim. 2018. "A Word from Hashem El Nahas." www. ismailiafilmfest.com.

Nas al-Fann. 2006. www.nesselfen.org.

Nornes, Mark. 2011. "Bulldozers, Bibles and Very Sharp Knives: The Chinese Independent Documentary Scene." In *Film Festival Yearbook 3: Film Festivals and East Asia*, edited by Dina Iordanova and Ruby Cheung. 101-109. St. Andrews: St Andrews Film Studies.

Salti, Rasha. 2006. *Insights into Syrian Cinema: Essays and Conversations with Contemporary Filmmakers.* New York: ArteEast.

Van de Peer, Stefanie. 2012. "The Moderation of Creative Dissidence in Syria: Reem Ali's Documentary *Zabad.*" *Journal for Cultural Research* 16, no. 2–3: 297–317.

Van de Peer, Stefanie. 2017. *Negotiating Dissidence: The Pioneering Women of Arab Documentary*. Edinburgh: Edinburgh University Press.

Zakariya, 'Isam. 2017. "No Change in the Competitions of Ismailia Film Festival." February 27. www.ismailiafilmfest.com.

10

NEGATIVE/POSITIVE: NEWSREELS IN NASSERITE EGYPT AND THE CRAFTING OF NATIONAL IDENTITY

Yasmin Desouki

Imagining time lost and spent is more often than not an exercise in empty nostalgia, rather than the true reconstruction of an era, with all its hurt and complicated realities. Past narratives are often privileged in the minds of the general public, and disparate visual iconography survives far longer than the written record. This is especially true of the past one hundred or so years, wherein the moving image has arguably formed the most salient point of reference in cultural memory.

Still, a somewhat indulgent exercise in remembrance can be withstood for a moment. Imagine going to the movies in early 1960s Egypt, in one of the major metropolises.[1] The rarefied halls were, back then, the center of how the nation understood itself, and the ceremony of going to see a film—punctuated with smart ties and jackets for the men, dresses for the women, followed by ice cream and a stroll later in the evening—was an indelible experience for a large swath of the country, regardless of social standing or personal circumstance. Once the audience was seated in the cinema, the lights would dim, and the first images would reveal themselves in the hushed dark. Before the night's main feature a newsreel would debut, documenting Egyptian accomplishments, the nation still basking in the warm glow of revolutionary ideals. Soon after, the film would start: the propagator of ideology followed by the container of those ideologies.

Newsreel films were a vital form of early cinema. Their functionality seems rather straightforward: news in the form of moving images, diluting the human experience onto celluloid. But stylistically they had a profound influence on the history of cinema, and more so on the public that was exposed to them.

Newsreels in Egypt—as in most countries, particularly those in the throes of constant revolution—possess a long and intricate history. Most film researchers have conflated accounts of newsreel production with

177

documentary filmmaking at large, and with good reason. The lines delineating one form of image making from the other are frequently blurred, in terms of both their production and the figures controlling their creation. Mohammed Bayoumi is, of course, a pivotal figure, but so are Hassan Murad, Hussein Hilmi al-Muhandis, and Ahmed Kamel Awad, among others. Each era of the newsreel's life cycle varies aesthetically in accordance with the concurrent managerial structure of the entities churning them out for public consumption, and the general cultural mood at the time.

Arguably, the apotheosis of the newsreel—not just as a form of "news," or information, but rather as a particular kind of documentary filmmaking emblematic of its time—was reached during Gamal Abd al-Nasser's reign as president. Nasser was a famous cinephile, and he deeply understood the power of the image. While he is mostly remembered for his rhetorical brilliance, his administration's celebration of the arts, and cinema in particular, carries with it a long-standing reinterpretation of film history and industry that is often underexplored or misunderstood.

Nasser's socialist regime was in the business of selling national personhood. What is remarkable about viewing many of the films, newsreels, and advertisements produced during this era is the stark revelation of his regime's consciousness—their knowledge that the public needed ideas to be sold to them via capitalistic packaging. Therefore, the socialist-romantic melodrama of Youssef Chahine's *The People and the Nile* (*al-Nas wa-l-Nil*, 1964–72),[2] detailing the controversial building of the Aswan High Dam, is given a story of strident nationalism and pride told through the prism of young love, which in turn is meant to symbolically represent national unity. Many other state-produced films have followed suit, and not just genre-oriented features. While documentaries still possessed a niche audience, their production increased dramatically during this time, with a number of well-known filmmakers getting their feet wet in this particular arena of production. Likewise, advertisements were of incredible importance, particularly with the advent of television. The Ahram Advertising Agency diligently trained its staff to draw upon song, dance, poetry, and other lyrical traditions as forms of inspiration to better sell their products[3]—to say that part of the Nasserite legacy is a fluent understanding of the nation's mood and mentality is an understatement.

Needless to say, newsreel production flowered considerably during this time, with full support from Nasser's administration in terms of finance and visibility: no inauguration of an iron-rolling plant or calligraphy exhibition opening would be complete without cameras eagerly capturing the astonishing pace of industrialization and art production in the country. Contrary to current perception, newsreels were not dedicated solely to documenting major political events, but rather occasions as seemingly innocuous as horse races, Alexandrians enjoying a day at the beach, diplomats visiting the country's ballet institute, different tourism initiatives, and so on, were captured on film. This is indicative of both the government's budgetary capacities at the time, and an overarching interest in bringing Egyptian citizens onboard with their conceptualizing of a broader national identity. The cultural import of newsreels, especially during the 1960s, is crucial to understanding cinematic trends in subsequent decades.

Avant-garde and experimental movements in documentary filmmaking in the 1970s and 1980s can be traced to the unwavering influence of the newsreel, in terms of both its formal and its political qualities. There is a case to be made for the medium's contemporaneous relation to documentary filmmaking writ large, with its introduction of iconic imagery and an almost surrealist penchant for symbolism steeped in the oblique "messaging" of Nasser's administration, especially as exemplified by the works of Shadi Abdel Salam, Madkour Thabet, Ahmed Rashed, and the postmodern thrust of Hossam Ali's oeuvre, alongside a younger generation of documentarians.[4] The aim of this research has been to uncover that which is typically mired in traditionally nationalist narratives of Egyptian film history, by underscoring the somewhat underrated influence of newsreels not just on documentaries but on moving-image history in general.

The starting point is a question: What is the negative image, and what is the positive iteration? Which developed first, and what was the end result?

Variations on a Theme

On the banks of the river Nile, Egyptians recorded their history and built their civilization. The glorious monuments they created left behind a lasting legacy, bearing witness and documenting all forms of life for future generations . . . the Egyptian Cinematic Newsreel[5] reflected the people's humanity . . . and total awareness of the importance of preserving it as a part of our identity and heritage for younger generations. (Abu Sir 1995, 1–3)[6]

The State Information Service published its first (and perhaps only) compendium detailing the newsreels produced from 1955 through 1995, in celebration of the moving image in Egypt and its perceived technical accomplishments. The uninspired prose reveals the gilded terms through which cinephiles have historically viewed the newsreel, and, perhaps more importantly, its specific place within the realm of state-approved art as popular media.

Of course, newsreel production and its dissemination in Egypt began well before 1955.[7] However, the key figures (both individual and governmental) who played an enormous role in their production changed consistently from the early 1920s onward, reflecting the country's upheaval and major spurts of radical energy, particularly with the revolutions of 1919 and 1952.

While the films of the Lumière Brothers, and their contemporary Alexandre Promio, were screened in Egypt at the turn of the century (encapsulating what can now be considered the earliest forms of documentary filmmaking), it was not until the restless artist Mohammed Bayoumi laid claim to the filmic medium that it could be said that Egyptians started producing newsreels, let alone cinema.

Despite the gloom enveloping much of Europe in the wake of the First World War, Bayoumi, like many ambitious souls before and after, traveled abroad to try his hand at studying visual art. He returned home a few years later, after the revolution against British colonial rule, with a diploma in cinematography from Austria.

Inspired by the tremendous societal change overtaking the country, Bayoumi endeavored to start Amun Film in 1923, with the first images captured on film being the return of political leader Sa'd Zaghlul from exile on September 18, 1923. According to scholars Ibrahim al-Disuqi and Muhammad al-Qalyubi—both of whom dedicated much of their research to exploring Bayoumi's career[8]—the inauguration of the Amun newsreel was a conscious attempt to document the momentous change in Egyptian politics and the country's concurrent independent sensibility to the outside world. No doubt influenced by those early screenings of the Lumière Brothers' works in the late 1800s, Bayoumi was also exposed to other filmmaking pioneers who made enormous headway in the realm of newsreels (and later became part of the same school), such as Germaine Dulac, who worked for Pathé Films, and Dziga Vertov's Kino-Pravda. While perhaps the respective filmmakers' aesthetic sensibilities did not significantly alter the dynamic of what Bayoumi created onscreen via Amun Film, his work can be seen as part of a broader global wave indicating the transformative power of the newsreel when capturing political events, especially during revolutionary movements (Schefer 2016, 61–70).

In the subsequent year, Amun Film produced at least fifteen other newsreels, all of which documented the nascent country's work in building its infrastructure after dispelling the specter of colonialism.[9] Governmental activities such as the inauguration of the Egyptian parliament in 1924 and the opening of Banque Misr were filmed, alongside the unlocking of King Tut's tomb—which, in its own way, is notable, given that it is sometimes forgotten that Egyptians also documented this moment for themselves and claimed it as their own, not just Howard Carter and his associates.

The work of Amun Film continued as an almost entirely independent venture until the Egyptian Company for Acting and Cinema (al-Sharika al-misriyya li-l-tamthil wa-l-sinima) founded Misr Newsreel (Jaridat Misr) in 1935, thereby taking over Amun Film, and appointing Bayoumi as supervisor of its operations alongside his then assistant, Hassan Murad.

Perhaps not so surprisingly, what is now considered by a number of historians to be the first autonomous iteration of newsreels (or documentary filmmaking more generally) on the African continent is ignored by much of the foreign press of the time. In a 1952 report published by UNESCO titled "Newsreels Across the World," Egypt is chosen as a case study alongside France, the United States, Uruguay, and India. Amun Film is never mentioned, and some statistics are given regarding the output of Misr Newsreel. What the study highlights more than anything is the distributive flow of foreign newsreels such as Actualités françaises, Fox Movietone News, Paramount News, and Gaumont-British News, which were imported on a nearly weekly basis, in addition to a few Greek newsreels brought in for exhibition once or twice a year (Baechlin and Muller-Strauss 1952, 57–58).

While UNESCO's report can be interpreted in different ways, any inherent prejudice or unwitting ignorance takes a back seat to the hard numbers it plainly presents: it is clear that in the wake of the Second World War especially, foreign newsreels were being screened in Egypt at a remarkable pace, which can be seen as a logical extension of the country's geographic imprint at the time; it was crucial to both the Allied forces and German troops, and caught in the middle of intractable conflict. In parallel, much of the research published in Egypt in recent years regarding the history of newsreels implicitly notes the slowed output of Misr Newsreel during this period.

This, in turn, can be taken to imply a multitude of meanings. Perhaps it reflected King Fu'ad's kowtowing to Western interests, thus the financial investment in Misr Newsreel went to subtitling foreign-produced newsreels. Or Egyptians were eager to understand the war that was starting to impinge upon their interests, forcing local news to take a back seat as other countries moved front and center. Most likely, the truth lies somewhere in between. Regardless, tracing the evolving nature of newsreels in Egypt, and the ways in which they were distributed, is incredibly vital to understanding what took place during Gamal Abd al-Nasser's years. This means not just properly contextualizing their manufacture and distribution, but understanding the visual baggage brought along with them: the stylistic sensibilities that inevitably filtered their way into the newsreels of later decades, and the ways in which the Egyptian public viewed them.

Shortly into Misr Newsreel's young history, its name was changed to Jaridat Misr al-natiqa, roughly translated to "Misr Newsreels with Sound." Soon after the 1952 Revolution, in which a military junta overthrew King Faruq's monarchy, the ownership of Misr Newsreel was transferred to al-Hay'a al-'amma li-l-isti'lamat, or the State Information Service. The company structure was reorganized by developing its managerial and technical capacities, as the government readily granted it new equipment and a bigger budget.[10] In 1960, the state-sponsored newsreel underwent another transformation, with its name changed to The Arab Newsreel (signifying the creation of the United Arab Republic, Egypt's short-lived political union with Syria), and its production was transferred to the Egyptian State Television in 1963.[11]

In July 1971, early in the Sadat administration and as part of his initial efforts to reorder much of the media and the Ministry of Culture, the ownership of the Arab Newsreel was transferred to the State Information Service, until November 1971. During this brief interlude, the newsreel's name reverted to Misr Newsreel (or Egyptian Cinematic Newsreel; both translations had started appearing by this point, and have been used interchangeably), and its production was returned to the auspices of State Television until 1980. Finally, from 1980 through 1995, the newsreels were produced solely by the State Information Service, and premiered on television—at this juncture, they essentially became long-form news reportage, and their aesthetics changed dramatically from their antecedents in the Nasserite era.

Choreography of the Image

The newsreel is life transmitted. The newsreel is the machine that writes history.[12]

Early in Gamal Abd al-Nasser's administration, the state attempted to further codify its relationship to cultural production by instating the now-familiar dominant discourse conflating nationalism with the arts. Little space was left for alternative narratives, and—in keeping with the socialist ideology of the time—strident individualism was generally frowned upon, as Egypt saw itself at the vanguard of a greater struggle for freedom in the region. As such, national unity overrode personal liberty.

It is little wonder, then, that key figures within the Egyptian arts scene at the time understood the inherent power contained within the newsreel as a tool to help educate the general public—both locally and abroad—on Egypt's newfound sense of place in the world. While the implied connection between newsreel production and revolutionary politics was initially explored in Bayoumi's work, the Nasserite administration arguably took it one step further by redesigning its language and setting it in stone. Key elements of the newsreel's identity were maintained—a detailed credits sequence at the beginning, the trumpet-inflected music announcing the arrival of something "important," the authoritative voice-over, carefully selected subjects, and so on. However, other visual indicators of the newsreel were introduced during this period, including very self-aware and deliberate compositions of movement captured within the frame; 1960s pop-art inflections such as inserts of squiggly lines, dancing circular objects, and fade-ins/outs to indicate a break in the montage of a clip; and—perhaps most tellingly—the introduction of newsreels in English, indicative of the administration's strong awareness that part of their "messaging" needed to be made palatable for other nations, especially Western ones.

The aesthetic developments that began to appear in Egyptian newsreels during the late 1950s and 1960s underscore several crucial points. First and foremost, the influence of slightly Westernized mainstream fare (if only in terms of the visuals used), with the deft combination of Soviet-inspired rhetoric and topical concerns, are emblematic of the period's cultural shift, a sublime sense of confidence conveyed in the slick packaging of socialist ideals. Second, the wide-ranging influence of various art movements and cinematic trends, namely Italian neorealism, pop art, and—perhaps most importantly—the Second World War–era newsreels from Great Britain and the United States, which were still fresh in the minds of filmmakers and the wider populace at that time.

That is to say, none of this happened in a vacuum. Newsreels can and should be viewed as not only one of the first and most constant forms of cinema produced, but also an early mode of communication that rendered the distance between time and space rather insignificant. From here, it makes sense to again draw upon the influences of significant players such as Dulac and Vertov; their work presents two distinct modes of practice that nonetheless ran in direct opposition to the American and British newsreels produced during that time, and would have likely played an almost subliminal role in the evolution of the medium and its reinterpretation by countries undergoing revolutionary change, such as Cuba and, of course, Egypt.

Charles Pathé gave the newsreel its initial shape in 1911, during which the informative aspect overrode its formal qualities. But true innovation within the medium began when filmmakers were commissioned by private or governmental entities to aid their production, or filmmaking collectives took the initiative and created something different altogether.

The first example of the latter is Dziga Vertov, who started the Kino-Pravda ("Film Truth") newsreel series in 1922,[13] with the intention of capturing fragments of everyday life (including both politically significant events and portraitures of daily routine), emphasizing the ways in which they were shown together to reveal a deeper truth heretofore unseen by the naked eye. His work foregrounded the importance of the "camera-eye," and is understood in some ways to be a precursor to the *cinéma vérité* movement. Primarily an independent venture undertaken by Vertov and his collective, Kino-Pravda nonetheless influenced many of the state-produced newsreels of the USSR's Moscow's Newsreel Studio,[14] particularly through the ways in which montages were employed.

While Vertov's work eschewed propagandistic tendencies, the formal innovation apparent in his dedication to the theory and practice of the "camera-eye" were vital in introducing a new storytelling approach within the newsreel format. The didactic editing and carefully structured shots were oftentimes less like reportage and more akin to mini–thesis statements on the state of the world, and the position of the masses within it.

Not terribly far from the tremendous wave of change occurring in Russia, Germaine Dulac also began to make headway within the realm of newsreels as of 1930. A French filmmaker and theorist known for her surrealist films *The Smiling Madam Beudet* (*La souriante Madame Beudet*, 1922–23) and *The Seashell and the Clergyman* (*La coquille et le clergyman*, 1928), Dulac worked for Gaumont and Pathé during the 1930s, until her death in 1942. Another sharply aware filmmaker involved in creating commercial newsreels during a troublesome period in Europe's history, Dulac devoted much of her later work to writing about the importance of newsreels, and shaping its aesthetic qualities to curtail the darker tendencies of the rise in media-savvy fascist governments.

While her legacy is perhaps lesser known today than Vertov's, the fact that she committed much of her theoretical vision of newsreels as "social educators" to films that crossed the seas and were shown on a large scale necessitates a brief exploration of her style. Dulac's approach was more spontaneous and less constructed than Vertov's, and was seen as a "concrete stylistic precursor of 'direct cinema' of the late 1950s and early 60s" (Williams 2014, 166). Her theories on "pure cinema" are heavily documented, and she wrote extensively on her view of "the newsreel as an ideal cinematic form" (Williams 2014, 178). Dulac believed that the lack of participation on the part of the newsreel director contributed to the peculiarity of this type of cinema: its aura of objectivity and ability to reveal the truth. Throughout her work with Actualités francaises, what is immediately apparent is her aversion to more bourgeoisie concerns and a lack of sensationalism, which runs counter to the overall style of newsreels at the time. The grand parades of power and wealth were never really her purview, and she understood the ways in which newsreels could be used for propagandist purposes. Dulac saw the newsreel director as a journalist-filmmaker, which is notable given the modernity implicit in such a vision and "the larger view of the newsreel in a shifting international context" (Williams 2014, 187).

Although other newsreel directors no doubt informed the technological and stylistic innovations that became apparent in the format throughout the ensuing decades, the influences of Vertov and Dulac are important to note for their rather hidden effect throughout history. The two pioneers absorbed different cinematic trends and political concerns, while deftly diluting them into a very specific kind of documentary filmmaking. Egypt's appropriation of the newsreel after Bayoumi's transformative undertaking reveals an amalgam of influences, through which major filmmakers—both foreign and Egyptian—helped to create a particular kind of storytelling that perfectly encapsulated the ideologies of the time, and a keen knowledge of how to communicate this to the public.

It is also worth reiterating that the form's introduction in Egypt came part and parcel with a sense of radical politics, and the resulting aesthetics are virtually inseparable from—in fact, they are a reflection of—revolutionary sentiment. The newsreel as first initiated by Bayoumi, then later in the Nasserite period, and even as adopted by countries like Cuba, Jordan, and Palestine, do not reflect the interests of the ruling power in the same ways often attributed to Western newsreels. In the public's imagination, the people became the ruling power, and likewise the newsreel attempted to adopt this view.

Further, while these pieces are usually denigrated as nothing more than eminently state-produced propaganda, it is important to note that this assessment is not in keeping with the general mood of the time. The naiveté inherent in much of the discourse in the newsreels produced during Nasser's presidency is insidious and has continued to have a profound effect on the nation's psyche. But none of it was played for irony. Perhaps there was a performative, slightly playful insouciance in some of the dialogue of the voice-over, or the ways in which certain scenes were shot, but this is reflective of the all-encompassing tone of confidence much of the country's media enjoyed at the time.

A single frame excerpted from a newsreel is in some ways more revealing of the nation's sense of self than an entire film could ever be from that decade. Take, for instance, one notable reel featuring Gamal Abd al-Nasser visiting a new iron-rolling plant in the industrial city of Helwan in the mid-1960s (*Opening of New Iron-Rolling Plant*, 1966). The opening musical score is akin to something Henry Mancini would have come up with, and the establishing shot entails an image instantly familiar from newsreels featuring the former president: Nasser, walking slightly ahead of his entourage of ministers and handlers, wearing a smart suit and sunglasses, peering at the massive steel edifices, coolly assessing their prowess. Cut to the factory workers, enthusiastically cheering the president as he walks by, waving and smiling. The cold remove of the iron pipelines and machines figures prominently, revealing a fascination with their mechanics that is representative of the era—an era in which Egyptians expected that they could manufacture and export everything from cars and home goods to a short-lived dream of building shuttles transporting them to outer space.

10.1. a-d Screenshots revealing the tight choreography of imagery in the newsreel "Opening of New Iron Rolling Plant," in Helwan. *Arab Newsreel* (1966) by Hassan Murad (1966).

The montage employed in the clip underscores who the keys players are in the narrative of the manufacturing industry: the president and the workers. Deliberately moving from one strategic shot to another, then back again, with the slightly bombastic voice-over coloring the event with tinges of national pride, it all points to a glowing belief in pan-Arab nationalism as a project—which should be the takeaway after viewing this. Each frame is tightly controlled, and even when things veer into the slightly absurd or cloyingly sentimental, the film never deviates far from its central message.

Newsreels that do not depict a major socioeconomic event convey a similar mise en scène when it comes to the masses and the ways in which they are captured on film. Be they laborers, audience members at a concert,

10.2. a-d Picture top left features Gamal Abdel Nasser behind the podium, which is draped in signage noting, "Work is honor, work is duty, work is a right, work is life." In this newsreel celebrating Labor Day, the cameraman is featured prominently, alongside the sound engineers recording the speech for posterity. Screenshot bottom right shows workers enthusiastically greeting the president and his message on the rights of workers. *Arab Newsreel* (1968) by Hassan Murad.

or families relaxing on the shores of Alexandria, carefully constructed sequences of people either cheering or smiling politely are prevalent. This is indicative of a newfound love for real, on-the-street accounts of what was happening, a sort of *cinéma vérité* inflection seeping into the newsreel. But it can also be seen as an awareness that the newsreel's function during Nasser's time was to reveal a silent agreement with the regime and its central ideology, a pact between those who were once deemed "background players" and the government.

Other self-aware stylistic flourishes often found in the newsreels of the 1960s were the sudden cutaways from a scene involving, say, Nasser in the middle of a speech, to a cameraman documenting the event. This is especially evident in a newsreel from 1968 covering Labor Day celebrations in Helwan (*Labor Day*, 1968). The staging itself is echoed in the meticulously edited sequences featuring signage celebrating Nasser's achievements, the importance of workers, oft-repeated shots of crowds from diverse backgrounds ecstatically cheering, and the cameramen hard

10.3. Hassan Murad

at work to capture the celebration in all its glory. The question arises here: who was the intended audience? Interestingly, this particular newsreel's voice-over is in English, adding another layer of meaning. No doubt it was one of the many pieces meant for foreign distribution—the disparate iconography emphasizing the full weight of those supporting Nasser's presidency, from art cultural producers to his cabinet and the large swaths of workers.

Media deemed to be propaganda are only revealed as such once the people realize they have been lied to. But again, to dismiss the newsreels produced in Nasser's era as mere propaganda is to discount full-bodied sentiments within the culture that remain very much alive in the public's memory.

For the first time, Egyptians had centered their own destiny as a people, and the country made headlines the world over. Nasser was beloved in Spain, Africa, and the USSR, and greeted as part of an international liberation movement. The idea that Egyptians were stars of world news made them consumers of the news. Therefore, they devoured newsreels, newspapers, radio broadcasts, and other forms of media with true hunger. Not all was disingenuous, and to indicate that the politics of the time were indeed representational (to some extent) is important. The newsreels indicate one of the first times Egyptians truly saw themselves onscreen. Nasser's administration only hastened to tighten the narrative.

In parallel, Egyptians watched American movies and were exposed to newsreels steeped in Second World War rhetoric. Hence, they possessed an acute self-awareness in their understanding of the discourse and how to spin it, especially when it came to fighting wars against the British and French in the Suez Crisis of 1956, and later in the Arab–Israeli War of 1967.

The influence of newsreels on Egyptian cinema during this time is especially noteworthy. One example is the film *Life or Death* (*Haya aw mawt*, 1954), directed by Kamal El-Sheikh. The first few minutes of the movie—a now classic, neorealist social melodrama—features aerial shots of modern-day Cairo, and a haunting voice-over that ruminates on the nature of time, fate, dreams, and the deep economic troubles of "the people." The starring actors do not appear onscreen immediately, and the camera glides along, capturing images of busy Downtown streets and Tal'at Harb Square, conveying a fascination with public spaces and filming them. The prologue ends, finally, when the camera settles on the film's titular patriarch peering with considerable longing through a shop window at a dress he is desperate to purchase for his daughter.

Significantly, this segment of *Life or Death* engages with some of the more austere elements of documentary style, which could be seen as partly influenced by the language of newsreels. Or, in a broader sense, it could be part of the newfound interest in claiming ownership over image making and the ways in which Egyptians are depicted onscreen—an extension of the newsreel's central driving sensibility. And, to complete the picture, films like *Life or Death*, which centered primarily on familial concerns, could be read as an extended analogy of Nasserism and its central tenets: no unit is more important within the framework of a socialist regime than the family. Here, cinema renders ideology manifest.

The works of other major filmmakers changed considerably during this time. One example is Youssef Chahine, who moved from rather mainstream musicals and romantic-melodramatic fare toward a more socially engaged kind of cinema, which ran parallel to Nasser's administration and the overall socialist messaging of the time. In fact, Gamal Abd al-Nasser practically commissioned the filmmaker to put the struggles of Algerian activist Djamila Bouhired on film, resulting in *Jamila, the Algerian* (*Jamila al-Jaza'iriya*, 1958). The Algerian "cause" was very much on the minds of the public during this time, and the fascination deepened when Gillo Pontecorvo's *Battle of Algiers* was released in 1966 (which in and of itself was in some ways a radical reappropriation of the newsreel form, as posited by Bill Nichols [Nichols 2009]). In keeping with a prevalent trend, Chahine became famous for filming important events as they happened, for example Umm Kulthum's and Nasser's funerals, and the student protest movement of the 1970s.

Experimental short films and even long-form advertisements (roughly six- to nine-minute works produced primarily for television consumption) were directly influenced by the proliferation of newsreels. Madkour Thabet's short film, *Revolution of Machinery* (*Thawrat al-makan*, 1969) was made in the wake of the disastrous defeat of the 1967 War. Meant to be a testament to the strength and will of the people in overcoming adversity, the film consists primarily of close-ups on machines working almost autonomously, a show of strength in the face of calamity. It echoes different newsreels, including the one previously mentioned depicting the inauguration of a new iron-rolling plant. The sense of awe at the performance of cold steel, symbolizing the country's strengthening infrastructure, is strongly felt in Thabet's film, and can be read as a metaphor for the country's resilience.

Interestingly, many of the same people who worked behind the scenes shooting newsreels were also involved in advertising, as was Ahmed Kamel Awad. The overlap in aesthetics between one form of media and the other becomes rather self-evident, and points to the small circle of influencers working within the medium. Awad's short advertisement/film *A Conversation Between Two Generations* (1969) combines elements of drama, musical, and documentary to help promote a new engineering institute that would ostensibly help the country's industry flourish. The first portion of the advertisement features well-known actors and dancers praising the institute in its rather stilted dialogue, and ends with considerable portions of what was once newsreel footage of factories in Helwan, adapted for a slightly different purpose.

Before Awad led the Ahram Advertising Agency over the course of four decades, he worked extensively as a director of newsreels. The repurposing of documentary footage initially meant for newsreels in advertisements (or, in this case, a kind of precursor to promotional video) was therefore incredibly common. It is one of the few ways in which the influence of newsreels on the culture at large is made tangible; filmmakers migrated freely from one form of media to another, bringing with them their specific branding and know-how.

While the production of newsreels during Nasser's time is indicative of a wider renaissance concerning documentary in general, it is important to dwell a bit on the era's burgeoning, fashionable obsession with the "live" element in popular entertainment. At around the same time the newsreel as a format was becoming more widely produced and consumed by the general public, radio was making exceptional headway, and it punctuated much of Egyptian daily life. Documentary-driven news programs, such as *Majallat al-hawa'* (loose translation, *The Live Magazine*) became incredibly popular, mixing reportage with interviews and with live on-the-street commentary from ordinary people. Other shows followed suit, such as *Around the Streetcorner ('Ala al-nasya)* and *Who Is the Killer? (Mann al-qatil?)*, which was a docu-drama, true crime series. This, coupled with the mandatory listening to Umm Kulthum's concerts every Thursday evening, and hearing Nasser's speeches as they were given live, could all be seen as a pure translation of the newsreel aesthetic permeating other parts of the culture.

That being said, if forced to pinpoint one defining characteristic of the newsreel in Nasser's era, it would be—again—the overwhelming sense of confidence and assurance that pervaded the tonal shifts and visual characteristics. However, this would change somewhat after the 1967 War, and even Nasser's own body language altered subtly to reveal a vulnerability and modestly rarely depicted previously. Newsreels would continue to be produced in virtually the same way, with a distinctly "cinematic" feel, throughout the earlier part of Sadat's era, but the language slowly changed. It would move from being the harbinger of pan-Arab nationalism and romanticism to something less strident and authoritative. The topical undercurrents would progress toward more open-market concerns, and the slow but steady privatization of the media sector signified the end of one era, and the precarious move into another.

Breakdown of Language

> "Dedicated to that miserable word, Honesty; to The Ego that manu-factured this film, and to all who supported this experiment in art—I offer this modest attempt."
> —Introductory inter-title to the film, *The Story of the Original and the Copy (Hikayat al-asl wa-l-sura)* (Thabet 1971)

While the 1967 War represented perhaps the biggest shift in the Egyptian psyche, the true rupture came with the passing of Gamal Abd al-Nasser. His legacy, fraught and deeply problematic as it was, nonetheless provided the central unifying spirit behind which much of the nation rallied. The years 1970 through 1973 signify a nadir of sorts, as the ghosts of revolutions past haunted popular discourse, and hovered like a dreadful pall over much of the intellectual output of the time. An era of stagnation was broken only (albeit briefly) by the 1973 October War. The country remained on edge during this brief interlude, wherein the collective destiny seemed hazy, and paranoid politics became the dominant frame of mind.

Central precepts of Arab nationalism were questioned in cinema, as in Tewfik Saleh's *The Dupes (al-Makhdu'un*, 1972), which features several sequences of newsreel/documentary footage intercut with the film's central narrative, as part of an acute meditation on Palestinian destiny, while also interrogating Nasserite ideology. Chahine's work shifted once again during this period, with his film *The Choice (al-Ikhtiyar*, 1970). Inspired by film noir, *The Choice's* starting point is a murder, and twin brothers who seemingly meld their persona(s) into one another—the resulting mystery being, who was the original, and who was the copy? A metaphor for the schizophrenic relationship between the country's intellectual elite and the proletariat, the noir-ish style encapsulated Egyptians' broken psyche against the backdrop of a deceitful and decadent political stalemate.

Arguably, no other filmmaker embodies the major change in tone and approach within documentary and avant-garde cinema during this time more than Madkour Thabet. His oft-neglected experimental film, *The Story of the Original and the Copy*[15] (1971), based on a story written by Naguib Mahfouz and produced for television, represents the paranoid nightmares of literati in stasis. Simultaneously nonsensical and an odd summation of the cinematic movements that came before, the film explores the aftermath of a murder, in which everyone from local law enforcement to journalists and members of the bourgeoisie are implicated. Combining documentary footage of Cairene streets alongside deeply stilted acting (to be fair, it seems partly intentional), and a film crew heavily prefiguring the creation of a film-within-a-film, *The Story of the Original and the Copy* represents an odd break in the predominant norms of narrative filmmaking. The director's attempt to create something new altogether—by frequently breaking the fourth wall, and combining traditional storytelling tropes inspired by *One Thousand and One Nights*—points to a new wave of documentary filmmaking which in turn represents the dialectical shift and breakdown of Nasserite ideology. The world no longer made any sense, and there was no central "message" or thesis statement that could bring together the fragments left behind. In a rather bittersweet development, Madkour Thabet would go on to produce several television documentaries celebrating the heyday of the newsreel, when "honesty" was not always such a "miserable word."

This collapse in what could be considered the common language of the documentary—which first appeared in its most coherent form, the newsreel—would continue well into the early 1980s. Despite there being a number of truly avant-garde filmmakers who left an indelible mark on the documentary genre,[16] perhaps no one could be considered more postmodern than Hossam Ali, who foresaw the significant shift in the medium's aesthetics, and its progression into the digital age. Through films such as *The Exhibition* (1985) and *The Harvest* (1987), among others, he predicted the onset of the digital format, and the influence of video art: a single shot expressing more sardonic commentary than the exasperating wails of a violin or other sonic "techniques" endemic to documentary film styles of the 1960s and early 1970s. The singular framing of newsreels produced during Nasser's time would be broken down into its most elemental fragments, devoid of an overarching voice-over, and a desire to move away from telling the audience how and what to think.

The legacy of Nasser's ideology and the ways in which it was portrayed on film was thus turned on its head, and the inversion is exemplified by a new language that shuns easy conclusions.

Postscript

While filmmakers such as Hossam Ali worked in their own quiet and diligent way to rejuvenate the documentary form, the newsreel as it was once known became the province of television. But instead of the slickly produced works that progenitors such as Hassan Mourad worked so hard to create within a governmental framework, they turned into hour-long segments, completely devoid of character, with no real antecedents in cinema history. This development mirrors in many ways the nature of Hosni

Mubarak's presidency, an arid study in governmental condescension that did not even pretend to offer any thoughtful observation on the nation's destiny. Documentaries featuring archival footage were prevalent in 1990s television, but they usually focused on the October War or the 1952 Revolution, and painfully little else. The sense of pageantry as evidenced in the newsreel footage of Hassan Murad's death in 1970 (*Hassan Murad in Memoriam*, 1970) was all but gone, and in place of earnest, cheering crowds were paid extras disguised as peasants—the carefully constructed mise en scène of the newsreels as created in Nasser's era were stripped of any latent sincerity and instead diminished to cheap props bolstering a morally and intellectually corrupt regime.

Serious documentarians who continued to work during Mubarak's era began to focus their energies elsewhere. For instance, 'Atiyyat al-Abnudi's *Permissible Dreams* (*al-Ahlam al-mumkina*, 1983) was an important breaking point in her career, in that it was the first film she attempted to sell to the BBC and other European networks. The mid-1990s were a significant period of paralysis, and television production dwindled tremendously, as did cinema. It is no wonder then, that the compendium detailing the life of the newsreel mentioned earlier here notes its end date as 1995. The need for alternative voices, or even clever marketing for the regime's policies, was not considered important, thus forcing filmmakers to look elsewhere for funding and support. Egyptians were no longer the target audience for documentary cinema, and even proper news reportage became the domain of private satellite television stations or foreign entities. The thinking among a broad spectrum of filmmakers still working within the realm of documentary filmmaking was that their work could debut abroad, and then be seen by the Egyptian public two or three years later on a private channel, if at all. The crafting of a national identity was no longer a driving concern. And in direct opposition to the past inclination to capture major events "live," or include vibrant pictures of Cairo's bustling streets, the people's sense of ownership over their own filmic depiction dissipated, much like everything else.

Somewhere along the line, Bayoumi, who first pioneered the form and had stopped cooperating with Misr Newsreels, mentions in his memoir, *The Unknown Soldier: Diaries and Colloquialisms*, the production of newsreels—his first passion project—was unlawfully taken from him by the government, and he was eventually forced out of his own enterprise. Bayoumi, a documentary filmmaker who represented the first true wave of revolutionary thinking, was stuck in a no-man's land, his desire to create completely independent work portraying the reality of his fellow countrymen consistently thwarted. He plaintively wrote on November 21, 1946:

The first cry is against the oppressors and dictators,
The second cry from losing your rights and lawsuits,
The third cry when time forsakes us.

His career having suffered tremendously at the hands of the state, his final denouement here eerily echoes the frustrations of other filmmakers who later followed in his footsteps, trapped in the twilight between state-produced media—with all their dangers and pratfalls—or no production at all. Like much of Egypt's film history, the negatives have been destroyed, and we have been left with the positive iterations, which tell only half the story. But from the remaining shards time has thought not to forsake, the reclamation of national personhood was, for a brief moment, not a fairytale.

References

Abu Sir, 'Abd al-Halim. 1995. *Jaridat Misr al-natiqa 1955–1995*. Cairo: State Information Service.

Baechlin, Peter, and Maurice Muller-Strauss. 1952. *Newsreels Across the World*. Paris: UNESCO.

al-Disuqi, Ibrahim, Muhammad al-Qaylubi, and Hilmi Sami, eds. 2010. *al-Sinima al-misriya al-samita al-watha'iqiya (1897–1930)* [Silent Egyptian Documentary Cinema (1897–1930)]. Cairo: Ministry of Culture.

Hassan Murad in Memoriam (Zikrat Hassan Murad). 1970. Arab newsreel. Director unknown. Tape Ref. No. 94/17655. Cairo: State Television.

Labor Day ('Id al-'ummal). 1968. Arab newsreel. Directed by Hassan Murad. Tape Ref. No. 94/17655. Cairo: State Television.

Mar'i, Diya'. 1979. "Tarikh al-jarida fi Misr." Master's thesis, High Institute of Cinema, Cairo.

Baratiera, Daniela. 2009. "Terrorists and Veils. *The Battle of Algiers* Four Decades Later" In *Rethinking Third Cinema: The Role of Anti-colonial Media and Aesthetics in Postmodernity*, edited by Frieda Erkotto and Adeline Koh. 11-31. Berlin: LIT Verlag.

Opening of New Iron-Rolling Plant in Helwan (Iftitah masna' li-darfalat al-hadid fi Hilwan). 1966. Arab newsreel. Directed by Hassan Murad. Tape Ref. No. 94/17655. Cairo: State Television.

Schefer, Raquel. 2016. "The Return of the Newsreel (2011–2016): Contemporary Cinematic Representations of the Political Event." *Cinema Comparat/ive Cinema* 4, no. 9: 61–70.

Thabet, Madkour. 1971. *Hikayat al-asl wa-l-sura*. Cairo: State Television.

———. 1998. *Sihr ma fat fi-kinuz al-mar'iyyat*. Cairo: State Television, Ministry of Culture.

Williams, Tami. 2014. *Germaine Dulac: A Cinema of Sensations*. Urbana: University of Illinois Press.

11

FROM POETICS OF REVOLUTION TO THE POETICS OF THE HUMAN: VOICE-OVER IN EGYPTIAN DOCUMENTARY, 1956–82

Viola Shafik

The gap between image and voice breeds ideology. (Chanan 2007, 129)

I n 1957 French filmmaker Chris Marker directed *Letters from Siberia (Lettres de Sibérie,)*, what I would call a documentary parody in which he repeated the same film sequence of found material three times, each time equipped with another voice-over commentary, different in tone and content (Chanan 2007, 128). He thus gave the viewer a profound lesson in how "the semantic domination of the voice imposes itself on the image" (Chanan 2007, 129), or in other words, the extent to which a commentary can fundamentally alter the perception of one and the same identical piece of film. Consequently, Marker made each of the different segments convey a totally different ideological message, while the same set of images of people, nature, and city life in Yakutsk, Siberia remained unaltered.

In the following analysis of a small, selected, rather exemplary number of Egyptian documentaries, I will argue that the ideology generating fissure between voice and image may be a useful way to understand and dissect the opposing attitudes and aesthetic choices of so-called revolutionary[1] and postrevolutionary, Nasserist and post-Nasserist documentary filmmakers in Egypt in the time span between 1952 and 1982, and their relation to the concurrent political leadership. In the framework of this generational and ideological gap, the use, or conversely the waiving, of the anonymous voice-over commentary or so-called Voice of God became a major field of contestation, as well as an ideological marker setting apart the new documentary school in Egypt from what came before, with regard to the modernist project as it developed in the framework of the anticolonial struggle for independence, advocated by the post-independence regime.

One major impediment to the study of this work, it should be added, is the fact that many films from this period have been lost, destroyed, or made inaccessible. The most prominent causes of this loss are two fires: one at Studio Misr—an important center of production of the time, consuming most of the prerevolutionary production—and a second in a temporary storeroom of the public Arts Department (Maslahat al-funun). The latter wiped out some of what had been produced after independence until 1967 (Mar'i 2003, 29–30). Not less impactful on the loss of, or difficulty in finding, films from that period is the still ongoing negligence and state bureaucracy with regard to much of what was produced after 1952, due to the fact that the state and its different organs were the main producers of the format (cf. Mar'i 2003). Some of the films discussed here seem to have survived only as digitized versions of run-down VHS copies.

Film and Ideology

But what is ideology in the first place and how is it translated into film? Ideology is certainly more than an expression of false consciousness along Marxist lines (Rodriguez 1997, 260), even if it contributes to "play a part in a situation of domination" (Rodriguez 1997, 268). If equated with moral beliefs, shaping opinions, and the "texture of social conduct," it does not necessarily exclude rational considerations (Rodriguez 1997, 266–67), nor is there a critical position above ideology. In other words, my own analysis here may be methodological but is not unaffected by ideology. I am guided by my wish to reevaluate positions in certain Egyptian documentaries within their sociopolitical context, to search and speak for an aesthetically liberated and liberating cinema. Without wanting to pit the rhetorical or expository mode (Nichols 1981, 172ff) against more emancipatory forms, I would like to mention briefly Jacques Rancière's often-quoted triad of the "regime of the Arts" as it inhabits the realm of politics (Muhle 2008, 8–10). Rancière perceives a division into three historically consecutive yet not radically separated regimes: the ethical (didactic), the representational (hierarchic), and the aesthetic (emancipatory, revolutionary) (Muhle 2008, 12–13).

With regard to the two waves of Egyptian documentary filmmaking in question here, I would argue that those of the post-1967 generation struggled to liberate themselves from the stifling ethical and representational regimes of the Nasserist era, and shifted toward more expressive and at times postmodernist modes of representation, without being able to fully establish a connection to this new aesthetic regime. The basic dilemma of the first generation of documentary filmmaking in Egypt that began to emerge in the 1950s is that the most active filmmakers considered themselves revolutionary, but at the same time were embracing an evident didacticism and fostered state-modernism. Hence, in the eyes of the young generation the founding fathers became guilty of a collaboration too close to the regime, which rendered their work a celebration of the revolution and "the role of the state instead of those who carried out the labor" (Ramzi 1988, 31).

Indeed, much of what was produced in the field of nonfiction from the 1940s onward—if we review and believe the records comprising financiers, titles, and brief synopses of mostly perished works—was concerned with national, cultural, and technological progress and development, all of which is integral to modernist ideas. A great many of them had been commissioned by enterprises or ministries, or later produced by public entities concerned with documentary film production.[2] Modernism in this respect does not denote the artistic modernism of twentieth-century arts but rather the defensive flip side of colonialist Orientalism, namely, the dualism of progress and underdevelopment as based on the presumed civilizational gap between the strong, powerful West and its subject colonies.

Post-independence Nasserism made use of this particular defensive modernist stance as it expressed itself not only in film but more generally in contemporary popular Egyptian culture (cf. Armbrust 1996; cf. Shafik 2007). It was enriched with populist, socialist, and anti-imperialist elements, particularly after the so-called Tripartite Aggression against Egypt following Nasser's nationalization of the Suez Canal in 1956 and the country's turn toward the Soviet Union in search of technical and political assistance that would permit the realization of the biggest national project of the time, the construction of the Aswan High Dam. The objective of collecting and regulating the waters of the Nile was meant to enhance agriculture but also to provide the electricity that would boost industrialization, including heavy industry such as steel and iron production, and consequently bring prosperity to and improve the living conditions of all Egyptians. The price to be paid in return, namely the dislocation of Nubian tribes and the destruction of ancient monuments, was downplayed if not disregarded.

However, idealism and hopes of social justice and national sovereignty associated with this movement and its ideology collapsed in the aftermath of the 1967 defeat against Israel, at a time when the dam had not been fully completed. The strong disillusionment that followed al-naksa, or "the setback" as the defeat was called, and Nasser's death in 1970, coincided with the appearance of a new generation of filmmakers who slowly turned their focus away from imperialism and technical progress toward Egyptians themselves and, consequently, to questions of cultural identity. Moreover, while the pioneers had called for state intervention and were instrumental in creating a public cinema infrastructure, subsequent, largely locally trained documentarists had to deal with the negative side effects of state involvement. Particularly as times and politics changed under the new president, Anwar al-Sadat, they struggled to survive economically and artistically.

Voice-over and Ideology

The essential query is, of course, why in the 1970s did some Egyptian documentarists start to reject the hitherto prevalent voice-over? One possible yet incomplete answer is that the general trend in the evolution of cinema worldwide also reflected positions developed in Egypt, particularly if we consider the fact that the most influential representatives of the first generation had strong ties to the foundational British documentary movement initiated by its architect, John Grierson. For this movement but also elsewhere, the "disembodied" voice-over was one of the big challenges (but also continuation of illustrated lectures) since the introduction of synchronous sound to film theaters in the late 1920s, and reflected decisively on the formal choices made for documentary (cf. Öhner 2013; cf. Wolfe 2016).

In an era when simultaneous sound recording outside the studios was still costly and complicated, and thus the use of direct testimonies rare, the motivation to inform, educate, and mobilize was on the rise. The spoken commentary facilitated these tasks enormously. Hence, as Grierson admitted in an interview, which in turn was used by Bill Nichols to interpret his school as primarily "expository," the documentary film "ceased exploring into the poetic use of documentary with us in the 30's" (Nichols 1981, 171). In line with this argument, some have suggested that, typically, these oratory formats resorted to an "invisible voice that inflects the film's whole mode of address" (Chanan 2007, 116). Consequently, the voice-over came to be seen as a locus of ideological transmission. Since the 1960s, new avant-gardist and leftist-oriented artistic waves, such as the French cinéma verité or the politically active American direct cinema, followed this logic and discredited almost entirely the so-called disembodied and "omniscient" Voice of God as "overwhelmingly didactic," "supposedly authoritarian yet often presumptuous" (Nichols 1988, 48).

It is evident that related debates and attitudes to the use of the voice-over have been tainted by their own ideological blind spots and tended to disregard the actual creative use that was made of voices and orators in combination with image and music in many early sound films. This includes those directed or produced by Grierson, which even Bill Nichols admitted later could be also "poetic and evocative" (Nichols 1988, 48). As much as these productions pursued "sociological rather than aesthetic aims," according to Paul Rotha, a colleague of Grierson, they strove for a "creative treatment of actuality" (Bruzzi 2006, 121). With their reform-oriented intentions, however, they were marked for some by their ambivalent if not paternalistic attitude toward the working classes (cf. Winston 1988). Notwithstanding, in a number of classical 1930s documentaries, it is precisely what Charles Wolfe prefers to call the "voice-off" that induces moments of subjectivity, body, and a location from where to speak through the way in which voices are cast and how they perform (Wolfe 2016, 273).

The Griersonian model played a crucial role in Egyptian development, due to the direct link between British and Egyptian documentary filmmaking. The latter—and this needs to be underlined—evolved in a colonial moment when Egypt was still under de facto British rule, while anticolonial nationalist and patriotic sentiments among many Egyptians were at their highest. Little wonder that a number of the first-generation documentarists in Egypt received training at the hands of the British and felt indebted to Grierson and his school, most prominently Saad Nadim, one of the founding fathers of Egyptian documentary. This did not, however, prevent him and others from attacking British politics, particularly after 1956.

Saad Nadim, in fact, is said to have coined the Arabic term *al-film al-tasjily* (*sajala*, "to record") for documentary (Ramzi 1988, 28) that is often used either synonymously with, or in opposition to, *al-film al-watha'iqi* (*wathaqa*, "to document"). In 1946, Nadim was able to convince the Studio Misr administration of the necessity of the Short Film Unit because of a script he wrote for a documentary and thirty meters of film he shot privately of the fishermen at al-Mattariya village in al-Daqahliya (Ramzi 1988, 9ff), and was consequently put in charge of Studio Misr's documentary film unit. Later, in 1950, he was sent to Britain for further training. The studio's previous documentaries had focused on spectacular events, such as the wedding of Princess Fawziya to the Shah of Iran in 1939, but these were no more than "trial runs" (Ezz Eldine 1962, 2). Moreover, in the years of the Second World War, from 1939 to 1945, Studio Misr had hosted the production of the Cairo-based British War Pictorial News (*Jaridat al-harb al-musawara*), which was, according to other sources, issued from 1940 to 1946 (Mar'i 2003, 67).

During his time in Britain Nadim met Paul Rotha, and attended lectures by Carel Reitz and a training program run by John Grierson (Ramzi 1988, 18). Even though he did not witness firsthand the deposing of the Egyptian king in 1952, his earlier vita and his subsequent films show that Nadim must have admired and shared the patriotic and anti-imperialist orientation of Nasser, who finally came to power in 1953. As a student he was politically active, attended demonstrations (Ramzi 1988, 5) and later is said to have been a member of the Avant-Garde of the Socialist Union

(Mar'i 2003, 128). His ardent patriotism is more than evident in his iconic 1956 production *Let the World Witness (Fa li-yashhad al-'alam)*, which was translated into eight different languages and, most importantly, created a stir in Great Britain itself for being a successful propagandistic counterattack vis-à-vis the Nasserist regime (Ramzi 1988, 23).

The film denounces the destruction of Port Said as a result of the Tripartite Aggression by Israel, France, and Great Britain in 1956, after the nationalization of the Suez Canal the same year. It starts first by portraying Port Said before the attacks, praising its modernity, the infrastructural achievements, and its ethnic and religious diversity, and then moves on to depict the horrific effect of the warfare through images of fire, destruction, and mutilated bodies. The main vehicle for the argument of the film in conjunction with this frightening visual account is indeed the accusatory commentary, which at one point forthrightly describes the British involvement as a crime, while the city of Port Said "embodies the fight of the nations for their liberation" because it resists "foreign forces who want to impose slavery and to terminate life." The film offers a clear political argument that explains the source of the conflict and incites sentiments against the aggressor.

The orchestral music contributes to an emotionally affective atmosphere, for example in a scene in which the construction of modern buildings is depicted while we hear a joyful piano staccato. The voice-over claims this was a housing project for workers, then continues concomitantly with a pictorial depiction of modern schools that form part of the public education plan, of churches and mosques that underline religious coexistence, electricity and sewage plants, summer beaches and playgrounds and parades, where—according to the commentator—locals and foreigners enjoy themselves side by side. We see ships making their passage through the canal as the commentator mentions its nationalization, explaining that the British claimed this would disrupt use of the waterway until October 29. One quick animated white explosion disrupts the flow of images at this point and is followed by shots of destroyed bridges and sunken ships. Here, the narrator turns to accuse the British themselves of having disrupted navigation through the canal by their military aggression.

This was not the only agitprop film Nadim authored. *The Road to Peace (al-Tariq illa al-salam,* 1966), on poverty in the world and the immense costs of war, earned him an award at the GDR Leipzig Film Festival from the Union of the Friendship of the People. Nadim was only one of several transmitters of British documentary conventions in Egypt. Another important catalyst was the Shell Oil Company Film Unit, which came into existence in 1952 and remained active until its nationalization in 1959. It issued a newsreel called Pictures of Life, which became the training ground for two of the subsequently most important "old-school" documentary filmmakers, Salah al-Tuhami and Hasan al-Tilmisani, among others. One of its episodes, *Renaissance of History (Ba'th al-tarikh)*, was directed by Salah al-Tuhami in 1955, and features the spectacular transportation of the Ramsis II colossus from Memphis to the center of Cairo. Its classical Arabic commentary is illustrative and interpretative at the same time. It comments, for example, on the workers' efforts to move the colossus: "In the sacred precinct of the statue the workers started to pave the way, to design the course of labor, self-assured and faithful, sensing how it is enveloped by history."

11.1. *Renaissance of History* (1955), directed by Salah al-Tuhami.

11.2. *Renaissance of History* (1955), directed by Salah al-Tuhami.

11.3. *Renaissance of History* (1955), directed by Salah al-Tuhami.

Watching the workers in their worn-out attire supervised by the well-dressed engineers, surrounding the machinery that drags the statue while they try to catch a glimpse of the camera, leaves us to question if they indeed *felt* that sense of history which the orator so eloquently invokes. Not all films from this period display such a direct and verbally suggestive mode of address. Some produce a rather sophisticated and at times also poetic interaction among commentary, voice, music, and editing, like *O Nile* (*Ya Nil*, 1963) by Hasan al-Tilmisani—in essence an audiovisual ode to the Nile—based on an idea by Saad Nadim, who also produced it.

In fact the commentary in this film is a colloquial poem conceived and read by Salah Jahin, who was nicknamed the "poet of the revolution" (Radwan 2012, 126). He speaks to the river directly, praises its existence and its history, goes on to explain the annual alternations between flood and drought, pleads with the river to be gentle and to save the harvests, while we observe images of crops, fields, and peasants trying to reinforce dams. He addresses "the thirsty land that has been cracked open, each crack like a lip crying for the Nile, O Nile," and a chorus responds singing the poem's refrain, "Ya Nil" (O Nile). "Don't worry," the poet continues,

> patience has an end. Red water is coming, rose syrup, sweet for drinking. Water is running agreeably, its taste will fill you, earth, to the top with love and odes, brought by your beloved Nile. It's bringing you a gift, a green scarf to adorn yourself after it has stayed away for so long, longing for you. O fasting earth! Patience desists.

A popular workers' song gets interjected: "Hala hala, salli 'ala al-nabi" (Praise the Prophet!). Then we see a stunning scene of a dam breaking to let through the dark fertile waters. Finally, the poet, mourning the loss of the annual disappearance of the waters into the sea without being held back, leads to shots displaying the construction of the High Dam.

Like other documentaries of the period, poem and film advocate the construction of the dam but, in this case, in a rather creative, visually and rhythmically stylized manner. As such, it recalls Basil Wright's lyrical *Song of Ceylon* (1934), a Grierson production that similarly juxtaposes a modernist stance, advertising trade within the empire with a poetic form that describes a premodern situation. The accompanying illustrative orchestral music in *O Nile*, composed by Sulayman Jamil, mimics with its specific recurrent motifs the actions and movements in the frame, such as the flow of the waters or the workers' endeavors to reinforce the shores. Much like the oratory, the music maintains a close relationship to the visuals as it responds periodically to the spoken word with a sung refrain.

Within the framework of recent Western perception, poetry is likely to be seen as a "species of composition which is opposed to works of science by proposing for its immediate object pleasure, not truth" (Renov 1993, 14). Yet in his discussion of the poetics of documentary, Michael Renov recalls the etymological roots of the Greek "poesis," which means "active making," which was originally linked to knowledge production and "couched in the active mood of scientific inquiry in the way it addressed the aesthetic domain with an epistemological urgency" (Renov 1993, 16). Following this logic, Renov proposed to analyze documentary as well through the lens of poesis and suggested four fundamental "poetic" documentary tendencies, namely to record, reveal, or preserve; to persuade or promote; to analyze or interrogate; and finally, to express.

One is tempted to dissect *O Nile* as an expressive documentary. However, its ending shows that it clearly also intends to promote the High Dam and persuade audiences of its necessity. It juxtaposes ancient history, as represented by the Nile and its untamed natural forces, on the one hand, and the need for technological control and progress, in the shape of the High Dam, for the sake of the nation's welfare on the other. Poetry here shifts from being an aesthetic expression and alternative form of knowledge production to an evident will to persuade and promote a modernist project at the very heart of this postcolonial national formation. This adds a very specific notion of national and cultural identity to its use of verbal poetry.

Even though its author and reciter is never seen in person, his recognizable voice adds a personalized, if not subjective, perspective to the film. It equips it with a very specific locus and locality with which it contradicts, even subverts, one of the main political cornerstones of Nasserism, namely pan-Arabism. This ideological movement, which was actually born in the nineteenth century, had its heyday in Egypt with the unification agreement between Syria and Egypt under the umbrella of the United Arab Republic. It was proclaimed in 1958 and ended in 1961, two years before the making of *O Nile*. Jahin's poem, however, is composed entirely in Egyptian colloquial Arabic, as it has been spoken in the country's main metropolis, Cairo, and more generally in Egyptian cinema since the 1930s. It thereby embeds itself in a specific cultural context and unique locality, namely the Nile Valley, with its Ancient Egyptian roots so distinct from other Arab countries.

It is noteworthy that since the 1950s, Jahin had contributed decisively to the promotion of colloquial Egyptian poetry (*shi'r al-'ammiya*). More recently, this poetry has been regarded as one strand of modernist Arab poetry (Radwan 2012, 38ff) that departed from the highbrow canon of *fusha* (classical Arabic) poetry. Apart from formal and thematic differences, the first is characterized by a lack of authoritative tone. The poet has ceased to be an advisor, critic, or hero (Radwan 2012, 62); he is "part of the world, deeply affected by its ills and virtues. While the 'Voltairean poet' only 'acts upon events,' the modernist poet is 'acted upon by them'" (Radwan 2012, 63). In juxtaposing the colloquial to poetry and to documentary, whose commentary had been hitherto confined to classical Arabic, the film discursively unsettles the symbolical order and its hierarchies without necessarily contradicting the core arguments of official modernist ideology. Moreover, it also adds a level of subjectivity that is expressed in the simplicity and loving tenderness audible in Jahin's voice and words, which defy any possible authoritarian mode of address or revolutionary fervor.

The Second Generation: Toward a Postmodern Poetics?

In April 1967, two months before the defeat, the documentary filmmakers Fouad al-Tuhami, Hasan al-Tilmisani, and Saad Nadim, who were members of the Avant-garde of the Arab Socialist Union (the ruling party at the time), submitted a petition asking for the foundation of a National Documentary Film Center (al-Markaz al-qawmi li-l-aflam al-tasjiliya), a demand which was granted the same year. Soon after, in 1969, the National Documentary Film Center was restructured into two entities, the Arab Agency for Cinema (al-Wikala al-'arabiya li-l-sinima, 1969–71) and the Experimental Film Center (EFC, also Experimental Film Unit), directed by filmmaker and production designer Shadi Abdel Salam. The first was supposed to foster commercial production and distribution, while the second was meant to boost the arts of nonfiction.

In 1971 the National Documentary Film Center (NDFC) was nominally reinstalled with the declared task of producing and distributing documentary, short film, and animation, while the Experimental Film Center remained active for a while. Simultaneously, at least until 1973, the financial responsibility for the NDFC was shuffled around between the Ministry of Culture, the General Film Organization, and the Cinema Body (Hay'at al-sinima). Even after the responsibilities were settled, the NDFC's production was still in jeopardy because of recurrent financial crises. In 1977 only four films saw the light, after an average annual output of twelve films in the five preceding years. In comparison, Abdel Salam's short-lived EFC produced even less, a total of only six films between 1969 and 1974 (Mar'i, 2003, 41–46).

In this period of political and administrative turmoil, and against all odds, a handful of exceptional works by aspiring young directors started setting a new tone, indirectly criticizing the social and political system. They tackled persistent "underdevelopment," complained about deficient governmental services, and highlighted the huge amount of social injustice that had not diminished despite Nasser's quasi-socialist experiments, and even more so in the light of the subsequent reorientation toward the West and neoliberal economy under Sadat after he took power in 1970. The inadequate financial means these filmmakers were offered, and the huge administrative obstacles they had to face due to the very same governmental institutions, unquestionably affected the technical and artistic standard of their output. Because of the outmoded equipment and the very limited quantity of film stock they had at their disposal, their works needed to be tightly scripted beforehand. Also, sound and image were to be recorded separately. Despite all the difficulties, particularly those films produced or inspired by the EFC exhibited their own unique style and departed from the previous documentary modes significantly.

Shadi Abdel Salam served as the Center's director from 1969 to 1975, most probably at the instance of the then minister of culture, Tharwat 'Ukasha (in office 1958–70), who was himself an ardent defender of film arts as opposed to commerce ('Ukasha 1990, 770ff). He tried to set the standard for a new approach to documentary. Abdel Salam was an acclaimed set and costume designer and innovative filmmaker, whose film *The Mummy*, also known as *The Night of Counting the Years* (*al-Mumya'*, 1969), won top awards at the Venice Film Festival; it remains, to date, the most celebrated art house film in Egyptian film history. Moreover, he was a personal friend of Roberto Rossellini, and, most importantly, a strong spokesman for dropping the voice-over completely, focusing on the image as a major means of expression.

A prime example of his artistic orientation is his nonfiction film *Horizons* (*Afaq*, 1972), an audiovisual symphony devoid of any narration (the only spoken words are a theater scene from Shakespeare's *Hamlet* performed in Arabic). The film is dedicated to Egyptian arts and artists as they presented themselves in the year 1971. Despite being a state production, his film has an implicit anti-government attitude. As the director recalls, officials had asked him to portray the activities of the Ministry of Culture; in other words, he was supposed to deliver an "information film" (*film i'lami*), a request he first resented and eventually subverted.

> The country was in a state of grief and disgust because of the defeat. I realized that, except for institutions, it was first of all individuals and children who were culturally active. I started to discover that there is an ongoing life despite the nightmare. I realized that the film is giving me the opportunity to show beautiful things in our lives that are hidden because they are far from any spotlights without anyone to discover them. . . . I made the film without a word of commentary and did not try to enforce a connection between the twelve elements which the film displays within 40 minutes. ('Abd al-Rahman and Mar'i 1994, 16–17; author's translation)

The film required one year of editing. On the sonic level, it weaves in and out of music, uses sound bridges, starts for example with a classical music rehearsal at the opera and moves on visually, while the music lingers to become extradiegetic. Visually it uses smooth transitions, first and foremost with camera movements like slow tracking, and pans to switch from one space, one form of art, to another. Sometimes this strategy is used within one and the same environment, as in the historical library where the camera tours through the aisles just to meet the eye of a second camera. In another instance the camera enters the studio of a modern painter, who then is followed to his window where he starts playing with a small sailboat, a traditional paper-and-wood toy, on which the take ends. This interplay merges all types of art production, from weaving to painting, from sculpting to brass handicraft, from lute to orchestral music, bringing together the modern, traditional, popular, classical, foreign, local, highbrow and lowbrow threads. *Horizons* does not just produce a hodgepodge of these aspects, but in fact subverts the categories and their attached hierarchies through its equalizing aesthetic representation, and in so doing, it seems to acquire a rather postmodernist stance, making it quite a unique piece, even in comparison to other works of the same period.

While the Experimental Film Center's productions often focused on art and monuments (for an example of monuments, see for instance Samir 'Uf's *Pearl of the Nile* (*Lu'lu'at al-Nil*, 1972) on the Philae Temple), and were thus more plainly interested in history, a variety of other productions took a considerable interest in the life and work conditions of the rural population and the lower classes, in another departure from the developmental and populist stances of the previous generation. The most notable examples here are Attiat El-Abnoudi's student film *Horse of Mud* (*Husan al-tin*, 1971), and Hashim al-Nahas' *The Nile Is Fortunes* (*al-Nil arzaq*, 1972), produced by the NDFC. They adhered to the methods of observational direct cinema and set aside the oratory voice-over entirely.

In addition, al-Nahas avoided synchronous sound and speech. Dialogue or songs performed by protagonists did not serve as auxiliary to the images in his films; rather, he regarded them as independent elements, weaving them into an expressive fabric or contemplative "mosaic" (Nichols 1981, 211). He did this, to use Renov's words, in a way in which "each sequence [is] a semi-autonomous, temporally explicit unit in itself, contributing to an overall but non-narrative depiction of the filmed institution" (Renov 1993, 25), through which he could comment on social conditions in a nonverbal manner. Al-Nahas, who recounts analyzing some of Eisenstein's montage scenes meticulously, seems to have followed the ideas of early Soviet and British sound documentary, which opted for the creative, contrapuntal rather than synchronous use of sound to enhance its poetic and expressive potential (Öhner 2013, 100–101).

The Nile Is Fortunes is a case in point. Shot in black and white, it focuses on the bodily movements related to physical labor performed on the Nile and its shores, as can be seen in the opening montage of men and women rowing, fishing, watering the fields, climbing the mast of a sail boat. It continues with diverse shots of ships on the Nile, sailing, docking, ferrying people; the loading and unloading of goods like gravel, stones, hay; the ancient brick production; and the dam construction. This is accompanied by close-ups and short observations of people: passengers, workers, fishermen and their families, ending with the latter eating, and the washing, mending, and eventually throwing out their fishing nets to harvest what the river offers them. At this point comes a sudden change of scenery: from a fish caught in the nets, the film cuts to fish being prepared and grilled to be offered to the customers at a fish restaurant, followed by close-ups of a bourgeois couple enjoying their leisure time with a common meal, a scene which is accompanied by mundane electronic music that stands in stark contrast to the discreet non-diegetic melody of a guitar inserted intermittently during the rest of the film. After this intermezzo, which is certainly to be read as a commentary on class difference in Egypt, the film closes with pictures of the same set of people seen at the beginning, most notably a fisherwoman—still rowing the boat—breastfeeding her child.

Hashim al-Nahas has remained quite faithful to his style over the years, despite criticism. *The Nile Is Fortunes* was praised by fellow filmmaker Sami al-Salamuni as a "new model of Egyptian documentary," but dismissed simultaneously for its "lack of opinion and commentary on what

11.4. *The Nile is Fortunes* (1972), directed by Hashim al-Nahas.

happens," or in short for its "descriptiveness" (Abu Shadi, n.d., 63). *The Well* (*al-Bi'r*, 1982), also by al-Nahas, shows the same "descriptive" inclination. Shot in color a decade later, it depicts the daily life of a tribe located in the Western Desert, in Marsa Matruh province near the Libyan border. In this undeniably ethnographic account, al-Nahas does not contextualize his observations historically, nor are his protagonists personalized, nor does he compare the conditions to other places in Egypt as he did in his previous film. He focuses solely on a cultural depiction through work and habits, meaning that it may be easily read as the kind of observational cinema that, in echoing a critique leveled at Malinowski's anthropological work, was compared by David MacDougall with a "descriptive synthesis of events" that "lacks theoretical integration" (MacDougall 2016, 568). Interestingly, al-Nahas' declared concern has been the "Egyptian human,"[3] and, consequently, his country's cultural identity. This orientation may also be detected in his parallel work as a researcher, editing and writing film books, such as his pivotal publication, *The National Identity of Arab Cinema* (*al-Hawiya al-qawamiya li-l-sinima al-'arabiya*, 1986). The mere interest in these marginal communities and the implied humanism in the wake of the Nasserist era and after the implementation of Sadat's Open Door Policy is a statement in this regard.

Unlike Hashim al-Nahas, other directors who worked with the EFC, most prominently Daoud Abd El-Sayed, who later became an acclaimed fiction filmmaker, reacted ironically to the new dictum of visual supremacy. In 1975 Abd El-Sayed authored an effusive parody of the didactic voice-over instead of relinquishing it. His *A Wise Man's Advice in Matters of Village and Education* (*Wasiyyat rajul hakim fi shu'un al-qarya wa-l-ta'lim*, 1975), in fact an early "mockumentary," introduces an off-narrator who enthusiastically warns of the negative effects of modern school education and literacy in the Egyptian countryside and replaces the modernist developmental discourse with a solely class-defined bourgeois perspective. As in the previously mentioned film by Chris Marker, it is the rhetoric of the narrator that redefines the observational images of the village and its inhabitants.

In contrast, around the same time, Khairy Beshara, who later also turned to fiction film, delivered a highly sensitive and poetic portrait of a *Village Doctor* (*Tabib fi-l-aryaf*, 1976) that scrutinizes the role of the educated urban elite and its ambivalent relationship to the rural masses. The film was produced by Saad Nadim and the re-established NDFC, which means it came after Abdel Salam's short intervention through the EFC, yet it makes a highly personalized use of the voice-over delivered by its main protagonist, a countryside doctor. Dr. Khalil Muhammad Fadil runs the medical center at al-'Amariya al-Sharqiya village in al-Minya province (Upper Egypt) and shares his experiences as the doctor of this small village. The film shows him struggling to secure the necessary medications from the state bureaucracy, examining the sick at the clinic, and socializing with his assistants during his leisure time. From his narration we understand that he is of urban origin but has deliberately chosen to move to the countryside. The film ends with him traveling back home to marry and bring his future wife to the village.

The film's introductory voice-over narration is spoken by the doctor in semi-classical Arabic while the camera pans from the silent filmmaker, who is seated on one side of a table, to the doctor on the other. In the shot that follows, the protagonist is seen in full action while he is receiving medicines from the provincial city depot. The ensuing dialogue between the doctor and the depot employee, who explains that he cannot have the desired amount, discusses bureaucratic deficiencies. This conversation is conducted entirely in colloquial Egyptian Arabic. In the course of the film, the dialogue and the doctor's commentary, which provide the narrative framework, keep switching between these two "jargons."

It can only be speculated as to why the director and his protagonist chose to use a more "elevated" language, which is still not the purely classical Arabic used by the media of the time. It unambiguously introduces the doctor as a man of letters, educated, distinct from the people to whom he caters. Hence it demonstrates the "developmental" or civilizational gap between the intellectual and the common people, a fissure that also extends to the visual representation: each time the doctor needs to cross to the other side of the river, he is carried on the shoulders of boatsmen dressed in the traditional *gallabiya* to or from the shore, in order not to wet his shoes and trousers. That this difference is one of the main themes of the film is underlined by the already mentioned introductory speech that sounds like a declaration of intention, and at the same time burdens the intellectual with the modernist civilizational duty.

> The reason for my work as a doctor in the countryside is my feeling that we, as children of this people who grew in its womb and emerged from its loins, are not supposed to play the role of a lame son who endures for the sake of labor. We should not wear the robes of pain and seem to be sent from one people to the other to fulfill a difficult task.

As in Nahas' films, the soundtrack has been heavily manipulated in postproduction, most likely to compensate for technical deficiencies. Some scenes lack the original soundtrack to the extent that the interaction seems muted; only a few synchronized words, mainly the voice of the doctor and his assistant, accompany the apparently staged action, as suggested by the continuity editing of the scenes in question. Occasional lute music and two extradiegetic local songs addressing a doctor are used to tie the sonic level to the region.

Compared to Abdel Salam's and al-Nahas' poetic approach, Beshara's film and its concern with verbal expression have an almost restorative consolidating character. It certainly pictures and problematizes the ambivalent role of the intellectual in the framework of the modernist project, but it does so without leveling out the basic hierarchies between the educated and the uneducated. It fosters, on the one hand, an almost nostalgic vision of rural life in Upper Egypt and its local culture, such as hospitality, feasts, and songs. This strongly collides with the harsh realities as expressed in the prevalent physical ailments and numerous infections of the villagers, particularly the children—some caused by lack of information and education—and which can doubtless be interpreted as signs of underdevelopment.

Moreover, it privileges the doctor's story by installing him as the sole personalized narrator, speaking from the perspective of his learned expertise, similar to the premodernist poet. True, his speech lacks the promotional, if not propagandistic, rhetorics of *O Nile* or *Let the World Witness*; however, in proposing yet again an ethical solution to the problem of underdevelopment as represented in the attitude of the intellectual, it does not really allow the expressive poetics of documentary to unfold. In other words, despite its skepticism toward the state, this film turns to modernist ideology as a promise for national salvation, and it does so formally in its particular uses of the voice-over as an important vehicle to convey its ideological message.

11.5. *Village Doctor* (1976), directed by Khairy Beshara.

In conclusion, it seems indeed that the first wave of documentaries, despite being produced at a time when fervent revolutionary ideals were still omnipresent, had little in common with revolutionary aesthetics in the sense of Rancière, not least because they were eager to promote, persuade, and represent, a mode to which the voice-over was instrumental in different ways. Only after the defeat of 1967, and particularly in the work of Shadi Abdel Salam and Hashim al-Nahas, were the expressive potentials of documentary, or its "poesis," explored in the decided absence of any spoken non-diegetic narration.

Thanks go to Magdy 'Abd al-Rahman for sharing his film collection, and to Alisa Lebow for revising this text.

References

'Abd al-Fattah, Mohammed. ed. 2016. *Hashim al-Nahas: 'Umq al-ru'ya wa sihr al-ru'ya*. Cairo: al-Jam'iya al-Misriya li-Kuttab wa Nuqqad al-Sinima.

'Abd al-Rahman, Majdy, and Salah Mar'i, eds. 1994. *Shadi 'Abdel Salam. Shu'a' min Misr. al-Qahira* 145 (December, special issue). Cairo: al-Hay'a al-Misriya al-'Amma li-l-Kitab.

Abu Shadi, Ali, ed. n.d. *al-Film al-tasjili fi Misr: Liqa'at. Dirasat*. Cairo: al-Thaqafa al-Jamahiriya.

Armbrust, Walter. 1996. *Mass Culture and Modernism in Egypt*. Cambridge: Cambridge University Press.

Bruzzi, Stella. 2006. *New Documentary*. London: Routledge.

Chanan, Michael. 2007. *The Politics of Documentary*. London: Palgrave Macmillan.

Ezz Eldine, Salah. 1962. *Report: Arab Documentary Film Production and the Use of Music in Arab Films*. UNESCO. unesdoc.unesco.org.

MacDougall, David. 2016. "Beyond Observational Cinema (1975)." In *The Documentary Film Reader: History, Theory, Criticism*, edited by Jonathan Kahana, 565–70. Oxford: Oxford University Press.

Mar'i, Diya'. 2003. *Tarikh al-sinima al-tasjiliya fi Misr*. Alexandria: Bibliotheca Alexandrina.

Muhle, Maria. 2008. „Einleitung", in: *Jacques Rancière. Die Aufteilung des Sinnlichen. Die Politik der Kunst und ihre Paradoxien*. Berlin: b-books Verlag.

Nichols, Bill. 1981. *Ideology and the Image*. Bloomington: Indiana University Press.

———. 1988. "The Voice of Documentary." In *New Challenges for Documentary*, edited by Alan Rosenthal, 48–63. Manchester: Manchester University Press.

Öhner, Vräth. 2013. "Suggestive Klänge, störende Wirklichkeiten: Die britische Schule und der Realismus des Geräuschs." In *Ton: Text zur Akustik im Dokumentarfilm*, edited by Volker Kaminsky and Julian Rohrhuber, 98–109. Berlin: Vorwerk8.

Radwan, Noha. 2012. *Egyptian Colloquial Poetry in the Modern Arabic Canon*. New York: Palgrave Macmillan.

Ramzi, Kamal. 1988. *Sa'd Nadim: Ra'id al-sinima al-tasjiliya*. Cairo: Wiz-arat al-Thaqafa/al-Markaz al-Qawmi li-l-Sinima.

Renov, Michael. 1993. "Toward a Poetics of Documentary." In *Theorizing Documentary*, edited by Michael Renov, 12–36. London: Routledge.

Rodriguez, Héctor. 1997. "Ideology and Film Culture." In *Film Theory and Philosophy*, edited by Richard Allen and Murray Smith, 260–80. Oxford: Oxford University Press.

Shafik, Viola. 2007. *Popular Egyptian Cinema: Gender, Class and Nation*. Cairo: American University in Cairo Press.

'Ukasha, Tharwat. 1990. *Mudhakirati fi-l-siyasa wa-l-thaqafa*. Cairo: Dar al-Hilal.

Winston, Brian. 1988. "The Tradition of the Victim in Griersonian Documentary." In *New Challenges for Documentary*, edited by Alan Rosenthal, 269–85. Manchester: Manchester University Press.

Wolfe, Charles. 2016. "Historicizing the Voice of God: The Place of Voice-over Commentary in Classical Documentary (1997)." In *The Documentary Film Reader: History, Theory, Criticism*, edited by Jonathan Kahana, 264–77. Oxford: Oxford University Press.

12

FROM SILHOUETTES TO SUPERSTARS: DOCUMENTING HIV/AIDS IN EGYPTIAN CINEMA

Hend F. Alawadhi

The doctor told me, "You've got AIDS; this means you are not a good person."
— Woman living with HIV, Tunisia (UNAIDS 2012, 32)

Perhaps the most unfortunate current just-world assumption is that AIDS is a moral judgment on homosexuals and intravenous drug users. (Thomson 1997, 37)

Introduction

In the latest report issued by the Joint United Nations Programme on HIV and AIDS (UNAIDS), it is estimated that 11,000 adult Egyptians were HIV-positive in 2015 (UNAIDS 2015, 2). According to the report, an estimated 230,000 people (with a possible range of 160,000 to 330,000) were living with HIV in 2016 (UNAIDS 2017). Although these statistics are some of the lowest in the world, the number of new infections in MENA rose by 52 percent between 2001 and 2012, "the most rapid increase in HIV among world regions" (Setayesh et al. 2014, 3). However, because HIV is mistakenly associated with homosexuality and recreational drug use, many people who are HIV-positive choose to keep their condition private (UNAIDS 2010, 10). Fear of discrimination, compromised anonymity, loss of employment, and lack of treatment options contribute to a widespread reluctance to even get tested. Objective, not to mention sympathetic, discussion of HIV/AIDS is so unheard of in Arab social spheres that it was not until 2012 that a public figure in the Arab world openly announced his struggle with the virus to the media. He has since disappeared into obscurity (Viney 2012).

This chapter looks at representations of HIV and AIDS in Egyptian media, focusing specifically on director Amr Salama's documentary

AIDS HIV+ in Egypt (al-Muta'ayishun ma' fairus al-AIDS fi Misr), 2007, and his subsequent feature film *Asmaa (Asma'*, 2011) (Salama, 2011). By contextualizing it among earlier films from the 1980s and 1990s, as well as contemporary media and official health publications addressing HIV/AIDS, I argue that *Asmaa* subverts the stereotypes and ideological connotations typically associated with HIV/AIDS, and critically interrogates the tropes present in Salama's earlier documentary. Although HIV/AIDS is rarely addressed publicly in the Arab world, this chapter demonstrates how the film *Asmaa* represents a shift in attitudes toward people living with HIV/AIDS (referred to hereafter as PLWHA), despite the persistence of deeply entrenched stigmas and misinformed ideas. The first section of the chapter provides a thematic analysis of the documentary and film, vis-à-vis selected accounts from contemporary media. The second section is dedicated to the cinematic techniques and conventions that *Asmaa* utilizes to clearly establish its departure from previous representations of HIV/AIDS in Egyptian cinema, focusing on certain documentary and melodrama conventions, as well as the use of flashbacks. Finally, the chapter will move beyond textual analysis in order to focus on how shifting discourses affect contemporary sociopolitical attitudes. In contrast to earlier representations in both feature films and documentaries, *Asmaa* is unique in that it attempts to dismantle the stigma that PLWHA face. There have been next to no unbiased representations of PLWHA in mainstream media, and thus *Asmaa* is uniquely positioned to change public awareness by subverting common misconceptions about HIV/AIDS.

Cultural Politics of AIDS in the Arab World

In December 2013, Qatar-based Al Jazeera, one of the world's most followed news networks, published an Arabic-language article online entitled "AIDS in the Arab World: Terrifying Numbers and Sad Facts (AIDS fi al-'alam al-'arabi, arqam mur'iba wa haqa'iq muhzina)" (Al Jazeera 2013). The article called for immediate government action, citing a 100 percent increase in AIDS cases. Engendering fear and paranoia, the article notes that AIDS is especially dangerous because it only needs to affect a small number of people before it becomes an epidemic. In a familiar pattern, the article continues to associate AIDS with homosexuality and what it considers to be indecent sexual and social behavior. It classifies the highest-risk groups as follows (in order of declining risk): gay men, sex workers and their customers, drug users, and prison inmates. However, when the article lists the "terrifying" numbers and "sad" facts about AIDS, it mentions that women are the most likely group to "get AIDS," through sex with their husbands—80 percent of HIV-positive women contracted the disease through intercourse with their husbands—thereby contradicting its previous identification of high-risk groups. The article uses reductive and confusing statements, starting with the erroneous claim that AIDS (rather than HIV) is a virus that can be caught from others. The regional media and, in turn, the general public's attitude toward HIV/AIDS are steeped in and fueled by fear, discrimination, and ignorance.

On the rare occasions that HIV/AIDS campaigns exist in the Arab world, this tendency to ignore or stigmatize seems to prevail. By default, HIV/AIDS is associated with particular frowned-upon sexual constituencies.[1] A mixture of religious and cultural conservatism, as well as influence from Western campaigns, creates a reluctance to disseminate information about how to prevent HIV transmission, such as safe-sex practices. To many conservative minds, simple solutions like distributing free condoms to the public at health clinics are seen as advocating extramarital sexual relations or, even worse, homosexuality. Male homosexuality continues to be an extremely contested and taboo issue in the Arab world. There are very strong cultural and religious connotations that put gay men at risk of social stigma and persecution. Often, homosexuality itself is not illegal, but individuals are frequently persecuted under debauchery laws. One such case was publicly filmed by Mona Iraqi, an Egyptian journalist whose television show is titled *The Hidden (al-Mistakhabbi)*. In December 2014, Iraqi went undercover to expose a bathhouse in Cairo. The resulting three-part series collapsed homosexuality, sex work, sex trafficking, and the AIDS "virus" into one threatening concept. Nearly everyone in the bathhouse was arrested publicly during a raid, with Iraqi orchestrating and filming the entire event. The episodes, although quite disturbing to watch, are available on YouTube (Iraqi 2014a; 2014b; 2014c).

Against this backdrop, Amr Salama released a short web documentary in 2007 titled *AIDS HIV+ in Egypt* in which he interviews several PLWHA. Upon their request to remain anonymous, the voices of the interviewees were modified and their faces silhouetted. The PLWHA describe the moment they discovered they were HIV-positive and their experiences with the healthcare system, family, and friends. One man recounts an incident with a doctor who refused to treat him, asking him to seek help from a pharmacy instead. They all describe the shock and isolation they experienced, citing a need to remain anonymous to protect their families and employment status. Salama also interviews Mervat al-Geneidi, a doctor working for the National AIDS Program (NAP), an initiative supported by the Egyptian Ministry of Health and Population. She is filmed talking to PLWHA in a support group in conversation about the exorbitant price of antivirals, and the difficulties of finding employment. The scene is interjected with several people explaining the importance of having support networks such as the group being filmed, where they find a rare sense of emotional connection and solidarity. Salama also interviews random pass-ersby and asks them whether they think they might be HIV-positive. Their responses reveal a physical abhorrence to the thought; some even chastise him for merely asking. This reaction extends to the hypothetical presence of PLWHA in their lives. They answer with, "I would stay away from him," "cut all relations with him," and "I would visit but keep a distance."

The documentary is roughly divided into sections through title screens that display text in English and Arabic: "What's your perspective on HIV/AIDS?!," "Fear . . . or Horror?!," "Are you HIV-positive?!," "The shock," "The need for a new world," "isolation," and "support groups." The text is accompanied with images of frustrated and worried-looking individuals, set against a vacant black background. Working within a general style of made-for-TV and web documentaries about HIV/AIDS that attempt to break stigma and provide educational interventions about testing and pre-vention, *AIDS HIV+ in Egypt* received very little traction in the Arab world. The PLWHA are filmed in darkness (to protect their anonymity), their voices distorted, and they aren't seen outside confined domestic spaces. In effect, these documentaries and reports recreate the very isolation of PLWHA that they speak against. They rely on stigmatizing tropes such as the pitting of "healthy" people against PLWHA, and allow the former to openly express fear, disdain, and a need for separation.

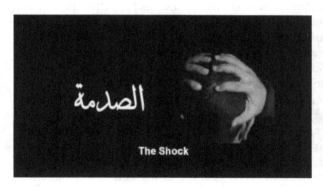

12.1. *Asmaa* (2011), directed by Amr Salama

On Amr Salama's YouTube channel, the documentary has only received 22,000 likes since December 2007. Meanwhile, copies of *Asmaa* illegally uploaded on YouTube (and often taken down) usually garner hundreds of thousands of views. Comments on these videos range from heartfelt thanks to Salama and the main protagonist, superstar Hend Sabry, for making *Asmaa*, to PLWHA looking for partners who are also HIV-pos-itive. The Arabic hashtag أسـماء_فيلم (Asmaa_film) was trending on Twitter in Egypt after it was screened on the Egyptian broadcast channel CBC

(Capital Broadcasting Center).[2] The hashtag is still active today, six years after the release of the film.[3]

What made *Asmaa* resonate so much more with its audience? Why was a docudrama more successful than a documentary in effecting change, changing at the very least people's perception of PLWHA? How was this change documented? How has *Asmaa* shifted the representation of HIV/AIDS in Egyptian media?

Positive Bodies, Contagious Stigma

Based on true events, *Asmaa* explores the traumatic circumstances that Asmaa, an HIV-positive woman, has to navigate in present-day Egypt.[4] When she develops a severe gallbladder infection, she is unable to find a doctor willing to operate on her due to cultural contempt and misinformed fears of contamination. Throughout the film, Asmaa struggles against the stigma of living with HIV in a Muslim/Arab society, and confronts her own fears of familial rejection. By focusing on an HIV-positive, working-class woman, the film attempts to dispel the connection between serostatus and moral judgment or, to phrase it differently, between "innocent HIV/AIDS" and that which is divine punishment. *Asmaa* also demonstrates how the state renders bodies marked with stigma—in this case, HIV/AIDS—as disabled and relegates them to the outskirts of society.

Asmaa is set in contemporary Cairo, Egypt's populous capital. Asmaa, played by superstar Tunisian actress Hend Sabry, hides her HIV status from everyone, including her only daughter, her father being the sole exception. From the beginning of the film, the viewer bears witness to the discrimination that Asmaa has to navigate in everyday life. A hospital employee, whom Asmaa has to bribe to schedule her for a gallbladder operation, asks her not to disclose her serostatus to the operating doctor. He tells the surgeon that "she only has hepatitis C." When Asmaa tells the surgeon, "I have AIDS," minutes before the operation starts, he refuses to operate on her.[5] At work, her manager presses her for medical examination results. She reminds Asmaa that she hired her before receiving the reports as an act of faith but that Asmaa must turn them in to retain her job as a cleaner at the airport. When Asmaa eventually and reluctantly hands in her papers, her manager is visibly appalled. Unable to fire her legally, she resorts to blackmailing Asmaa emotionally by exposing her serostatus to all of her colleagues and asking them—in front of Asmaa—whether they would want an HIV carrier to work among them. Their negative response causes Asmaa to "quit" her job.

Due to her constant fear of being exposed, Asmaa lives in self-imposed isolation, cut off from any friends or family. When she is approached by a friend from her past, Asmaa pretends she cannot hear her. Her only social activity appears to be a regular meeting group hosted by the Friends of Life Society (Jam'iyat Asdiqa' al-Haya), a vaguely titled organization for PLWHA. The film opens with Asmaa introducing herself for the first time at one of these meetings.

> My name is Asmaa. I'm forty-five years old. I have a daughter, Habiba. . . . My father and I are originally from Banha. . . . I have a good, respectable job. . . . I'm a bit overwhelmed because it's my first time, but I'm glad I came. It's the first time I'm meeting people *like me*. I don't take any medication; my immunity is okay I guess. But I have a gallbladder problem. An operation, as you know . . . would be difficult.

When the organizer of the group learns of Asmaa's medical condition, he introduces her to Ayten, the programmer of a popular reality TV show called *Hot Tin Plate (Safih sakhin)*, which deals with everyday events in Egypt. Ayten (Samia As'ad) and Muhsin (Majid al-Kidwany), the obnoxious host of the show, offer to expose the difficulties and harassment that Asmaa continuously experiences. By doing so, they hope to appeal to a doctor or an official who will intervene in her seemingly simple situation. The proposed episode would be devoted entirely to HIV/AIDS in Egypt, but Asmaa finds herself conflicted when they ask that she give up her anonymity and reveal her face on air. Seemingly in direct response to the documentary *AIDS HIV+ in Egypt*, Ayten tries to convince Asmaa that revealing her identity will help give HIV/AIDS a "personal face," thereby making it possible for the average viewer to relate to PLWHA.

> When people are silhouetted to speak on TV, people are scared of them. It will backfire and increase the stigma. Is this what you want? Your case will cause an uproar. Imagine what happens if you go on TV, and say you've been thrown out of the operating room. And that doctors, who should know better, wouldn't do the operation? It's a real opportunity. It's a lifetime opportunity. I know you have a daughter to raise.

But it is precisely Asmaa's concern for her daughter, Habiba (Fatima Adil), and how Asmaa thinks Habiba will react upon finding that her mother has HIV, that leads Asmaa to refuse to reveal her identity on the show. The film culminates with Asmaa appearing on the show with her face hidden and her voice altered, while Muhsin receives calls from viewers commenting on whether PLWHA "deserve" treatment or not. Habiba, however, soon realizes that the guest is actually her mother. She then calls the show and asks Muhsin to help her mother in any way he possibly can. Habiba's call leads Asmaa to uncover her face on live television, announcing to the world that she is Asmaa Hosni and that she is living with the "AIDS virus."

I argue that *Asmaa* resonated so much with its audiences because of Salama's use of certain cinematic techniques that established a connection with the spectator in ways that the documentary failed to do. One formal aspect of *Asmaa* that shaped its effect on viewers is the use of documentary conventions. The opening sequence that announces that the film is based on real events, as well as the closing titles that mention the demise of the actual person upon whose story the film was based, allows the spectator to perceive *Asmaa* as part documentary rather than pure fiction. This establishes what Vivian Sobchack calls a "documentary consciousness" in the audience. Sobchack defines documentary consciousness as a "particular mode of embodied and ethical spectatorship that informs and transforms the space of the irreal into the space of the real" (Sobchack 2004, 261). The use of certain stylistic documentary conventions in the diegesis, however, also emphasizes the documentary space, or the "charge of the real," that moves the audience from fictional into documentary consciousness. It instills an "ethical charge" into the narrative, one that Sobchack argues "calls forth not only response but also responsibility—not only aesthetic valuation but also ethical judgment" (Sobchack 2004, 284). This comprises the direct address of the on-screen characters to the camera and audience; the use of handheld cameras that produce a shaky, out-of-focus effect on the image; and the use of visual materials that are considered "documents," such as medical forms, the photograph of Asmaa's wedding night, the elaborate studio in which the live interview takes place, and the realistic opening title sequence for *Hot Tin Plate*. The end credits also inform the audience that some of the actors who appear in the Friends of Life Society meetings are not actors but in fact PLWHA.

Asmaa begins and ends with the textual emphasis that the story is based on real events in order to situate a documentary consciousness in the viewer, but it is the casting of Hend Sabry, an immensely beloved and respected female star, and the use of melodramatic conventions that truly establishes a connection with the character of Asmaa. In her essay "Melodrama Revised," Linda Williams argues that the operative mode of a film is melodrama "if emotional and moral registers are sounded, if a work invites us to feel sympathy for the virtues of beset victims, [and] if the narrative trajectory is ultimately more concerned with a retrieval and staging of innocence than with the psychological causes of motives and action" (Williams 1998, 42). As a film, *Asmaa* assumes the form of a melodramatic narrative based on real events. The viewer is constantly invited to oscillate between feelings of pity and outrage for Asmaa—a position that was difficult to inhabit for spectators of the documentary. The feeling of empathy that Asmaa engenders in viewers due to the unnecessary suffering she experiences is precisely what defines the film as (part) melodrama. For example, several scenes focus on Asmaa struggling with her gallbladder pains; she is seen panting, exhausted, and unable to walk. In one particularly charged scene, she faints on a crowded bus and gets pickpocketed. The film also positions the spectator directly in Asmaa's body, with shots that emphasize searing pains (complete fade-out/white-out of the screen), double vision, and blurriness. The camera shifts, tilts, loses focus, and changes into a deathly pale color. The audience is thus positioned to feel Asmaa's experience of pain vicariously. This is also emphasized in the contrast between current scenes, which are tinted with gray and bluish overtones, and scenes from her past, which take on a warm, sepia-toned palette. The use of melodrama, as well as the construction of Asmaa as a victim/hero in order to grant the film moral legibility, is central to the theme and message of *Asmaa*. By positioning Asmaa as a victim of stigma and the state's legal bias, the film effectively invites the audience to recognize and feel Asmaa's victimhood through pathos.

If you exceed the dose, you could go on a trip.

12.2. *Asmaa* (2011), directed by Amr Salama

However, *Asmaa*'s use of melodramatic conventions in order to establish a moral good—the right to healthcare, at the very least—is not without complications. Although the film invites the audience to pity and condemn Asmaa's suffering of HIV-related stigma and pain, its use of the female body to represent an illness via displays of weakness and suffering also perpetuates some of the most basic cinematic tropes of the feminized body. In stark comparison, the male characters in *Asmaa* are unaffected by HIV/AIDS. They don't exhibit any signs of illness. Asmaa's husband dies quickly and is not rendered pathetic. Shafiq, an HIV-positive man who figures prominently throughout the narrative as he attempts to help and impress Asmaa, does not exhibit any signs of pain or illness, unlike Asmaa and Farida, another HIV-positive female character. Farida, who is hospitalized at one point during the film, speaks about her estranged son endlessly, wanting to impress him with new clothes she buys and recipes she learns in case he chooses to visit her. Shafiq, on other hand, contracts HIV by "cheating left, right, and center" and subsequently infects his wife. He lives, while she dies. Asmaa suffers, and her pain is precisely what induces sympathy from the audience. The masculine body, on the other hand, is not reduced to an "excess" of pain or emotions. It does not break down nor does it suffer even when it is HIV-positive.

As Linda Williams has argued, pathos in melodrama is triggered not merely by the suffering of the characters but emerges from the very precise moment when "the characters in the story catch up with and realize what the audience already knows" (Williams 2009, 615). This produces a "too lateness" in temporality, a moment that reveals a (futile) desire for a reversal in time, to get back to the moment before it was "too late." In *Asmaa*, however, the audience does not know more than the characters. In fact, it is Asmaa who knows more, and the spectator who has to catch up. The narrative in *Asmaa* utilizes flashbacks, jump-cut scenes of the past that depict Asmaa's life with her husband in Banha, a small village in the Egyptian countryside. There, the pre-HIV Asmaa is depicted as a strong and unconventionally defiant woman, fighting tradition to keep a stall in the male-dominated marketplace where she can sell her hand-woven carpets. These scenes are juxtaposed with her current situation: struggling with the pain of a gallbladder infection, unable to find a doctor willing to operate on her, and in constant fear of being exposed. She has sporadic access to painkillers, when she has cash. For example, when her colleagues give her a handout after her forced dismissal from work, she immediately buys extra-strength painkillers on the black market. The rural flashbacks in the film also are in direct contrast to the urban scenes in Cairo, emphasizing the disadvantages of Asmaa's class background and, in turn, offering another critique of the healthcare system. For example, in one flashback, Asmaa's doctor in the village tells her that she can have an HIV-negative child and also prevent herself from being infected by her husband if she's "careful" enough, but does not offer her any medication. This stands in contrast to the wealthy Muhsin, who would "go abroad for medical care if he had the common cold."

Flashbacks, according to Maureen Turim, occupy a "hermeneutic" space and offer "way[s] in which narrative organizes the exposition of events so as to keep interest invested in a posed question, the answer to which is delayed" (Turim 1989, 11). Through the flashbacks, the viewer discovers that Mus'ad, Asmaa's husband, contracted HIV after being sentenced to prison for killing a man who assaulted Asmaa verbally and physically in the market. The flashbacks also slowly reveal how Asmaa contracted HIV. The central question in *Asmaa* is how she became HIV-positive. The answer, portrayed in a series of flashbacks, does not emerge until more than halfway into the film. The first of these flashbacks depicts Asmaa walking home in tears, clutching medical reports, and telling Mus'ad that she has contracted the virus. Only then is he willing to engage in any sexual activity with her.

Toward the end of the film, the same flashback is presented with an additional few minutes preceding it: We see the doctor telling Asmaa she does not have HIV, but he advises her against trying to get pregnant. The scene that follows is repeated: Asmaa walking home in tears, clutching medical reports, and telling Mus'ad that she has contracted the virus. It is now clear that she is not actually HIV-positive at this point. In this same flashback, Asmaa proceeds to convince her husband to have a child with her, one who will "inherit the land and the legacy." What is clear about Asmaa's decision to have unprotected sex with her husband is her desire for him and for intimacy. After he resists her sexual advances on the grounds of not wanting to infect her, she tells him, "Why should you have something I don't have? Isn't it enough that you went to prison alone? You also want to carry your illness alone?"

The flashbacks do keep the spectator engaged until the mode of Asmaa's HIV infection is revealed, but by the time it is revealed, it does not really affect or justify her receiving or not receiving medical care, employment, and support from her community. The film presents Asmaa as HIV-positive from the beginning, and by the time the viewer discovers how Asmaa acquired the virus, identification with Asmaa has already been established. The circumstances under which she acquired HIV are irrelevant, and the idea of her being refused treatment because she refuses to disclose how she became HIV-positive seems extremely unjustified. The flashbacks reveal the answer to the question of "How?," while also making the spectator aware of just how unnecessary the investment in that posed question is. They also instill a sense of complicity in Asmaa's deteriorating health because they "self-consciously position the cinema audience, calling attention to their role as spectators" (Horeck 2004, 105).

Thus we find that the flashbacks intervene in the ideological structures of the film. Usually, flashbacks reveal the answer or the cause to something after the viewer knows the effect. In *Asmaa*, that function is altered. The flashbacks not only reveal a different answer from the one the audience was expecting, but they are also positioned temporally in such a way that they lose their conventional qualities of shock and revelation. They also work against the conventions of melodrama, wherein the audience knows what the protagonist doesn't. Here only the protagonist knows, but because the flashbacks are anticlimactic—promising revelation but not delivering—they contribute, on both the narrative and formal levels, to the film's intervention in the moralistic ideology surrounding the causes of HIV/AIDS. Rather than providing an answer to the spectator's question of "How?," the flashbacks pose another, more important question to the spectator: "Why ask how?" This reversal, or relocation of investment onto another posed question, arrives in the narrative at the critical moment when it becomes clear that Asmaa knowingly exposed herself to HIV. Precisely because the film works to undermine the narrative investment in how Asmaa became HIV-positive, the implications of her choice are similarly emptied of moral significance and set beyond the realm of moral judgment.

It has nothing to do with religious habits, or traditions.

12.3. *Asmaa* (2011), directed by Amr Salama

A series of scenes that directly confront the audience occurs toward the end of the film, during the filming of *Hot Tin Plate*. One important aspect of the TV show is that it takes calls from viewers. Random people, including a cleric, a doctor, and a former minister, all call to weigh in about whether HIV/AIDS patients should be entitled to equal treatment. Highlighting television as a site for civic engagement and social consciousness by having spectators actively argue for or against treatment, *Asmaa* compels viewers of the film to also think about their own civic duty and implication in such matters. The narrative here turns to the spectator and asks: What do *you* think? Do *you* see how your support (or the lack thereof), whether as a doctor, a religious authority, or even a layperson, affects those whose lives are hanging on the delicate thread of state benevolence and the availability of resources afforded to them? Through the position of the camera, Muhsin faces the audience of the TV show and, more importantly, the cinematic audience. The film thus forces the audience to confront its involvement in critiquing the healthcare system, as well as instilling an "ethical charge" that invokes responsibility and a demand for change.

Asmaa ends with an especially charged scene, in which Asmaa directly accuses the audience of effectively killing her through complicity and silence. During the previous scenes with Asmaa's employer and Muhsin, in which Asmaa briefly addresses the camera, the frame always includes some diegetic element, such as actors or a camera. However, the scene of Asmaa on *Hot Tin Plate* contains no diegetic elements interfering with the frame, just Asmaa looking at the cinematic spectator, saying, "If I die, it won't be from a disease I have. It will be from a disease *you* have." Here, Asmaa echoes disability scholar Lennard Davis's argument that "the 'problem' is not the person with disabilities; the problem is the way that normalcy is constructed to create the 'problem' of the disabled person" (Davis 1995, 24). She once again looks directly at the screen at the very end of her walk home after the *Hot Tin Plate* filming, saying, "I don't want to be afraid of people. I don't want to be afraid that they know. I don't want to be afraid of what they'd do to me if they knew. . . . If I stopped fearing all these things, maybe then I'd feel alive."

I'll die of a disease you have.

12.4. *Asmaa* (2011), directed by Amr Salama

Local Reception

Given its cultural context, *Asmaa* was considered controversial simply by addressing HIV/AIDS—automatically invoking associations with homosexuality and promiscuity. Several film set locations refused access to their premises, and the actresses and actors had to consider the possibility that they would be less marketable in the future. Nonetheless, *Asmaa* was awarded eighteen Egyptian, Arab, and global awards since it premiered at the 2011 Abu Dhabi International Film Festival, where it claimed the award for Best Arab Director (Ramchurn 2013). More importantly, the popular reception of the film in the Middle East has been immensely successful, indicating a general interest in discourse on HIV and AIDS. In fact, a small online study of *Asmaa*'s effects on Egyptian audiences conducted by UNAIDS shows that 61 percent of respondents would positively respond to Asmaa in all scenarios of social interactions that the study poses (and wouldn't have before) (El Beih et al. 2012). In Egypt, TV represents the single most important source of information on HIV/ AIDS for more than 90 percent of the population.[6] As mentioned earlier, the film elicited thousands of responses on Twitter after being screened on CBC. Along with the hashtag, Twitter users shared screenshots as well as moving quotes from the film. It is thus highly likely that *Asmaa* will help improve the public's general knowledge on the topic—unlike earlier Arab films and contemporary reports and documentaries about HIV/ AIDS, which misinformed and horrified audiences, causing them at one point to walk out of theaters.

In earlier films from the 1980s and 1990s, HIV/AIDS operated as a metaphor for perversity, deviance, and Western foreignness, propagated through the allure of the abject, horrific, or diseased subject. In 1989, Ali Abdelkhaleq directed *Rape* (*Ightisab*) shortly after the first case of HIV/ AIDS was reported in Egypt. The narrative revolves around three men who attempt to rape a nurse. When she momentarily escapes them and finds shelter in an army base, the men proceed to spread the rumor that she has AIDS, resulting in the soldiers sending her away, afraid to even touch her. Two other early examples were released in 1992: Ahmed Fouad's *Love in Taba* (*al-Hub fi Taba*) and Karim Diaa Eddine's *Love and Terror* (*al-Hub wa-l-ru'b*). *Love in Taba* follows three friends as they vacation in Sharm al-Sheikh, a popular area for tourism in Egypt. Here they meet three women from Europe, who convince the men to join them on a road trip to Taba. During their time together, all three men engage in sexual activity with the women. When the women leave Taba, they leave behind individual letters addressed to the men, in which they disclose that they have AIDS. Upon their return to Cairo, the men get tested and confirm they are all HIV-positive. Overtaken by sheer terror, they all see their lives fall apart before their eyes. *Love and Terror* functions similarly. The narrative focuses on a beautiful single mother named Hind, who contracted HIV from her now-dead husband. After a night of heavy drinking in bars, a man rapes Hind. She seeks refuge at the apartment of Ahmad, a former lover. Although she is visibly intoxicated, Ahmad has sex with her. When she tells him that she has AIDS the next morning, he immediately gets tested and is told that he is HIV-positive. Moreover, the doctor urges him to "turn in" Hind, as a woman like her is "a menace to society."

These early films on HIV/AIDS were not well received by the public. According to one author, audiences found these films depressing and immoral, causing them to walk out of theaters (al-Mahdi 2014). At the time that these films were released, fear and paranoia had a firm hold on the media and, in turn, on the public. Cinematic presentations of HIV/AIDS only cemented this fear and perpetuated misinformed ideas as common knowledge, contributing to a deeply entrenched stigma against PLWHA and a binaristic discourse pitting "innocent" against "guilty" victims.

Sanitizing AIDS?

In *Asmaa*, there is considerable emphasis—especially at the Friends of Life Society meetings—on PLWHA carrying out day-to-day activities, such as putting on makeup, thinking about clothes, taking cooking classes, and considering remarriage. The group's conversations reinforce the idea that having HIV/AIDS is not a death sentence and that being HIV-positive is not equivalent to being ill. These meetings provide a much-needed space for attendees to talk freely about pain, stigma, medicine, estranged family members, and so forth. They also provide an "in-between" space, where new meanings of selfhood—singular and communal—emerge and new signs of identity are initiated, while also serving as innovative sites of collaboration and contestation (Bhabha 2004, 2). Indeed, throughout the film there is a strong emphasis on the importance of marginalized groups forming collectives for social and political reasons. Collectively identifying as members of a group who share the social oppression of disability and the stigma of having HIV/AIDS in the Arab world has vital political meaning. In her book *The Body in Pain: The Making and Unmaking of the World*, Elaine Scarry points out that because pain is invisible, unverifiable, and unrepresentable, it is often subject to misattribution or denial by those who are not experiencing it (Scarry 1985, 14). Many PLWHA do not really exhibit any external symptoms (unless they are in the late stages of AIDS), which grants them one layer of invisibility. Because many people in the Arab and Muslim world(s) are reluctant or unwilling to seek help, they seal themselves in another layer of invisibility. There are also no visible coalitions for PLWHA in the Arab world, which unfortunately contributes to the governmental reluctance to address the lack of resources, funds, and drugs available to PLWHA as a legitimate problem.

Yet the group's focus on "life" in turn excludes "sick-looking" people. In *Asmaa*, all the PLWHA *appear* healthy. The film takes HIV/AIDS away from the virus and lab, offering a rather sanitized depiction of HIV/AIDS. There is no classic deathbed scene; only the pains of Asmaa's gallbladder infection are visible to the viewer. This seems to be an unavoidable marketing strategy to draw in the spectator, who already has experienced a barrage of negative imagery about how PLWHA look. Had Salama tried to offer an unbiased depiction of PLWHA, in addition to focusing on the excruciating bodily pain that is inflicted throughout the course of the syndrome, he might have alienated audiences. This is especially evident when Muhsin begins the episode of *Hot Tin Plate* by saying, "Tonight, we will be discussing AIDS. But before you change the channel, let me assure you that the character we have with us tonight is not depressing at all." This is perhaps another meta-cinematic reference to the documentary—which does indeed rely on rather depressing and somber imagery—as well as earlier feature films that featured HIV-positive characters in disparaging contexts.

However, it is also important to note that the film does not use a reductive "positive image" approach to PLWHA, offering a character who is somewhat sanitized according to mainstream values in order to redeem public prejudices. Asmaa occupies a precarious position as an HIV-positive woman. She is not the "innocent victim" who gets infected unknowingly, but neither is she the drug addict, prostitute, or sexually promiscuous woman. As the flashbacks show, Asmaa chooses to become HIV-positive. They also show how Asmaa's character is substantially different from the other women in her village. She actively earns a living by selling hand-woven carpets at the local market, marking a contested presence in a male-governed space. The film does not use the image of the "good woman" or "mother" to temper the meanings associated with HIV/AIDS, nor does it cast Asmaa in the category of people who "deserve" to get AIDS because of their lifestyles. Asmaa does not fall into either of these binary categories; she occupies both spaces.

The closing titles of *Asmaa* state that the actual person on whom Asmaa is based did not experience the saccharine ending that she receives in the film. They abruptly interrupt the film's somewhat "feel-good" ending, disclosing that the actual person did not reveal her face on screen, did not receive treatment for her gallbladder infection, and ultimately died from those complications. While the film does not show Asmaa receiving any treatment after the show, the ending scene delivers an optimistic picture to the viewer: Asmaa walks home defiantly amid passersby who seem to recognize her from the show, directly suggesting to the spectator that without fear of pain, medicine, and stigma, she would truly be able to live. This scene invites the spectator to occupy Asmaa's position, in order to feel, for a few long seconds, the social stigma and compromised anonymity of having HIV/AIDS.

By presenting to the viewer two juxtaposed realities—a hopeful one in which an HIV-positive person receives attention, medication, and equal rights, and a bleak one in which an HIV-positive person dies from an easily treatable gallbladder infection—the spectator is made acutely aware of the life-saving possibilities that are denied PLWHA due to stigma, corruption, and homophobia.

Conclusion

The films discussed in this chapter represent a historical moment in relation to HIV/AIDS, but they also produce that historicity. As Douglas Crimp argues:

> AIDS does not exist apart from the practices that conceptualize it, represent it, and respond to it. We know AIDS only in and through those practices . . . If we recognize that AIDS exists only in and through these constructions, then hopefully we can also recognize the imperative to know them, analyze them, and wrest control of them. (Crimp 1988, 3)

Thus, analyzing these films helps to deconstruct how HIV/AIDS has been produced discursively in Egypt and the Middle East. *Asmaa* adds nuance to a one-dimensional and monolithic narrative of patients struggling with HIV/AIDS in the Arab world, blurring the distinction between "innocent" and "guilty victims." By challenging dominant accounts of HIV/AIDS in the media, *Asmaa* represents a defining moment in the Egyptian and Arab canon, as the implications of the stigma that PLWHA face are finally addressed. The "burden of proof" is upon films like *Asmaa* to represent "a disturbing social reality" to an Arab—and perhaps a larger—audience (Walker 2005, 54).

Through its distinct representation of illness and suffering character(s), *Asmaa* presents a positive change in the representation of HIV/AIDS in Arab (and specifically Egyptian) cinema, especially in comparison to earlier examples that relied on biased and stigmatizing "outbreak narratives." The use of documentary consciousness and flashbacks, as well as the pathos invoked from melodrama, both mediates viewer identification and entreats the audience to consider their own position toward PLWHA. This is achieved in a number of ways. First, by utilizing the "charge of the real," *Asmaa* instills a documentary consciousness in the audience. By fictionalizing the stigma of PLWHA and projecting it onto the body of Hend Sabry, *Asmaa* exceeds the limits posed on maintaining the anonymity of actual PLWHA in documentary filmmaking. The pathos invoked by the melodrama aesthetic and techniques enables a connection to the lived experience of PLWHA, demanding an ethical response from the spectator. Additionally, the use of carefully placed flashbacks effectively undermines the audiences' negative preconceptions about HIV/AIDS and morality. As HIV/AIDS continues to be a foreign sign of otherness in the Arab public's eyes, it is through Asmaa's character that the audience is invited to embody that otherness.

References

El Beih, W., A. Salama, H. Sabry, A. Morgan, and G. Crescenzi. 2012. "Role of 'Asmaa' Feature Film in Egypt in Addressing HIV Related Stigma and Discrimination and Creating Public Debate." Poster presented as AIDS 2012: Nineteenth International AIDS Conference, Washington, DC, July 22–27.

Bhabha, Homi K. 2004. The Location of Culture. London: Routledge. Originally published 1994.

Crimp, Douglas. 1988. "AIDS: Cultural Analysis/Cultural Activism." In *AIDS: Cultural Analysis/Cultural Activism*, edited by Douglas Crimp, 3–16. October Books. Cambridge, MA: MIT Press.

———. 2002. *Melancholia and Moralism: Essays on AIDS and Queer Politics*. Cambridge, MA: MIT Press.

Davis, Lennard J. 1995. *Enforcing Normalcy: Disability, Deafness, and the Body*. London: Verso.

Deif, Ingy. 2015. "HIV/AIDS in Egypt: Facts, Numbers, and Challenges." Interview with Ahmed Khamis. Ahram Online, September 6. www.english.ahram.org.eg.

Horeck, Tanya. 2004. *Public Rape: Representing Violation in Fiction and Film*. Sussex Studies in Culture and Communication. London: Routledge.

Al Jazeera. 2013. "AIDS fi al-'alam al-'arabi, arqam mur'iba wa haqa'iq muhzina (AIDS in the Arab World: Terrifying Numbers and Sad Facts)." December 3. www.aljazeera.net.

al-Mahdi, Ahmed. 2014. "Aflam al-AIDS fi al-sinima: al-jins huwa al-sabab (AIDS in the Movies: Sex is the Cause)." DotMSR, December 1. www.dotmsr.com.

Ramchurn, Rakesh. 2013. "Egyptian Filmmaker Amr Salama Confronts Attitudes to HIV and AIDS." *Your Middle East*, October 28. www.yourmiddleeast.com.

Scarry, Elaine. 1985. *The Body in Pain: The Making and Unmaking of the World*. New York: Oxford University Press.

Setayesh, Hamidreza, Farzaneh Roudi-Fahimi, Shereen El Feki, and Lori S. Ashford. 2014. *HIV and AIDS in the Middle East and North Africa.* Washington, DC: Population Reference Bureau. www.prb.org.

Sobchack, Vivian. 2004. *Carnal Thoughts: Embodiment and Moving Image Culture.* Berkeley: University of California Press.

Thomson, Rosemarie Garland. 1997. *Extraordinary Bodies: Figuring Physical Disability in American Culture and Literature.* New York: Columbia University Press.

Treichler, Paula A. 1988. "AIDS, Homophobia, and Biomedical Discourse: An Epidemic of Signification." In *AIDS: Cultural Analysis/ Cultural Activism,* edited by Douglas Crimp, 31–70. Cambridge, MA: MIT Press.

———. 1999. *How to Have Theory in an Epidemic: Cultural Chronicles of AIDS.* Durham, NC: Duke University Press.

Turim, Maureen. 1989. *Flashbacks in Film: Memory and History.* New York: Routledge.

UNAIDS. n.d. "Countries." www.unaids.org.

———. 2010. "National AIDS Program Egypt: UNGASS Country Progress Report: Arab Republic of Egypt, January 2008–December 2009."

———. 2012. *Standing Up, Speaking Out: Women and HIV in the Middle East and North Africa.* Issues brief. July. UNAIDS/JC2388. www.files. unaids.org.

———. 2014. "Fact Sheet 2014." www.files.unaids.org.

———. 2015. "National AIDS Program Egypt: National HIV Programme Situation and Gap Analysis, Egypt." April. www.unaids.org.

———. 2017. "Data 2017." Joint United Nations Programme on HIV and AIDS. www.unaids.org.

Viney, Steven. 2012. "A Year after Announcing He Had HIV, Maged El Rabeiy Is Fighting On." *Egypt Independent,* September 24, 2012. www.egyptindependent.com.

Wald, Priscilla. 2008. *Contagious: Cultures, Carriers, and the Outbreak Narrative.* Durham, NC: Duke University Press.

Walker, Janet. 2005. *Trauma Cinema: Documenting Incest and the Holocaust.* Berkeley: University of California Press.

Watney, Simon. 1994. "AIDS, 'Moral Panic' Theory, and Homophobia." In *Practices of Freedom: Selected Writings on HIV/AIDS,* 3–14. Durham, NC: Duke University Press, 1994.

———. 1996. *Policing Desire: Pornography, AIDS, and the Media.* 3rd ed. Media and Society. Minneapolis: University of Minnesota Press.

Williams, Linda. 1998. "Melodrama Revised." In *Refiguring American Film Genres: History and Theory,* edited by Nick Browne, 42–88. Berkeley: University of California Press.

———. 2009. "Film Bodies: Gender, Genre, and Excess." In *Film Theory and Criticism: Introductory Readings*, edited by Leo Braudy and Marshall Cohen, 602–16. 7th ed. New York: Oxford University Press.

Filmography

Abdelkhaleq, Ali, dir. 1989. *Ightisab*. Egypt.

Diaa Eddine, Karim, dir. 1992. *al-Hub wa-l-ru'b*. Egypt. 88 mins.

Fouad, Ahmed, dir. 1992. *al-Hub fi Taba*. Egypt. Dokki: El Sobki. Vidiyu Film. DVD, 105 min.

Iraqi, Mona. 2014a. "Silsilat kashf tijarat al-jins al-jama'i wa intishar al-AIDS fi Misr." *al-Mistakhabbi*. Originally broadcast by al-Qahira wa-l-nas. YouTube video, 27:44. Posted by "Mona Iraqi," December 10.

———. 2014b. "Silsilat kashf tijarat al-jins al-jama'i wa intishar al-AIDS fi Misr: Part 2." *al-Mistakhabbi*. Originally broadcast by al-Qahira wa-l-nas. YouTube video, 27:39. Posted by "Mona Iraqi," December 18.

———. 2014c. "Silsilat kashf tijarat al-jins al-jama'i wa intishar al-AIDS fi Misr: Part 3." *al-Mistakhabbi*. Originally broadcast by al-Qahira wa-l-nas. YouTube video, 29:23. Posted by "Mona Iraqi," December 20.

Salama, Amr, dir. 2007. *al-Muta'ayishun ma' fayrus al-AIDS fi Misr*. YouTube video, 9:47. Posted by "Amr Salama," December 25.

———. 2011. *Asmaa*. Cairo: New Century. DVD, 96 min.

13

ME AND NOT ME:
THE PERSONAL-COLLECTIVE VOICE OF
FIRST-PERSON FILMS FROM THE
EGYPTIAN REVOLUTION

Alisa Lebow

When thinking about films made during times of revolutionary insurrection, many different styles and approaches come to mind. In the Soviet Union Eisenstein innovated his theory of montage and Vertov worked with his Council of Three to perfect his 'camera eye' in the service of revolutionary truth (Eisenstein 2010; Vertov 1984). In the 1960s and '70s, the Palestine Film Unit made countless films mostly in the newsreel and training film vein, while in Argentina, a theory of Third Cinema was being developed by Octavio Getino and Fernando Solanas with a set of guidelines for militant cinema that ranges from the long form fiction film to the short, sharp intervention of a film 'pamphlet' (Solanas and Getino 1969/2014; 1971/2014). Around the same time, Jean-Luc Godard, in his most militant phase, renounced individual authorship altogether and worked in collaboration with Jean-Pierre Gorin for a number of years under the collective named The Dziga Vertov Group. In none of these disparate cases does one ever see any emphasis on the individual, whether in the development of psychologically complex characters or the emphasis on the subjectivity of the filmmaker.

For reasons that may be too obvious to dwell on, it was nearly always the case that filmmaking strategies were developed to work against any type of individualism that might have been considered anathema to a collective mass struggle.[1] The revolutionary filmmaker was not meant to emerge as the subject of their film, and such an act of idiosyncratic singularity would surely have been decried by their comrades if they had. There have even been points along the span of twentieth-century revolutionary filmmaking where filmmakers were indeed singled out and isolated for their formal innovations, with accusations of pursuing a type of "petty bourgeois individualism."[2] For instance, Dziga Vertov, working feverishly in the first decades of the Soviet Revolution, was roundly criticized by his filmmaking peers, including Eisenstein, and eventually his idiosyncratic style was denounced precisely for being too subjective. He was eventually sent to work in the backwaters of Ukraine, and his documentary approach was sidelined in favor of the more "objectivist" stance of Esfir Shub and her compilation films (Malitsky 2004; Yampolski and Spring 1991).

Knowing this history made it all the more surprising to find, while conducting research for my project *Filming Revolution* in winter 2013 and spring 2014, several film projects, either recently finished or still in production, foregrounding the subjective view of the filmmaker in unexpected ways. I had traveled to Egypt to investigate the approaches to filmmaking of independent, mostly documentary, filmmakers in the wake of the momentous historical events that began in 2011. My initial contention was that for the entirety of the twentieth century, revolutionary unrest constituted a remarkably fertile ground for new approaches and thinking in cinema, and that here was an opportunity to understand what might be unfolding right before our eyes in this new century. What I had absolutely not expected was to encounter so many personal films. Admittedly, few of the filmmakers I met were making claims about innovating a new form of revolutionary cinema, nor were they necessarily concerned with such questions. Some were new to filmmaking, others were experienced filmmakers, and most were simply trying to use film as a way to make sense of their relationship to the events around them. As Viola Shafik states in an interview conducted in May 2014, "[m]ajor historical events throw people back on themselves," and it then becomes their task to understand better what happened and what their role was in it. As she says, the revolution was a "moment of truth, and in that moment of truth, you want to know more about yourself . . . not just as an individual, but as a society."[3]

Before entering into a discussion of the films themselves, a note about first-person film may be in order.[4] In general, I will be speaking about the first-person modality in documentary, rather than in fiction film. The emergence of the overtly subjective perspective in documentary, something that was always there but was actively repressed in all but the most autobiographical of documentaries, initially ran counter to the carefully constructed illusion of objectivity pursued in the majority of cases. The first person may have been an available mode of address for experimental filmmakers and video artists, but documentarians took much longer to foreground their own perspective and point of view, preferring to hide it up their rhetorical sleeves. Whether this has more to do with left-wing affinities or journalistic aspirations (or both) is an open question. What is apparent, however, is that first-person documentary came to prominence, at least in North America and to a lesser extent in Europe, in parallel with the rise of identity politics and the demise of the organized left, leading me to consider, in an article entitled "First Person Political" (Lebow 2013), whether there wasn't perhaps a direct correlation between these phenomena, and to wonder what the politics of first-person films might be said to be.

In a cynical vein, one might be tempted to ask whether this turn to the first person in Egyptian documentary is not a sign of the neoliberal demands and dreams of the revolution, neoliberalism revering the individual more as a consumer than a revolutionary, and going some way to prepare the ground for individualistic ideas and pursuits. Surely, if we follow a strain of thinking that suspects the West of a particular investment in developing a compliant consumer rather than a collective actor, we can imagine the drive toward more individualist concerns would fit this picture perfectly. After all, many of the funding and training initiatives that have supported these recent film projects come from abroad (including IDFA in Amsterdam, Bertha Foundation in the United Kingdom, the Canadian Foundation AlterCine, the Doha Film Institute, AFAC in Lebanon, and more), and there are certainly currents that might have influenced the modes of narration in these films, possibly impelling them toward the personal or testimonial vein. We know that there is a conflation between individualism and a certain vision of democracy, and we know too that the West's overt "democratization" campaigns tend to derive their definition of democracy straight from the IMF and the World Bank.[5]

Even if first-person documentary, as it began to be practiced in the West sometime in the late 1980s or early 1990s, may have been directly influenced by post-leftist identity politics whose main innovation was the departure from the objectivist pretenses of the documentary dogmas of an earlier age, its emergence in the Middle East can be traced to much more directly political phenomena. We see the earliest signs of it coming from Palestine (years after the demise of the Palestine Film Unit), Lebanon, and a bit later Iraq; countries and cultures in conflict that suffered from a type of journalistic over-mediation of their crises with a dearth of images made from the perspective of those living the consequences of these struggles. I have suggested elsewhere that first-person films emerge in the region at a point where their expression is a sign of resistance—resistance to the dominant media, to the othering gaze of international journalism, to over-determined readings, to the absence of any alternative perspective (Lebow 2013, 261) In other words, I argue that there are certain conditions in which the first-person film can be understood as necessarily more than an individualistic or narcissistic gesture, drawing on and in collectivities and communal identities that have profound political potency and potentiality.

Further, even while recognizing that some aspect of the shift to first-person filmmaking broadly speaking may reflect a loosening of the political commitment to a type of collective action, it can also be seen to be much more closely allied with a post-structuralist and postcolonialist turn away from the Enlightenment stance on rationality and objectivity, and the universalism that such positionalities hoped to represent. If there could be no universal speaking subject, or rather, if such a subject position constituted an exclusionary illusion in the service of a dominant imperialist and masculinist project, then surely it should not be considered a vehicle for liberatory, revolutionary politics.

In turning my sights to filmmaking in Egypt, and unexpectedly encountering a raft of first-person projects, I became interested in the ways in which the first-person film might indeed become a vehicle for politically engaged filmmaking and constitute a contemporary approach to speaking cinematic truth to power. In the research for the interactive documentary project *Filming Revolution*, I interviewed approximately thirty filmmakers, and a full 30 percent of the film projects discussed turned out to be first-person films. This by no means suggests that 30 percent of all independent film projects in Egypt since the revolution were personal films. Their preponderance in my research may have simply been a coincidence. However, it is undeniable that such a modality has become an acceptable and even fairly common form of filmmaking, especially documentary filmmaking, in Egypt today.

What were the projects I was introduced to in the editing suites and home offices of countless filmmakers who had all been actively involved in the revolution—or the uprising—and were all in the process of making sense of it? A young feminist activist and filmmaker, Nada Zatouna, was beginning to explore her roots as a half-Nubian Egyptian, prompted by the racism she had encountered during her active participation in the revolution.[6] Ahmed Nour, in his film *Waves* (*Mawj*, 2014) explores his, and his city's, experience of the revolution as a young Suezi who grew up in the era of Mubarak, having known no other leader for his entire life. Viola Shafik (a German-Egyptian) attempts to make sense, in her film *Arij: Scent of Revolution* (2014), of a revolution that appears to her to be as much a calamity as a liberation, in part by trying to take account of relevant histories. Nada Riyadh, hailing from Alexandria, talks about the revolution as a kind of idealistic passion and, in her film *Happily Ever After* (*Nihaya sa'ida*, 2016), suggests parallels between the idealism represented by the revolutionary yearnings on the streets and the idealism of romance in her personal life. Her friend Mohammed Rashad made his film *Little Eagles* (*Nusur saghira*, 2016) in part to investigate the lack of political education in Egypt's working classes, and in part an effort to make sense of his own unpreparedness to act politically when so many of his friends in Cairo—many of whom come from the Egyptian intelligentsia and the left—seemed to have a ready-made revolutionary vocabulary right from the start of the uprising. While I won't discuss every film mentioned above, and will actually discuss some films I learned about well after the research for the *Filming Revolution* project had concluded, I bring these projects to mind because of the diversity of issues they, as an aggregate, manage to address: culture, race, ethnicity, regionalism, migration, history, generational memory, class, gender, education, politics, eros—all find their way into these personally inflected films.

In this chapter I will discuss five first-person films from Egypt, all completed between 2012 and 2016. The films are: Safaa Fathy's *Mohammed Saved from the Waters (Muhammad yanju min al-ma'*, 2012); *Arij: Scent of Revolution* by Viola Shafik; Ahmed Nour's *Waves; Happily Ever After* by Nada Riyadh; and Mohammed Rashad's *Little Eagles*. I will discuss these films in two main groupings: the first two made by veteran filmmakers, as films that had been started before the revolution and transformed to one degree or another once the revolution exploded in Tahrir; and the latter three, all made by younger filmmakers, very much in the aftermath of, and as reflections on the effects of, those events. Of course there are other first-person films that have been made by Egyptians since the revolution and some will be mentioned along the way,[7] but it is the analysis of these five to which I turn now. At times I will depend on the words of my interviewees for the *Filming Revolution* project, in an attempt to collectively decipher this trend.

Mohammed Saved from the Waters and *Arij: Scent of Revolution* were both projects that were in production prior to the revolution's start. Or to be more precise, the first was already in production and continued its trajectory, incorporating the events of the revolution along the way, and the second was meant to be a different film before the revolution and shifted significantly in its aftermath. In Fathy's film, the revolution is just a fact, something that was happening while the last part of filming a long-term project was being completed. In Shafik's film, the fact of the revolution seemed to challenge all previous facts, requiring a complete re-evaluation and rerouting of the project to reckon with the current transformative crisis. In short, one film retained its focus and incorporated the revolution in its stride, while the other appears to have been utterly derailed by it.

And yet, to say that *Mohammed Saved from the Waters* is unmoved by the revolution would be a step too far. It is a film that, while appearing to be a chronicle of the filmmaker's younger brother's kidney disease, actually all but calls for the revolution and appears to be fully prepared for it when it comes. *Mohammed* is one of the few first-person documentaries I've seen from Egypt that is able to draw together so many of the factors (economic, environmental, social) that led to the uprising against the Mubarak regime in the first place. At the start of the film Fathy's brother, a man of just forty, is afflicted with a type of kidney disease common in Egypt, attributed to the extreme pollution of the Nile. In the film we learn that there are sixty-seven sewage canals discharging directly into the Nile. It goes on to suggest a negative reciprocity, in that the lack of respect shown to the Egyptian life-force that is the Nile is being returned by the indomitable river in the form of humiliation of those who depend on it, cutting them down in their prime. As Mohammed's disease progresses, we also learn of the collapse of the government-supported healthcare system, forcing Fathy's family to rely on private treatments which are much more expensive. In the process of documenting the beloved brother's irreversible descent into illness, and his extraordinary rationale that leads him to reject a transplant until it's too late (he doesn't want to exploit someone in need, nor is he easily convinced that it's not "haram" to buy or sell organs), the filmmaker seamlessly weaves in the family's fury about the systemic government neglect and a politics of resistance that seems to be shared by friends and relatives alike. Of all the films I discuss here, *Mohammed* is the one that penetrates closest to the bone, unflinchingly documenting a painful personal loss with a poetic stoicism that displays great skill and restraint. Yet despite the deep affective register that could have easily overwhelmed the project and made it a narrowly cast domestic drama, it manages to make profound connections with the social and political circumstances in which it is filmed.

Arij: Scent of Revolution is a very different type of first-person film. It does not involve family members or close friends as is typical of this mode, but engages a range of seemingly unconnected interlocutors in the filmmaker's quest to understand something about the upheaval the country has just gone through. It turns out the characters are connected in a typology of mourning, each representing an essential stage in the process of grieving after a traumatic loss: oblivion (the Islamist), anger (the activist), preservation (the collector), and depression (the author), though this schema is nowhere indicated in the film itself. Originally a film about history—in particular, the ambitious construction project around the main archaeological sites of Luxor in Upper Egypt, designed by the government to turn it into what some have disparagingly called "Vegas on the Nile" (Hauslohner 2010)—it still retains vestiges of this initial focus, while also exploring related and unrelated themes via the four characters. There is the young veiled woman, Awatef Mohammed, who, for reasons that I have not fully untangled, stands in for "oblivion," and has created a virtual Tahrir Square using the Second Life platform, for women to visit if (forbidden by relatives or husbands) they're unable to reach the actual square; a Coptic shopkeeper who doubles as a human-rights activist and advocate for his community (anger); a tour guide and collector of historical photographs who is nearly drowning in his own unarchived collection (preservation); and finally and most poignantly, the well-known Egyptian author Alaa El Deeb, whom Shafik interviews about his 1978 novella *Lemon Blossoms*, which he has only the vaguest memory of having written, though it holds many important insights for the current age of newly minted (failed) revolutionaries. Shafik tells us in her interview for *Filming Revolution* that the film, not unlike El Deeb's book, had a difficult birth, as it was born of the trauma caused by the degree of destruction produced by the dictatorship and made evident in the moment of revolution. In the interview, Shafik appears to be well aware that her film doesn't fully cohere and in fact justifies this as a symptom of the moment, where it was "impossible to tell a coherent narrative of the revolution" (Lebow 2018).

It is clearly the interview with El Deeb and his writings that anchor the otherwise disjointed narrative. His warning, borrowed from the Cuban author Desnoes, about the need to remember and preserve one's history if one hopes to become civilized, resounds in the contemporary context, not only because of the crass money-making schemes visited upon heritage sites by the Mubarak regime, but because of the new revolutionary circumstances that almost seemed to want to wipe the historical slate clean. In fact, both *Mohammed* and *Arij* draw on the ancient history of Egypt as the bedrock foundation from which to make sense of the present, and El Deeb acts in *Arij* as the wise fool who, while he can't remember the contents of the story he wrote, nonetheless knows that one needs to remember the contents of one's history.

The three films that were begun after 2011 concern themselves exclusively with modern Egyptian history, going back only as far as Nasserism and the Suez Canal, in the case of Ahmed Nour's *Waves*, and back to the insurrectionary movements of the 1970s in Egypt, in the case of Mohammed Rashad's *Little Eagles* and Nada Riyadh's *Happily Ever After*. Perhaps the concern with the recent rather than the ancient past has something

13.1. *Arij: Scent of Revolution* (2014), directed by Viola Shafik.

to do with the immediacy of the struggles, turning only to what appears to be the most pertinent history to help think through the challenges of the present. It may also have to do with the relatively young age of the three filmmakers (all around thirty at the time of production). Either way, it's as if history has been reduced to the time just before they were born, before the ego was formed, a referentless point that is as unfathomable as it is near. As Barthes neatly mused about a photograph of his mother from a past he could just barely imagine, it represented "History" with a capital "H," characterized as "the time when my mother was alive before me." The historical point of reference most important for these filmmakers is that which is closest to them: that of their parents' generation, which leads directly to Barthes' parenthetical add-on, referring to that time as "the period which interests me most historically" (Barthes 1981, 65). In this way, most of these first-person films touch on history and attempt to understand its legacy, but only as far back as the filmmakers' parents generation, and the ways in which this relatively recent, lived history may or may not have affected their own identifications and associations.

The first-person films of this latter grouping that are most concerned with a generational inheritance, especially in political terms, are those, coincidentally, made by the two Alexandrian filmmakers: Nada Riyadh's *Happily Ever After* and Mohammed Rashad's *Little Eagles*.[8] Riyadh's film, ostensibly about how to maintain long-distance relationships (including the one in which she finds herself), eventually reveals itself to also be about how to live with political defeat. After several detours into other people's stories of long-distance love lost or maintained, we get to the heart of the

13.2. *Happily Ever After* (2016), directed by Nada Riyadh.

film, where we learn that Riyadh's parents, before moving to the Gulf to make money and raise a family, had been politically active in the 1970s and had, at least in their daughter's view, left Egypt with their tails figuratively between their legs before the job of system and regime change was finished. When the stakes are revealed, all of the film's handwringing about leaving or staying suddenly makes sense. This young revolutionist does not want to leave with the job half finished, and can't abide by her boyfriend's prioritizing his own career and education over the nation's future. And when it becomes clear that they may indeed not succeed in their revolutionary aims, she is forced to reconcile with her parents, judging them less harshly, and her partner too, for their personal priorities in the face of forces well beyond their control. The intimate style of the film often feels too insistent, even to the point of insensitivity, as Riyadh frequently films herself and boyfriend in what appear to be quite unguarded and sometimes quite trying conversations. Though the film can be cloying at times, in the end it allows us to witness a subtle shift in her perspective, a softening and an acceptance that in effect chronicle her transformation into a mature and nuanced adult.

With Mohammed Rashad who, incidentally appears in some of the group gatherings in Riyadh's film, the situation is slightly different. His film *Little Eagles* was made precisely because he did not have political parents, never even knew that such a thing existed, and come the revolution, felt woefully underprepared in comparison to many of his Cairene friends, who seemed to know exactly what to do and how to be in the unprecedented situation, as if they had been trained from a young age, which it turns out they had. He learns that many of his friends at the forefront of the movement to occupy Tahrir grew up in a social sphere comprised of predominantly middle-class left-wing parents, who set up a youth group called al-Nusur al-Sagira, translated variously as Young Eagles or Little Eagles, hence the title of the film. The Little Eagles, set up by 1970s activists, was essentially a left-wing equivalent to the Scouts, with meetings and summer camps that taught the young members survival skills, as well as educating them on political issues such as human rights and their rights as children. Not only did membership create a tight social network, it also proved to be excellent preparation for the revolution, preparation that Rashad noticed he was sorely lacking.

While the film may expose the painfully unresolved dynamics between a father and son, with Rashad in voice-over almost cruelly expressing his desire for a better caliber of father, it also shines a light on the class distinctions that run right through the core of Egyptian society. These are precisely the distinctions that enable a small, educated elite to imagine another kind of world, while the vast underclass of ordinary Egyptians toil away in dead-end

13.3. *Little Eagles* (2016), directed by Mohamed Rashad.

jobs (in the case of Rashad's father, working as a clothing presser), while never for a minute daring to dream of even the slightest change or improvement in their lot. Rashad may be the only working-class filmmaker in all of the first-person films I've seen from Egypt made in this period, and the only one who is thus able to express the dimensions and frustrations of this experience. Had the film taken a more collective view of that experience, insisting that Rashad's perspective, and not the Little Eagles', is the one shared by the vast majority of Egyptians, and thus the one most in need of attention if such collective revolutionary aspirations are ever to succeed, this film would have accomplished much more than it currently does. As it is, Rashad may have been too caught up in the personal need to avenge himself against his workaday, lackluster father, returning the disappointment he faced all his life as the too "artistic" (code for "effeminate"?) and idealistic embarrassment of a son. Nonetheless, the film reveals the wide chasm between the classes in Egypt that needs somehow to be bridged if any real change is going to happen, and in this the film is uniquely positioned.

Ahmed Nour's *Waves* is an important film in terms of diversity, given that it is made from the perspective of someone from Suez, far outside of the capital and center of all art and film production (Alexandria is really the only alternative film scene in Egypt, with Cairo as the unrivaled center), reminding the viewer that the revolution was literally and figuratively ignited in this neglected industrial backwater. In a country where "Cairo" is a metonym for "Egypt" and vice versa, it is important to remember the provinces and to differentiate the experiences of those living outside of the megalopolis, far from Tahrir, yet nonetheless absolutely essential to the nation's fortunes. Without the oil from the Suez region, and of course the revenue from the Suez Canal, a major international shipping zone, the Egyptian economy would suffer major losses. Yet we are all too rarely exposed to the vantage point of a Suezi.

Nour's film is structured as a series of "waves" which function like chapters, except that they don't necessarily add up so much as randomly process information and emotion through which meanings ebb and flow rather than accrue. At the outset of his film, there is a series of portraits of people in Suez, followed by a brief introductory monologue that has Mubarak coming to power in the 1980s, just as Nour's generation is born in Suez, tying their fates together while immediately situating the film in a broad historical context. The very next image after the title is that of Nour's baby niece, born a month before the start of the revolution, tying her generation to the new, post-Mubarak era. The footage of the weaning infant is intercut with images of the burning streets of Suez, the city credited with igniting the January 2011 revolution. There is a clear association being made between the individual, the new generation, and the political conditions into which these individuals were born. No one simply stands for him- or herself. And the emphasis on the neglected residents of Suez, their rage at the injustices visited historically upon the city, finds its analogy in the stories Nour chooses to tell based on his childhood and adolescent recollections. His experience, then, stands in synecdochically for the experience of those of his generation born in Suez. He makes a point of saying that the film is "personal and not personal," adding that, "if the film were just about myself, I wouldn't have made it" (Lebow 2018).

This leads me back to the point with which I began, about a collectivist

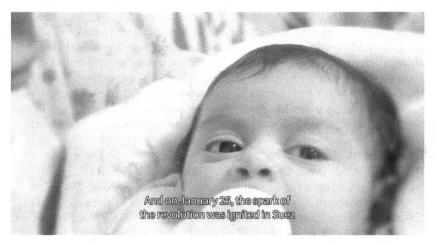

13.4. *Waves* (2013), directed by Ahmed Nour.

notion of the first person in most Egyptian first-person films emerging since the revolution. Viola Shafik, in her *Filming Revolution* interview, coins the phrase "personal-collective" to describe the introduction of her own individual subjectivity as as being more widely representative of a larger collective. In Shafik's words, "the 'I' that is speaking there, that's not Viola. It's actually me and the others who have the same problem of trying to understand the Revolution and the history of the country." This "personal-collective" voice represents the "me and not me" of such an endeavor (Lebow 2018). The implication of positioning oneself at the apex of such an association does assume an affinity with a collective that may not be fully formulated, and is certainly not fully representative. Having already raised the issue of class omissions that a film like *Little Eagles* implicitly underscores, it is not unproblematic for the predominantly middle-class filmmakers in this brief study to assert their commonalities with the Egyptian people as a whole, nor is there some neat mathematical equivalence that would translate divergent experiences of gender, race, educational level, religious beliefs, or political affiliation, making them one unified whole. That said, we must not discount the relevance of the emergence of the personal voice, as it models a type of citizenship and activism that can potentially affirm and inspire others, given the identificatory power of film. It may even be said that the more collectivist approaches to revolutionary cinema of the past constitute a failure on the part of cinemas of revolution, some of which tended to alienate viewers and fail to connect. Could it be that the effort to personalize and account for the experiential dimension of revolution is precisely what these Egyptian documentaries contribute to the history of revolutionary cinema? In the case of the Egyptian first-person films discussed here, I want to propose that rather than standing *out* from the crowd to emphasize a personal, individualistic point of view, they are precisely standing *with* the crowd, being willing to stick their heads above the parapet and be counted as one of the many, the millions who took to the streets to fight for change. Thus it is the collective spirit of these first-person films, even when they veer toward the intimately personal, that not only saves them from a myopic inwardness, but may in fact signal a new turn in twenty-first-century cinema of revolution.

References

Barthes, Roland. 1981. *Camera Lucida*. New York: Hill and Wang.
Berg, Andy, Jonathan Ostry, and Jeromin Zettelmeyer. 2006. "What Makes Growth Sustained?" IMF Working Paper, November. imf.org.
Eisenstein, Sergei. 2010. "The Dramaturgy of Film Form." In *Sergei Eisenstein: Writings 1922–1934*, edited and translated by Richard Taylor, 161–80. London: I.B. Tauris.

Hauslohner, Abigail. 2010. "Egypt's Plans for Luxor: Vegas on the Nile?" *Time Magazine*, October 21. http://content.time.com/time/world/article/0,8599,2026394,00.html.

Lebow, Alisa. 2008. *First Person Jewish*. Minneapolis: University of Minnesota Press.

Lebow, Alisa, ed. 2012. *The Cinema of Me: Self and Subjectivity in First-Person Documentary Film*. London: Wallflower Press.

Lebow, Alisa. 2013. "First Person Political." In *The Documentary Film Book*, edited by Brian Winston, 257–65. London BFI/Palgrave.

———. 2018. *Filming Revolution*. Palo Alto, CA: Stanford University Press. filmingrevolution.supdigital.org.

Malitsky, Joshua. 2004. "Esfir Shub and the Film Factory-Archive: Soviet Documentary from 1925–1928." *Screening the Past* 17. tlweb.latrobe.edu.au.

Solanas, Fernando, and Octavio Getino. 1969/2014. "Towards a Third Cinema: Notes and Experiences for the Development of a Cinema of Liberation in the Third World." In *Film Manifestos and Global Cinema Cultures: A Critical Anthology*, edited by Scott MacKenzie, 230–50. Berkeley: University of California Press.

———. 1971/2014. "Militant Cinema: An Internal Category of Third Cinema." In *Film Manifestos and Global Cinema Cultures: A Critical Anthology*, edited by Scott MacKenzie, 256–58. Berkeley: University of California Press.

Vertov, Dziga. 1984. *Kino-Eye: The Writings of Dziga Vertov*, edited by Annette Michelson, translated by Kevin O'Brien. Berkeley: University of California Press.

Yampolski, Mikhail, and Derek Spring. 1991. "Reality at Second Hand." *Historical Journal of Film, Radio and Television* 11, no. 12: 161–71.

14

GARDENING A PITILESS MOUNTAIN: TRANSCRIPT OF A LECTURE PERFORMANCE, 2011

Oraib Toukan

BACH SCENE 1

Every second humans are awake their eyes produce tears.[1] These tears contain fighters which resist foreign objects. Blinking spreads them over the surface of the eyes, and tears get sucked back through two small holes in the corner of our eyelids. These two openings are called puncta, and they are there to drain our tears.

14.1 Jerash, Jordan, 1971. 19 seconds dedicated to a flower and a sign. The sign reads that this flower grew in front of the PLO headquarters in Gaza Refugee Camp, Jordan.

While looking at this sequence, something—the flower, the subtitle, or the signpost—made me want to weep.[2] Admittedly, I did not weep at all, but I did start to wonder whether there is a relation between crying and landscapes. It was at that point that I chanced upon the Stendhal Syndrome in Andrea Fraser's seminal essay "Why Does Fred Sandback's Work Make Me Cry?" (Fraser 2006). The Stendhal Syndrome describes spurts of dizziness, heart palpitations, confusion, and sheer exhaustion after the ecstasy of being exposed to the "grandeur" of European art and heritage. It was apparently particularly noticeable among American tourists in Florence, and Japanese tourists in Paris, and was coined by the Florentine psychoanalyst Graziella Magherini in 1979 while studying groups of tourists, some of whom were admitted into psychiatric wards. More specifically, the Jerusalem Syndrome is said to be a form of confusion—and sometimes delusion—triggered by a visit to the city of Jerusalem. The syndrome does not explain weeping but does account for emotional exhaustion to the point of a breakdown of one's logical capacities. It could explain the inability to decipher meaning in the aftermath of visiting Palestine, even when one hasn't visited it.

There are three films relating to representation, revolution, and landscape that I will be borrowing from in this lecture, and they are by a group of filmmakers and writers who either lived in or traveled to Jordan to capture the Palestinian Revolution. These films are Masao Adachi and Kôji Wakamatsu's *Red Army/PFLP: Declaration of World War* (1971); Jean-Luc Godard's *Ici et Ailleurs* (1976) (initially with the Dziga Vertov group, then with Anne-Marie Miéville); and Mustafa Abu Ali's *They Do Not Exist*.

BACH SCENE II

Masao Adachi's *Red Army/PFLP* is a newsreel on the Marxist-Leninist revolutionary movement of the Popular Front for the Liberation of Palestine (PFLP) and their place in global anti-imperial struggles. Officially, the film was a collaboration between the Red Army Faction of Japan's Revolutionary Communist League and the PFLP, and was co-shot and produced with Koji Wakamatsu.

Adachi and Wakamatsu, like other Maoists at the time, stopped in Beirut on their way back from the Venice Film Festival in 1971. They exemplified a larger Third Worldist trend in the late 1960s that mobilized people like Jean Genet, Jean-Luc Godard, Jean-Paul Sartre, and Simone de Beauvoir to the Middle East (though the latter two had to be encouraged by the Beirut-based writer and publisher Suhail Idriss to give refugee camps in Gaza a chance while they were meeting with Gamal Abd al-Nasser in Cairo).

While in Lebanon, Adachi and Wakamatsu met with Leila Khaled and Ghassan Kanafani, who offered access to PFLP activities in the Saida and Shatila refugee camps. They then traveled to Jordan to shoot in the training camps of the northern border mountain area of Jerash, in its Gaza refugee camp, and in the city of Salt, followed by the Syrian–Israeli border. In spite of the disillusionment fellow French vanguardists began to feel for the violence these revolutionary movements entailed,[3] Adachi moved to Beirut in 1974 to "commit himself to Palestine." He stayed until he was arrested in 1997; in September 2001 he was handed over to the Japanese by Jordanian intelligence to be imprisoned for another two years in Japan.

My specific entry into the question of landscape and representation simmered in exactly nineteen seconds during the introductory sequence of this film: the camera pans across laundry-lined rooftops in a refugee camp, and cuts to a woman in yellow placing a tray on a rooftop. It was here that I recalled my grandmother saying she would leave a pot of *maglubeh* for fighters hopping from rooftop to rooftop in Jabal al-Weibdeh, targeting Jabal al-Qala'. Because the camp also overlooked an airport, I therefore (subconsciously) concluded that this scene was shot in Amman, and probably in Jabal Hussein refugee camp.

Adachi's shot list, however, confirms that this woman was not in Amman, but in Shatila camp in Lebanon. She may have been placing food, but she was more likely feeding the birds, or drying sage. Neglecting any kind of affinity I, or Adachi, or the PFLP may have to pan-Arabism, I pettily begin to figure out what was shot in which neighboring country until I realized it did not matter, for they were shot as one ubiquitous landscape representing: "Palestine."

This translation of landscapes into stages of political commentary is in fact Adachi's formal contribution to film theory. After his collaborative release of *AKA: Serial Killer* in 1969, *fukeiron* was coined to describe a rising movement of Japanese filmmakers with a formal propensity toward shooting event-less landscapes as eventful political shots in their own right. Though Adachi sees the *Red Army/PFLP* film as the beginning of his transition from Landscape Theory to newsreel films, traces of *fukeiron* still strikingly dot the film: traveling shots of roads and olive groves, fragmentary images of forests and barren mountaintops, banal and ordinary landscapes, all intercut with the everyday life of Palestinian guerrillas training to fight.

And though these scenes were geographically set in the north of Jordan and the south of Lebanon, they became de facto *about* "Palestine," both for Adachi and for the viewer. In interviews with Adachi, as well as in conversations among Go Hirosawa, Takashi Sakai, Shiro Yabu, or Harry Harootunian and Sabu Kohso, there is inadvertent talk of "going to Palestine," of "being in exile in Palestine," and so on, when actually Adachi was in Jordan and Lebanon. In the end sequence, a Japanese Communist League Red Army soldier states: "I think the purpose of my coming to Palestine involves a question of how we grasp the worldwide revolutionary war in our theoretical struggle." Indeed, in various synopses across the web, the film is often noted as being shot in Palestine.[4]

Here one may recall an article by Ahdaf Souief, published in *Al Ahram Weekly* in 2003, on Jean Genet's book *Prisoner of Love*, playfully entitled *Genet in Palestine*. Like Adachi, Genet was not in Palestine when he experienced "Palestine." Genet slowly wrote *Prisoner of Love* years after scribbling his thoughts among the Palestinian resistance in the landscapes of Ajloun and Jerash and the Beka'a camp in Jordan. This is the polar opposite of what W.J.T. Mitchell described as a Mark Twain syndrome of "the innocent abroad." a pilgrim (like, say, Pier Paolo Pasolini) who feels disenchanted if the landscape looks like Nevada when it's supposed to be biblical. In a way this landscape, be it Jordan parodying Palestine or Palestine parodying itself, has acted throughout as a mnemonic device for anyone outside of Palestine to help retain the memory of Palestine, one, as it is supposed to have existed, and two, in order to exist.[5] This idea of "Palestine as metaphor" was beautifully cast by Rasha Salti as the idea of there being "'many Palestines': Whether remembered, dreamed, or imagined in a life of forced exile within 'historic' Palestine" (Salti 2012, 19).

In 1982 the filmmakers Jean-Marie Straub and Danièle Huillet shot the film *Too Early, Too Late* in Egypt and France. Like many of their films, the horizon is used as the film's formal space to explore time and revolution. In a diptych they read excerpts of letters from Friedrich Engels to Karl Kautsky, against slow pans and static shots of rural France, followed by readings from Mahmoud Hussein's *Class Struggles in Egypt* that are set against Egyptian landscapes. In defending their film against charges of "landscape excess," the couple remark: "Yes, there are landscapes, and they are treated exactly as if they were people." The hero figure, the protagonist, is therefore the land, and it gets flipped into a subjective being in order to hold it accountable for its class-based representations.

In English, "landscape" was originally a painters' term, and though it derives from *landschap* (literally, land condition), it was commonly used in reference to paintings that "represent natural scenery." Arguably, European landscape painting evolved from romanticism to realism to impressionism in a struggle to locate subjectivity in the world itself. From Turner to Courbet, landscapes swayed between matters pertaining to light, planes, and perspectives, to that which became instrumentalized for articulating national sentiments. What was often bypassed altogether was a reading of these images in terms of class representations of an industrial and economic system that made these various scapes desolate, hollow, or sprawled in the first place (Bermingham 1994).

There are essentially two words in Arabic that denote landscape: *manzar* and *mashhad* (Latiri 2001). Both words point to the experience of seeing the representation of a framed scene. Subjectivity is encapsulated in the word, where what is being represented is likely to be analyzed, perceived, and described. There are numerous examples in contemporary representations of the Palestinian struggle where the word *ard* (terrain, earth) is imbricated within the word "Palestine" to form a particular understanding of the meaning of Palestine itself. Mahmoud Darwish's poem "On This Earth What Makes Life Worth Living" is just one example of Palestine and landscape being interwoven to mean one and the same thing (Said 1994). Similarly, the hills, in Palestinian poet Ibrahim Toukan's work "Mawtani" (My Homeland), which has now become the national anthem of Iraq, is an instance of the appropriation and reappropriation of landscape as hero and symbol of civil strife. Other examples could even include film titles in the 1960s and 1970s in the Arab world: *al-Tariq ila al-Quds, Imra'a fi al-tariq, Ithnayan `ala al-tariq, Sira' fi Jirash, Watani habibi*, and so on.

Adachi's contribution to revolutionary film, therefore, was to use that landscape as a backdrop to the everyday of militarism and not to center on narrative, or on the dramatic and epoch-making moments that filled militant filmmaking at the time (Furuhata 2007) (cf. "the camera as the inexhaustible expropriator of image-weapons; the projector, a gun that can shoot 24 frames per second"[6]). Even spectacular events, like the Dawson's Field operation, when five aircrafts were hijacked and rerouted to a small landing strip in Jordan, become rather subdued. The "everyday" was represented here as women learning to use artillery, men cooking, and men and women collectively reading Mao, all leading up to a long finale accompanied by the sound of the *Internationale*.

Though the montage of these images reeks of propaganda, the film never claimed to be otherwise. The fedayeen were undeniably created to construct an image for a Palestinian revolution; they were a conscious, concerted effort to create a locality in the act of representing it. Jean Genet twice recounts in *Prisoner of Love* a woman telling him the Palestinian revolution means "to have been dangerous for a thousandth of a second, to have been handsome for a thousandth of a thousandth of a second, to have been that, or happy or something, and then to rest—what more can one want?" (Genet 1986, 268).

Marking an antagonism to the newsreel formats of fellow Maoists like Adachi, Godard argues in *Ici et Ailleurs* that the anthem of the *Internationale* is being played too loud in general, and in his own film, to the point where he can't see the images he shot any more. In fact his whole film unfolds into the choice of making a film that problematizes the very idea of representing a Palestinian revolution in the first place.

Although Godard and Jean-Pierre Gorin arrive in Jordan before Adachi in 1970, to film *Until Victory* for the PLO, Godard only revisits and deconstructs this footage five years later on the editing table. In three separate segments, and by way of first-person voice-over, we unpack what happens to hearing and seeing when shifts in time and space entirely change the original premise on which the footage was built. Only then does Godard title the film *Ici et Ailleurs*, and uses Mieville's voice in the third part of the film, to have a conversation on the film as a critique of its own making.

In the Brechtian vein of activating viewers to decode meaning for themselves (Emmelhainz 2012), Godard essentially ends up silencing his footage to the point of misinformation. Crudely speaking, *Ici et Ailleurs* is often analyzed from the perspective of "May '68 in France vis-à-vis Palestine," from the perspective of Godard's disenchantment with "staged" material and "blatant lies," from the perspective of "reframing an unfinished film about Palestine" or of the naivetés in "protest aesthetics," and so on (Sheikh 2010; Steyerl 2002). What ultimately resonates most, though, is the imagination of sounds and pictures angrily protesting against their unjust employment in the parallel histories of cinema, Palestine, and resistance.[7] Protesting, perhaps, against Palestine as a *mise en abîme* of its own image from early European photography of the Holy Land until today; against Palestine's automatic mnemonic button when its contemporary problems are so much bigger;[8] against a surprised intellectual left that the images the resistance ultimately chose in their game of mass media.

In this manner, Godard created an assembly line of sorts, as Hito Steyerl seminally proposed in 2002: a chain of production of pictures and sounds that are strategically organized, edited, and arranged to articulate protest in montage, and montage of protest. Steyerl concludes by asking a few questions: "What if the 'and' in this 'here and elsewhere,' in this France and Palestine, does not represent an addition, but rather a subtraction?" So what, I would ask, is one to make of Godard's choice of subtracting a context entirely from these images?

In one scene, Godard and Miéville critique a character they call "a little girl from Fateh," who is dressed in a military outfit and is standing on the ruined landscape of al-Karameh while impeccably reciting a poem by Mahmoud Darwish. Miéville interrupts the girl and analyzes her performance as staged (whether by a political faction or by Godard and Gorin, we are not told), and declares that this form of political theater is very familiar in the context of the French revolution: "She is innocent, but maybe not this form of theater." Though the girl's gestures may indeed feel familiar to my own experience of first-grade Arabic classes (pre-Oslo), her performance transcends theatrical and aesthetic analysis, given the delicate and ephemeral context in which she is standing, and the landscape she is reciting from.[9]

But Godard left that landscape entirely decontextualized, even though, paradoxically, the girl's performance encapsulates that key moment in which the image of a Palestinian revolution was born; the kind of image that prompted the likes of Godard, Genet, and Adachi to come and represent it as it was being made on celluloid. Godard was well aware of that, but, ironically, he chose the aesthetics of the landscape over its politics, to address the very paradox of the role of the intellectual in activism/nationalism.

Al-Karameh is actually a small town in Jordan, close to the Israeli border, with a Palestinian refugee camp that stationed many guerrilla fighters, including a headquarters for the PLO. Although several guerrilla factions had been formed in the late 1950s, it was not until the 1967 war that fighters streamlined their representation until the actual coining of the term "fedayeen" (fida'iyyin; literally, "the sacrificers") in refugee camps in Jordan (Massad 2001).

In March 1968, Israel crossed into Jordan to crush the resistance at that very site where the girl is standing. Joining forces with the Jordanian army, the fedayeen went into battle with the Israeli army head to head for the first time. Although the Israelis leveled the town, they equally suffered heavy damages and ultimately withdrew. According to Joseph Massad, and depending on whose account one reads, the al-Karameh battle was the single most influential event in creating and then representing the Palestinian revolution. It was the first victory, after which thousands of Palestinians (and Jordanians) volunteered to join the guerrillas, and caused King Hussein's famous quote of May 1968: "There will come a day when we all shall become *Fida'iyyin* in that part of the world" (Massad 2001).

The battle was ironically also the single most important historical event for King Hussein and the Jordanian army, but also for a generation of Jordanians on the quest to nationhood (Massad 2001). A closing scene in Abdallah Kawash's film *Watani habibi* (*My Beloved Homeland*, 1964) exemplifies this: the main character's son surprises his father by wearing a little army outfit, his father embraces him in pride, and the film ends.

That year, Hani Jawharieh, who was working as a wedding photographer in his brother's studio, teamed up with Sulafah Jadallah and Mustafa Abu Ali to form what later became the Palestine Film Unit of the PLO. The unit was so makeshift it camped out in a kitchen in Amman, drying films with primitive machines that ran on kerosene (Habshneh 2008). And thanks to this, Jawharieh claims,

> the pictures of Palestinian fedayeens spread throughout the world, especially those pictures that portrayed the al-Karamah Battle of March 1967. A group of young, high-spirited nationalists toiled round the clock to print, develop, and magnify posters of the Fedayeen. Posters were hung in big tents in al-Wihdat Refugee Camp in Jordan. That was the first exhibit in which the Palestinian people saw themselves in pictures that spoke of their national cause and revolution. For the first time they could *see* Palestinian youth fighting against the Israeli Army. (Habshneh 2008)

Their success led to a spurt of units that used film for mass media: "the PFLP Central Media Committee in 1971 (for whom Adachi worked), the PLO Cultural Media Department in 1972 (for whom Godard was filming), the PDFLP Central Media in 1973, Palestine Cinema Group/Palestine Research Center in 1973, and Samed for Cinema Production in 1976" (Habshneh 2008).

The popularity of the guerrillas became such a challenge to Jordanian rule (and to faction heads themselves, who could not control the public rights that some fighters were arrogating to themselves [Massad 2001]), that by September 1970, the tensions culminated in a two-week period of blood-shed,[10] killing thousands of Palestinians and forcing thousands more into exodus.[11] Mustafa Abu Ali, Sulafah Jadallah, and Hani Jawharieh left this chapter of their film unit and became part of that exodus at different points.

Jean Genet writes, "If I have to say why I went with the Fadayeen, I find the ultimate explanation is that I went for fun. Chance helped a lot. I think I was already dead to the world. And very slowly, as if of consumption, I finally died altogether."

BACH SCENE III

The three-part Bach scene that has structured my lecture is borrowed from Mustafa Abu Ali's film *They Do Not Exist* (1974). Abu Ali uses Bach's Violin Concerto in e minor, structured in three separate movements, to form a three-part sequence of the Israeli air raid on Nabatieh Camp on May 16, 1974. Bach's concerto is played against silent footage of the air raid, while the sound of the raid is placed against text quotes from Golda Meir and Moshe Dayan.

If you place the piece in voice recognition software, you can confirm that this particular work was extracted from the following record:

The piece was first recorded in 1972 in London, at Abbey Studios, by the Israeli trio, Itzhak Perlman, Pinchas Zukerman, and Daniel Barenboim. I am not entirely sure if Abu Ali intentionally chose an Israeli version of this oft-recorded Bach piece. But thirty years later, as a symbolic example of just how radically different the fabric is now, Mustafa Barghouti and Edward Said (who created the Barenboim-Said Foundation for music with Barenboim) lobbied for Barenboim to become the first Israeli to be granted Palestinian citizenship from Mahmoud Abbas, as a reward for his solidarity with Palestine (Haas 2008).

14.2 Cover of Barenboim Bach's 1972 Recordings at Abbey Studios.

Nevertheless, in one scene, Abu Ali seamlessly draws that very "theater" that Godard and Miéville critique: a man leaves the camps with gifts, and enters the next scene where he is in the mountains handing out these gifts to the fighters. The character so happens to be in both places, from the doorbell to the training camp, from the refugee camp to the revolution, in consecutive seconds.

In another scene, another character called Aida writes a fan letter to the fighters. In fact Aida has often spoken:

14.3 Aida speaks in a letter in the *Arab Weekly*.

Here I find her in an archival issue of *Arab Weekly* described as follows: "Another young Arab girl looks for a means to donate to the heroes of the armed resistance. Aida has come from her homeland in Saudi Arabia to the *Arab Weekly* offices in Beirut offering her hair for sale, the proceeds of which will go to the heroes of the armed resistance. Aida is willing to immediately cut it off for any willing and able person who would purchase it for the sons of the Arab World."

Jean Genet writes: "It was the Palestinian phenomenon that made me write this book, but why did I stick so closely to the obviously crazy logic of that war? I can only explain by remembering what I value: one or another of my prisons, a patch of moss, a few bits of hay, perhaps some wild flowers pushing up a slab of concrete or granite paving stone. Or, the only luxury

I'll allow myself, two or three dog roses growing on a gaunt and thorny bush" (Genet 1986, 386).

So, if we remove the event from the landscape, will we find that these images were ever about Palestine to begin with? If we remove the sound from Abu Ali's testimonials in Nabatieh Camp, can we better hear his characters? And if we subtract the sound and the event from Adachi's timeline, what will ultimately become of it?

References

Alessandrini, Anthony. 2011. "The Elsewhere of Our Here." Review of John E. Drabinski, *Godard Between Identity and Difference* (New York and London: Continuum, 2008). *Jadaliya*, October 13.

Barthes, Roland. 1982. *Camera Lucida: Reflections on Photography*. 2nd ed. New York: Hill and Wang.

Bermingham, Ann. 1994. "System, Order, and Abstraction: The Politics of English Landscape Drawing around 1795." In *Landscape and Power*, 2nd ed., edited by W.J.T. Mitchell, 76-98. Chicago: University of Chicago Press.

Emmelhainz, Irmgard. 2009. "Before Our Eyes: les mots, non les choses: Jean-Luc Godard's *Ici et Ailleurs* (1970–74) and *Notre Musique* (2004)." Master's thesis, Department of Art, University of Toronto.

———. 2012. "Between Objective Engagement and Engaged Cinema: Jean-Luc Godard's 'Militant Filmmaking' (1967–1974)." *E-flux Journal* 34. e-flux.com.

Fraser, Andrea. 2006. "Why Does Fred Sandback's Work Make Me Cry?" *Grey Room* 22 (Winter). 30–47.

Furuhata, Yuriko. 2007. "Returning to Actuality: Fûkeiron and the Landscape Film." *Oxford Journals, Screen* 48, no. 3 (Autumn), 345–362. doi.org.

Genet, Jean. 1986. *Prisoner of Love*. 2nd ed. New York: NYRB Classics.

Haas, Amira. 2008. "Honorary Citizenship of the Moon." *Haaretz*, January 16.

Habshneh, Khadija. 2008. "Palestinian Revolution Cinema." *This Week in Palestine* 117. January. thisweekinpalestine.com.

Hirasawa, Go. 2003. Hirasawa's *Cinema/Revolution*. bordersphere.com.

Al-Khalili, Yazan. (2010) "Darkness Against the Landscape: De-familiarizing the Image." Centre for Research Architecture, Goldsmith. www.yazankhalili.com.

Latiri, Lamia. 2001. "The Meaning of Landscape in Classical Arabo-Muslim Culture." *European Journal of Geography* 196 (October 16): 1-17.

Massad, Joseph. 2001. *Colonial Effects: The Making of National Identity in Jordan*. New York: Columbia University Press.

Salti, Rasha. 2012. "I Am So Lonely: Palestine as a Metaphor." In *Tin Soldiers*, edited by Ala' Younis, 18-35. Gwanju Biennale, Korea.

Said, Edward. 1994. "Invention, Memory and Place." Critical Inquiry 26: 175–192.

Sheikh, Simon. 2010. "Positively Protest Aesthetics Revisited." *E-flux Journal* 20 (November). e-flux.com.

Steyerl, Hito. 2002. "The Articulation of Protest." republicart.net.

15

THE ARAB–JEW AND
THE INSCRIPTION OF MEMORY

Ella Shohat

Recent years have seen a renaissance of Mizrahi and/or Arab-Jewish cultural practices related to identity and belonging. These practices too must be seen against the backdrop of contested histories and terminologies. The identity crisis provoked by the rupture of Jews from their largely Arab/Muslim countries is reflected in a terminological crisis in which no single term seems to fully represent a coherent entity. The very proliferation of terms suggests the enormous difficulties of grappling with the complexities of this identity. To name a few: "Sephardim," "Jews of Islam," "Arab–Jews," "Jewish–Arabs," "Middle Eastern Jews," "Asian and African Jews," "Non-European Jews," "Third World Jews," "Levantine Jews," "Bnei Edot Ha-Mizrah" (descendents of the Eastern communities), "Blacks," "Mizrahim" (Easterners), "Iraqi–Jews," "Moroccan–Jews," "Iranian–Jews," "Kurdish–Jews," "Turkish–Jews," "Palestinian–Jews," and so forth. Each term raises questions about the implicit discursive politics that both generated the terms and made them catchwords at specific conjunctures. Each term encodes a historical, geographical, and political point of view. Prior to their arrival in Israel, Jews in Iraq, for example, regarded themselves as Jews, but that identity was diacritically positioned in relation to other communities. Within a transregional space that extended from the Atlantic through the Mediterranean to the Indian Ocean, Jews retained a Jewishness that was culturally and socially interwoven into Islamic civilization. Shaped by Arab–Muslim culture, more specifically, they also helped shape that culture, in a dialogical process that generated their Judeo-Arab identity. The proliferating hyphens, in this sense, highlight a complexly embedded identity that must be articulated in relation to multiple communities and geographies.

The rise of Zionism and Arab nationalism, along with the implementation of partitions as a colonial solution for regional conflicts, inevitably

259

impacted the identity designations of Jews in the Arab Muslim world. Arabness came to signify a national identity, requiring a realignment of Ottoman definitions. Their religion (Judaism) rapidly became a national marker in the international arena, conflicting with their Arab civilizational belonging. They came to occupy an ambivalent position vis-à-vis both Zionism and Arab nationalism. The explosive political situation subsequent to the partition of Palestine and the establishment of the state of Israel produced a new context, rendering their existence in Arab countries virtually impossible. Upon arrival in Israel, Arab–Jews entered a new linguistic/discursive paradigm, shaped by geopolitical (the Israel/Arab conflict), legal (Israeli citizenship), and cultural (East versus West) forces. The normative term became "Israeli," not merely a signifier of a new passport, but also an indicator of a new cultural and ideological formation.

Whereas Jewishness in Arab/Muslim spaces formed part of a constellation of coexisting and complexly stratified ethnicities and religions, Jewishness in Israel was now the assumed cultural/political "dominant." Arabness became the marginalized category, while the religion of Arab Jews, for the first time in their history, came to be affiliated with the dominant state power and attuned to the very basis of national belonging. Their cultural Arabness, meanwhile, was transformed into an embarrassing excess, a marker of ethnic, even racial, otherness. If in the Arab world it was their Jewishness (associated now with Zionism) that was subjected to surveillance, in Israel, it was their affiliation with an Arab cultural geography that was similarly disciplined and punished. The processes of spatial rupture and cultural displacement, in this sense, have impacted and shifted the identity labels.

[. . .]

Another aspect of this terminological problematic is how to verbally convey the unprecedented movement across borders of West Asian/North African Jews in the wake of the partition of Palestine. Nationalist paradigms cannot capture the ambivalence of this historical movement, particularly for Arab Jews. Given the idiosyncratic situation of a community trapped between two nationalisms—Arab and Jewish—each term used to designate the displacement seems problematic. Terms such as *"aliya"* (ascendancy), *"yetzia"* (exit), "exodus," "expulsion," "immigration," "emigration," "exile," "refugees," "expatriates," and "population exchange" do not seem adequate. In the case of the Palestinians, forced into a mass exodus, the term "refugee" is appropriate since they never wanted to leave Palestine and have steadfastly nourished the desire to return. In the case of Arab–Jews, the question of will, desire, and agency remains highly ambiguous. It is not only a matter of legal definition of citizenship that is at stake, but also mental maps of belonging within the context of rival nationalisms. Did Arab–Jews want to stay? Did they want to leave? If so, did they want to leave for Israel or elsewhere? Did they exercise free will in deciding to leave? Once in Israel, did they want to go elsewhere, or go back to their countries of origin? Were they able to do so? And did they regret the impossibility of returning? Different answers to these questions imply distinct assumptions about agency, memory, and space.

The official term *aliya*, meanwhile, is misleading on a number of levels. It suggests a commitment to Zionism, when, in fact, the majority of Jews— and certainly Jews within the Levant—were hardly Zionists in the modern nationalist sense of the word. Zionist discourse normalizes the telos of a Jewish nation-state; any move toward its borders is represented as the ultimate Jewish act. When the actual departure of Arab–Jews is represented on the screen, it is usually narrated as an act of devotion. In the controversial TV series produced for Israel's fiftieth anniversary, *Tkuma* (1998), images of Yemeni Jews arriving at the camps set up by the Jewish Agency are juxtaposed with a voice-over that reductively speaks of persecution and Messianic will.[1] The Yemeni Jews are represented as voluntarily crossing the desert and sacrificing their lives to get to the Promised Land, which the film implicitly equates with the state of Israel. Zionist writings often naturalize the inevitability of this destination while erasing the diverse Zionist tactics to actively dislodge these communities, including false wrappings of the nation-state with the "coming of the Messiah." This *aliya* metanarrative at times is axiomatically assumed even within revisionist films, as when David Belhassen and Asher Hemias' documentary *Ringworm Children* (Yaldei Hagazezet, 2003) begins its arrival story with a voice-over that describes "the wave of massive *aliya* knocking on the gates of the land."

Critical films, such as David Benchetrit's epic scale documentary *Kaddim Wind: Moroccan Chronicles* (2002), rewrite the foundational *aliya* discourse. The film begins with the Moroccan national anthem on the soundtrack, thereby acoustically counteracting the assumption that Moroccan Jews by definition belonged to Israel. Through the archival footage of departing vehicles, we glimpse the moment of rupture for Moroccan Jews, narrated with an almost dirge-like elegy. The testimonial interviews with diverse Moroccan-Israelis address their confused reasons for moving to Israel, which for the most part do not reflect a Zionist desire, as well as their initial traumatic encounters with the Ashkenazi-dominated Israeli apparatus. Whether through archival material or contemporary interviews, the film, in a kind of a double movement, interweaves nostalgic memories of the Moroccan past with the shock of arrival in Israel. Deconstructing the metanarrative of modernization, revisionist cinema fills in an important representational gap—the challenge of being at once of the larger Middle East and living within the boundaries of Israel. Instead of constituting merely a euphoric beginning of modern Jewish life, here Israel constitutes a topos of loss, including the loss of Jewishness as lived and known before the arrival of Zionism in the region.

Critical Mizrahi work has called attention to the chasm between official discourse and the actual experiences of Middle Eastern Jews, both in terms of the before and the after of their arrival in Israel. (Here I use "Mizrahi" less in the sense of origins and more in the sense of conveying a critical perspective.) Revisionist films do not view Arab-Muslim spaces through the prism of pogroms and the Holocaust; instead, they interrogate the dominant paradigms. Some even go as far as to articulate the latent "what ifs" of history, expressing a forbidden desire for a lost Arab homeland. A few documentaries capture moments where interviewees express regret over their destination of ending up in Israel, or reveal, however unrealistically, a desire to return. An unofficial chronicle of Moroccan Jews, *Kaddim Wind* orchestrates a polyphonic conversation with a variety of interviewees from the Moroccan-Israeli political spectrum, including politicians, activists, writers, scholars, and religious leaders, such as Erez Bitton, Reuven Abergel, Shlomo Ben Ami, Arieh Der'i, Sami Shalom Chetrit, and Ovad Aboutbul, who arrived in Israel at a young age. Diverse in terms of class, status, occupation, and residency, as well as in terms of ideological perspectives, they all recount a traumatic first encounter with Israel and an ongoing struggle for equality. A deep nostalgia for Morocco is often expressed, at times even moving toward a beyond-the-pale potential affiliation with Palestinians and Palestine. One sequence, shot in the *moshav*[2] town Mevasseret Zion, near Jerusalem, follows homeless families and squatters protesting discriminatory policies on land and housing. They report having asked for asylum from Yasser Arafat's Palestinian Authority in Jericho. Benny Torati's *Barzent Roofs* (1994), meanwhile, documents a southern Tel Aviv tent "settlement" camp protesting housing policies and angrily promising an "intifada" (using the Arabic word in Hebrew) worse than the Palestinian intifada. (That year-and-a-half-long protest, like many, was completely crushed.) In these instances, "Palestine" signifies crossing the outer limits of a licensed imaginary; it points to an emotional exhaustion point, to the failure to contain Mizrahi anger and a refusal to be "bad children," to evoke Golda Meir's condescending 1970s phrase about the Black Panthers.

The Mizrahi/Palestinian nexus is explored in Nizar Hassan and Danae Elon's documentary *Cut* (2000), which recounts the 1950s settlement of the Palestinian village 'Agur with largely Kurdish Jews from Iraq and Turkey. The residents describe the reasons for their departure for Israel: "It was not Zionism; it was religion, and therefore we kissed the earth." When Hassan asks if they wish to return, they respond that their Iraqi departure document stated "*ruha bala raj'a*" ("leaving without returning" in Iraqi Arabic dialect). In fact, the laissez-passer issued by the Iraqi monarchy stated: "La yasmah li-hamilihi bi-l-'awda ila al-'Iraq batatan" (the [document] holder is definitively not permitted to return). Yet the interviewee's rendering of the laissez-passer's idiom as a colloquial expression, "*ruha bala raj'a*," actually a curse, echoes the morbid sentiment around departure. At the same time, one of the residents admits with visible emotion: "To return would have been the greatest pleasure of my life . . . but to live there, I wouldn't want it. Can't even think of it . . . It's impossible to leave. To visit, I did visit. My uncle who converted to Islam became the sheikh of the village. . . . I visited the grave of my father." Throughout, the film captures an existence caught between the anxieties of the Israeli/Palestinian conflict, on the one hand, and Arab spaces of nostalgia, on the other. On the soundtrack, the contemporary moment is largely evoked by the Iraqi music of Ilham al-Madfai, who emerged onto the music scene almost two decades after the departure of Iraqi Jews. Syncretizing traditional Iraqi songs with jazz and salsa, the film's non-diegetic music invokes Iraq in the past and present tenses. The soundtrack registers multiple dislocations and exoduses from Iraq (al-Madfai has been residing in Jordan), producing diverse Iraqi diasporic syncretisms. At the same time, Israel/Palestine is evoked through the recurrent sounds and images of military helicopters. Under the shadow of the conflict, the residents recall their desperate struggle to survive in Israel: hunger, joblessness, crowded shacks, lack of electricity, protests and clashes with police, along with fatal confrontation with *mistanenim/fida'iyun*. Symptomatically, they oscillate between Hebrew and Arabic when they refer to the Palestinians who crossed back across the borders, whom the Israelis called "infiltrators," and the Palestinians "men of sacrifice" or "freedom fighters"—an instability having to do with the anxiety of both Israeli and Palestinian addressees.

Partly narrated in Arabic, using Arabic text in the prelude and deploying Arabic subtitles throughout, *Cut* attempts to mediate the story of Arab–Jews for Palestinians in Israel. The filmmakers, furthermore, incorporate their own presence into the story, addressing the residents' anxiety over the filming. Hassan challenges the interviewees when they use the Hebrew pronunciation 'Agur (pronounced with a hard "g") to refer to their *moshav*, reminding them that prior to filming they consistently used the Arabic name 'Ajur (pronounced with a soft "g"). The presence of non-Mizrahi filmmakers, it could be argued, provokes Mizrahim to become self-aware and relay the official discourse, virtually performing docile citizenship. Numerous anti-occupation films use the hostile dark faces of Mizrahim to represent the oppressive nature of occupation. Their aggressivity toward the interrogative camera and their hands covering the lens tend to underline the Euro-Israeli image of Mizrahi fanaticism or even fascism. Yet, without romanticizing Mizrahim—or any community, for that matter—what such representations do not acknowledge is the underlying Mizrahi class/ethnic hostility to the privileged Euro-Israeli filmmaker, whose camera, car, and body language communicate an assumed authority or entitlement over the space. Such tensions go unmarked in such anti-occupation documentaries as Amos Gitai's *Field Diary* (1982), where the soldier–filmmaker friction is framed as merely about the occupation, between the enlightened camera and the (dark) forces that close off its view. *Cut*, in contrast, reflexively narrates a triangular encounter between a Euro-Israeli filmmaker (Elon) and a Palestinian filmmaker (Hassan), on the one hand, and Arab–Jews on the other. It calls attention to the process—from the suspicion with which the filmmakers are greeted to their bonding with some of the interviewees. The film itself relays an edifying story of building trust—of hopeful possibilities and anxious impossibilities. Thus, while subjectivizing the Mizrahim, *Cut* ends with an appreciation of the limits of trust in the war zone. The concluding acknowledgment—"This film would not have been possible without the love and the trust of 'Agur's residents"—is cut short by the aggressive acoustic and visual presence of the military helicopters.

The interviews with Arab–Jews in *Route 181* (2004), similarly, reveal an intricate relationship to Israel/Palestine on the part of individuals entangled in a war situation but also imbued with memories of life in the Arab world. In the "North" chapter, the filmmakers interview North Africans, who speak of a Moroccan or Tunisian past, which would seem out of place given their fraught situation near the Lebanese border. A Tunisian woman, who lost a son in a war, expresses a longing for her former life in Tunisia, thus illuminating the Arab/Jewish interfaces that were much more likely before 1948. The Iraqi–Jews in Samir's *Forget Baghdad* (2002), similarly, some of whom were communists in Iraq and never actually intended to move to Israel, shed light on the circumstances that dislocated them, asserting that Israel would not have been their preferred destination had there been other options. Indeed, the writer Samir Naqqash stubbornly continued to write his novels in Arabic even after moving to Israel, crafting a heteroglossic array of Iraqi ethnic, religious, and regional dialects, while Sami Michael and Shimon Ballas shifted to Hebrew, but continued to write about Iraq or about Iraqis in Israel. The protagonists of Michael's *A Handful of Fog* (*Hofen Shel Arafel*, 1979), which is set in Iraq, are communists who belong to diverse ethnicities and religions. Ballas's *Outcast* (*Ve-Hu Aher*, 1991), meanwhile, recounts the case of a Jewish–Iraqi scholar who stayed in Baghdad after the Jewish community's departure and converted to Islam.[3] The treatment of the Arab–Jew in literature and cinema thus offers the reader/spectator an imaginary voyage into the past, prior to the severing of the Arab-Jewish body, and hints at the possibility of reclaiming the Arab–Jew for a reconfigured future. "Arab" and "Jew" are revealed to be contingent signifiers rather than essential categories. Home and homelessness, meanwhile, do not coincide neatly with the boundaries of the nation-state or with official documents of citizenship. The figure of the Arab–Jew, in this sense, transcends past fixities and blurs contemporary boundaries.

15.1. *Route 181* (2004), directed by Michel Khleifi & Eyal Sivan.

15.2. *Forget Bagdad* (2002), directed by Samir.

Above and beyond the initial rupture, whether contested, mourned, or celebrated, recent displacements represent an end to an era that elicits potential allegorical readings of the earlier displacement. The representation of recent dislocation poses a retroactive question of whether Jews could, should, or would have remained in the Arab/Muslim world. Against the backdrop of the "return from exile" operation, which brought elderly Iraqi Jews to Israel following the outbreak of the Iraq War, Inigo Gilmore's *The Last Jews of Babylon* (2003) tells the story of eighty-five-year-old Ezra Levy's journey from Iraq to Israel. In Baghdad, where he feels at home in his spacious house, he longs for his family and for his lost love Daisy, whom he last saw more than fifty years ago at the departure of the majority of the Jewish population. The cross-border move that began with the excitement of reunification ends with an elderly man alone in his narrow living quarters, visibly depressed. In one sequence, Ezra visits an Israeli school, where he answers (in English) rather prejudicial questions about Iraq. A sense of alienation emerges even with the Iraqi-Israelis, the decades of separation lived in different worlds having created a gap that seems unbridgeable. Through Ezra's unique perspective, the spectator reflects on the measure and the degree of the acculturation of his old Iraqi acquaintances in Israel. Whereas he had lived as a Jewish minority in a Muslim space, Ezra begins to live as an Iraqi minority in a Jewish state. In Israel, his joyful moments are visible in Palestinian spaces; in a Jaffa café or at a Palestinian wedding, dancing to Arab music. While the film revolves around the theme of *aliya*, it does not replicate the *aliya* discourse, performing neither the rescue of the Baghdadi Jew, nor the happy end of a homecoming among fellow Jews, even, for that matter, with fellow Iraqi–Jews.

[. . .]

Recent Mizrahi cultural practices invoke Arabic or Middle Eastern culture as inhabiting the present-day Mizrahi body, liminally figuring life on the edge of the intimate and the distant, of home and exile, state citizenship, and cultural belonging. The question of the Arabic language—a mother tongue for Arab–Jews but also Israel's enemy language—has thus become a metonym and metaphor for the displacement. Arabic, in this context, is not merely a language but a trope that evokes the dilemmas of continuity and discontinuity between past and present where one's previous homeland has become the enemy of the current one. In contrast to Mizrahi literature, where Hebrew occasionally stands in for Arabic, and where Arabic phrases are sometimes written in Hebrew script, cinema as a multitrack medium has made it possible for Arabic to neighbor and intersect with Hebrew—both written and spoken. The celluloid inscription of Arabic, along with Mizrahi-accented Hebrew, relocates the Mizrahim within cultural contexts and historical moments that transcend nation-state boundaries. Unlike literary texts, films allow for the literal registry of the multiplicity of dialects in Israel and the diversity of Mizrahi and non-Ashkenazi accents in Hebrew (inflected not only by Arabic but also by other tongues, such as Turkish, Farsi, Ladino, Georgian, and Amharic). Mizrahi cinema, in this sense, tends to deploy a multi-accentual soundtrack. The broken Hebrew of the older generation and the broken Arabic of the younger generation no longer signifies inferiority, but rather a culturally dense fault-line existence. (At times, a single sentence features multiple languages, rendered comprehensible with the help of subtitles). Eschewing the generic "mark of the plural," Mizrahi cinema thus orchestrates the variety of Mizrahi voices, invoking multiple geographies and diverse classes. Mizrahi subaltern proletarians, without access to upwardly mobile institutional spaces, gain access to a space of representation. Repressed memories, whether of Muslim spaces or of the immediate aftermath of the arrival to Israel, are reenacted and documented, generating a new Mizrahi testimonial cinema. In a vital audiovisual revisionist project, critical cinema revisits the literal polyglossia that informs the intricate social-cultural space of Israel/Palestine.

The Mizrahi project of reclaiming "Arabness" and "Easternness," whatever its political implications, has cumulatively redefined the cultural parameters of an Israel that is no longer merely a prolongation of Europe "in" but not "of" the Middle East. Over the past decade, Mizrahi literature and cinema of the second and third generation have been engaging the departure from the Arab world and the move to Israel, whether in semi-autobiographical fiction or in autobiographical documentaries. Duki Dror's *My Fantasia* (*Fantazya sheli*, 2001) traces the story of the filmmaker's family in Iraq and Israel using the family's Hanukkah menorah workshop as a backdrop for probing conversations. Rami Kimchi's *Cinema Egypt* (2003) cites Egyptian cinema to rekindle memories of a lost Egyptian past that continues to survive in present-day Israel. Interviewing his mother about her life in Egypt and in Israel, Kimchi screens one of her favorite Egyptian films, *Leila the Village Girl* (1941), directed by the Jewish-Egyptian Togo Mizrahi, and starring the Jewish-Egyptian movie actress Leila Mourad. These autobiographical documentaries go down film's memory lane, as it were, in order to paint a cosmopolitan portrait of Egypt. Other films, meanwhile, recount literal return journeys. In Duki Dror's *Taqasim* (1999), the Egyptian Israeli musicians visit their old Cairo neighborhood and friends, while in Asher de Bentolila Tlalim's *Exile* (*Galoot*, 2003), the filmmaker returns to Morocco, to the family's house in Tangier. Return, whether literal or symbolic, has become a common motif within a process of reflection triggered by the search for "roots."

15.3. *Café Noah* (1996), directed by Duki Dror.

15.4. Poster of *Taqasim* (1999),
directed by Duki Dror.

Documentaries such as Eyal Halfon's *Chalery Baghdad* (2002) and Duki Dror's *Taqasim* and *Café Noah* (1996) are devoted to the music of the dislocated generation, specifically the story of Arab-Jewish musicians who ended up in a country that disdained their Arabic music, denying them access to funding and public outlets. While *Taqasim* follows the voyage of the musician Felix Mizrahi to Cairo, where he grew up, *Café Noah* tells the story of the consumption of Arabic music in Israel by Arab–Jews throughout the 1950s and 1960s. Other films shed light on Arab-Jewish writers and Mizrahi literature, delving into the linguistic rupture for writers whose mother tongue is Arabic. David Benchetrit's documentary, *Samir* (1997), focuses on the Iraqi-Israeli writer Sami Michael, who, along with other writers such as Shimon Ballas, made a conscious decision to shift from writing in Arabic to writing in Hebrew, while Samir Naqqash, as we have seen, continued to write in Arabic. The homage to Sami Michael attempts to recuperate the place of the Arab-Jewish/Mizrahi writer within the Hebrew literary canon.

The surge in memoirs and personal essays, in autobiographical and diary documentaries, and in the performing and visual arts' incorporation of familial memorabilia must all be seen as part of a desire to reconfigure a conflictual Mizrahi identity.[4] Films such as Simone Bitton's *Yoredet* (1989), Yochi Dadon-Spigel's *Gifted* (2000), Serge Ankri's *Mama's Couscous* (1994), Sini Bar David's *The South—Alice Never Lived Here* (1998), David Benchetrit's *Kaddim Wind*, Rami Kimchi's *Cinema Egypt* and *Father Language* (2006), Sigalit Banai's *Mama Faiza* (2002), Duki Dror's *My Fantasia* (2001), Sarit Haymian's *Gole Sangam* (2007) "out," as it were, the formerly closeted Arab, Iranian, Sephardi, or syncretic Mizrahi cultures, which had been rejected and therefore confined to the private sphere of the home. Even mundane activities, such as cooking, singing, and dancing, form part of an effort to recuperate rejected home culture associated with "the enemy" across the border. Such films explore, often through a cross-generational encounter, the fault line between the Arabic/Middle Eastern world of the parents' generation and that of their now adult children shaped by new Israeli cultural paradigms. *Mama Faiza*, for example, follows the career of Faiza Rushdi, an Egyptian-Jewish singer, who continues to sing in Arabic in Israel, accompanied by Arab-Jewish musicians. This story is filtered through the daughter, the actress Yaffa Tusia Cohen, who is shown not only in her everyday life but also on stage, where she offers a wrenching theatrical version of their intergenerational relationship.

Mizrahi narratives dissect the pain of dislocation that had been kept until recently in the shadows of an Euro-Israeli façade. Sini Bar David's *The South* (1998) offers an introspective voyage through the story of the dislocations of the filmmaker's grandmother, who reflects on a communal history that spans cross-border movements between Turkey, Greece, and Bulgaria after the Second World War and Nazi deportations, ending in Israel, in a south Tel Aviv neighborhood bordering on the mixed Jewish/Arab city of Jaffa. In the slum, in the morbid vicinity of Tel Kabir's Forensic Institute, the grandmother lives a confined existence, echoed by both Bar David's own childhood experiences and those of the present-day younger generation. Slow-motion sequences at the beginning and the end portray a young girl playing hopscotch and jumping rope in an empty street full of shuttered storefronts. A no-exit situation is also portrayed in films made by non-Israeli Arab–Jews; for example, in Mary Halawani's *I Miss the Sun* (1984), which tells the story of the filmmaker's Egyptian-Jewish grandmother, chronicling the exodus from sunny Egypt in 1956 to grim Brooklyn, where the Passover ritual of commemorating the biblical Exodus clashes with the grandmother's deep sense of loss and of missing Egypt. Nostalgia and claustrophobia are intimately linked in Arab-Jewish exilic narratives.

[...]

For Mizrahim, the Israeli experience has not been conducive to success. Many families who led prosperous lives in Egypt, Iran, Iraq, Morocco, or Tunisia encountered a social crisis in Israel. In a short period, the identity of Middle Eastern Jews was fractured, their life possibilities diminished, their hopes deferred. Thus, in the Mizrahi cinema of displacement, the question of memory is embedded in a sense of geographical dislocation, of loss without gain. What may be termed Mizrahi displacement cinema relays a skeptical or ambivalent relation to the official account, disrupting its totalizing coherence through a paradoxical poetics of exile in the Promised Land. In many ways, such cultural practices, in tandem with sociopolitical struggle, point to a dystopian take on the utopian project of the "ingathering of exiles." Euro-Israeli ideologues promoted the myth of the melting pot in the wake of mass *aliya* in the 1950s and 1960s, but cultural mixing did not take place exactly in the ways foreseen and imagined by the dominant Euro-Israeli institutions. In the working-class neighborhoods, Mizrahim of Arab or Turkish or Iranian origin acquired new multiplicities, the product of a new historical encounter of cultures. They quickly learned slang and recipes from other "Oriental" countries. While they experienced delegitimization by Euro-Israel, they were also only marginally connected to an Arab world that knew little of their new existence. In Mizrahi neighborhoods in the 1950s and 1960s, the radio dial was turned to Arab music. They continued to listen to Umm Kulthum and Nazim al-Ghazali, and, in the age of television, especially since the 1970s, when Mizrahim en masse began purchasing TV sets, they viewed Arabic programs and films from within cramped living rooms.

Hybrid identities cannot be reduced to a fixed recipe; rather, they form a changing repertory of cultural modalities. Occupying contradictory social and discursive spaces, the Mizrahi identity, like all identities, is dynamic and mobile, less an achieved synthesis than an unstable constellation of discourses. Mizrahi popular culture has clearly manifested a vibrant dialogue with Arab, Turkish, Greek, Indian, and Iranian popular cultures. Despite the separation from the Arab world, Mizrahi culture has been nourished through the enthusiastic consumption of Egyptian, Jordanian, and Lebanese television programs, films, and music video performances that have ruptured the Euro-Israeli public sphere in a kind of subliminal transgression of forbidden reminiscences. In fact, some Mizrahi music is produced in collaboration with (Israeli) Palestinians, as is the case with the musicians working with Yair Dalal. The Moroccan-Israeli musical group Sfatayim was one of the first to travel back to Morocco to produce a music video sung in Moroccan Arabic against the scenery of the cities and villages that Moroccan Jews have left behind, just as Israeli-born Iraqi singers, such as Ya'aqub Nishawi, sing old and contemporary Iraqi music. This yearning for a symbolic return "to the Diaspora" results in an ironic reversal of the conventional narrative of "next year in Jerusalem," as well as a reversal of the biblical expression that substitutes "Babylon" for "Zion": "By the waters of Zion, where we sat down, and there we wept, when we remembered Babylon."

[. . .]

Despite shared leitmotifs, the Mizrahi cultural movement is thus not at all monolithic, given the undergirding political rifts around the historical Middle Eastern Jewish relation to Zionism and the place of Mizrahim vis-à-vis the state. The distinct narratives and genres also relay different sensibilities, investments, and negotiations vis-à-vis the hegemonic Euro-Israeli culture, on the one hand, and the marginalized Arab culture, on the other. While some films assume a nationalist framing of Mizrahi dislocation or belonging, others—for example, Simone Bitton's *Yoredet*, Eli Hamo's *New Direction*, Benny Zada's *Hamara: A Place near Life* (1999), David Benchetrit's *Kaddim Wind*, and Eli Hamo and Sami Chetrit's *The Black Panthers [in Israel] Speak* (2003)—cast doubt on the Zionist master narrative.

Revisionist Cultural Practice

If diasporic Palestinian cultural practices explore the shock of departure from Palestine, Israeli Mizrahi practices address the shock of entry to Israel. Many Mizrahi films, whether explicitly or implicitly, have as their reference point the traumatic period of arrival in Israel. The past two decades have brought a significant increase in documentaries that challenge Orientalist representations and inscribe an alternative Mizrahi perspective. Critical Mizrahi cinema (even, at times, when not made by Mizrahim) is embedded in a long sociopolitical struggle. The past two decades have seen a surge in revisionist accounts of history, explicitly tackling discriminatory state and establishment policies and practices during the period of the *ma'abarot* (transit camps), including the controversial subjects of the Kidnapped Yemeni and Mizrahi Babies and the Ringworm Children. Archival footage and historical research are central to what can be called a revisionist Mizrahi cinema. Here "Mizrahi" stands less for the origins of the makers than for a sociopolitically critical perspective.

Ayelet Heller's *Unpromised Land* (*Dekel shfal tzameret*, 1992), for example, follows the story of Yemeni Jews who during the Ottoman period settled in the Sea of Galilee area and cultivated the land, largely as part of a messianic vision of the vision of the Promised land. Yet in 1914, the land became "unpromised," when a group of Ashkenazi pioneers, the well-known founders of Kvutzat Kinneret, took their land away, leading to the Yemenis' dislocation. One of the elder Yemenis weeps as he recalls the disrespect and the humiliation, countering the kibbutz's claim of an exclusively Ashkenazi "development," denying Yemeni labor. The camera follows the Yemeni descendants mourning their loss and confronting the kibbutzniks who have erased their presence from the official history, now conveyed by tour guides, which glorifies the (European) founding fathers. While rewriting this history, the film frames the ethnic division of labor within the Jewish settlement without relating it to the question of Palestine. The socialist Zionist ideal of "Hebrew Work" was partly realized in the form of the exploitation and discrimination of Yemeni workers, called "Jews in the form of Arabs," a concept crucial to the colonization of Palestine. Films such as Tali Shemesh's *White Gold/Black Labor* (2004), meanwhile, examine continued labor discrimination in the contemporary era, in this case, in a development town in the south, revealing the persistence of an ethnic division of labor within Jewish Israel.

Some documentaries perform historical research, uncovering erased moments in the repressed history of Arab–Jews' arrival to Israel. Some films deal with the still buried story of the kidnapping of Yemeni and Mizrahi babies from the late 1940s to the early 1960s. Disoriented by the new reality in Israel, Yemenis, as well as Jews from other Arab and Muslim countries, fell prey to the state's welfare institutions, which provided babies for adoption largely in Israel and in the United States while telling the biological parents that their babies had died. Over several decades the government has ignored or silenced Mizrahi demands for investigation. Kidnappings were at least in part a result of a belief in the mission of Western "science and progress," operating on a continuum with the reigning academic discourses of the time. In this intersection of race, gender, and class, the displaced Jews from Muslim countries became victims of the logic of progress, bearing the marks of its pathologies on their bodies. In 1986, "Mabat Sheni," a TV program on the subject, denied and downplayed the historical veracity of the accusations, producing Orientalist narratives about neglectful child-breeding parents. Documentaries such as Tzipi Talmor's *Down a One-Way Road* (1997) and Uri Rozenwax's *Fact* (Channel 2, 1996)[5] raise questions about this still unresolved episode. The topics are also dramatized in Yamin Messika's fictional film *The Vineyard of Hope* (1997), about an American woman who comes to a south Tel Aviv neighborhood in search of her biological parents, only to find out that she was never willingly given up for adoption, and that she is one of the kidnapped Yemeni babies.[6]

The investigative testimonial documentary *Ringworm Children* (2003), by David Belhassen and Asher Hemias, opens up another suppressed chapter—the case of the X-ray radiation, said to be a treatment for ringworm, administered to approximately 100,000 children, primarily from North Africa, in the early 1950s. The radiation resulted in high rates of mortality for children and fatal or chronic diseases for the survivors, including excruciating headaches, infertility, epilepsy, amnesia, Alzheimer's, psychosis, cancer, and sexual dysfunction, along with psychological scars resulting from their changed appearance. According to officials, the medical establishment was concerned with the severe danger to public health posed by ringworm, but was unaware of the grave consequences of the treatment itself. A minor skin or scalp problem, which used to be treated in their home countries with vinegar, was "treated" in Israel with X-ray radiation doses surpassing 35,000 times the maximum recommended—in an era, as the film shows, when the dangers of radiation were already known to the medical community. At times, children without any manifestation of a ringworm problem also received the X-rays. Thousands of the children died shortly thereafter, while thousands of others perished as a result of cancers and other disorders, and others are still dying up to the present.

As with other charges against the state apparatus, the official response is to claim that the calamity was unintentional. The film argues, in contrast, that the X-rays formed part of an experiment to test the effects of large radiation doses on humans. The program was apparently funded by American sponsors who supplied outmoded X-ray machines and made large payments to an Israeli government that could not have otherwise afforded the treatment/experiment. Whereas such experiments were no longer legal within the United States, they were still possible in Israel. A key official facilitator of the experiment, the director general of the Israeli Health Ministry, Dr. Chaim Sheba, according to the film, had opposed the "bringing" of North Africans to Israel on the basis of their supposedly contagious diseases being a threat to public health. After their arrival, Dr. Sheba's rhetoric continued in the same vein; he spoke of the war against ringworm as an "epidemic extermination." The film includes archival footage, interviews with government officials, survivors' testimonials, and written texts, all orchestrated to demonstrate the logic of racism. *Ringworm Children*'s examination of the Israeli-U.S. scientific institutional links evokes other documentaries on eugenics, such as *La Operación* (1982), which details the experimentation with birth control pills and forced sterilization on women in Puerto Rico. In the case of the ringworm children, it was the vulnerable "Third World" of Israel that was made available for medical experiments. The argument made throughout is that the children were deliberately poisoned, within an institutional racism that disregarded non-European lives, all carried out by the "Division for Social Medicine," a euphemism for eugenics.

Revisionist documentaries contribute, then, to the Mizrahi testimonial narrative. As with the documentaries about the kidnappings, some of the interviews with the ringworm survivors take place at the trauma site, for example in Sha'ar Aliya (The Gate of Aliya) near the Haifa port. The film recalls the event from the point of view of the children, now adults, their bodies ravaged by time. The interviewees, addressing their testimonials to the camera, speak of their experiences, including having their heads forcibly "scalped," being "plucked like chicken," and being "tied like sacrifice," before being placed under a heavy machine without anti-radiation protection and left alone for the duration of the radiation. They confess their resentment at their parents for permitting such an action, only to realize that, on the radiation day, the parents had been told that the students were being taken on a school trip. The non-diegetic music of Shlomo Bar and "The Natural Alternative"—a syncretic East/West musical ensemble associated both with protest and with recovering the Eastern dimension—underlines the larger historical and social pain. As with the kidnappings, the ringworm case has been suppressed for decades. The film tracks down the administrative processes that usually lead to the rejection of cases for "lack of proof," but in the Ringworm case, in 1995, after a long struggle led by a few Mizrahi Knesset members, the Knesset passed a law mandating government compensation for the victims. (The "Ringworm Law," however, did not include any admission of governmental wrongdoing.) The film intercuts scenes of official defenders of the government with the interviewees, in shots showing them both as individuals and as a collective. As the children of the 1950s continue to suffer and die, the film's investigation reveals the extent to which information about such cases has been buried. This documentary, it is implied, has only begun to scratch the surface, highlighting the urgent need for more revisionist Mizrahi histories.

In many ways, such films denaturalize and disrupt the discourse of *aliya* and the teleological narrative of the Jewish nation-state. While it has been common in official political discourse, as well as in artistic and scholarly practice, to separate the Mizrahi question from the Palestinian question, and even sometimes to posit them as simply in conflict (by stressing the eternal persecution of Jews in the Arab world, or the putative ingrained tendency of Mizrahi to hate Arabs), such hegemonic narratives have been increasingly challenged. Directed by the Jewish-Moroccan filmmaker David Benchetrit, the documentary *Through the Veil of Exile* (1992) follows three Palestinian women as they narrate their experiences under Israeli occupation in Gaza and the West Bank. But in this instance, the exile of Palestinians and their dispossession comes to illuminate the subject position of the filmmaker himself, whose exile as a Moroccan–Jew in Israel is allegorically displaced through the Palestinian narrative. In *Kaddim Wind*, as we have seen, Benchitrit narrates the nightmarish Moroccan experience in Israel as having begun already in Morocco, with the lure of Zionism. The archival footage that shows vehicles transferring Moroccan Jews to waiting boats revisits moments of traumatic separation. The sense of uprootedness is thus visually performed at the very overture of this epic documentary. The acoustic presence of the Moroccan national anthem on the soundtrack, meanwhile, stages the very question of living in between nation-states and the sense of a return to a taboo belonging in Morocco.

Mizrahi cultural practices revisit the traumatic moment of entry into Israel that redefined a new collective identity born on the ruins of a hasty departure from one geography and a disturbed entrance into another. It is perhaps not a coincidence that, time and again, Mizrahim have returned to this primal scene—the moment of landing in the Holy Land, only to be sprayed by government agents with the disinfectant DDT. Already in 1974, Sami Michael's novel *All Men Are Equal—But Some Are More* registered that paradigmatic moment of arrival when the protagonist's father, full of dreamy hope, is met with DDT. Literary fiction legitimated an experience that formerly had only been part of oral narratives, discussed in Mizrahi homes and neighborhoods. Three decades later, a new literature and cinema has emerged centering on the shocking moment of arrival, but this time actively shaping the visual and oral archive.

Revisionist Mizrahi cinema has invariably depicted the impact of this history on the lives of Mizrahim. While some of the films form part of a broader intellectual project critiquing Euro-Israeli historiography, others take this history and the struggle on the "periphery" as a backdrop for captivating dramas or autobiographies of the protagonists of Mizrahi struggle, as in films like Amit Goren's *6 Open, 21 Closed* (*6 Patu'ah, 21 Sagur*, 1994), David Ofek's *No. 17* (*Ha Harug Ha*, 2003), Nissim Mossek's *Have You Heard About the Black Panthers?* (*Shamata Al Ha Panterim?*, 2002) and *Who Is Mordechai Vanunu?* (*Mi Ata Mordechai Vanunu?*, 2004), and David Fisher's *Buried But Alive* (1996). Mossek's *Who Is Mordechai Vanunu*, for example, tells the story of the Moroccan-Israeli nuclear whistle-blower who was recently released after eighteen years in solitary confinement, in a context where Vanunu had been vilified as the enemy of the people. Told against the backdrop of the Black Panther rebellion of the 1970s, *Buried But Alive* narrates the story of Mazal Sa'il, wife of Dani Sa'il, an *'aguna*[7] who fights the rabbinical establishment in a convoluted case involving a Black Panther who vanished, or was perhaps made to "disappear." Although Dani Sa'il declared his intention to return to the "enemy country" of Iraq in the late 1970s, his whereabouts and trajectory have yet to be revealed. Caught in the gears of the rabbinical state apparati, Mazal Sa'il has lived in legal limbo for about twenty years.[8] Also, in Nissim Mossek's *Have You Heard About the Black Panthers?* (2002) the Black Panthers' past looms against the present, with Mossek incorporating his own 1973 footage of Jerusalem's Musrara neighborhood and of the young rebels from his earlier documentary *Have You Heard About the Panthers, Mr. Moshe?* The quoted film becomes a steppingstone for a contemporary journey for the older Black Panthers—notably Charlie Bitton, Sa'adia Martziano, and Kokhavi Shemesh—who remained on the political scene even after the dissolution of the movement. In a kind of Black Panther road movie, the film travels across the country in search of other former members. Many members still live in poverty; some continue in the same activist path, while others have found solace in religious mysticism, as in the case of 'Amram Cohen, who relocated to the ancient city of Safad. The spectator comes to reflect on the passage of time—their language, discourses, and faces that no longer correspond to the iconic images of the young Panthers. Providing the narrative's organizational principle, the journey thus metaphorizes the long road traveled since the heydays of Sephardi rebellion.

Eli Hamo and Sami Chetrit's *The Black Panthers (in Israel) Speak*, meanwhile, pays homage to the egalitarian vision of the Black Panthers, elucidating the radicalization of the Mizrahi struggle. The film offers a sociopolitical analysis through interviews with leaders of the movement—Charlie Bitton, Sa'adia Martziano, Kochavi Shemesh, Reuven Abergil, and also including Haim Hanegbi of the leftist Matzpen group.[9] Seeing themselves as the children of earlier protests, and especially of the 1959 Wadi Salib rebellion, they address some of the movement's better-known symbolic actions, such as removing milk bottles from the rich Ashkenazi neighborhood and distributing them to the residents of the Mizrahi working-class neighborhood in Jerusalem. For the Ashkenazim, they left a provocative flyer: "We're taking your milk today in order to give it to people in need. We assume this milk was for your cats and dogs." And to the Mizrahim, the milk arrived with the message: "We managed to get milk for you today, but don't get used to it. If you'll join us, we'll do a lot more together." The film also examines the movement's relation to the Palestinian struggle, reminding viewers that the Black Panthers had already met with the PLO leaders in 1972 and recognized them as the leaders of the Palestinian people, in a period when Golda Meir used to say that there was no such thing as the Palestinian people. In line with subsequent Mizrahi leftist movements, which have emphasized the interdependency of Palestinian and Mizrahi issues, the film offers a retrospective prism that simultaneously engages the present. Lamenting the Shas Party's destructive impact on the radical Mizrahi struggle,[10] the film addresses the negative role of diverse Sephardi/Mizrahi establishment-dominated organizations, while offering an ideological analysis of the emergence of anti-racist struggle in Israel.

[. . .]

These variegated texts and cultural practices allow elisions and ambivalences to emerge in full force. Against this backdrop, revisionist Mizrahi cinema has interrogated the doxa of official History, posing questions about the "what ifs" and the haunting silences of history. The potency of such work ultimately lies in the poetics of dissonance that facilitate a reading of Arab-Jewish/Mizrahi narratives beyond the boundaries of Israel, accentuating multidirectional regional connectivities. Whether in cinema, literature, or the visual arts, Arab–Jews narrate their memory of their Arab past, reinscribing the hyphen, as it were, between Jews and Arabs, and at times between the Jew and the Muslim. Political geographies and state borders, in sum, do not always coincide with imaginary geographies, whence the existence of "internal émigrés," nostalgics, and rebels—that is, groups of people who share the same passport but whose relationship to the nation-state is conflictual and ambivalent. Within a situation where the state created the nation, the educational and social apparatus was mobilized to enforce an adherence to narrowly defined notions of Jewishness and Arabness. Yet, despite the efforts to transform Middle Eastern/Arab Jews into Israeli Jews, Mizrahi Israeliness remains complex, ambivalent, and contingent, and now expressed in a new sense of cultural politics.

This chapter is an abridged version of Ella Shohat's postscript to the twentieth-anniversary edition of her 1989 book *Israeli Cinema: East/West and the Politics of Representation* (London: I.B Tauris, 2010).

This essay is dedicated to the memory of the documentarists David Benchetrit and Eli Hamo.

References

Saranovitz, Eric. 2006. "Negotiating History in an Era of Globalization: The Production of Narratives of a Nation's Past in the Israeli Media." PhD diss., New York University.

Shohat, Ella. 1989. *Israeli Cinema: East/West and the Politics of Representation*. Austin: University of Texas Press.

16

LACAN, SONTAG AND ISRAEL ON SCREEN

Hanan Toukan

I n 1973, Susan Sontag, the visual critic and essayist, traveled to the Middle East to film in Israel, just before the end of the October War that saw Egypt and Syria uniting to launch a surprise attack in retaliation for the colossal losses of the 1967 war.[1] To watch Susan Sontag's *Promised Lands* in April 2012 as part of the London Palestine Film Festival, playing to a full house, may be read a testament to the changing mode of representing, framing, and ultimately grappling with Israel as a political, cultural, and social construct and reality in Western cultural capitals today. The experience was also arguably an entirely different aesthetic, intellectual, and emotional experience than viewing the film when it first premiered in 1974 in New York City might have been. It is impossible to engage this film today, along with others such as *L'Olivier* (*The Olive Tree*, 1976) and *Lacan Palestine* (2012) that were shown at the same festival in London in 2012, without contextualizing them against the backdrop of the shifting politics of representing Israeli politics in liberal and more progressive circles in Western capitals, across the twentieth and twenty-first centuries.

16.1. *Lacan Palestine* (2012), directed by Mike Hoolboom.

Against Interpretation? The Politics and Poetics of Israeli Trauma

Upon its release in 1974, *Promised Lands* was banned in Israel. This ban was not a result of fear of the Palestinian perspective, for there is hardly any of this in the film. Sontag was more interested in capturing the vulnerability of Israel, as she and her liberal New York intellectual cohort understood it, during the period from the foundation of the state in 1948 to 1974, when the film was released. This was a period when the "Palestinian," and the very idea of "Palestine," was either nonexistent or simply a synonym for "terrorist" in mainstream Western (especially American) society. Through a collage of images of a fearful, traumatized, and insecure nation, *Promised Lands* could be read as an early attempt to uncover the young Israeli state's narrative of a heroic national liberation. This was a narrative resting on a deep belief—ironically held by many supporters of anticolonial nationalist struggles prominent in the leftist intellectual New York circles of the 1960s and 1970s—that a civilized and Western Jewish state was liberated from Arabs by Holocaust survivors against all odds, rather than that the Arab population was forcefully expelled by colonial settlers armed with the latest in European military technology and racist ideology.

16.2. *Promised Land* (1974), directed by Susan Sontag.

The film was barred from being shown in Israel for the very simple reason that it does not partake in what Ella Shohat has termed the "heroic nationalist" genre of Israeli cinema: the genre defined by the representational framework through which the Israeli–Zionist ideology and narrative has been reproduced and perpetuated, both within Israel and outside of it by its supporters (Shohat 2010). Rather, in what seems to be an attempt that is decidedly "Against Interpretation" (to quote the title of Sontag's classic 1966 essay), the film sets out to observe Israel through a poetic lens, rather than offer commentary. The result is a Godard-influenced lamentation of the psychological effects of the multilayered complexities binding the Israeli state. These include above all the collective consciousness of a beleaguered, paranoid, and terrified nation grappling with the traumas of persecution, war, pain, and death. Like the form used in Godard's *Ici et*

Ailleurs (*Here and Elsewhere*, 1976), released a few years later and embodied in the images and sounds received by the television-watching French family from a faraway place called "Palestine," Sontag's film also experiments with a similar formal language. This language is transmitted through what is received from another place, an exotic milieu, out of place and out of time from where she comes.

The camera's silent surveying includes daily life in the marketplaces and on the streets, decorated with posters from Israeli popular culture and marked by American-style supermarket chains, which mirror the shift from the early socialist rhetoric to a growing capitalist consumer reality. Other shots portray prayers at the Wailing Wall, a service at the war cemetery, and a wax museum that memorializes the nation's violent military history and concurrent socialist imaginary of the emancipated laborer building the nation. The camera pauses on the wreckage of cremated tanks and scorched corpses, surrounded by dried blood and swarming flies against a backdrop of vast arid earth, which interrupt these semblances of "normalcy" in a militarized society. Most disturbing of all is Sontag's venture into a psychiatric ward for shell-shocked war veterans. Under her silent gaze, this closing scene of the experimental treatment that recreates the battlefield stands as an allegory of a truly tormented nation. The veterans' loud cries and squirming body movements embody the claustrophobia of a tragic nation caught between a rock and a hard place. "Israel fights because Israel cannot lose," claims one of Sontag's protagonists.

Yet by Sontag's refusal to interpret or mediate what she sees, the film leaves one wondering about what is lost through the process and if it was in fact able to do what it set out to do. Sontag's film could be about Israeli society in particular, or it could be a poetic approach to representing the absurdity of war through the use of Israel as a case study. In both cases, an attempt to enable the subjective interpretation of the object of study is made by employing only faint narrative, as in the genre of poetic modes of documentary more generally: events and characters are purposely kept underdeveloped, in order to generate affect. But in *Promised Lands*, narrative content is never abandoned altogether; it is there, albeit sporadically. More, the narrative is strategically drawn upon to explicate what the affective mode seamlessly transmits to the viewer about the absurdity of the violence Israel is "forced" to contend with.

No Palestinian or female voice is ever heard in the film. Save for one mundane shot of Palestinian men and women crossing the Allenby border from Jordan and having their luggage searched by the Israeli Army border patrol, they are hardly seen, not even in the background. But they are "spoken" about. Israel's narrative of victimhood, and the subsequent justification for the siege mentality that results from it, is essentially represented by the deliberations of two Israeli Zionists that run intermittently throughout the length of the film. The first is Yuval Ne'eman, a physicist and a pioneer of Israel's nuclear technology program, who presents his version of Arabs' and Muslims' supposedly deeply entrenched loathing of Jews by reading from Jordanian and Egyptian school books to prove his point. The second is Yoram Kanium, a liberal writer who expresses what he sees as the Palestinian narrative ("we are right, and they were right," he observes) but who also bemoans the perpetual cycle of conflict as a deadlock from which there is no escape, precisely because of the tragic predicament of the Jews, which leaves them no alternative but the present one.

Sontag's reconstruction of fragments of sound reinforces both these narratives. The soundtrack of the film includes sounds of prayer, running footsteps, women wailing, radar beeps, explosions, machine-gun fire, and, most significantly, the Voice of Cairo's English radio broadcasts addressing the question of Palestine and Israel's role in the region in a propagandist tone. Yet, despite the fact that the film relies more heavily on everyday sound and images than words, the words that are uttered reinforce the arresting mood of fear conveyed throughout the film, rather than interrogate it. More insidiously, Sontag's decision to generally leave Palestinians outside her camera frame reinforces the Zionist claim that Palestine was "a land without a people for a people without a land."

For all her insistence not to interpret, Sontag's greatest achievement in *Promised Lands* was to document the fallacy of the heroic Israeli state through a poetic mode that (ironically) depended on her aesthetic and subjective visual interpretation of the political situation. Hence, while the emphasis is indeed on the film's form—an approach that arouses the senses so that we ultimately "learn to see more, to hear more, to feel more," as she explains—it is unable "to show how it [the subject matter] is what it is, even that it is what it is," as she insists this technique might do (Sontag 1961, 23). This is because, as her own writing in *On Photography* (1977) and then *Regarding the Pain of Others* (2003) later insisted, images must be measured against the misperceptions they sometimes propagate, as well as the restlessness they might provoke, the exploitation they might enable, and the latency they may engender. In other words, narrative and framing are central to the reception of images insofar as they ultimately confer meaning on what it is that we are looking at. In this light, *Promised Lands* is equally valuable as an archival document of the New York liberal intellectual elite's historically sympathetic yet largely uninformed understanding of the Israeli state's self-perpetuated predicament. The fact that the film steered clear of confronting, either aesthetically or through narrative, the role, place, and effect that Israel's paranoia has had on the Palestinians most implicated in it is symptomatic of what Joseph Massad has argued more generally about Western liberal intellectuals' inability to transgress the boundaries set out by the hegemonic Israeli and U.S. discourse on victimhood and self-defense by refusing to disconnect the experience of the Holocaust from the racist and paradoxical nature of the concurrently Jewish and "secular" state (Massad 2000).

What may be interpreted here as a retrospective attack on Sontag's inability (or unwillingness) to confront the complexity of the Israeli situation in its entirety should not be read as a dismissal of her contribution in terms of aesthetic experimentation and political inquiry, nor a lack of appreciation for how bound she was by her own cultural and political moment. What is being questioned, rather, is the way in which certain aesthetic conceptions of protest and dissent may end up being organized by hegemonic discourses. This convergence between protest and power is most obvious in Sontag's attempt to visually critique the Israeli predicament through a supposedly neutral and silent lens. But in doing so, Sontag falls victim to the labyrinthine structure of deception that so defines the mainstream representation of the Palestinian version of history. This is a powerful reminder that the absorption of protest often holds most for the political forms that are most at ease in and most celebrated by circuits of global power.

Interpreting Israel Anew

When Sontag was in the process of editing her film, Maxime Rodinson had already broken a taboo against criticizing Israel with his seminal *Israel: A Colonial Settler State?* which first appeared in English in 1973. In this slim publication, based on an article initially published in Jean-Paul Sartre's *Les temps modernes* in 1967 as "Israel: Fait Colonial," Rodinson documented the racist logic that infused Zionist ideology and praxis (including even its socialist branch). The Zionist leadership, he argued, manipulated the Jewish people into identifying with a fabricated nationalist ideology and thus into Judaizing Arab land at the cost of expelling, excluding, and dominating the local Palestinian population.

Along these lines, and two years after the release of *Promised Lands* in 1974, the Parisian Maoist collective Groupe Cinéma Vincennes, formed after the events of 1968, released *L'Olivier*. Shot in 16mm and in formal documentary mode, this monochrome film, which was recently "rediscovered" by Subversive Film Ltd and shown for the first time by the London Palestine Film Festival, boldly locates the territorial dispute that defines the Palestine/Israel conflict within the history of European racism, and shows that the two are inextricably intertwined. If *Promised Lands*, as described by Sontag, was an attempt to "present a condition rather than an action," then *L'Olivier*, quite obviously influenced by French existentialism and specifically Jean-Paul Sartre's call for *l'art engagé*, was very much an appeal to a rising revolutionary consciousness in order to counter the distortions produced by the twin effects of imperialism and capitalism.

Many of the issues raised in *L'Olivier* are not only still relevant, but also more consolidated by almost forty more years of occupation. The film reveals the systematic land confiscation, forced displacement, resource plundering, demolition of housing, collective punishment, arbitrary detention, and construction of illegal settlements occurring under the guise of Israeli self-defense, often with direct approval and support from Western governments. None of what is represented in the film in terms of history or Zionist policy practice comes as news to those working in solidarity with the Palestinian resistance to Israel, whether in 1976 or today. In fact, films such as Mustafa Abu Ali's *No to a Peaceful Solution* (*La li-l-hall al-silmi*, 1968), *With Our Blood with Our Souls* (*Bi-l-rawh bi-l-damm*, 1971), and *They Do Not Exist* (*Laysa lahum wujud*, 1974)—as well as later features also produced by the PLO Film Unit, such as Iraqi director Qasim Hawal's *Return to Haifa* (*'A'id ila Haifa*, 1982), and other independents like Heiny Srour's feminist take on the Arab/Israel conflict in *Leila and the Wolves* (*Layla wa-l-dhi'ab*, 1984)—are already part of an archive documenting the Palestinian version of history and the reasons for continued anticolonial struggle. Often didactic in form and emphasizing linear representations of history, these compelling films rely heavily on narration and how the perceiver actually encounters it, as well as the use of stills, slogans, poetry, and songs as material; they are directed as much at the Arabic-speaking world as at anti-imperialist struggles elsewhere.

L'Olivier is similar in content and form to films like these. Yet what makes it all the more powerful as a historical document is its refusal to couch the Jewish experience (or even the Palestinian one in which it is by extension imbricated) in the universal language of suffering and pain without first interrogating it. Through its rhetorical content, the history of the territorial conflict is revised with the aim of provoking spectators into awareness of the existence and effectiveness of the dominant frames that represent the conflict in terms of Israel as passive victim and the Palestinian as mindless perpetrator of violence, and consequently to engender a critical attitude toward these frames. This contrasts starkly with Sontag's film, which critiques, through its affective language, a state of paranoid psychosis resulting from being located in a historical moment that has victimized European Jews.

Despite its sometimes didactic narration, *L'Olivier* manages to avoid the traps that would lead it to merely sentimentalizing the story of a people, ruthlessly expelled and then occupied. It takes a different route and focuses instead on the existential crisis of European Jewry vis-à-vis notions of identity, the nation, memory, and how the question of Palestine is ultimately incriminated in the manifestations of this crisis. "What did it mean being a Zionist?" one man filmed at an anti-Zionist rally in Jerusalem asked. Pondering his own rhetorical question, he continued: "It was very different from how the state interpreted it. It was based on an interpretation, in my opinion, that the essential problem was a Jewish one. I want to say here that there wasn't a Jewish problem. However, everything was explained through this interpretation. The simple solution was for all Jews to go to Israel and there were people to arrange this. This brings me to the conclusion that I was played."

Since the productions of *Promised Lands* and *L'Olivier*, the conflict has undergone some dramatic developments, with major consequences for Israel's claims to victimhood and self-defense. These changes have witnessed the eruption of two intifadas, the U.S.-led sham "peace" process and its consequent collapse, the rise to power of Benjamin Netanyahu's Likud-dominated government, and the growing power of ethno-religious parties, violently articulating itself amid a larger global movement of right-wing populism and white nationalism. The building of the illegal Segregation Wall and the rise of the international solidarity movement for the liberation of Palestine have posed previously unimaginable challenges to Israel. Against this backdrop, both films can be read as documentation of the conflict itself as well as its aesthetic representation during certain historical moments. The shot of Palestinians crossing an unthreatening-looking Allenby Bridge in 1973 in *Promised Lands* has today metamorphosed into a monstrous complex of security with airport-like terminals and machinery to filter out not only Palestinians, but anyone else deemed to threaten the state through pro-Palestinian sentiment or activity. Similarly, the narrative of the wives of prisoners held without trial in *L'Olivier* are no different from those of hunger strikers languishing without trial in Israeli jails today. This shows just how much more of the same there is when it comes to Zionist policies and practices.

Yet, because each film represents and uses the category of history differently, in political, conceptual, and cinematic terms, so each also conceives of and uses the concept of representation differently. Accordingly, we as spectators are able to look for our own causal, spatial, or temporal links to understand what we can of the conflict. It is here that the biggest challenge to the visual representation of the conflict lies. In the same way certain formal devices in filmmaking—such as closure, linearity, and objective narration—can serve ideological ends, so can diffuse strategies and fragmentary approaches. This matters a lot when it comes to visually documenting Israel's historical subjugation of Palestinians on screen, for this particular conflict is as much about the exercise of military and economic imperial power as it is about narration, documentation, and representation.

Re-presenting History

It is thanks to the curatorial competence of the organizers of the London Palestine Film Festival that Mike Hoolboom's *Lacan Palestine* may be read as an attempt to visually re- present past interpretations of Israel. Hoolboom's striking skill in grappling with the birth of Israel in his stunning work is testament to cinema's ability to deconstruct dominant cultural representations without compromising either political or aesthetic values. It is also a tribute to the world community's growing recognition that the Palestinian plight is indeed valid, genuine, and justified, and that the call to revise the history of the conflict can no longer be ignored.

Using as a starting point Lacan's psychoanalytic theory of the "mirror stage" and the "alienation" it results in, which describes the early shaping of the ego in response to a clash between one's self-perceived ideal visual appearance and one's actual emotional experience, Hoolboom stunningly juxtaposes the trauma of the ancient Judaic experience against the contemporary pain of the Palestinian one. He hints throughout that while unraveling the layers of history does indeed put in perspective the decisive moments we experience, the moment of trauma when it occurs can never be reduced to mere historical occurrence, precisely because of what are ultimately our "singular" experiences. By stitching together visual imagery already etched into our minds and nestled in our subconscious, Hoolboom prods his spectators to reconstruct the layers that constitute our understanding of nation, community, and tribe. Central to his cinematic essay is the vast archive of visual material reassembled by him into a heart-wrenching story of human pain. Included in this are: epic American Civil War films, scenes from violent Crusader wars, Hollywood productions bursting with Orientalist overtones, and even shots from more recent experimental films such as Sontag's *Promised Lands* and video art works by Velcrow Ripper, Elle Flanders, and Dani Leventhal, sometimes superimposed over the voices of Edward Said and others. The dizzying pastiche of footage is interwoven with iconic images of Israel's brutal occupation, such as the Israeli Army's beating of Palestinians with truncheons dictated by Yitzhak Rabin's "break the bones" policy in the first intifada, and the horrifying destruction of Gaza in 2009. Ben-Gurion's proclamation of the establishment of the Jewish state standing under a statue of Theodor Herzl, the founder of Zionism, and accompanying street jubilations are also part of the assembled footage. These images then metamorphose into scenes from films depicting the hedonistic celebrations of the Roman Empire's ruling elite.

A large segment of the film is dedicated to uncovering Britain's role in the violent inception of the state of Israel. In one sequence, Hoolboom takes his spectators on a journey through the passion, drama, secrecy, and tragedy of the interwar mandate period. This is done through assembling maps, voice-overs, and news footage, such as that of King Abdullah of Transjordan standing alongside British mandate officials, in a nod to the collusion between the two over the carving up of Palestine. Other footage recalls BBC commentary from the interwar period affirming British interest in ensuring a friendly (Jewish) population on the historical land of Palestine at the expense of marginalizing its original inhabitants (Palestinians).

This dizzying series of images is interspersed more than once with the quintessential British icon of drama and conspiracy: the Rolls-Royce "Spirit of Ecstasy" mascot adorning one car driving freely against a backdrop of an ongoing British imperial pomp ceremony. As if adding insult to injury and in a breathtaking end to the sequence, Hoolboom presents us with a shot of two men, one naked, the other in a British army uniform, locked in a passionate embrace lying atop a Union flag. Hoolboom's choice of footage here compellingly recalls British prime minister David Cameron's suggestion that British aid be cut from those countries with anti–gay rights records, indicating, as sharp criticism warned, a contemporary repeat of imperial Britain's civilizing mission.

"What are these guys doing in jazz combos?" asks filmmaker Mike Cartmell in a voice-over monologue reflecting on his painful personal life experiences by mapping them onto collective ones. He goes on: "Coltrane, no one could play like that. Elvin Jones, nobody could drive a band like that. Each one of these guys is playing something different, but together there is a coalescing of these quite discrete, quite radically different singular expressions."

There is a mismatch between how the British Empire, and the violent birth of Israel it helped bring into being, perceive themselves, and the reality of the "singular" painful experiences they engendered as a result, Hoolboom seems to be saying. His point is movingly driven home through his Lacanian visual interpretation of the manly outer demeanor of a fearful and timid young Palestinian boy woken up in the early hours of the morning by his mother and forced to board a bus full of adults to see his imprisoned father in an Israeli jail.

Despite what may be interpreted as his collapsing of the collective and the singular into a morass of parity through his choice of visualizing ancient and more recent history, the sheer brilliance of Hoolboom's film lies in the fact that he never once loses sight of the reality of the conflict today. Despite never stating it, he is clear on who the perpetrators are and who the victims are in the contemporary conflict in Palestine. He reminds us throughout that history is always part of a living consciousness that pulls together past and present as a way of remaking, reclaiming, and reimagining what we think we already know. And this he does without ever shying away from interpreting the history of a conflict that is in dire need of being reread and retold, if it is ever to end.

References

Massad, Joseph. 2000. "The 'Post-colonial' Colony: Time, Space, and Bodies in Palestine/Israel." In *The Pre-occupation of Postcolonial Studies*. Edited by Fawzia Afzal-Khan and Keplana Geshadri-Crooks. Durham; London: Duke University Press.

Rodinson, Maxime. 1973. *Israel: A Colonial Settler State?* New York: Monad Press.

Shohat, Ella. 2010. *Israeli Cinema: East/West and the Politics of Representation*. New ed. New York and London: I.B. Tauris.

Sontag, Susan. 1961. *Against Interpretation*. New York: Dell Publishing.

———. 1977. *On Photography*. New York: Farrar, Strauss and Giroux.

———. 2003. *Regarding the Pain of Others*. New York: Farrar, Strauss and Giroux.

17

POLITICAL ISSUES IN TUNISIAN WOMEN'S CINEMA

Mathilde Rouxel

Introduction

Many of the first images of Tunisia were shot by settlers, as the landscapes and patrimony were an ideal setting for dramas of all types. When the Tunisian people proclaimed their independence in 1956, no infrastructure existed for cinematographic creation. The Cinema Department (S.A.P.T.E.C, Société Anonyme Tunisienne de Production et d'Expansion Cinématographique) was created in 1957 by the Secretariat of State for Information, which was the first step toward the creation of cinematographic institutions.[1] Besides the official circuit, the Tunisian Federation of Amateur Cinema was created in 1959, and took on an important part in the history of Tunisian cinema, starting with documentary.

In 1966, ethnologist Sophie Ferchiou became the first woman filmmaker in Tunisia. She gave a visual depiction of the results of her studies on Tunisian workers, both men and women. A long line of women filmmakers followed in her footsteps and began filming in order to denounce society's status quo, the state negligence toward minorities, or the rise of religious extremism.

From the beginning, documentary films made by women in Tunisia discussed politics. I define "political cinema" by following the French essayist Nicole Brenez, who argues that the main issue for political cinema is "historical efficiency" (Brenez 2012, 23). More than fiction, documentary cinema must produce its own norms to deal with reality. The movies I analyze that are made by Tunisian women depict politics in many different ways. They all deal, however, with the question of the relationship between the individual and the collective, from the very first 1970s films that question the establishment to movies shot during and after the 2011 revolution. As François Niney recalls, documentary film is not only an eyewitness account but also "a symbolic language . . . engaged on singular

289

realities" (Niney 2002, 14). The political nature of these movies will also be defined in this study by its capacity to carry a different message from the official narrative: to name the alienations is to name the possibilities of the riposte. Brenez affirms the omnipresence of cinema alongside oppressed people: working on a cinema that is being produced outside the formal circuit or in the shadow of a more mainstream cinema means working on a cinema that accompanies emancipation struggles (Brenez 2014, 32).

In the 1960s, Tunisian festival director and film critic Tahar Chériaa wrote that Arabic cinema "will be militant, it will above all be a cultural act, it will above all have a social and political value. . . or it will be nothing" (Khayati 1996, 56). It appears that a history of Tunisian women in film bears testament to this aspiration: Sophie Ferchiou's works present a reality erased from common narratives and challenge the policies led by Bourguiba and the spreading patriarchal conservatism in Tunisian society. As noted by sociolgist Sarah E. Gilman, Bourguiba's "paternal mission" to support women's liberation was not "bubbling up from below," and "lacked direct participation of Tunisian women or anyone else outside Bourguiba's circle of political elites" (Gilman 2007, 97). Selma Baccar's famous *Fatma 75*—the first film made for Tunisian cinema by a woman—also attempts, in a different manner and through specific aesthetic choices, as will be described later, to rewrite history in opposition to the official narrative. This first generation of women filmmakers, whether feminist or leftist, do not hesitate to take risks in order to highlight taboo topics, and were part of a movement that was widespread throughout the Maghreb and Egypt in the 1970s, according to Noureddine Saïl. They were the generation that wanted to show "real problems," as "cinema was a voluntary act seen by filmmakers as a necessity" (Saïl 2012, 20).

The generation that followed would not give up the fight. The iconic filmmaker Nadia El Fani—who started directing in the 1990s—is, in this regard, a reference for this kind of militant social-minded filmmaking. She stood throughout her career as a disruptive voice against the established order, challenging gender relations, communist activism, and the role of Islam in Tunisian society.

In order to establish a thorough overview without offering a mere chronological interpretation of the role of women in the history of Tunisian cinema, I will discuss these politically engaged documentaries via three separate approaches. First, I will question the boundary between documentary and fiction and analyze the transition from the 1970s ethnographic approach to the affirmation of subjective creation through satirical mockumentaries in 2010. I will then linger on the quintessential political moment that was the 2011 revolution, started by riots and gatherings that sent dictator Zine El Abidine Ben Ali on the run to Saudi

Arabia. Then I will study revolutionary and postrevolutionary movies in order to define the aesthetic means used by young women filmmakers to establish, through images, the possibility of a new voice for the Tunisian people. Finally, I will attempt to broaden the study by breaking away from strictly political movies and engaging with seemingly apolitical films. To do so, I will study patrimonial documentary films, for which I postulate a political value in the underlying tension that pitches local popular culture against the growing standardization of a fully Western-oriented Tunisian society.

From the Ethnographic Documentary Movie to the Mockumentary: Evolution of Aesthetic Forms in the Service of Political Discourse

According to Denise Brahimi, Tunisian cinema of the 1970s and 1980s "endeavors to speak up about the dysfunctions of a highly conformist society that is more repressive than it appears and often harmful and sometimes lethal for individuals who, in one way or another, live outside society's standards" (Brahimi 2009, 12). These standards have remained very patriarchal, despite some progress in women's liberation. Brahimi's observation thus also resonates with depictions of women at the margins of society in films by Tunisian women.

There are many examples of societal critique by Tunisian women filmmakers, from Ferchiou's ethnographic documentary movies in the late 1960s to Kaouther Ben Hania's mockumentary *The Challat of Tunis* (*Shallat Tunis/Le Challat de Tunis*, 2013). From their first images, through classic documentary perspectives or more bold and experimental choices, criticism against the state of society has become sharper. Some filmmakers have not hesitated to voice their criticism, blurring the line between fiction and documentary, and several have risked censorship for speaking up—what could be more politically oriented than a documentary film made under an authoritarian regime?

Tunisian women, as noted by Tunisian filmmaker and academic Sonia Chamkhi, benefit from a "singular status, where social policy marked the lives of women well beyond the elite circle" (Chamki 2012, 28). Ever since its independence, Tunisian society has participated in moves toward women's liberation in an exceptional fashion for the Arab world: the Code of Personal Status, enacted in 1956, protects Tunisian women against polygamy and repudiation, and offers them the same rights as men in terms of divorce and religiously mixed marriage. Bourguiba imposed mandatory education for girls and made it not mandatory for them to be veiled. Despite the modernization, however, Tunisian society under Bourguiba's regime had its critics.

In the late 1960s, Ferchiou made her foray into filmmaking via her background in anthropology. She stands out as the first female filmmaker in the history of Tunisia with a series of ethnographic documentary movies. Ferchiou took an interest in traditional practices and ancestral Tunisian customs. Despite the informative aspect of her movies, true criticisms against Bourguiba's system in her oeuvre appeared only at the end of the 1970s, especially with her exposure of women's work on farms in *The Mistresses of Agriculture* (*Rabbat al-manzil fi-l-filaha/Les Ménagères de l'agriculture*, 1975). The movie begins with these words: "In Tunisia, the woman is the most active element in agriculture. But integrated in the predominant family production structure, her work is often unpaid and symbolically linked to her inferior status" (1:20). Ferchiou's critique is clear from the first sentences of the movie, which are swiftly followed by a series of examples showing the hierarchical division of work that dominates the patriarchal system of agricultural environments. "For olive-picking, whether in Sahel or way down south, the sexual division of labor is very clear. The man, whose status is superior, stands on a ladder and shakes the olive branch in a frenzy while the crouching woman picks up the fallen olives one by one" (5:35). Women take up the most screen time and are depicted working in fields and kitchens alike while taking care of the children playing around them. They never look at the camera. Women hoe, dig, pick, and bundle up harvested vegetables and then work to clean up these vegetables at the well. "But this strictly female-oriented work is not regarded as an agricultural task. It is categorized as household work, similar to laundry." The movie is traditionally made as a voice-over in "direct-address style,"[2] which adds additional information about life in the fields. But these twenty-six minutes of documentary contradict the official message on gender equality that Bourguiba's political campaign was trying to broadcast both nationally and internationally. By narrating the voice-over herself, Ferchiou is directly criticizing the system. In an article published in 1996 titled "Féminisme d'État en Tunisie: Idéologie dominante et résistance feminine" (State Feminism in Tunisia: Dominating Ideology and Feminine Resistance, 122), she asserts that Bourguiba launched his program of reforms in women's rights upon gaining national sovereignty, but the state feminism he supported was not a response to feminist considerations.

Three years earlier, on the occasion of International Women's Day 1975, Habib Bourguiba ordered a movie to be made on the history of feminism in Tunisia by the Tunisian Women's Union, an association close to the regime described by Sophie Bessis as a "transmission belt of the regime discourse in female environments" (Bessis 1999). The purpose of this work was, naturally, to shed a positive light on Bourguiba's measures, which were intended to place Tunisia on the map of progressive countries. This work fell to Selma Baccar, who, after making her debut at the Tunisian Federation of Amateur Filmmakers, took directing classes in Paris and started working in television after her return to Tunisia. With *Fatma 75* (1976), the final product of this official order, Baccar was the first Tunisian woman to direct a film for the movie theater. In spite of this exceptional position offered to her, she did not abide by the party line, and made an audacious movie in both background and shape, thus resulting in its censorship in Tunisia for more than thirty years. Even more clearly than others, this movie meets Nicole Brenez's definition of political cinema as the place where political stakes interact dynamically with creative stakes. Baccar chose formal creativity to serve a strong political comment: her radical narrative choices allowed her to rewrite official history. *Fatma 75* tells the story of a young student, Fatma, whom the university asks to create a presentation on the history of feminism in Tunisia. This presentation is an opportunity to retrace a social history of women from the Queen of Numidia, Sophonisbe, to the contemporary age. In an innovative format between documentary and fiction, Fatma travels through reconstituted ages to show the progress of the twentieth century—but also to show that the struggle is far from over. The historicity suggested by Baccar did not gain approval from Bourguiba's officials. The way she presented Tahar Haddad's theories was notably divisive. Born in 1899 and active until 1935, this unionist thinker was one of the first to commit himself to women's liberation in Tunisian society, in particular by calling for the abolition of polygamy.[3] By showing Haddad as a forerunner, Baccar denied Bourguiba's claim to be the father of reform ideas concerning personal status laws. Baccar also did not accept the rewrite of the story suggested in the official narrative, which made Bourguiba's wife out to be a feminist activist early on, while Bchira Ben Mrad—founder of the Muslim Union of Tunisian Women in 1936, and active until independence—was erased from the official history. This film, with the help of French cinema critic Guy Hennebelle, managed to cross the border and land in a feminist film festival in Holland. A copy subtitled in Dutch toured the world until the censorship was lifted in 2006.

Tunisian women's rights are a subject of both pride and debate for the Tunisian people. Filmmakers are bound to defend them in a region where women's liberation is far from a priority and is increasingly perceived as a danger by societies ever more strongly influenced by Islam. This subject is often addressed in TV documentaries. Even if these documentaries are of a more traditional style and sold worldwide, they perpetuate in their own way the social documentary movement. They meet the need to accompany struggles and the importance of filming a political experience, in order to oppose Benjamin's assertion that "History is written by the victors" (Benjamin 2006) by writing another memory. The Franco-Tunisian director Feriel Ben Mahmoud uses women's liberation as a recurrent theme in her movies, most notably in *Tunisia: A History of Women* (*Tunisie, une histoire de femmes*, 2005), the premise for *Feminism Inshallah: A History of Arab Feminism* (*Révolution des femmes: Un siècle de féminisme arabe*, 2014). In 2013, when the Islamist Ennahda Party secured a place in the Tunisian government, Ben Mahmoud filmed the much more critical *Tunisian Women: On the Front Line* (*Tunisiennes, sur la ligne de front*) with the intention of defending freedom for women against the turn to religion in Tunisian society. Religion is a sensitive topic in Tunisia, especially under Ben Ali's dictatorship, which sought to standardize a model society. Filming permits for Nadia El Fani's movie *Neither Allah nor Master* (*La'ikiya insha' Allah/ Laïcité Inch'Allah*[4]) were delivered only because she lied about the title and content. Shooting started in August 2010 during Ramadan, with the aim of proving that Islam's prohibitions were far from being respected by the entire Tunisian society, despite appearances given by the empty streets of Tunis and its closed shops. From the beginning of the film El Fani appears on screen rather than staying behind the camera. This allows her to question society without endangering her interlocutors, since she chose her interlocutors to fit and lend legitimacy to her personal ideas.

The call for a secularization of Tunisian society was amplified by the outbreak of the first anti–Ben Ali demonstrations, which led the dictator and his wife to flee to Saudi Arabia on January 14, 2011. The opportunity for a democratic debate was finally at hand for El Fani. The second part of the movie illustrates these unprecedented discussions, giving a glimpse into the depth of upcoming changes in Tunisian society. The revolution marked a turning point in the movie: people who were hiding to eat during Ramadan in the first part of the movie demonstrated and risked their lives to get the opportunity to build a new model of society. But the secularists were not the only ones in the ranks of revolutionaries. The theater release of El Fani's film provoked the wrath of Islamic fundamentalists, who attacked the cinema showing the movie (Malterre 2011) and threatened to kill the filmmaker for her atheism (Martin 2013, 273). In this way El Fani became a participant in revolutionary struggle.

Despite the violence, El Fani kept denouncing the failings of society. In her 2013 film *No Harm Done* (*Même pas mal*), she associated her own cancer with the religious extremist tendencies that had spread since Ben Ali's departure. The comparison sparked a massive outcry.

El Fani's films do not meet the requirements of the classic documentary movie. Highly subjective, filmed in the first person, they express uncompromisingly the filmmaker's radical point of view. She states in her own words, in the voice-over: I am Tunisian, a woman, a lesbian, and an atheist. The struggles she portrays in her movies become hers. She stages herself speaking out and provoking the conservative middle class and the hypocrisy of "decency" in not speaking out. She never hesitates to put herself at risk, even by risking exile: a trial for "violations of the sacred, of customs and religious precepts" (El Hammi 2011) prevented her from entering Tunisia as a free woman for six years (2011–17).

Other strategies have been used to denounce the excesses of religion, defend the freedom of women, and speak out against institutional censorship. An example is Ben Hania's mockumentary *The Challat of Tunis* (*Le Challat de Tunis*, 2013), which features fictional characters. As defined by Craig Hight, a mockumentary "is popularly understood to be a fictional audio-visual text . . . which looks and sounds like a documentary" (Hight 2015, 26). Ben Hania picks up on a news item from 2003, the thread of an urban legend about a biker called "The Challat" (The Blade) who roams the streets of Tunis slashing women's buttocks with a razor blade. She interviews people, particularly men, about the case and about their opinions on how women "should" dress in order to command respect, using this strategy to show that the normative role of women in society is understood by her interlocutors to be established and more or less unquestionable.

The discourse drawn by these fictive interactions shows how nonfiction can be used to document a certain reality. Through a casting exercise to find an actor to play "The Challat" in the film, Ben Hania further combines fiction and reality. The audience is no longer entirely sure whether an actor who shows up and presents himself as "The Real Challat" has been directed as part of the film to do so or not.

Ben Hania also depicts an encounter with the authorities who prevented her from filming in some of Tunis' neighborhoods. Even after the revolution, cameras were perceived as enemies. Viola Shafik recounts "the three corners of the Arab taboo triangle" (Shafik 2007a, 251) that put people at risk of censorship and intolerance: sexuality, religion, and politics. Reinforced under Ben Ali, censorship and control over creativity contributed to a nation's exasperation. Inevitably anger broke out during the 2011 revolution, and with it hundreds of images were circulated, many of which were created by women.

Revolutionary and Postrevolutionary Movies: Creating a Citizen's Voice under Ben Ali (1987–2011)

Women documentary filmmakers partly vanished from the scene under Ben Ali, and it became increasingly difficult to make films about contemporary Tunisian society. "I was afraid that the film could not go to committee and that it could not be edited,"[5] director Kalthoum Bornaz said in the media after the revolution about her last feature film *The Other Half of the Sky* (*Shatr mahaba/L'Autre moitié du ciel*). Nonfiction seemed even more dangerous than fictional stories, and screenplays were meticulously controlled. Selma Baccar, who made a few heritage documentary films in the early 1980s, also worked in television, producing[6] and directing fictional TV programs. Sophie Ferchiou only made two movies after 1980: *Stambali* (1996) and *Sculpted Words* (*Paroles sculptées*, 2005), both of them again addressing Tunisian patrimonial customs. Only Nadia El Fani, who started her cinematographic career in 1990, made a few politically and socially themed documentary movies, concurrently with her shorts and feature fictional films. *Sons of Lenin* (*Awlad Lenin/Ouled Lénine*, 2007) is perhaps the most ambitious, as she attempts, through her father's life, to trace the communist movement in Tunisia before its ban by Bourguiba after independence.

A quick glance at the catalog of documentary movies made by women and released during the years of dictatorship allows us to assess the weight of the lead blanket that crushed artists and filmmakers at that time. After Ben Ali's departure and the lifting of institutional censorship, the contrast in terms of freedom of speech is extreme. Post-2011, cinematographic production increased to an unprecedented degree, in an attempt to respond to the issues of the moment. Though the films produced during this period differ in perspective, they all show a blatant disruption to the filmmakers' conceptions of both the world and the use of cinema, and those set within historical context appear more informed. In 2011's *My 14th* (*Arba't 'ashr, Mon 14*), Ismahane Lahmar desired that every Tunisian be able to express themselves freely. Relieved by Ben Ali's flight, the filmmaker sought to give a voice to skilled workers, students, and Tunisians who were willing to express their experiences of January 14. There are multiple testimonies that follow one another, making it seem as though the entire Tunisian people, both united in revolt and adamant in their demands, are speaking out in this movie. In reality, cameras brandished under the dictatorship were only shooting certain oppressed categories of the population. A new expression of "tunisianité"—a term invented by Kmar Kchir-Bendana in her inquiry on the ideological identity of Tunisian cinema (Kchir-Bendada 2003)—appeared. Building a torn society back up, the people must be the only one choosing new tools in order to define itself.

The theme of rebuilding a society that collapsed is also engaged in Nadia El Fani's movie. The film opens with democratic debates held in the aftermath of the dictator's flight. El Fani's film is the first example of this passion of women filmmakers for the establishment of a democratic government. Most were personally involved, outside of their work as artists, in laying the foundations of a new society. Film editor and director Kalthoum

Bornaz also used her talent to further democracy, making portraits of politicians she supported during presidential, legislative, and municipal elections. She created short activist movies, such as *Fadhel Moussa, Strength and Determination* (*Fadhel Moussa, force et détermination*, 2014), which appears as both a campaign advertisement and an ode to a long-awaited democracy. Selma Baccar, who ran and won a campaign to become the representative of her region, placed her camera in the cause of revolution: she went to the south of Tunisia to help refugees fleeing the chaos of post-Gaddafi Libya. In *Refugees of Both Sides* (*Réfugiés des deux rives*, 2011), she showed the terrible reception conditions in a refugee camp in Ben Gardane. In this short movie, which she shot alone with one camera operator, Tunisia is critically depicted as a country that had already suffered the backlash of revolution and seen the rise of Islamic fundamentalism.

Though women filmmakers had already represented the Tunisian people under Ben Ali— as seen in *From the Side of Women Leaders* (*Du côté des femmes leaders*, 1993), in which El Fani presented and staged women politicians throughout the country—the revolution allowed them the right to claim a place and a role in political debate. Thrilled by the transformation of the political establishment to a democratic regime, Sonia Chamkhi made a documentary movie about the electoral campaign, *Women Activists* (*Munadilat/Militantes*, 2012), which followed women who tried to encourage others to vote. Individuals and party representatives tell stories of oppression and liberation. Their attitudes are the result of a long struggle against the patriarchy, and their traditional values remain apparent. The revolution, for female politicians and filmmakers alike, has also been the opportunity for changes to women's emancipation. The rising power of the Islamic Ennahda Party was a roadblock on the way toward social and political change, but it did not keep the movement stagnant. The resistance of these women and their will to speak up was evident once again in Feriel Ben Mahmoud's *Tunisian Women on the Front Line* (*Tunisiennes, sur la ligne de front*, 2013).

Women fighting not to be forgotten by the revolution enjoyed unprecedented attention in the media and movies in postrevolutionary society. Yet others found it difficult to come out of the shadows—too oppressed to find their place in the struggle for freedom of speech. This is the subject matter of Hinde Boujemaa's *It Was Better Tomorrow* (*Ya man 'ash/C'était mieux demain*, 2012). The movie introduces us to Aïda, a woman who tried to find shelter during the revolution. Accompanied by her son, who is a violent adolescent, she knocked down the doors of empty flats and settled in squats in front of the filmmaker's camera. Boujemaa chooses to move away from the demonstrations to take an interest in the margins of the revolution and to find hope there for social change. A sexually abused mother of three, without financial or physical security, Aïda never ceases fighting. Her two youngest children are placed in foster care. The revolution doesn't change much for her, apart from temporarily distracting the authorities from her small illegal activities. Once again, a woman takes center stage—a worthy protagonist, who refuses to give up and allows herself to be carried away by the fervor of a people by whom she had always been excluded.

Most Tunisian women documentary filmmakers chose to take up the challenge of social reorganization and attempt to create innovative images of a new Tunisian society. Others maintained a critical distance and continued questioning the political agenda.

By shooting these movies in the heat of a thrilling actuality, the filmmakers become "archaeologists of the present" (Ben Ouanès 2012, 93), to use Kamel Ben Ouanès' phrase. They reposition the question, which "is not about being (who am I?) nor about having (what do I own?) but about belonging to a national entity" (Ben Ouanès 2012, 99), which we defined as "tunisianité." To remain at the forefront of events, in most of the cases I have detailed here, women filmmakers started filming before obtaining funding. Some of them, like Sonia Chamkhi's *Women Activists*, Selma Baccar's *Refugees of Both Sides*, or Kalthoum Bornaz's *Fadhel Moussa, Strength and Determination*, were funded by their directors' own resources. Such self-reliance was made possible by the democratization of digital technology in the early 2000s. Women, rather than accepting loss of control over their work, self-produced and continued to question the world they were living in. The revolution thus allowed, as phrased by Olivier Barlet, to "draw from the creativity of the work, which didn't appear on its own during the revolution: it existed already underground" (Barlet 2012, 271). Women took up the image and used it as a weapon, introducing alternative images of their societies.

Political Stakes in the Patrimonial Documentary Movie: Views on Popular Culture against Standardization and Radicalization in Society

Habib Bourguiba's views on Tunisian society have always been clear. While he led the struggle for independence and then ruled the country from 1956 to 1987, his commitment to secularism, advancements in women's rights, and the Westernization of Tunisian culture and values formed the basis for his creation of a new nation-state until Ben Ali's rise to power. However, as has been highlighted, filmmakers were critical of the state for some time before Bourguiba's dismissal. In the aforementioned movies, they denounced the gap between the official discourse and reality, including challenging projections of an ideal society internationally. With the advent of Ben Ali and the reinforcement of police control, freedom of speech was even more threatened. Nevertheless, opening up to Europe still appeared to be the main political line. It was a new relation to the "tunisianité" as an expression of national identity, developed during the 2011 revolution, that exposed more clearly the limits of Ben Ali's party line in films. Testifying to the omnipresence of these critics against the state in national cinema, Denise Brahimi (2009, 51) suggests reading *Le Désenchantement national* (National Disenchantment, 1982) by Tunisian philosopher Hélé Béji to explain this Tunisian peculiarity—the disappointment by the promises of a post-independence nation-state, which remained on paper and was never fully and democratically carried out.

It is important to set this politically charged expression via cinematographic images in a broader context, and to examine the political aspects of heritage films made by women. Sonia Chamkhi, herself interested in Tunisian patrimony in her cinema, wrote that Tunisian women filmmakers took an interest "from the 1970s . . . in questions arising from social and cultural anthropology—most notably about patrimony and craft" (Chamkhi 2012, 29). This interest is also part of a political agenda. Such filmmakers stage and utilize Tunisian customs as a form of cultural resistance to a government that is encouraging Western influence.

Ways of life and traditions were highlighted from the very first movies by Tunisian women: Sophie Ferchiou's *Chechia* (*Chéchia*, 1967), presented the history and manufacturing processes of national headwear in Tunisia. This movie accompanied a study that Ferchiou published as part of her research work named *Technics and Society*, published in 1971. The following year, Ferchiou took an interest in the nomad's feast of Zarda—*Zarda: A Nomadic Tribe's Feastday* (1972); wedding celebrations in the central region of El-Sabria—*Wedding in Sabria* (*al-Zafaf fi Sabria*, 1974); and the potter's village of Guallala on the island of Djerba—*Guallalla: A Potter's Village in Tunisia* (1975). During the following decade, Selma Baccar made *The Land of Tarayoun* (*Fi bilad al-Tarayoun/Au pays de Tarayoun*, 1986), a documentary film about the craft of weaving the traditional Tunisian dress *(tarayoun)*. In the 1980s Baccar also created a series of TV reports titled *Tunisian Craftsmen*. She took a particular interest in glass painting and pottery techniques in the Sahel. In 1988, Fatma Skandrani made a very personal documentary movie on her perception of Tunis' old town, titled *Medina . . . My Memory (al-Madina . . . dhakirati/Médina . . . ma mémoire)*, then created during the 1990s several films about traditional Tunisian patrimony and artistry: *Tunisian Painters (Les peintres tunisiens*, 1995) and *Tunis' Medina: Traditional Housing in Africa (Tunis la medina: habitat traditionnel en Afrique*, 1996).

Beyond their folkloric appearance, the subject matter of these movies allowed for the affirmation of a historically strong Tunisian culture. The political aspects were sometimes more obvious. Some of Kalthoum

Bornaz's documentary movies aimed to counter a political decision: *Three Characters in Search of Theater* (*Trois personnages en quête d'un théâtre*, 1988) was, for example, made to counter a project to destroy the municipal theater of Tunis, a big structure built in the early twentieth century by the Bey's family architect under the protectorate. In this film where fiction and reenactment are combined, the filmmaker paid tribute to the most renowned theater in Tunisia, and to all the stars it had presented. This movie made such an impact that the building was preserved; the heritage had been saved thanks to its appearance in a film.

When shooting *El Medfoun Forest* (*Ghabat al-madfun/La forêt d'El-Medfoun*, 1998), Bornaz aimed for a similar goal: to showcase a natural landscape that president Ben Ali wanted to destroy in order to build tourist resorts. The project was halted as a result of economic recession and the 2011 revolution.[7] There was also a form of political activism at stake in *Wedding Nights in Tunis* (*Nuits de noce à Tunis*, 1996). Although religious fundamentalism was gaining ground in society, Bornaz decided to aim her camera at dancers practicing their art in spite of the extremist condemnations. Following the rhythm of the voice of Bornaz talking about her Tunis, this movie depicts a dancer who travels by night from wedding to wedding to enliven the celebrations. The film has a tone of nostalgia as it laments the disappearance of rich traditions. Against the urban elitism of Tunis' cultural circles, Chamkhi endeavored to present another image of the margins of society, capturing the way of life of Douz's Bedouins in *Douz, the Sahara's Gate* (*Duz, bab al-sahra'/Douz, la porte du Sahara*, 2003), featuring the camel drivers and their expertise. She later took an interest in popular music with *Mezoued Art* (*Fann al-mizwad/L'Art du Mezoued*, 2010), depicting music played on traditional instruments across the country during weddings or popular celebrations, but rarely studied. Chamkhi aimed to give these largely overlooked musicians a platform, in contrast to the influence of Western music in Tunisia at the time. Through these patrimonial movies, another history of Tunisia appears, one that goes back to the foundations of Tunisian culture, its traditions, its art, and its crafts. Tunisian women documentarians refused from the very first day to follow a political discourse that did not offer concrete answers and opportunities to people in their everyday lives. They struggled against the odds to film and spread their conception of "tunisianités" as citizens, speaking more to a local than to an international audience and attempting to rekindle aspects of Tunisian society that have been lost.

Conclusion

Tunisian women, as this chapter has shown, have been making eminently political films—both documentary and fictional—since the 1970s. This has been credited by some analysts to the advent of personal status laws under Bourguiba. Yet the examples cited here demonstrate the deeply subversive nature of such works, which challenge the patriarchal system to its core, and even in some cases put the filmmaker in precarious positions vis-à-vis state and society.

Although the 2011 uprising provided a window of opportunity for societal challenge, the political nature of films made by Tunisian women long before this, in which the filmmakers themselves often speak through voice-overs to personally challenge normative contexts, show how provocative the medium of women's documentary filmmaking has been in Tunisia for decades. Notable examples, such as Sophie Ferchiou's *The Mistresses of Agriculture*, Nadia El Fani's *Secularism Inshallah*, Sonia Chamkhi's *Women Activists*, and Hinde Boujemaa's *It Was Better Tomorrow*, illustrate the ways in which Tunisian women have used their own voices in documentary filmmaking to denounce inequalities in society.

References

Barlet, Olivier. 2012. "Le cinéma tunisien à la lumière du Printemps Arabe." In *Les Cinémas du Maghreb et leurs publics*, edited by Patricia Caillé and Florence Martin, 270-280. Africultures 89. Paris: L'Harmattan.

Béji, Hélé. 1982. *Le Désenchantement national*. Paris: Maspero.

Benjamin, Walter. 2006. "On the Concept of History." In *Walter Benjamin: Selected Writings*, Vol. 4: 1938–1940, edited by Howard Eiland and Michael W. Jennings, 450-457. Cambridge: Harvard University Press.

Ben Ouanès, Kamel. 2012. "Rhétorique de la rupture dans le cinéma maghrébin." In *Les Cinémas du Maghreb et leurs publics*, edited by Patricia Caillé and Florence Martin, 92-101. Africultures 89. Paris: L'Harmattan.

Bessis, Sophie. 1999. "Le féminisme institutionnel en Tunisie." *Clio: Histoire, femmes et sociétés*. clio.revues.org.

Bourguiba, Sayda. 2013. "Finalités culturelles et esthétiques d'un cinéma arabo-africain en devenir: Les Journées Cinématographiques de Carthage. PhD diss., Université Paris 1-Panthéon Sorbonne. tel. archives-ouvertes.fr.

Brahimi, Denise. 2009. *50 ans de cinéma maghrébin*. Paris: Minerve.

Brenez, Nicole. 2012. "René Vautier: Devoirs, droits et passion des images." *La Furia Umana* 14. Ourense: Duen De Bux.

———. 2014. "Two Lovers—Cinema and Revolution." *La Furia Umana* 19. Ourense: Duen De Bux.

Caillé, Patricia, and Florence Martin, eds. 2012. *Les Cinémas du Maghreb et leurs publics*. Africultures 89. Paris: L'Harmattan.

Chamkhi, Sonia. 2012. "Du discours social au discours de l'intime ou de la démystification de la violence." In *Les Cinémas du Maghreb et leurs publics*, edited by Patricia Caillé and Florence Martin, 28-39. Africultures 89. Paris: L'Harmattan.

Denoix, Sylvie, ed. 2013. *Cinémas arabes du XXIe siècle: Nouveaux territoires, nouveaux enjeux.* Revue des mondes musulmans et de la Méditerranée. Aix-en-Provence: Presses Universitaires de Provence.

Ferchiou, Sophie. 1971. *Techniques et sociétés: Exemple de la fabrication des chéchias en Tunisie.* Paris: Institut d'ethnologie.

———. 1996. "Féminisme d'État en Tunisie: Idéologie dominante et résistance féminine." In *Femmes, Culture et Société au Maghreb 2: Femmes, pouvoir politique et développement*, edited by Rahma Bourqia, Mounira Charrad, and Nancy Gallagher, 134-138. Casablanca: Afrique Orient.

Gabous, Abdelkrim. 1998. *Silence, elles tournent! Les femmes et le cinéma en Tunisie.* Tunis: Cérès.

Gilman, Sarah E. 2007. "Feminist Organizing in Tunisia: Negotiating Transnational Linkages and the State." In *From Patriarchy to Empowerment: Women's Participation, Movements, and Rights in the Middle East, North Africa and South Asia*, edited by Valentine Moghadam, 97-119. Syracuse: Syracuse University Press.

Haddad, Tahar. 1930. *Our Women in the Shari'a and Society.* Tunis: Nirvana.

El Hammi, Emna. 2011. "Liberté d'expression en Tunisie: La justice, nouveau fer de lance de la censure"? *Nawaat*, December 30. nawaat.org.

Hight, Craig. 2015. "The Mockumentary." In *Contemporary Documentary*, edited by Daniel Marcus and Selmin Kara, 26-41. London: Routledge.

Kchir-Bendana, Kmar. 2003. "Ideologies of the Nation in Tunisian Cinema." In "Nation, Society and Culture in North Africa," edited by James McDougall. *Journal of North African Studies* 8, no. 1: 27–34. London: Routledge.

Khayati, Khémais. 1996. *Cinémas arabes: topographie d'une image éclatée.* Paris: L'Harmattan.

Leclère, Thierry. 2011. "C'était quoi, être artiste sous Ben Ali?" *Télérama*, January 28.

Malterre, Ségolène. 2011. "Attaque du cinéma Africart par des islamistes: La vie culturelle tunisienne est-elle en danger?" *Les Observateurs, France 24*, June 28. observers.france24.com.

Martin, Florence. 2013. "Nadia El Fani, cinéaste de la contestation." *Studies in French Cinema* 13, no. 3: 273-280.

———. 2007. "Tunisia" in Hjort, Mette, and Duncan Petrie, eds. *The Cinema of Small Nations*. Edinburgh: Edinburgh University Press: 213-228.

Nichols, Bill. 1983. "The Voice of Documentary." *Film Quarterly* 36, no. 3: 17-30.

Niney, François. 2002. *L'Épreuve du réel à l'écran*. Paris and Brussels: De Boeck.

Pallister, Janis L., and Ruth A. Hottell. 2005. *French-Speaking Women Documentarians: A Guide*. New York: Peter Lang.

Saïl, Noureddine. 2012. "Journées cinématographiques de Carthage 2010: Allocation d'ouverture du colloque." In *Les Cinémas du Maghreb et leurs publics*, edited by Patricia Caillée and Florence Martin, 18-27. Africultures 89. Paris: L'Harmattan.

Shafik, Viola. 2007. *Arab Cinema: History and Cultural Identity*. Cairo: American University in Cairo Press. Originally published 1998.

18

MEMORIES AND LEGACIES OF ALGERIAN WOMEN'S STRUGGLES DURING AND AFTER INDEPENDENCE

Olivier Hadouchi

A number of Algerian documentaries, filmed from the end of the 1970s onward, highlight an oft-overlooked, even forgotten, aspect of the country's history: the involvement of women in the fight for national independence.* The position held by women in Algerian society has evolved since independence; there has been progress as well as setbacks, and fights have been fought for the advancement of women's rights that continue today. "Women have always protested, whether it was wartime or not... There is a continuity. Women have always been there. And depending on the circumstances, they were brought to the fore, or pushed to the back," declares Habiba Djahnine in *Letter to My Sister* (*Lettre à ma soeur*, 2006), dedicated to her sister, a leftist feminist activist who was assassinated by Islamic fundamentalists in Tizi Ouzou in 1995, during the black decade.[1]

In order to establish a link between the struggles of the past and those of today, several documentarians have turned to the Algerian War of Independence and the role women played in this (re)formative fight for their country. Other films have established this link in an attempt at advocacy in terms of gender relations and women's rights today.

In certain wartime news footage, one could sometimes glimpse a female nurse or uniformed combatant, for example *Algeria in Flames* (*L'Algérie en flammes*, 1958) by René Vautier, but it was quite rare. During the Battle of Algiers, the FLN[2] enlisted women as liaison officers to gather and circulate information, and as combatants, since they did not hesitate to transport weapons or carry out bombings because it was easier for them to cross the French army's roadblocks. In fact, several subsequent documentaries have reused footage from Gillo Pontecorvo's famous narrative film *The Battle of Algiers* (La Bataille d'Alger, 1966).

---

* translated by Kevin St. John

Shot on location and inspired by the aesthetics of reportage, the film features women taking part in urban guerrilla warfare. Meanwhile, Youssef Chahine filmed *Djamila* (*Jamila al-Jaza'iriya/Djamila l'Algérienne*, 1958) to show his solidarity (and the solidarity of Nasser's Egypt) with Djamila Bouhired, who had been arrested after a bombing attack and subsequently sentenced to death. This led to a far-reaching campaign, which eventually allowed her to escape execution. During the 1960s and 1970s, the war had a large presence in film because it served as a source of legitimacy for the powers that be—powers that did not hesitate to erase certain historical figures from the "official" accounts of events. Despite the war's large presence, women were very rarely featured in film, except as mothers of courage or victims of the conflict.

The first female Algerian director, Assia Djebar, had been known as a novelist for more than two decades when she decided to film *The Nouba of the Women of Mount Chenoua* (*Nubat nisa' jabbal Shinuwwa/La nouba des femmes du Mont Chenoua*, 1977–78).[3] Shot in her family's home region of Cherchell, this narrative film is punctuated with numerous documentary sequences. The filmmaker dedicates the *nouba* of the title, a North African genre of music, to the Hungarian composer Béla Bartók (who drew inspiration equally from "academic" music and folk traditions) and to "Yamina Oudai—known as Zoulika—who in 1955 and 1956 coordinated the national resistance in the city of Cherchell and its surrounding mountains. . . . Arrested in the Maquis[4] at forty, she was never seen again." This war veteran lives on today in the stories and popular memory of this region. Djebar asserts the legacy of this martyr-soldier, along with those who preceded her—particularly the women who fought against the colonial conquest during the Insurrection of 1871—and those who followed. In doing so, she threads a continuity (characterized by a fight for liberation) through several generations—achieved though oral transmission—as well as individual and collective pursuits. At several points she draws a parallel between women of several generations (grandmothers, mothers, and daughters), who are ultimately united in the cave sequence in the last part of the film, to dance and sing together (with lyrics written by the novelist-filmmaker herself), affirming their desire to break free from the yoke that oppresses women today just as it did in the past: "Oh, you the viewer/Oh you who are surrounded by darkness . . . Now begins the time for liberty."

After this, other Algerian filmmakers—Djamila Sahraoui, Yamina Bachir-Chouikh, Fatima Sissani, and Nassima Guessoum (the latter two being part of the Algerian diaspora, living in France but returning regularly to their home country), as well as men such as Hassen Bouabdellah, and later Amine Rachedi—sought, in their respective films, to gather the testimony of women who had participated in the Algerian War of Independence.

Barberousse, My Sisters (*Barbarus akhawati/Barberousse, mes sœurs*, 1985) by Bouabdellah is another important documentary (produced by Radio Télévision Algérienne, which also produced the earlier works of Assia Djebar). The film is based on a simple premise: in 1982, Hadj Rahim made a narrative film called *Serkadji* (after Serkadji Prison, formerly Barberousse Prison) to depict the lives of the prisoners during the war, or rather, the male prisoners, since he entirely overlooked women prisoners in the film. Meanwhile, several of these overlooked women (Zohra Drif, Jacqueline Guerroudj, Baya Hocine, Djamila Bouhired, etc.) were sentenced to death. So Bouabdellah decided to display the reactions of these former women prisoners during a screening of *Serkadji* that he had organized at the Alger Center. In the film, the screening is sometimes interrupted by their commentary, which serves to correct one or another aspect of the film (for example, the prisoners did not say "oui, chef" ["yes, boss"] to their guards). Sometimes it is punctuated by their cries, or even the fainting of one of the women during a sequence showing a guillotine intended for an execution. *Barberousse, My Sisters* interweaves many types of media (newspaper clippings, photos, letters from the prisoners to their families and their lawyers, etc.) with the reactions of the women watching—women who were in reality (sometimes forgotten) actresses, acting out a story. Thus the women find a plural existence, an identity, a face, a voice, and a message that invites us to understand their (singular and collective) stories, imploring us to (re) consider and record these stories in a more fair and just manner—all while knowing that "words, and even images, are inadequate when describing these moments," as stated by Djamila Bouhired, facing the camera. "Prison is never the same; from one moment to the next, from one year to another, from one month to the next. It's not fixed. Everything depends on the political situation, on the outside," explains another prisoner.

These documentaries were produced by Algerian filmmakers, or in the form of coproductions, sometimes even with French production companies (there are more than a few examples of this), or with Misr Films (an Egyptian company)—as was the case with Amine Rachedi's *Woman Is Courage* (*Femme Courage*, 2003). This film sometimes incorporates narrative effects that seem quite televisual (a sort of lightning bolt flashing into the frame for dramatic effect), and other effects that borrow from video reportage. Certain images (documentaries and news footage shot at that time) reappear in several other films. Film director Fatima Sissani explains during a televised interview that she tried to balance the scales by exclusively featuring the voices of women in *Women Resistants: Your Untangled Hair Hides a Seven-Year War* (*Résistantes, tes cheveux démêlés cachent une guerre de sept ans*,

2017). The film focuses on Eveline Safir-Lavalette, Zoulikha Bekkadour, and Alice Cherki (Sharqi), three women, all born in Algeria, all from different backgrounds (the first having European origins, the third being of Jewish heritage), but who all fought for Algeria's independence. Two of them remained in Algeria, while the third left the country yet maintained ties to her homeland, returning regularly. The passing down of a memory, the writing of history in lively and concrete terms, is carried out through oral testimonies that will go on to form future audiovisual archives that document the women who played a role in the history of their countries. Besides, "what reason do we have to falsify history?" notes Bekkadour, thus advocating for a calmer and more just approach—an approach different from the rigid dogmas and the deliberately myopic, false perspectives: an approach that has room for the convictions of all, insofar as they are not a hindrance to historical knowledge.

For several years now, and in direct proportion to the time that has elapsed since 1954–62, the search for testimonials from, and depictions of, women activists and combatants in the war seems more urgent than ever, now that they have grown older. These women are passing away, and even sometimes pass away during the making of films dedicated to them. This was the case, to name just two examples, with Eveline Safir-Lavette, who died before Fatima Sissani had finished *Women Resistants*, and Nassima Hablal, a former activist with the FLN. Hablal, born in 1928, is the primary focus of Nassima Guessoum's documentary, titled *10,949 Women* (*10949 femmes*, 2014), a reference to the number of women registered as veterans with Algeria's National Organisation of Mujahideen. This underappreciated and forgotten heroine passed away before Nassima Guessoum had finished her film: the director shows us images of her burial, but then opts to finish her film with earlier images of the former combatant, as though she had not died. Thus the film concludes with a sequence in which the former activist points out to the filmmaker (thus making the viewer a witness of sorts) that they share the same first name, creating a kind of mirror effect that enables an intergenerational transfer, as if one were the daughter or the granddaughter, and thus her successor of sorts.

10,949 Women opens with a TV broadcast of an official commemoration of independence; next, the one-time heroine opens the doors of her modest home to the young filmmaker, who has come to hear her story and immortalize not only her image but everything concerning her as a person (her long-lost hopes, her disappointments, even her taste in songs, and her elegance)—all of this thanks to the existence of film recording and the cinematic apparatus. In this way, the film establishes an exchange (in a casual, intimate mode) with a war veteran who is clearly named and identified during ceremonies, surrounded by the pomp of official commemorations, replete with an orchestra, fireworks, and the laying of a wreath before the official monument called the Martyrs' Memorial (Maqam al-Shahid), overlooking Algiers. Nassima Hablal is direct and speaks frankly, like the majority of women in our corpus: she starts by inviting Guessoum (and the audience, in a symbolic sense) to drink a coffee and to join her in her daily life. This kind of approach allows Guessoum to humanize Hablal, avoiding the kind of "heroine worship" that surrounds the petrified figure of the "hero in marble" found in certain socialist-realism depictions. These women's testimonies (about their past deeds, their views on the evolution of society, and the present day) become all the more precious, marked with a real urgency just before the end of their lives, acquiring even the gravity of a will and testament.

Made in 1995, in the middle of the "black decade," the film *Half of Allah's Sky* (*La moitié du ciel d'Allah*, 1995), by Djamila Sahraoui, does not hesitate to stand up for women and their struggle—women being among the first victims of fundamentalism—nor does it hesitate to directly provoke the viewer with these words: "You all cry out for my honor, and yet no one remembers my rights." After independence "women didn't leave the political arena; they were pushed out," asserts a female activist, later in the film.

This documentary offers a careful arrangement of sequences dedicated to the memory of the women who fought in the War of Independence. The female narrator immediately assumes this lineage: "I was a child, and I remember you," along with the remarkable nature of their journey. This arrangement is made in order to place their struggle back into perspective, as well as to reinforce the call for women's rights by first contemplating the actions of those who suffered oppression under the colonial regime, followed by the actions of women (often from later generations) who fought against the 1984 Algerian Family Code, which curtailed the rights of women in society, and then, finally, by observing those who fought the rise of fundamentalism. However, we learn at the film's end that the director decided to go into exile, leaving her country, yet maintaining solidarity with her fellow countrywomen with whom she asserts a sisterhood: "This film is for you, my sisters, who confront the horror on a daily basis." These words slide onto a black screen just before the closing credits begin to roll. A historical continuity begins to form, little by little, thanks to the narration that unfolds through a dynamic montage of images (using a rich archival reservoir, namely the war photographs from the personal collections of Djouher Akrour and Djamila Amrane,[5] two veterans of the Zone d'Alger), accompanied by overlaid sounds, as well as the frequent use of songs whose lyrics are often stirring and eloquent. Female veterans of the War of Independence such as Myriam Benhamza, who was a member of the French Federation of the FLN, participate in an association called "SOS Women in Distress." Formed at the beginning of the 1990s, the association is dedicated to providing shelter to women who have been thrown out by their families or husbands. Shot more than ten years after that of Sahraoui, Faouzia Fekiri's documentary *The Fire-Bearers*[6] (*Les Porteuses de feu*, 2007)[7] makes the argument (in its closing sequence) that these women whom she calls "the fire-bearers" (thus lending them a promethean glow) were not born warriors. Rather, it was the circumstances of the War of Independence and their personal choices that turned them into fighters (be it with weapons, information gathered from the enemy, or by acting as liaisons between other FLN activists). "They would have rather cradled a baby in their arms," claims the voice-over, returning them to their roles as mothers and bearing witness to a willingness to endorse, once more, the traditional conception of the family in an attempt to reestablish stability in a society still in the process of rebuilding itself after a period of gross mismanagement and unrest during the years of the black decade. The last words of the closing sequence claim that these women "played a role in the evolution of women in society" (through their actions, carried out alongside men). The role that women played in the evolution of Algerian society during the war—in total flux at the time—was it truly taken into account once independence was gained, or during the 1960s, 1970s, 1980s, and beyond? In later years, this participation was likely tinged by a sense of unfulfillment.[8] A former activist with the French Federation of the FLN's task force, who were sent as envoys to Tunisian refugees, shares her feelings with us, based on her personal experience, in *Women of Algiers* (*Femmes d'Alger*, 1992) by Kamel Dehane—a documentary that also lends a voice to Assia Djebar, among others. According to her, the *moudjahidates*[9] had achieved equality with men in the years of the War of Independence in the name of a united front, but they were pushed out afterward, relegated to their homes, and their fighting was forgotten.

Certain testimonies and admissions revealed in *Yesterday . . . Today and Tomorrow* (*Aujourd'hui . . . hier et demain*, 2010) by Bachir-Chouikh—just to cite one among many documentaries—inform us of the numerous difficulties and the many kinds of violence these women had to face during the war. Even then, in the face of sometimes brutal, not to mention traumatic, experiences (arrest, torture, rape, death sentences, and more), these former Algerian combatants were able to maintain their dignity and fight for their physical and mental well-being with great modesty and devotion, just like their male counterparts. They felt that they were doing their duty as Algerian women, regardless of their social or "ethnic" backgrounds, and ultimately we know just how effectively they fought colonialism. Not all the women react the same way before Fatima Sissani's camera, though. Eveline Safir-Lavalette makes it clear that she does not want to talk about her experience of being tortured, whereas Louisette Ighilahriz recalls the deplorable state her torturers left her in, recounting details that reveal the monstrosity of her situation—she was tied up, sitting in her own excrement, and what is more, she tells us, she was menstruating. That was until she was saved by a doctor, a man she would attempt, over the course of many years, to find and thank in person. How did she endure the torture? She explains that she would frequently shake her head in order to put herself in a daze and thus forget the pain and the fear. The question of portraying, depicting, or even recounting torture clearly raises ethical and artistic issues for filmmakers.

What is to be done with all these examples of resistance and courage in a modern context that differs, in certain ways, from that of times past? My viewing and study of this corpus of documentaries dedicated to this multifaceted memory—a memory that stands in solidarity with the struggles of women during the War of Independence—made me aware that this memory remains vivid and very fertile. The current struggle for liberation continues, to this day, to revisit those that came before, in an effort to extend them, to update them, and even to use them (by means of cinematic language and artist expression) as models for the present day—all in an attempt to promote a society in which gender relations between men and women will be more and more equal and harmonious, without sacrificing the culture or identity (interpreted in a plural, open fashion) of the country.

References

Amrane, Djamila. 1991. *Les femmes algériennes dans la guerre*. Paris: Plon.

Amrane-Minne, Danièle-Djamila. 1994. *Des femmes dans la guerre d'Algérie*. Paris: Karthala.

Armes, Roy. 2006. *Les cinémas du Maghreb: Images postcoloniales*. Paris: L'Harmattan.

Brahimi, Denise. 2009. *50 ans de cinéma maghrébin*. Paris: Minerve.

Calle-Gruber, Mireille. 2001. *Assia Djebbar ou la Résistance de l'écriture: Regards d'un écrivain d'Algérie*. Paris: Maisonneuve et Larose.

Foloppe, Virginie, and Nassima Guessoum. 2017. *De Nassima Hablal à Nassima Guessoum, D-Fiction*. http://d-fiction.fr/2017/03/de-nassima-hablal-a-nassima-guessoum/

Hadj-Moussa, Ratiba. 1994. *Le corps, l'histoire, le territoire: Les rapports femme-homme dans le discours algérien*. Montreal and Paris: Éditions Balzac and Publisud.

Shafik, Viola. 1998 (2016). *Arab Cinema: History and Cultural Identity*. Cairo: American University in Cairo Press.

Tamzali, Wassyla. 1979. *En attendant Omar Gatlato*. Algiers: ENAP.

Vince, Natalya. 2015. *Our Fighting Sisters: Nation, Memory and Gender in Algeria, 1954–2012*. Manchester: Manchester University Press.

Filmography

Bachir-Chouikh, Yamina. 2010. *Hier. . . aujourd'hui et demain.*

Bouabdellah, Hassen. 1985. *Barberousse, mes sœurs.*

Dehane, Kamal. 1992. *Femmes d'Alger.*

Djahnine, Habiba. 2006. *Lettre à ma sœur.*

Djebbar, Assia. 1978. *La Nouba des femmes du Mont Chenoua.*

———. 1982. *La Zerda ou les chants de l'oubli.*

Dols, Alexandra. 2007. *Moudjahidates.*

Fekiri, Faouzia. 2007. *Les Porteuses de feu.*

Guessoum, Nassima. 2014. *10949 femmes.*

Lallem, Ahmed. 1966. *Elles.*

———. 1998. *Algériennes 30 ans après.*

Rachedi, Amine. 2002. *Femme Courage: Louisette Ighilahriz.*

Sahraoui, Djamila. 1995. *La moitié du ciel d'Allah.*

Sissani, Fatima. 2017. *Résistantes: Tes cheveux démêlés cachent une guerre de sept ans.*

19

SPACES OF DISPOSSESSION: EXPERIMENTS WITH THE REAL IN CONTEMPORARY ALGERIAN CINEMA

Peter Limbrick

I n recent years, a number of new Algerian documentaries have achieved success in international festivals like FIDMarseille, Medfilm, and the Toronto International Film Festival. While it would be foolish to try to characterize all of them as possessing some unifying theme or style, they reveal the dedication of a new group of filmmakers to find new means of expressing the complexities of contemporary life in Algeria, whether by addressing the movement of exile and return, or through quiet observation of unusual or marginal characters and situations. *Ask Your Shadow* (*Demande à ton ombre*, 2012), by Lamine Ammar-Khodja, for example, is the diaristic chronicle of its filmmaker's return to Algeria in 2011, after eight years of exile, just as political protests broke out. Ammar-Khodja uses cellphone footage to construct an urgent, fractured montage and mise en scène that explores the contemporary political situation. Karim Sayad's *Of Sheep and Men* (2017) received support from European and Gulf sources and follows two young men in the Algiers neighborhood of Bab El Oued who train sheep—destined for sacrifice at Eid al-Adha—to become fighting rams. *A Roundabout in My Head* (*Fi rasi rond-point/Dans ma tête un rond-point*, 2015), by Hassen Ferhani, intimately observes and interacts with the workers at an abattoir. And *Samir in the Dust* (*Samir dans la poussière*, 2016), by Mohammed Ouzine, a filmmaker who grew up in France but returned to his family's village in Algeria for the making of the film, traces the life of a petrol smuggler—the nephew of the filmmaker, we eventually learn—who criss-crosses the Moroccan–Algerian border.

This chapter isolates just two of these films for further examination. In comparing *A Roundabout* and *Samir in the Dust*, I will develop an argument about the construction of space in both films and about their discourses on masculinity and dispossession, which I regard as constituting a common rhetoric. In so doing, I will compare the two films to other experiments by Algerian filmmakers who usually work in the domain of fiction rather than documentary to show how all these films complicate and even problematize the relationships among realism, fiction, and documentary form. At the same time, I will reach back further than the recent present to think about Arab cinema more generally and its relationship to masculinity and ideas of defeat, a relationship signaled by Nouri Bouzid's essay on the new Arab cinema of the 1960s and 1970s. These recent Algerian films have some precedent, I will argue, in a longer cinematic history that treats the question of defeat in the wake of revolutionary hope.

Both *A Roundabout* and *Samir* could be said to have a comparable aesthetic, in that each is constructed with long-take cinematography that is content to let the camera stay on a scene in which relatively little action occurs. Yet while the style of the two films may appear similar, their respective constructions of space are quite different and illustrate the ways that each approaches the question of masculinity and dispossession. *A Roundabout* opens with a kind of mid-credit prologue, a decontextualized shot of a winch handle on the bloody wall of the slaughterhouse around which the entire film takes place. A young man enters the frame, his shirt stained with blood and grime, and, with his back facing the camera, begins to turn the handle of the winch. The physicality of the gesture is immediately evident; he needs his whole body weight, not just his arms, to turn the winch. This is work, work that seems already to be dirty and perhaps dangerous. The soundtrack captures the squeak of the winch as it turns the cable, hoisting something that is still held offscreen, beyond our vision. We see cause, but not effect; or, perhaps, we see the effect of the work on the worker, but not the thing that causes it (which, we retrospectively deduce from a scene referred to below, is the winching of a newly slaughtered beast above a slaughterhouse floor). There is already in the scene a sense of something being tightly wound to breaking point, something that, as viewers, we don't really know or understand. Gradually, we are given more of the scene of the slaughterhouse, such as a shot of Youssef, who will become a central character, moving cattle skins around, or another shot—the widest of the first five minutes of the film—that reveals the verandah and partial exterior of the slaughterhouse, and which eventually is the basis for the title and director credit. The entire film is set in the vicinity of this slaughterhouse in Algiers, but we have remarkably little context for it. Ferhani's only establishing shot is ten minutes into the film, and barely gives a sense of scale. For the most part, the space of the film is the immediate space around the characters: the slaughterhouse floor, the porch outside, the alleyways and access lanes around the buildings.

The development of such a mise en scène functions in two ways. First, it throws our attention to the interaction of the documentary subjects (developed more and more as characters) with the space that they inhabit. In the absence of factual and explanatory details, the location becomes a kind of abstract stage for the conversations and interactions that we see there. Second, because the film never extensively explains the kind of work they do in this setting, the space itself comes to signify a kind of mental state, as if the characters interiorize the death and dismemberment by which they are surrounded. The film's perplexing title, "A Roundabout in My Head," which is not explained until some time into the film, resonates with this sense of interiorization: in this film, the external becomes subjective.[1] In constructing this kind of troubled subjectivity for its characters, the film oscillates between an observational style in which the camera explores the space from a mostly static position and a more interactive style in which characters speak to the camera in long interviews. Observationally, while it shows the men in the context of their work environment, *A Roundabout* eschews any detailed description of what these men actually do. We never really understand work done by Hossein (Husain; often referred to simply as "the Kabyle"), and we see little of Youssef's, which seems to consist of attending to the skins of the carcasses. As many critics have pointed out, for a film set in an abattoir there is relatively little gore, although two scenes in particular point to the stark realities of what happens in the abattoir while also—like so much else in the film—acting as metaphors for the kind of lives led by the men who work there.

In the first of these scenes, Ferhani's camera follows a game of football that is being watched on a small portable television. The camera is situated behind a group of men who jostle for space, seated on low stools across an area of tiled floor, watching a television that is stationed in the doorway of a small room opposite. In between the TV and its viewers, we begin to see other men working in a kind of tug-of-war with something or someone offscreen that drags them back and forth as they pull tight on a rope. Eventually a bull enters the frame to the right, the same rope attached to its head, fighting the pull of the abattoir workers who try to draw it toward slaughter. There is something potentially shocking about the casual indifference of the football viewers to the life-and-death struggle going on between them—they just want to see the match!—but the contrasting planes of action here are crucial to what the film establishes about their world. Like the enigmatic opening sequence with its steadily cranked winch, the literal tensioning that occurs inside the frame is an external signifier of what becomes subjective for the young workers who perform the work.

A second and related scene in which the stark realities of the abattoir are revealed is when we see a cattle beast—perhaps that same one, now having truly met its match—suspended by one hind leg, its throat slit so that its body can slowly bleed out after death in the manner of *halal* slaughter. As the animal occupies the right of the frame, occasionally convulsing, a man with his back to us to the left of the frame reads a newspaper, seemingly waiting for the process to finish. Again, the apparent indifference may strike some viewers as shocking, but in the affect generated by the spectacle of the dead or dying animal strung up by its slaughterers, there is an echo of the kinds of dead-end existence and exploitation that have, by now, been expressed by the film's workers in their conversations with each other and their interviews to the camera.

In one sense, then, the film becomes expressionistic to the extent that the external qualities of its mise en scène are indicative of the state of mind of its characters. But it also relies on two levels of interactivity: one between the characters themselves, and the other between the characters and the camera. The emotional center of the film is found in the interactions between Youssef and Hossein, both around twenty years old, who speak variously of love, everyday political realities, and the prospects for change in Algeria; ultimately, it is Youssef's subjectivity that structures the film and gives it its title. While the observational elements of the film do little to reveal his job, the way in which he interacts with his friends tells us much about him. In one scene, he discusses a woman whom he loves and with whom Hossein encourages him to elope; later, they declare that they're sick of women. Ferhani also includes a long sequence in which the two men converse largely out of sight of each other, and never in the same frame for the viewer. Hossein sits in a plastic chair on his own, looking over to his left as Youssef washes himself from a plastic bucket, his body mostly hidden by a wall from which he only occasionally emerges. He suggests he would kill himself but for his mother, who would be the only one touched by his death: he fears her response to a suicide, but not God's (for whom it would be a sin). "Too many sons of bitches don't give a shit about me. Fuck this shit, that's no life! I would prefer to get punished up there by God than get bored here with them." The scene thus establishes in dialogue the extent of his despair.

His most significant speech, however, is what follows immediately after. Youssef says to his friend, "In my head is a roundabout with ninety-nine paths and I don't know which one to take!" Hossein replies, "There are no roundabouts with ninety-nine paths!" But Youssef continues, "My head is like that. I'm talking about the one in my head, not on the road." He goes on to elaborate all the normative dreams that he has (marriage, a car, family, travel), but we gain the impression that these exist only in the context of suicide or migration, the two choices he describes with a passion shortly afterward. We are left, then, with the image of a young mind absolutely overloaded with negative possibility. As we will continue to learn,

19.1. "In my head is a roundabout with 99 paths and I don't know which one to take!" *A Roundabout in my Head* (2015), directed by Hassen Ferhani.

this sense of impossibility is one that the film connects subtly, yet firmly, to the political space that these men inhabit.

Samir constructs a different economy of scale within its construction of space but, ultimately, develops a similar tone of despair, leavened, like Youssef's seemingly impossible dreams of marriage and travel, with flashes of possibility that seem far-fetched or fictional. In contrast to *A Roundabout* with its restricted point of view and framing, *Samir* alternates between numerous wide, extreme long shots of the landscape around the border region of Morocco and Algeria, near the Mediterranean coast, and an intensely claustrophobic interiority. The border is essential to the film's narrative—it is where Samir crosses to take contraband gasoline from Algeria into Morocco—yet we apprehend it in only the vaguest terms; Ouzine, the filmmaker, denies us any visual drama or even knowledge of what it looks like. While Samir gestures toward the border in one shot, saying it's "*hnak*" (over there), the camera still refuses to isolate it exactly and we are left with the vaguest sense of where it actually runs (somewhere in the valley between the foreground and background of the shot). Indeed, in a shot where Samir approaches the camera or, later, when he sets out on one of his missions, the camera often seems to have trouble racking focus between the various planes of the image in which the border appears. Ouzine also builds a series of long takes framed in extreme long shot that are very often static and that depict the areas around where Samir lives, on his family's land, with his mother. These also map out an ambiguous terrain: despite the family connections, there is no romanticism about this land for Samir, who finds it bleak and desolate. At one point early in the film he even taunts the filmmaker, his uncle, by saying, "I see you filming the cactuses, the river, the mountain and all that. I can't figure out what you see in this mess, in this country, in this filth . . . I don't know."

The film is, in these moments, as much a documentary about the return of someone exiled in France who knows nothing of the country that he is shooting in, as it is about its subject in Algeria. As Samir maps the landscape and surrounds for the unseen filmmaker (in the same sequence where he points to the border), he also gestures across the Mediterranean and, as he does so, says "there's your country . . . France." The sense of a conjoined Mediterranean landscape where Morocco and Algeria touch, with their common footholds in the Rif Mountains, is palpable, as is the proximity to France and Europe, but the spatial disconnect between France and Algeria is just as tangible as it is in *A Roundabout*. France here represents everything that Algeria is not, everything that Samir doesn't have. Thus, in the dichotomy established between the filmmaker and his subject, we better understand the film's construction of space. The wide landscape shots and long takes of barrenness seem a reflection of Ouzine's attempt to come to terms with the scale and nature of the landscape. This external space is not suggestive of Samir's subjectivity in the way that the enclosed spaces of *A Roundabout* hem in that film's characters and express their anxieties; it is, instead, the intense darkness of the many interior interview sequences that suggest Samir's suffering. The construction of external space corresponds very much to the perspective of someone trying to analyze its nature, just as with the character of Kamel, played by the director Rabah Ameur-Zaïmeche, in *Back Home* (*Bled Number One*, 2006), a film to which I turn in more detail below.

19.2. *"Bladak...shuf!"* (There's your country, look!). France offscreen, in *Samir in the Dust* (2016), directed by Mohammed Ouzine.

Yet unlike *A Roundabout*, which remains in the claustrophobic scale of interiority but for a couple of establishing shots, *Samir* alternates between the more objective, external scale I have just described and a contrasting subjective scale of extreme intimacy. It opens with a radically decontextualized sequence that is both claustrophobic and sinister. His body and face lit in extreme low-key lighting (as Ferhani sometimes uses for his figures in *A Roundabout*, but here even more intense), Samir lies propped up in his room smoking a cigarette, the intermittent glow of which is seemingly the only source of light in the frame. In a gravelly mumble, Samir relates to the camera the violent story of two mules, probably high on fumes from the petrol that he smuggles across the border, locked in combat with each other. When the owner of one of the mules tries to separate them, the animal grabs the man's neck in its jaws and snaps it, holding on to the broken column until the man is dead. Given the circumstances of how the scene is shot, the story functions less as a social revelation of the difficulty of life there and more as the indication of a subjective state of fragility inflected with the inevitability of violence and horror (such as was manifest in the *décennie noire* or "dark decade" of the 1990s). Thus, even as it evokes the externality of landscape and space in suggesting the point of view of the filmmaker, *Samir* is also adept at constructing visually the state of mind of a character who seems to be almost without hope.

But not entirely: in one of the film's enigmatic contrasts, Ouzine introduces a lengthy sequence at a beach. Samir, clothed in a wetsuit, launches an inflatable dinghy in which he powers out into the Mediterranean. As if the sudden sight of him with a boat were not uncanny enough, the soundtrack is manipulated at this point so that all we hear is the gentle lapping of water, even as we see onscreen the surging wake of an outboard motor whose sound is completely withheld. There is a cut, and Samir emerges from the water with a diver's mask on his head, holding a fish that he slaps onto the side of the boat. As the chuckling of the water on the boat's hull continues, we see Samir sit on the gunwale and pray, and the scene cuts to the next. The short scene on the water suggests something we have not yet been aware of: that Samir has the wherewithal for a small boat and motor and gear for fishing. Despite the apparent bleakness of his life as we've experienced it so far, he still has access to commodities. In the next scene, he arrives at the beach in a Volkswagen and, with the car parked at the high-water mark, he flips through radio stations before landing on a station playing an Edith Piaf song ("La Foule").

Here emerges one of the film's most performative moments thus far. Samir starts to hum to the song (a humming we hear as external diegetic sound, confirmed in the frame by the movement of his lips). The song continues, however, across a cut as we see Samir standing in the shallows, talking to the camera and pointing out to sea, moving his mouth in speech but with the words absent from the soundtrack; instead, we hear Piaf's voice with Samir humming over it. Samir continues to smoke and talk to the camera, and then over another two shots we see him first rolling back with laughter and leaning into the camera to joke with the unseen cinematographer and then, in medium close-up, draping a piece of seaweed over his lip to make a dangling handlebar mustache, hamming it up for the camera with music that he cannot hear. The scene has a lightness to it while also existing as a formal jolt to the simplicity of the on-camera discourse that has dominated thus far. The sheer silliness and performativity of the sequence offer a new and different side to the character that we have not yet witnessed and prefigures the next scene, in which the truth quality of the documentary is further called into question and its expression of internal subjectivity is heightened even more.

19.3. Samir performs "La Foule." *Samir in the Dust* (2016), directed by Mohammed Ouzine.

Shortly thereafter, in voice-over, Samir talks about a girlfriend whom we see in a small keyhole lit within the frame, as if peeping through a door. She is wearing a headscarf and passes back and forth between the iris created by the cinematography. It is the first time we have heard anything about a lover, and the story is fanciful, suggesting that her father is a customs agent who disapproves of the relationship because of Samir's trade. Then we cut to a bokeh-filled, kaleidoscopic view of foliage, then to another, similar, shot with Samir's head in it, and finally to an uncanny tracking shot with an oddly fragmentary frame rate, following Samir and his girlfriend as they ride a motor scooter around deserted country roads. The film's deployment of sound is paramount here, as an abstract soundtrack—with a wind sound and a minor-keyed chord made up of chiming, ethereal tones like those produced by a glass harp—complements the kaleidoscopic frame and shallow depth of field. The film thus takes the viewer from the objective, wider perspective of an observational documentary to an intimacy that is suggestive of subjectivity, dreams and the unconscious, and fiction.

The possibility of fiction in *Samir* is furthered by the film's earlier gesture of performance, one that is Rouchian in its associations. In films like *Jaguar* (1957–67), *Me, a Black Man* (*Moi, un Noir*, 1958), and *Little by Little* (*Petit à petit*, 1968–69), Jean Rouch experimented with fictional strategies that saw his subjects playing roles that they would make up before the camera or, indeed, playing versions of themselves. Steven Feld identifies several elements typical of Rouch's unusual mode of ethnographic cinema, in particular "his extensive use of fiction formats for revealing ethnography, his use of surrealist and dream techniques, and, perhaps most significantly, his blurring of the very cinematic distinction between documentary and fiction film in favor of a more ethnographic and imaginative integration" (Feld 2003, 17). There is a strong debt to such a tradition in both *Samir* and *A Roundabout*. The performative element of the seaweed-mustachioed dance to Edith Piaf makes us think of the characters adopted in *Me, a Black Man*, with names like Edward G. Robinson, Tarzan, and Dorothy Lamour. Indeed, the development of a sparkling, surreal scene on the beach, followed by another in which Samir's (imaginary) lover is introduced, is reminiscent of scenes like the astonishing sequence in *Jaguar* where Rouch's three collaborators, Damouré, Lam, and Illo, dance about in the waves as the camera moves around them. It is a scene of play of the kind that Rouch loved and that Ouzine freely repeats.

A similar dynamic can be observed in *A Roundabout*. Here, even more than in *Samir*, we have the sense that there is an interactive individual behind the camera whose presence, questions, and responses are central to what unfolds before the camera. Moreover, several sequences reveal the limits and possibilities of the film's representation. As mentioned already, there are many scenes in which Ferhani's characters speak directly to the camera, responding to unknown questions or even engaging the camera/filmmaker without prompting. Such interaction is especially notable in the sequences with Amu—who is middle-aged, resembles Saddam Hussein (as he is continually reminded by his workmates), and keeps a bird that he says stowed away on a boat from England to Algeria. From the outset, he interacts with the unseen filmmaker: his first utterance is directed to the camera, when he asks, "Is everything ready?" Over the course of several interviews, he develops what becomes a motif in the film: the phrase

"I don't lie, but I don't come upon the truth, either." The self-reflexive possibilities of the phrase are present throughout, but they are developed to their fullest across two key scenes. One takes place shortly before Eid al-Adha, when we see a TV news crew bustling its way through the abattoir and interviewing people it encounters. We might even wonder if this were the *Roundabout* crew itself, except that everything about the energy and affect of the team seems wrong; their bravado is nothing like the quiet interaction that the film itself develops with its subjects. The difference is registered in Amu's speech when he asks the camera, "Did you film the sheep? The guts and entrails?" The filmmaker's voice replies, "We filmed the journalists." Amu says he didn't see them himself but continues: "Maybe they'll come and we'll tell them they only come on *eid* and never any other time. We'll tell them they don't lie but they don't come upon the truth either." A little later, he talks to the filmmakers about how much work they have left and whether they're likely to make another film in the future. Amu then suggests that his catchphrase about lies and truth might even become the title of their film. "Everyone can take it how they wish." Prompted that it might be too long for a title, he replies "It has to be long! Then think for yourself, with your head. One must invent. If you've understood the meaning . . . it's simple. It's all lies, the truth doesn't exist. People talk, you think they've understood. But in fact it's not so!"

These scenes make clear the film's interactive engagement with its characters and, as Marie Pierre-Bouthier has pointed out, such a strategy was manifest throughout the history of the film's production: Ferhani has described that he went into filming with few preconceived ideas, save for the idea of taking his camera with him at all times so that he and the men he interviewed would become comfortable around each other. Scouting his locations at the same time as he shot footage, Ferhani developed intimacy and ease between the abattoir workers, his sound engineer, and himself as cinematographer (Pierre-Bouthier 2016, 2; Letoré 2016). That rapport, according to Pierre-Bouthier, meant that his documentary subjects accepted their transformation into characters who could participate in the work in a new way, not only to "inform the film with their imaginary, but also to its process and its specificity—a first step in the reappropriation, if not of their destiny, then at least of their image" (Pierre-Bouthier 2016, 5; author's translation).

If Ferhani was working, consciously or not, in a profoundly Rouchian manner, then he is not alone among Maghrebi or Maghrebi-diaspora filmmakers. Rabah Ameur-Zaïmeche's *Back Home* starts from opposite pole from Ferhani and Ouzine's films: while *Back Home* appears as a fiction film, Ameur-Zaïmeche allows elements of documentary to also inflect it. The film begins with Kamel (played by Ameur-Zaïmeche) returning to his family's village in Algeria, having been deported from France. Ameur-Zaï-meche here plays the same character as in his first film, *Wesh Wesh (Wesh Wesh: qu'est ce qui se passe?*, 2001) and, while the sequence of events is left open, it appears that the story takes place either after, or possibly before, the events of the earlier film. The village and family that Kamel returns to are the filmmaker's own, and the film thus includes many actors who are non-professional and are, in effect, family members playing themselves. As Gilles Mouëllic notes, the film has in common with *Wesh Wesh* and the later *Aden (Dernier maquis*, 2008) a mode of production where Ameur-Zaï-meche and his small crew begin with a written scenario but then consult it as little as possible during the actual shooting, letting the crew immerse itself in the setting and allowing for familiarity and improvisation (Mouël-lic 2011, 60); one is reminded of Ferhani's approach to *A Roundabout*. *Back Home* has many remarkable sequences that are testament to this manner of working. Perhaps the most memorable is the sequence of the *zerda*, a custom where the men of the village slaughter a bull and butcher it for the entire community, setting out small parcels of meat on the ground for each family. Gilles Mouëllic also notes the importance of this scene as an indicator of the way in which Ameur-Zaïmeche crosses the borders of fiction and documentary in the most profound ways, allowing for new perspectives to emerge that either mode on its own could not as effectively capture. Mouëllic argues that, for this moment in the film:

> There was no a priori mise-en-scène: Ameur-Zaïmeche replaced the marriage planned in the initial screenplay with this ritual, orga-nized to honor the crew, which becomes one of the most important moments of the film. But filming all the while with great attention to the successive steps in the ceremony, from the putting to death of the beast to the sharing of the meat, he doesn't hesitate to have the characters of the fiction intervene in the heart of the ritual. (Mouëllic 2011, 61–62; author's translation)

This intervention occurs after Kamel is told that he must not mingle with the women of the village who are approaching the ceremony. Ignoring the command (and thus continuing the plot line where "Kamel la France," as they call him, is out of step with the practices back in the *bled*), he goes down the hill to visit them as they approach in a procession. "This crossing of the territorial limit between the men and the women," argues Mouëllic, "is also a way of blurring the frontier between fiction and documentary, and contesting at the same time the inalterable character of the ritual" (Mouëllic 2011, 62). The Rouchian character of the filmmaker's approach is thus much more than style: rather, it is an ethics of engagement that allows the filmmaker to immerse himself in an environment in order to better reveal its character and question its customs and suppositions.

Tariq Teguia's films have also utilized this kind of improvisational manner. Of particular interest here is Teguia's film *The Fence* (*Hasla/La clôture*, 2004), for its portrait of young men in Algiers who, like those in *A Roundabout*, seem to be in a state of subjective and social crisis. The film gives the impression of being an interactive documentary. Young men from around the area of Bab El Oued speak directly to the camera about their lives, the bleakness of opportunity that they experience, and their frustration and anger with the state of their country. This kind of direct address is juxtaposed to sequences shot in the local streets, and Teguia thus builds up a portrait of a generation of dispossessed young men in a space that seems to offer them no hope. But the film is not a documentary; rather, it works across the space between documentary and fiction. Teguia shot the "interview" sequences as performances but without a real script and with as few retakes as possible. According to him, "It was not really written. We proposed ideas: 'There'll be that, that, and that. You say that, your name. You state your intentions, your suffering, your job, where you are in life.' There weren't really any textual details. We did a take and if it didn't work, we did another." At the same time, he said, it was not really performed, either: "It's not that . . . I don't know what it is. Each time I asked for a performance, I wanted them to give the impression of doing it the least amount possible" (Gravayat and Haddadi 2010, 58). Indeed, the film leaves few, if any, traces of the gap between the performance of subjective realities for the camera and the direct expression of them, a situation which prompts us to appreciate that even an interactive, interview-based documentary is just as much in debt to strategies of performance and self-presentation as a film like Teguia's.

The question of direct address to the camera, however, can send us to an even earlier precedent in which the questions of fiction, performance, and reality are raised. The subjects of *A Roundabout*, *Samir*, and *The Fence* recall a much earlier Algerian film that also presented a direct-to-camera discourse reminiscent of the documentary interview. As Omar Gatlato narrates his life and experiences for the camera, Merzak Allouache's 1976 film of the same name traces the lost hopes of a young Algerian man whose failed attempts at connection with women expose the deeply gendered segregation of Algerian society. The film begins with a sequence in which Omar addresses the camera directly while sitting on his bed and moves to other sequences where he narrates or reflects upon what we see in voice-over. In the first few minutes, this voice-over combines with a dispassionate, omniscient view of the housing projects in Bab El Oued where Gatlato lives, and in these sequences Allouache consciously evokes documentary strategies. Yet he also takes pains to signal that this is a fiction film, not only through a disclaimer in the credits but by directing other scenes that clearly rely upon fictional, non-realist elements (Armes 1998, 10–11). Omar's testimony before the camera reveals that, like the protagonists of *A Roundabout*, *Samir*, and *The Fence* many years later, he is unable to directly feel any positive impact of the liberation from colonial rule. In a decade when the glory of the Algerian revolution had faded into the realities of disenfranchisement and lack of education, *Omar Gatlato* (*'Umar qatalthu al-rujula*) articulated the rising social tensions of the moment, as James McDougall has noted (McDougall 2017, 263–64), and the later films continue to articulate this hopelessness in term that are exclusively masculine. Omar's failed attempts to meet Selma, with whose voice he falls in love after he discovers a cassette tape that she recorded, are registered in the contrast between the extreme long shot of him abandoning the meeting and walking away from her into a chaotic crowded street scene, and the 360-degree handheld medium close-up shot that circles around him and Selma. That remarkable shot, with its different color tint and dramatic drumming on the soundtrack, constitutes an alternate fantasy realm in which he is able to converse with her, just as *Samir*, almost forty years later, constructs an equally implausible fantasy sequence for its male protagonist.

All of this is reminiscent of what Nouri Bouzid diagnosed in 1988 as a "defeat-conscious cinema." Taking stock of the films that had appeared from the late 1960s across the Arab countries, Bouzid suggested that some were characterized by a new kind of response to the current realities of the post-independence states. Such a response, he argued, was typified by three key motifs, all of which pertained to gendered relations. With respect to masculinity, Bouzid argued, first, that "the male is not strong as he is traditionally portrayed. On the contrary, he is lost and confused and is plagued with a set of dilemmas that shake him to the core." In addition, he proposed that, in these films, "the projected image of a constantly victorious and honourable Arab hero has been abandoned. Admitting defeat, the new realism proceeds to expose it and make the awareness of its causes and roots a point of departure" (Bouzid 1995, 249). Bouzid, of course, was speaking of the aftermath of 1967 where the traumas of that year—the loss of Palestine and the resignation of Gamal Abd al-Nasser—became a watershed moment for Arab thought and cultural expression. In the present context, that defeat-consciousness is further contextualized by the loss of faith in the memory of the Algerian revolutionary war and in the subsequent traumas of the 1980s and 1990s, including the events of "Black October" 1988 (when five hundred protestors were killed by state forces) and in the "dark decade" of the 1990s where civil war led to further despair and suffering. The aftermath of these losses are felt in Ferhani's, Ouzine's, and Teguia's films by the characters' expression of a potent combination of *hogra*—the Algerian *darija* term for the contempt and marginalization exacted on the population by *le pouvoir* or ruling power— and entrapment. Here is Vader, thirty-two years old, in *The Fence*:

> You need to find a solution. Go? Stay? Stay or go? The solution—you don't find it. People are suffocating. They daze themselves in drugs, drink, delinquency. If you don't want us, tell us! If you don't want Algerians to live, then don't show us that there's something better. Show us that the world is ruined, don't show us that there's a better life than we're living. Remove the satellite dishes, remove whatever is outside. Remove this word "liberty" from our heads![2]

Vader's impassioned plea is uncannily close to the testimony of the much younger Youssef, who declares:

> Three things exist in Algeria; any twenty-year-old will tell you the same thing. Three things happen to any young Algerian: either commit suicide, fill your head with weird stuff (drugs) and become the living dead, or go do the *harga*.[3] Any young person will tell you same thing. Being a man from a respected family and working hard, that doesn't exist. Insha'Allah, I won't be a thief or druggie, but a *harga*, that I'll do. I'll leave or kill myself. This plays like a loop in my head. Cross the sea or kill myself.

Complicating the defeat-consciousness that Bouzid described, these films also demonstrate a particular sentiment of entrapment germane to the Algerian situation. Austin, for example, finds a similar dichotomy of entrapment in Merzak Allouache's 2009 film *Harragas* (a *harraga* is one who performs the *harga*), where a character despairs that "if I leave, I'll die; if I stay, I'll die; so I will leave, and die" (Austin 2012, 139).[4] If some of the films that Bouzid cites depicted doomed protagonists, they at least despaired and died in the context of public political life that the films could articulate, what Bouzid called a "passage from the private and the particular (the characters) into the public and the general (political events)" (Bouzid 1995, 248). This is not always the case in the more recent films. Hossein and Youssef have a heated discussion about the possibility of a unified Arab/Kabyle uprising, after which Algeria "would never be the same." But Youssef shoots this down immediately, saying that those in power send in the army and then "go to France and come back when things are better. We stay and eat each other alive. . . . Even if everyone rises up together, people like us will lose, Algeria will be lost just like Egypt and the others." Notably, Youssef's statement does not preclude the possibility of revolutionary protest or uprisings in Algeria. Rather, it forecloses on what he fears as the inevitable outcome of any such movements: the survival of *le pouvoir* and the ultimate triumph of the state. That is the outcome he identifies as that of "Egypt and the others" in the wake of the so-called Arab Spring and it is an outcome that he cannot see beyond. The domain of revolutionary politics no longer holds any hope of success for these characters, just as Islam—the political solution for some of the population in an earlier time—is never mentioned, either. What is left is just evidence of the futility of a life that seemingly cannot be transformed.[5]

A Roundabout in My Head and *Samir in the Dust* express the defeat-consciousness of a new Algerian generation. It is a consciousness that is articulated in both films through the relationship of space to the subjectivities constructed for the characters and even for the filmmakers. In *A Roundabout*, the internal anguish of the characters emerges in close relationship to the claustrophobic and mortal intimacies of the space. While the filmmaker is engaged with and immersed in that space, the subjectivities revealed are those of the workers. In *Samir*, there is a tension between the subjectivity of the character or documentary subject—Samir himself—and the filmmaker. While the film's unseen filmmaker seems to reckon with the external nature of the space, Samir reveals, in the intimacy of the dark, chiaroscuro-lit room, the violence and seeming despair of his situation. As he says to the camera, the conditions that led Ouzine's father to emigrate to France are the same ones that play through his own head. *Back Home*, despite its revelations of the harshness of domestic and political violence in the village, still allows some hope for transformation in the space of the psychiatric institution where Louisa (Meriem Serbah) ends the film (Higbee 2013, 142). But in the masculine world of *A Roundabout*, *Samir*, and, before them, *The Fence*, there is little chance of redemption; in its place, there is a recognition of the intransigence of contemporary life and its seemingly repetitive cycle of labor, dispossession, violence, and defeat.

References

Armes, Roy. 1998. *Omar Gatlato*. Wiltshire, U.K.: Flicks Books.

Austin, Guy. 2012. *Algerian National Cinema*. Manchester: Manchester University Press.

Bouzid, Nouri. 1995. "New Realism in Arab Cinema: the Defeat-Conscious Cinema." *Alif: Journal of Comparative Poetics* 15: 242–50.

Brahimi, Denise. 2017. "Réflexion sur des jeunes documentaristes algériens." *Huffpost Algeria*, May 6. huffpostmaghreb.com.

Feld, Steven. 2003. "Editor's Introduction." In *Ciné-ethnography*, by Jean Rouch, edited and translated by Steven Feld, 1-25. Minneapolis: University of Minnesota Press.

Gravayat, Jérémy, and Noria Haddadi. 2010. "Dans le blanc des cartes: conversation avec Tariq Teguia." *Dérives* 2: 47–69.

Higbee, Will. 2013. *Post-beur Cinema: North African Emigré and Maghrebi-French Filmmaking in France since 2000*. Edinburgh: Edinburgh University Press.

Letoré, Nathan. 2016. "*Dans ma tête un rond-point*: filmer les ouvriers des abattoirs d'Alger." *Orient* 21 (February 5). https://orientxxi.info/lu-vu-entendu/dans-ma-tete-un-rond-point-filmer-les-ouvriers-des-abattoirs-d-alger,1181.

Machta, Insaf. n.d. "De la porosité des régimes de l'image dans *Samir dans la poussière* de Mohamed Ouzine." *Dissonances*. https://nachaz.org/de-la-porosite-des-regimes-de-limage-dans-samir-dans-la-poussiere-de-mohamed-ouzine/.

McDougall, James. 2017. *A History of Algeria*. Cambridge: Cambridge University Press.

Mouëllic, Gilles. 2011. *Improviser le cinéma*. Crisnée, Belgium: Yellow Now.

Pierre-Bouthier, Marie. 2016. "Dans les abattoirs, un rond-point." *Trafic* 98: 1–5.

Rouch, Jean. 2003. *Ciné-ethnography*. Edited and translated by Steven Feld. Minneapolis: University of Minnesota Press.

20

THE DARING LYRICS OF WOMEN MUSIC DOCUMENTARY FILMMAKERS IN THE MAGHREB

Florence Martin

There is no shortage of literature on the movies from the Maghreb that tell stories about a return to the past. However, the studies on documentaries made by women directors from the same region are few and far between—especially studies of the films focusing on musical traditions. And yet, Algeria, Morocco, and Tunisia have produced a considerable number of films in this domain. This chapter highlights the main features of this particular genre of documentaries. It focuses on three documentaries on music by three women directors: Izza Génini's series *Maroc: Corps et âme* on Moroccan music; Sonia Chamkhi's medium-length movie *The Art of the Mezwed* (*Fann al-mizwad/L'Art du mezoued*, 2010), and Safinez Bousbia's feature film *El Gusto* (2012), on the Algerian popular music known as *chaâbi*. Once contextualized against the production of musical documentaries in the region, these three works are analyzed as exemplars of women's musical documentaries. The author also shows that, beyond its focus on local history and cultures, this documentary genre may fall under the category of world film production for two reasons: firstly, its mode of funding exceeds the traditional postcolonial circuits, and secondly, the themes of its movies—preservation and renewal of a particular musical tradition—redefine the notions of world music and diasporic music.

When writing about women's filmmaking in the Maghreb, critics concentrate on fiction films that flash back to a more or less distant past,[1] but seem to shun the documentaries about music made by women directors from the region. And yet, these documentaries strive to both preserve a musical heritage threatening to fall into oblivion and trace the multiple meanders of its complex, multicultural history. This apparent initial focus often changes, however, from historico-folkloric to historico-political: women directors then sketch the outline of a new historical account that undermines former certainties about the cultural heritage of the region or of each nation in the Maghreb; corrodes the foundation of the official, masculine nationalist *grand récit* that followed independence; and ends up shaking up the mono-lithic, often ethnocentric discourse of state authorities.

In this chapter, I examine three documentaries about music, made by three women directors—one from Morocco, one from Tunisia, and one from Algeria. Izza Génini, a pioneer of Moroccan documentary films, directed a series of eleven twenty-six-minute films titled *Morocco, Body and Soul* (*Maroc, corps et âme*, 1987–93), which she then edited into one docu-mentary, *Voices of Morocco* (*Voix du Maroc*, 2003). In *The Art of the Mezwed* (*Fann al-mizwad/L'Art du mezoued*, 2010), Sonia Chamkhi explores this popular music of Andalusian origin still in existence, albeit clandestinely so, in Zine El Abidine Ben Ali's Tunisia. Between 2003 and 2012, Safinez Bousbia researched and shot *El Gusto*, a documentary about the *chaâbi* music of Algiers. During the many years of her filmmaking, the direc-tor brought back together the *chaâbi* musicians who had left Algiers after 1962 (for the suburbs of the city, the Algerian countryside, or France) and helped organize an international tour by the reunited orchestra of *chaâbi*.

In the three films, the directors start with local musical production, explain its components, and then trace the history of the local music back to a larger, repressed history of music and rhythm with which the power and ideology in place in Algeria, Morocco, or Tunisia are not ready to engage. Thus, starting from a humanist-feminist position which consists of extending feminist solidarity and inquisitiveness to all oppressed groups, each filmmaker explores the history of traditional music and reaches the same conclusion: the traditional music of the Maghreb is not only Arabic, of Muslim inspiration, or Amazigh, but also shares its roots with the music of the Jewish community, settled for centuries in the Maghreb.

Production Circumstances

These three films from diverse directors (from different countries, gener-ations, and training) illustrate the diversity of Maghrebi cinema (whether fiction or documentary).

Born in Casablanca, Izza Génini, who directed *Voices of Morocco* (2003), left her native Morocco in 1960 with her parents to live in Paris, as did numerous Jewish families after Moroccan independence (1956). She stud-ied at the Sorbonne and at the Institute of Oriental Languages, and became involved in cinema early on. First, she worked for festivals in Tours and Annecy, and in 1973, together with Louis Malle and Claude Nedjar, she founded the SOGEAV company in order to buy a screening room, promote Moroccan film, and support the export of a selection of films to West Africa (such as Euzhan Palcy's *Black Shack Alley*, 1983). SOGEAV also became a production company and produced, for instance, fellow Moroccan Ahmed

El Maanouni's musical documentary *Trances* (*al-Hal/Transes*, 1981). *Trances* has enjoyed a long critical career: it was selected in Cannes when it came out, got the audience award at the first Moroccan National Film Festival in Rabat in 1982, was eventually selected by Martin Scorsese as the first film the American director presented at Cannes International Film Festival in 2007 to launch his Cannes Classics—World Cinema Foundation in 2007, and has since then become a Criterion classic.

Génini's experience with El Maanouni marked a sharp turn in her career: returning to Morocco for the first time since her family's exodus to produce *Trances*, listening to and recording music from her native land, and watching Nass El Ghiwane (the group El Maanouni was filming) up close showed her what she really wanted to do. As a result, in 1987, Izza Génini started producing her own films and directed a series of shorts on Moroccan traditional music. Her training in literature and linguistics as well as in production led her to a reasoned cinematographic approach to documentary filmmaking: her films are beautiful to see and allow the viewer to sense her commitment to issues that extend beyond the scope of the screen proper. Hailed as a *grande dame* of Moroccan cinema,[2] she has continued her humble, patient labor of documenting and showing the intricate, multicultural musical traditions of Morocco. Her last eighty-minute documentary at the time of writing, *Nuba of Gold and Light* (*Nûba d'or et de lumière*, 2008), explores the traces of the Nuba music of the Andalusian tradition.

Tunisian Sonia Chamkhi received a much more formal training in film. Awarded a PhD in film and audiovisual arts at the Sorbonne, she published a remarkable study of Tunisian cinema, *New Tunisian Cinema: A Different Take* (*Cinéma tunisien nouveau: parcours autre*, 2002), followed by *Tunisian Cinema in the Light of Modernity* (*Le Cinéma tunisien à la lumière de la modernité*, 2009). She teaches audiovisual techniques at the Institut Supérieur des Beaux Arts in Tunis. She first directed two short films: a work of fiction, *Normal* (*Nesma wa Rih/Normal*, 2002), and a documentary, *Douz, the Gate to the Sahara* (*Douz, la porte du Sahara*, 2003). Her short fictions that followed, *Borderline* (*Wara' al-balayik/Borderline*, 2008), and *The Making of* Life Is a Dream *by Hacen Mouathan* (*Making of* La vie est un songe *de Hacen Mouathan*, 2009), won critical acclaim. *The Art of the Mezwed* confirms her status as a solid filmmaker: in it, she is able to bring her expert skills and nuanced approach to bear on both the subject to be filmed (a popular musical tradition that has gone more or less underground) and the filming of it. The making of the film occurred during the last years of Ben Ali's dictatorship, when the veneer of a peaceful Tunisian society was beginning to show serious cracks. The film came out in 2010, and it would only take one more year for the Arab Spring to erupt in Tunisia and Ben Ali to be booted out of the country on January 14, 2011. When she investigated the art of the *mezwed* (the folksy bagpipe musical tradition), she collected both expert and controversial views on the topic by instrumentalists, singers, and composers. Her political views are known: after the revolution, she made a documentary about women activists who had stood up to Bourguiba's and then Ben Ali's regime, *Activist Women* (*Munadilat/Militantes*, 2012), before she launched into her first fiction film, *Narcissus* ('*Aziz rawhu/Narcisse*, 2015), on the micropolitics of oppression.

The third and youngest director in this study, Safinez Bousbia, has forged her own unique path to filmmaking. Born in Algeria, she spent most of her life in Ireland, where she obtained a master's degree in architecture. She began making her film almost by chance: while walking in the Kasbah of Algiers, she stopped at a small shop to buy a mirror, and started to chat with the vendor, who recounted his experience as a *chaâbi* musician before 1962. Intrigued by his story, she decided to gather the musicians who had been dispersed in the wake of the Algerian War of Independence and film them. Completing her work took seven long years, during which she came up against all sorts of obstacles: some of them financial, others thrown her way by people and governments. This young woman, equipped with remarkable resilience and an acute sense of space and of how to organize it, had to learn how to make a film while directing her first film, which ended up being nominated at several festivals and receiving two awards at the Abu Dhabi Film Festival: the FIPRESCI prize and Best Director from the Arab World in 2011.

Just as each director followed her own discrete career path, the mode of production and the financing of each film were quite different. Izza Génini, the most senior of these filmmakers, produced her own series of documentaries on the musical traditions in Morocco in the 1980s through the SOGEAV production company, of which she was a co-founding executive. This company is now known as OHRA (the company having changed names in 1987). However, because some of these short films had been aired on French and then Moroccan television channels (2M), she also received funding from both TV companies, which meant that she could reissue her documentaries as commercial DVDs and also finance her latest film on Nuba music, *Nuba of Gold and Light*, coproduced by OHRA, 2M, Sigma Productions, and SACEM (Society for Authors, Composers, and Publishers of Music in France). The same companies provided funding for the production of the documentary under discussion: *Voices of Morocco* (2003). Thus, even though Izza Génini films her documentaries in Morocco, her main sources of funding (apart from 2M) are still French. This funding setup seems surprising, given that the Moroccan Cinema Center (CCM) has a policy of supporting locally made films—contingent on a submitted proposal (complete with a script and a detailed financial dossier), which is reviewed by a commission.

The Tunisian Sonia Chamkhi lives in a country where film production is usually funded by state subsidies allocated by the government via a commission headed by the audiovisual department of the Ministry of Culture. Under that system, funding comes from a grant awarded on presentation of the proposed film's script. This can be supplemented with funding for postproduction, for use at a later stage.[3] She received such funds from the Ministry of Culture for her prior short films (from 2000 to 2009) and, like almost all filmmakers in the Maghreb, created her own production company, Moustaches, in order to produce her films. And yet she did not receive any funding from the state for her film on *mezwed* music. "I made the film with my own savings. I filmed it during the former dictatorship and didn't even have a permit to film."[4] Furthermore, although it had promised Chamkhi some financial backing further down the line, the state-run broadcasting company never delivered. The success of the project seems to have relied mostly on an immense amount of good will, lightweight digital filming equipment, and a flexible production team.

In contrast to the narrative of tenuous funding of these two films, Safinez Bousbia's film—the only feature-length film in this corpus (2 hours and 35 minutes)—has a unique profile. Bousbia is half Algerian, half Irish, and was living in Ireland at the start of her project. It was from her Irish base that she assembled a financial structure for the backing of her film, through her own production company, Quidam. However, her search for the musicians who had been students of *chaâbi* music at the Conservatoire in Algiers until 1962 took the director to the four corners of Algeria, as well as to Marseille and Paris in France, thus increasing the cost of production significantly. In order to shoot and edit her film, she used up all her savings (she even sold her own house!), and applied to both the Irish Film Board (the Irish national funding body) and the Algerian National Broadcasting Corporation (she also obtained archival footage from this body) for subsidies. After a while, though, she still ran out of money.

> I met the mirror guy in autumn 2003, I started pre-shooting in 2005, because it took me two years to find them, and then in 2006 I found the budget to begin. The concerts were in 2006, that's when I started shooting. But there was a bombing in Algiers, we would not have been able to bring the Jewish musicians back so after spending all our money, I mean I was literally ruined by then, it was either we finish the film saying that only the Muslim musicians reunite or what do we do? That's when I decided to go for a new film and find funding again, a year later, and that's when the concerts started in 2007, the ones you see in the film in Marseille and Bercy. In 2008, as I was editing, I got cancer, so I had to stop. I stopped for two years, and when I

got back I didn't have any money, so I applied for the Abu Dhabi Film Festival and that's how I got the funding for post-production. They helped in a major way to finish the film. (Rothe 2012)

Her financial setup, rather than a typical transnational, postcolonial film funding scheme, is, in part, akin to a "translocal" one, the structure of which depends entirely on the director's dual nationality and links to both countries, which provided funding at a micro level. Here, we are not talking about an arrangement that would include drawing from a postcolonial transnational fund (e.g., Fonds Sud Cinéma or Hubert Bals), but about a funding structure that brings two distinct communities together through the comings and goings of a new *cinéaste de passage* (as Merzak Allouache is fond of describing himself; Higbee 2015) in a "translocal" funding scheme. The term "translocality" is used as soon as two or more production areas work together at a local level (Dublin and Algiers, for instance) rather than on a national level.

> *Translocality* prefers place-based imagination and reveals dynamic processes of the local/global (or glocal)—processes that involve not just the dynamic traffic of capital and people, but that of ideas, images, styles, and technologies across places in polylocality. Moreover, translocal traffic is rarely a one-way street. On the contrary, polylocality allows for the reconfiguration of different spaces and patterns of collaboration, competition, contestation, and contradiction. (Zhang 2010, 136–37)

Recognizing that this mode of film production is based on an exchange of human and financial resources in a *translocal* rather than transnational context changes how the film is regarded. In the initial production phase, we are no longer dealing with the classic neocolonial system of funding but with a network of relationships. We should add that this type of translocal production has already been used by others, most notably Moroccan director Farida Benlyazid, for instance, in the making of *The Wretched Life of Juanita Narboni* (*La Vida perra de Juanita Narboni/La Chienne de vie de Juanita Narboni*, 2005), coproduced by a local entity in Spain and another in Morocco.

The postproduction funding from Abu Dhabi points to a recent development in Arab filmmaking: the availability of funds for Arab directors to finish their films that helped a number of Maghrebi filmmakers during the short-lived existence of the Abu Dhabi Film Festival (ADFF, 2007–14). To wit, between 2010 and 2014, the ADFF helped finance—via Sanad ("support" in Arabic) grants—the development and/or postproduction of no fewer than eleven films from Moroccan directors alone.[5]

Each distinct mode of funding of these three documentaries mirrors the fundamental independence of the individuals who directed them. For Génini and Chamkhi, it meant making a film on a shoestring budget—or close to it—about subversive music; for Bousbia, it meant making a film for which the sources of funding largely avoided the countries involved in the Franco-Algerian split, and stating a position on the 1962 dispersals of peoples: that of a director's intent on bringing a style of music and the members of a disbanded orchestra back to life. The filmmakers operated within an open space of freedom since they were not dependent on any governmental or political decision makers to do their work. They created a new cinematic language to recount the history of each style of traditional music, a history that had been frayed over time.

Film Structures

If we believe Michel Chion—who admittedly studies the music used in fictional films rather than documentaries—the image–music dyad in film offers genuine semantic parallels and cross-checks: under the pulsations of the rhythms that they share, they can complement each other, oppose each other, or harmonize with each other. When the film's topic is the music itself (as is the case in these documentaries), the viewer attends a mediated performance of a piece of music (or at least parts of a performance), which imprints its rhythms and harmonies on the visual filmic narrative on screen. According to Chion, the primary function and effect of a film showing a musical performance is that "[we] feel as though we are present at the miraculous creation, amidst the disorder of the world, of order and harmony" (1995, 267) This alignment, entirely created by music that guides our listening and viewing, echoes Noureddine Saïl's definition of film:

> The film—not cinema—orders life. The way in which the director, when he looks at me in the audience, directs what I see, in line with what he sees . . . , this ability he has to align my view to his, I know of no other art capable of doing this. (Saïl 2012, 22)

A documentary on music brings together these two ways of realigning the gaze and listening to the narrative suggested by the music on screen: if we follow both Chion and Saïl, then a documentary on music is a film par excellence! To create one thus requires a narrative and editing strategy that allows the director to conduct an ensemble in which the featured music is both seen and heard in the final product by the extradiegetic audience. What narratives do our filmmakers employ in their films about local music? And how are they structured and edited?

Voices of Morocco, a montage of several documentaries about traditional styles of music into a single film, begins with a filmed concert: mid-shots of the group alternate with close-up shots of each musician.[6] Once the concert clip is over, the camera cuts to a wide panoramic shot of the countryside with a voice-over (that of Izza Génini's daughter) saying, "The light, the people, the history of Morocco make it a country of images and music. The worlds of the Berbers, of Islam, of South sub-Saharan Africa, of Judaism, of Andalusia, all of them pass through it." From this opening on the various roots of Moroccan music, Génini singles out seven distinct musical traditions emanating from seven different places: the music of the rural Berber in the Atlas Mountains, the sacred music of Islam played in the holy city of Moulay Idriss, the Andalusian Judeo-Islamic songs heard in Tetouan, the *malhoune* of the Menara in Marrakesh, the *aita* played along the fantasias in Moulay Abdallah, the regional music of Marrakesh, and lastly, the rhythmic music of the Gnawas who came from south of the Sahara desert. These seven sections of the film blend into one another to form one sound continuum.

The sound recordings and shots of each musical tradition (with its musicians, its instruments, its voices and subtitled songs) are complemented by a discreet commentary explaining the characteristics of each musical style, its origins, and the specific location where it flourished. For instance, as the *malhoune* is introduced, we hear: "The *malhoune* is a collection of poems in Moroccan *darija*, composed by craftsmen and played by passionate amateur musicians at musical gatherings like this one at the Menara in Marrakesh around the singer Boucetta." The voice-over is informative but remains unobtrusive. This kind of voice over that comes out of what Deleuze (1985, 258) called the "relative off-screen" (the off-screen space into which what we see/hear on screen can extend) plays the role of an aural inter-title: it underscores what is seen or heard, or adds information to it. It shapes the order of our viewing. The visual gives way to the sound and vice versa on screen, while regular switches between shots of the group and close-up shots of each artist were added at the editing phase. Clearly, the documentary here goes from the group to the individual and back, in order to show the group's performance *and* highlight each musician's particular brand of virtuosity, with no perceptible hierarchy. This is a highly democratic documentary, classically shot, aiming to capture on camera the fleeting moment of a specific type of musical performance with an uncertain future. The rhythm of the alternating shots also recalls the structure of Andalusian Nuba music (*nuba* means "to each his turn"), during the performance of which each musician in turn plays a solo, as I have described elsewhere.[7]

In *The Art of the Mezwed* Sonia Chamkhi adopts a different approach to show another musical tradition also threatened with extinction: the *mezwed*, a musical repertoire played by an ensemble comprising a bagpiper (*mizwad* is the Arabic term for bagpipes), a singer, and various drummers (playing *bendir*s, tambourines, *darbuka*s). The lyrics of these proletarian songs are bawdy at times and describe the lives of the destitute and the disenfranchised: *mezwed* is a kind of Tunisian blues which both condemns social injustice and sings of pain. The music follows the thirteen *maqamat* (melodic modes) of the Andalusian Nuba: each *maqam* has its specific rhythm and key that the musician must know. It is a musical form that is at once very sophisticated (originating in a long musical tradition with noble roots in Andalusia) and quite folk-oriented (it is intended for celebrations and festivals, and is played, for instance, at weddings).

The film is structured along a framed narrative. It opens at a wedding reception, as the guests wait for the singer and his band to start the party and the dancing; it ends with a return to the wedding reception as *mezwed* singer Salah Farzit (seen in various interviews during the film) arrives and starts to perform with his band in front of a joyful, dancing crowd. What is framed between these two scenes is an exploration of *mezwed* music: the construction of its bagpipes, its distinctive musical style, singers, composers, bagpipers, drummers. There is no voice-over narration in this film.

The individuals file on screen one after the other, their monologues edited into a logical pattern. The narrative moves in stages: first from the making of the bagpipes by a craftsman, then to the reputation of the *mezwed* as a popular musical form not recognized by the classical traditional musical establishment, then again to the distinctive drums used according to specific rhythms, to eventually expose the existence of a double discourse on the *mezwed*. On the one hand, a famous *mezwed* player chronicles its history and highlights its noble roots in the long tradition of Andalusian Nubas (which was court music) brought to Tunisia after the expulsion of the Muslims and the Jews from Spain at the turn of the sixteenth century; on the other hand, Salah Farzit claims that "*mezwed* music has been banned on several grounds" in contemporary Tunisia (under Ben Ali) without ever clearly stating what these "grounds" were, although the film subtly suggests a couple of them. The film structure, apart from its framed narrative, calls to mind that of a woven fabric, the threads of which (in this case, the lives of the singers and musicians) are entwined, or pulled apart. The focus shifts from one individual to the next, and from one period to the next, rarely stopping to provide an overall perspective. Rather, it gives us elements and expects its extradiegetic viewers to organize the polyphonic history of the *mezwed* and fill in the gaps.

Finally, *El Gusto* follows—and completes!—the chronicle of a *chaâbi* orchestra. During a holiday visit to the medina in Algiers, Bousbia met a Mr. Ferkioui, who showed her his mementos of the time when he studied *chaâbi* music at the Algiers Conservatory and later played with his fellow musicians in the cafés of the city. All his friends scattered outside Algiers: the Jewish *pieds-noirs* moved to France in 1962; most others moved away either at the demand of the state—which renovated the crumbling Kasbah and relocated its inhabitants to more salubrious suburbs on the outskirts of the city—or because of the various twists and turns their individual lives took. Bousbia decided to find the musicians in Algeria and reunite them. She then did the same with the musicians in France, and ended up organizing a meeting of the two groups in Marseille, which culminated with a concert at the Théâtre du Gymnase. The latter was so successful (the orchestra enjoyed a tremendous reception in Marseille) that the musicians went on to play at the Bercy stadium in Paris, produced a CD, and undertook an international tour.[8]

El Gusto presents a double temporary structure: its present-day narrative is linear (we see the progressive reassembling of the orchestra, then attend its first two concerts and witness the emotions felt by the musicians upon being reunited), but it is interrupted by deep plunges into the past, as each musician tells his story in front of the camera. There is no flashback per se, but instead, running commentaries and explanations about old Algiers coming from each artist. In one instance, a musician is filmed in a taxi in Algiers pointing out the cafés, now closed and boarded up, in which he and his friends used to play music, party, and drink a lot. A third structural element also comes into play: the editing of the film that splices the voices of the members of the orchestra in Algeria and the voices of their counterparts in France, giving the impression of a trans-Mediterranean dialogue. The topics they discuss (the *chaâbi* music they used to play together, the youth of these now aged men) provide an aural and thematic continuity throughout the film, steeped in nostalgia. We follow the reassembling of the orchestra step by step, all the way to the end of the film and to the concert with all members of the orchestra from both sides of the Mediterranean together.

Interestingly enough, gender in these musical documentaries receives unequal treatment. Génini is the only one who shows men and women musicians playing traditional music (in Morocco). *Mezwed* (in Tunisia) and *chaâbi* (in Algeria) are both predominantly male musical practices. At the same time, however, these documentaries might be casting the question of gender in a new light in the postcolonial era. Cinema, in this way, seems to illustrate the theory of postcolonialism (rather than the condition of postcolonialism, haunted as it is by the ever-present ghost of neocolonialism), as it imagines a redistribution of power and projects the images of new forms of resistance to the national and/or neocolonial *grand récit* in a near or mythical future:

Film (and media generally), because they can deal in fantasy and the imaginary, project new possibilities of resistance and subversion, particularly through the prisms of micropolitics and aesthetics. The *grands récits* break down opening space for the infinite specificities that refract larger, often repressed, miswritten, and unofficial histories of the nation, communities, classes, genders, and subaltern groups. (Ponzanesi and Waller 2012, 9)

From this postcolonial perspective, the three musical documentaries can be read as accounts given by subaltern voices. Hence, the voices heard are not those of experts in ethnomusicology, but those of Mohsen Matri, *mezwed* music and lyric composer; of Abdelkarim Benzanti or Toumsi, both of them *mezwed* singers; of Mehrez, a craftsman who fashions beautiful bagpipes, or of Moustapha Gattel Essid, virtuoso bagpiper and occasional musicologist and historian. These voices mingle, call and respond, and even sometimes contradict one another in Chamkhi's film. The words of the *mezwed* people are often spoken from the very places where the music was born: from poor neighborhoods with overflowing dustbins, from inside modest homes, and from trash-strewn waste grounds.

Similarly, Izza Génini films and records the *aita* musicians and the Gnawas without an ethnomusicologist to introduce their performances in learned terms. The (diegetic) audience is seen participating in the musical performance. In the *aita* section, the film takes us inside a home where Fatma Bent El Houcine, its famous diva, is leading a call and response song with the women around the table, each of them clapping or beating on a plastic bottle in rhythm, all of them recording the changes in rhythm effortlessly. The documentary thus provides us with an intimate glimpse into the women's quarters, as well as into a spontaneously improvised musical number that conveys a sense of familiarity in sharp contrast with concert stages. Here, the song, known by all around the table, shows that the sharing of music no longer divides space between stage, proscenium, and audience space, but democratizes the musical performance into the joyous and convivial performance of a community.

Finally, *El Gusto* ("fun" or "pleasure" in Algerian slang) offers a view of *chaâbi* music on par with other musical forms, and also performed in interstitial or peripheral spaces in the twentieth century. In fact, the French occupier had accepted its entry into the Conservatory as an object of study, but only if classes and rehearsals took place in a small room in the basement of the building. Yet *chaâbi* had its moments of glory: Ferkioui remembers that the musicians had performed at the Opera House in Algiers in 1957. After independence, the FLN (Front National de Libération/National Liberation Front) reinstated *chaâbi* as part and parcel of Algeria's national musical heritage—El Hadj Mohammed El Anka, a great *chaâbi* master, was regularly broadcast on the radio, for example. But such national glory was short-lived, in both official venues and more modest ones, as shown by the camera, which follows the old musicians wandering in the city and pointing to the places where *chaâbi* used to be played, including popular cafés in the medina and brothels in the port of Algiers—all of them since closed. This festive music, with its noble Andalusian legacy, had nevertheless been shared, sung, and danced to by several communities.

Postcolonial and Transnational Political Significance

What kind of meaning does a Maghrebi (whether Moroccan, Algerian, or Tunisian) documentary on music produce? For what purpose or purposes?

Cecilia Mangini, the first woman documentarian after the Second World War, who collaborated with Pasolini (Garson 2011, 62), defined documentary as "a third eye to grasp what is behind reality." Indeed, a documentary usually reveals what is not immediately visible, or unearths a buried story. According to Rochdi El Manira: "A documentary helps, among other things, to give voice to silences and to throw light on the phenomena of the real world that transform the latter by showing them or denouncing them, or, as is often the case, both simultaneously" (El Manira 2014, 43). But what is silenced in music? What remains unsaid in this explosion of sounds? How does the third eye—or is it a third ear?—uncover what is silenced beneath, what has been muted?

Obviously, what is at stake in a Maghrebi documentary on music is also what is at stake in a postcolonial documentary. A postcolonial documentary on a type of music that is possibly on the verge of extinction—or at the very least marginalized away from conventionally accepted musical styles—seems inspired by the agenda of postcolonial feminists in its very attempt to revive its lyrics and music with aging musicians, outside the commercial networks of entertainment. Just as postcolonial feminists reimagine and inscribe in the public sphere the female body that has long been confined to the private sphere, documentary cinema is able to transpose it from the private sphere (Fatma and her sisters around the family table in *Voices of Morocco*) to the large screen, to a public display of women making music collectively. Likewise, filming working-class areas in *The Art of the Mezwed*, or the erasure of the places where *chaâbi* used to be played in *El Gusto*, or yet again the artisanal, rough instruments used by the Gnawas in *Voices of Morocco*, imbues the musical narrative with a sense of human-feminist empathy that proclaims: one cannot be a woman without being in solidarity with other humans whose voices have not been taken into account in the history of music—the poor, the oppressed, the other silenced peoples of the world.

These three documentaries about music loudly project styles that are on the verge of being forgotten on the big screen; they record and broadcast the voices of grassroots music, not the voices of famous musicologists on the topic. Giving voice—literally—to these musical styles constitutes a democratic gesture in tune with the global postcolonial movement, since it hands the microphone over to the subaltern, and no longer heeds the voices of power. This first political move on the part of the documentaries that record music with apparent urgency (What if this music were soon to disappear? What if the musicians could no longer train others in these musical styles?) points to another political move which is just as significant: that of democratic listening. The documentaries make it possible for audiences to listen to music that is no longer the sound sanctioned by the Algerian state or the *makhzen* in Morocco as *the* expression of national cultural heritage in either country, and prefer to focus on music previously *unheard* (in both senses of ignored and not understood) by those in power. Such is the case with *mezwed* music, a musical style of ill repute, with its sometimes bawdy love lyrics ("Aouicha, I will never give you up!") and social commentary on, for example, the response to immigrants in France ("Foreigner! They said: foreigner, get out!"). This double gesture that makes room for the other in cinema and deconstructs the clichés around him or her is also practiced by Farida Benlyazid, a director of both fiction and documentary films.

> The perspective through which I make films reveals another form of thought that is neither better nor worse but one that makes us ponder another possible becoming for the human being—outside stereotypes and preconceived ideas. (Bâ and Higbee 2012, 223)

Human-feminist postcolonial cinema works from the exact same perspective as it changes the old, known focal point; hence, over the span of a documentary, the undervalued musician becomes the star, his/her presence fills the screen and the soundtrack, outside the social categories of class and classical education.

Further, these three documentaries restore the genealogy of the three musical traditions on film. In each case, after having investigated the local expression of that musical tradition, the film takes the viewer/listener deep into its history. The latter transcends the local, the national, and the regional, as it clearly shows that the music belongs to both the Muslim community and the Mediterranean Jewish community. Such a perspective runs counter to local or even national politics. In its compelling reassertion of the cultural diversity of the Maghreb in the harmonies of its musical traditions, it also corrects a few thriving separatist preconceptions in the region that paint a definitive split between Jewish and Muslim cultures, when both communities suffered the same wrenching dispersal from Spain in the sixteenth century, and both share the same Andalusian cultural heritage. In the end, after starting a thorough investigation of local music, obtaining production funding in idiosyncratic ways, and filming and structuring their narratives along new, distinctive models, the three documentaries point in the same direction—to the deeply intertwined Judeo-Muslim roots of today's Maghrebi musical culture.

References

Armes, Roy. 2006. *African Filmmaking: North and South of the Sahara.* Bloomington: Indiana University Press.

Bâ, Saër Maty, and Will Higbee. 2012. *De-Westernizing Film Studies.* London and New York: Routledge.

Boym, Svetlana. 2002. *The Future of Nostalgia.* New York: Basic Books.

Chamkhi, Sonia. 2002. *Cinéma tunisien nouveau: Parcours autres.* Tunis: Sud Éditions.

———. 2009. *Le Cinéma tunisien à la lumière de la modernité.* Tunis: Centre de Publication Universitaire.

Chion, Michel. 1995. *La Musique au cinéma.* Paris: Fayard.

Deleuze, Gilles. 1985. *Cinéma 2: l'image-temps.* Paris: Éditions de Minuit.

Dönmez-Colin, Gönul, ed. 2007. *The Cinema of North Africa and the Middle East.* London: Wallflower Press.

Garson, Charlotte. 2011. "Cécilia Mangini, le troisième œil." *Cahiers du Cinéma* 665 (March): 62.

Gugler, Josef, ed. 2011. *Film in the Middle East and North Africa: Creative Dissidence.* Austin: University of Texas Press.

Higbee, Will. 2015 "Merzak Allouache: (Self-)Censorship, Social Critique, and the Limits of Political Engagement in Contemporary Algerian Cinema (Algeria)." In Josef Gugler, ed. *Ten Arab Filmmakers: Political Dissent and Social Critique.* Bloomington: Indiana University Press: 189-212.

Hjort, Mette, and Duncan Petrie, eds. 2007. *The Cinema of Small Nations.* Edinburgh: Edinburgh University Press.

El Manira, Rochdi. 2014. "Femmes à la caméra: trois voix aux chapitre du documentaire." *Revue marocaine des recherches cinématographiques* 2: 42–56.

Martin, Florence. 2011. *Screens and Veils: Maghrebi Women's Cinema.* Bloomington: Indiana University Press.

———. 2007. "Tunisia" in Hjort, Mette, and Duncan Petrie, eds. *The Cinema of Small Nations.* Edinburgh: Edinburgh University Press: 213-228.

Martin, Florence, Kamel Ben Ouanès, and Patricia Caillé, eds. 2012. *Les Cinémas du Maghreb et leurs publics*. Dossier Africultures. Paris: L'Harmattan.

Ponzanesi, Sandra, and Marguerite Walker, eds. 2012. *Postcolonial Cinema Studies*. London and New York: Routledge.

Rothe, E. Nina. 2012. "Safinez Bousbia's *El Gusto*: Film as a Movement to Change Lives." *Huffington Post*, May 17. huffpost.com.

Saïl, Noureddine. 2012. „Journées cinématographiques de Carthage 2010: allocution d'ouverture du colloque". In *Les Cinémas du Maghreb et leurs publics*. Dossier Africultures edited by Florence Martin, Kamel Ben Ouanès, and Patricia Caillé, 18-26. Paris: L'Harmattan.

Zhang, Yingjin. 2010. "Transnationalism and Translocality in Chinese Cinema." *Cinema Journal* 49, no. 3 (Spring): 135–39.

Filmography
Safinez Bousbia, Algeria
El Gusto, 2011 (Best Director and Audience Award, Abu Dhabi Film Festival, 2012; Audience Award, Arabian Sights Film Festival, Washington DC, 2012)

Sonia Chamkhi, Tunisia
Narcissus (*'Aziz rawhu/Narcisse*, 2015), fiction
Militants (*Munadilat/Militantes*, 2012), documentary, 52 minutes
The Art of the Mezwed (*Fann al-mizwad/L'Art du mezoued*, 2010), documentary
The Making of Life is a Dream *by Hacen Mouathan* (*Making of* La vie est un songe *de Hacen Mouathan*, 2009), 52 minutes
Borderline (*Wara' al-balayik/Borderline*, 2005), fiction, 21 minutes
Douz, the Gate to the Sahara (*Douz, la porte du Sahara*, 2004), documentary, 35 minutes
Normal (*Nesmah wa rih/Normal*, 2002), fiction, 20 minutes

Izza Genini, Morocco
Documentaries:
Morocco's Percussions (*Maroc tambours battants*, 1998)
For the Pleasure of the Eyes (*Pour le plaisir des yeux*, 1997)
The Citrus Route (*La route du cédrat, le fruit de la splendeur*, 1997)
Voices of Morocco (*Voix du Maroc*: montage of the *Morocco, Body and Soul/ Maroc, corps et âme* series, 1995), 60 minutes
Concerto for 13 Voices (*Concerto pour 13 voix*, 1995), 90 minutes
In Search of Ouled Moumen (*Retrouver Ouled Moumen*, 1994), 50 minutes. Prix du Festival de Film Historique, Pessac (Historic Film Festival Award in Pessac)

Morocco, Body and Soul (*Maroc, corps et âme*, 1987–92); Jules Vernes Award
    in 1991. Series of twenty-six-minute episodes:
Aïta (*Ayta*)
Songs of Praise (*Louanges*)
Of Lutes and Delights (*Des luths et délices*)
Gnawas (*Gnaouas*)
Malhun (*Malhoune*)
Marrakesh Rhythms (*Rythmes de Marrakech*)
Songs for Shabbat (*Chants pour un chabbat*)
Embroidered Hymns (*Cantiques brodés*)
Vibrations in High Atlas (*Vibrations en Haut Atlas*)
Wedding Music in the Mid-Atlas (*Nuptiales en Moyen Atlas*)
Festivals (*Musem/Moussem*)

Ahmed, El Maanouni, Morocco
Trances (*al-Hal/Transes*, 1981)

21

THREE HUNDRED KILOMETERS SOUTH OF MARRAKECH: IMIDER, ARTIVISM, AND THE ENVIRONMENTAL DOCUMENTARY IN MOROCCO

Jamal Bahmad

From August 2011 to late September 2019, the Amazigh-speaking community of Imider in southeastern Morocco staged a long-standing sit-in against the degradation of its natural environment by Africa's biggest silver mine. Since 2015, the Moroccan activist filmmaker Nadir Bouhmouch has worked with the community to produce films on the ongoing standoff with the authorities, to be used in this epic battle for land and water. Bouhmouch made three documentary films about the protest. His documentary films about Mount Alebban are illustrations of "artivism" (the combination of art and activism), and are significant in terms of the future of Moroccan cinema and documentary, environmental politics, and the aesthetic intersections between the two.

Assamer (southeast Morocco) is not only an arid region severely hit by climate change in the form of water scarcity, but also home to many of Morocco's most profitable mines. The natural resource bonanza has been a curse to the region because most mines heavily rely on water to process the extracted underground wealth. The mines and their processing plants are also the primary cause of water and air pollution in Assamer. This has created tensions between the predominantly private mining companies and the local inhabitants. The native language of the locals is Tamazight (Berber), which has long been suppressed by the Moroccan regime. This has compounded the question of the region's exploitation by the neoliberal economic and political establishment in Rabat. Little wonder that Morocco's longest-running sit-in took place on Mount Alebban hilltop (Tinghir province), which overlooks Africa's most productive silver mine, located in the municipality of Imider. The occupation started in 2011 alongside the Arab Spring uprisings, but is a continuation of a long-standing battle with Moroccan authorities that began in 1996. The protesters camping on Mount Alebban from 2011 to late September 2019, when the camp was voluntarily broken up, have been filming their everyday lives and protests against the repression of the authorities, who have arrested and imprisoned many activists over the years. The Mount Alebban sit-in also attracted the attention of a young Moroccan documentary filmmaker.

Morocco is well known for its rich mineral resources. Even though it is neither an oil-producing nor a natural gas–producing country like neighboring Algeria, the country is home to over 70 percent of the world's phosphate reserves. The national economy has relied on mines, international tourism, remittances by Moroccan immigrants overseas, and agricultural exports to guarantee social peace and relative economic development since the introduction of market reforms in the 1980s. The neoliberal nature of the economy, however, has meant that regional disparities and social inequalities have soared in the country (Cohen and Jaïdi 2006). This has led to frequent street protests and episodes of police violence to crush popular demands for social and spatial justice (Zemni and Bogaert 2009, 103–104). Fishmonger Mouhcine Fikri died tragically on October 28, 2016, after a policeman confiscated five hundred kilograms of his swordfish, leading to the El Hoceima events in the Rif region. The subsequent Rif revolt attracted global attention following the violent crackdown on protests and mass arrests since May 2017. Less known is the story of the country's longest running sit-in, on Mount Alebban in southeastern Morocco.

The silver mine of Imider, about three hundred kilometers south of the city of Marrakesh, is one of the most profitable mining sites in the country. It is Africa's most productive silver mine, in fact, the seventh-highest in the world, according to the Environmental Justice Atlas.[1] Silver has been extracted from it since the seventh century. It is currently exploited by La Société Métallurgique d'Imiter (Imiter Metallurgical Company, SMI), a subsidiary of Managem S.A., the country's main mining company. Managem is owned by the Société Nationale d'Investissement (National Investment Company, SNI), a private holding company that is mainly owned by the Moroccan royal family (Houdret 2012, 289). The mine began to be exploited in 1969, with intensive silver extraction beginning in 1978. According to the website of the operating company, the mine has an annual output of 300,000 tons of silver metal today, with a purity rate of 99.5 percent (Managem, n.d.). What the website does not mention is how the mine has contributed to the rapid depletion of underground water resources and their pollution in Imider.

The first protest took place in 1986 when the mining company started digging a well to supply the mine with water for the onsite processing plant. The inhabitants were worried about the well's negative environmental and social impacts on Imider's scarce underground water resources in this desert region. However, mine officials went ahead with their well-digging program. Twenty-three protesters were arrested, and six of them were jailed for one to two years on charges of staging "a revolutionary rally in order to attack the authorities" (Amussu n.d.). The second most notable protest took place over forty-five days in 1996 when SMI was privatized. On March 10, 1996, the police violently repressed the protest on National Road No. 10 (N10), resulting in one civilian casualty, Lahcen Usbddan.

Peaceful protests reoccurred in 2004 after SMI decided to dig a new well to supply the mine with more water to meet its increasing production levels. The mine's water usage in 2018 was estimated at more than 1,383 cubic meters per day, which is twelve times more than the consumption of the seven Imider villages (six thousand people). The *khettarat* (traditional irrigation systems) in the area have been drastically affected by the mine's overexploitation of underwater reserves. This has led to olive, apricot, and almond trees dying because of the lack of water or the impact of toxic wastewater from the mine, which has polluted the soil and underground water reserves of Imider. Villagers have also reported cases of livestock fatalities suspected to be related to the toxic air and water pollution from the mine. In protest against this environmental degradation, the Imider villagers cut the water supply to the mine for a week in 2010. Promises were made by the authorities to find solutions to the environmental damage and social problems caused by the silver mine, but all in vain.

In the early summer of 2011, the villagers decided to take their decades-long mobilization and protests against exploitation and pollution to a new level. The protests were led by university students returning to spend the summer holidays in Imider in the wake of the popular uprisings in North Africa and the Middle East that year. They applied for internships and summer jobs at the silver mine as usual, but the mine officials kept them waiting for too long. Things took a new turn when drinking water cuts started to happen frequently in Imider that summer. The villagers blamed the mine for the water shortages. Led by the students and unemployed youth, who were armed with a strong awareness of their rights and an indigenous Amazigh civil rights consciousness, the Imider community wanted to give international visibility to its long struggle against SMI's water overexploitation, air- and water-polluting landfills, toxic waste treatment, uncontrolled dumping sites, and environment-unfriendly mineral processing practices. On August 1, 2011, they set up a protest camp on Mount Alebban and cut off one of the two water pipes supplying the mining plant. Protest action led to a drop in SMI's processing capacity by 40 percent in 2012 and 30 percent the following year. The protest camp was set up on Mount Alebban hilltop, which is 1,524 meters high in the Atlas mountains overlooking the silver mine. Protesters created a dialogue committee to negotiate a solution to the environmental and social issues with the authorities, who reacted by intimidating, arresting, and imprisoning many protest leaders on flimsy charges in the months that followed. For example, Mustapha Ouchtoubane was sentenced to four years in prison on the trumped-up charge of stealing eighteen grams of silver from the mine (Amnesty International 2015, 35–36). As an act of solidarity with the Occupy Alebban protest camp and to demand better educational infrastructure and conditions, primary and junior-high school students from Imider went on strike and boycotted school in 2011–12. The students returned after a gap year in which they were neglected and left to themselves by the Ministry of National Education.

In further action against the silver mine exploitation, activists organized artistic and creative activities, such as guerrilla theater, the creation of murals, and an annual film festival on Mount Alebban. They also regularly marched along N10 (the main road linking Tinghir to Ouarzazate), hoping to attract the attention of passing international tourists and fellow Moroccans. Protesters have also been very active on social media, using the name of the movement, "Amussu: Xf Ubrid n 96" (Movement on the Road of '96), in reference to the 1996 revolt against the mine that led to a number of casualties. The movement's slogan—"To Exist Is to Resist"—echoes the voice and struggle of many communities around the world who find themselves at the mercy of big mining companies backed by neoliberal states and their security forces. The Movement on the Road of '96 linked up with similar grassroots movements around the world such as Standing Rock, which began in early 2016 in opposition to the approved construction of Energy Transfer Partners' Dakota Access Pipeline in the United States (Ilnyckyj 2017, 4–5). Standing Rock and Imider activists marched together during the United Nations Climate Change Conference (COP 22), which was held in Marrakech from November 7 to 18, 2016.

During COP 22, as well as in their protests on and around Mount Alebban, the Imider protesters highlighted the environmental costs of the silver mine. They raised awareness about the mine's liability for biodiversity loss (wildlife, agro-diversity), soil contamination, loss of landscape and its aesthetic degradation, waste overflow, food insecurity (crop damage), groundwater pollution and/or depletion, and the large-scale disturbance of hydrological and geological systems in the area. The protesters also highlighted the health risks associated with the mine, where many villagers have jobs, including exposure to radiation, accidents, deaths, occupational diseases, and mental health issues such as stress, depression, and suicide. Moreover, the protest movement pinpointed many negative social and political impacts of the mine. As reported by the Environmental Justice Atlas (EJA), these include land dispossession, corruption and co-optation of different local actors, lack of job security at the mine, unemployment of local youth, loss of livelihood, militarization and increased police presence, and human rights violations (EJA, n.d.).

While the mine administration has largely kept quiet about these issues, except to deny activists' allegations, the authorities have often reacted with violence, and thirty-three people were imprisoned between 2011 and the end of the protest camp in September 2019. Some of those detained include Mustapha Ouchtoubane, Hamid Ouberka, Ichou Hamdan, Omar Moujane, and Mustafa Faska. This did not dissuade protesters from continuing their sit-in on Mount Alebban. As proclaimed on the website of the Movement on the Road of '96:

> The silver mine is poisoning our lifestyle and our existence, it threatens our survival and our land through water and air pollution, through disease and repression of our demands with the silence and the constant intimidations by the authorities. At the same time, the policies of marginalization and exclusion still continue without change and more and more aggressive and negligent against the protesters of the Movement, in an attempt to break the spirit of struggle and the continuity of the sit-in. (Amussu, n.d.)

The protesters were demanding an independent study of the environmental impact of the mine, better infrastructure in Imider (hospitals, schools), and that 75 percent of jobs at the mine be allocated to the villagers, who suffer the highest levels of unemployment and poverty in Morocco although they live next to the most profitable silver mine in Africa.

Culture as a Means of Resistance

The marches included twice-weekly gatherings in which villagers discussed their demands and made decisions following the *agraw* system, a traditional form of local democratic government among the Amazigh people in North Africa. "After each meeting held at the foot of the hill," as the *New York Times* correspondent reported in January 2014, "the villagers walk back home holding up three fingers—one for the Berber language, one for the land and one for mankind—hoping for someone to hear their call" (Alami 2014). Participation in the *agraw* is open to all six thousand men, women and children from the seven villages of the Imider municipality.

The Movement on the Road of '96 deployed cultural symbolism in its struggle for environmental justice: the walls of the little stone buildings on Mount Alebban were decorated with graffiti protest messages. In addition to a painted portrait of former prisoner Mustapha Ouchtoubane (arrested on October 5, 2011 and released on October 10, 2015) next to the logo of the protest movement, there were also sayings by Mother Teresa and Martin Luther King, among others. The protest outpost had a makeshift school where Imider children learned writing and reading. They were also schooled in their history and struggle for social and environmental justice. The students were made aware of the importance of their surrounding environment and the role of civic activism in reclaiming their rights to clean air, water, and land. Despite the difficult weather conditions in this arid desert region, with its cold winters and extremely hot summers, the protesters organized sports events and competitions to provide some entertainment for themselves and to stay healthy in what turned out to be the longest sit-in in Moroccan history. They also partnered with various organizations from Morocco to provide training sessions for men, women, and children.

The Mount Alebban protest camp inspired dozens of songs in southeast Morocco. Modern protest music began to emerge in the region in the late twentieth century, with singers like Moha Mallal and Mustapha Elouardy, who followed in the footsteps of the *imdyazen*, the famous bards who have existed in the region and across North Africa for centuries. *Imdyazen* like Zaid Oubjna, Hmad Ou Hachem, and Moulay Ahmed Ou Taher, to name but a few, have composed and sung poetry addressing political, social, and cultural issues. Using their lyrics and sometimes accompanied by traditional musical instruments such as the violin, flute, and tambourine, *imdyazen* have chronicled and commented on the various transformations of their society and the world. Their oral poetry is an inspiration to contemporary singers like Mallal, who have used modern instruments and rhythms to sing about love, reflect on social change, and spread the messages of the Amazigh civil rights movement among youth in southeast Morocco and beyond. The region has witnessed a boom in protest music in recent years, following the Amun Style first created and perfected by Mallal, who in turn was drawing on world music and the modern Kabyle musical scene in Algeria and the diaspora. The Assamer singers often find inspiration in the problems of their communities, hence protest music is the most dominant music genre in the region today.

The experience of Imider has inspired many singers in the municipality and all around Assamer. Mallal was among the first to contribute to these Amazigh blues of resistance. In his song "Inkerd Imider" (Imider Is Rising, 2012), the veteran of Amun Style chants the unity and resistance of Imider people against Managem. Posted on YouTube on February 4, 2012, the video clip of the song opens with the footage of a demonstration by Imider protesters at the foot of Mount Alebban. Their chants smoothly give way to the music of Mallal's "Inkerd Imider." As the music unfolds, the video shows more footage of hundreds of protesters marching along N10. Women, men, and children are chanting slogans and demonstrating peacefully without blocking road traffic. They carry banners, posters, Amazigh flags, and the Moroccan national flag. There is also footage of an *agraw* meeting and people resting under tents on Mount Alebban. With the exception of two short scenes of the singer toward the middle of the video, the clip uses real footage of Imider protests from beginning to end. One scene shows a security helicopter trying to intimidate the protesters, who fearlessly stand their ground until the aircraft abandons its hopeless act of provocation. The lyrics commend the people of Imider for taking a strong stand, and critique the mining company for its extraction of enormous mineral wealth from Imider and leaving the community in poverty without even enough water to drink. Mallal also denounces the high level of youth unemployment in what should have been the richest municipality of the region and perhaps all of Morocco. History, he says, will remember this stalwart rebellion against social and environmental injustice. Mallal calls on the Amazigh people to show solidarity with Imider and with other struggles, to be the agents of their own history again. The video clip significantly zooms in on Imider school children chanting revolutionary slogans as they walk back to Mount Alebban camp after the day's march along N10. This signifies that they are likely to continue the battle in the future, since they are the first victims of the silver mine's violations of human and environmental rights.

In "Albban" (2013), 'Abdu Ummad and his three-person band sing about the suffering and hopes of the people of Imider. Using guitars, the trio from Imider speak in the name of their people and lament the fact that their struggle has not attracted much solidarity from other people in Morocco and beyond. With a portrait of Che Guevara in the background, the Amazigh singers explain how the silver mine and the powers of oppression it represents have stolen land and history from Imider and the Amazigh people. The lyrics then speak about how Ayt Imider (the people of Imider) are demanding their share of their land's natural wealth and social and economic development. 'Abdu Ummad and his companions conclude their song by saying that they are not afraid to write their history with their own blood, meaning that they are ready to die for the sake of saving the environment and achieving their rightful demands.

Beyond the CCM

Since its creation by the French colonial authorities in 1944, the Centre Cinématographique Marocain (Moroccan Cinema Center, CCM) has played a major role in fashioning the identity and evolution of Moroccan colonial and postcolonial cinema. The CCM survived Moroccan independence in 1956 and has maintained its role as the main player in Moroccan cinema from production to exhibition. The center is in charge of granting or refusing permission for the production of films in Morocco. It also administers the public fund system through which the majority of films in Morocco are partially made. To be funded or simply authorized by the CCM to shoot a film, the filmmakers need to submit their scripts and professional identity cards to the center's Film Production Commission. Made up of representatives from the Ministry of Interior, the Ministry of Finance, the Ministry of Communication, the CCM, and the film production sector, the committee has the power to approve or block any film project. This power makes the CCM both the facilitator and the censor of Moroccan cinema. It has used this power to censor films from being produced or distributed in the country. A recent example is *Much Loved* (*Zin li fik*, 2015) by Nabil Ayouch. In addition, the obligation for Moroccan film professionals to apply for and regularly renew their CCM professional identity cards is an effective means of censorship. It is almost impossible for Moroccan film professionals to make films, or apply for healthcare or visas to travel abroad, without these cards. Nadir Bouhmouch's experience at the Dutch embassy in Rabat illustrates this barely veiled censorship system. This is the full exchange he had with the visa officer (his personal Facebook account, October 23, 2017).

> Bureaucrat: What is your job?
> Me: Filmmaker.
> Bureaucrat: Do you have proof?
> Me: I can show you my films.
> Bureaucrat: Do you have a paper from the Ministry of Culture?
> Me: No, but do you want me to show you my films?
> Bureaucrat: Do you have a card from the National Cinema Center?
> Me: No, but do you want me to show you my films?
> Bureaucrat: So you have no proof?
> Me: ....
> Bureaucratic lesson of the day: having made and making films does not make you a filmmaker, the state does.[2]

The censorship mandate of the CCM has pushed many film directors to seek alternative ways of making films in Morocco. A few film directors have gone underground to make their movies, thus both risking their own safety and denying their films public funding through the CCM. Bouhmouch is a case in point. This young Moroccan filmmaker has made all his short and feature documentary films without permission or funding from the CCM.

He launched his filmmaking career in 2011, when he was a film student at San Diego State University in California. The 2011 protests in Morocco and across North Africa and the Middle East led him to return to the country. Bouhmouch made his first film about the protests in Morocco. His *My Makhzen and Me* (*Ana wa makhzani*, 2012) tells the story of Morocco's "Arab Spring." It covers the demonstrations in many cities and follows February 20 Movement activists in an attempt to explain the genesis, development, and aftermath of Morocco's unfinished revolution.

Bouhmouch savvily benefited from the opportunities offered by the digital revolution, using small cameras to shoot films and release them on alternative distribution networks. Bouhmouch made *My Makhzen and Me* in 2012 with his own small means and distributed it online free of charge. This helped his film attract broad audiences despite dwindling cinema attendance (Bahmad 2016, 90–92). Bouhmouch knew how to play these factors to his advantage and thus made films beyond the traditional CCM circuit and its censorship. The digital revolution has not only caused immense disruption to traditional modes of filmmaking and viewership, it has also provided new opportunities for making a new kind of cinema. This is especially helpful to activist filmmakers in countries where production means are limited and censorship rampant. He has made many other films, including *473* (2013) and his two documentaries about Imider.

300 Km South

While films about the natural environment have been made in Morocco for decades, the "environmental documentary" generally demonstrates an acute awareness of climate change and the social, political, economic, and ethical challenges it has created. Although not considered a major contributor to climate change, Morocco is one of the most vulnerable countries in terms of its impact. The country is already suffering from increasing droughts, water shortages, flash floods, heat waves, and desertification. The environmental documentary in the age of climate change draws attention to the human destruction of the planet and to attempts to save what can be saved. This genre also foregrounds grassroots and alternative ways of seeing and living on a planet increasingly suffering from natural disasters and diminishing resources. It is in this context that I will explore Bouhmouch's two short environmental documentaries about Imider, namely *300 Km South* (2016) and *Timnadin n Rif* (Rif Blues, 2017).

Bouhmouch is an activist filmmaker who brings fresh perspectives to disturbing questions, and gives a voice to people who are denied one in Morocco. He illustrates the structural reasons behind the suffering of large classes of Moroccan society. His real-life characters range from February 20 Movement activists to female victims of rape who are forced to marry their rapists, to Imider's poor population, which has to live with the environmental damage caused by the mining company. He combines art and activism to unveil myriad forms of injustice in Morocco.

Bouhmouch the activist seized the occasion when Morocco hosted the United Nations Climate Change Conference (COP 22) in Marrakech from November 7–18, 2016. One of the conference sponsors was Managem, which operates the Imider silver mine through its SMI subsidiary. The filmmaker made and released his four-minute documentary *300 Km South: Imider Has a Speech* to draw global attention to the standoff between Imider and Managem, and Morocco's contradictory discourse on climate change. While the country has one of the most ambitious renewable energy programs, building gigantic production projects such as the Noor solar power plant in Ouarzazate (just 130 kilometers south of Imider), Morocco is also causing harm to the environment in other sectors, for example mining. The film was widely shared on social media and was used to contradict Morocco's and COP 22's greenwashing discourse. In fact, the film title became a hashtag (#300kmSouth) and was widely used by activists on social media during COP 22. World leaders traveled to Marrakech to take part in the U.N. summit, and so did protesters from around the world. Activists from Imider demonstrated outside the COP 22 village to denounce Managem's anti-environmental activities in Imider. They were joined and supported by environment activists from other parts of the globe. Bouhmouch's film was screened in Marrakech and used as a protest tool against the official discourse of the U.N. summit, which was sponsored by big companies with a dark record of damaging the planet. The "300 Km" in the title refers to the distance separating Imider from the U.N. environment conference venue in Marrakech. The film was also screened on Mount Alebban as part of the first International Imider Environmental Justice Film Festival (November 8–12, 2016).

300 Km South opens with scenes of arid land, with a young female narrator speaking in Tamazight and challenging the audience with rhetorical questions about this desert landscape. She says that the audience would think this is a desert, and that the land is useless and produces nothing. However, she clarifies, "this land is our land and it is generous. It has fed this community for centuries. Besides, it is rich in natural resources." As she utters this, the film shifts from arid landscapes to green fields and abundant water running in traditional irrigation ditches. The ditches are part of the *khettarat*, a traditional and economical system of water management using underground canals. People are shown in the green fields living in harmony with Mother Nature. The film then shifts back to aridity and the narrator demands to know if her motherland will continue to have water and therefore life in the future. She explains that she is doubtful because Managem has taken land away from the people and polluted it with toxic chemicals, in addition to the overexploitation of underground water resources. Bouhmouch shows the silver mine and its problematic water pipes. Scenes of dried-up land and dead trees are also depicted, and the narrator asserts that Managem is behind this drought and toxicity of soil and water. The next scenes are of people marching along N10 in a peaceful demonstration. The narrator tells us that her people have had enough of futile conferences and false promises. She says that COP 22 will not solve their problem because solutions to climate change cannot come from the top. "The solution will not come from those who created the problem, those who profit from the problem," she explains. "So what is the solution?" The answer is provided by footage of Mount Alebban protesters marching along N10. This means that solutions to environmental injustice issues in Imider and beyond can come only from grassroots and social movements that bear the voices of their communities regardless of repression and the high price of social activism. "The answer is with us," confirms the narrator, who appears for the first time in the film. The young girl emerges from among the attendees of an *agraw* gathering. She tells us that her people live three hundred kilometers south of COP 22. This message is addressed to the U.N. environment summit in Marrakech and to the world. The film credits roll and we learn that the people of Imider are the producers of the film, with Bouhmouch behind the camera.

The film was conceived and written by the Temporary Cinematographic Committee of the Movement on Road 96. The direct style of the documentary and its short duration reflect the ends to which it was made—to spread the word far and wide about Imider vs Managem. The film was used for this purpose during COP 22 and at other environment film events in Morocco and abroad. The success of *300 Km South* has encouraged Bouhmouch to make more films about Imider and environmental and social problems in Morocco and North Africa. Thus one of his documentaries, *Paradises of the Earth (Jannat al-ard*, 2017), focuses on environmental and social problems in Tunisia created by the greed and irresponsible behavior of neoliberal corporations and governments.

Rif Blues

Bouhmouch's second environmental documentary was released in June 2017, just as the Rif region of Morocco was in turmoil due to intensive protests, heavy security presence, and bloody repression of peaceful demonstrations in El Hoceima and other towns and villages. Subtitled "a film in solidarity with our siblings in the Rif," *Rif Blues* brings two historically rebellious regions of Morocco together in one short documentary focused on struggle and solidarity. The seven-minute film is a poem dedicated to the activists in the Rif in their fight for their right to jobs, social justice, and dignity. The short documentary follows a prominent poet and activist from Imider as he chants his *tamnat* (lyrical poem) in solidarity with El Hoceima protesters and prisoners. Alternating between Mount Alebban and other iconic protest sites in Imider on the one hand, and El Hoceima's rebelling streets on the other, the film weaves a poetic-realist narrative of resistance. It is the resistance of ordinary people attached to their environment and conscious of their rights against a regime that is not willing to share the natural wealth of the country with its people.

The film is motivated by the human rights violations in Imider for over six years and in the Rif since the tragic death of Mohcine Fikri in October 2016. Bouhmouch sees both struggles as one fight against oppression. The state's security approach to protest movements has resulted in tragic deaths and dozens of prisoners. This approach has failed to solve the question of social and environmental justice at the heart of the protests. In fact, things have only got worse in both Imider and El Hoceima. The film shows the solidarity of the people of Imider with their brothers and sisters in the Rif as both fight for their socioeconomic, environmental, and cultural rights, and for a better Morocco. Produced by the Movement on the Road of 96 and directed by Bouhmouch, the collective production is a visual poem with far-reaching messages for both the activists and the state that has oppressed them. The poetry of *timnatin* (or *timnadin*) is a traditional form of Amazigh blues. Accompanied by visually sublime long shots of Mount Alebban and El Hoceima's rebellious streets, the film blends the lyrical depth of *timnadin* with the art of cinema in what is also an homage to the bard tradition of *imdyazen*, who sang the resistance of the indigenous Amazigh people against colonial and postcolonial oppression. The film reclaims this dying tradition and thus stages a double resistance against oblivion and the neoliberal state. The bard tradition has been in decline due to rapid social changes, but also because of the Moroccan state's censorship.

Conclusion

Nadir Bouhmouch's two films are pioneers of the environmental film wave in Morocco, where the documentary tradition has been historically weak. The young citizen filmmaker has used digital means of production and distribution to his advantage. He is armed with a strong social justice ethic, has defied the censorship board of the CCM, and has made films that have enjoyed wide acclaim among audiences in Morocco and abroad. His first two documentaries about Imider are eloquent illustrations of how environmental and social justice are intertwined in a neoliberal state.[3] Fighting for one is impossible without the other. Climate change has deepened the crisis over natural resources and will shape the future of Morocco and the entire region. People are increasingly left with only one choice: to resist or die. They are choosing the former. Bouhmouch has led the way in making his camera a voice by and for the people. His Guerrilla Cinema project, particularly his cooperative work with the Imider social movement, demonstrates how Moroccan cinema can make itself useful in an age when the traditional functions of cinema are disappearing or being eroded by other media.

References

Alami, Aida. 2014. "On Moroccan Hill, Villagers Make Stand Against a Mine." *New York Times*, January 23. https://www.nytimes.com/2014/01/24/world/africa/on-moroccan-hill-villagers-make-stand-against-a-mine.html.

Amnesty International. 2015. *Shadow of Impunity: Torture in Morocco and Western Sahara*. Amnesty International.

Amussu: Xf Ubrid n 96—Imider (Movement on the Road of '96). n.d. "Our History." http://imider96.org/about-us/our-history/.

Bahmad, Jamal. 2016. "The Good Pirates: Moroccan Cinema in the Age of Digital Reproduction." In *The State of Post-Cinema*, edited by Malte Hagener, Vinzenz Hediger, and Alena Strohmaier, 89–98. New York: Palgrave Macmillan.

Cohen, Shana, and Larabi Jaïdi. 2006. *Morocco: Globalization and Its Consequences*. New York: Routledge.

Environmental Justice Atlas (EJA). n.d. "Imider Silver Mine, Morocco." https://ejatlas.org/conflict/imider-silver-mine-morocco.

Houdret, Annabelle. 2012. "The Water Connection: Irrigation and Politics in Southern Morocco." *Water Alternatives* 5, no. 2: 284–303.

Ilnyckyj, Milan. 2017. "Networks and Frames in Pipeline Resistance." *Canadian Political Science Association (CPSA) Conference, Ryerson University Toronto, Ontario*, vol. 30, 1–22.

Managem Group. n.d. "Mine d'Imider." http://www.managemgroup.com/Activites/Operations/Mine-d-Imiter.

Zemni, Sami, and Koenraad Bogaert. 2009. "Trade, Security and Neoliberal Politics: Whither Arab Reform? Evidence from the Moroccan Case." *The Journal of North African Studies* 14, no. 1: 91–107.

22

SCREEN FIGHTERS: FILMING AND KILLING IN CONTEMPORARY SYRIA

Donatella Della Ratta

"Politics in the Middle East is now *seen*" (Khatib 2012, 1).[1] Lina Khatib's remark about the markedly political visual culture that has (re)surfaced in the Arab region since 2011 is nowhere better illustrated than in Syria, where a tiny mobile camera phone defiantly held against a gun has become iconic of the peaceful phase of the March 15, 2011 revolt. The use of the camera phone as a counterpart to weapons—which symbolically makes it into a weapon in its own right[2]—is so intrinsically intertwined with the imagination of the Syrian conflict that a little girl can surrender to a camera, thinking it is a gun.[3] This widely circulated image suggests the extent to which protest culture in the country has embraced the visual form.

The mobile camera phone *is* indeed a gun, the only tool an unarmed protester has to shoot back at his killers, "trying to provoke them into producing an image of *his* death, so that at least there will be some evidence of their murderousness" (Snowdon 2016, 92). In this way the protester and his murderer are jointly condemned to the immortality of images, Snowdon remarks. Yet, as Dima Hamadeh's fascinating analysis suggests, "the threat that the protesters pose by parading cameras against the Syrian armed forces" might be read less as a defiant gesture of documenting the violence against civilians and more as "an act of rebellion" against the "practice of disappearance" from public spaces and collective memory that has been systematically carried out by the regime (Hamadeh 2016, 17, 35, 36). The most (in)famous symbol of this joint erasure of dissent—from both the physical and the immaterial space of Syria's collective imagination—is undoubtedly the 1982 massacre perpetrated by the Syrian armed forces against a Muslim Brotherhood–led rebellion in the city of Hama, during which between ten thousand and forty thousand people were killed, in the complete absence of any recorded evidence or visual documentation

(Hamadeh 2016, 25). Such was the climate of fear that parents would hardly talk to their children about what they dared to refer to only as "the Events" (Omareen 2014), without giving any more specific name to the bloodshed: an "*obliteration*" of the visual and of language that resembles what Georges Didi-Huberman defined as a "machinery of *disimagination*" (Didi-Huberman 2008, 20) when describing the Nazis' systematic project of destroying all evidence of the violence committed in order to deny its historical existence. In this "world that the Nazis wanted to obfuscate, to leave wordless and imageless," four photographs were "snatched from hell" by brave members of the Sonderkommando[4] (Didi-Huberman 2008, 20, 3): four blurred, undefined, almost unrecognizable frames from Auschwitz that Didi-Huberman calls "images in spite of all," because, "in spite of their low technical quality, their lack of framing, and their blurriness, they stand as powerful evidence" (Della Ratta 2017, 116) of what the Nazis attempted to eradicate from collective memory and imagination.

Syria's pixelated, mobile-generated, blurry frames are indeed images *in spite of all*; images that have been shot and uploaded in spite of the danger and against all the odds, like "signals to be emitted" (Didi-Huberman 2008, 5) to the outside world in order to resist oblivion. Before serving as evidence-images (Didi-Huberman 2008, 90; Della Ratta 2017) and seeking to become historical testimony—even in such a fragmented, unfinished way—the Syrian frames produced since the beginning of the uprising are counter-actions to the regime's project of removing any trace of dissent from public spaces and from the space of history: a resurgence, as Hamadeh calls it, in the "virtual space inaugurated by the act of filming,"[5] "of what was determinately erased in full presence somewhere else" (Hamadeh 2016, 17). The videos themselves become substitutes for a space that was violently subtracted and appropriated by the ruling power; they turn into the quintessential place to perform and manifest dissent, making the latter visible not only to other Syrians and to the entire world, but also to the person simultaneously filming and live-witnessing the events filmed (Hamadeh 2016; Rich 2011).

The question of visibility is crucial in reading Syria's uprising video archive as a collective "statement against this forced disappearance" that the regime has condemned its people to since "the Events" in Hama (Hamadeh 2016, 36). In the eyes of the ruling power, Syrians who oppose the regime simply do not exist, they have no visibility in public space; and if they do manage to gain this visibility, as during the 2011 uprising, then they should be treated as "conspirators" (al-Assad 2011), or individuals whose "Syrianness" is to be questioned and denied.[6] From this perspective, "the lives of those who dared to desacralize the national ideal had no critical mass, no political visibility, no representability, and thus their extermination held no ethical claims or consequences." Unlike the Nazis' disimagination strategy, erasure from the public space in Syria does not serve "to cover the traces of a despicable crime, but as [a] negation" of the very fact that those lives have ever existed (Hamadeh 2016, 14). Hence, before being a "rational act of a 'citizen journalist'" (Snowdon 2016, 91) determined to capture evidence-images, the compulsive, nonstop filming inaugurated in 2011 stands as a powerful reaction to the decades-old denial strategies of the ruling power: the denial of public visibility, and the denial of "Syrianness" in those whose values of nationhood and identity diverge from the mainstream narrative.

The first citizen-generated videos casually filmed during the spontaneous protest of February 17, 2011 in a central Damascus market already demystify these two strategies. Firstly, the footage shot by unknown citizen-protesters in itself represents a reclaiming of stolen visibility, as it testifies to the *being there* of the people in that very moment. Yet visibility is not only regained through the frames documenting protests as the main object of the filmed material, but also by virtue of the fact that the footage itself is the living testimony of more people filming, as active subjects in the unfolding of the events. Here visibility is multiplied, expanded, as it concerns the visibility of the crowd: not that of an isolated person filming as "a spectacular, narcissistic thing," but that of the individual *"being there* together with others" (Snowdon 2016, 68, my emphasis). Secondly, the collective, spontaneous chant—"the Syrian people will not be humiliated"—as the immediate reaction to the police brutally beating a fellow citizen reaffirms an idea of "Syrianness" in which a shared identity *in defiance* is shaped in contrast to the blind acceptance of the abuses perpetrated by the ruling power, defined by the crowd as "humiliation."

After this first wave of spontaneous, grassroots videos, the footage filmed by unknown protesters throughout 2011 has often emphasized these two recurring elements: the (re)establishment of the visibility of the crowd, in combination with a different, defiant idea of "Syrianness." A protest pattern can be clearly identified in the Syrian uprising: the simultaneous surfacing of a network of sporadic and loosely connected demonstrations,[7] at first exclusively on Fridays, and later spread throughout the entire week. Unlike the Egyptian uprising, in which Tahrir Square served as a centralized and monumental protest and filming hub, in Syria's heavily surveilled public space protesters had to reinvent the time and space of the political protest, at the same time as finding new ways of documenting it. The new formats of the *muzahara tayara*—a flash demonstration starting unexpectedly and lasting only a few minutes—and of the *i'tisam manzili*—a home sit-in organized mostly by women fearing the danger of being in the streets—are innovative responses to the violent repression perpetrated by the Syrian armed forces and secret services since March 2011. The act of filming takes center stage in forging these emerging practices on the aesthetic level, as it shapes a visual culture of dissent which is peculiar to Syria, establishing its own sort of grammar, creating its own tropes, formats, and genres for documenting political activism. More importantly, it operates at a political, symbolic level by creating a "virtually augmented space of contention" (Hamadeh 2016, 18) that extends much further the tiny alley where the flash mob happens, or the secret home in which the sit-in is held; once uploaded and injected into the realms of web 2.0, in fact, the filmed material finds a new online life—an *onlife*—as it circulates and is recirculated by thousands of unknown users.

22.1. Syrian video-activist Basil al-Sayed's camera (courtesy of Rami Jarrah).

The videos thus perform an operation of (re)connection at a double level. On the one hand, they reunite visually what the regime has historically worked to isolate spatially, in order to avoid the formation of a cross-cultural and interreligious solidarity across very diverse cities that would threaten the mainstream narrative on minorities in the country (also perpetuated through TV drama). Finally, in 2011, Syrians managed to talk to each other through protest videos. The chant "by our blood, by our souls we will defend you, O Daraa"[8] resonates in the footage filmed in Damascus, Baniyas, and other protest sites since the first demonstrators were killed in the southwestern city on March 18; and it reaches out to its population once the material is uploaded and circulated on the web.

Thanks to the uploaded video footage, in a spontaneous domino effect, after one city had somebody killed during a protest—its own martyr[9]—the material filmed in other parts of Syria would feature a crowd chanting "By our blood, by our souls, we will defend you," followed by the name of the martyr's city, in a sort of endless and fascinating "intertextual visuality" (Hamadeh 2016, 21) between cities that were once divided, geographically and culturally. On the other hand, once uploaded to the internet, the footage connects the Syrian space of contention with the broader networked space of the web 2.0, linking it to other spaces, people, and data, and circulating it within a much wider, transnational spatial dimension. This way, the symbolic and political function of reclaiming visibility performed by these videos vis-à-vis the Syrian ruling power meets with their communicative and informative function directed toward a more general, international public.

Together with (re)establishing the visibility of the Syrian people, at both a local and an international level, the 2011 protest videos work to affirm a different idea of "Syrianness" in stark contrast to that of the regime. The video shot in Damascus on March 15—which has become iconic as it marked the official "start" of the uprising[10]—features a small crowd of about fifty people descending on the tiny alleys of Suq al-Hamidiyya (a famous market in the Old City) and chanting "the Syrian people are one," a recurrent slogan both in later demonstrations and in the footage documenting them. "One hand" is another chant often resonating in 2011 videos, sung by crowds that progressively increase in size, by hundreds, then by thousands, sometimes managing to take control of a public square and stage a sit-in, as happened in the city of Homs.[11]

These slogans, and the way in which they are bodily performed in the protest videos, testify to the participants' desire to inject into the public space—both the physical space of the protest and the virtual space of its video documentation—an alternative idea of Syrian identity. Whereas the regime's rhetoric asserts the impossibility of Syrian religious and ethnic minorities living together in peace and stability, other than under the leadership of al-Assad's family,[12] these chants suggest that demanding a civic state and the rule of law is, in fact, a common and shared request across the Syrian cultural mosaic. At a time when the ruling power widely disseminates the words *fitna* (a Quranic expression evoking sectarian divisions) and *ta'ifiya* ("sectarianism") in the public space—from Butheina Shaaban's first speech after the uprising (al-Marashi 2011) to street billboards[13]—as a strategy to suggest that protest will lead the country into chaos and conflict, the protest videos uploaded across the country testify to a very different situation on the ground. The protesters hold the regime accountable for having generated fears and anxieties over sectarianism in order to justify the tight surveillance and the continuous abuses perpetrated by the secret police, and they respond by demanding instead the establishment of a "civic state" (*dawla madaniya* [civic state] is in fact another recurrent expression in the footage documenting the protests).

The idea of "Syrianness" emerging from the protest videos is that of a mature population wanting to live together despite the cultural and religious differences, and to do so not under authoritarian rule, but governed by the rule of law—a vision in stark contrast with the *tanwir*[14] ideology supported by the political and cultural elites. It is not by chance that *tanwir*-inspired TV drama has tried, since the outbreak of the uprising, to lampoon the idea of unity in diversity emerging from the protests. In the 2012 episode of the multi-season television series *Buq'at al-daw* (*Spotlight*), with the telling title "Id wahda" ("One Hand"), the protagonist seeks to convince his fellow citizens to act together and stay united, only to discover, on "the day of his death, that he has been totally left alone by society" (Della Ratta 2012). Several other episodes of the same TV series—widely deemed progressive and cutting-edge—also try to debunk the idea that the Syrian people are ready to live in a multicultural, multi-religious society regulated by the rule of law, as the protesters demand (Della Ratta 2012). This does not necessarily indicate the drama makers' full support for the regime, but it does signal the patronizing attitude vis-à-vis Syria's population that is widespread among the country's elites.

This scepticism toward the protest movement and, more generally, toward the capacity of Syrian society to embrace a political path leading to the establishment of a civic state is not, however, shared by the entire drama-maker community. The videos Fadwa Suleiman recorded from her hiding place during the peak of demonstrations in the city of Homs, defiantly talking to the camera about the civil rights brutally stolen from Syrian citizens, stand as a striking counter-narrative to that of the political and cultural elites; even more so as the actress belongs to the Alawite community, the same religious minority as the al-Assad family. In stark opposition to the idea of a society deemed backward and not ready for political reform, such protest videos finally conquer a physical and immaterial space of dissent. For the first time in Syria's history, they manage to inject into the public space a portrayal of society that is radically different from regime-sanctioned elite communications. Through these videos' pixelated frames, Syrian society finally (re)gains visibility, as much as a public, markedly political space.

Filming and Killing, Dying and Filming in Contemporary Syria

Since those very first grassroots videos, spontaneously surfacing from the February 2011 protest in a Damascus market, a smartphone protest culture has taken over in Syria. Protesting and filming, filming and protesting, have become dramatically intertwined activities, mutually influencing each other. A "new protest culture has developed . . . through images and sounds" (Boëx 2013),[15] as image-making in Syria has finally found an opportunity to flourish in the realm of politics in the guise of a collective life activity accessible on a mass scale.

Once the project to keep technology in the "safe hands" of the upper middle class had fallen apart, and the "quintessentially social world"[16] of commodified urban experiences imagined by regime-backed spin doctors had collapsed, the activity of filming—completed by networked processes of uploading and sharing—lost its elitist nature as an art separated from life, and eventually turned into an ordinary matter of the everyday. In his seminal manifesto "For an Imperfect Cinema,"[17] Cuban filmmaker Julio Garcia Espinosa defines this process of life reappropriating art as the latter's disappearing "into everything" (Espinosa 1979). "Cultivated art," as Espinosa calls it, traditionally referred to an individually centered, unique occupation, directed toward self-fulfilment and carried out as labor, unlike "popular art," which was just an activity among other life activities, where the line between "creators" and "spectators" remained blurred. In a perspective on art understood as a continuous life activity, cinema also has to transform itself, and become "imperfect" by virtue of the fact that it becomes "committed":[18] no longer preoccupied by the aesthetic qualities of images, its raison d'être now lies in using the latter to serve revolutionary goals.

As much as in Cuba in the 1970s, in Syria in the 2010s filming seems to have become an ordinary, ongoing life activity.

> Peaceful activists, street protesters, regime officials, torturers, armed groups, unknown citizens; everyone films and everyone is a filmmaker in contemporary Syria. All relationships—whether political, material or human; whether within Syria or between Syria and the outside world—have been shaped and processed by images and through images. Filming literally disappeared into everything, as Espinosa envisioned." (Della Ratta 2017, 114)

This *everydayness* of filming is powerfully rendered by Oussama Mohammad's[19] *Silvered Water: Syria's Self-Portrait* (*Ma' al-fidda*, 2014),[20] co-directed with Wiam Simav Bedirxan, in collaboration with "1001 Syrians," as the credits acknowledge, paying tribute to the thousands of unknown filmmakers whose anonymous YouTube uploads appear in the film. "It is Syria filming herself" (Badt 2014), Mohammed declared, underlining the Syrians' compulsive practice of video recording every routine action in a time of war, from the brutal torture inflicted inside the prisons, to protesters running away and filming, filming and running away, during street demonstrations that quickly resulted in bloodshed.

Yet, far from removing the aesthetic from the everydayness of filming, or ascribing the latter's potential to the realm of the political and the revolutionary—as Espinosa does—throughout *Silvered Water* Mohammed's voice-over is haunted by the cinematic language powerfully yet unconsciously emerging from those anonymous shots abruptly taken from the flow of life. Only after watching—and making us watch, as powerless spectators—thousands of anonymous frames rescued from YouTube does the director finally realize that the *murderer* and *murdered* make two very different cinemas.

> Only those who commit a crime, in fact, have the time to look for the most spectacular angle, fix the camera, and finally render their violence into an aesthetic performance that can be reproduced and re-enacted for the sake of the camera-eye. The protester, the tortured, the victim, must run away in an attempt to escape death; their cameras are shaky, their images blurry. It's the "cinema of the murdered" versus the "cinema of the murderer"—ultimately, the luxury of a static shot belongs to those who perform violence, not to those who risk their lives to document it. (Della Ratta 2017, 115)

In post-2011 Syria, the image has dramatically taken center stage in the execution of violence as well as in its denunciation. On the one hand, the gaze of the perpetrators—like those who mercilessly torture a young kid in the opening sequences of *Silvered Water*—is complacent: their "on-screen boasting" reflects "their cinematic fantasies to dramatize their roles in the killings" (ten Brink and Oppenheimer 2012, 9–10).[21] As a Syrian filmmaker who was jailed in the first phase of the uprising has remarked: "They dress up to torture, as for a day of feast; they are brutal and have no mercy on you, but some of them, after their shift is over, come to see you, as if nothing had happened. They look completely different."[22] This performance-like aspect of torturing aesthetically translates into sophisticatedly filmed static shots in which the camera surgically records the execution of the violence, step by step. The static shot, or "caught on tape" form, as film studies scholar Catherine Zimmer notes, is a common aesthetic trait both of the early cinema and of contemporary surveillance cameras (Zimmer 2015, 8). It lies at the "intersection of spectacle and surveillance" (Zimmer 2015, 15), in between the amazement caused by the first public projections of the Lumiéres' *Arrival of the Train at La Ciotat* (L'arrivée d'un train en gare de La Ciotat, 1895),[23] and the anxiety of being constantly followed and watched that surveillance cameras, so dramatically familiar to contemporary global cities, generate. The mix of spectacle and surveillance aesthetically conveyed by the "caught on tape" shot embodies the quintessential visual mode of "a decade politically and culturally saturated by the 'war on terror'" (Zimmer 2015, 53). Terror is the politics behind the static shot;[24] vice versa, the latter aesthetically transposes the logic, rhetorics, and tactics that, since 2001, have occupied a key place "in the world's political reality, not to mention its imaginary" (Zimmer 2015, 32)—an imaginary that, thanks to mass media and networked communications technologies, has circulated globally, thus normalizing and standardizing the imagination and the performance of violence worldwide.[25]

On the other hand, the protester also films. He/she does so in an unprecedented way, performing several roles at the same time: the role of the victim and that of the hero, as he/she is able to move the camera away from the crowds demonstrating on the streets and turn it toward himself/herself, filming his/her own death. *He shoots while being shot at,*[26] producing blurred, shaky, pixelated images that are the stylistic trait of the condition of emergency in which they were generated.[27]

22.2. Syrian video activist Bassel Safadi with his camera (picture by Kristina Alexanderson, licensed under Creative Commons CC BY 2.0).

As Jon Rich has poetically put it, "the protester in Syria is simultaneously a victim of bare repression and a historian . . . who writes history with his own blood" (Rich 2011). This (re)gained agency, even at the time of his own death, is probably the most significant achievement of the Syrian protester; finally, nobody is entitled to speak for him, "neither the Syrian regime nor the western reporter/spectator," because he has succeeded in "appropriating the double enunciation as victim and historian" (Hamadeh 2016, 26). The "three-dimensional presence" of embodying at once the victim, the narrator, and the spectator constitutes, as Hamadeh observes, a "complex layering of viewing perspectives" that stands in stark contrast and blunt opposition to the oversimplified "monocular voyeuristic view" (Hamadeh 2016, 27). Perhaps this constitutes the tragedy of the Syrian image: because it (re)acquires its own agency and takes control of self-narration even when death is at stake, it "confronts the spectator with the impossibility of being Syrian" (Rich 2011), whether victim or killer, let alone the videographer who is simultaneously the viewer of the narrated events. This simultaneity of performances, this "inter-changeability of positions" (Hamadeh 2016, 27) and the multilayered perspective it offers, powerfully opposes a "politics of producing and consuming death imagery, what Hannah Arendt calls a *"politics of pity"* (Hamadeh 2016, 26, my emphasis), preventing viewers from identifying with Syrians.[28]

In short, from the perspective of both the perpetrator and the victim, the camera is a weapon. For the former, it serves the spectacular goal of documenting his own performance of violence; for the latter, it captures that very performance on a film whose blurry frames will remain as a living testimony to the condition of emergency and fear in which they were produced, sometimes at the cost of the narrator's own life. One films his own death, the other films the death of others. One films with the aesthetic perfection of the static shot—"the static shot is beautiful," Oussama Mohammad tells his protester friend, before realizing that it embodies the gaze of the murderer (Della Ratta 2017, 114–15). The other creates *images in spite of all*, like the undefined, barely recognizable frames produced by the Sonderkommando in Auschwitz.

Yet, although they seem so diametrically opposed, the first-person-camera aesthetics of self-representation and that of the objectified, static, "caught on camera" shot characterizing surveillance actually converge in what Zimmer calls a culture of "compulsive documentation" (Zimmer 2015, 78). The global diffusion of consumer recording technologies—the pervasiveness of the smartphone protest culture—implies, among other things, that everything can be documented by everyone; this peer-to-peer surveillance is ubiquitous, reproducible, and accessible on a mass scale. As such, power—the state, the media, *the killer* —is no longer the only subject entitled to surveil and punish, to manage violence and render its performance in the objectified gaze of the static shot; other agencies—individuals, citizens, *the victim*—have their own ways of striking back, thanks to the pervasiveness of the amateur video gaze. Aesthetically, this convergence between self-representation and surveillance cultures signals a "mingling of explicitly subjective perspectives"—such as the blurry frames captured on the move by a camera phone—"with more traditionally 'objective,' evidentiary representational forms" (Zimmer 2015, 78)—as in the "caught on camera" genre.

This mixing of languages and perspectives is naturally encouraged by the techno-human infrastructure of the web 2.0, as the sharing and participatory cultures shaped by the latter promote the nonstop production of self-representations in order to boost an economy increasingly driven by the commodification of self-disclosed data and ubiquitous peer-to-peer surveillance (Zimmer 2015, 113). The prosperity of a social networking environment is intimately connected to the rise of compulsive documentation cultures enabled by forms of live recording and sharing, such as the smartphone, that have turned into "stand-ins for existence itself" (Zimmer 2015, 93). Real-time updating has become the other side of nonstop surveillance, which is, again, intimately related to the post-9/11 logic of terror, from the very first user-generated mobile camera shots that randomly captured the collapse of the Twin Towers (Berg 2011) to Osama Bin Laden quietly talking with an AK-47 on his back, in the most sinister static shot cinema has ever produced.

The logic of commodification and terror, of self-documentation and surveillance, smoothly captures "whatever" (Dean 2010, 61–90) content is produced in the ever-circulating stream of data supporting the economic infrastructure of networked communications technologies, thereby assimilating "what could be resistance back into an increasingly totalizing system" (Zimmer 2015, 114). In the end, even the heroic gesture of the Syrian videographer filming and narrating his own death is caught in this logic of compulsive documentation that finally nurtures profit and communicative capitalism. In the context of the latter, the exchange value of a message, "its contribution to a larger pool, flow, or circulation of content" (Dean 2009, 27), acquires more prominence than the *meaning* of the content itself. From the perspective of the circulation and reflexivity that defines the infrastructure of web 2.0 (Dean 2010), the use value of a message injected into the data stream—even that of a video documenting the cruel spectacle of the filmer's own death—does not really count, since "a contribution need not . . . be understood," but only "repeated, reproduced, forwarded" (Dean 2009, 27).

The increasingly commodified aspect of the networked environment in which Syrian acts of rebellion and defiance are injected and circulated together with "whatever" other messages requires us not only to focus on the fascinating aesthetic questions raised by the Syrian images, but also to reflect on the material and political implications of the act of filming, understood as a continuous life activity. As Tarnowski rightly points out, the dichotomy, upon which several readings of Syrian image-making are based, between "the elusive, revolutionary, low-res image and the commoditized, compromised, high-res image" (Tarnowski 2017) does not account for the complexity of the situation in which those images were produced. Not only can several subjects—such as the market, the state, international NGOs, and foreign journalists, appropriate, make, and remake the blurry, pixelated revolutionary aesthetics, using them to serve their goals and agendas;[29] the pixelated images can also be the result of a supply and demand process even when generated by anonymous citizens and videographers, uploaded and shared free of charge on social networking platforms.

The Syrian documentary *Jellyfish* (*Qandil al-bahr*, 2015)[30] sheds light on the heavy commodification of citizen-generated content that was once deemed innocent, by showing the extent to which amateur protester-videographers got caught up in a commissioning process where several subjects, from international NGOs to the armed forces, from media outlets to medical associations, all requested tailor-made videos to serve their purposes and agendas. Tarnowski (2017) refers to a similar process when remarking that a U.K.-founded organization helped create a centralized media office for the Free Syrian Army, whose job was to commission and package user-generated videos for their YouTube page.

Just as much as the seemingly objective "caught on camera" shot, the pixelated, low-fi image can no longer be deemed innocent. Its charming aesthetics, its poetic value, the sense of emotional proximity it renders, so close to the *being there* of its filmer, might distract from the exceptional material conditions in which it was generated, diverting attention from the power struggles it conceals, and of which it is a result. These seemingly innocent blurry clips are "commodity images, active in the economy of war, and contributing directly to it" (Tarnowski 2017). Finally, the everydayness of filming in Syria seems to have resulted in its inevitable hyper-commodification. Part of the catastrophe of Syria's imperfect cinema is that it no longer serves the revolutionary goal, as Espinosa and the original amateur videographers had wished, but rather other, more opaque and still to be unveiled projects.

References

al-Assad, Bashar. 2011. "Speech at Syrian People's Assembly." Voltaire Network. voltairenet.org.

Austin, Jonathan. 2016. "Torture and the Material-Semiotic Networks of Violence Across Borders." *International Political Sociology* 10, no. 1: 3–21.

———. 2017. "We Have Never Been Civilised: Torture and the Materiality of World Political Binaries." *European Journal of International Relations* 23, no. 1: 49–73.

Badt, Karin. 2014. "Filming Killing: *Silvered Water, Syria Self-Portrait* by Oussama Mohammad and Wiam Simav Bedirxan." Huffington Post. huffingtonpost.com.

Berg, Alex. 2011. "9/11 Attacks Seen by First-Person Footage." The Daily Beast. thedailybeast.com.

Boëx, Cécile. 2013. "La grammaire iconographique de la révolte en Syrie: Usages, techniques et supports." *Cultures & Conflicts* 91/92: 65–80. journals.openedition.org.

Boëx, Cécile. 2014. *Cinéma et politique en Syrie: Écritures cinémato-graphiques de la contestation en régime autoritaire (1970–2010)*. Paris: L'Harmattan.

Dean, Jodi. 2009. *Democracy and Other Neoliberal Fantasies: Communicative Capitalism and Left Politics*. Durham, NC: Duke University Press.

———. 2010. *Blog Theory: Feedback and Capture in the Circuits of Drive*. Cambridge: Polity Press.

Della Ratta, Donatella. 2012. "Syrian TV Drama Provides Ineffective Release Valve." Al Jazeera. aljazeera.com.

———. 2017. "The Unbearable Lightness of the Image: Unfinished Thoughts on Filming in Contemporary Syria." *Middle East Journal of Culture and Communication* 10, no. 2–3: 109–32.

———. 2018. *Shooting a Revolution: Visual Media and Warfare in Syria*. London: Pluto Press.

Didi-Huberman, George. 2008. *Images in Spite of All: Four Photographs from Auschwitz*. Chicago and London: University of Chicago Press.

Donati, Caroline. 2009. *L'exception syrienne: Entre modernisation et résistance*. Paris: La Découverte.

Elias, Chadi, and Zaheer Omareen. 2014. "Syria's Imperfect Cinema." In *Syria Speaks: Art and Culture from the Frontline*, edited by M. Halasa, Z. Omareen, and N. Mafhoud, 257–68. London: Saqi Books.

Espinosa, Julio Garcia. 1979. "For an Imperfect Cinema." *JumpCut* 20: 24–26. ejumpcut.org.

Hamadeh, Dima. 2016. *Syrians Revolting Against Immortality: The Politics of Filming One's Own Death*. MA thesis, University of Amsterdam.

Khatib, Lina. 2012. *Image Politics in the Middle East: The Role of the Visual in Political Struggle*. London: I.B. Tauris.

Leenders, Reinoud. 2013. "Social Movement Theory and the Onset of the Popular Uprising in Syria." *Arab Studies Quarterly* 35, no. 3: 273–89.

al-Marashi, Ibrahim. 2011. "The Strange Logic Behind Syria's Culture of Conspiracy." *The National*. pressreader.com.

Omareen, Zaher. 2014. "A Bedtime Story for Eid." Words without Borders. wordswithoutborders.org.

Ranciére, Jacques. 2013. *The Politics of Aesthetics*. London: Bloomsbury.

Rich, Jon. 2011. "The Blood of the Victim: Revolution in Syria and the Birth of the Image-event." e-flux 26. e-flux.com.

Snowdon, Peter. 2016. *The Revolution Will Be Uploaded: Vernacular Video and Documentary Film Practice After the Arab Spring*. PhD diss., University of Hasselt.

Tarnowski, Stefan. 2017. "What Have We Been Watching? What Have We Been Watching?" Bidayyat. bidayyat.org.

ten Brink, Joram, and Joshua Oppenheimer, eds. 2012. *Killer Images: Documentary Film, Memory and the Performance of Violence*. London and New York: Wallflower Press.

Wedeen, Lisa. 1999. *Ambiguities of Domination: Politics, Rhetoric, and Symbols in Contemporary Syria*. Chicago: University of Chicago Press.

Zimmer, Catherine. 2015. *Surveillance Cinema*. New York: New York University Press.

23

JEAN CHAMOUN AND LEBANON'S
SUSPENDED HISTORY

Hady Zaccak

The New Lebanese Cinema

On August 9, 2017, Lebanese cinema lost one of its icons, who was deeply committed to documentary cinema and to the fight for greater rights and freedoms—Jean Chamoun.*

Chamoun belongs to a generation of filmmakers to emerge at the beginning of the Lebanese civil war in 1975. This generation—including Borhane Alaouié, Maroun Baghdadi, Jocelyne Saab, Randa Chahal, and others—made cardinal changes in Lebanese cinema. Most of them studied in France or Belgium and returned to Lebanon to make their films. They were known for their political orientation, their commitment to the Palestinian cause, and close ties with the Lebanese national movement—which was hoping to bring about a secular rather than sectarian state. Their first films were produced during an era of change in the Arab world, amid the emergence of revolutionary movements, when discussions about alternative Arab cinema—a cinema with political and social awareness that is committed to societies' problems and questions—had just begun.

With the beginning of the civil war, documentary ceased to serve merely touristic or institutional purposes, and became more cinematic, seeking to reveal the complexities of reality—sectarianism, the situation in the Palestinian camps and south Lebanon, class differences, the eruption of Lebanese unity, the destruction of Beirut, and the daily suffering of the people.

The Lebanese cinema of the 1950s, and more particularly the 1960s, was dominated by a drive for entertainment that lacked identity. This changed with the advent of the civil war, with films reaching beyond the news and folklore to attempt to approach the people and make sense of the reasons for the war.

---

* translated by Najat Abdulhaq

373

This is the context in which Chamoun (born in the Beqaa, 1944) returned to Lebanon in 1974, on the eve of the civil war, after completing his studies between Beirut and Paris. In 1976, he directed the documentary film *Tel al-Zaatar* in cooperation with Mustafa Abu Ali and Pino Adriano, about the Palestinian refugee camp Tel al-Zaatar, which surrendered on August 12, 1976, after a long and hard siege by the right-wing Christian militias.

Commitment to the Palestinian Cause

Since the early seventies, the Palestinian Cinema Institute in Beirut (Mu'asasat al-Sinima al-Filastiniya) was actively producing documentary films about the Palestinian cause, the ongoing struggle, and the situation in the camps. These films were directed by Palestinian filmmakers like Mustafa Abu Ali—who was head of the institute between 1971 and 1980, and one of the founders of revolutionary Palestinian cinema—and other Arab filmmakers like the Iraqi Qasim Hawal and the Lebanese Jean Chamoun. The cooperation between Lebanese and Palestinian filmmakers culminated in *Tel al-Zaatar*, which was a collaboration between Mustafa Abu Ali and Jean Chamoun, coproduced by the Palestinian Cinema Institute and Unitel Film.

Tel al-Zaatar depends on witness accounts from citizens, fighters, political figures, soldiers, and physicians, who were in the camp during the fights that took place between June 17 and August 12, 1976. The interviews are inserted between scenes from inside the camp, which was established in 1950 and inhabited mainly by Palestinians forced to leave Palestine following the Nakba in 1948. They were joined by numerous poor Lebanese citizens from the south who worked in the factories near the camp. The siege of the camp started in April 1975 after the bus incident in Ain El Remmaneh, which killed a number of Palestinians, all of whom were residents of Tel al-Zaatar. The intervention of the Syrian army in Lebanon in 1976—eventually giving the green light to the right-wing militias— contributed to the elimination of the camp from Christian territory. The eastern area "was to be cleaned," according to the terminology that was used back then, from all strongholds of armed enemy—the Karantina area was first, followed by the Ras al-Naba'a, Dbayeh, and Jisr al-Basha camps, and ending with Tel al-Zaatar.

The film *Tel al-Zaatar* is a product of that moment and the feelings of the massacre survivors: the perspectives of those who witnessed the horrible elimination of men, the raping of women, various methods of torture, and mass death. Needless to add that these massacres—the embodiment of hatred in the extermination of the other—dominated the War of the Two Years (1975–76), starting with the Black Saturday, Karantina, Ras al-Naba'a, and Damour massacres, and didn't differentiate between Lebanese or

Palestinian, nor between Christian or Muslim. In that moment, as is made clear by the voice of the commentator and the interviews, the wider context of the war was not apparent to the observer. This was a war in which the Palestinian resistance and the Lebanese national movement were unified against the "isolationist forces"—as the Lebanese right-wing Christian militias were called then—as well as a mixture of coalitions who intervened based on political interests, Syria and Israel in particular. Jean Chamoun holds his microphone and interviews people with clear sympathy, as he did in all his subsequent films. There are bodies scattered on the ground, preparing us to see even more of them in *Under the Rubble* (*Taht al-anqad*, 1983). A beautiful woman arrives with armed men to look at the bodies, as if she is visiting a museum of heroism; children carry weapons, and we later witness their alteration throughout the course of the war in *Beirut, a War Generation* (*Beirut, jil al-harb*, 1989). Such films come to bear witness to key moments and become documents that may serve as a source of historical research, a history that is difficult if not impossible to write officially. In fact, modern Lebanese history in school curricula stops by the end of the French mandate in 1943 and the departure of foreign troops in 1946. Thus, the documentary films by Chamoun's generation, and those that followed, may be considered a chapter of a history book that goes beyond mere descriptiveness, deploying audio and visual elements to prompt necessary dialogue and a closer analysis of events. This is not to say that we should ignore the context in which the films were produced, by whom they were produced, and the biases of their directors.

Not only do Chamoun's films help to address official amnesia, he is one of the few among his generation who stayed in Lebanon during the war; thus he was able to cover the various phases of Lebanese contemporary history from the 1970s until 2009. *Beirut, a War Generation* (1989) is an important film in this respect, as it is the last filmed documentary during the war, while *Suspended Dreams* (*Ahlam mu'alaqa*, 1992) marks the beginning of the new postwar and hesitant peace era.

Tel al-Zaatar was followed by the short film *Hymn for Liberty* (*Nashid al-huriyya*, 1978), which was also produced by the Palestinian Cinema Institute in the same frame of commitment toward the Palestinian cause and the revolutionary movements. It was screened at the 11th World Festival of Youth and Students, held in Cuba in the summer of 1978. The festival's theme was "Solidarity Against Imperialism for Freedom and Friendship," with participating delegations from Palestine (represented by Yassir Arafat) and Lebanon. *Hymn for Liberty* includes archival segments of the revolutionary movements in Africa, Latin America, the Arab world, and Iran, and shows how the CIA interfered to eliminate several symbolic figures of these revolutions, like Ernesto Ché Guevara and Salvador Allende. The revolutionary songs in the film are loud, and evocative of a revolutionary momentum that seems so far away, especially in the Arab world, where we moved from the leftist and secular context to a more religious perspective, and have been trapped in civil wars for decades.

After *Hymn for Liberty* and the Israeli invasion of Lebanon in 1982 came a new era of Lebanese documentary films, marked with the clear signature of Palestinian filmmaker Mai Masri, who married Jean Chamoun in 1986, commencing a journey in film together that would span three decades and a number of wars. The cooperation between Chamoun and Masri ensured that the complexity of the Lebanese–Palestinian relationship was depicted in their work, beginning with the emergence of the Palestinian resistance after the 1967 defeat, and the start of Palestinian military operations in south Lebanon, followed by the Cairo Agreement in 1969—when operations had to be coordinated with the Lebanese state—up until the Lebanese civil war in 1975, in which the Palestinians were major players. Chamoun and Masri carried their shared experiences of war, imprisonment, and displacement into these films. In practical terms, they complemented each other and shared production tasks. When Chamoun was author and director, Masri would take on production. Masri contributed a particular sensitivity to *Wild Flowers: Women of South Lebanon* (*Zahrat al-qandul*, 1985) and *Beirut, a War Generation* (*Beirut, jil al-harb*, 1989) that is not perhaps as visible in some of her subsequent works. She edited *Under the Rubble* (1983) and *Wild Flowers*, as well as *Beirut, a War Generation*, and recorded the sound for *Under the Rubble* with Chamoun.

The Cinema of Jean Chamoun and Mai Masri

The significance of shooting in 16mm, as the couple did in the 1980s, lies in the depiction of a reality different from what may be achieved by the pale video format. Their cinematic quality sets these films apart from those that followed, where at times an investigative reportage style dominated—zooming in on and directly illuminating protagonists, quick discontinuous editing instead of long takes that preserve the spatial and temporal unity of a scene.

Female characters take on cardinal roles in the Chamoun–Masri films, starting with *Wild Flowers*, as they discuss various forms of resistance— from humanitarian work to military activity and social and cultural aspects. Women are shown resisting the occupier amid sexual discrimination and the limited perspectives of traditional society. The female protagonists play a very important role as mediators, introducing the themes of the films, and with each film we empathize with them more. The close relationships built between Chamoun and these protagonists shows the trust they had in him. As Masri recalls: "Jean Chamoun has a character that people loved. We as a couple helped to build this trust with the people."[1]

In fact, with his last two films, Chamoun created sequels to his former works, introducing some of the same characters again. Thus, *Longing for the Laurel* (*Hanin al-ghurdil*, 2008) represents the second part of *Wild Flowers*, while *Lanterns of Memory* (*Masabih al-dhazira*, 2009) is a continuation of *Suspended Dreams*.

Generally, Chamoun's films may be divided into two categories. First, there are the films that document the reality of the city between war and peace, showing the ongoing traces of the war, as in *Under the Rubble* and *Suspended Dreams*. Second, there are films on resisting and the combatant south, reflecting the reality of the occupation in southern Lebanese society. These films document the main phases of the political struggle with Israel, the invasion of 1982, the withdrawal in 1985 until the aggression in 1993, the liberation in 2000, and the war in 2006. Here the protagonists (all of them women) are mixed, Lebanese and Palestinian, and depict different ways of resisting the occupation.

Under the Rubble

Under the Rubble (1983), jointly directed with Mai Masri, is an important documentation of the Israeli invasion of Lebanon, particularly Beirut in 1982. From the beginning of the film, the voice of commentator and director Jean Chamoun is heard for around forty minutes. The text was written by author and theater director Roger Assaf. *Under the Rubble* documents the suffering of the people and their ongoing displacement from Tel al-Zaatar, Ras al-Naba'a, Chyah, and the villages in south Lebanon. Each chapter of the war forced people to move from one place and camp to another. The year 1982 was a tragic year of Israeli airstrikes, involving the use of internationally prohibited bombs and the massive devastation of West Beirut. The number of victims is scary: twelve thousand children, nine thousand women, and eight thousand men. In West Beirut the victims were Palestinian and Lebanese, poor and rich, who were forced to watch their city being destroyed under siege and held together in solidarity by huge resistance. Beirut became "the last bastion of Arab dignity." *Under the Rubble* captures this threat of complete annihilation. An eight-storey building disappears after being shelled by an Israeli fuel-air bomb while 137 people were in the building; a French resident of Beirut shouts, "It's a war against the dead," as she wanders in a graveyard destroyed by tanks; and the film ends with silent images of Sabra and Shatila victims. These "traces" of history, all these bodies under ruins, had to be filmed and documented, but what about those who watch these images? How should they deal with this kind of material?

Chamoun speaks of the film as a book documenting images of the living and the dead: "In south Lebanon, images accumulate and seek a history book to hold them,"[2] he says, mentioning also the difficulty of filming such moments, and of feeling paralyzed while doing so.

In recent years, audiences have become more used to seeing such images in the news, especially from the Arab region, but the significance of *Under the Rubble* is that it documents the momentum of reality, and shows the destruction of humanity and its effects, leading to substantial changes in society, which Chamoun addresses in his subsequent films.

Beirut, a War Generation

Beirut, a War Generation, co-directed with Masri, is one of the cardinal films made at a time in which the number of Lebanese documentary films was decreasing. This is another historical documentation of the damage inflicted on subsequent generations by war, its uselessness, and the bankruptcy of political actions that turned war into a game played by adults and children alike.

The film commences in 1988 at al-Mathaf checkpoint on the border between East and West Beirut. Children are shown imitating the militia by making checkpoints and carrying arms. We get to know a group of them (a car mechanic and a street trader) who were forced to start work early, and through their stories we learn about the harsh realities of life in a city that is dominated by arms. One of the most memorable moments in the film is a scene in Saroula Cinema in al-Hamra Street, where one of the children is watching an American action film and the audience gets excited about it. The children later reenact the film, role-playing the scenes they relate to. The story then moves on to a teenaged Christian militia fighter with the Lebanese Forces (Forces Libanaises, known as FL), who uses his gun as a toy. The list of enemies is long: Palestinians, Shia, Druze, Socialists, and Kurds. The young militant is ready to eliminate them all if they attempt to enter the east side of the city, but he assures viewers that he believes in God and in the protection of Saint Elias, whose image is tattooed on his breast, and the peace sign on his arm. Things become even more absurd and darker when the youngsters share a joint at the cease-fire line, and others swim in the garbage at the Normandy beach area. In the end, there is no difference in the degree of poverty for any of those living in Shatila or any of the other camps, whether Palestinian or Lebanese. Then come those who grew up during the war and were armed, seeking to fulfill their dreams of changing the system and as a reaction to economic and social realities. They cheered when the Saint George and Holiday Inn hotels were ablaze during the "hotel battle" (1975–76). But what is left of those dreams, and what changed in reality?

After thirteen years of war, it seems that the damage is all-embracing, particularly the psychological damage, and nobody knows when and how the war will end. The film closes at the cease-fire line between the two sides of the city, where we follow a conversation on the front lines between enemies—a conversation that evolves beyond dialogue to gunfire. Jean Chamoun told me they waited four days to capture this conversation, and during an exchange of gunfire a microphone was shot. The film shows a city that is trying to catch its breath, but is a graveyard of dreams, leading us directly to Chamoun's other titles, such as *Suspended Dreams* and *In the Shadows of the City* (*Tayf al-madina*, 2000).

Suspended Dreams and Lanterns of Memory

It is a good idea to watch *Suspended Dreams* directly after *Beirut, a War Generation*. We have seen how the latter ends with a heated conversation at the front lines. *Suspended Dreams* begins with the meeting of Nabil (the Muslim fighter) and Rambo (the Christian fighter), who become friends and set about restoring demolished houses as if they are miniature images of the country. Yet the picture is not this idyllic, as we see through the female protagonist Wedad Halawani, whose husband was kidnapped in 1982 and never returned. By the time she became head of the committee of kidnapped and missing persons, the number of the forcibly disappeared was estimated to be seventeen thousand.

Halawani returns to her home in Ras al-Naba'a, which was destroyed during the war. Nabil, who is carrying out the restoration, says to her: "I destroyed my country and now I am restoring it." But is the rebuilding of stones enough? What about those who were kidnapped and who are still missing? Will there be a general amnesty? Will the warlords be held to account?

It seems to me that these questions are accompanied by persistent fears that the peace era is a mere cease-fire, while the country is still contaminated by its bloody history, just like its beaches, which were turned into garbage dumps during the war. The image of a future Beirut is closer to advertisements than to the stark realities of the city. It is completely different from that of the ruined theater in which the actor Rafik Ali Ahmed is walking around, where the seats look like the corpses of all those who fell during the war. *Suspended Dreams* tackles the questions and fears experienced in Lebanon at the time, many of which are still felt.

This is what motivated Chamoun to represent the characters of the film again in 2008–2009, in *Lanterns of Memory*, which starts with the return of Samir al-Quntar and his comrades from Israeli prisons after years of detention. During the official ceremony for their arrival at Beirut airport on July 16, 2008, Wedad Halawani also made a reappearance. She confronted the country's leaders, most of whom were warlords, about the fate of those who were kidnapped or disappeared during the war. The only one who came close to a response was the minister of internal affairs, the then young lawyer and activist Ziad Baroud, who represented a minority of civil society outside the traditional set of politicians.

Even though *Lanterns of Memory* gets off to a strong start, it is dominated by a more television-type style that reduces its imagery to mere illustrations, and obstructs the drama with its use of music and lighting. Remarkable characters like Wedad, Nabil, and Rambo lose impact in this film, in comparison to *Suspended Dreams*. Having said this, it is a continuation of Chamoun's attempt to collect and portray traces of war.

The Combatant and Resistant South
Wild Flowers and Longing for the Laurel

In *Wild Flowers*, Chamoun and Masri show the role of women in resisting the occupation. Shot after the partial Israeli withdrawal from the south in 1985, when the consequences of the Israeli invasion in 1982 were still present, the film represents another important historical document through which we come to understand the impact of the occupation, especially on the Shia community in the south. It pictures the participation of women in direct resistance, throwing stones at Israeli soldiers, carrying arms, and planting bombs. Yet it also shows, in contrast to previous films on the south, the extent to which women have turned to the veil. *Wild Flowers* seems like a window through which we watch a society involved in its entirety in resistance, where a wife is imprisoned together with her husband by the occupier. The last scene is of a flower emerging through a rock to assert the will for life, and reiterate the image of the resistant woman. Generally the film takes a humanitarian approach that departs clearly from the exploitative stance of the political parties, who seek to monopolize resistance. As we watch the portraits of martyred women from different religious sects and parties (communist and nationalist) that carried out operations against the occupation, we also follow scenes from southern villages, reminding us of the film *Ma'rakah* (Battle, 1985), directed by Roger Assaf.

As we discuss the images in this film, it is again important to remember the magic of the 16mm images (Mai Masri's signature), which makes the characters, especially at the beginning, look like those from a feature film whom we follow through their diaries. This image is clear and cinematic at a time in which video was emerging as a means of making TV reports, even suicidal attacks, like the operation of Hassan Quasir, who blew up himself and his car as an Israeli envoy was passing. The film lacks a main character, however, which means the theme is central and the protagonists become a means to an end. This approach repeats itself in Chamoun's subsequent films, which follow other women characters in the south, as in *Hostage of Time* (*Rahinat al-intizar*, 1994), *Women Beyond Borders* (*Ard al-nisa'*, 2004), and *Longing for the Laurel* (2008). In the latter, we again meet Khadija, the heroine of *Wild Flowers*, after more than twenty years, following a new war with Israel in 2006. Khadija loses her son during the war, a member of Hezbollah who was following the path of resistance taken by his parents. This is another example of how Chamoun keeps following his characters over the years. He met Khadija in the eighties, when she married Ahmad, and featured her in *Wild Flowers*; then he maintained contact with her.

In *Longing for the Laurel*, we see how the Shia community became more organized during the war with Israel, building its own institutions. We also follow other female artists like Susan Ghazawi, who lost her house and her paintings during the Israeli strikes on Beirut's southern suburb. The scene in which the corpses of her paintings are excavated from the ruins is one of the most remarkable moments in the film. Ghazawi's husband picks up a painting he made of his grandmother, who was killed, torn apart by the Israeli invasion in 1978. She then had her painting destroyed and "torn apart" in 2006, just like the destruction of the museum which kept the memory of occupation and torture at the al-Khiam detention camp in the south. There is also Khairat Alzein, another artist who exhibited her colorful paintings among the ruins of Beirut's southern suburb, emphasizing the ongoing march of life. Traces vanish, but these films are witnesses and remain important documents of memorialization.

Hostage of Time

After *Wild Flowers* we go back to the Lebanese south with *Hostage of Time* (executive producer Mai Masri, 1994); thus the cinema of war has not ended, as Israeli operations continue in the south, with the then most recent attack in 1993, the consequences of which are seen in this film. We follow Layla, a physician who looks after the health of women. Through her diaries, we witness the role of the resistance movement and engage with the model of the "Islamic revolution" in Iran, personified by Hezbollah (through the character of Layla's fundamentalist brother). In contrast, Layla herself is a secular, unveiled physician, who educates other women on matters of life and sexuality. She represents a society that is resisting the occupation and political Islam with all means possible.

Women Beyond Borders

With *Women's Land* (executive producer Mai Masri, 2004), we continue to follow the path of women of the resistance through the struggle of the Palestinian Kifah 'Afifi, who was detained in al-Khiam prison for six years. Through 'Afifi we get to know other women of the Palestinian resistance who shared her fate in prison. Soha Beshara is one of them, providing important documentation of the joint Lebanese–Palestinian resistance, and shedding light on Chamoun and Masri's relationship, which marks their films. In the last scene of the film, we see 'Afifi with her husband, who was also arrested. They have a staged conversation for the camera, which ends with 'Afifi looking into the lens and asking if the shoot is done. This final look and smile highlight the crossover between filming reality spontaneously with a hidden camera, and filming reenactments where the protagonists are transformed into actors.

'Afifi shows up again in *Longing for the Laurel*, where, after the 2006 war, she visits the ruins of al-Khiam prison where she was detained, and where the images of *Women Beyond Borders* were filmed. The Israelis, for the second time, had eliminated all traces of the prison. But the spirit of victory dominates in this film, as the resistance is ongoing.

Chamoun and *In the Shadows of the City*

Chamoun's documentary heritage is clear in his only fiction film, *In the Shadows of the City* (2000). This film covers three decades of Lebanese history by following the story of a family that found refuge in Beirut in 1974. It bears witness to the preparations for war, its outbreak, the Israeli invasion in 1982, and the postwar era, in which the militia leaders took over the reconstruction of the city and dominated the economy. This essence was crystallized in the archival snapshots Chamoun uses: the waves of displacement, the Israeli airstrikes, and the destruction that is seen in previous documentary films. Some of the film's characters are already known from his documentaries, even though they are played here by actors: for example, the role of Siham, played by Christine Choueiri, is inspired by Wedad Halawani, the hero of *Suspended Dreams*, who leads the Committee of the Families of the Kidnapped and Disappeared during the Civil War. It is a striking decision to place Halawani together with Siham, putting real and fictional figures side by side in a demonstration that Siham organizes to demand more information about the fate of the disappeared. The exchanges of cursing at Beirut's cease-fire line are also familiar from the documentary *Beirut, a War Generation*.

Transforming this kind of documentary heritage into fiction using more stylized camera shots and lighting, and casting actors in roles, somehow simplifies the story of war and condenses its different phases. As Chamoun told me, he was not aiming to chronicle the war in *In the Shadows of the City*. Though this approach loses some of the multifaceted details of the conflict and the spontaneity of the moment, it is constructed and reconstructed with Chamoun's careful commitment to humanity, daily life and problems, and his own ambitions and resistance. It respects the concept of cinema that Chamoun holds to, as having a role in developing society. "Our role is to help the human; otherwise what else is the artist's responsibility?"

Chamoun's works cover four decades of modern Lebanese history and its wars, making war cinema a continuous process that interacts with the present and the sedimentations of the past, and continues to do so, even though Chamoun himself has passed away. Thus, after Maroun Baghdadi, Randa Chahal, and more recently Jocelyne Saab and Borhane Alaouié, another representative of this generation has left us, a generation that laid the foundation of the Lebanese experiment in documentary film, which goes on witnessing our suspended history.

24

PAPER AIRPLANES: AN INTERVIEW WITH AKRAM ZAATARI

Dore Bowen

24.1. *Letter to a Refusing Pilot,* Venice Biennale Installation (2013), by Akram Zaatari.

Letters and Photographs

Dore Bowen: As a founder of the Arab Image Foundation, and as an artist who interrogates images, letters, video, and films, you've thought about documents from numerous angles.[1] Frequently, in your work, the photograph is paired with the letter. The two have many similarities. Like letters, photographic negatives are generally printed on paper, and the print has defined the medium until recently, when digital photography replaced analog photography.

The letter and photograph are contrasted in your 1997 video *All Is Well on the Border (al-Sharit bi-khayr)*. For example, the letters written from Nabih Awada (under the name of Neruda) to his family, and narrated in the film, say everything and nothing about his experience in prison. The photographs taken in the prison were attached to the letters sent home. Presumably the photograph provided a different kind of testimony, contrasting with Awada's flowery letters.

What does the photograph provide that the letter doesn't? And conversely, what does the letter provide that the photograph doesn't? When the two are attached, does the photograph supplement the letter or threaten to replace it with its visual detail? Can you explain how you intermingle or contrast the letter and photograph?

Akram Zaatari: In its primary function, the letter is an address intended from a person or a group to another, and thus intended as a form of communication. A photograph is at first a description. In its primary function, it invites the viewer to look at it, and because of that agency can be used for documentation, for archiving, for copying, and can be turned into a tool for communication. Many families in the nineteenth and early twentieth centuries went to photographers to have their portraits made, and then sent them to relatives abroad, as a sign of affection, maybe, but also as a simple way of communicating how they were. Portraits functioned in so many different ways and sometimes accompanied letters. For example, in 1993, after a series of hunger strikes, Arab political prisoners in Israel were granted many of their requests, including the right to be photographed once every six months. Since then, more than ten thousand prisoners in Israel have been allowed to exchange pictures with their families and with other prisoners. I gained access to the entire collection of Nabih Awada's materials, which consists of portraits of his fellow inmates, and Palestinian, Syrian, and Lebanese prisoners detained in Israel for security-related matters. Photographs accompanied letters or carried dedications on the back. The pictures and accompanying letters were sent in and out of prison through the Red Cross, but were checked by the prison authorities. The letters were supposed to include only content of a strictly personal nature. This is why the text communicated very little actually beyond missing family, as opposed to pictures that, no matter how staged, carried a trace of a familiar beloved face.

Similarly, a postcard binds a line of words with an image of something or somewhere pictured on its reverse. It allows an individual to personalize a standard vista by adding a message on its back, and to send this to a friend or family member. Similarly, millions of newspapers match a current event photograph with a written headline.

The photograph and the letter are an obvious match; but it's too reductive to think of them as supplements to each other. They belong to different traditions, different practices. In their most "noble" being, both can be forms of poetry, but most of the time they are simply receipts of transactions.

DB: Today, both letters and photographs have "gone digital." I'm thinking of your collage of YouTube videos in *Dance to the End of Love* (2011). Do you find that these digital videos are part of a history of image making that began with analog photography (which much of your work investigates)? Or is it of an entirely different order?

24.2. *Dance to the End of Love*. Installation at Moderna Museet Museum, Sweden (2011), by Akram Zaatari.

AK: We still do not know how the digital archive of the future will be organized or accessed. There is a liberating aspect in the absence of a potentially sacred or speculated-over original, and there are various benefits in "the cloud" that keeps everyone's personal photographs or films and preserves access to them. But to go back to your question, people used the photographer when they did not have a camera, or when they did not want to go through the hassle of taking pictures that may or may not be successful. So they solicited this "medium," that's the photographer, to make their pictures for them. On Instagram, on Facebook and YouTube, you need no medium any more. Everything is set up for you, and with the camera on your laptop or mobile phone your videos may go viral and you can seduce the world. So *Dance to the End of Love* is about that. It is about people who are alone at home communicating with the world, trying to impress the world. I hate to call it a collage. It is an orchestration of various videos that people took of themselves—acting in front of the camera to seduce others they do not know with their voice, with their dancing, with their muscular bodies, with how they ride cars, and so on.

I find it fascinating that with the same tool that we use for writing, a computer for example, we can also take photographs, make films, and make calls. Indeed, we're back to communication—photography and writing. And the same goes with a telephone. Now all professional cameras for photography record HD or sometimes 4k resolution movies, so the boundaries between photography and cinema are gone. Film still refers to analog material, but terms like "cinema" and "movie" refer to a movement. So I prefer not to use terms like "video" and "film" any more, because they are rooted in traditions that don't reflect cinema recordings nowadays.

The work is supposed to be seen on the four walls of a room, so one never sees the whole at once, but one needs to turn around to view the screen in the back, and so forth.

Documentary Veracity

DB: A number of your works seem to present photographs and letters as expressions of the desire for freedom through fantasy, rather than a testament to historical truth. In such cases, the document carries the possibility of transcending history, religion, even geography. I sense this in the story of Mohammed Assaf—in *All Is Well on the Border*—who escapes from al-Khiam Detention Center, due in part to his having been obsessed by the 1963 film *The Great Escape*. And the idea of photographic truth is undermined in your work in yet another way. Often the narrative, or text, puts the image in question. For example, in *This Day* (*al-Yawm*, 2003), the narrator, Norma Jabbur, points out that the figures in the photographs taken for her grandfather's 1988 book on Bedouins are actually relatives trying on Bedouin costumes for the first time. Here, does the familial knowledge of the narrator undermine the photograph as a reliable document of Bedouin life? If so, is this underscored by the imagery in the video?

I'm also thinking of your interest in the staged photographs by Hashem El Madani from his studio Scheherazade, particularly the photos of kissing same-sex couples and the posed Palestinian resistance fighters. In these images what we are seeing is not a couple, or necessarily a resistance fighter, but a dream, or in the case of the same-sex couples, a prohibition on heterosexual couples kissing in the studio.

Can you explain why in *This Day* you include information that ultimately challenges the documents you present in the video? What are we to take from this? What is the value of the document in such cases in terms of truth-telling? Are we to doubt its veracity? Accept that all documents are staged and have complicated lives, like people?

AK: The "stage" is an essential element in photography, even in landscape photography. What a photographer does is "staging" at its best. Throughout my research on vernacular forms of photography, I was interested in photographs that reveal their fabrication. I was interested less in perfect, seamless photographs, and more in situations that revealed staging for the camera. I believe that one needs to construct a certain knowledge about a photograph, knowledge about its context and period, to be able to deconstruct it and reveal its fabrication. Very often it's a creative process. I'm not interested in this process as an investigation about evidence in photographs, for I do not believe this opposition of document vs. fiction could add anything to the understanding of documents. I'm simply interested in how these deconstructive elements could inform us about the photographer and the social context of a photograph.

In the nineteenth and most of the twentieth century, people dressed up to be photographed, or at least chose to be photographed when their appearance was uncommon, "out of the ordinary," or on a special occasion that doesn't occur every day. Implicit in this practice is the idea that everyday moments may be forgotten, but special moments need to figure in some photographic register. Therefore, the history that made it into the photographs from the nineteenth and most of the twentieth centuries records out-of-the-ordinary moments, which historians often rely on to represent a particular time. We look at them often as evidence of what was once there. My work simply tries to unpack that construction.

In *This Day* I travel to al-Qaryatayn in Syria to meet Jana Istfan, who was photographed by Jibrail Jabbur and Manoug in the fifties holding a jar on her head. I wanted to interview her because I was interested in the two photographers, and I was trying to reveal the playful fabrication in their photographs. I did not do that because I wanted to prove them as "fabricators." It goes without saying that photography is fabrication. I did it because the details of that fabrication are part of the missing record I was interested in. I am a historian of missing records, such as how photographers made decisions and who influenced them. This would lead me to understand more about Jibrail Jabbur and his entourage. Jabbur was born in 1900 in al-Qaryatayn. In the introduction to his book he writes about the threshold moment when he realized that the Bedouins, whom he knew and feared as a child while growing up on the edge of the desert, represented a distinguished culture that was worth studying and documenting, particularly as he saw it gradually disappearing. It's only after he studied abroad that he came to realize this. So he returned with an anthropologist's interest, along with a photographer that he brought with him from Beirut named Manoug. Jabbur's awakening is very similar to the awakening of Wanis, the main character in Shadi Abdel Salam's 1969 film *The Night of*

Counting Years (al-Mumya'), when he suddenly realizes that the reliefs covering the playgrounds of his childhood are historical records by ancestors to be read and interpreted, and not pure decoration. *This Day* dedicates itself to those moments when one returns to the most banal—which one never thinks of as worthy of any historical record—and takes a picture of it. *This Day* is about what triggers that desire to record the banal, the daily. So it is about writing diaries, recording audio, recording the news, sending emails, etc. Communicating with an unknown reader or viewer is very present in my work, hence my interest in time capsules!

Tomorrow Everything Will Be Alright

24.3. *Tommorow Everything Will be Alright* (2010), directed by Akram Zaatari.

DB: For me, a touching investigation of the document occurs in your video *Tomorrow Everything Will Be Alright* (*Ghadan sawfa yakun kullu shay' bi-khayr*, 2010), in which we see only a dialogue scrolling across a typewriter. It is between ex-lovers who make contact ten years after their sudden separation. The protagonist's dialogue is typewritten in red, one letter at a time, sticky keys and all. His ex-lover's lines, however, appear in black, all at once, similar to the way text appears on a computer screen, and this gesture mimics his sudden appearance and disappearance in the protagonist's life (which we learn about as the narrative unfolds). Here, as in *This Day*, the weight of historical ("real") knowledge is contrasted with the hope symbolized by the ex-lover's flirtatious dialogue, which seems to magically appear on the typewriter. *Tomorrow* ends on an upbeat note as the estranged lovers plan to meet again.

Do you feel this work expresses hope about the possibility of creating associations by way of letters and photographs across deep divisions without minimizing these divisions?

AK: This work is one of the few times when I wrote fiction, as script, before filming it. It is a work I made for a very specific commission by LUX in London and the ICO (Independent Cinema Office) in the United Kingdom. The short film was supposed to screen prior to feature films in commercial theaters across the United Kingdom, as a way to introduce art films. I see it as a site-specific piece for the cinema space.

DB: Yes. The hopeful conclusion to this story seems to be manufactured from bits of film culture. The ex-lovers agree to meet at sunset at the site of their first meeting, *le rayon vert*—a reference to Eric Rohmer's film, which is about the desire for connection. In conclusion, the typewriter pounds out "an Eric Rohmer film. Forget your tears. Everything will be alright." We see the sunset, a car driving through a tunnel, and then a sunset with the date stamp "31 DEC 1999." Is this montage suggesting that in fact what we are witnessing is a loop of desire created by film and expressed through a typewriter and video camera? Is this an expression of the desires manufactured by modernity?

AK: On December 31, 1999, I took my camera and went to film the last sunset of the millennium. I had no concrete objective apart from capturing a legendary sunset that was like any sunset, except that I could not forget that it was the last one in a millennium. I kept the film aside until 2010 when I decided to use it for this work. In a way, the film is conceived around this footage and written as a prelude to it. The unfolding story brings the viewer to experience this sunset footage from a very specific angle and therefore to read it in light of a love story, thus bringing into the picture also a legacy of romance films set around an omnipresent sunset, notably in Yusuf al-Sibai's love story *Among the Ruins (Bayn al-atlal)*, in which two lovers, no longer together, still think of each other at every sunset. The novel was the basis for two important and extremely popular romance films in Egypt: *Among the Ruins* (Ezzeddine Zoulfiqar, 1959) and *Remember Me* (*Uzkurini*, 1978) by Henri Barakat.

Like the text typed on an analog typewriter, the video camera is also a tool for writing. This film is thus an exercise in writing, dedicated to the idea of script, withdrawing actors yet bringing emotion, love, and desire through a machine, replacing the main two actors with red ink and black ink. In classic love stories, audiences get attached to actors, even to their physical features. You go back home after you watch a film with a face or a body in mind with an unsatisfied desire to meet with that actor again. Maybe it's what drives you to go see the actor's next movie. It is this desire that I wanted to try and reproduce without using human subjects.

The typewriter I used in the video is featured in many of my photographic works. It is the typewriter that my father gave me when I turned sixteen. Using it today is using a device that belongs to the early eighties to write a script that belongs to the internet age. It produces something surreal and enforces the ghostly presence of the absent actors. A log of their chat unfolds on paper as their conversation takes place. It's unfolding on a machine traditionally known for script writing in the form of a dialogue. The intention was to strip cinema of its actors, from mise en scène, and to bring it back to one of its roots—the textual script.

DB: Given that the story unfolds through words, the gender of the two protagonists could have been concealed. Why did you decide to confirm it, and therefore confront the viewer with the fact that these are male lovers?

AZ: Love in the history of film is dominated by heterosexual romance. References to pop culture are also dominated by gender polarity. Only recently can stories about same-sex love be seen in mainstream cinema, and then only in a few cultures, where same-sex love is accepted socially. I thought it was important to introduce that gender twist to romance in cinema, and make it an uncommon love story that nevertheless refers subversively to the same heteronormative pop culture. However, the gender identity of the protagonists isn't confirmed until halfway through the film. By then, the viewer has maybe already imagined it differently. For some it is a disappointment, for others it pushes the romance in a social-political direction.

Machine Vision vs. Intimate Vision

DB: The contrast between personal and official knowledge is often expressed in your work. For example, in *Letter to a Refusing Pilot*, the rumor concerning a pilot that refused to bomb a school in Sidon, Lebanon turns out to be true. The pilot, it seems, did not see the building as a "target" but instead, due to his personal experiences there, as a school. His intimate contact with the site altered his view of it as a target. What the pilot saw was a habitation—a place with stories, people, and a history.

This makes me think of a scene in Harun Farocki's 1989 film *Images of the World and the Inscription of War (Bilder der Welt und Inschrift des Krieges)*, which focuses on a black and white photograph taken by a Nazi soldier of a Jewish woman preparing to board a train (that will take her to the camps and presumably to her death). In this photograph, the photographer's erotic gaze interrupts the cold eye of the Nazi death machine, and the film parallels this view to the similarly "objective" gaze of the Allied forces, who were unable to "see" Auschwitz in aerial photos of the area and thus bombed it. The film suggests that, unlike the objective gaze that sees only targets, this photograph shows a human encounter. The woman returns the admiring gaze of a photographer. Can you discuss *Letter to a Refusing Pilot* in terms of what is seen by whom in the aerial photograph of the school in Sidon?

Also, in terms of paper airplanes (the title of this interview), you incorporate *Le Petit Prince* into the introduction to the film, a book written by a pilot. And the film includes beautiful scenes on the topic, including a paper airplane floating above a city; a boy making a paper airplane; three figures sending paper airplanes off a balcony, with another shot of the planes circling above the city like fighters. Can you explain what these scenes mean for you in the context of the film about the refusing pilot?

AK: This is a possible and interesting reading of Hagai Tamir's refusal to bomb. Hagai's cognitive agency was indeed informed by the architectural education he got following his release from the army in the 1970s. When he was called from the reserve to join the Air Force again in 1982, he was already in disagreement with the motivation behind the war. He did not bomb, not because he feared destroying a building, but because his recent education was acting on him to reject the values of the military machine and instead to join the values of humanity. His refusal was triggered by the sight of that building, but could have been triggered by any other "familiar" element that could have given him a reason not to bomb. I would say he would not have done the same ten years earlier.

Hagai's desire to join humanity reminds me of the angels' desire to become human in Wim Wenders's film *Wings of Desire (Der Himmel über Berlin)*, and also in Peter Handke's poem "Song of Childhood" ("Lied vom Kindsein"), which is integrated into the film. For me, a refusal to join war is also about going back to childhood, parting with the corrupt world of grownups. And this is the primary reason why St.-Exupéry's *Little Prince* is referenced, not because he was an aviator, although the fact that he was an aviator also supports the association with Hagai, or maybe with me too. In the first part of the twentieth century, one very often finds practitioners of various professions with a passion for flying. It's a penchant that was associated with modernity and that imposed a different perspective on the experience of nature, cities, and time. For someone who traveled for the first time, let's say from London to Paris, the short duration of the trip must have been like an ellipsis in a film.

Nevertheless, the film is not about the pilot Hagai Tamir. The film is made for him, in response to his refusal, thirty years later, by someone who lived in Sidon, in that urban fabric that Hagai certainly flew over. The film is written from the perspective of the "bombed"—from the point of view of the ground as opposed to the sky. This is where bringing up Farocki's work—and I think also of his 2003 *War at Distance* (*Erkennen und Verfolgen*), which analyzed footage recorded from the point of view of machines, moving missiles, and robots—makes total sense. It's only humans that can disrupt the execution of a machine-operated mechanism. From the military-machine point of view, Hagai represents a failure, or maybe an imperfection that needs to be eliminated, hence the invention of unmanned airplanes—the drone.

In establishing the two points of view from the sky and from the ground, the film also has to do with reversing age. If children represent innocence, then Hagai's decision not to bomb is a way of returning to childhood.

Only people like Hagai or St.-Exupéry are capable of longing for humanity, perhaps because they have experienced war from the sky.

Time Capsules and Potential History

DB: According to Noah Simblist, the document, in your work, is a testimony to what is no longer there. The document never seems to find its appropriate time. It either arrives too late (after the destruction of that which it documents), or too early (before the event it captures can be assimilated).

The photograph that functions this way can be placed in a time capsule for the future, however, and your 2005 video *In This House (Fi haza al-bayt)* provides an interesting example. We watch the exhumation of a letter that the current occupants of the house may not be ready to read, from a radical resistance group that once occupied the house for seven years. The letter was buried in the garden inside the empty case of a B-10, 82mm mortar. We hear shouting off-screen; there is resistance to locating the letter.

This sense of sending a message to the future can be read alongside the notion of "potential history" articulated by Ariella Azoulay, particularly her claim that there are forms of "being together"—of racial and religious mixing—that can only be understood as such when the history on which such a mixing is predicated is validated. If at all, that time will be in the future.

It seems to me that *In This House* shows how difficult this process actually is, this idea of potential history. The letter is a testament to "being together," but one that is not easily exhumed. In this video, the unearthing of the letter is presented as work. Can you talk a little bit about the process of digging in this piece? As well, the time capsule pertains directly to your 2012 installation at Documenta (13) [titled *Time Capsule*, this installation was inspired by the fact that the National Museum in Beirut sealed its collections at the outbreak of the civil war in 1975]. Can we think about these works in terms of potential history?

AK: I am interested in archaeology as a research tool, therefore digging, in its literal and also metaphorical sense. Digging is researching, trying to identify composition and looking to identify what happened in the past, looking partially for objects that could testify to that past, but sometimes looking for stories and identifying rumors and creating registers for them so they inhabit history. However, this process is not always mono-directional. I am interested in archaeology and what its reverse might be.

A time capsule is a testimony (or sometimes a letter) produced in a specific time, but the reading of which is deferred until a time in the future. It is exactly like a picture taken on a film stock that is never developed, but that could be developed at a future time. In other terms, it is produced, but it is withdrawn or made inaccessible, intentionally, for a reason. The fact that it is a withdrawn testimony does not make it nonexistent. Not being retrievable does not mean it does not exist, and it does not mean either that it is a ruin. It is a trace of some presence, or evidence of some act or fact that would disturb its period, or that is in conflict with its period, so it seeks to inhabit a future time. To produce a time capsule is to reverse the act of excavation. If archaeology intrudes upon the past, imposing on it in order to reveal itself, creating a time capsule and burying it is a way of reflecting on a record, but only by a future reader, hence indeed potential history.

Documentary Practice

DB: Your interest in resurrecting the studio culture that produced a photograph stands in stark contrast to many documentary films. Yet, *28 Nights and a Poem (Thamaniyat wa 'ushrun laylan wa bayt min al-shi'r)* does not show us much of the studio life that produced Hashem El Madani's stunning studio photographs. Much of the film shows him watching—something out the window, dance shows on his television, for example. We also see the television shows screened on your laptop. And at the end of the film we see the two of you together with disco-like lights illuminating the studio behind as you both (presumably) face a screen.

What is the role of watching in this film? How does it relate to the studio practice the film concerns?

24.4. *28 Nights and a Poem* (2015), directed by Akram Zaatari.

AK: Photographs invite you to look, and, in a way, this is their primary function. From my current position in time, I consider photographs and moving images as one entity. On one hand, the legacy of a photo studio is so much informed by popular attitudes, and is therefore a form of popular visual culture. On the other hand, the idea of the photographic archive includes, nowadays, both moving and still images. This is why my film addresses both. The film is not about Hashem El Madani and his work only; it is about the technology of producing images and of diffusing them, and the position the photographic studio occupied in the lives of millions of users in the 1950s and 1960s. It is about broadcast technology, the archive, and access to it. It is also about all the links that tie images to one another through the transmission of fashion, of modes of living, of melodic tunes, and it is about the performance of all of those. Performing elements of an archive is essential for understanding how the archive functions, of how elements are retrieved and how they affect our gestures, our imagination, and our processes of identification. I hope the film presents all of that. What would be the equivalent of upload and download, now common in the internet age, in the analog age? I want the viewer to ask that question, and get a feel of how older machines worked with the logic of today, exactly like what I did in *Tomorrow Everything Will Be Alright*.

A key to understanding this film is Yoko Ogawa's 1994 novel *The Ringfinger* (*Kusuriyubi no hyōhon*), which takes place in a conservation institute that samples all sorts of specimens. However, this sampling takes place following the dictates of the professor in charge, who extracts the essence from the specimens in order to preserve them. I was struck by this when I read the book in 2011, and I believe it helped me enormously to identify my discomfort with scientific norms of preservation when applied systematically to objects without being attentive to the specificities of objects, to their histories, and to the emotional registers they may carry, or had carried.

The last scene is key to understanding that while looking in a direction, we always miss so much of what's happening in the background, the counter-shot of an image. There is so much that we don't know and that we will not grasp while looking at a document because we do not have the tools to decode it, or because we are not ready to understand it, or because we are looking for something specific in the picture, so other elements don't reveal themselves to us. A document lives longer than humans, and is most likely to cross different periods, encountering different social and political climates in which it would be seen differently. We need to be generous with a photographic object in order to start seeing different aspects of it. We need to put aside our convictions, our education, our visual training, so we can see subtleties that others can't yet see. In the scene where El Madani and I sit side by side looking at the screen of a laptop, the contents of which are not revealed to the camera, the spectacle takes place behind us and we are not aware of it.

DB: Also, your studio is clean with technologically up-to-date equipment. We see only your hands on a keyboard or operating a recorder. By contrast, El Madani's studio is cluttered with books, photographs on the wall, and furniture. He sips tea. Can you talk about this contrast in studio environments?

AK: You are talking about the conservation space at the Arab Image Foundation, which is a neutral and sterile space, where archivists work on collections. This is how it should be in a conservation institute, and the AIF is one. The film is consciously oscillating between two locations: The Madani Studio, and the AIF, where El Madani's collection is now located. I claim that the two locations are linked. It is the same link that ties a museum displaying an archaeological object with the place where the object has been excavated. Whereas that link may not be obvious when one visits either of the spaces, I make it visible through a dramaturgy of actions that occur between these two locations, notably actions that take place in the AIF and that trigger other actions in Madani's studio—actions like playing a song on my mobile phone in the cool storage space in the AIF, which triggers the playback of the same song on El Madani's phone in his desk drawer, and other actions follow the same logic.

Audience

DB: Although your work primarily concerns Lebanon and the surrounding region, many of your works incorporate English subtitles. Who do you conceive of as your work's audience? Has your imagined audience changed over the past twenty years? Do you conceive of multiple audiences? A future audience?

AK: I hate to say I do not think of audience, but this is how it is. Of course I do care that my work finds those who may find it useful, but I do not cater my work to the tastes and concerns of a particular audience. Many of the topics I work with are very local, but I hope that this locality connects to a larger concern. I like saying that I produce the work that I desire to encounter but that I find missing.

Akram Zaatari - Film and Videography

The Landing (al-Hubut, 2019)
On Photography, Dispossession, and Times of Struggle (2017)
Twenty-eight Nights and a Poem (Thamaniyat wa 'ushrun laylan wa bayt min al-shi'r, 2015)
Beirut Exploded Views (2014)
Letter to a Refusing Pilot (Risala li-tayyar rafid, 2013)
HER + HIM (Hiya wa huwa, 2012)
On Photography, People, and Modern Times (2010)
Tomorrow Everything Will Be Alright (Ghadan sawfa yakun kullu shay' bi-khayr, 2010)
Tabiah Samitah (Tabi'a samita/Nature morte, 2008)
Video in Five Movements (Video fi khams harakat, 2008)
In This House (Fi haza al-bayt, 2005)
This Day (al-Yawm, 2003)
How I Love You (Shu b-hibbak, 2001)
Her + Him VAN LEO (Hiya wa huwa Van Leo, 2001)
Red Chewing Gum (al-'Alka al-hamra', 2000)
All Is Well on the Border (al-Sharit bi-khayr, 1997)
Majnounak, Crazy of You (Majnunak, Crazy of You, 1997)
Teach Me ('Allimuni, 1996)
Countdown (Mashahid mawquta, 1995)
Mourning Images (Ghuna' buka' suwar futughrafiya, 1995)
Reflection (Nur, 1995)

Akram Zaatari - Selected Publications

Against Photography. Barcelona: MACBA, 2017.

A Conversation with an Imagined Israeli Filmmaker Named Avi Mograbi. Aubervilliers: Les Laboratoires d'Aubervilliers; Paris and San Francisco: Kadist Art Foundation; Berlin: Sternberg Press, 2012.

Hashem el Madani: Studio Practices. Beirut: Mind the Gap; Arab Image Foundation; London: The Photographers' Gallery, 2004.

Mapping Sitting, with Zeina Maasri and Karl Bassil, in collaboration with Walid Raad. Beirut: Mind the Gap; Arab Image Foundation, 2002.

The Vehicle: Picturing Moments of Transition in a Modernizing Society. Beirut: Mind the Gap; Arab Image Foundation, 1999.

Portraits du Caire: Van Leo, Armand, Alban. Beirut: Arab Image Foundation; Arles and Paris: Actes Sud, 1999.

Another Resolution. Beirut: Mind the Gap, 1998.

Akram Zaatari - Solo Exhibitions

Against Photography: An Annotated History of the Arab Image Foundation. Sharjah Art Foundation, United Arab Emirates, 2019.

The Script. New Art Exchange, Nottingham, England; traveled to Turner Contemporary, Margate, England; Modern Art Oxford, Oxford, England, 2019.

The Third Window. Sfeir-Semler Gallery, Beirut, Lebanon, 2018.

Against Photography: An Annotated History of the Arab Image Foundation. National Museum of Modern and Contemporary Art, Korea, 2018.

Letter to a Refusing Pilot. Moderna Museet, Malmö, Sweden, 2018.

The Fold. Contemporary Arts Center, Cincinnati, OH, USA, 2018.

Against Photography: An Annotated History of the Arab Image Foundation. MACBA, Barcelona, Spain; K21, Dusseldorf, Germany, 2017.

Unfolding. Galerie Sfeir-Semler, Hamburg, Germany, 2017.

Double Take: Akram Zaatari and the Arab Image Foundation. National Portrait Gallery, London, England, 2017.

Letter to a Refusing Pilot. Thomas Dane Gallery, London, England, 2016.

Tomorrow Everything Will Be Alright. Galpão VB: Associação Cultural Videobrasil, São Paulo, Brazil, 2016.

This Day at Ten. Kunsthaus Zürich, Switerland, 2016.

Akram Zaatari: The End of Time. The Common Guild, Glasgow, Scotland, 2016.

The Archaeology of Rumour. British Institute, Rome, Italy, 2016.

Akram Zaatari. SALT, Istanbul, Turkey, 2015.

Unfolding. Moderna Museet, Stockholm, Sweden, 2015.

Akram Zaatari: All Is Well, curated by Vicky Moufawad-Paul. Carleton University Art Gallery, Ottawa, Canada, 2015.

Akram Zaatari: This Day at Ten. Wiels Contemporary Art Center, Brussels, Belgium, 2014.

Akram Zaatari: The End of Time. The Power Plant, Toronto, Canada, 2014.

On Photography, People, and Modern Times. Thomas Dane Gallery, London, England, 2013.

Letter to a Refusing Pilot. Lebanon Pavilion, 55th International Venice Biennale, Italy, 2013.

Project 100: Akram Zaatari. MoMA, New York, USA, 2013.

This Day at Ten. Sfeir-Semler Gallery, Beirut, Lebanon, 2013.

ALL IS WELL. Agnes Etherington Art Centre, Kingston University, Ontario, Canada, 2013.

Akram Zaatari. Liverpool Biennial, Liverpool, England, 2012.

The End. Sfeir-Semler Gallery, Hamburg, Germany, 2012.

Tomorrow Everything Will Be Alright. MIT List Visual Arts Center, Cambridge MA, USA, 2012.

The Uneasy Subject. MUAC, Mexico City, Mexico, 2012.

This Day at Ten. Magasin—Centre National d'Art Contemporain, Grenoble, France, 2012.

Akram Zaatari. Museum of Contemporary Art, Chicago, Illinois, USA, 2012.

Composition for Two Wings. Kunsternes Hus, Oslo, Norway, 2011.

The Uneasy Subject. Museo del Arte Contemporáneo de Castilla y León, Spain, 2011.

This Day. Moderna Galerija Ljubljana, Ljubljana, Slovenia, 2011.

Play van Abbe Part 3. The Politics of Collecting—The Collecting of Politics. Van Abbe Museum, Eindhoven, Netherlands, 2010.

Earth of Endless Secrets. Kunstverein München, Munich, Germany, 2009.

Sfeir-Semler Gallery, Beirut, Lebanon, 2009.

Ludlow38, New York NY, 2009.

Galerie Sfeir-Semler, Hamburg, Germany, 2007.

ART Basel, ART Statements booth with Sfeir-Semler Gallery, Basel, Switzerland, 2007.

Hashem el Madani: Promenades and Studio Practices. La CaixaForum, Barcelona, Spain, 2006.

Mapping Sitting (collaboration with Walid Raad). Grey Art Gallery, New York, USA, 2005.

Unfolding. Portikus, Frankfurt, Germany, 2004.

Photographers' Gallery, London, England, 2004.

Mapping Sitting: On Portraiture and Photography (in collaboration with Walid Raad). Centre Pour l'Image Contemporaine, Geneva, Switzerland, 2004.

Musée Nicéphore Nièpce, Chalon-sur-Saône, France, 2004.

Mapping Sitting: On Portraiture and Photography (in collaboration with Walid Raad). SK Die Photographische Sammlung, Cologne, Germany; Palais des Beaux Arts, Brussels, Belgium, 2002.

The Vehicle. The Townhouse Gallery, Cairo, Egypt, 2000.

The Vehicle. Darat al Founoun, Amman, Jordan, 1999.

Goethe Institute, Beirut, Lebanon, 1998.

References

Cotter, Suzanne. 2009. "The Documentary Turn: Surpassing Tradition in the Work of Walid Raad and Akram Zaatari." In *Contemporary Art in the Middle East*, edited by Paul Sloman, 50–57. London: Black Dog Publishing.

Feldman, Hannah. 2009. "Excavating Images on the Border." *Third Text* 23, no. 3 (May): 309–22.

Latimer, Quinn, and Akram Zaatari. 2014. *Film as a Form of Writing: Quinn Latimer Talks to Akram Zaatari*. Brussels: WIELS Contemporary Art Centre.

Moufawad-Paul, Vicky, and Judith Rodenbeck. 2014. *Akram Zaatari: All Is Well*. Kingston: Agnes Etherington Art Centre; Ottawa: Carleton University Art Gallery.

Westmoreland, Mark. 2012. "In This Field: Akram Zaatari's Ethnographic Excavations." *Cairo Papers in Social Science* 31, no. 3/4: 128–48.

Wilson-Goldie, Kaelen. 2009. "On Resistance and Retirement: Still, Silent Lives of Former Fighters in Nature Morte." In *Akram Zaatari: Earth of Endless Secrets*, edited by Akram Zaatari and Karl Bassil. Frankfurt, Hamburg, and Beirut: Portikus, Sfeir Semler Gallery, and Beirut Art Center.

Zaatari, Akram. 2007. *Hashem El Madani: Promenade*. Beirut: Arab Image Foundation and Mind the Gap.

———. 2011. *el molesto asunto/The Uneasy Subject*. León: MUSAC, Museo de Arte Contemporáneo de Castilla y León; México: MUAC, Museo Universitario Arte Contemporáneo; Milano: Charta.

———. 2013a. "Against Photography: Conversation with Mark Westmoreland." *Aperture* 210 (February): 60–65.

———. 2013b. *Time Capsule*. Milan: Mousse Publishing.

Zaatari, Akram, and Karl Bassil, eds. 2009. *Akram Zaatari: Earth of Endless Secrets*. Frankfurt, Hamburg, and Beirut: Portikus, Sfeir Semler Gallery, and Beirut Art Center.

Zaatari, Akram, and Hannah Feldman. 2007. "Mining War: Fragments from a Conversation Already Passed." *Art Journal* 66: 48–67.

25

CATASTROPHE AND POST-CATASTROPHE IN THE FILMS OF KAMAL ALJAFARI

Nadia Yaqub

In *Empathic Vision: Affect, Trauma, and Contemporary Art,* Jill Bennet writes of the danger of "colonizing" another's traumatic experience—that is, claiming the right and ability to represent such experience and communicate it to others (Bennet 2005, 7). Works that avoid such appropriation succeed by creating an empathic affect without seeking to produce secondary trauma within the spectator. They do not aspire to show the spectator what trauma looks like, to uncover the "secret" that trauma sufferers possess as a result of their experiences. Instead, they recognize the unbridgeable gap between survivors of an event and those who can know it only through mediation. They create empathic unsettlement, that is, "the aesthetic experience of simultaneously *feeling for* another and becoming aware of a distinction between one's own perceptions and the experience of the other" (Bennet 2005, 8).[1] They avoid identification with the victim of trauma, while creating a point of encounter between the inside (the secret of the traumatic experience that can be referenced but not represented; what Bennet, following Charlotte Delbo, calls sense memory) of an experience and its outside (common memory—the narrated history of events). The affect sparked within spectators through this encounter elicits thought rather than the emotions of sympathy, shame, or guilt that mimetic images making claims about violence are likely to arouse.

Bennet's concept is useful for understanding a strand of filmmaking that addresses Palestinian experiences with violence and dispossession without employing a witnessing mode of address.[2] In such works—essay and experimental films, art videos, non-narrative fiction—filmmakers do not seek to inform viewers about events and contexts, but rather to communicate affect or comment ironically on events and conditions. They do not supplant the extensive documentary work that continues to be made by and about Palestinians. In fact, their efficacy often depends on their viewers' prior knowledge of the events and conditions they treat, knowledge obtained from either personal experience or watching or hearing the witnessing of others. Thus, these films work alongside, rather than in place of, informative documentaries. Films of this sort from the Arab world are not limited to the Palestinian context, but the long-standing nature of the Palestinian condition (stretching back at least to the 1948 war or *Nakba*) and the plethora of films that have been made about it render Palestinian cinema a particularly rich area for such works. In this chapter I analyze a trilogy of films by Palestinian artist and filmmaker Kamal Aljafari through the lens of empathic unsettlement as a way to both understand the efficacy of his work and extend Bennet's concept. While the first two films in the trilogy—*The Roof* (*al-Sath*, 2006) and *Port of Memory* (*Mina' al-dhakira*, 2009)—use empathic unsettlement as a strategy for attending to the Palestinian condition of ongoing dispossession, the third—*Recollection* (*Istidhkar/ isti'ada*, 2015) engages in a type of radical empathy whereby viewers are not just invited into empathic unsettlement but called to experience the possibilities inherent in a time of post-catastrophe—that is, the coming-to-terms with existence that must be undertaken when one understands that one's world has been irrevocably altered. In the temporal mode of post-catastrophe neither mourning nor human rights claims are productive. Empathy results from a sharing that is related to the present and the future rather than the past. In *Recollection* Aljafari offers Jaffa as a vanguard into the post-catastrophe that is in store for all of us.

In *The Roof* and *Port of Memory* Aljafari arouses empathic unsettlement primarily through two strategies: refraction and opacity. I use the term "refraction" to designate a cluster of techniques that redirect viewers' perspectives of events, people, places, and conditions. Generally, refraction avoids direct representations of violence because of the distance these create between characters and viewers (they are suffering and I am not), and the false sense of identification (I now know what they have experienced) that they produce. Like a prism that bends a ray of light, films that refract offer viewers new, often unexpected perspectives on a subject. Refraction comes into play at a number of levels, including form, structure, and content. Significantly, filmmakers offer this new perspective not by providing new information or explanations, but rather by giving spectators a new experience such that they arrive at an affective understanding of a particular circumstance or event. Refraction can encompass different forms of counter-hegemonic practices. It can deconstruct or queer dominant discursive practices. Through refraction filmmakers can circumvent the discourse of claims-making that viewers have widely come to expect in the Palestinian context, instead creating a point of encounter through which characters and viewers can meet on the basis of equality (Yaqub 2014).

The concept of opacity was developed by the Martiniquan writer Edouard Glissant to address the epistemic violence underlying relations between colonial metropoles and their peripheries.[3] Opacity challenges the notion that any culture can be transparently translated and comprehended through the colonial gaze. However, by opacity Glissant does not mean that there is an essential, hidden core to colonized cultures that is inaccessible, difficult, or unfathomable. Rather, opacity refers to "an interplay of differences whereby no culture may claim to have incorporated any other within its own epistemological projects" (Figueroa 2009, 20). Opacity is, of course, a feature of all culture, but Glissant also uses the term to refer to a stance or representational strategy assumed by a group in order to prevent or counteract epistemological appropriation related to postcoloniality. It is in this context that Glissant writes of demanding "the right to opacity" (Glissant 1997, 190). That is, opacity is not just something out there in the world; it is something to be practiced, cultivated, and protected. Works can be evaluated on how much they encourage or undertake such practices.

Three aspects to opacity are relevant to Aljafari's work. First, opacity addresses the problem of excess: no representation or communication can ever be complete or completely understood. Opaque works draw attention to that fact in some way. Works of film and photography are particularly useful in this regard because both their physical and temporal frames are visible, reminding spectators that what they are seeing has been selected. The indexicality of film and photography also necessarily introduces the notion of excess: one can never know everything about what appears within the image because it consists of a trace of an object, person, and/or place in the real world that will always exceed representation.

Secondly, opacity is a form of protection from appropriation. If a text defies full explication, if its representational inadequacy is recoverable, then it can avoid the violence of transparency. Those depicted within the text retain their human complexity through the mystery and density that is communicated but not penetrated. This is not to say that such works always attempt to represent what cannot be represented, or that they always eschew familiar structures (e.g., narrative), but rather that such works resist leaving viewers with a feeling of full understanding or identification. They may illuminate situations, points of view, feelings, or affects at the same time that they raise questions (or a feeling of wonder) about them. They may, at times, be puzzling, but they are not puzzles; they are not necessarily even "difficult." "Difficult" texts often invite explication, which can position the scholar in a hierarchical relationship to the text, its author, and her reader or viewer: only the scholar has the requisite knowledge and intelligence to complete the communicative act that the author and audience attempt to engage in. Betsy Wing (1997) uses the metaphor "rock" to describe opacity. It is that sort of physical density, rather than the metaphorical notion of "dense or impenetrable prose" to be deciphered, that is applicable here. Just as one can only penetrate the density of a rock by disfiguring or destroying it (drilling through it or blowing it up), the act of attempting to fully grasp an opaque text is akin to violating it in some way. Instead, a viewer or reader cultivates a quality of openness and curiosity vis-à-vis the text that does not require complete comprehension.

Finally, opacity thematizes the encounter created by the act of representation between those who appear within the text and those who interact with the text—in this case, between the Palestinians who appear in the films and their spectators. Glissant speaks of "the penetrable opacity of a world in which one exists, or agrees to exist with and among others" (Glissant 1997, 115). Artists and writers create texts that discourage readings for transparency, but readers and viewers, by also approaching texts without seeking to comprehend them transparently, by accepting ambiguity and resisting the types of close readings and explication that scholars are trained to produce, cultivate a respect for the protected depth of the other that is as precious and unknowable as one's own.[4]

In *Recollection*, the third film of the trilogy, Aljafari takes these strategies to their logical conclusion. Utterly devoid of characters and narration, he does not use refraction or opacity in creating relationships, but rather inserts the viewer herself into a world he has created in the film. The unsettlement that arises from the work is based not on empathy (arriving at an understanding of another's condition) but on sharing (post-catastrophe envelops us all). In what follows I outline in detail how these techniques work in each of Aljafari's films.

The Roof

The Roof contests the erasure of Palestinians in Israel from history. Aljafari's subject is not the *Nakba* as an event from the past that is remembered. Rather, he remains rigorously focused on the present. Like the trauma art that Jill Bennet analyzes, *The Roof* treats the present experience with memory rather than the pastness of particular events. When Bennet distinguishes between common memory and sense memory, she defines the former as a discursive framework through which events are transmitted and understood. While that process is psychologically and socially valuable, through that transmission, traumatic events are consigned to history, as if they are over, even though for survivors their effects live on into the present. Thus, common memory is always partial (Bennet 2005, 25). *The Roof* acts as an intervention into common memory, inviting viewers to share in an affective understanding of the ongoing *Nakba* as it is experienced by Palestinians living in Israel today.

Because the film's characters are Palestinian citizens of the state of Israel, the affective understanding developed in the film queers the Israeli nationalist narrative (Limbrick 2012, 106). Significantly, the common memory in that narrative does not just consign the experiences of Palestinians in Israel to the past, it actively removes them from history. In *The Roof*, refraction occurs as viewers are given an affective experience allowing them to see the constructed nature of the Zionist discursive framework in which the film's characters live their lives. At the same time, through an opacity created through stillness and inscrutability, Aljafari strips these characters of almost everything except their presence, intimating but not definitively identifying their discursive erasure as the foundation for their ongoing physical erasure from Israeli cityscapes.

The Roof is structured largely as a poetics of the Aljafaris' home. In a voice-over at the start of the film, the director states that in 1948 family members who failed to leave were forcibly resettled into the houses of residents who fled. The Aljafari home consists of a ground floor where his family resides, and the bare walls of a second floor which the previous owners had been in the process of building. This second floor/roof appears repeatedly throughout the film—as a backdrop to opening and closing credits, as a site where Aljafari's mother sits contemplating the town around her, and as the object of the filmmaker's obsessive camera. The interior is also interrogated; there, viewers see family members engage in the activities of daily life. Static shots of the empty family room invite viewers to contemplate its narrowness, its high windows that admit diffuse daylight but offer no view to the outside, and its television whose flickering contrasts with the quiet of the rooms themselves. The life Aljafari portrays within the rooms is of a piece with this mood: three sisters nap in their bedroom, and various configurations of family members silently watch television. Even a dinner scene with eight family members gathered around the table is notable mainly for its quiet. Almost no conversation takes place. Instead the soundtrack, as with much of the film, is dominated by the ambient noise of clinking spoons, scraping chairs, and television music (Yaqub 2014, 164).

Aljafari makes liberal use of haptic images (Marks 2000, 162). His repeated slow panning shots of the concrete block walls of the unfinished second floor and long photographic shots of the family's homes in al-Ramlah and Jaffa might at first suggest an attempt to interrogate or penetrate, to reveal to viewers the significances and associations these spaces and objects have for their owners. However, Aljafari's work teases the viewer by simultaneously suggesting the auras of the roof and the home beneath it but refusing to reveal their secrets. In a practice he repeats in other home spaces featured in *The Roof*, the close survey of the filmmaker's home includes a series of photo-like shots of details within each room: a pendulum wall clock, a dresser top full of cosmetics, photographic snapshots tucked into the frame of a needlepoint panel on the wall, a wedding photograph, curtains, and a canary in a birdcage. The effect is to suggest, but not actually convey, intimacy. Aljafari appears to offer up his Arab family's most private spaces to the gaze of outsiders, but these images obscure as much as they reveal. People and objects are mute. Viewers can confidently infer that the nail polish and hairbrushes on the bedroom dresser are used by the young women napping on the room's narrow beds, but know almost nothing about where, when, or why they might do so. The photos are clearly of family members, but one cannot be sure of who is who or why these particular photos were chosen for display. These private objects surely possess auras of experience and contact for the residents of the house, but Aljafari resists revealing them.[5] The effect is one of inscrutability, of the impossibility of viewers ever sharing the experiences of those who appear in the film.

Moreover, object-like characters in *The Roof* are marked by an almost alarming passivity. Over and over one sees shots of people in states of rest or inactivity. When they work (e.g., the sister chopping tomatoes, the brother mounting a car tire), they do so silently and without visible personal engagement. In scene after scene characters sit, either staring into space or watching television. However, as is the case with the mute objects that Aljafari patiently offers up to a viewer's gaze, characters are protected by an avoidance of emotion or meaningful disclosure. Within the mundane chronicling of the family's daily life, gestures reveal no more than their surface meanings. How characters may feel about their lives or each other, their strategies for coping with the alienation that permeates the film, their frustrations or failures, is not revealed.

All these windows, I made with my bare hands.

25.1. The cinematic occupation of Jaffa in *Port of Memory (2009)*, directed by Kamal Aljafari.

Passive people and mute objects add up to a depiction of characters and lives stripped of the justifications or claims that would otherwise clutter and hence obscure a central point of the film: it is the mere existence of Palestinian Arabs within the state of Israel that gives the lie to the Zionist narrative and reveals the racism at its core. Viewers are made to pay attention not to characters' actions, accomplishments, relationships, or injuries, but rather to their obdurate and impenetrable *presence*. In this regard Aljafari's use of language is also of critical importance. Televisions screen Arabic-language shows from the surrounding Arab countries, not Israeli shows.[6] The characters' Arabic is also almost entirely free of the Hebrew that usually peppers the speech of Palestinians in Israel. Hebrew and English appear in the film, but circumscribed within contexts of nationalism (a magazine article about soldiers in the Israeli army, Aljafari's driver's license application, and the song "I Believe") and of colonialism (an audio tour recounting a history of Jaffa). Finally, the extradiegetic music of the film, much of which appears over smooth, tracking shots of the walls of the family home, is made up of well-known Arabic songs from the 1940s to the 2000s. Arabic, then, is ostentatiously present in the film. This choice has ramifications that go beyond the experience of Palestinians to gesture toward another major erasure that grew out of the creation of the state of Israel and continues in the sense memory of many of its citizens, namely the violent erasure of the Arab-ness of Israel's Arab Jewish citizens.

While Aljafari protects characters from false intimacy, his pacing creates empathic unsettlement by offering viewers an affective experience akin to that created by the existential position of the film's characters. The panning shots and lingering on static scenes place viewers in a position of suspended, ironic contemplation, which itself mimics the subject position of the characters within the film vis-à-vis the Israel mainstream. Like Aljafari and his family, viewers gaze at something of which they are not a part, sitting before a screen, their immobile bodies suggesting suspension rather than action. Stillness, slowness, and inscrutability, then, create refraction, carefully preparing viewers for a confrontation with the Israeli Zionist discursive framework that appears later in the film.

A climax of sorts occurs when Aljafari visits the Azrieli Center Tower in Tel Aviv. There, he engages in encounters utterly alienating in their insistence on Jewish Israeli-ness. He picks up a book titled *How to Make a Jewish Movie* and sugar packets emblazoned with the images of Jewish Israeli leaders. He gazes out the windows of the tower at the city of Jaffa, dwarfed and hemmed in (another visual reference to imprisonment) by the high-rises of Tel Aviv. He listens to an audio tour in English that completely elides Jaffa's Palestinian history. In a final shot Aljafari sits slumped and immobile in an armchair in a lobby, while the English lyrics "I exist,

I exist, I'm the son of Israel" from the nationalist song "I Believe" fill the soundtrack. This last shot is heavily ironic, of course; the lyrics clearly are not intended to include Aljafari and other Palestinian citizens of the state, and yet there he is, incontrovertibly existing before the viewers' eyes. Moreover, the contrast between the quiet practice of Arab Palestinian life that has permeated the film up to this point with the noisy assertion of nationalist and ethnic identity in this section of the film make manifest the constructed nature of the latter.

The placement of this segment near the end of the film, after nearly forty-five minutes dominated by the contemplation of silent objects and mostly impassive figures, is the key to its power. Up until this point, viewers have been conditioned to inhabit a perspective of ironic distance and temporal suspension—as Bennet would put it, to come into contact with a sense memory, in this case one arising from the Aljafari family's experience with the *Nakba* and its ongoing effects (Bennet 2005, 44). Israeli nationalist discourse is suddenly not just visible but experienced from a perspective of silencing and exclusion. There is an irony, then, to the opacity with which the Palestinian characters are treated in the film: it is through that opacity that the violence inherent to Israeli nationalist discourse is rendered transparent (Yaqub 2014, 166).

Port of Memory

Like *The Roof*, *Port of Memory* takes as its subject matter the ongoing *Nakba* as experienced by Palestinians living in Israel. It also picks up and focuses on a theme raised in that earlier film, namely the ongoing erasure of Palestinians from the Israeli landscape through the destruction/construction of housing. The film focuses on the eviction of two small Palestinian families from their homes in Jaffa. Salim, the main character, has received a notice contesting his ownership of the home where he lives with his sister and their aged mother. A second family, the Hamatis, consists of an elderly woman and her middle-aged daughter, who lead their quiet lives in the midst of the construction noise of rapid gentrification. Non-narrative in structure, the film consists largely of a series of uneventful vignettes in the lives of the two families. Thus, the film treats not the violence of war and occupation, but ethnocentric laws and capitalist development, key tools in the process of displacement/replacement that underpins Israel's settler colonial project. Viewers learn of Salim's predicament when he visits his lawyer, who has lost the documents that attest to his ownership of the house. The best option he can offer is a settlement with the real estate development company that seeks to expropriate the house. His second option is a court case which, without documents, he is likely to lose. As he did in *The Roof*, in *Port of Memory* Aljafari uses opacity and refraction to generate in viewers an affective experience such that difference between the lived experiences of characters and viewers is maintained. In this case, however, the distance between them is bridged mainly by a shared relationship with moving images.

While *The Roof* addresses the marginalization of Palestinian life in Israel, *Port of Memory* is bleaker, taking as its subject not just its marginalization but its active, ongoing erasure from the landscape. The families profiled in the film are dying: each consists of an elderly parent who is cared for by unmarried, middle-aged children. There are no young people or children. References to social and biological reproduction appear in family photographs and the work of Salim's sister (she creates flower bouquets for wedding receptions and wedding procession cars), but such socially reproductive practices are engaged in by others, not by the members of these families. Moreover, characters carry out their daily routines and non-productive conversations with an impassivity that suggests the paradoxical aftereffects of trauma as described by Jill Bennet—a simultaneous "It hurts. I can't feel anything" (Bennett 2005, 34). They wait, they carry out the small routines of a regulated life, and they engage in conversations that reflect their fundamental lack of agency: Amidar Development Company claims they do not own the house. They claim that they do. The papers are lost and so, apparently is the cause. "What is to be done?" Fatima asks her brother. "What are we supposed to do?" he retorts, "Just give them the house?"

Like *The Roof*, *Port of Memory* engages opacity to prevent the spectators from easily identifying with the characters. As in the earlier film, Aljafari makes ample use of slow panning shots of old walls and beach rubble, a suggestive soundscape, and repeated still shots of cherished and intimate household items and photographs that remain stubbornly enigmatic to viewers. Mysteries are left unsolved; who, for instance, is Samir, the character who never appears in the film but whom Salim regularly feeds? Twice Salim fills a plate of food and leaves it on a doorstep for him, calling his name but never receiving a response. The film is replete with faintly strange and utterly unexplained images and vignettes. Salim's lawyer uses a white shower curtain for an office door. Men sit nearly immobile in a café inexplicably rubbing thumb and index finger together. Another man in the café plays with the glowing coals of a charcoal fire, repeatedly lifting one with tongs and holding it against his throat in what appears to be a ritual of daring, healing, or exorcism. Salim dines alone at a small table facing a wall, rather than with his mother and sister. None of these scenes is explained or fully explicable.

Some of the characters display a degree of eccentricity that tips over at times into madness. Fatima responds to each stressful encounter with the pending eviction from her home with an obsessive practice of hand-washing. The reclusive Samir who eats Fatima's cooking but never shows his face, the silent, still men rubbing fingers in a café, the café owner's obsession with fire, even the excessive religiosity of the Hamati family, all suggest underlying stresses that have no outlet. Three times in the film, the characters' emotional responses to moments of bitter absurdity (including the eventual eviction of the Hamati family from their home) are represented by a scene in which an unknown man rides a motorcycle into the camera's still frame, throws his helmet to the ground, and raises his head in maniacal laughter.

Port of Memory is also similar to *The Roof* in that Aljafari does not represent people and places as they ordinarily appear or behave. In the films Jaffa and al-Ramlah have been stripped of their usual bustle and depicted as almost ghost towns. Individuals or small groups of nearly immobile people inhabit empty streets lined with crumbling buildings. In *Port of Memory* the ordinary liveliness of Jaffa's Ajami neighborhood, where the film takes place, has been relegated to the soundtrack, where the sounds of traffic and, most significantly, of continual construction appear as a world that impinges on characters' lives but in which they play no part.

Where *Port of Memory* differs strategically from *The Roof* is in its refraction of the accumulated stresses of the characters' lives through cinema. As in *The Roof*, the characters' lives are saturated with still and moving photographic images. While still images consist mostly of family photographs that gesture to the love and sociality that is a significant part of the characters' lives, even though they are not represented in the film, moving images are sites of fantasy and desire. In *The Roof*, characters, counterfactually, watch Arabic-language television almost exclusively, a significant contribution to the Arabic soundscape Aljafari constructs in that film.[7] Arabic television contributes to the dissonance of the main character's alienating Israeli/Jewish/Hebrew encounter at the Azraeli tower near the end of *The Roof*. In *Port of Memory*, the women of one family watch dramatizations of the life of Jesus, while those of another watch sappy programs about love, marriage, and weddings. Refraction occurs through what Aljafari has termed the cinematic occupation of Jaffa. The Ajami neighborhood of Jaffa was, for some decades, used frequently as a set for both Israeli and American films. Aljafari plays with this film history first with a scene in which the Hamati family are seen confined to their bedroom, the mother with a coat over her shoulders as if she is about to depart the house, while a film crew shoots a scene in their living room. "All of these windows I built with my own hands," an actor is made to repeat over and over again in Hebrew until he can put the appropriate emphasis on the word "my." The irony is clear: within the constructed world of cinema, any claim is possible, but it must be practiced and inhabited to become convincing.[8] In this scene, viewers are aware of the Palestinian family behind the closed door whose home is being claimed through this repeated practice.

25.2. Figures come into focus in *Recollection (2015)*, directed by Kamal Aljafari.

The cinematic occupation of Jaffa appears again at the café where silent men sit and watch *Delta Force* on a small television.[9] Viewers are invited to consider the contrast between the empty and quiet Jaffa created by Aljafari, and the noisy and frenetic version on the screen, to note the frenetic movement of bodies and cars on screen as viewed through the eyes of still and silent men in the café. If subjectivities are created in part by what one sees, what relationships are created between these Palestinian viewers of the appropriation of their neighborhood to represent the violent Beirut of an American imagination?

The cinematic occupation of Jaffa takes over most forcefully near the end of the film. Salim walks through town to the cemetery overlooking the city. As he gazes at the view before him, a Hebrew song appears on the soundtrack and clips of the popular 1974 Israeli film *Kazablan* come into view. In the song, the eponymous main character, a Moroccan Jewish immigrant to Israel, sings longingly of "a place beyond the sea where the sand is white and home is warm" (that is, Morocco) as he walks through the streets of Jaffa, the hometown of Salim. Aljafari manipulates the footage such that after a few seconds the character Kazablan is excised and Salim inserted in his place. In other words, Aljafari digitally reappropriates Jaffa for Salim, whose avatar is made to walk through the virtual (but indexical) streets of Jaffa of the early 1970s. The clip suggests a truth within the filmic image that can be retrieved through careful viewing and imagination.

However, Aljafari does not overstate the power of this cinematic reappropriation. He cuts from the *Kazablan* footage to a panning shot of the rubble at Jaffa's beach, where the remains of destroyed houses of Palestinians forced to leave in 1948 intermingle with trash. The concrete, material dispossession of Palestinians cannot be undone with green screens and digital technology. Salim next walks down from the cemetery back into Ajami, straight into a violent clip from *Delta Force* in which two blond, blue-eyed American film stars careen through the narrow streets of the town, shooting buildings and Arabs with wild abandon. Salim's world continues to be shaped by the physical and representational violence of settler colonialism.

When we next see Salim he is napping on a narrow bed, dreaming that his lawyer has found his house documents. The remainder of *Port of Memory* consists of images of continued dispossession: A wall of signs in Arabic stating "We miss you," similar to others shown earlier in Hebrew asking about properties for sale in the neighborhood, the fading into black of a still shot of the Hamati family accompanied by the sound of frantic construction; the man on the motorcycle issuing one last maniacal laugh; a last shot of Salim's living room, empty of people and with bedding the women used earlier for napping rumpled along the sofas; one more compulsive handwashing by Fatima; and finally, a shot at dusk with the Hamati family furniture strewn in the road.

Recollection

In *The Roof* and *Port of Memory* Aljafari is concerned with the ethics of the encounters between viewers and characters that his film sets up, but the goal is less to thematize an encounter than to convey an affect, to create a connection between viewer and viewed that is built on a bodily experience with a particular Palestinian structure of feeling that emerges from the experience of ongoing dispossession (Tawil-Souri 2014).[10] In *Recollection*, Aljafari starts from a different temporal position, picking up where *Port of Memory* left off. Its temporality is post-catastrophe—not the ongoing *Nakba* that is the subject of most Palestinian films. Jaffa has already been lost, destroyed, appropriated, and redeveloped for others. What is left for Palestinians are images. In his intensive engagement with those images Aljafari has created a surprisingly optimistic film. There is life, work, and subjectivities to be formed even after the collapse of an aspiration.

In the press kit for *Recollection* there appears in large-font italics the sentence, "I'll let you be in my dream if I can be in your dream." The statement is an assertion of equality, humanity, and survival, an invitation, and a framing of the film as a work of the imaginary, the hoped-for, and the subconscious. It is in these qualities that the film's optimism lies. Its dissidence arises not from any resistance or working in opposition to another, but rather in its use of aesthetic precarity—blurriness, glitches, a jerky camera, odd framing, and indistinct sound—as tools to reconfigure the attempted erasure of Palestinians into the material from which an agential intervention in representational practices surrounding Israel/Palestine can be undertaken.

Built primarily out of footage from Israeli and American movies shot in Jaffa from the 1960s through the 1980s, Aljafari removes the actors from the foreground of these films to reveal the destruction of the city that these works could not help but document, and to find the Palestinian residents of Jaffa and traces of their lives that lurk as "mistakes" in the background of these films. Aljafari created postcards from the film footage that blurrily document figures and architectural details of Jaffa and its environs. Much of the film consists of a refilming of these stills and the manipulated Hollywood/Israeli footage. Through this refilming Aljafari trains the viewer to look at the images in a new way, to search along with his camera for the alternative characters (and perhaps their narratives) that are embedded within.

Recollection's assertion of agency lies in its thematization of image-making itself, in its willful manipulation of the imbrication of history and fantasy that the Jaffa films with which Aljafari works inadvertently captured, and its audacious and virtuoso performance of a deliberate uncovering of history and its reconfiguring as fantasy to arrive at a truth. However, Aljafari's purpose is not simply to uncover what has been erased. By playing with blurriness, close-ups, and framing, he reveals something of the complexity of the relationship between the foreground and the background, between the Palestinian and the Israeli, the marginalized and the centered, and their respective narratives. Proximity and enlargement are necessary to reveal the hidden Palestinian characters, but they disappear again into abstraction if the zoom is too radical. In other words, the precarious subject becomes visible after the excision of the foreground, but remains precarious, fleeting, blurry, and partial. At the same time, the training of the viewer's eye that constitutes much of the first part of the film normalizes the blur, the jerk, and the un-centered frame. Viewers, whose perspective is that of a visitor walking through this post-catastrophic dreamscape, grow so accustomed to the precarious image that clarity and centering, when they appear, are rendered jarringly artificial. The move echoes the impact on viewers of the Azrieli Tower scene in *The Roof*.

Recollection is not only a virtuoso performance of forensics, however. A forensics of old footage can assert a presence, but its claims will always be about the past. Having staked out the world of images and the imaginary as his area of intervention, Aljafari addresses the possibilities within the virtual in a post-catastrophe manipulation of the Palestinians, who, as he puts it, "smuggled themselves into the images." Through animation he takes the dozens of Palestinians he has found in film backgrounds and places them in the foreground of his own film. En masse, they move eerily through one of the dilapidated streets. The movement of the characters imbues them with life, foreclosing the association with death that characterizes the still photograph. By moving these phantoms of an alternative narrative from the background to the foreground, he undoes the marginalization that arises in part from their fixity in the framing created for Hollywood and Israeli movies. As with the earlier passages, this animated sequence is reshot with a handheld camera that sometimes veers up to reveal the sky, rooflines, and just the tops of peoples' heads, and sometimes angled down at their walking feet. The camera asserts its presence—its capacity for framing and focusing—and thereby prevents viewers from forgetting the constructed nature of its images.

The footage is accompanied by one of the rare passages of extradiegetic music in the film, a feature that helps to transform these figures from accidental documentary traces to characters in a cinematic and imaginative work. It ends with the marchers coming suddenly into sharp focus. In post-catastrophe Jaffa, there is no *essential* difference between these figures and the actors Aljafari has excised from the footage. Palestinians, like their Israeli and American counterparts, can also be the subjects of fiction, just as Israelis and Americans, like Palestinians, can be erased. "I'll let you be in my dream if I can be in your dream."

Aljafari continues to play with footage in an increasingly outrageous fashion during the last minutes of the film. An improbable car chase ends in a manic dash through a cornfield. Ominous music underlies an upside-down clip of the Israeli singer Ofra Haza as she walks apprehensively through an old building, picks up a white rabbit, pulls aside a red curtain, and then runs outside. Aljafari's montage makes it appear as if she is startled to find herself entering the dream-world of grainy Palestinians that Aljafari has been constructing for his viewers over the course of the past hour.

Through this blatant manipulation of found footage, Aljafari lays claim to fiction and the imaginative, transcending (without abandoning) the evidentiary mode that can always be answered with a counterclaim (the "greater" trauma of the Holocaust that justifies the violence and dispossession of Palestinians, the recent development of a human rights movement for Israeli settlers, and right-wing challenges to the evidentiary force of

B'Tselem videos, to name a few salient instances) (Gordon 2014; Perugini and Gordon 2015). It makes manifest the constructed nature of cinema (a constructedness that is particularly apparent after spectators have been trained throughout the film to "watch" images in entirely new ways); most importantly, it interjects into a Palestinian film the pure joy of constructing a narrative through the manipulation of the indexical image.

Conclusion

What can one do once one realizes the inevitability of one's own dispossession? How can one remain truthfully engaged with one's past, one's environment, the fate of one's family without giving in to despair? How can one create a cinema that goes beyond the melodramatic temporality of "too late," or that avoids the false optimism of resistance after it has become evident that resistance, whether violent or otherwise, will not undo the ongoing processes of theft and erasure that underpin every settler colonial project? These are the questions that Palestinian filmmakers face today. Aljafari's films are not a "solution" to conflict, occupation, or dispossession. They do not address the problems of refugees; of bombings and shootings by Israeli settlers, police, and military; of house demolitions, checkpoints, and walls. Rather, through their empathic unsettlement, they are expressions of a Palestinian agential subjectivity that simultaneously cedes no rights but make no claims. They do not ask for equal rights for Palestinian citizens of Israel, for half of Jerusalem, or one, two, or more states, Jewish, secular, democratic or otherwise. Instead, they are enactments of an ability to create and manipulate images in a world that is increasingly dominated by the visual.

"[H]istory has been made out of man's need to detach and project fabulous images, to send them as delegates into the future to act in the very long term, after death," says Jean Genet in *Prisoner of Love* (Genet [1986] 2003, 301). Gazans, Palestinian filmmaker Abdelrahman Shehadah warns us in his film *To My Father* (*Illa abi*, 2008), must attend to the nature of the images they create because of the powerful connection between archives and the subjectivities of the future. "A picture lasts longer than a human being," Aljafari writes in the text that scrolls like idiosyncratic credits at the end of *Recollection*. It is in the realm of images that Palestinians, Israelis, and Americans can meet as equals. It is therefore in the realm of images that this dissident idea can be enacted and alternative subjectivities forged.

References

Abounaddara. 2017. "Dignity Has Never Been Photographed." documenta14.de.

Azoulay, Ariella. 2008. *The Civil Contract of Photography*. New York: Zone Books.

Bennet, Jill. 2005. *Empathic Vision: Affect, Trauma, and Contemporary Art.* Stanford, CA: Stanford University Press.

Berger, John. 1980 [1972]. "Photographs of Agony." In *About Looking,* 37–40. New York: Pantheon Books.

Demos, T.J. 2013. *The Migrant Image: The Art and Politics of Documentary During Global Crisis.* Durham, NC: Duke University Press.

Emmelhainz, Irmgard. 2009. "A Trialogue on *Nervus Rerum*: Irmgard Emmelhainz and the Otolith Group (Kodwo Eshun and Anjalika Sagar)." *October* 129: 129–32.

Fassin, Didier. 2008. "The Humanitarian Politics of Testimony: Subjectification Through Trauma in the Israeli–Palestinian Conflict." *Cultural Anthropology* 23, no. 3: 531–58.

Feldman, Allen. 2004. "Memory Theaters, Virtual Witnessing and the Trauma-Aesthetic." *Biography* 27, no. 1: 163–202.

Figueroa, Victor. 2009. *Not at Home in One's Home: Caribbean Self-Fashioning in the Poetry of Luis Pales Matos, Aime Cesaire and Derek Walcott.* Madison, NJ: Fairleigh Dickinson University Press.

Genet, Jean. [1986] 2003. *Prisoner of Love.* Translated by Barbara Bray. New York: New York Review of Books.

Glissant, Edouard. 1997. *Poetics of Relation.* Translated by Betsy Wing. Ann Arbor: University of Michigan Press.

Gordon, Neve. 2014. "Human Rights as a Security Threat: Lawfare and the Campaign Against Human Rights NGOs." *Law and Society Review* 48, no. 2: 311–44.

El-Hassan, Azza. 2002. "Art and War." In *Unplugged: Art as the Scene of Global Conflicts = Kunst als Schauplatz globaler Konflikte,* edited by Gerfried Stocker and Christine Schöpf, 280–83. Ostfildern: Hatje Canz.

Hochberg, Gil Z. 2015. *Visual Occupations: Violence and Visibility in a Conflict Zone.* Durham, NC: Duke University Press.

Keenan, Thomas. 2001. "Publicity and Indifference (Sarajevo on Television)." *PMLA* 117, no. 1: 104–16.

LaCapra, Dominick. 2001. *Writing History, Writing Trauma.* Baltimore: Johns Hopkins University Press.

Lebow, Alisa, ed. 2012. *The Cinema of Me: The Self and Subjectivity in First Person Documentary Films.* London: Wallflower Press.

Limbrick, Peter. 2012. "From the Interior: Space, Time, and Queer Discursivity in Kamal Aljafari's *The Roof.*" In *The Cinema of Me: The Self and Subjectivity in First Person Documentary Films,* edited by Alisa Lebow, 96–115. London: Wallflower Press.

Marks, Laura U. 2000. *The Skin of the Film: Intercultural Cinema, Embodiment, and the Senses.* Durham, NC: Duke University Press.

Perugini, Nicola, and Neve Gordon. 2015. *The Human Right to Dominate*. Oxford: Oxford University Press.

Rancière, Jacques. 2009. *The Emancipated Spectator*. Translated by Gregory Elliott. London: Verso.

Sliwinski, Sharon. 2011. *Human Rights in Camera*. Chicago: University of Chicago Press.

Sontag, Susan. 1977. *On Photography*. New York: Farrar, Straus & Giroux.

———. 2004. *Regarding the Pain of Others*. New York: Picador.

Stocker, Gerfried, and Christine Schöpf, eds. 2002. *Unplugged: Art as the Scene of Global Conflicts = Kunst als Schauplatz globaler Konflikte*. Ostfieldern: Hatje Canz.

Tawil-Souri, Helga. 2014. "Cinema as the Space to Transgress Palestine's Territorial Trap." *Middle East Journal of Culture and Communication* 7: 169–89.

Torchin, Leshu. 2012. *Creating the Witness: Documenting Genocide on Film, Video, and the Internet*. Minneapolis: University of Minnesota Press.

Williams, Raymond. 1977. *Marxism and Literature*. Oxford: Oxford University Press.

Wing, Betsy. 1997. "Introduction." In *Poetics of Relation*, translated by Betsy Wing, x–xx. Ann Arbor: University of Michigan Press.

Yaqub, Nadia. 2014. "Refracted Filmmaking in Muhammad Malas' *The Dream* and Kamal Aljafari's *The Roof*." *Middle East Journal of Culture and Communication* 7, no. 2: 152–68.

26

SYRIA PORTRAYED IN TWO
DOCUMENTARIES BY OMAR AMIRALAY

Ahmad Izzo

This paper examines two documentary films by the Syrian filmmaker
Omar Amiralay: *Everyday Life in a Syrian Village* (*al-Haya al-yawmiya
fi qarya suriya*, 1972/74) and *The Chickens* (*al-Dajaj*, 1977), in which
he addresses 1970s Syrian society. Film critics generally regard Amiralay
as the first documentary filmmaker in Syria (Salti 2012), or, more eloquently, as the "craftsman of documentary in Syria" (Valassopoulos 2013,
195). For Amiralay, making films is not just an artistic project, but rather
constitutes political involvement, by which means he organically inserts
himself into the everyday lives of people (Yakoub 2006) and deals with the
complexities of life, or, as he stated, "Contact and exchange with people
as well as engagement with reality transformed this choice into a deep
convention, and I have come to believe, that mere mortals such as myself
could not imagine a fiction with characters and a plot more enchanting
and powerful than that which happens in the crucible of the everyday"
(Amiralay 2006a, 97).

Amiralay shares to a large extent the theoretical view of Friedmann
and Morin with regard to filmmaking (2010 [1952], 22): that film makes
it possible through its aesthetic characteristics to recreate a microcosm
of society and thus to represent the images of the same society, which is
why films can be regarded as social documents (Hennebelle 1976). That
does not mean, however, that the term *documentary* is synonymous with
objectivity—on the contrary. Based on this, the filmmaker's political stance
is of major importance when it comes to creating stories that are selected
from a non-filmic reality and transformed into a filmic reality (Roscoe
and Hughes 1999, 143; Escher and Zimmermann 2001). Amiralay's role
is analogous to that of a cartographer, in the sense that the final product,
be it a film or a map, positions the recipients not only geographically but
also ideologically.

Omar Amiralay: A Biographical Introduction

Amiralay was born in Damascus in 1944; his father was an Ottoman military officer and his mother was Lebanese (Ginsberg and Lippard 2010). Initially he had studied fine arts at the University of Damascus, before he began his studies at the French film school La Fémis in Paris in 1967. The students' protests that broke out there in May 1968 provided Amiralay with an initial opportunity for filming such events (Soueid 2006). Transforming the political act into a cinematic project motivated him to make documentaries: "I do not know why I dedicated myself to documentaries from the very beginning. But politics certainly played a role: When I left the film school in Paris in 1968 to learn filmmaking on the street, my first contact with cinema was inevitably political and politicized" (Forum Transregionale Studien 2015 [2007]).

Immediately after returning to Syria, he eagerly took the first steps to realizing his documentation project. This resulted in the *Film-Essay on the Euphrates Dam* (*Film muhawala 'an sad al-furat*, 1970), which is more like "a modernistic song praising the construction of the Euphrates Dam" (Arnold 2015). At the same time his positive attitude toward the Ba'thist state changed, as will be explained later when analyzing his two films from that period, *Everyday Life in a Syrian Village* and *The Chickens*. In 1974, Amiralay and the Syrian director Mohammad Malas founded the Damascus Cinema Club (Nadi Dimashq al-sinima'i) (Wright 2006, 49; Ginsberg and Lippard 2010, 382) as an alternative film institution, in order to liberate themselves from dependence on the National Film Organization (Ginsberg and Lippard 2010, 264). In the 1980s, the director lived in exile in France (until 1991) after his films were subjected to harsh censorship by the Syrian regime (Armes 2010, 66; Dickinson 2012; Van de Peer 2013).

While the topics that make up Amiralay's documentaries do vary, they generally focus both on the underlying social and political conditions in Arab countries and on the balances of power at various levels and directions. For instance, he made the socialist revolution that was taking place in Yemen a topic in his *On a Revolution* (*'An thawra*, 1978) (Armes 2010, 66). On the other hand, his film *Love Aborted* (*Al-hubb al-maw'ud*, 1983) focused on the social position of women in Egypt, taking the country as a paradigm for an entire Arab society in which patriarchal power mechanisms evoke variable tensions between men and women. Another of his films addressed the Lebanese civil war and its uncontrollable violence: *On a Day of Ordinary Violence, My Friend Michel Seurat . . .* (*Fi yawm min ayam al-'unf al-'adi, mata sadiqi Michel Seurat*, 1996) deals with the abduction of a French sociologist, who died while in captivity during the so-called Western hostage crisis in Beirut in the 1980s (Ginsberg and Lippard 2010, 29). In addition, Amiralay addressed the charismatic image of the traditional ruler in *The Man with the Golden Sole* (*Al-rajul dhu-l-na'l al-dhahabi*, 2000), painting a biographical portrait of Lebanon's late prime minister Rafiq al-Hariri (1944–2005), who had initiated far-reaching urban planning measures in Beirut immediately after the Lebanese civil war in order to build a neoliberal city. The film challenged Amiralay's political beliefs, since he seemed to have veered from the views of convergence between documentary film and documentary filmmaker, and those who possess power and authority. In one scene, three key Lebanese intellectuals, Fawwaz Traboulsi, Samir Kassir, and Elias Khoury, offer scathing criticism of Amiralay. Their criticism is based on the assumption that the film would be viewed as a declaration of capitulating on the alleged truth in favor of monetary power and corruption.

Amiralay's political involvement for public issues is not limited to the cinematic portrayal of social topics. At the beginning of President Bashar al-Assad's term in office, Syria experienced a relative political openness (from July 2000 to February 2001), which became a part of the so-called Damascus Spring. Amiralay and other Syrian intellectuals made a constructive contribution by publishing, among other things, the "Statement of 99" *(Bayan al-tis'a wa-l-tis'in)* within the framework of this democratic atmosphere (Helberg 2012, 86; Schneiders 2013; Boëx 2014, 14-15; Jaki 2014, 49-50.). In this statement the intellectuals called for ending the state of emergency that was declared in March 1963, urgent reforms of the political system, and releasing the regime's political opponents from prisons (Jaki 2014). After the Syrian regime suppressed the Damascus Spring, Amiralay saw this as a sign of the continuation of Syria's political system via succession of power from father to son. He attached great importance to the view that the totalitarian measures of the Ba'th Party would not save the governmental system in Syria from ruin (Amiralay 2006a). In his last film, *A Flood in Ba'th Country* (*Tufan fi bilad al-ba'th*, 2003), he presented stagnation at the political and social levels, and the entrenchment of ideological rigidity. To do so, Amiralay did not just rely on his voice-over comments in order to unequivocally expose his position regarding the Syrian regime, he also used his camera to ascribe symbolic importance to people and critical structures of power—the Madafah (hosting place for dignitaries) and the school and its local representatives; the *mukhtar* and his nephew, and the headmaster of the village school. The uniqueness of these elements and their presence in a small and neglected place like al-Mashi helped Amiralay to recreate a symbolically identical image of the political and social status quo in Syria—increasing corruption and cronyism and the personality cult of Hafez al-Assad. The story of al-Mashi is the story of Syria—a country that, at the time of production, has not witnessed any democratic transfer of political power for nearly half a century. Amiralay focused on the metaphorical meaning of the flood threatening the country because of the possible collapse of the Euphrates Dam in order to simulate another flood in a different sense—fear of the fall of the Assad regime and the imminent collapse of social structures.

Amiralay's sudden death from a heart attack on February 5, 2011 shocked Syrian intellectuals; they had been expecting him to follow the protests against the Ba'th regime with his camera. He was buried in Damascus.

Everyday Life in a Syrian Village: Exploring the Terra Incognita of Syria's Ba'thists

Everyday Life in a Syrian Village is the product of the invaluable collaboration between Amiralay and Syrian playwright Saadallah Wannous (1941–97), which they considered to be a fundamental re-evaluation of the Syrian regime (Al-Hajj 2015). Its objective was to highlight the problematic living conditions of people in eastern Syria, who should have experienced a supposed prosperity (or self-sufficiency at least), especially in the agricultural sector, based on the economic reforms announced by the government under the Ba'th Party in March 1963. From Amiralay's perspective, the village of Mwaylih embodies the perfect example of this. His experience of Mwaylih was analogous to the discovery of a terra incognita in Ba'thist Syria, the existence of which the official propaganda agency tried to conceal.

The circumstances surrounding filming were not easy. The crew visited Mwaylih three times but had problems understanding the locals and, in turn, were perceived and treated by the villagers as outsiders. Being Syrian had no significance at all in Mwaylih (Kennedy-Day 2001, 394). Moreover, the locals initially distrusted Amiralay, his camera, and his constant questions, since they saw the sign of the official car in which Amiralay and his crew arrived in Mwalyih: it belonged to the National Film Organization (Hennebelle 1976).

For Amiralay, this documentary film was a personal attempt to atone for making his first film, *Film-Essay on the Euphrates Dam*, in which he presented propaganda for the construction of that huge project: "*Everyday Life in a Syrian Village* was my own political redemption from prior sins, because I had not paid attention to the tragedy of people" (Soueid 2006, 107). Direct interviews conducted with some villagers allow viewers to form a clear impression of the regional status quo in Syria in light of the local socioeconomic variables, while the images show the extent to which the gap between the government's discourse—which was tireless in promoting the nationalist identity—and the complicated living conditions of underprivileged villagers had become irreconcilable.

Thus the film introduces a group of landless peasants in Mwaylih who are mercilessly thrown around by various powers. The statements provided both by them and by the opposing authority figures, which describe how a tribe called al-Hefl gained observable ascendancy in the region, identify the village as a center of contested tribalism. *Tribe* and *state* can be perceived here as conceptual spaces (Zimmermann and Escher 2005), between which there is tension because of the agricultural policy adopted by the Ba'thists. On the one hand, the state strives to eliminate the *imperium in imperio*, or state-within-a-state, model (Chatty 2010, 29) that is forming due to the unstoppable increase of tribal power. On the other hand, the tribe sees the activities of the general peasants' union, by which the supposedly socialist ideology and the modern conceptualization of land reform and distribution of land ownership infiltrated into the region, as an attack by outsiders against powerful sheikhs who saw themselves as the only *internal* actors in the region.

When the inhabitants of Mwaylih join the general peasants' union, it has thus been interpreted by al-Hefl as crossing the boundaries of local tradition, which is primarily based on loyalty to the tribe's orders. As stated in Amiralay's interviews with some peasants, the tribe aggressively attempted to prevent them from joining this "foreign entity" and thus becoming outsiders.

It is also noticeable in the film that the effectiveness of the government as an administrative and normative apparatus of power, which is represented by official institutions, remains weak with regard to resolving critical internal conflicts within the society. The peasants express doubt as to whether the power mechanisms of the modern state could be effectively activated in the region, since the dynamics of the traditional authority of the tribe are still active, with the systematic seizure of properties among other acts. The central state of Syria is hence not confronted with individuals in this region but rather with the entire tribe, whose members are loyal to the tribalistic orders and values, especially when threatened by *outsiders* (i.e., the state) (Batatu 1999, 22).

The lack of intervention by the state caused a growing hopelessness among the peasants of Mwaylih, leading them sometimes to doubt their identity and their sense of belonging to the country. It is apparent that a peasant commonly interprets the neutral attitude of the state toward the local conflict with al-Hefl as intentional neglect that is based on the weakness of the state apparatus: "Today all the peasants are holding onto their homes. If they think that we're Israelis, they should make us leave! If we're Muslims and citizens of this country, the government should find us a land, or deport us to another country. But where will we go?" he tells Amiralay. The peasants were promised heaven on earth by the revolutionary authorities. These promises turned to sand, which was dispersed by the dry wind.

The state and tribe failed to satisfy the peasants' desire for social recognition. The mosque therefore served as a refuge in the film, a place for immersion in religious ritual in order to forget about this horrible experience. In his portrayal of the mosque Amiralay used montage and camera perspectives to link this place of action with its narrative function as a location of spiritual shelter. The Sufi ritual of *dhikr* offered believers burdened with social misery a mythical space in which ceremonial acts could be designated as magical communication with God, unaffected by the reality of the living world. The practical teachings of the Rifa'iya Sufi order in the form of *wajad*, where the believer is no longer anonymized or marginalized but rather finds God and is at the same time found by God, gave the peasants the sense of social status and recognition that they were missing. They attached special significance to the Islamic mystic Ahmad al-Rifa'i (died AD 1183), since he himself came from a village and his Sufi practices focused primarily on the peasantry (Batatu 1999, 105 ff.). Ahmad al-Rifa'i does not throw sand in the eyes of poor villagers; or at least, his religious teachings do not call villagers "a bit evil," as the police station's chief described their behavior to Amiralay.

Everyday Life in a Syrian Village also approaches the question of social discrepancy between the rural and the urban, which occurs not only at the regional, but also at the national level. *Village* and *city* appear in the film as two spatial dimensions that are charged with opposing meanings, in which *village* represents mainly the dystopian and *city* the utopian.

The view of Mwaylih is presented after the opening credits with different definition settings, camera positions, and perspectives in order to create a cinematic overview of the village. The brief, extreme long, wide, and medium-long shots present Mwaylih as a spooky, remote, and isolated place that is dominated by sand and wind: adjacent mud homes; an empty tavern or an animal-powered mill that are buried by sand dunes; unpaved streets that are virtually deserted. The unescapable harshness of the desert is noticeable in the opening scene. Another important technique for visualizing the dystopian significance of the film space in Mwaylih is the recourse to certain objects in the non-filmic reality. An empty sardine can, the legs of a dead animal, an animal skull lying under rubber tires, gain a narrative function to evoke the symbolic quality of the dystopian in the village. The portrayal of the desert with a wide shot ensures an aesthetic form of remoteness of a village located in eastern Syria. One thing that stands out in the frame is the proportional ratio of people to the filmed landscape, which creates a sense of people becoming lost within the unending expanse of the barren desert landscape. Another example that shows Mwaylih as an isolated space, where people live apart from others, is conveyed through a short scene: A young shepherd lets his flock graze beside a road that runs past the village. Meanwhile, a small, fast-moving car can be seen, while something edible is discarded from the car window. The shepherd, shrouded in a tunic, quickly picks up the thrown-away food and eats eagerly.

Compared to this less-than-appealing presentation of Mwaylih as undesirable living space, the *city* has a utopian character, which is presented on a dual level. On the one hand, the interviews conducted with some people describe the city as a reliable space in terms of the services offered. On the other hand, Amiralay depicts in one scene how the villagers of Mwaylih have gathered on the village green to see a short film, titled *The Syrian Arab Homeland in Good Images (al-Watan al-'arabi al-suri fi laqatat jayyida)*, in which the quality of urban life on the beach in western Syria is presented. The scene starts with a public official who is tasked with organizing this event in Mwaylih by the Syrian Ministry of Culture and National Orientation. Before screening the film, he gives a short speech to the villagers, in which he elucidates the importance of cinema from the state's point of view. For the state, he explains, there is no doubt at all that the mass dissemination of cinematically reproduced events leads to the systematic distribution of its own political ideas. In this way, the cinematic depiction of urban space in this short film bears not only an aesthetic quality, but also a practical value, serving the ideological hopes and expectations of the Ba'th state (Posner and Schmauks 2004).

The people presented on the beach in that short film are shown as strangers within the meaning of Simmel, who are in principle characterized as an "element of the group itself" (Simmel 1958, 509). They are not put in the "unknown" category, but rather in the "intruder" category (Stenger 1998, 24). One thing they share with the inhabitants of Mwaylih is the common status of having the same nationality and living within the same state borders. At the same time, they differ from one another with regard to their way of life, because each group follows different cultural and social discourses: on the one hand, the Bedouin-influenced village tradition, and, on the other hand, a discourse that strives to emulate the West and urban modernity.

The experience of otherness elicited by the film allows the inhabitants of the remote village of Mwaylih to enter a different world through media (Waldenfels 2011).With that, the people depicted on the beach intrusively enter the rural community with their modern notion of culture. The villagers experience on a visual level the modern values of urban life, which are ascribed the connotation of goodness and beauty by the state, in the form of women dressed according to the latest fashion at that time and behaviors that indicate an ability to relax on the beach and the wharf. In addition, the use of the non-diegetic jazz piece "Polvere di Stelle" by Fausto Pappetti does much to strengthen the impression of a comfortable atmosphere at the auditory level. These two minutes alone can challenge what is shown about Mwaylih in the entire film.

Everyday Life in a Syrian Village reaches the end with the scene of a slim old man ripping his clothes angrily. He cries out: "We're hungry and dying!," giving the last statement of Mwaylih's inhabitants, who are forgotten in Syria's eastern desert, suffering from the consequences of aridity, oppression of tribal power, and the absence of any fundamental solution from the republic of the revolutionary Ba'thists.

The Chickens: Melodies of Village Bourgeois

In an interview conducted during the International Film Festival in Berlin in 1979, Amiralay addressed the real reasons behind the production of *The Chickens* (*al-Dajaj*, 1977). His third documentary might be considered as a response to the official Syrian press, which received *Everyday Life in a Syrian Village* with bitter criticism. The starting point of this criticism was the assertion that Mwaylih could in no way represent the situation in Syria, because Amiralay deliberately chose a remote, underdeveloped village to make general statements about daily life in rural Syria. He ironically notes: "[I] [had] chosen another, very exemplary 'case,' a model example on the Damascus–Aleppo national road, a region that has everything to become a 'Syrian Normandy'" (Amiralay 1979).

Amiralay also describes how he had noticed during his periodic visits to the village of Sadad that keeping chickens evolved from a family-organized gainful activity to an out-of-control phenomenon, as chicken operations spread rapidly, with one or two rooms in a home devoted to the endeavor (Amiralay 2006b). Such hasty ambition had an impact on traditional village activites, such as the marginalization of agriculture and abandonement of loom weaving, as well as on the intimacy of the family home. Consequently, both villagers and filmmaker see Sadad as a repulsive place, due to social disarray and economic failure. As a result, young people in particular chose to escape to the city. On the other hand, the city is constructed within the context of the film as a competing space, as an antithesis, that mercilessly draws the vital lifeblood of Sadad.

Considering Amiralay's sarcastic remarks about a Syrian "Normandy," it is not surprising how Sadad is presented to viewers in the film. In contrast to *Everyday Life in a Syrian Village*, in which the cinematically depicted topographies of Mwaylih indicate a dystopian space from the first shot, Amiralay presents a view of the village of Sadad as a space characterized by rural idyll. The view of the village shown at the beginning of the film is created by inside and outside shots of different dimensions such that the representation of Sadad is diametrically opposed to that of Mwaylih. The camera blurs the boundaries between private and public to create a correlation between the village and casual intimacy. This intimacy and rusticity unfold more clearly through close-up shots of Sadad's older women. In this case, the recipient encounters a facial image that cannot be separated from the semantic composition of Sadad as a familiar space at the beginning of the film. The facial expressions captured in close-ups, whether of women or of the man dancing cheerily in front of the camera, exude happiness, joy, and spontaneity. They are aesthetic elements that do not apply to Mwaylih.

The sequence of shots making up the opening scene is accompanied by an *'ataba*, a song genre popular in the region whose text describes the close ties that inhabitants have with their village.

> Nothing in the world can match a speck of soil from Sadad,
> We'll stay here,
> We won't leave our Sadad,
> Where land's more precious than gold.

At first glance, the images suggest that there is nothing that could disrupt the harmonious life they depict. Then a direct reference is made, on the auditory level, to the existence of a threat or uncertainty in Sadad. The use of an *'ataba* (monodic folksong in colloquial Arabic) per se, which can be interpreted more as an implicit chastising within the context of the non-diegetic song, serves as a poetic expression for a social crisis that the village is likely to suffer. The lyrics insinuate that the singer chastises those who have left Sadad. In this context, it should be noted that this genre of songs is imbued with a sentimental correlation in the Arab world, evoking in particular nostalgic memories of a homeland left behind (Asmar and Hood 2001).

Although the idyllic, positive image of Sadad presented at the beginning of the film does not convey the same fateful impression as Mwaylih, it is still necessary to examine the nature of the crises that the inhabitants of Sadad are facing. To do so, Amiralay divides the narrative structure of the film into three sections according to the economic activities in the village: agriculture, weaving with looms, and chicken farming.

In the light of failed agriculture, villagers have to find their way through everyday life by searching for solutions to survive—either the traditional trade of weaving, which has appropriated a space within people's homes, or the emergence of raising chickens as a new opportunity for supposedly gainful activity.

The village, which is mentioned in the biblical book of Numbers (34:8, where it is called Zedad) as part of the description of the borders of Canaan, has a long history of emigration, as an old minister tells Amiralay. Sadad can be thought of as a "mother" village, since around twenty new villages formed as a result of the long periods of drought suffered during the course of history. According to a peasant, the cultivated land in Sadad symbolizes the result of family solidarity of the Christian village community, whereby the peasant families managed to scare off the local feudal lords from appropriating the land (Wirth 1965, 270). The increasing aridity was the main factor in the disappearance of this spirit of solidarity over time, as another inhabitant says. At this point a series of images of graves, abandoned buildings, cracks in the ground, and damaged windmills is followed by an explanation of the economic crisis in the village.

One of the specific features of the aesthetic presentation of economic structures in Sadad, which is characterized by the juxtaposition of traditional and modernized mechanisms of economic production, is indicated through the dramaturgical use of sound: the sequences that show farming and weaving pass with quiet tones, while those showing chicken farming are synchronized with loud squawking.

Amiralay's narrative and aesthetic style, which relies for instance on the utilization of sarcasm for presenting decisive facts, becomes visible when he strives to metaphorically place the spotlight on the sudden emergence of chicken farming in Sadad. To do so, he uses the narrow streets of the village. With his handheld camera, he advances through the streets, thus evoking the entrance of chickens into the village. The images of the streets shown in this sequence are provided in this context with the non-diegetic sounds of military marching. Amiralay benefits from the moment when many inhabitants look with deep skepticism at the new conquerors, that is, the chickens. The camera then captures, with a wide-angle lens, the exterior of a chicken farm, which consists of isolated structures standing next to one another at the edge of the village. The buildings, which are architecturally similar and resemble a military camp, create the absurd impression of being able to profoundly counter the idyllic images and sounds presented at the beginning of the film.

The belief that is anchored in the collective consciousness of the farmers, that raising chickens could be the last resort for escaping the economic dilemma, is in keeping with the gradual disintegration of the spirit of solidarity. The increasing rise in the individual interest that is fed by the power of the capitalist way of production was not just elaborated on through interviews. Attention was also focused on four ideological elements, whose indexical, symbolic, and metaphorical qualities are purposefully used: excerpts from 'Abd al-Wahab's songs, intertitles, camera perspectives, and the metaphorical comparison of the hen mentality with that of the chicken farmers. Amiralay justifies resorting to this with the following comment: "One has to destroy their image, not as people, but rather as deformed representatives of a choice that they did not make. And not only at the level of village, but the entire country" (Amiralay 1979).

The decontextualization of the lyrics of 'Abd al-Wahab's songs occurs in such a manner that the song lyrics can no longer be considered in the context of a romantic relationship. Instead, they correspond from a symbolic perspective with the general sentiment of the chicken farmers, while associated with the operations of raising chickens—an optimistic sentiment that is largely linked with the expectation that all of the current threats might be overcome through chicken farming. In this context, chicken farming is to be understood as a desired magic, supplanting strenuous work in cultivating fields or weaving, by means of which the villagers—who are normally recognized as peasants or craftsmen—evolve into small capitalists. The excerpts of songs by the Egyptian singer that were used in the film belong to the 1930s and 1940s, and reflect the then-dominant cultural ideology of the national bourgeoisie in Egypt (Giant 1997, 50), "conveyed an individualistic mentality to the masses" (Amiralay 1979). Thus the filmmaker proclaims his own vision of the recontextualization of the songs: "I have used all of the sentences that express this mentality as sound for the intertitles" (Amiralay 1979). The use of songs by this singer can also be interpreted from another perspective, where the focus is placed on the importance of 'Abd al-Wahab's personality itself. In Arab popular culture he is regarded as a symbol for the intercultural interaction between East and West or tradition and modernity: "the 'modern' Abd al-Wahab contrasts with the 'backwardness' of the cultural milieu from which he rose" (Armbrust 1996, 69). As a result, it is possible to interpret the selection of 'Abd al-Wahab as a symbolic presentation of the cultural contrast between two opposing mentalities that Amiralay encounters in Sadad, namely the mentality of the urban bourgeoisie and that of village peasants.

Since not all of the chicken breeders could be grouped together on one level in a social sense, this contrast was supposed to be cinematically implemented based on the size of their capital. In this context, the camera has the role of aesthetically conveying the filmmaker's intended reference to the size of the operations of the large chicken farmers. It is remarkable how Amiralay incorporates the large owners with his camera using a frog's-eye view so that their power is emphasized visually.

The emergence of a capitalist activity, and the accompanying rise of an individualistic mentality on the part of the breeders, is therefore not derived from taking the content of the interviews literally. Instead, a conceptual analysis of this situation explores an interpretation of what was said in the interviews and what was captured by the camera's lens based on metaphorical correlation. The intended individualistic mentality, which dominates Sadad after the establishment of a new economic activity, is metaphorically implied by way of example in the following statement made by a small farmer: "The chickens crowd together, like anything that's hungry . . . . When you put down the feed, they start running right away and crowd up together. This one hits this one and that one hits another. The one that's first is the one that's strong." The chickens, which crowd together in certain locations in order to feed or lay eggs and thus shove and jostle one another, largely serve in the context of the film as a metaphor for the individualized tendency to dominate and prevail. Given the fact that the chickens are rivals in relation to one another, where "the survival of the fittest" plays an integral part in their mentality, it can be stated that they become metaphors in this manner for the human relation of the bourgeoisie: the fittest chicken overcomes and eliminates the weakest.

Sadad is depicted in the film as a prime example of a Syrian village that has been losing its potential workforce for the benefit of areas beyond its boundaries. The cinematic portrayal of the migration phenomenon affecting Sadad is of primary interest. Amiralay associates the photos of trucks loaded with young people with this phenomenon. The trucks pass through the entire frame and disappear at the top of the picture. They transport people who want to escape a location that suffers from repellent economic forces.

Due to the development policies pursued by the Ba'th Party, particularly in urban centers in Syria, the chicken farmers appeared as if they suffered from an immovable city complex. Besides the interviews, the significance ascribed to the city is also constituted through the presentation of various images and sounds intended to indicate the urban: the distinct trademark of Mercedes Benz and Le Meridien Hotel, as well as the images of the hotel building in close-ups and wide shots; multistory residential buildings under construction; stacked egg cartons and chickens being roasted on skewers over a grill. The city is depicted as a visualization of what the chicken farmers verbally tell Amiralay. Moreover, city and state are shown as symbolically linked. The visual use of the Mercedes star can be interpreted in two ways. On the one hand the star, together with the M of the Meridien Hotel, is in an indexical relation to the city as a center of capital accumulation and service; on the other hand, the Mercedes star attains an additional symbolic value because of its association with the Ba'th Party. High-ranking officials in the state authorities, in the party, and in the army enjoy privileges (such as Mercedes cars) that essentially contradict the ideological principles of a "revolutionary party" (Batatu 1999, 175).

Sadad represents a demonstrative character of the rural economy, based on a hybrid model that is symbolically anchored in the Arab world with modern mechanisms and economic structures existing alongside traditional structures (Sharabi 1988, 42). This centers around an intentional material lack of systematic organization of farmers in the form of a collective or trade association, due to the increasing individualism that is sustained by their capitalistic tendencies. In this context, Amiralay states, "They wanted to sell everything to the capital, without giving a damn about establishing a production cooperative, not even a capitalistic cooperative" (Amiralay 1979).

The chicken farmers recognized the discrepancy between the state's promises and deeds. In the closing scene of the film, they express not only their implicit fears about their fate in the country, but also an awareness that the economic policy of the Ba'th Party is fundamentally not based on revitalizing rural areas. It was used as a political slogan, behind which the real intentions of the Ba'thists remained concealed: "'Revive the country-side' is their slogan, so we don't move to cities. It's all just talk, because when the conditions dictate, we'll leave for the cities," says a large-scale farmer. After another farmer says the last sentence in the film, "These days, we're afraid," the overlapping voices of men are suddenly transformed into the loud squawking of chickens. In the last shots, the camera backs away from the squawking farmers. Amiralay finally positions the camera at the main entrance to an empty chicken farm, and captures the moment when the iron gate of the farm building closes.

Conclusion

Amiralay's attempts to capture the everyday dynamics of Syrian society in film documentation and present it for discussion are far from banal. Despite his heavy reliance on the interview format as a conventional means of drawing viewers into the story, he also makes significant use of the camerawork, montage, and non-diegetic sound. These elements are successfully used to evoke the symbolic dimension of each of his films. Moreover, Amiralay's political opinions, which were contradictory to those of the Ba'th Party, permitted him to sharply criticize authority figures who represented official and traditional powers, and to acknowledge the lives of subjugated peoples.

His films about Syria might be thus interpreted as counter-propaganda, through which he was able to challenge the myths about Syria constructed through official propaganda. This may be why Amiralay's documentary films are banned in Syria.

Although *Everyday Life in a Syrian Village* and *The Chickens* present two different villages, in each of them the narrative focuses on daily issues that concern the locals. Amiralay dedicated his cinematic projects in Mwaylih and Sadad to trying to expose the experiences of inhabitants who faced the consequences of corrupt policies enacted by totalitarian authorities. He felt that the "ideal worlds" created by the nationalistic and/or religious ideologies should be undermined, at least cinematically. According to Amiralay, this is not possible if the filmmaker deals with material imposed from above (by God, state, sheikh, and so on) as an unquestionable fact.

> My engagement with cinema has also been animated by a different creative input, namely, a search for understanding guided foremost by doubt and skepticism. That skepticism I deem to be one of virtues, not a coin for sin, like those who have relegated their quest for understanding to absolute truth-values laid out in books. The truth in every fact or postulate is suspicious, ambivalent, relative, and ought to be subjected to the test of investigation, history, and accountability. This is one of the reasons my films lie in the liminal space between documentary and fiction; they are crafted with a compulsion to coax ambivalence and titillate doubt. (Amiralay 2006a, 97)

References

Amiralay, Omar. 1979. "*Al Dajaj/Die Hühner.*" *Arsenal Berlin*. arsenal-berlin.de.

———. 2006a. "Were It Not for Cinema." In *Insights into Syrian Cinema: Essays and Conversations with Contemporary Filmmakers*, edited by Rasha Salti, 95–98. New York: Rattapallax Press.

———. 2006b. "Omar Amiralay: aflam tasjiliya ashbah bi-tajarib hayya [Omar Amiralay: Documentary Films Which Are Similar to Live Experiences]". *Al Jazeera*, April 10. aljazeera.com.

Armbrust, Walter. 1996. *Mass Culture and Modernism in Egypt*. Cambridge: Cambridge University Press.

Armes, Roy. 2010. *Filmmakers of the Middle East: A Dictionary*. Bloomington: Indiana University Press.

Arnold, Andrey. 2015. "Filmmuseum: Auf der Leinwand hat Syrien Kraft." *Die Presse*, June 5. diepresse.com.

Asmar, Sami, and Kathleen Hood. 2001. "Modern Arab Music: Portraits of Enchantment from the Middle Generation." In *Colors of Enchantment: Theater, Dance, Music, and Visual Arts of the Middle East*, edited by Sherifa Zuhur, 297–320. Cairo: American University in Cairo Press.

Batatu, Hanna. 1999. *Syria's Peasantry, the Descendants of Its Lesser Rural Notables, and Their Politics*. Princeton, NJ: Princeton University Press.

Boëx, Cécile. 2014. *Cinéma et politique en Syrie: Ecritures cinématographiques de la contestation en régime autoritaire (1970–2010)*. Paris: L'Harmattan.

Chatty, Dawn. 2010. "The Bedouin in Contemporary Syria: The Persistence of Tribal Authority and Control." *Middle East Journal* 64, no. 1: 29–49.

Dickinson, Kay. 2012. "The State of Labor and Labor for State: Syrian and Egyptian Cinema Beyond the 2011 Uprising." *Framework: The Journal of Cinema and Media* 53, no. 1: 99–116.

Escher, Anton, and Stefan Zimmermann. 2001. "Geography Meets Hollywood: Die Rolle der Landschaft im Spielfilm." *Geographische Zeitschrift* 89, no. 4: 227–36.

Forum Transregionale Studien. 2015 [2007]. "Omar Amiralay: Documentary, History and Memory." vimeo.com.

Friedmann, Georges, and Edgar Morin. 2010 [1952]. "Soziologie des Kinos." *Montage/av: Zeitschrift für Theorie und Geschichte audiovisueller Kommunikation* (February 19): 21–41.

Giant, Rami. 1997. *Egypt's Incomplete Revolution: Lutfi al-Khuli and Nasser's Socialism in the 1960s*. London and New York: Routledge.

Ginsberg, Terri, and Chris Lippard. 2010. *Historical Dictionary of Middle Eastern Cinema*. Lanham: Scarecrow Press.

Al-Hajj, Yazan. 2015. "Understanding *Everyday Life in a Syrian Village* Forty Years After Its Production." *Alakhbar English*, February 11. english.al-akhbar.com.

Helberg, Kristin. 2012. *Brennpunkt Syrien: Einblick in ein verschlossenes Land*. Freiburg: Verlag Herder.

Hennebelle, Guy. 1976. "Ein Gespräch mit Omar Amiralay." *Arsenal Berlin*. www.arsenal-berlin.de.

Izzo, Ahmad. 2017. "Die syrische Gesellschaft in den Filmen von Omar Amiralay." publications.ub.uni-mainz.de.

Jaki, Julia. 2014. *Kurzer Frühling in Damaskus: Die syrische Zivilgesellschaft nach Baschar al-Asads Machtübernahme*. Hamburg: Disserta Verlag.

Kennedy-Day, Kiki. 2001. "Cinema in Lebanon, Syria, Iraq and Kuwait." In *Companion Encyclopedia of Middle Eastern and North African Film*, edited by Oliver Leaman, 364–405. London and New York: Routledge.

Posner, Ronald, and Dagmar Schmauks. 2004. "Die Reflektion der Dinge und ihre Darstellung in Bildern." In *Bild—Bildwahrnehmung—Bildverarbeitung*, edited by Klaus Sachs-Hombach and Klaus Rehkämper, 15–31. Wiesbaden: Springer.

Roscoe, Jane, and Peter Hughes. 1999. "Die Vermittlung von 'wahren Geschichten': Neue digitale Technologien und das Projekt des Dokumentarischen." *Montage/av: Zeitschrift für Theorie und Geschichte audiovisueller Kommunikation* (January 8): 134–53.

Salti, Rasha. 2012. "Shall We Dance?" *Cinema Journal* 52, no. 1: 166–71.

Schneiders, Thorsten Gerald. 2013. "Der Arabische Frühling Syriens: Hintergründe, Strukturen, Akteure." In *Der Arabische Frühling: Hintergründe und Analysen*, edited by Thorsten Gerald Schneiders, 231–52. Wiesbaden: Springer.

Sharabi, Hisham. 1988. *Neopatriarchy: A Theory of Distorted Change in Arab Society*. New York: Oxford University Press.

Simmel, G. 1958. *Soziologie: Untersuchungen über die Formen der Vergesellschaftung*. Berlin: Duncker & Humblot.

Soueid, Mohammad. 2006. "Omar Amiralay: The Circassian, Syrian, Lebanese." In *Insights into Syrian Cinema: Essays and Conversations with Contemporary Filmmakers*, edited by Rasha Salti, 99–111. New York: Rattapallax Press.

Stenger, Horst. 1998. "Soziale und kulturelle Fremdheit: Zur Differenzierung von Fremdheitserfahrungen am Beispiel ostdeutscher Wissenschaftler." *Zeitschrift für Soziologie* 27, no. 1: 18–38.

Valassopoulos, Anastasia, ed. 2013. *Arab Cultural Studies: History, Politics and the Popular*. New York: Routledge.

Van de Peer, Stefanie. 2013. "The Moderation of Creative Dissidence in Syria: Reem Ali's Documentary *Zabad*." In *Arab Culture Studies: History, Politics and the Popular*, edited by Anastasia Valassopoulos, 190–209. New York: Routledge.

Waldenfels, Bernhard. 2011. "In Place of the Other." *Continental Philosophy Review* 44, no. 2: 151–64.

Wirth, Eugen. 1965. "Zur Sozialgeographie der Religionsgemeinschaften im Orient (The Social Geography of Religious Groups in the Near East)." *Erdkunde* 19, no. 4: 265–84.

Wright, Lawrence. 2006. "Disillusioned." In *Insights into Syrian Cinema: Essays and Conversations with Contemporary Filmmakers*, edited by Rasha Salti, 45–65. New York: Rattapallax Press.

Yakoub, Hala Alabdalla. 2006. "Interview with Omar Amiralay." In *Insights into Syrian Cinema: Essays and Conversations with Contemporary Filmmakers*, edited by Rasha Salti, 113–17. New York: Rattapallax Press.

Zimmermann, Stefan, and Anton Escher. 2005. "Spielfilm, Geographie und Grenzen: Grenzüberschreitungen am Beispiel von Fatih Akins Spielfilm *Gegen die Wand*." *Berichte zur deutschen Landeskunde* 79, no. 2/3: 265–76.

27

THE BERLIN ASHLAA INCIDENT

Stefan Pethke

A Letter to Filmmaker Hakim Belabbes, Written in September 2011; Author's Comments Added in January 2018

Dear Hakim,
A short introduction of myself:

My name is Stefan Pethke, I am based in Berlin.

We met during the Marrakech Film Festival in 2006, where I had come to represent the Berlinale Talent Campus (now: Berlinale Talents), one of the sections of the Berlin Film Festival.

Another section of the Berlinale, the International Forum of New Cinema, is organized by the Arsenal—Institute for Film and Video Art, which has historically evolved out of a somewhat complicated organigram of the German Cinematheque, and which also runs a movie theater with two screens.

You have surely heard of the Arsenal's showing of a series of nine Moroccan films last week, as your film *Ashlaa* was part of that special program.

At the beginning of September 2011, the Arsenal cinema presented "Upheaval and Diversity—The Moroccan Film Days," a program of nine Moroccan films produced between the years 2001 and 2010. It was curated by Birgit Kohler, co-director of Arsenal—Institute for Film and Video Art, in collaboration with Sonja Hegasy of the Leibniz-Zentrum Moderner Orient.

I went to the *Ashlaa* screening on Friday, September 2, and I would like to share with you a few impressions:

437

Of the six films I could watch from the whole program, yours was the most accomplished work, the most thought out, and the most radical, too!

Your perseverance as a filmmaker goes beyond personal or artistic obsession: In your case, cinema becomes a tool of research, with research results that reveal something. I didn't perceive you as someone preoccupied by esthetical considerations—the beautiful frame—but rather by necessity—the right frame. Your father in a close-up shot in the foreground, and the audiovisual setup—hence: yourself!—in the background, seen through a mirror, is an exemplary framing in that respect.

There are many like you in the Arab-Islamic World who wanted to be film-makers.

27.1.

The above-mentioned Sonja Hegasy uses a very similar film still in her text "Transforming Memories: Media and Historiography in the Aftermath of the Moroccan Equity and Reconciliation Commission" (Hegasy 2017). In this text, Hegasy focuses on the political issue of disappearances in Morocco during the country's notorious Years of Lead, and a short paragraph is dedicated to *Ashlaa (Ashla'/In Pieces/Fragments)*, among others (Hegasy 2017, 89–90). Although illustrating her topic with an image from a dialogue on very personal matters might not serve her actual purpose, it proves two aspects central to the film: the alluring power of Belabbes' aesthetics of subjectivity, and the specific relevance of one sequence in *Ashlaa* where we meet a family of Amazigh people—which sparked off the idea for this very letter, as one can read below.

The presence of your camera is surprising: You have a way of "diving in" into the activities and interactions of your protagonists which remains very natural and fluid, even when it is annoying and insisting.

Your timing is excellent, too, in the camera movements as well as in the editing: When there is a duration shot, duration is needed to see something unfold itself: the poorness of the old uncle; the loneliness of the dying man—both scenes showing the harsh aspects of getting old, a topic that you treat from yet another angle when you show the efforts undertaken by a whole family—yours—to take care of a very much weakened father of yours . . .

The cuts in your film always come at the right moment: They place emphasis, make a comment, or give an idea. In the circumcision sequence, it becomes "Soviet montage," parallelizing the boy's resistance with the beating wings of the sacrificed chicken . . .

I also found it interesting how you play with perspectives in your film, for instance when you adapt one of the "classical" scenes of ethnological film, the killing of the sheep, by turning your camera away from the act itself to the little "American" girls watching it: What a show on their faces! What a beautiful statement about the relation of two different concepts of society, and about bi-nationality!

- The little Americans are asking a lot of questions.
- They've never seen a sacrifice before.

27.2.

Hakim Belabbes was a student of American and African literature at Rabat's Mohamed V University, then left Morocco for film studies, first in Lyon, and finally at the Columbia College in Chicago, where he has lived since the late 1980s. Because the United States has a policy of birthplace nationality, Belabbes' children have American passports, hence the reference to the "little 'American' girls."

Needless to say, Belabbes' travels reflect migratory movements characteristic of all the stages of globalization since the era of decolonization. What the resulting complexity of relations does to the individual has been categorized unsatisfactorily ever since, from the dubious "metropolis/periphery" dichotomy and the moral blackmail of "braindrain" to more up-to-date suggestions of flexible identities.

In any case, I find your film extremely precise in terms of its autobiographical approach. Against the backdrop of the many navel-gazings, which continue to multiply exponentially with the easy access to digital image production, it is very reassuring to re-discover to what extent the personal message can be the source of basic information—provided its means and rules have previously been examined with care.

Indeed, your film is an open meditation on cinema and the very diverse forms it can have: There are different ways of staging—your work seems to cover a wide range of them. There are different ways of looking, first of all technically speaking, including watching images on a laptop. Also, a history of technology becomes visible, with the different video formats that you used, showing through in different "grains" or "textures" of the images that you produced over the years.

On March 16, 2013, Belabbes gave a lecture at Shangri La—Museum of Islamic Art, Culture & Design, in Honolulu, Hawaii, USA, to celebrate his residency as part of the Caravanserai 2012–13 film residency tour (see reference list). In this seventy-two-minute speech, with film excerpts bearing the title "Autobiographical Strategies: Writing with Images," Belabbes also elaborated on criticism he was constantly confronted with, according to which his films lacked contact with the modern, the contemporary—and he seemed to show some kind of understanding when he related his film-making approach to his hometown Boujad in central Morocco, described by him as "not ceasing to die."

I want to object definitively to that kind of criticism. Firstly, for what has long become commonplace in the humanities: instead of ONE modernity, we rather deal with "mutually constitutive modernities," as the Moroccan-American anthropologist Tarek Elhaik suggests (even though in the very different context of contemporary arts in Mexico; Elhaik 2016, 47). Elhaik is not only a pupil of Paul W. Rabinow (who counts as one of today's anthropologists most actively working on the notion of contemporaneity—and who, by the way, started his academic career with fieldwork in Morocco); he also is a longtime confidant of Belabbes, with whom he shares a basic biographical element: both left Morocco for the United States in their twenties.

But, more importantly, I would like to argue that Belabbes is utterly modern/contemporary not because of WHAT he films, but because of HOW he films. Regardless of his specific topics, he does not cease to remind us of the notorious range of devices of cinema: His films are crowded with visible arrangements for camera and sound and actors/protagonists, team instructions on and off screen, jump cuts, tech failures, and so on—everything that is violently made invisible by the motion picture machine, and that has been explored by a branch of experimental film focusing on the margins of the standard frame, on the fringes of the apparatus, on the Off to the manufacturing of meaning in the movie industry. Also, Belabbes can combine documentary and fiction in the same film, use the same footage over several films, and mix media. In other words, he resorts to a wide range of the postmodern vocabulary of audiovisual gestures. By doing so, he makes the visibility of his means of artistic (and intellectual) production an essential part of his work, documenting the process of filmmaking itself—and the claim that shooting film should be a praxis inseparable from personal life seems almost palpable. By not only involving, but even exposing himself, he delivers his very own version of the romantic struggle for the unity of life and art: full of pathos and contradictions, torn between ambition and self-questioning, shuttling between country of origin and home of choice, and always aware of what his toolset is, he seems to become the author of his own transnational filmmaker self.

So, time passes by, which is the central pillar of more then one family saga . . . . But *Ashlaa* is a film about a family which spares us the anecdotal. It arranges its ingredients so that the representation of a specific family network comments on the generic concept of family itself. Far from being a family like any other (which is made clear very soon), your family reflects nonetheless the circumstances of its existence, i.e., the larger contexts, generally called "society" and/or "era."

How could it be otherwise, anyway? Reflection—what makes your film so strong is its radical subjectivity as well as its radical visuality/cinephilia, although your images strictly insist on the impact of the generic conditions defined by the bigger structures, for instance the political ones.

This is why the central scene of *Ashlaa*, at least in last Friday's projection at the Arsenal, happened to be the one where you broaden your horizon of introspection, where you open your field of vision to that other family of Amazigh (formerly known as Berbers) who grieves for thirty years over the disappearance of their son/brother/uncle.

By the middle of the film, the mood, which is already very charged with emotions, thanks to what the film has already accomplished to get there, is now even stressed by the dignified despair of these very modest people. Then, another man joins the scene, a man who was in prison for ten years, a survivor. He tries to give his account, asking to be excused for his nervousness—and we can sense that he also asks to be excused for having survived, to be there instead of the other person, the missed one.

In this very moment, we start to hear a very strange noise: someone is exhaling heavily. For a few seconds we look for the sound's source inside the image, but quickly the crescendo of the hyperventilation resolves all doubt: this sound of excessive empathy emerges from the audience. It goes on to get louder and louder, to culminate in a never-ending series of high-pitched female sobs, now entirely dominating the film's soundtrack. All of us in the theatre are baffled and frozen: What is happening? When the image turns lighter from time to time, we scan the seats. We see two persons bent over an apparently empty seat between them, and we understand: Someone has collapsed there, the pain is two-fold, probably, as a feeling of fresh shame adds to an old wound. After a while, someone leaves the room: to look for help? The sobs go on, transforming into sighs and, very slowly, calming down. Meanwhile nothing else happened: no doctor, no intervention at all, by no one from the audience nor the theatre staff. Total paralysis! The film moves on, pityless. The sequence ends, followed by darker images. Three individuals abruptly get up from their seats and hurry to the exit. Suddenly there's a bright frame in the film. The three runaways are caught in the projector's beam, for everybody to see: It's three young men. How on earth the sound we all had heard just a few moments ago could have emanated from a male body, the rest of the audience seems to wonder, in collective awestruck silence.

You don't need to have studied psychology to assume that an effect of identification had occurred; undoubtedly, the sequence had triggered the memory of a similar experience. Considering the young age of the three "fugitives," we might have witnessed the affective outburst of other uncles, cousins, brothers.

Please forgive us. We've burdened you with our story.

27.3.

Belabbes had *Ashlaa* structured in fifteen chapters. With the exception of the introductory sequence, each of these chapters is preceded by a title card–like chapter heading.

The disappearance sequence is the central chapter of *Ashlaa*. The whole film is eighty-eight minutes long, and this chapter, titled "Weight of the Shadow," starts at 40'19, close to the middle of the film.

The sequence is also central in the sense that it runs for more than fifteen minutes. Thus, it is—by far—the most extensive chapter of *Ashlaa*.

Also, it triggered the production of another feature-length film by Belabbes, bearing the same title. The film *Weight of the Shadow* was released five years later (see filmography).

This being said, *Ashlaa* is obviously a film about a father, and a work of mourning about his death.

Oh, film and its relation with ghosts/spectres! I did not need this incident to happen to appreciate your film. But what the incident definitively could do for me, was to confirm the film's conceptual strength, its massive energy of empathy, with the potential to crack up more than one!

I thank you for this film, which goes very far on many levels: There is the level of great personal honesty, the level of lucid perception of the world with its rites of social cohesion, last but not least the level of know-how in filmmaking, a logical mastery of the cinematographic machine. All of this results in an act of emancipation of a person (yourself) and the one of an art form (cinema), not limiting itself to naively celebrating the little individual soul, but staying conscious of the fact that the self is an indispensable starting point. From there, from the exploration of the intimate, you reached out very far, discovering the world!

Ashlaa is an extremely encouraging film. It calls to be followed: It is still possible to want to make films!

Thank you and all the best,

Stefan[1]

Belabbes' reply to my email was laconic. It said: "A brother!" Now, years later, I can hear in that reply a strange echo resonating in the vast space between (at least) three continents, and through the mysterious, maze-like corridors stretching through centuries of time, when Rabinow opens his *Reflections on Fieldwork in Morocco* (1977) with a famous Charles Baudelaire quote: You know him reader, that refined monster,—Hypocritish reader,—my fellow,— my brother!

Hakim Belabbes Filmography

(Overseen and completed by the filmmaker, February 1, 2018)

Sweat Rain/'Araq al-shitta/Pluie de sueur
Morocco 2016, 126 minutes
Weight of the Shadow/Thiqqal al-zill/Le poids de l'ombre
Morocco/United Arab Emirates 2015, 82 minutes
(feature-length documentary tale about one character of *Ashlaa*'s epyno-
  mous chapter)
*Defining Love: A Failed Attempt/Muhawalattun fashila li ta'rif al-hubb/Une
  vaine tentative de définir l'amour*
Morocco/USA 2012, 90 minutes
Faces/Wujuh
Morocco 2012, 40-episode documentary series for Moroccan TV Net-
  work Al Aoula, 26 minutes per episode
Boiling Dreams/Shi ghadi wa shi jay/Rêves brûlants
Morocco 2011, 102 minutes
Children's Games and Dreams/Al'ab wa ahlam atfal/Jeux et rêves d'enfants
Morocco 2011, 52 minutes
In Pieces/Ashlaa (ashla')/Fragments
Morocco/United Arab Emirates 2010, 88 minutes
These Hands/Hazihi al-ayadi/Ces mains-ci
Morocco/United Arab Emirates 2008, 120 minutes
Why, O Sea?/'Alaysh al-bhar?/Pourquoi, Ô mer?
Morocco/United Arab Emirates 2006, 87 minutes
Threads/Khait al-ruh/Les fibres de l'âme
Morocco 2003, 92 minutes
Tell the Water/Ihki li-l-bahr/Raconte à l'eau
Morocco 2002, 20 minutes
A Witness/Shahid/Témoin
Morocco 2001, 15 minutes
R'maa/'Ubaydat al-rami/R'maa
Morocco 2001, 30 minutes
*Three Angels, No Wings/Thalathatu malai'kattin bi-ajnihattin mutakassira/
  Trois anges aux ailes cassées*
Morocco 2001, 30 minutes
Whispers/Hamasat/Chuchotements
Morocco 1999, 15 minutes
A Shepherd and a Rifle/Ra'in wa bunduqiyya/Un berger et un fusil
Morocco 1998, 50 minutes
Still Ready/Nisa'un muqawimat/Toujours prêts
Morocco 1997, 60 minutes

Bound: A Nest in the Heat/Bu-Jad: 'ushunn fi-l-qayd/Boujad, un nid dans la chaleur
Morocco 1992, 45 minutes
Sources for a Hakim Belabbes filmography, none of them perfectly
   accurate:
http://www.imdb.com/name/nm1485865/?ref_=nmbio_bio_nm
https://mubi.com/cast/hakim-belabbes
https://iffr.com/en/persons/hakim-belabbes

References

Arsenal—Institute for Film and Video Art. 2011. "Upheaval and Diver-
   sity—The Moroccan Film Days." arsenal-berlin.de.
Belabbes, Hakim. 2013. "Autobiographical Strategies: Writing with
   Images." https://vimeo.com/62822443.
Elhaik, Tarek. 2016. *The Incurable Image: Curating Post-Mexican Film and
   Media Arts*. Edinburgh: Edinburgh University Press.
Hegasy, Sonja. 2017. "Transforming Memories: Media and Historiog-
   raphy in the Aftermath of the Moroccan Equity and Reconciliation
   Commission." In *The Social Life of Memory: Violence, Trauma, and
   Testimony in Lebanon and Morocco*, edited by Norman Saadi Nikro and
   Sonja Hegasy, 83–112. Cham: Palgrave Macmillan.
Rabinow, Paul W. 1977. *Reflections on Fieldwork in Morocco*. Los Angeles:
   University of California Press.

28

THE UAE'S NUJOOM ALGHANEM: THE PAST, THE PRESENT, THE NATION, AND THE INDIVIDUAL

Alia Yunis

One of the most often repeated quotes from the founder of the United Arab Emirates (UAE), Sheikh Zayed bin Sultan al-Nahyan, is "A nation without a past is a nation without a present or a future. Thank God, our nation has a flourishing civilization, deep-rooted in this land for many centuries." Numerous UAE heritage festivals, as well as corporate films, museum exhibitions, and even restaurant menus, are working these days toward validating Sheikh Zayed's words. Indeed, if there is a trending buzzword in the UAE in recent years, it has been "heritage."

Dubai-born director Nujoom Alghanem's works are often seen as films about fading traditions, such as fishing, camel racing, beekeeping, and herbal medicine. Three of her films actually use heritage festivals as sets in the structuring of the stories. Always soft-spoken but sure of herself, she bristles at this idea. "I don't make films about heritage," she told me during a recent conversation over Skype. "I make films about characters."

28.1. Hamama making her medicines. *Hamama* (2010), directed by Nujoom Alghanem.

Alghanem's films are indeed not cut-and-paste TV documentaries about cultural traditions. Her films deal with a more subtle side of the making and losing of heritage, one that has evolved naturally from the people to whose stories she is attracted. She uses the word "character" rather than "subject" because of her beginnings in narrative film during her studies in the United States and Australia—and because each of her films focuses on one person whom she captures over time in a raw and emotional state. This is not an easy accomplishment in the UAE, where people, particularly women, are reluctant to speak on camera, let alone allow a multinational camera crew into their world in the intimate way her films often do.

When one looks at Alghanem's films collectively, the common themes are aging, lost love, and the determination not to lose the present or the past because of other people's plans for the future. All these things together speak to a subtle but profound loneliness. However, this loneliness is not only a sorrow but also a virtue, a reminder of what we give up without our heritage to cling to, not only as a nation but also as individuals.

Loneliness in her body of work becomes part of the UAE's collective memory—it is personal, but it is also national. And her films show that this is felt across generations, saved from the pain of irretrievable loss through kindness between generations, and to a lesser degree, between different nationalities, and more often than not, the generosity of the ruling sheikhs.

For most of her characters, unappreciated or unexpected change comes with acceptance of the higher power of God's will. In *Hamama* (2010), the title character, a healer, refuses to move, even though a road is planned to run right through her home. In *Honey, Rain & Dust* (*'Assal wa mattar*, 2016), elderly 'A'isha, a beekeeper, waits for the long-absent rain to arrive as a pack of expat bikers rides by her farm. "Look at the dust they are bringing," she says. "But what can we say? We should be nice to outsiders. That is our way." In *Sounds of the Sea* (*Sawt al-bahr*, 2014), a younger man tries to coach music out of the nearly toothless mouth of the fisherman who sang the best love songs. In *Red Blue Yellow* (*Ahmar azraq asfar*, 2013), Najat, a contemporary visual artist, continues to live on her own despite being the last Emirati in her faded Dubai neighborhood—because without this family house, she would really be alone. In *Amal* (2011), the title character, a Syrian actress in Dubai, struggles with her conflicted feelings about living away from home. In a country in which more than 80 percent of the population is from abroad, *Amal* is also the only UAE feature film with a fully developed expatriate.

For many of Alghanem's characters, there is a current absence of a romantic partner, children, and friendly neighbors. These things are all part of the past for them.

But these circumstances are not projections of Alghanem's own life. She is the mother of three adult daughters, and her husband, the esteemed Emirati poet Khalid Abdalnoor, is her producing partner. They connected through poetry, as Alghanem is also a respected poet, which comes across in her films' reliance on landscapes that reveal unspoken details and the visualized silences of her characters.

That Alghanem even has a body of work makes her a rare filmmaker in the UAE. In 2008, the UAE government launched Image Nation, a film production company with a fund of US$1 billion committed to creating a local film industry. In reality, a fledgling UAE film community already existed, begun at the grassroots in the mid-1990s by a collective of determined Emiratis who would show their films, mostly to each other, at the annual Emirates Film Competition. Alghanem came of age as a director with these filmmakers. However, these early Emirati filmmakers mostly made short narrative films, were male, didn't stay in film for the long haul, and, aside from Nawaf al-Janahi, did not go on to make feature-length films.

Now in her early fifties, Alghanem is the only Emirati director who has quietly established herself in feature-length documentaries. Her first documentary film, *Between the Two Banks* (*Bayn al-dufatayn*, 1999), a black and white film about Dubai's last local boat rower, became the first UAE film to play beyond the Arab world when it debuted at the Yamagata International Documentary Film Festival, and it has played around the world ever since. It is a short film, and she has gone on to make seven feature-length films, as well as a short narrative.

Alghanem recognizes that her audience is not at the UAE's multiplexes, which are programmed primarily with Hollywood blockbusters. "When the footage is cinematic and so is your structure, TV is just a possibility but it is not the target," she says. "I work on my films to have them in film festivals. I learned that when I was a film student in Griffith University. My professor encouraged me to try to find the right film festivals for my films, so this is always on my mind. Only recently, local television offered to air two of my documentaries, and I've had opportunities with Etihad, Emirates, and Turkish Airlines."

But as she travels, Alghanem doesn't want to carry the female Emirati label any more than the heritage label. "I'm always responsible for making a good film, an interesting film, this is the technical and aesthetic responsibility," she says. "As for the fact that I'm a woman and Emirati, this is my role in society. I'm just open to interesting people, and I'm always searching for them."

She attributes her ability to get her subjects to open up to her years working as a reporter at UAE's *Al-Ittihad* newspaper. But she cringes at the

28.2. Poster of *Nearby Sky* (2014), directed by Nujoom Alghanem.

thought of making TV films, or reportage, although she has discovered many of her characters after seeing them at events on TV.

While her first films were based on male characters, she finds it easier to work with women. "Maybe it's because the women are more serious," she says. "Because when the women say, 'Yes, I will do this film,' they are very serious. And you can trust them, and you can rely on them. I don't find it the same with men. They have their own conditions. They are also more conservative than women. For example, when women open the door, they allow you to meet the children, the spouses, but the men have conditions. They have boundaries. They say, 'I can meet you outside of my house, but you can't come inside.'"

The UAE, and the Gulf in general, is a TV culture. "So the characters think about you as someone who is coming from TV. They think you will spend a couple of hours with them and leave. Then the next day it will be on air, and they can show it to their friends on YouTube. Film is another process. To go deeper, you need to take time. And this is a new culture for them. Even if the character has been on TV, their style of speaking is like preaching and describing—you need to spend time with them to change this style."

Proof of her words is reflected in her films. *Hamama* was the quickest film she made—shot and edited within a year because she had sufficient funding after receiving significant prize money for *al-Mureed* (*al-Murid*, 2008). While she does capture the heart of Hamama, the healer, the camerawork is less cinematic than her other films, and there are elements of television style, such as a sit-down interview with a medical doctor and a healing session that looks staged, with a female patient dressed as an Emirati woman. But her other films have taken her much longer, up to five years, in an odd way benefiting from the slow process of getting funding to get even closer to her characters, without needing to create material not intrinsic to the setting.

She estimates her documentaries cost on average US$140,000, no matter how long they take to make. She gets the money in bits and pieces from the UAE's handful of governmental and semi-governmental arts organizations, including the now defunct Abu Dhabi Film Festival's Sanad Grant.

"This isn't a healthy way to make films," she says. "And it's not just about money." Skilled crewmembers are not based in the UAE because there is not enough work to sustain them all year long. "I go into very difficult locations and I need people who can do handheld camera because my shooting style requires that," she says. "I've tried to use people living in the UAE, but unfortunately they're not skilled enough. Maybe they are good for stationary cameras, but you have to be on boats, deserts, mountains—you have to go with your equipment, and you don't want to bring bad footage to the editing room. For example, I needed the rain for *Honey, Rain & Dust*, and when the rain came, my cinematographer was not in the UAE, so I had to hire a person living in the UAE. The footage I came back with was very hard to use, and the rain part was so important to the film."

I suggest that maybe her subjects are freer to speak knowing that she is the only one among the crew who can understand them. She agrees, but then adds, "It puts a lot of pressure on me. Because the cameraman doesn't know the language, he doesn't know what they are saying, so I have to be with the people and have to direct the camera through these very intimate or emotional moments. And if that character says something that is a mistake, the audio guy doesn't know what is missing."

Even though Alghanem and I both live in the UAE, when we speak for this article she is in Marseilles, where she has been for the last couple of months, editing her eighth documentary feature, about the late Emirati contemporary artist Hassan Sharif, a loner, a maverick, and a mentor to her.

Then she is heading to Washington, DC, where *Nearby Sky* (*al-Sama' al-qariba*) will play. The film is about Fatima al-Hameli, a widow who decides to enter her camels in the UAE's annual camel beauty competition, the first woman to do so, much to the amusement and frustration of others. This film has played abroad more than Alghanem's others, perhaps because it fulfills expectations of what a UAE film is supposed to be—camels, sand dunes, women struggling against a patriarchal society. After the Washington screening, Alghanem will undertake the color and sound corrections in Thailand for the new cut of *Honey, Rain & Dust*.

Stepping away from films based on one character, *Honey, Rain & Dust* revolved around three beekeepers in the northern UAE. It premiered at the Dubai International Film Festival (DIFF) in 2016. But after a 2017 screening at New York University in Abu Dhabi, Alghanem asked the mostly expatriate audience what they liked or did not like about the film. In her head, she was already planning on re-editing, and she just wanted a little confirmation that that was the right choice. The audience, with their expatriate gaze on the exotic, had nothing but praise for the film and its sweeping wide shots capturing this fading, rural landscape of the UAE, which most of them did not even know existed.

But Alghanem was disappointed when that film was submitted to the Carthage Film Festival and the committee couldn't tell the two female characters apart. "I realized that they were confused because of the *burqa* (the traditional face veil that many of the women in her films wear). Even though one had henna and the other was older, they couldn't tell the difference. Also, one of the women, Fatma, wasn't that cooperative, and she was nervous at the end. So I thought for the future of film it is better to make it about only two characters—'A'isha, collecting honey with just Mother Nature's help, and Gharib, a more resourceful beekeeper trying to keep himself in business. Both of them came to see the film at DIFF, and they loved their roles. They asked me to come back so they could talk more, and I wanted to include more about the environment and climate change. My husband was very helpful and generous, and he is the producer as well. He told me that we can handle this—just go ahead and make it stronger. So I took the risk, and I know it is a very weird situation."

It's a weird situation that has paid off. The new version is her most cinematic film. It is also the most poignant, along with *Red Blue Yellow*, which is based on Najat Makki, a pioneer in contemporary visual arts in the UAE. She is also Alghanem's aunt, which is not revealed until the closing credits of the film.

"*Red Blue Yellow* is one of my favorite films," says Alghanem. "And I was completely free when I made this film. I could go deeper into art and her life creating this medium's symbolic language. I was able to play with the sound and inner elements of the artist—I enjoyed shooting this film, I enjoyed editing this film, even though it was also painful. I made it when my mother (Najat's sister) was very ill. She was struggling with cancer, especially in postproduction—that was toughest time. I wanted to interview her but she refused." In fact, in the film there is a scene where Najat's nephew tells the camera that he tried but his mother is refusing to speak on camera about Najat, whom she helped raise. While watching, we do not know this is Alghanem's brother speaking about her mother.

28.3. On the water in *Sounds of the Sea* (2014), directed by Nujoom Alghanem.

Najat deserved to have a film made about her, Alghanem says, but for her the film is about freedom. "Freedom. This is a serious thing," says Alghanem, who has an appreciation for experimental film. "To think freely but also to experiment freely. Sometimes the subject matter forces you to keep a certain way of telling the story. The style has to go with the story and the character. You can't be very experimental with someone like Fatma al-Hameli, although you can be symbolic. But when you make a film about an artist, the artist's world is sophisticated. It gives you the chance to dive in and explore the inner self, the inner peace, the inner questions—how this artist recalls the figures, how she draws the shadows, how masks and spaces appear in this artist's work. When I was working on Najat's film, I also found my own memories. She is a female artist, and she also had the problem of freedom. She encountered the frustrations I encounter as a director."

Alghanem delves even further into the complex inner world of artists with *Sharp Tools* (*Alat hada*, 2017), the film she was editing when we talked. The main subject, the contemporary UAE artist Hassan Sharif, makes no compromises to keep his freedom, including never marrying, a very rare thing for a man in UAE culture. Although he inhabits a solitary world, like many of her other subjects, he stands out for claiming to have no need for the past or for nostalgia. Filmed after Sharif knew he was dying, and with his stipulation that no one else be interviewed, the narrative is built around his interviews and poetry written by Alghanem and her husband. The result is a provocative film that pushes deep into the soul of a prolific artist whose work is physically and emotionally made of sharp objects—his art in the film unapologetically lacks anything that could be called "Emirati," in a country in which nation branding is a daily activity. His moments of affection are for Alghanem, when he speaks to her during filming. She only appears in the film in photos taken years earlier with him.

Even when telling a story of the past—of the collective heritage of the UAE—the cultural pressures that are also a part of Emirati heritage force Alghanem to think symbolically. "In *Sounds of the Sea*, when the guy is talking about the wedding night, I had to use sea creatures and show how they are mating to go deeper into that dimension."

This can be positive, leading to more creative, magical filmmaking. As another example, in *Honey, Rain & Dust*, she couldn't show the factory that is changing the environment. "You see the dust coming from it—you can you see when the car is passing it, and you can you hear the factory, but I couldn't approach the factory closely."

There isn't always a symbolic solution. "We are part of a conservative society but cinema is art—cinema needs strong stories, needs emotional stories, and real stories," she says. "If we take into consideration our conservative society and the censorship and that you are not allowed to tackle this issue or that issue, this can make the films almost corporate. So I compromise, not only on quality but on topics and the issues I discuss in my films. I'll find something that is so critical for the film, very strong, and I can't include it . . . sometimes you also need to have the freedom of going securely straight forward on certain issues."

Government censorship aside, the cultural heritage of the region makes many subjects taboo—and limits what the society collectively discusses and what they share with the outside world, including on film. But as she perseveres in her work, Alghanem keeps in mind that documentary can fall flat if it doesn't tell the untold.

"Documentary is based on truth. You have to say the truth," she says fiercely. "If you don't show the truth, what are you going to show?"

(This interview was conducted on June 21, 2017.)

References

Dickinson, Kay. 2016. *Arab Cinema Travels: Syria, Palestine, Dubai and Beyond*. London: BFI/Palgrave Macmillan.

Hambuch, Doris. 2018. "Furrows and Forks in Emirati Short Films." *Canadian Review of Comparative Literature* 45, no. 3 (September): 396–410.

Hudson, Dale. 2017. "Locating Emirati Filmmaking within Globalizing Media Ecologies." In *Media in the Middle East: Activism, Politics, and Culture*, edited by Nele Lenze, Charlotte Schriwer, and Zubaidah Abdul Jalil, 145-163. New York: Palgrave.

Yunis, A. 2014. "Red Carpet Education." In *Film Festival Yearbook 6*, edited by Stefanie Van de Peer and Dina Iordanova, 271–80. St. Andrew: St. Andrew University Press.

———. 2015. "The UAE Goes to the Movies." *CineJ* 2, no. 3: 49–75.

Yunis, A., and G. Duthler. 2011. "Lights, Camera, Education." *Journal of Middle East Media* 7, no. 1: 26–35.

29

IRAQ WAR HOME MOVIES: ABBAS FAHDEL'S SLOW DOCUMENTARY *HOMELAND (IRAQ YEAR ZERO)*

Shohini Chaudhuri

The Iraq War has been the topic of numerous cinematic depictions, from Hollywood films such as *Green Zone* (Paul Greengrass, 2010) and *American Sniper* (Clint Eastwood, 2014), through U.S. and British documentaries such as *Iraq in Fragments* (James Longley, 2006) and *Battle for Haditha* (Nick Broomfield, 2007), to documentaries by Iraqi expats such as *Return to the Land of Wonders* (2004) by Maysoon Pachachi, *Life After the Fall* (*Haya ma ba'd al-suqut*, 2008) by Kassem Abid, and *Iraq: War, Love, God and Madness* (*Harb. Hubb. Rabb wa junun*, 2011) by Mohammed al-Daradji.[1] Several of these films try to reveal what was left out in highly mediated Western news coverage, where the war was transformed into a pyrotechnic show of military assault to avert viewers' attention from its effects, while ordinary Iraqis were rendered invisible, only permitted to appear in displays of exaltation after the fall of Baghdad to U.S. troops. The military campaign was followed by a full-scale occupation of the country, unleashing further violence and deprivation on the local population, effects that were also elided by mainstream U.S. and U.K. news media, showing that they held Iraqi lives to be worth less than American or British ones. As Christina Hellmich and Lisa Purse remark, "Film form permits rhetorical strategies of framing, selection, narrativisation, immersion and erasure to work on the viewer over longer durations" (Hellmich and Purse 2017, 2). This chapter concerns itself with one film by an Iraqi exile, *Homeland (Iraq Year Zero)* (*Wattan (al-'Iraq al-sanna sifr)/Homeland (Irak année zéro)*, 2015) by Abbas Fahdel, which has a considerably longer duration than the others.

Fahdel, an Iraqi-born filmmaker who has lived in France since he was eighteen, has made most of his feature films to date in Iraq. In his first documentary, *Back to Babylon* (*al-'Awda illa Babil*, 2002), he explored the parallel destinies of his childhood friends who had stayed in Iraq while

Everyone is afraid... of the invasion.

29.1. Haider tapes the windows of his house in *Homeland (Iraq Year Zero)* (2015), directed by Abbas Fahdel.

he left for a life in exile. Together with his second documentary, *We Iraqis* (*Nahnu al-'Iraqiyyun/Nous les Irakiens*, 2004), which focuses on his compatriots as they prepare for an imminent war, it directly overlaps in its content and concerns with *Homeland*, while his fictional feature *Dawn of the World* (*Fajr al-'alam/L'aube du monde*, 2008), although taking a more fantastical tone, is also preoccupied with the effects of war on Iraqis, and is set in the Iraqi marshlands during the 1991 Gulf War. To date, only *Yara* (2018), a slow, observational romance, takes place outside Iraq.

On January 29, 2002, U.S. president George W. Bush gave his "axis of evil" speech portraying Iraq as a major threat to world peace, making the case that it was developing weapons of mass destruction, which laid the justification for war (although such weapons were later found to be nonexistent). It was shortly after this that Fahdel returned to the country to film his family and acquaintances over the course of a year and a half, resulting in a five-and-a-half hour documentary that became *Homeland*. Consisting of two parts, *Homeland* presents the Iraq War as a home movie from an Iraqi perspective. The first part, "Before the Fall," focuses mostly on domestic scenes of the family, neighbors, and friends, documenting daily life under Saddam Hussein's dictatorship, before enlarging its scope to show cultural parts of Baghdad, the city in which they reside. Part Two, "After the Battle," surveys the city's altered landscapes in the immediate aftermath of the invasion, exploring the effects of the war and occupation on the family and other Iraqi citizens. The division into two parts marks the upheaval that the war caused for ordinary Iraqis, not only producing a clear "before" and "after" but also a hiatus for the invasion itself, which is not depicted in the film. The decision to divide the film into two was also driven by its unusual length, so that the two parts can be shown with a break. Revisiting the footage after several years and realizing that the film would be "too long to screen or broadcast in a conventional way," Fahdel wrote, edited, and produced it himself, without any industrial support (Cutler 2015).

Homeland is an important document of the period before and after the invasion and occupation of Iraq. Having screened at film festivals, and also made available for home viewing on Netflix, it has received critical acclaim in the form of the Best Feature Film Award at Visions du Réel Festival and favorable reviews, but to my knowledge no scholarly attention to date. In reviews and director interviews, it has raised a number of comparisons with other long-format documentaries dealing with historical violence or marginalized communities, such as *Shoah* (Claude Lanzmann, 1985) and *Tie Xi Qu: West of the Tracks* (Wang Bing, 2003), while Fahdel has likened its portrayal of a war-devastated landscape to "the Zone" in Soviet director Andrei Tarkovsky's fictional feature *Stalker* (1979).[2] While, on the one hand, *Homeland* bears similarities to a home movie, on the other, it belongs to and claims lineage from a filmic movement hailed in critical discourse as "slow cinema," encompassing films of a "slower than average pace, or longer than average duration," a durational aesthetic that marks a "divergence" from mainstream practice (Stringer 2016, xx). Given Fahdel's preferences for extended takes unfolding in real time, statically framed tableau shots, and focus on everyday and apparently insignificant moments, observed in minute detail, this chapter argues that the home movie and slow cinema provide pertinent theoretical and genre frameworks for understanding not only *Homeland*'s stylistic choices, but also its cultural politics, as it mobilizes these formats to address what is out of the frame in mainstream (Western) depictions of the war, namely its lived experience and consequences for ordinary Iraqis.

Writings about slow cinema tend to dwell on particular shot types, such as long takes, referring incidentally to running time rather than analyzing it as part of the film's cumulative durational experience. Meanwhile, in reviews of *Homeland*, its long duration is frequently perceived as a problem for distributors and audiences, rather than a quality crucial to the film's meaning and effect. As Fahdel explains, "Each film must have its own time to breathe. Some works only need five minutes to express themselves, while others—such as Wang Bing's *Tie Xi Qu: West of the Tracks* or *Homeland*—need more" (Cutler 2015). This chapter gives critical prominence to length, an underexplored aspect of slow cinema, as a means of forging a sense of intimacy and connection between spectators and the diegetic space, resulting in an extended encounter with people about whom (most) Western audiences have little knowledge except through the clichés of TV news and Hollywood movies. The invasion and occupation were initiated without an understanding of the country and its people, their society, history, and culture, or their views or aspirations. My analysis, therefore, focuses on sensations of space and time created by the film as it strives to unearth another reality of Iraq that was lost on the country's Anglo-American invaders.

The chapter is divided into two sections. The first section will situate *Homeland* in relation to both the home movie and slow cinema movements, and will argue that Fahdel's formal choices can be read as a refusal of the expedient political rhetoric of the Iraq War and accompanying media representations, as well as of commercial dictates that require films to fit established formats, such as the standard one-and-a-half hour documentary. The second section will examine the film's portrayal of war-destroyed landscapes, focusing on its use of ruins and a peripatetic "road movie" style to reflect on the catastrophic state of postwar Iraq in ways that resonate with Tarkovsky's *Stalker*, a film whose durational experience similarly defies any attempt to condense it and which likewise explores a ruined landscape in search of a promised future that fails to materialize.

The Home Movie and the Long Format Slow Documentary

I begin with the caveat that *Homeland* is not an actual home movie. According to a definition offered by documentary theorist Patricia Zimmerman, the home movie is a kind of amateur film "located within individual and/ or familial practices of visual recording of intimate events and rituals and intended for private usage and exhibition" (Zimmerman 2008, 8). In contrast, Fahdel is a professional filmmaker, imparting a strong sense of directorial intent through his framing and other stylistic devices. And while the home movie's traditional "space of communication" (Odin 2014, 15) is within the family, made inside the home and destined for the ritual of home screening, Fahdel (2016) has stated that his family does not, due to the tragic turn of events, wish to see *Homeland*; the film's primary audience is external rather than internal to the family.

Nevertheless, *Homeland* is marked by a number of qualities that make it comparable to a home movie. Although not made by an amateur, it lacks the visual polish of documentaries such as *Iraq in Fragments* and *Iraq: War, Love, God and Madness*, which capture the fierce beauty of Iraq's landscapes and sunsets through their saturated color palettes, and Hollywood movies, which depict the country as an alienating environment, drained of color, through an equally stylized bleach bypass process.[3] Despite its division into two parts, *Homeland* feels relatively unstructured, seemingly possessing what the filmmaker Péter Forgács calls the home movie's "intrinsically naïve quality of capturing whatever is before it" (Forgács 2008, 47). Indeed, the presence of these "imperfections," with minimal postproduction manipulation, which give *Homeland* its raw, unembellished features, adds to its power and credibility. But, like a home movie, it is constructed from a vast archive, one that is by necessity incomplete and fragmented, since it is itself culled from an infinitely larger flow of time whose totality the filmed moments cannot capture.

Homeland's other obvious similarity with the home movie is its intimate first-person documentation of everyday family life and activities: a record of ephemeral and apparently unimportant moments. Its use of the home-movie format to represent the Iraq War should be regarded, however, as a political (not merely personal) intervention, offering (as Zimmerman says of the home movie movement in general) "visions of history and culture that would otherwise go unseen and unknown by the general public" (Zimmerman 2008, 22). The home movie's historiographic import lies in documenting what professional journalists or historians have not officially documented. Contrasting with their history of the Iraq War told largely "from the top," following the actions and decisions of policy-makers, politicians, and generals, *Homeland* instead chronicles a different type of history "from below"—the hidden, everyday history of war and occupation through the experiences of ordinary people. Larger historical changes are placed in dialogue with daily events, as life goes on in front of the television and the family engages in conversations about larger, public events. Through its home-movie format, which constitutes a different order of what is "worth" filming from elite movie-making practices, *Homeland* questions accepted ideas of who or which subjects are worthy of our attention and concern.

Homeland begins with a black screen and howling wind, a harsh, baleful sound which can retrospectively be understood as the "seed" of the tragedy of Part Two.[4] The wind subsides to sounds of the ambient environment both inside and outside Fahdel's family house in Baghdad. The metronomic ticking of a pendulum clock situates us in the everyday sounds and rhythms of a middle-class family home, the lack of added musical score or explanatory voice-over helping to accentuate the sensory materiality and lived time-space of the world depicted onscreen. Filming with a portable DV camera, Fahdel does not physically appear in the movie. His family members are introduced to us with onscreen captions designating their relation to him: "My brother Ibrahim," lying on the carpet watching TV; "My sister-in-law," seen through the window, hanging the laundry; "My niece Kanar," still asleep in bed, rolling over moodily when Fahdel urges her to get up; "My nephew 'Ammar"; "My niece Ithar"; and "My nephew Haidar," a smart, lively, charming eleven-year-old, who has just woken up and who later emerges as a lead character in the film.

Homeland creates an immersive experience through intimacy with the family in their domestic setting. The opening scene contains the first of several prolonged tableau shots of the TV set juxtaposed with shots of the family watching. With them, we watch Saddam greeting the nation at the start of the Eid festival in February 2002, marking an important time in the life of the community as well as the official timeline of the Iraq War. Saddam scorns the "childish" beliefs of his enemies who think he has weapons of mass destruction that he will pass on to terrorist organizations. The fact that he is incessantly on TV attests to his self-glorification and extravagant displays of power. Unimpressed, having seen such displays many times before, Fahdel's cousin Madhat changes the channel—one of the small gestures of noncompliance possible under Saddam's dictatorship, when all media were under state control. Part One closes with television news headlines on March 20, 2003, the day of the invasion: "World condemns attack on Iraq." The perspective of the Iraqi News Agency, then Iraq's sole news network, offers a contrasting view from Western media portrayals, stating that the invasion was an attack on a sovereign state, carried out without legitimate international support. Its official rhythms and ideologies are juxtaposed with the everyday rhythms and concerns of ordinary Iraqi people. In scenes unfolding in real time, we watch the family watching TV, linger on their faces and bodies at rest, and listen to their silences and conversations, restoring the intimacy of bodily engagement absent from both official Iraqi and Western coverage.

Part One preserves a sense of the ordinary in extraordinary times, including the family's attitudes to the impending war. They feel like they have been through this already—the 1991 Gulf War having occurred relatively recently, followed by a crippling twelve-year regime of U.N. sanctions that, apart from blocking imports, affected the maintenance and supply of vital services such as electricity, water, and sanitation. Early in *Homeland* we see the family installing a well in their garden in anticipation of the coming war and further water shortages. But they also react to their adverse circumstances with humor, perhaps as a coping mechanism. In one scene, Ithar demonstrates to Haidar and Kanar how diapers can be repurposed as gas masks in the event of a chemical attack, a proposition that has them all collapsing into giggles. The film details the effects of the U.N. sanctions on ordinary people's lives. A family gathering at a relative's house in the provincial city of Hit is interrupted by an electricity cut, one of several power cuts shown in Part One. In preparation for the war, we see 'Ammar on an errand to stock up on basic food supplies from a small neighborhood warehouse, comparing the prices of the food rations and those of the same items on the black market.

True to the home-movie genre, *Homeland* even contains a video of a wedding, which appears toward the end of Part One, marking the midpoint of the whole film. A joyous occasion, the wedding is that of the daughter of actor Sami Kaftan, whose theater also appears in the film. On the dance floor, a group of young women line up for the *dabke*; a song, performed live by pop star Souad Abdallah, announces the shift to *choubi* (چوبي) music (a mix of pop and folk), to which even the toddlers dance enthusiastically, mimicking the singer's routine. The wedding encapsulates the joie de vivre that marks Part One, despite life's hardships and the impending war. The high spirits contain an element of defiance: that America can attack if it likes, but life will go on.

Less than halfway through Part One, Haidar is shown taping the windows of the house to stop them from shattering during the expected bombardment. Traces of the tape from the previous Gulf War remain, like a ghostly palimpsest beneath the new layers of the tape that he plasters over them. Then the shock comes, unanticipated and unbidden, with an onscreen title soberly announcing Haidar's death in the aftermath of the invasion. This is the first of several onscreen texts telling us which characters will die, long before the deaths happen in the narrative, creating a sense of disjointed time and foreknowledge that imbues our experience of the remaining film. Fahdel has explained that when Haidar was killed, "I felt unable to continue, to the point of not being able to look at the rushes I had shot for over a decade before eventually returning to find a film in them" (Cutler 2015). The film reveals itself as a tracing of an unresolved trauma that is still being worked out in its home-video form, recovering images of those who have passed away, in an act of mourning and marker of loss—"ghosts" who become real again through their rematerialization in the playback of the film. Similar to the Jewish family, the Peerebooms, whose Second World War home movie Forgács reworked in his film *The Maelstrom: A Family Chronicle* (1997), the fate of Fahdel's family was unforeseen and unknown by them, given that they were only living their everyday lives. The future was equally invisible and unimaginable to Fahdel as he recorded his family, for he could not predict Haidar's death nor other calamities that befell Iraq.

The onscreen title, "Haidar will be killed after the invasion," acts like a flash-forward. As we watch, we gain a sense of the irrevocable alteration of Iraqi lives; meanwhile, the impending war, anticipated by the opening baleful wind, draws closer in Part One and so does the fate that awaits Haidar, visualized by darkness in Part Two—forces that pull at the characters, reconfiguring their lives. From the start, the tension exists—the film heightens our awareness of it through onscreen titles, endowing us with knowledge about the family's history that they themselves do not have. The precariousness of life and poignancy of these moments are highlighted through the haunted quality of the footage—as we are watching, Haidar is already dead. Our sense of the ephemeral and the contingent becomes intertwined with a sense of unswerving fate.

The slow cinema movement, consisting of narrative fiction, documentary, and experimental film, is said have emerged since the turn of the millennium in opposition to a culture of speed apparent in the fast cutting and "camera ubiquity" conveyed by news bulletins and Hollywood cinema (Ellis 2012, 84). In their anthology, *Slow Cinema*, Tiago De Luca and Nuno Barradas Jorge observe that cinematic slowness tends to emanate from places neglected by globalization and attends to experiences of marginalized people who are "invisible" on that dominant map. Furthermore, slowness, an inherently subjective category, is laced with questions of value: "what is worthy of being shown, for how long . . . [and] what is worthy of our attention and patience as viewers and individuals" (De Luca and Jorge 2016, 14). Writing about slow documentary, John Ellis finds that the genre "insists that time should be taken, that the evidence should be weighed up by the viewer, and that instant reactions are to be distrusted" (2012, 94). Although slow cinema is labeled a contemporary movement, it has precursors in the work of earlier filmmakers and theorists. As will be shown in the rest of this section, the stylistic and theoretical specificities of slow cinema as a form of cultural resistance can further illuminate *Homeland*'s approach.

If *Homeland* has a "trademark" camera style, it is the slow zoom-out and pan to produce an almost panoramic view, in order to show what is otherwise not in the frame. In the Baghdad souks, Fahdel creates portraits of sellers and wares in their stalls, panning across them at a glacial pace, as if attempting to inscribe a 360-degree reality, reminiscent of what the film theorist André Bazin called an aspiration toward "a total cinema" which offers a "complete illusion of life" (1967, 20). In *Homeland*, slowness can be understood as a means to make sense of change, but also to preserve life as lived: "By filming my loved ones on the eve of a new war, I maintained the hope of preserving them from harm," Fahdel says (Cutler 2015). "To preserve . . . is to snatch . . . from the flow of time, to stow . . . away neatly . . . in the hold of life" (1967, 9), Bazin tells us, aptly describing the psychological impulse behind *Homeland*. Slow cinema is a revival of Bazin's principles, indebted to the philosopher Henri Bergson's concept of duration: an inner experience of time in which the past is prolonged into the present and future (Bergson 1911, 2). Quintessentially for Bazin, cinema answers a desire for preservation, lending us an image of the duration of objects and people—"change mummified" (Bazin 1967, 15). The act of preservation relies on an indexical bond between object and image which the digital, capable of simulating people and places that were never in front of the camera, is said to have broken. However, contemporary slow cinema itself is a product of cheaper, more flexible digital camera technology, capable of recording more affordably for longer periods, showing that "the digital can be applied to *resist*, as much as to elicit simulation" (Nagib 2011, 7).

Bazin praised the use of depth of field and long takes to cover whole scenes, and a preference for panning shots rather than montage in the films of Jean Renoir, Orson Welles, and Italian neorealism—techniques that he believed laid bare the reality of people and things while safeguarding their inherent unity. Claiming that "depth of focus brings the spectator into a relation with the image closer to that which he enjoys with reality," he suggested that this style invites viewers to take a more active role, instead of having their attention guided by montage (Bazin 1967, 35). Similarly, in *Homeland*, rather than being steered toward the significance of scenes through voice-over commentary and frequent cuts, the viewer must mostly respond to audiovisual cues from within the action, which makes it a demanding film to watch. Ellis claims that slow documentary's radical approach is that it "throws the viewer's attention back onto the events that took place, rather than the filmmaker's subsequent construction of meaning from them" (2012, 94). It thereby addresses some of the criticisms to which news and documentary are susceptible, namely that they have "'left out' vital details, or have distorted the viewer's conception of events and people by too much elision" (Ellis 2012, 97). Like other slow films, *Homeland* leaves in the "dead moments" that mainstream news and cinema edit out, moments that lack official significance, yet form the background for official events and impart to viewers a more palpable sense of characters and their circumstances, as when the camera rests on 'Ammar's face while he watches on TV the preparations to mobilize the Iraqi army into which he himself will be conscripted.

Homeland's observational aesthetic does give priority to the image over the edit shift, holding its attention on characters and objects in their world for longer than their informational value seems to warrant, our eyes given time to wander across the frame, inhabiting the space and absorbing more about the characters and their context. If each cut is a shift of attention, then the film's unhurried pace – staying with the characters, settling on them in moments of relative inaction, listening to their views—conveys thoughtfulness and patience, suggesting that more time needs to be given to them. The opposite of a manufactured, sensationalized, conventional "war movie," *Homeland* attempts to illuminate their reality and thereby refresh perceptions of Iraq and Iraqis. Furthermore, as Ellis remarks of slow documentary in general, it "concentrates on the absolute particularity and individuality of person, place and moment," rather than generalizations or reduction to types, "leaving significance to emerge gradually" (2012, 95). This attentiveness to lives in their singularity is also, of course, a stylistic device for activating empathy.

Part One is suffused with a feeling of waiting, as the family awaits the impending war. The film shows extended periods of actual waiting; in this sense, length is the very substance and subject of the film. They involve multiple durations: the family's own and the external duration of the official buildup to war from February 2002 to March 2003. We feel the time that everyday and official actions take, and characters' bodies, captured in a state of waiting, likewise register passing time in shows of anticipation or weariness. In his writings on film, Tarkovsky defined cinematic time in terms of "the pressure of the time" in the shot (Tarkovsky 1986, 117). Taking Bazin and Tarkovsky as his starting points, the film philosopher Gilles Deleuze created the concept of the "time-image" to describe how "'a little time in the pure state' . . . rises up to the surface of the screen," becoming palpable to viewers (Deleuze 1989, xi). Although he mostly applies it to European postwar modernist cinema, the time-image acquires further relevance here.

Like Bazin, Tarkovsky saw film as uniquely positioned among the arts in its ability *"to take an impression of time"* (Tarkovsky 1986, 62). Cinema imprints time in the form of the "factual," that is, "simple, direct observation" of an event, person, or object (Tarkovsky 1986, 63, 66). Although renowned for his fiction films, Tarkovsky hailed documentary chronicle as the "ultimate cinema" (1986, 65). But, rather than real time, he emphasized cinema's freedom to enhance and elongate our experience of time through the way it selects and combines "facts taken from a 'lump of time' of any width or length" (Tarkovsky 1986, 65). In this way, *Homeland* can be understood as creating its own time (and space), a reconfiguration of reality which, over time, mingles with our own spatial and temporal awareness. When one enters that world, one also enters an intersubjective bond with the characters that deepens and grows in the course of the film, creating a feeling of "being-with" them. Tarkovsky writes that "the time we have lived settles in our soul as an experience placed within time" (Tarkovsky 1986, 58). Furthermore, the time we have watched a film "not only enhances" but makes our experience "significantly longer" (Tarkovsky 1986, 63). By Tarkovsky's reckoning, a standard one-and-a-half hour film "settles in our soul," but his statement arguably pertains even more to a much longer film, such as *Homeland*, with a greater potential to enhance and expand our experience.

The sound of howling wind, with which *Homeland* begins, returns toward the end of Part One, when Fahdel visits al-Amiriyyah Shelter, which was bombed by the United States in 1991, killing at least four hundred civilians. Now a devastated chasm, the shelter has been turned into a memorial, with Haidar acting as our guide. The howling wind and the bombed shelter form the "seeds" of the new war devastation to come. In Deleuze's theory of the time-image, time is no longer subordinated to movement; instead, it "gives rise to *false movements*" (1989, xi), such as asynchronous image/sound combinations (like the sound of wind over otherwise still and serene scenes), and irrational cuts in which time is disjointed, revealing the coexistence of different durations. In these moments, time flicks forward, announcing the untimely arrival of the harmful events of Part Two.

Ruined and Unsafe Spaces in Iraq's Post-conflict Landscape

"After the Battle," Part Two of *Homeland*, begins in April 2003, two weeks after the invasion. Fahdel's nephews and nieces have returned to Baghdad after having been evacuated to the provinces during the bombardment. In the provinces, they stayed with their uncle in Hit, although that city too was bombed. "Operation Iraqi Freedom," the military campaign to remove Saddam, was swift but, as we see at the level of everyday Iraqi experience in Part Two, it was conducted without any viable plans for the post-conflict period. The U.S.-led occupation officially ended in June 2004, when the Iraqi interim government was inaugurated, although large numbers of U.S. and U.K. troops remained in Iraq years longer to deal with the protracted aftermath. *Homeland* covers the beginning of this period, when widespread tolerance of the occupation among ordinary Iraqis subsided into anger and resentment, as the U.S./U.K. coalition's woefully inadequate governance became apparent.

In *Homeland* Part Two, we observe the effects of the occupation. On the one hand, there is greater freedom of expression. Under Saddam, satellite dishes were banned, but now, Haidar tells us, showing us the newly installed dishes on the family home's roof, "everyone has one or two." The changes are visible in the customary long takes of the family watching TV. Instead of state TV, programs from all over the world are beamed into their home: American music videos, Bollywood films, Al Jazeera news. As Madhat says, in one of many scenes shot from inside a car, driving around the changed landscape, "For over thirty years, Iraqis"—including journalists, writers, and historians—"lived in a state of schizophrenia, saying one thing in front of Saddam and the opposite behind his back! A discourse at home, another one in public. Because if one dared to say a part of the truth about the regime, he ran the risk of disappearing forever. In Iraq, because of oppression and censorship, we have become schizophrenic." Dealing with a transitional political landscape, *Homeland* gives attention to ordinary Iraqis voicing, perhaps for the first time publicly, their reflections and grievances about their past ruler as well as their present occupiers. In the climate of relative openness, regime atrocities are unearthed. The remains of Mohsen, Fahdel's childhood friend, are found in a mass grave— he had been missing at the time of Fahdel's previous film, *Back to Babylon* (2002), but back then it was too risky for interviewees to say that he had been arrested by the regime.

On the other hand, infrastructural problems, consisting of food short-ages and failures in electricity and water supplies, are much worse than under Saddam. According to international law, it is the responsibility of the occupying power to restore and maintain infrastructure, and keep law and order. However, in Iraq, the coalition did not seem to understand that electricity was crucial to restore normality to people's everyday lives, and their failure to deliver improvements in these vital services led to a rapid decline in the locals' tolerance of the occupation and to the growth of resentment (Gregory 2004, 223). In *Homeland*, we see the everyday ways in which a middle-class family is affected, as Fahdel's nieces are forced to do their homework by the light of hurricane lamps, and 'Ammar com-pares rationing before and after the invasion, the only difference being that the products are now better quality. Furthermore, we see and hear the fury of other Iraqi citizens whom Fahdel meets on the streets—not the extras of "America's Iraq" seen on Western TV news and Hollywood movies, but people with outspoken political views, angered by systemic failures and capable of distinguishing between occupation and liberation. One man says that the Americans did not come to free us but "to enslave us and exploit our country's resources," cutting through the occupier's lofty rhetoric of giving the Iraqis self-determination and control of their own resources which was later belied by the privatization of Iraq's state indus-tries and the handout of lucrative contracts to largely U.S. companies.

After the invasion, lawlessness ensued, including looting, robbery, murders, rapes, and violent attacks, which the occupying powers failed to crack down upon, as well as, in the longer term, an undermining of regional stability and border security that created a space for extremism to flour-ish (Chilcot 2016, 110). The Iraqi population felt this internecine violence more frequently and more directly than the occupying forces. Lawless con-ditions form the backdrop for *Homeland* Part Two as the family copes with the day-to-day practicalities of the situation. Just before the war, 'Ammar tells us, Saddam released criminals from prison, leading to the presence of dangerous gangs on the streets. Like many other ordinary Iraqis, 'Ammar has procured a gun to defend his house. People feel unsafe and believe that they have to arm themselves, because their occupiers do not provide them with security. As part of their policy of "de-Ba'thification" (removal of the

Ba'th Party's influence in the new Iraq), the coalition disbanded the military and security bodies who had worked under Saddam, leaving Iraq without a functioning police force or army to keep law and order. With prophetic words that identify humiliation and frustration as grounds for the subsequent popular revolt against the occupation, one Iraqi citizen interviewed in *Homeland* observes, "Iraqi resistance will be declared in response to the exactions of the U.S. occupiers. There's no government to protect citizens and their property, to provide them with water, gas, electricity, and medicine. All of this will exacerbate the anger of the Iraqis."

This part of the film was made under volatile, transitional political conditions that leave their traces on its style; therefore, it is not just through the content of the interviews, but also through formal elements such the use of space and landscape that the social and political implications are drawn out. The inspection of landscapes, along with a sustained focus on the views of the city's inhabitants, contrasts with the more intimate portrayal of the family in Part One—a shift from the personal to the geographical that helps to underscore the effects of the war and occupation on the population. There is a prevalence of traveling shots, filmed through car windows, as Fahdel roams around the city with Ibrahim or Madhat. The devastated and derelict topography of the city becomes the focus in Part Two, conveying a palpable sense of the changes the citizens have undergone, since space is not merely the backdrop against which things happen but rather a material form of duration.

In *Homeland*, we do not see the aerial bombing of the Iraq War, shown as a pyrotechnic display on Western news, but the aftereffects of its pounding on the city. Journeying by car, the film surveys the imploded and charred remains of government buildings as well as ordinary homes reduced to rubble: a ruined landscape. When we travel with Madhat into the ruins of the radio station where he worked, which was bombed twice even though it was a civilian building, the sound of wind can be heard again. These scenes raise parallels with *Stalker*, where both the monochrome world outside the post-apocalyptic wasteland known as "the Zone" and the verdant world inside it are dotted with ruins and haunted by the past—a landscape evocative of military and industrial catastrophe, as well as suffused with feelings of exile and nostalgia. The "stalker" is a character who guides others into the prohibited Zone in the quest to find a room where one's wishes will be fulfilled. In the absence of voice-over and the director's on-camera appearance, *Homeland* makes use of the device of the guide to the devastated area, a role performed by several characters, including the actor Sami Kaftan, who shows us the Office of Cinema and Theater, which was linked to the Ministry of Information. This is why, he tells us, it was set on fire by looters, like many other government buildings. Taking us into the Baghdad

Cinema Studios where ransacked reels of film have been unceremoniously dumped on the floor, Sami rails at the looters for stealing Iraq's heritage. Although the Ba'th Party controlled filmmaking prior to the war, he claims that films from the period constitute an important body of evidence about that history and culture. Therefore, he is relieved to find an archive of Iraqi documentaries, in neatly stacked cans, fulfilling Tarkovsky's dream of capturing and preserving time in metal boxes "theoretically forever" (Tarkovsky 1986, 62). Like the ruined buildings in the Zone in *Stalker*, the cinema archives hold the relics of a civilization. In a recuperative gesture, *Homeland* attempts to excavate elements of Iraq's rich past after its theft by looters who were condoned by Anglo-American invaders unaware of or indifferent to the country's past.

In *Stalker*, the Zone is an abnormal space where the parts are disconnected, where one cannot go back the same way one came: pathways can disappear, traps are always appearing or changing places. The journey to the wish room lasts hours, although it is only two hundred meters away. The Zone is cordoned off by the authorities; at a military checkpoint, guards shoot randomly at those who seek to enter. It resonates in multiple ways with the defamiliarized, displaced landscape of post-conflict Iraq. Here, with Ibrahim as our main guide, we travel by car around Baghdad, encountering roadblocks patrolled by U.S. soldiers who inform him that he cannot enter without a pass because it is a "military area," that is, a prohibited zone. The landscape is also reminiscent of checkpoints and "closed military areas" in occupied Palestine, underlining fears, expressed by several of the film's interviewees, that the U.S. occupation has created a Palestinized Iraq. The intrusive noise of helicopters hovering in the sky can be heard sporadically, sonically exerting U.S. control over Iraqi airspace. U.S. army trucks and armored vehicles line the streets, and one soldier sits in a tank parked at the entrance to the Iraqi national museum, which he appears to be guarding nonchalantly.

In Hollywood movies such as *American Sniper*, Iraq is constructed as an unsafe space, where snipers may be hiding on rooftops or guerrillas in alleyways. Iraqi cities are deadly labyrinths to be navigated with the aid of ultra high-tech surveillance. A different kind of unsafe space is conveyed in *Homeland*. As well as being militarized, the landscape is dangerous in countless everyday ways for Iraqis themselves. Fahdel's family members leave the house less often because of fear of armed attacks; in general, people are fearful of both Iraqi bandits and U.S. soldiers, who shoot indiscriminately. The film's two-part structure enables the spectator to understand how the space established in Part One is "being undone and ruptured by violence" (Cutler 2015). Daily routines, such as going to the market, have become almost impossible. In its typically understated fashion, *Homeland* shows how these public spaces have been destroyed by the invasion and occupation. Madhat drives the children to their schools, university, and workplaces, necessitating several trips a day: first, he drives Haidar and Kanar to school, then Manar and 'Ammar to university, and finally Ishtar to work. The sense of endangerment and concern for their safety are made palpable through this endless journeying. Ishtar explains there is no longer any shuttle bus and taxis are unsafe. As an additional measure, she carries a knife in her bag.

The private car seems the only safe space in which to travel and film, but not sufficiently so, as shown by *Homeland*'s final tragic scene. The unsafe spaces of the city are especially unsafe at night. In the last scene, Ibrahim takes some of his family members by car through an intersection at night which he knows is not entirely safe but it will shorten the journey. This "wrong" turn leads to Haidar's death at the hands of unknown gunmen and the film's abrupt ending. This is a death that cannot, of course, be represented—a real death. Darkness frames the scene, from which emerges the sound of gunfire and a muted cry of "wounded"—an abyss through which Haidar was lost and from which he can never return. The viewer is invited to feel that darkness: with the sound of bleak wind playing over his portrait, Haidar's absence is now as palpable as his earlier presence. The title card accompanying this scene offers no explanation; indeed, the violence remains unresolved: "A few months later, two of his cousins were killed in the same way." The film closes with this image of mourning: for both the lost homeland and the lost nephew.

Conclusion

With the Iraq War's repercussions still reverberating around the region, *Homeland* constitutes a crucial historical document, telling this history from below through the lived experience of a middle-class Iraqi family and other Iraqi citizens. The U.S. government's case for war was built out of expedience to justify intervention and regime change—priorities that were reflected in the mainstream media. *Homeland*'s stylistic approach bespeaks a refusal of this expedience: not only does it fill in the gaps of mainstream media, its unhurried pace and long duration require that we spend considerable time in its diegetic space, entering its world and inhabiting it with its characters. Through its home-video format and slow durational aesthetic, it reframes what is worthy of our attention, patience, and concern. Furthermore, its division into two parts, preserving and capturing the reality it observes, enables us to gain an intimate sense of life before and after the invasion, and absorb the everyday effects on the characters. In Part Two, the changes are materialized in the ruined and unsafe spaces of the city and the recourse to filming from the relatively safe interior of the car. As the film approaches its terrible conclusion, *Homeland*, with its everyday, even banal images, becomes a time capsule from a now-inaccessible world.

References

Bazin, André. 1967. *What Is Cinema?* Vol. 1. Translated by Hugh Gray. Berkeley: University of California Press.

Bergson, Henri. 1911. *Creative Evolution*. Translated by Arthur Mitchell. New York: Henry Holt and Company.

Chilcot, Sir John. 2016. *The Report of the Iraq Inquiry—The Executive Summary*. iraqinquiry.org.

Cutler, Aaron. 2015. "An Interview with Abbas Fahdel, Director of *Homeland (Iraq Year Zero)*." bkmag.com.

Deleuze, Gilles. 1989. *Cinema 2: The Time-Image*. Translated by Hugh Tomlinson and Robert Galeta. London: Athlone Press.

De Luca, Tiago, and Nuno Barradas Jorge. 2016. "Introduction: From Slow Cinema to Slow Cinemas." In *Slow Cinema*, edited by Tiago De Luca and Nuno Barradas Jorge, 1–21. Edinburgh: Edinburgh University Press.

Ellis, John. 2012. *Documentary: Witness and Revelation*. Abingdon: Routledge.

Fahdel, Abbas. 2016. "*Homeland (Iraq Year Zero)* Q&A." The New York Film Festival, May 25. youtube.com.

Forgács, Péter. 2008. "Wittgenstein *Tractatus*: Personal Reflections on Home Movies." In *Mining the Home Movie: Excavations in Histories and Memories*, edited by Karen L. Ishizuka and Patricia R. Zimmerman, 47–56. Berkeley: University of California Press.

Gregory, Derek. 2004. *The Colonial Present: Afghanistan, Palestine, Iraq*. Malden: Blackwell.

Hellmich, Christina, and Lisa Purse. 2017. "Introduction: Cinema and the Epistemology of War." In *Disappearing War: Interdisciplinary Perspectives on Cinema and Erasure in the Post-9/11 World*, edited by Christina Hellmich and Lisa Purse, 1–15. Edinburgh: Edinburgh University Press.

Nagib, Lúcia. 2011. *World Cinema and the Ethics of Realism*. London: Continuum.

Odin, Roger. 2014. "The Home Movie and Space of Communication." Translated by Barry Monahan. In *Amateur Filmmaking: The Home Movie, the Archive, the Web*, edited by Laura Rascaroli, Gwenda Young, and Barry Monahan, 15–26. London: Bloomsbury.

Stringer, Julian. 2016. "Foreword." In *Slow Cinema*, edited by Tiago De Luca and Nuno Barradas Jorge, xix–xx. Edinburgh: Edinburgh University Press.

Tarkovsky, Andrey. 1986. *Sculpting in Time: The Great Russian Filmmaker Discusses His Art*. Translated by Kitty Hunter-Blair. Austin: University of Texas Press.

Westwell, Guy. 2014. *Parallel Lines: Post-9/11 American Cinema*. London: Wallflower Press.

Zimmerman, Patricia. 2008. "Introduction: The Home Movie Movement." In *Mining the Home Movie: Excavations in Histories and Memories*, edited by Karen L. Ishizuka and Patricia R. Zimmerman, 1–28. Berkeley: University of California Press.

NOTES

Notes to Chapter 1

1 This guide was issued as one in a series of industry-concerned layperson handbooks. See Boughey 1921, 74.

2 Ali Abu Shadi, *Waqa'i' al-sinima al-misriya* (Damascus: Ministry of Cultural Press, 2004), 12.

3 It is worth noting that *jarida* is the colloquial term for "newspaper" in Egypt as well, rather than the rather exclusively formal *sahifa*.

4 Indeed, Pathé published *Pathé News* in the United States, *Pathé Gazette* in Britain, and the aforementioned *Pathé Journal* in France. See Boughey 1921, 75.

5 Boughey 1921, 76. Also see Hughes 1976, 56. To confuse matters, *magazine* is a term that turns up occasionally in reference to newsreels, likely because of the similarity between the two forms.

6 The screening took place in the hall of a club, not merely a bathhouse. See al-Hadari 1987, 29–30.

7 The page appears toward the end of what, at twenty-six pages of the issue's 110 pages, amounts to a promotional insert for Gaumont within the magazine. January 3, 1920, 92, http://archive.org/stream/exhibitorsherald10exhi#page/n105/mode/2up.

8 A similar promotional approach to that described in the previous note—the advertisement appears full-page within a twenty-five-page packet announcing Pathé's offerings in the coming year, heavy on variety and comedy. June 25, 1925, 56, http://archive.org/stream/e00newy#page/n257/mode/2up.

9 Mahmoud Ali addresses censure and censorship intersectionally in his expansive *Ma'at 'am min al-raqaba 'ala al-sinima al-misriyya* (Ali 2008b, 205–10).

10 Linda Griffith dubiously reports that her former husband D.W. had predicted that films would soon be exhibited on the very day they were produced, before reporting that she witnessed a "preparedness parade" in Manhattan of which she then saw footage the same night in a cinema on Broadway (Griffith 1917).

That may have been possible occasionally, especially when event and exhibition locations were so close to each other, but could not be sustained, judging by the fact that two of the most capitalized and established producers of newsreels, Pathé and Hearst, could not sustain their attempts at a daily newsreel for more than a few months. See Mould 1983, 34, 42.

11 I have been unable, regrettably, to identify this film. The publication source of the clipping is unidentified, though it is in Arabic (*The Memory of Modern Egypt* special collection).

12 Neither the publisher of the clipping nor the date of publication is identified, though it was likely during the Great War, in the latter months of 1918 (*The Memory of Modern Egypt* special collection). See "Duke Visits Battlefields" 1918.

13 I have identified over sixty domestically produced newsfilms during the decade of the 1920s, significantly more than the half-dozen or so Egyptian narrative features made during the same period.

14 Film historian Mahmoud Ali identifies fifty-one cinemas in Egypt in 1917 (Ali 2008a, 63–65).

15 I struggled to identify *Jaridat al-barq* (*Lightning Newsreel*), listed in the earliest exhibitor advertisement to appear in *Motion Pictures*, beginning in its second edition. The advertisement announced programs for two days, Monday and Saturday, which suggests it related to the coming week's planned screenings (*Motion Pictures*, May 17, 1923, 11). Through a process of elimination and considering the relatively scant appearance of commercial newsreels of the era, I at first thought this newsreel to be the Soviet national "flash newsreel," whose production Dziga Vertov had led, according to his own written recollection (Vertov 1984, 119).

16 *Ahli* is derived from the term *ahl*, meaning *family*. As such, *ahli* denotes both domesticity and association by blood. It warrants noting that the American Cosmograph was the site of nationalist activity of a non-cinematic variety, in that it was site of an important meeting of the union of tramway workers, who had gone on strike against the British-owned Cairo Tram Company (CTC) in 1919, a strike that shifted the locus of defiance of the 1919 Revolution from the streets of urban and rural Egypt to the country's institutions and organizations. For more on this fateful strike see Beinin and Lockman 1993, 395–428.

17 *Motion Pictures*, July 5, 1923, 22. I was able to correlate the two titles only when *al-Barq* was printed parenthetically following *Éclair*, several months later (March 20, 1924, 20).

18 This title card is cited by al-Qalyubi in his biography of Bayoumi when describing this film (al-Qalyubi 2009, 59). I have also seen the card in the opening credits to the copy I watched in the UCLA Film and TV Archive, University of California, Los Angeles.

19 This advertisement appears in *Motion Pictures* on August 23, 1923, 22.

20 For a complete list of films found or named in Mohammed Bayoumi's holdings, see al-Qalyubi 2009, 59–62.

21 "Nadi al-Suwar al-Mutaharrika (Motion Pictures Club)," *Motion Pictures*, August 23, 1923, 20.

22 The term often used to refer to films in *Motion Pictures* is *shara'it*, which literally means "strips."

23 The letter was to the "*Motion Pictures* Parliament" page, often referenced in this essay, January 24, 1924, 2. For a sample of these missives, see *Motion Pictures*' "*Motion Pictures* Parliament," August 2, 1923, 21.

24 See Davis 1983. For an examination of the Misr Company for Acting and Cinema, see Hasan 1986.

25 The term *wasfiya*, which means "descriptive," is one I have not encountered elsewhere, though is likely a documentary form, especially since in the same paragraph, the author refers to a film that documents the manufacture of sugar in a particular plant in Egypt. See "Bank Misr and Moving Images," 20.

26 These were not presented in order of production, since issue no. 19 of the Gaumont Journal (newsreel) appears in the May 7 issue of *Motion Pictures*, followed by issues 14, 15, and 16 successively in the three issues of the magazine in May 1925.

Notes to Chapter 3

1 Tracing the original titles for some of the films mentioned here is beyond the scope of this book, thus the titles of newsreels as written may not always be identical to the originals.

2 Due to the scarcity of sources, the dates of production for many films and newsreels in this chapter could not be traced.

Notes to Chapter 4

1 See, e.g., al-Ghul 2012; As-Safir 2012; Buali 2012; Darwish 2011; *Donia al-Watan* 2015; Fourest 2012; Habashneh 2008; Jacir 2007.

2 With the exception of Qasim Hawal's adaption of Ghassan Kanafani's novel *Return to Haifa* ('*A'id ila Haifa*, 1982), all PLO productions were documentaries. According to the international standard of that time, the films were of short to medium length.

3 All translations from German and Arabic by the author.

4 DEFA (Deutsche Film AG) was state run, or publicly owned, and the only film company in the GDR. It comprised the Studio for Fiction Film, the Studio for Documentary Film, the Studio for Animated Film, the Dubbing Studio, PROGRESS Film Distribution, DEFA-Foreign Trade, the National Film Archive, the Center for Film Technology, a Central Film Laboratory, two film laboratories at the studios, and its own school for vocational

training. The big studios were in Potsdam near Berlin, the previously famous UFA Studios, where films like *Metropolis* were produced and stars like Marlene Dietrich worked. The German state film archive was in the East, and hence the National Film Archive of the GDR contained the German film heritage since the beginning of German filmmaking in the late 1890s.

5   For the Hallstein Doctrine see, for example, www.konrad-adenauer.de/stichworte/aussenpolitik/hallstein-doktrin (all websites last retrieved February 2018); Grey 2003; "Bratpfanne vor der Sonne" 1965.

6   The German Democratic Republic (1949–90) had a population of 16 million, which was constant over forty years (as compared to 62 million in the Federal Republic of Germany during the same years). The Syrian Arab Republic's population was 4 million in 1956 and rose to 7.2 million by 1974. See, for example, www.populstat.info and www.populationpyramid.net

7   The beeline distance between Beirut and Damascus is 85 kilometers (53 miles).

8   The Department of Information and National Education is the same as the PLO Department of Culture and Information. The department's name varied during this time: Department of Information and Propaganda, Department of Information and National Orientation, Department of Information, or Information Department, are commonly used names. In 1984, the department was split into the Department of Information, led by Yasser Abed Rabbo, and the Department of Culture, led by Abdallah Hourani. The two departments were later reunited under the original name Department of Culture and Information. The current head of the Ramallah-based department is Hanan Ashrawi. With a few exceptions in Arabic, the documents in the archives are in German, translated by the author.

9   In April 1975, the civil war in Lebanon, in which the PLO was one party, began. It ended in 1990. In 1982 the Israeli army invaded Lebanon for the second time and reached Beirut. In summer 1982 it besieged parts of the city. The PLO had to pull out of Beirut and resettle in Tunis. After the departure of the PLO Lebanese Phalangist militia, allies of the Israeli Defense Forces committed the massacres of Sabra and Shatila.

10 The PLO had autonomy over the refugee camps in Lebanon at that time, and was the only power authorized to issue shooting permits.

11 Rafiq Hajjar (1947–2014) was a renowned Lebanese filmmaker. He was involved in over forty feature fiction films and more than thirty TV drama series, as well as several documentaries as director and/or writer. Before working on *Born in Palestine*, Hajjar directed the film *May . . . The Palestinians* (*Ayar al-Filastiniyun*, 1973), which won the award for the Best Short Film at the prestigious Carthage Film Festival in Tunis in 1974.

12 "Höre Israel" is the translation of "Shema Yisrael," or the Shema, the name of the central prayer of the Jewish morning and evening services.

13 It was common in the GDR state administration to send copies of letters to all offices that shared responsibility in a procedure. Here international relations, foreign currency, traveling abroad, international solidarity, and culture were involved. Today this helps to trace documents. When the Berlin Wall fell in November 1989, a windy and rainy month, millions of documents were literally thrown on the streets by both clerks and ordinary people. A few observers of such scenes started to collect papers, books, and film rolls from the asphalt or storage rooms. In the respective archives, professionals since then have sorted the documents, reconstructed folders, and prepared them for archival storage in order to make them accessible for historical research. Countless documents were lost or destroyed in those November days. On the Palestinian side, the access to documents is more difficult than on the German side, though not always impossible.

14 Kurt Tetzlaff (born 1933) started to work at the DEFA Studio for Popular Science in 1952, and was sent to study directing at the GDR film school in Potsdam-Babelsberg in 1955. After his graduation he worked at the DEFA Studio for Documentary Film until it closed in 1990. He taught at the GDR film school in the 1960s, was a member of the committee of the Leipzig International Filmweek for Documentary and Short Film from 1973 to 1984, and served as chairman of the Artistic Council of the DEFA Studio for Documentary Film from 1977. He directed about seventy films, among them fiction films and films for children, the bulk of his work being documentary films.

15 The Lion Cubs (Ashbal) is the children's and youth organization of Fatah, the largest party under the umbrella of the PLO. Before the disarmament of the PLO in the early 1990s it provided military and political training.

Notes to Chapter 6

1 Today it has become ECPAD (Establishment of Communication and Audiovisual Production for Defense–France).

2 The Battle of Algiers started in February 1957, lasting until September/October of the same year. René Vautier claims that this contact with Abane Ramdane took place after the Battle of Algiers, which would place it after September 1957, the date that Abane arrived in Tunis.

3 The DEFA (former East Germany public film company) was organized in production units. One of them decided to coproduce Vautier's film.

4 Not to be confused with *Algérie en flammes*, made in May 1958 by René Vautier.

5 It was in this center that the OAS had assassinated Mouloud Feraoun and his companions a few months previously.

6 *Révolution africaine* (April 18, 1964), 24.

7 Thirty years later, Ahmed Lallem met again with some of the protagonists of the first film (*Algériennes*, 1995, 50 min.). At the height of the war against

violent fundamentalism, Badra, Farida, Hassina, and Souad look back at their dreams, disillusions, and fight for equal opportunities.

8 Future director of *Nahla*, shot in 1979 in Beirut.

9 To understand Courrière's achievement, it should be noted that official French historiography at the time used the term "events of Algeria." The term "Algerian War" was not adopted until 1998 by a vote in the French parliament.

10 In Jean-Luc Godard's film *Pierrot le Fou*, Samuel Fuller describes the cinema in two words: *motion and emotion*.

11 Not to be confused with *Hors-la-loi* by Rachid Boucharef (2010).

12 The negotiations held in March 1962 between the French authorities and the representatives of the Algerian provisional government. These talks ended with a declaration of cease-fire on March 20, 1962.

Notes to Chapter 7

1 This research focuses on creative documentary film (*documentaire de création* in French; translator's note), or nonfiction film daring to present a subjective point of view and a personal style.

2 Ahmed Bouanani's book "La septième porte: Une histoire du cinéma au Maroc de 1907 à 1986" (The Seventh Gate: A History of Cinema in Morocco from 1907 to 1986), unpublished for decades, is finally in the process of publishing at Kulte Editions, Rabat. The quotes from it in this article stem from various versions, as the original manuscript was lost in a fire. Hence exact page indications for these quotes cannot be provided.

3 It is startling to observe the absence of mention of any Moroccan film in the last book dedicated to documentary film published in Morocco, and written in Arabic by Bouchaib El Messaoudi (El Messaoudi 2011).

4 I filmed interviews with Ahmed Bouanani during the last three years of his life. These filmed interviews were the foundation for the production of my film *Crossing the Seventh Gate* ('*Ubur al-bab al-sabi*'), completed in 2017. The interviews were published in their entirety as a book in 2018 and 2020.

5 The first Moroccan sultan whose portrait was officially circulated was Mohammed V (1909–61).

6 Note the absence of any written narrative tradition in Morocco, for either literature or theater. On the other hand, Moroccan culture is very rich in its oral heritage and non-figurative visual expressions.

7 Bouanani; see note 2.

8 cf. Ould-Braham 2012. I think I was able to track down these films at the French Institut National de l'Audiovisuel (INA) and at the archives of the Ministry of Defense of France, but their authentication requires additional expertise.

9 Bouanani; see note 2.

10 In detail: *The Rock* (*Le rocher*, 1958) by Larbi Benchekroun; *The Plague of the Century* (*La peste du siècle*, 1964) by Mohammed Ben Abdelouahed Tazi; and *Sin Agafaye* (1967) by Latif Lahlou.

11 Bouanani; see note 2.

12 In the Cannes Film Festival's archives, this film is listed in the category of feature-length competition films, whereas its only version available at the CCM is merely 35 minutes long, according to Ahmed Bouanani, who had watched it at the CCM.

13 Bouanani; see note 2.

14 Bouanani; see note 2.

15 The film's style strangely resembles that of Roger Leenhardt's *Mahmoud's Running Away* (*La fugue de Mahmoud*, 1955).

16 This film echoes a previous project of the author: *Siba or Morocco in Black and White* (*Siba ou le Maroc en noir et blanc*), which had never obtained the approval of the CCM's management; luckily, its manuscript is preserved in the Bouanani family archives.

17 The film has a second title: *Faces of Marrakech* (*Visages de Marrakech*).

18 Information received in a series of interviews with Mohamed Abouelouakar, in preparation for his and my participation in the project "Saving Bruce Lee—African and Arab Cinema in the Era of Soviet Cultural Diplomacy" at the Haus der Kulturen der Welt (HKW) in Berlin, January–February 2018.

19 The initial duration of *Memory 14* of 108 minutes was reduced by the censors to 24 minutes. Mohamed Abouelouakar may have had access to the censored reels since he joined the CCM in 1972, barely a year after the production of *Memory 14*.

20 Bouanani; see note 2.

21 The rushes of this project have just been found in a film library in Los Angeles. They exist in two versions—in color and in black and white—and both have been restored and digitized.

22 Bouanani; see note 2.

23 This film symbolically represents the merging of the "brief school" and the "school of sociology," since it was Majid Rechiche who was the cameraman.

24 Afifi is the only Moroccan director of this generation to show great interest in scientific films. In 1961, he was a founding member of the Cinémathèque Internationale Scientifique in Brussels, and became its vice president. At that point, he was already involved in the Paris-based Association Internationale du Cinéma Scientifique (International Association of Scientific Cinema), of which he was made first secretary general, then honorary secretary from 1960 to 1962.

25 *When the Dates Ripen* (*Hinama yanduj al-tamr/Quand mûrissent les dattes*) by Abdelaziz Ramdani and Larbi Bennani, 1968; *Conquer to Live* (*Intisar al-haya/ Vaincre pour vivre*) by Mohamed Abderrahmane Tazi and Ahmed Mesnaoui,

1968; *Spring Sunshine (Shams al-rabiʿ/Soleil de printemps)* by Latif Lahlou, 1969 (see below). These films were commissioned by the authorities to represent Morocco at the newly organized Festival de Cinéma Méditerranéen (Mediterranean Film Festival) in Tangier in 1968.

26 Mohammed Reggab and Abdelkader Lagtaâ have directed several television portraits of Moroccan artists for television—for example, *Mohamed Rabie and Abstract Arts (Mohamed Rabie et l'art abstrait)*, *Chaïbia* (both in 1984), *Kacimi or the Unveiling (Kacimi ou le dévoilement)* (in 1985; all three for the Moroccan television station TVM).

Notes to Chapter 8

1   Board member and former executive director of AFAC Oussama Rifahi acknowledges Arab filmmakers' precarious position, as they "compet[e] for funding from the Western non-profit sector and [are] frequently forced to tailor their creative output to the wishes of far-flung donors" (AFAC 2011, 10).

2   The Fund was restructured in 2017, but the old criteria remain available at Hubert Bals Fund, n.d.

3   That said, DIFF did support the Emirati fiction feature *City of Life* (*Dar al-hayy*, 2009) by Ali F. Mostafa, many of whose protagonists are foreign workers. For a fuller discussion of this narrative, see Dickinson 2016, 134–35.

4   So run the claims of the free zones' promotional materials, although such speed is certainly not afforded to personnel whose affiliations are considered "troubling" by the state. At the time of writing, for instance, a worker with identification papers labeling them as *shiʿa* (however secular they may actually be) are unlikely to pass through so easily.

5   For an elaboration of this argument as it plays out in film festival studies, see Falicov 2016, 210.

6   For an impressively thorough analysis of this regional market, see Mingant 2015, 73–87.

7   Since the time of writing this chapter DIFF has ceased to exist. Its last actual edition was in 2017.

Notes to Chapter 9

1   See, for example, Wang Bing's win of the Golden Leopard with his documentary *Mrs. Fang* at the 70th Locarno Film Festival in 2017. In Berlin in 2016, *Fire at Sea* by Gianfranco Rosi won top prize. Venice awarded *Sacro GRA* by Gianfranco Rosi in 2013. The Berlinale also included a prize for Best Documentary for the first time in 2017, and the award went to Palestinian Raed Andoni for *Ghost Hunting*.

2   See for example Yasmin Fedda's *Queens of Syria* (2014) winning at festivals like Abu Dhabi, the Human Screen Festival in Tunis, the International Festival of Women's Film in Salé, Morocco, and at Carthage in 2014 and 2015;

or Kaouther Ben Hania's first feature-length documentary, *Zaineb Hates the Snow*, winning the top prize at Carthage in 2016.

3   Compare this with the cine-mobile units in Morocco.

4   Leila Kilani's film *Our Forbidden Places* won the Etalon de Yennenga at FES-PACO in 2009 and was nominated for the Muhr Arab Documentary Award.

5   The AfricaDoc network also collaborates with other partners on the African continent, including: the Digital Mobile Cinema (Senegal and Tunisia); the master's program in documentary filmmaking at Gaston Berger University in Saint-Louis (Senegal); and the Cine Guimbi Theater in Bobo Dioulasso (Burkina Faso).

6   An earlier festival, which ran from 1971 to 1980, was also dedicated to documentary, but ceased to exist. In honor of this festival, run by Ahmad al-Hadari, Hashim al-Nahas referred to the first edition of the Ismailia festival as the eleventh, even if the two festivals were not the same.

7   The fact that the revamped Cairo International Film Festival was briefly presided over by Mohamed Hefzy, and has created a real buzz in the global festival scene because of its commitment to the 50/50 x 20/20 Pledge, shows how successful documentary specialists committed to democratic values can really inspire positive change on a transnational regional and globally significant scale.

Notes to Chapter 10

1   While reliable statistics detailing the exact number of cinemas in Cairo or other provinces at any given time throughout the country remain rather hard to come by, it can be accurately noted that as of the early 1950s there were 226 cinemas, in addition to 300 non-commercial halls in schools, ministries, and colleges, according to numerous reports put together by UNESCO. As part of the post-1953 revolutionary spirit, more cinemas came into existence, indicative of the rapid industrialization efforts—although specific statistics are rather murky, and virtually no study has been made of cinemas in provinces outside Cairo and Alexandria.

2   Chahine began shooting the film in 1964, as he was appointed to document the construction of the High Dam in Aswan, and meant to incorporate documentary footage into his film. However, the construction took years, and with the passing of Gamal Abd al-Nasser in 1970, which shook Egyptians to the core, the film was not released until 1972—by then, its initial message of national will and unity already a harbinger of nostalgia.

3   According to conversations with Ahmed Kamel Awad, who was head of the Ahram Advertising Agency for nearly forty years, and who worked as a journalist, lyricist, and screenwriter, in addition to being an ad man in the 1960s and 1970s.

4   For further reference: Hossam Ali's *Rafah Trilogy* (*Thulathiyyat Rafah*, 1982), *Harvest* (*Hisad*, 1987). Ahmed Rashed's *Port Said 71* (1971) is another

important documentary film attesting to the influence of newsreels on its aesthetics. The filmmaker was also of the Czech documentary school, which held the same belief in socialist ideals made palatable for the masses via the moving image as Nasser's administration.

5 Used interchangeably with the more official name *Misr Newsreel*, as explained later in this chapter.

6 Introduction from "Directory of the Egyptian Cinematic Newsreel with Sound 1955–1995" (*Jaridat Misr al-natiqa*), written by 'Abd al-Halim Abu Sir. This now out-of-print work was published upon the international celebration of one hundred years of cinema, by the State Information Service (al-Hay'a al-'Amma li-l-isti'lamat).

7 The timeline presented in the directory can be seen as indicative of two important details: (a) newsreel production as supported by the upper echelons of the state apparatus began in earnest with oversight from Gamal Abd al-Nasser's administration soon after the 1952 revolution; (b) accurate archival resources of work produced earlier in the century are rather disparate and quite lacking.

8 Much of the information presented here regarding Bayoumi's work is taken from El Dessouki, al-Qalyubi, and Sami 2010, 90–100.

9 A detailed list was published in Mar'i 1979.

10 As noted in Madkour Thabet's state television documentary on newsreels, *The Magic of the Past, in the Treasure of Visuals* (*Sihr ma fat, fi-kunuz al-mar'iyyat*, 1998).

11 With the increasing popularity of television in Egyptian households, many newsreels produced during this time were also screened for families at home, but this did not decrease their mass consumptions in cinema—on the contrary. It is also worth noting that many of those who worked in making newsreels during this time, especially Hassan Murad and Hussein Hilmy al-Muhandis, considered themselves filmmakers first and foremost, with their work meant for cinemas.

12 From Germaine Dulac's work, "La Question des actualités" (Williams 2014, 191).

13 Kino-Pravda ran from 1922 till 1925, producing twenty-three issues.

14 This entity appeared in different iterations as the government took on different shapes between 1931 and 1936.

15 The title can also be translated to *The Tale of the Positive and the Negative*.

16 Shadi Abdel Salam's Experimental Film Center produced several works that revolutionized documentary filmmaking, and numerous auteurs, such as Attiat El-Abnoudi, Hashim al-Nahas, Ali al-Ghazuli, and others have been equally instrumental.

Notes to Chapter 11

1 The 1952 coup and the following social and political changes initiated by Gamal Abd al-Nasser are commonly referred to as revolution. To assess the appropriateness of this definition exceeds the scope of this article.

2   I rely here on the film lists complied by Diya' Mar'i (Mari' 2003).

3   Interview with the author, Cairo, July 20, 2017.

Notes to Chapter 12

1   The only exception in the Arab world is the UNAIDS subgroup MENA-Rosa, which is designed to reach disenfranchised women and marginalized communities. See UNAIDS 2012, 6.

2   CBC Egypt, "#Asmaa_film tops #Twitter . . . To follow the live broadcast: cbc-eg.com/cbc/live-stream." 2 March 2016, 11:53 p.m. Tweet (author's translation).

3   Fathi, Shaker, "#Asmaa_film When I die, I won't die from a disease I have, but from the disease you have" 24 December 2017, 1:19 p.m. Tweet (author's translation).

4   The noun *asma'* means "names" in Arabic. Thus the film's title simultaneously indicates its focus on the protagonist, Asmaa, as an Arab woman living with HIV, while also drawing attention to the roles that names and name-calling play in stigmatizing and stereotyping.

5   In this scene, Asmaa says, "I have AIDS" in Arabic, but the English subtitles read, "I am HIV-positive." There is a constant slippage between the terms HIV and AIDS in the dialogue, pointing to what Paula A. Treichler calls an "epidemic of signification" Treichler 1988, 31–70).

6   UNAIDS 2012, 44. A similar argument is made regarding the international context by Paula Treichler (Treichler 1999, 178).

Notes to Chapter 13

1   There are, of course, exceptions, such as Tomás Gutiérrez Alea's *Memorias del Subdesarollo/Memories of Underdevelopment* (Cuba, 1968), which details the life of a bourgeois writer who has not fully adjusted to the ideological demands of the new revolutionary order. Many postrevolutionary Cuban films focused on individual characters and worked toward certain types of viewer identification with characters, so in this sense Cuban cinema stands as an exception to this unspoken rule. However, as it was a cinema emerging *post*-revolution, as opposed to most of the other militant movements mentioned here (from Palestine, France, Argentina), it was arguably made in a context that could emphasize the ideological implications of these choices. The Soviet Union, as the first revolutionary cinema–producing entity, took a much harder line toward such strategies, at least in the first few decades.

2   I am indebted to Ghalya Saadawi for reminding me of this period in the Soviet Union, where artists, including Brecht, were subject to the Stalinist–Zdhanovian suspicion and accusation of formalism as petty bourgeois individualism.

3   Viola Shafik, interview extract from Lebow 2018. filmingrevolution.supdigi-
    tal.org.
4   A good proportion of my scholarly research into documentary film has been in
    the area of first-person filmmaking. See, for instance, Lebow 2013; 2012; 2008.
5   For a compelling discussion about the definition of democracy as perpetuated
    by the IMF and the World Bank, and the implications for the revolution in
    Egypt, including the cultural dimension, see the interview with Irit Neidhardt
    in *Filming Revolution* (Lebow 2018). An example of this type of policy-related
    position can be seen in a November 2006 IMF working paper which directly
    associates democratization with longer spells of economic growth: "What
    Makes Growth Sustained?" (Berg, Ostry, and Zettelmeyer 2006).
6   This project remains unfinished.
7   It is not possible in this short chapter to discuss all of the first-person films
    that have been made since 2011. Some others include, in chronological order
    of their release: *Born on the 25th of January* (Ahmed Rashwan, 2011); *Cathar-
    sis* (Alia Ayman, 2013); *The Past Will Return* (Dina Hamza, 2015); *A Present
    from the Past* (Kawthar Younis, 2015); and *And on a Different Note* (Moham-
    med Shawky Hassan, 2015).
8   Other recent first-person films to touch on the recent past would include
    Dina Hamza's *The Past Will Return*, and Dina Hamza and Kawthar You-
    nis' *A Present from the Past*. Hamza's film is concerned with the passing of
    her father, Mohammed Hamza, a renowned poet who wrote for some of
    the most beloved singers of the previous generation and whose stirring
    nationalist songs were recently taken up by the younger generation of rev-
    olutionists in Tahrir. Younis' film concerns a long-lost love of her father's in
    Italy, with whom she facilitates a reconnection. In both cases, however, the
    father–daughter relationship is much more foregrounded (and in the case
    of Hamza, the father's successful career in the arts) than is any politically
    motivated generational connection or divide.

Notes to Chapter 14

1   This chapter was first published in *Tin Soldiers*, edited by Ala' Younis,
    Gwangju Biennale Foundation (2012).
2   In Roland Barthes' terms, it was "that accident which prick(ed) me [but also
    bruise(ed) me, is poignant to me] that drew me into either the sunflower or the
    subtitle on the sunflower, in that frame of a second" (Barthes 1982, 26–27).
3   In a conversation between Adachi and Takashi Sakai, Adachi notes: "God-
    ard seemed to have gone to Palestine as casually as I shot JRA-PFLP and
    witnessed the existence of the popular war line [?]—that which didn't exist
    in Europe—in the national liberation struggle" (Hirasawa 2003). For an
    analysis of the demise of Third-Worldism in relation to Palestine see chapter
    two in Emmelhainz 2009.

4   Beit in Bidoun, ubuweb, or YouTube commentary.
5   This is also what Elias Sanbar conceived as Palestine's predicament of being a figure of "her own imaging" (paraphrased from Irmgard Emmelhainz's wonderful chapter on the "Memory" of Godard's *Notre Musique* stemming from Elias Sanbar. See also al-Khalili (2010).
6   Furuhata (2007) quoting the Cuban filmmakers Solana and Getino.
7   Jean-Luc Godard in conversation with Daniel Cohn-Bendit, *Télérama* 3148 (May 13, 2010): "Palestine is like the cinema: it's searching for independence."
8   Here see both Elias Sanbar and Edward Said. The former was a longtime collaborator with Godard as an interpreter in *Ici et Ailleurs*, as well the channel for the idea of *Notre Musique*; the latter was an influence on Adachi for his relation to the role of the intellectual in nationalism.
9   For comprehensive treatment of this, see Alessandrini (2011; here too the author seems to refer to al-Karameh as being in Palestine).
10 Godard refers to this period as "Amman September 1970" in flashing text, followed with the statement "Death is represented in this film by a flow of images. A flow of images and sounds that suppress silence."
11 According to Massad (2001) the official number claimed was 1,500–2,000; foreign journalists claimed anything between 7,000 and 20,000.

Notes to Chapter 15

1   On the production of *Tkuma*, see Saranovitz 2006.
2   A *moshav* is a cooperative association of smallholders, somewhat similar to a kibbutz.
3   In the realm of film and music, Salima Mourad Pasha, an Iraqi–Jewish singer, and Leila Mourad, an Egyptian musical film star, both converted to Islam and stayed in Iraq and Egypt respectively.
4   One exhibition was dedicated to diaries written by Mizrahi women, curated by Shula Keshet at the Ami Steinitz's Gallery—Contemporary Art, 2000.
5   The research for the documentaries was prepared by Shoshana Madmoni-Gerber.
6   The screenplay was written by Yirmi Kadosh, Messika's longtime collaborator, and by Mizrahi activist Ilana Sugbeker.
7   In Jewish law, an *'aguna* is a woman who cannot be released from her religious marriage because it cannot be determined whether her absent husband is alive or dead.
8   After the completion of the film, some testimony suggested that Sa'il was buried in Baghdad in the early 1980s, although no witness claimed to have seen his body, and thus the full story of a person considered a traitor by the Shabak remains unknown. The filmmaker also traveled with Mazal Sa'il to Amsterdam to meet a newly arrived Baghdadi Jew who was able to testify and thus release her from the status of *'aguna*.

9   While Haim Hanegbi was not active in the Black Panthers at that time,
    he did participate in the 1989 Toledo meeting between Palestinians and
    Mizrahi intellectuals. In his speech, he brought up his Sephardi Hebronite
    background, at a time when some critical intellectuals were claiming their
    identity as Palestinian Jews to delegitimize the settlers' claim on the old city
    of Hebron (or al-Khalil in Arabic), supposedly in the name of the indigenous
    Hebronite Jewish inhabitants.

10 Eli Hamo has documented Mizrahi activism going back to the 1980s with
    Bimat Kivun Hadash in south Tel Aviv. Some of this filmic record can be
    found on the Kedma website established by Sami Chetrit, and dedicated to
    leftist Mizrahi perspectives. In conjunction with *The Black Panthers (in Israel)
    Speak*, Sami Chetrit and Eli Bareket organized an event dedicated to "30
    Years of the Black Panthers," in cooperation with Shatil and TZAH–Stu-
    dents for Social Justice at the Hebrew University.

Notes to Chapter 16

1   This chapter was originally published by *Jadaliyya* on September 3, 2012.
    jadaliyya.com.

Notes to Chapter 17

1   Bourguiba 2013. Read further on the beginnings of the cinema industry in
    Tunisia: Gabous 1998, 24; Shafik 2007, 17.
2   Nichols 1983, 17. The "direct-address style" is also described by the author
    as "the Griersonian mode." This kind of voice-over was the first thoroughly
    worked-out mode of documentary. It is mainly didactic and often dominates
    the visual.
3   Read further on this subject Haddad's book *Our Women in the Shari'a and
    Society*, published for the first time in Tunis in 1930.
4   Initially named *La Allah la sayyid* in Arabic and *Ni Dieu ni maître* in French.
    Nadia El Fani changed the title of her movie after the controversy started
    over its supposed atheist meaning. She chose to keep the original title for the
    English version.
5   Kalthoum Bornaz, interviewed by Thierry Leclère (Leclère 2001).
6   She was the first woman producer in Tunisian television.
7   Interview with the filmmaker, January 2016.

Notes to Chapter 18

1   Translator's note: The term *la décennie noire*, "the black decade," refers to the
    Algerian Civil War, an armed conflict between the Algerian government and
    various Islamist rebel groups that started in 1991.
2   Translator's note: FLN is short for le Front de Libération Nationale
    (National Liberation Front).

3   Next Assia Djebbar directed a montage film, *Zerda and the Songs of Forgetting* (*Zerda aw mawlid al-nisyan/La Zerda ou les chants de l'oubli*, 1982), and she also wrote texts that she read herself in *Algeria in Democracy, Women in Movements* (*L'Algérie en démocratie, femmes en mouvements*, 1991) by Merzak Allouache, alongside speeches by numerous associations fighting for women's rights at the time of the rise of fundamentalism and the beginning of the black decade.

4   Translator's note: The term *maquis*, French for "the bush" or "thickets," refers to bands of guerrilla Algerian Resistance fighters, as well as the remote terrain they often inhabited. The term was borrowed from the continental French term to describe guerrilla French Resistance fighters during the Nazi occupation of France in the Second World War.

5   Djamila Amrane (of European descent—her birth name was Danièle Minne) participated in the Battle of Algiers and planted bombs in areas that were frequented primarily by colonists, until her arrest in 1957. She later became a historian and obtained a PhD. She went on to write two books on the subject (Amrane 1991; Amrane-Minne 1994). She was the daughter of Jacqueline Guerroudj, who was another important activist in the FLN and was arrested by the French army and sentenced to death (though she was not executed). A French filmmaker, Alexandra Dols, shot the documentary *Moudjahidates* in 2007, a film that prominently features Djamila Amrane as well as several of her former (female) comrades in arms.

6   Translator's note: The word "Bearers" is feminine in French: *porteuses*, "the *female* fire-bearers").

7   Assia Djebar used this metaphor of "the fire-bearers" in her collection of short stories *Femmes d'Alger dans leur appartement*, published in 1980, as Mireille Calle-Gruber recalls (Calle-Gruber 2001).

8   This chapter, which is dedicated to documentaries that address the memory of these struggles, does not aim to study the question of the women's struggle, nor that of the woman's place in Algerian society as told through its cinema. However, the reader is referred to two films by Ahmed Lallem (Lallem 1966; 1998) that explore the place of women in society with great skill and subtlety. In fact, Nabila Djahnine, an activist who was assassinated in the 1990s, gives a speech in one of Lallem's documentaries: images of her speech can be seen in *Lettre à ma sœur* by Habiba Djahnine.

9   Translator's note: This term refers to female Algerian resistance fighters. It is the feminine plural form of *mujahideen*.

Notes to Chapter 19

1   As Ferhani pointed out in an interview: "It's a very difficult place, psychologically. To be around death, it weighs on you. And they are all precarious" (Letoré 2016; author's translation). I would like to thank Hassen Ferhani for access to the film.

2   The lines quoted here are my translation of the film's French subtitles.
3   Literally the "burning," the term *harga* is used in the Maghreb to refer to the act of crossing the Mediterranean with the purpose of migrating, without a visa, to Europe.
4   Austin notes that Allouache's character seems to echo the words attributed to the Kabyle poet Tahar Djaout: "Silence is death. If you stay silent, you die; if you speak, you die. So speak and die" (Austin 2012, 143). Djaout was assassinated by the Armed Islamic Front in 1993.
5   I would like to thank Muriam Haleh Davis and Thomas Serres for their comments on an earlier draft of this essay and for their thoughts on Algerian politics and history. The films were made and this essay was written before the advent of the *hirak* (literally "movement") or popular uprising that began in Algeria on February 22, 2019. While the outcome of the *hirak* is anything but clear as this book goes into production, months of ongoing peaceful protest have demonstrated the renewed creativity and tenacity of a population ready to seize political possibility even out of despair.

Notes to Chapter 20

1   For more on this subject, see Armes 2006; Dönmez-Colin 2007; Gugler 2011; Martin 2011; as well as the articles published in *Études Maghrébines*, *Journal of North African Studies* and recently the *Journal of African Cinema*.
2   She has received wide recognition: she was honored at the 2013 Film Festival of Tetouan, for instance; her documentaries have been awarded prizes at films festival in Valladolid (Spain) in 1988, Montecatini (Italy) in 1989, and Pessac (France) in 1995, and have been aired on several TV channels.
3   For a detailed description of the role of the Tunisian government in national film production, see Martin 2007.
4   Sonia Chamkhi, personal communication, March 2014.
5   Sanad Grants awarded to Moroccan directors between 2010 and 2014: 2010 Development
    • Ismael El Maoula El Iraki, *Zanka* (fiction)
    • Brahim Fritah, *Playground Chronicles* (fiction)
    2010 Postproduction
    • Leila Kilani, *On The Edge* (fiction)
    • Kamal El Mahouti, *My Brother* (fiction)
    • Faouzi Bensaidi, *Death for Sale* (fiction)
    2011 Development
    • Merieme Addou and Rosa Rogers, *Pirates of Salé* (documentary)
    • Faouzi Bensaïdi, *The Wall* (fiction)
    • Hicham Lasri, *99* (fiction)
    2013 Development
    • Karim Aïtouna, *A Place Under the Sun* (documentary)

2014 Development
- Daoud Aoulad-Syad, *The Birds of the Mountains* (documentary)
- Leila Kilani, *Joint Possession* (fiction)

2014 Postproduction
- Merieme Addou and Rosa Rogers, *Pirates of Salé* (documentary)
- Hicham Ayouch, *Fevers* (fiction)

6   In this particular way of opening her documentary, Génini seems to be quoting fellow Moroccan filmmaker Ahmed El Maanouni film *Trances* (1981), a film Génini produced and helped distribute. Yet she departs from El Maanouni's dizzying way of filming at close range (almost from within the circle of the musicians during performances), and adopts a more didactic approach with her camera at arm's length.

7   For a more thorough description of this musical structure, see Martin 2011, 43–62.

8   In this respect, *El Gusto* is akin to two other musical documentaries: the famous *Buena Vista Social Club* on Afro-Cuban music by Wim Wenders (1999), and *Kinshasa Symphony* on a classical music orchestra in Kinshasa, Democratic Republic of the Congo, by Martin Bauer (2010).

Notes to Chapter 21

1   Environmental Justice Atlas: https://ejatlas.org/conflict/imider-silver-mine-morocco

2   From Nadir Bouhmouch›s Facebook, posted on 23 October 2017.

3   He recently released a feature-length documentary about Imider called *Amussu* (2019). The film is traveling in international and local festivals and has not yet been released online like Bouhmouch's previous films. The film is produced by the Movement on the Road of '96 and partly financed by a postproduction grant from the Doha Film Institute.

Notes to Chapter 22

1   This chapter is an excerpt from "Screen Fighters: Filming and Killing in Contemporary Syria" from my 2018 book, *Shooting a Revolution: Visual Media and Warfare in Syria*. I wish to thank Pluto Press (www.plutobooks.com) for granting us the rights to republish this text free of charge, something that—sadly—happens very rarely in the publishing world.

2   "The filmer feels that the camera is *stronger* than the gun . . . by not only capturing the sniper's image, but by imitating his gesture as she does so, and turning it back against him, she feels that she is acquiring and exercising a kind of *mimetic power* over him" (Snowdon 2016, 92).

3   In March 2015, a four-year-old refugee girl, Hudea, surrendered to photographer Omar Sagirli's camera, thinking he was about to shoot at her.

4 The Sonderkommando was a work unit composed of Jewish prisoners who were forced under the threat of death to aid in the disposal of gas-chamber victims in the Nazi death camps.

5 Which she calls "cyber[riotal]space" (Hamadeh 2016, 13).

6 Calling fellow citizens "germs" or "insects" is a quite common trope in Arab authoritarian regimes: Qaddafi used the same expression in his speech after the outbreak of the Libyan uprising in 2011.

7 "Nation-wide protests did not 'diffuse' as much as they occurred in parallel" (Leenders 2013, 282).

8 This chant was traditionally used to hail Hafez al-Assad (bi ruh, bi damm, naf-dik ya Hafiz).

9 The Arabic word shahid, "martyr," is used here to refer to a person killed during the demonstrations.

10 Even if other sparks had manifested throughout February 2011.

11 For example, the "clock square" sit-in, April 18, 2011.

12 Under what Donati (2009) calls the "Syrian exception."

13 Regime-backed advertising campaigns that mushroomed in the streets of Syria in the second half of March 2011 featured colored posters stating "no to division," "no to sectarianism," as a way of reminding citizens not to protest.

14 Tanwir refers to a process of enlightenment inspiring a modernist ideology of progress and development through mass education and edifying media products.

15 In the original: "nouvelle culture protestataire qui s'élabore aussi dans les images et les sons" (author's translation).

16 On the "quintessentially social" smartphone campaign, see Della Ratta (2018, 125–31).

17 I am grateful to Chadi Elias and Zaheer Omareen (2014) for directing me to Espinosa's manifesto.

18 "Imperfect cinema is no longer interested in quality or technique. It can be created equally well with a Mitchell or with an 8mm camera, in a studio or in a guerrilla camp in the middle of the jungle. Imperfect cinema is no longer interested in predetermined taste, and much less in 'good taste.' It is not quality which it seeks in an artist's work" (Espinosa 1979).

19 Oussama Mohammad is a prominent Syrian filmmaker, living since mid-2011 in exile in Paris. For background information on his cinema, see Boëx 2014; Wedeen 1999.

20 The film premiered at the 2014 Cannes Film Festival.

21 Referring to the perpetrators of the Indonesian genocide.

22 Orwa al-Mokdad, personal communication, October 2012.

23 The first film in the history of cinema. During its first public screening the audience was reportedly in a state of panic because of the realism of the images.

24 On the politics of aesthetics, see Ranciére 2013.

25 On the global circulation of violence, torture, and the imagination of terror, see Austin 2016; 2017.

26 Many have reflected on this sort of "filming one's own death" genre. See Hamadeh 2016; Snowdon 2016.

27 "The Pixelated Revolution" (2012) is the telling title of Lebanese artist Rabih Mroué's lecture-performance on the Syrian user-generated videos.

28 "This is perhaps why the Syrian images did not proliferate, as did those of the Egyptian revolution, for it becomes very difficult to say, 'we are all Syrians,' as some would say we are all Palestinians or Egyptians" (Rich 2011).

29 As an example of a fake pixelated clip, see "Syrian Hero Boy," quoted in Tarnowski 2017.

30 The film was scheduled to premiere at the Berlin Film Festival in 2016, but a few weeks before the event the director decided to cancel the public screening due to security concerns regarding one of the activists featured in the film. However, other controversies seem to have later emerged and prevented the film from being shown in public, such as questions of ownership and copyright concerning some of the activists' footage included in the documentary. The director prefers not to address the issue in public. I wish to thank Khaled Abdulwahed for the opportunity to screen the film multiple times and discuss it with him. For more information about *Jellyfish*, see Della Ratta 2018.

Notes to Chapter 23

1 Interview by the author with Mai Masri during an event held in memory of Jean Chamoun on August 27, 2017.

2 Interview by the author with Jean Chamoun while shooting the film *War Cinema in Lebanon*.

Notes to Chapter 24

1 I would like to thank Viola Shafik for the opportunity to contribute to this volume, the Video Data Bank for extending online access to me, and Akram Zaatari for his work.

Notes to Chapter 25

1 Bennet borrows the concept from Dominick LaCapra (2001).

2 There is an extensive scholarship on the value and limitations of the witnessing mode dating back to early writings by John Berger (1980 [1972]) and Susan Sontag (1977) on images of violence. This literature, which addresses the limits and possibilities of the circuits through which such images travel (Abounaddara 2017; Keenan 2001; Sliwinski 2011; Torchin 2012), the effects of such images on distant spectators (Sontag 2004) and on photographed or filmed subjects (El-Hassan 2002; Fassin 2008; Feldman 2004), and the

relationships that develop between subjects that appear within such images and spectators who gaze at them (Azoulay 2008; Hochberg 2015; Rancière 2009), is too vast to summarize here.

3   Glissant uses the term within a postcolonial context and specifically in relation to language and literature rather than visual material. Thus, there is an element of translation and metaphorization involved in extending it to film. Language is by its nature more complexly rooted in specific cultures and subcultures such that opacity is a potential aspect of every verbal communication. Photographic and filmic images, on the other hand, often encourage the illusion of transparency, especially because the rapid viewing practices that our media cultivate encourage quick assumptions about their meanings.

4   The concept of opacity has been applied to a Palestinian context by others, most notably by the Otolith Group in their film *Nervus Rerum* (Demos 2013; Emmelhainz 2009; Hochberg 2015). However, they understand the term differently. The Otolith group emphasizes the refusal to bear witness for viewers, and, in fact, turning one's back on power (Emmelhainz 2009, 129). Glissant, on the other hand, does not advocate turning away, but rather an ethical practice of "turning toward."

5   See Marks 2000, 80-81 for a discussion of the aura of objects in films.

6   Aljafari himself has spoken of his own pleasure in constructing an Arabic mediascape within the film (personal communication, October 2009).

7   All the television is in Arabic, coming from either Jordanian or Egyptian channels, except for one scene in an auto repair shop, where men appear to be watching an American film or television show on break. Viewers hear dialogue in English, but the camera does not show them what the men are watching.

8   A subtle reference to the repetition within the film's structure. Characters do things over and over again, thereby constructing themselves. A hint of agency lies here. Aljafari, too, can use cinema to engage in the practice and repetition that underpins subjectivities, just as it underpins the nationalism that naturalizes the state of Israel for its Jewish citizens.

9   *Delta Force* is one of the American films shot in the Ajami neighborhood of Jaffa.

10 Helga Tawil-Souri applies Raymond Williams' (1977) concept of a structure of feeling to the Palestinian context as a means of analyzing the Palestinian condition as an evolving process rather than a state, and one that is not necessarily defined by the national. A Palestinian structure of feeling, she argues,

> is one of negotiating a shifting spatiality. This stems from the specific historical conflict over territory: from issues of control over specific locations, struggles over ownership of land and ability to reside on it, the process of exile, the desire to return, navigating shrinking territories, contending with the reality of your oppressor displacing

you in your own home, the desire for a future (or past) nation-state, the experiences of diaspora, and everything in between. This is the historical reality that Palestinians—no matter "where"—must continuously live with, experience, negotiate and make meaning out of. But we should not mistake the territory itself, nor its "loss," for the nation. (Tawil-Souri 2014, 173)

Notes to Chapter 27

1   This letter was initially written in French as an email, and translated to English by the author, with light edits to aid understanding.

The author would like to make it clear that Hakim Belabbes agreed to the publication of the letter within the framework of this volume, and he wishes to thank Laura Gribbon for overseeing its publication.

All screenshots stem from viewing links to *Ashlaa* made available by Hakim Belabbes.

Notes to Chapter 29

1   My thanks to Najwa Kadhim, who offered comments on an earlier draft of this chapter.

2   Fahdel also named his production company Stalker Production, after Tarkovsky's film.

3   For a detailed discussion of the stylistic approach of *Iraq in Fragments* and Hollywood Iraq War movies, see Westwell (2014).

4   A term taken from Gilles Deleuze's writings on cinema, a "seed" is something in the process of being made. Deleuze refers to the "virtual seed" of Rosebud and the paperweight as a crystalline seed in *Citizen Kane* (Deleuze 1989, 74).

CPSIA information can be obtained
at www.ICGtesting.com
Printed in the USA
JSHW021917290822
29841JS00002B/2/J

9 789774 169588